D0212571

FREEDOM
AND
DOMINATION

Alexander Rüstow

FREEDOM
AND
DOMINATION

A Historical Critique of Civilization

Abbreviated Translation from the German by
SALVATOR ATTANASIO

Edited, and with an Introduction, by
DANKWART A. RUSTOW

PRINCETON UNIVERSITY PRESS
PRINCETON, NEW JERSEY

From the German: *Ortsbestimmung der Gegenwart*, 3 vols.
(Erlenbach-Zurich and Stuttgart: Eugen Rentsch Verlag, © 1950, 1952,
1957)

CONTENTS

PART THREE   DOMINATION VERSUS FREEDOM

PREFACE TO THE ENGLISH EDITION

The following text represents a severely condensed translation of Alexander Rüstow's *Ortsbestimmung der Gegenwart*, which appeared in three volumes in 1950, 1952, and 1957, a revised edition of the second volume appearing shortly after the author's death in 1963. Salvator Attanasio, with rare erudition and tireless dedication, undertook the translation of the complete text from the German. Sheri Tierney assisted me in the laborious task of condensation. D. K. Moore's critical reading resulted in many invaluable suggestions in the final process of editing. The text as it appears here was freely revised by the editor, who must bear the final responsibility for any inadvertent departures from the original.

The three volumes of the original amount to 1,780 pages, of which 1,240 are text and the remainder, in smaller type, notes. To compress this material into a single volume, virtually all footnotes have been omitted except those that document quotations. This, I am aware, involves a serious distortion of Alexander Rüstow's erudite style. Footnotes to him served as guideposts as he crossed and recrossed the conventional boundaries of scholarly disciplines; as an occasion for celebrating those *qui ante nos nostra dixerunt*—that is, as a modest disclaimer of originality but also as a way of firmly embedding his own thinking in more than two thousand years of Western intellectual tradition; and as a means of expanding, elaborating, or embroidering the ideas in the text. The only apology that can be made for omitting this scholarly substructure from this English version is that, in this case, omission is not suppression. The notes range freely over literature and quotations in German, Greek, Latin, French, English, and occasionally Italian and Spanish, and over the many scholarly disciplines from ethnography to classical philology, from military history to dynamic psychology, whose boundaries the author felt compelled to cross. Readers in a position to do justice to this wealth of the footnotes, therefore, stand in no need of translation and should refer directly to the German-polyglot text.

But the text above the footnotes, too, has had to be condensed, by approximately one-half. Most of the appendixes that are inserted

between sections of the text have been omitted: "Research on Cultivated Plants and Prehistory" (vol. 1, pp. 56-57), "The Nomenclature
of Migrations" (vol. 1, pp. 72-73), "Significance and Derivation of the
Orphic Movement" (vol. 2, pp. 74-80), and "The Continuity in Intellectual History from Antiquity to Renaissance and Enlightenment"
(vol. 2, pp. 377-392). Chapter 4 of volume 1 ("Conditions of Survival
of Civilizations," pp. 259-277), which recapitulates much of the preceding and subsequent argument, has been omitted—as have three
short sections in volume 1 (chap. 2, sec. 6: "Superincumbency and
Popular Culture," pp. 122-123; sec. 9: " 'Chivalry,' " pp. 138-139; and
chap. 3, sec. 12: "Tendency toward Division of Labor and Specialization," pp. 249-250—the remaining sections having been renumbered
in the translation) and the postscript to the second edition of volume
2 (pp. 475-479). The appendix on "The History of the Superstratification Hypothesis" has been transposed from the end of volume 1,
chapter 1, to the end of the Introduction, where it follows immediately the only other appendix that has been included here, that on
"The Significance of Ethnography for the Science of History."

For the rest, Rüstow's outline of chapters and sections has been
left intact, although severe cuts have been made throughout by
omitting passages of several paragraphs or several sentences. Even
more frequently, we have cut a sentence here and there that elaborates or amplifies on the previous argument, or a phrase here and
there that reflects the more baroque customs of German scholarly
prose as against the terse imperatives of clear American English. It
should also be noted that what here appear as three "parts" originally were three separate volumes—which explains why the first
two parts each have their separate mottoes and the third a dedication.

No attempt has been made to translate the German title of the
work, which literally could be rendered as "Taking Bearings on the
Present." Instead, the title "Freedom and Domination" alludes to
the major theme of the work as stated in the titles of the three volumes. The subtitle, on the other hand, is taken from the original
("Eine universalgeschichtliche Kulturkritik").

Translation of the present work into English was made possible
through a generous grant from the Deutsche Forschungsgemein-
schaft. Thanks are due to Dr. Ursula Steinbrecher of the DFG, who
enthusiastically supported the project from its inception and
through many trials and delays; and to Dr. Philipp Schmitt-Schlegel
and Dr. Joachim Sartorius of the West German Consulate-General
in New York, who acted as intermediaries. Helen Ivanoff and Karen

Asakawa undertook the arduous tasks of typing, respectively, Mr. Attanasio's complete translation and the final, condensed text.

Special thanks are due to Dr. Eugen Rentsch, son and heir of the original publisher of the *Ortsbestimmung*, for generously making available the translation rights for this condensed English edition. For the editor, it is a pleasure to continue an association of nearly a quarter of a century with the Princeton University Press, most recently with Miriam Brokaw, Sanford Thatcher, and Margaret Case. On the part of the Press, the decision to bring out the present volume continues an honorable and devoted tradition of repatriating, on these American shores, continental European scholars ranging from Maritain and Jaeger to Einstein and Auerbach.

For the editor personally, publication of this volume is more than a son's act of piety: it is but a small repayment on the debt he owes to the most joyful, generous, and beloved of teachers.

DANKWART A. RUSTOW
April, 1978

ALEXANDER RÜSTOW (1885-1963):
A BIOGRAPHICAL SKETCH

When the present work was originally published in German in the decade after the collapse of Hitler's Third Reich, it was widely acclaimed by critics in Germany, and elsewhere in Europe, as a major contribution both to historical and sociological scholarship and to the moral regeneration and reorientation of which post-Hitlerite Germany stood in the profoundest need—and for which the survivors in neighboring countries only occasionally dared to hope. About the time of publication of the first volume, the author, at sixty-five years of age, was appointed to his first academic position in his home country—the chair of sociology at the University of Heidelberg that at one time had been held by Max Weber and later, until Hitler came to power in 1933, by his younger brother, Alfred Weber. In 1946 Alfred Weber, at seventy-eight, had briefly resumed teaching but then took great pride in securing the appointment of Rüstow as his successor.

Alexander Rüstow was born in Wiesbaden, in what was then the province of Hesse-Nassau, on 8 April 1885. The early influences that most clearly stood out in his oral reminiscences were a childhood of material austerity in a succession of Prussian garrison towns, a disciplinarian father, a sickly mother of pietist inclinations, long vacations of roaming through his maternal grandmother's small mansion and vast garden in an intimate town in the wooded hills of Thuringia, a quarrelsome sister three years younger, and two much smaller sisters and a brother who all adored him.

Attendance at the leading "humanist *Gymnasium*" in Berlin during his adolescence instilled a lifelong passion for classical Greece, its language and its philosophy, which in later years focused on the pre-Socratics, foremost the cheerful peasant-poet Hesiod. Graduation from the Bismarck *Gymnasium* (1903) led naturally to university study—in the history of philosophy and related subjects—at Munich, Göttingen, and elsewhere. In Munich he connected with a circle of cultural and intellectual rebels against Wilhelminian Germany of whom Max Wertheimer (1880-1943), the founder of *Gestalt* psychology, and Käthe Kollwitz (1867-1945), the sculptress, have become the best known. These were the early idealist days of the German "Jugendbewegung," long before its perversion to chauvinism, of which the author complains below (pt. 3, chap. 2, sec. 4).

His esthetic sensibilities were reinforced in his first marriage to a sculptress and painter nearer his own age, Mathilde Herberger. It finds expression, decades later, in several critical essays in the history of art, including a detailed monograph on the decay of architecture in Germany and Europe in the nineteenth century, and an article, "*Lutherana Tragoedia Artis*," on the chilling impact (as Rüstow sensed it), of Protestantism on Renaissance painting.[1]

At the University of Göttingen, he was strongly influenced by the rationalist philosopher Leonard Nelson (1882-1927), who revived the epistemology of Kant's disciple Jakob Friedrich Fries—a mentor and friend with whom Rüstow shared a passion for plain logic. (Rüstow himself, however, combined this passion with a sense of awe for "numinosity," as implied in one of the footnotes that this edition does not omit: pt. 3, chap. 1, n. 9.) Rüstow's doctoral dissertation, presented at the University of Erlangen in 1908, was entitled *Der Lügner: Theorie, Geschichte und Auflösung*. It was a philological and logical analysis of the classical Greek paradox of the liar (in paraphrase: Epimenides the Cretan says, All Cretans always lie: True or false?), and young Rüstow, along with furnishing a concise philological and historical disquisition, took pride in demonstrating the formal identity between this ancient conundrum and Bertrand Russell's paradox, recently discovered, in formal mathematics.

The six years from his promotion to the doctorate until the outbreak of the Great War of 1914 were divided between service as chief of the classics department of B. G. Teubner in Leipzig (then the leading publisher of Greek and Latin texts in Germany or, indeed, anywhere), and preparation of a *Habilitationsschrift* (on the epistemology of Parmenides), which, if completed, would have earned him the rank of lecturer (*Privatdozent*) in a Faculty of Philosophy of a German university.

But World War I intervened, and with it more than four years of service as a reserve lieutenant in the artillery branch, mostly on the German fronts against France and Russia. The war, to Rüstow, furnished not only proof positive of the logical contradictions and abject moral decay of the Second Reich of Bismarck and the two Williams; it also deflected him, irrevocably as it turned out, from the sheltered philological-esthetic path on which he had set out on his graduation from university.

The winter of 1918-1919 found him participating actively, if in minor roles, in the turbulent events in Munich and Berlin, Germany's closest approximation to a socialist revolution. An experience he would later recall with relish were long conversations with Karl Radek, who (others said) presided over Berlin's leading intellectual salon in the visitor's room of the Moabit prison.[2]

At the socialist meetings in Munich and Berlin he met his second wife, Anna Bresser, with whom he came to share a dedicated interest in ethnology (particularly the work of the "Vienna school" of ethnography) and prehistoric archaeology—two disciplines which, they believed, enabled the scholar, objectively and empirically, to search out "the basic dimension of that which, anthropologically, is of the human essence" (see Introduction, sec. 1).

By 1919, as the abortive "revolution" had simmered down into the precarious normalcy of the Weimar Republic, Rüstow took a post in the German ministry of economy in Berlin, as the official in charge of plans for the nationalization of the coal industry of the Ruhr. It was in this period that Rüstow developed a working grasp of economic theory, both liberal and Marxist, a ruthless political pragmatism—and, incidentally, a delight in drawing statistical charts and graphs that vividly demonstrated the contemporary play of forces in political economy. He also formed personal friendships with a group of socialist intellectuals, among which those with Gerhard Colm, Adolph Lowe, and Eduard Heimann proved to be the most enduring.[3]

The ministry of economy, headed, when Rüstow joined it, by Rudolf Wissell as minister and Adolf Trendelenburg as undersecretary, was one of the few that remained in Social Democratic hands throughout the precarious years of the early Weimar coalitions— the Kapp *putsch*, the assassinations of Erzberger and Rathenau, the Communist risings in Saxony and elsewhere, and the Ludendorff-Hitler beer-hall *putsch*. Yet the parliamentary maneuvering from coalition to coalition precluded any hope for implementing the plans for nationalization of major industries such as Rüstow was developing.

In 1924, he left the ministry of economy and accepted a position as director of political and economic research in the Verein deutscher Maschinenbauanstalten (VDMA)—the industrial association of the German tool and dye industry. This represented the turning point in an imperceptible conversion in economic ideology from socialism to liberalism—from advocacy of nationalization of industry to espousal of free, competitive enterprise. In later years Rüstow rarely talked about the detailed circumstances of this shift, which some of his more doctrinaire Socialist friends (not including those mentioned above) tended to resent as a defection. My guess is that he found it impossible to go on devoting himself to plans of nationalization that were doomed to remain all talk and no action, that he would rather be an honest liberal than a pretended Socialist, that he could not bear the implicit hypocrisy of the Social Democratic role within the Weimar Republic. This experience of disillusionment was common to a number of Rüstow's contemporaries among European intellectuals, including the German historian Arthur Rosenberg and the Swedish political scientist and journalist Herbert Tingsten.[4]

Nor, in immediate practical politics, did his shift imply any major realignment. The tool and dye industry was composed mainly of small firms, and the large coal and steel producers were their main suppliers. Rüstow was the VDMA's political strategist, and his major concern was to combat the oligopolistic and protectionist forces of the steel and coal industries and, by extension, of large industry in general and of the Junkers and other protectionist agrarians. ("*Ostelbier*," or "East Elbian," remained, in private conversation, one of Rüstow's bitterest words of abuse, foreshadowing the indignation against conquest, exploitation, and "superincumbency" fully articulated in the present volume.) The same criticism of monopoly, tariffs, subsidies, and all manner of deviations from full and fair competition is expressed in a number of essays and public lectures to political and academic audiences composed during Rüstow's later Berlin years.[5]

I once asked Theodor Eschenburg, an associate of Rüstow's at VDMA and later a professor of political science at Tübingen, how influential Rüstow's activity had been in those years. Eschenburg, after some reflection, answered that, of course, the tool and dye industry could not marshal the monetary or personnel resources of the big industrialist or Junker lobbies; yet the factual and analytic research on economic policy done by Rüstow's division at VDMA was so thorough and compelling (and the association's network of constituent firms so widely dispersed in Germany's smaller industrial centers), that officials in the relevant Berlin ministries would soon learn to be wary of taking the big lobbyists' advice without first ascertaining the VDMA's position.[6]

By the early 1930s the threat of Brown Shirts had overtaken that of tariffs or subsidies, and the rising tide of national socialism had swamped big industry and big landowners alike. With his Prussian family background, his sturdy liberal convictions, and his unrelenting political realism, Rüstow was one of the few figures able to

mediate or connect among the sparse forces of last-ditch defense of Weimar against the Hitlerite onslaught. These forces included staunch believers in the democratic *Rechtsstaat*, Socialist trade unionists who rebelled against the confusion and impotence of the official SPD leadership, and Prussian conservatives (including monarchists) who despised Hitler as an adventurist corporal. In the fall and winter of 1932-1933, Franz von Papen and Kurt von Schleicher were engaged in the petty and fateful maneuvers by which Papen in the end brought Hitler to power. A last minute list of a desperate anti-Hitler coalition cabinet (which never was formed) had Schleicher in the chancellor's place and Rüstow in that of minister of economy. Schleicher, it will be recalled, was murdered at Hitler's orders in June 1934.[7]

One of my own earliest political memories is a search of our suburban home in Berlin by the Gestapo in March 1933, which netted Hitler's secret police a starter's pistol (which my father kept by his bedside against possible nighttime intruders) and a box of file cards marked "SS" (for "Selige Sehnsucht"—or "Blessed Longing"—a Goethe poem from the *West-Östliche Divan* on which a younger sister of his had hoped to do a philological dissertation).

During the summer and autumn of 1933, Alexander Rüstow was frantically occupied, mostly in Switzerland, in trying to find a refuge from the "stifling atmosphere" of Hitler's Germany that "left me no air to breathe," as he says in the Foreword.

His gratitude to Atatürk's Turkey, which provided him and many other anti-Nazi German intellectuals with political asylum, and to the University of Istanbul, which from 1933 to 1949 appointed and reappointed him Professor of Economic Geography and Economic History, is recorded in the author's own Foreword.

Rüstow's departure from Germany for Turkey coincided with his third marriage, happiest of the three and the enduring one, to Lorena Countess Vitzthum von Eckstaedt. Her part, over many years, in stimulating, dreaming, prodding, coaxing, cajoling, disciplining, appreciating, and applauding the writing of this work was too private—and too well understood between author and wife—to be acknowledged in the Foreword.

While most of his closest friends from Germany had settled in the United States—the largest group among them at the New School for Social Research in New York—Rüstow spent most of his years of exile in relative isolation in the magnificent study with its magnificent bay window in Kadiköy, across the mouth of the Sea of Marmara from old Istanbul, reading compulsively and across the many petty frontiers of scholarship, writing not at all for years, haltingly for more years, and profusely at last.

During the years from 1937 to 1940, Rüstow, by correspondence and through several brief visits to Europe (including a longer stay in Geneva in 1939-1940), formed a close network of associations with a group of German and Austrian economists who came to be known as the neoliberal school. Among these he felt personally closest to Walther Eucken of the University of Freiburg and Wilhelm Röpke, earlier his colleague at Istanbul and since 1937 at the Institut de Hautes Etudes in Geneva; others included Friedrich A. von Hayek and Ludwig von Mises.

Neoliberalism, to many of its critics, has seemed little more than a revival of the old doctrine of *laissez-faire* with its onesided defense of business interests, and much in the writings of Röpke, Hayek, and Mises lends credence to that charge. But to Rüstow the qualifying prefix *neo-* was important. He was convinced that a free market must be free not only from market-distorting government interventions (such as protective tariffs or subsidies to business) but also from the no less distorting influences of private monopoly and oligopoly. This implied a strong rather than an inactive government, one that could interfere systematically so as to preserve the social and political framework for a fully competitive market. Rüstow had no difficulty in accepting differences, even steep differences, of economic reward as long as they reflected personal differentials in effort, risk-taking, or ingenuity. But an essential feature of his version of neoliberalism was his demand for *Startgerechtigkeit*, which implied not only full equality of educational opportunity but complete economic redistribution once every generation through a confiscatory inheritance tax.

Rüstow's first publications of the Istanbul period mostly concerned such economic themes, some of them starting as book reviews that grew into full-fledged essays.[8] But he soon began to connect his economic concerns with his more lasting interests in sociology and the history of ideas. The culmination of the series was an essay that, in successive drafts, grew to book size, and the very title of which suggests his sharp polemical edge against the palaeoliberalism of the Manchester school: *The Failure of Economic Liberalism as a Problem in the History of Religion*.[9] *Laissez-faire*, so his thesis may be restated in gross simplification, was a corollary of a metaphysical belief in preordained harmony that can be traced from Adam Smith, Bernard Mandeville, and François Quesnay all the way back to the Stoics—just as the fascination of classical eco-

nomics with occult quantitative rather than human-moral relations can be traced to Pythagorean and Orphic mysticism. And only by laying bare these metaphysical, pseudoreligious roots can a renewed liberalism free itself of their continuing and nefarious influence.

Other writings of Rüstow's of this period branched out more boldly into the problem of peace and international order, the modern ethic of work and duty (a restatement of Max Weber's thesis in the *Protestant Ethic and the Spirit of Capitalism*), the decay of architecture in the nineteenth century (already referred to), and solitude as a sociological affliction of modern mass society—an essay in which Thomas Mann found much affinity to the perspective of his *Doktor Faustus*.[10]

While part of Rüstow's time was occupied with these "exploratory drillings or probes," his major effort went into claiming the entire vast territory thus staked out, that is, into writing the present work. The first sketch, no more than a hundred or so pages of longhand on his favorite white octavo (about 5″ x 8″) writing pads, dates to 1937. Each successive version grew to about double the size of the last.[11] The most intensive writing effort began, as I recall, early in 1941. For nearly a decade the manuscript grew through inserts, added footnotes, afterthoughts, corrections, expansions, and revisions. (In a passage of the German Foreword not here translated, Rüstow refers to the many geological layers which the perceptive reader may discern in the work.) The working title of the early versions sounded academic and a little apologetic: "Zur geistesgeschichtlich-sozio-logischen Ortsbestimmung der Gegenwart" (roughly: "A contribution to determining the coordinates of the present in intellectual history and in sociology"). The Latin phrase *comprehendendo sol-vitur* ("through understanding it is solved"—Rüstow never succeeded in identifying its source), which now appears in the Foreword served as a motto. Later, the title was boldly, and perhaps a bit cryptically, shortened to its final form: *Ortsbestimmung der Gegenwart*, with a subtitle no less boldly proclaiming the book's historical sweep and moral aim: *Eine universalgeschichtliche Kulturkritik*.

The work's central concern was the question that had been tormenting that small, heterogeneous, but solid group of German (or German-speaking) intellectuals who had seen the writing on the wall before 1933 and who remained unyielding in their rejection of nazism. How was such a catastrophe *überhaupt* and *eigentlich* possible? How much of it was accidental, how much preordained? How much specifically German, more broadly European, or generally human? The answers have been many and varied: *Escape from Freedom* (Erich Fromm, 1941), *Behemoth* (Franz Neumann, 1942), *The Origins of Totalitarianism* (Hannah Arendt, 1951), *Capitalism, Socialism, and Democracy* (Joseph Schumpeter, 1942), *The Price of Liberty* (Adolph Lowe, 1937), *The Road to Serfdom* (F. A. von Hayek, 1944), *Permanent Revolution* (Sigmund Neumann, 1942), *The Mass Psychology of Fascism* (Wilhelm Reich, 1933), *Man and Society in an Age of Reconstruction* (Karl Mannheim, 1935, 1940)—to mention just a few in random order.

Rüstow's answer was broader and more complex—and for all that perhaps more deeply personal—than any of these. Its formulation took him ever deeper and wider into history, not just the three thousand years of which Goethe believed the educated man must be able to render an account to himself, but the ten thousand years since the advent of "high cultures," or advanced civilizations, and beyond. He kept asking, with the German romantic poet Hölderlin, "How did it begin? Who brought the curse?"[12] He went on to probe fully the height and width of the "culture pyramid": the sheer sadism of chariot-borne or tank-borne conquest—and the glories of leisure, freedom, and the liberating yet dangerous power of theoret-ical (and therefore thoroughly practical) thought. He continued to trace the ceaseless struggle of "freedom *versus* domination" throughout Western intellectual and social history since the ancient Greeks. He sought to sketch, in conclusion, an alternative and via-ble intellectual-political program that might bear fruit in Germany and elsewhere after the demise of nazism (which, through the dark-est days of 1940, 1941, and 1942, he never doubted was inevitable).

American readers may wish to be informed that, but for the many accidents of which the life of political refugees is replete, Alexander Rüstow might have arrived in the United States in person (rather than literarily and posthumously) in 1939, 1941, or 1943—when many of his friends at the Rockefeller Foundation and the New School, as well as Carl J. Friedrich at Harvard and Arnold Wolfers at Yale, endeavored to bring him to this country. Instead he re-mained throughout the war years in his Istanbul exile, writing at full speed in his study, recognized by then as the head of the German refugee colony in Turkey, cooperating to the best of his opportuni-ties and ability with such United States based organizations as the Office of Strategic Services and the International Rescue and Relief Committee—and muttering in helpless rage at Stauffenberg, that effete disciple of Stefan George, who in July 1944 had muffed the chance of shooting Hitler at point blank range.

Let what was stated initially in this biographical sketch be re-called, that the present work on its publication was well received in West Germany and neighboring parts of Europe. *Ortsbestimmung der Gegenwart* was hailed as "the most significant work in the his-torical and sociological literature of the postwar period in Ger-many," as "a scholarly and a moral event," and as a work likely to replace "the Cassandra-like panic about 'Decline of the West' with a healthy measure of dignity and reflection." Reviewers expressed admiration for the author's "militant humanism," his "courage in formulating the radical questions," and his "cheerful confidence" which ever "keeps him a step or two ahead of the bitterness of his insights." The three volumes were said to display "a structure of language and of mind of almost architectonic beauty," and to have been written with "a cool head and a seething heart." One reviewer professed himself astounded by "the wealth of deep and often star-tling insights that occur throughout the presentation," and another expressed confidence that Rüstow's *Ortsbestimmung* would take its place among the major syntheses of philosophy of history in the great European liberal tradition, including Jakob Burckhardt's *Re-flections on World History* and Benjamin Constant's *On Violence in History*.

On his return to Germany, the author from his Heidelberg base threw himself with sexagenarian, pent-up, youthful vigor into the fray of intellectual, economic, and political debate, doing battle for a *social* market economy (from his lips the adjective always carried more emphasis than from those of others), conferring, lecturing, writing, and attracting a widening circle of students, younger col-leagues, and political associates, and receiving awards and decora-tions. He became the founder of the Aktionsgemeinschaft Soziale Marktwirtschaft and its president from 1955 to 1962, and one of three trustees of the *Frankfurter Allgemeine Zeitung*, the leading German daily. Many German contemporaries considered him to have furnished the intellectual and philosophical foundations for Ludwig Erhard's "economic miracle," and one of the most charac-teristic provisions of the Bonn constitution, the so-called "construc-tive vote of no confidence," goes back in part to Rüstow's earlier critique of the Weimar constitution.[13] But Rüstow deeply resented what he considered Adenauer's undemocratic highhandedness and Erhard's excessive subservience to *Der Alte*. The Festschrift pub-lished on his seventieth birthday included contributions by the Fed-eral German Republic's first president, Theodor Heuss (like Rüstow himself of the social-liberal persuasion).[14]

He was instrumental in reviving the German Political Science Association, whose president he became in 1954-1956, and in bringing Carl J. Friedrich from Harvard and Dolf Sternberger from Frankfurt to fill the new chair in political science at Heidelberg. In 1962 the Free Hanseatic City of Hamburg awarded him its newly established annual Baron vom Stein prize; he accepted it with a lecture in which he sought to restate the promise and the failure of Prussian liberalism during Stein's great ministry after the military defeat of 1806 as a practical lesson for the Germany of the 1960s.[15]

This varied, at times frenetic, activity did not abate upon Rüstow's official retirement in 1956, at the age of seventy-one, from his university chair. But now he also found time to write more reflective articles full of disciplined passion. These turned out to be inspired, perhaps to his own surprise, not by his adult love for Hesiod or Parmenides, but by more deeply engraved childhood experiences like the tragedy of Lutheranism or the biblical succession from Abraham to Saint Paul.[16] One of the last was an essay on the correct philological interpretation of that mistranslated "passage dear to all of us [sic] from our youthful years from Luther's version of the gospels": Ἐντὸς ὑμῶν ἐστὶν.[17]

On 30 June 1963 Alexander Rüstow died in Heidelberg of complications of lymphal cancer only a fortnight after completing, on his sickbed, the page proof of the second edition of volume 2 of *Ortsbestimmung der Gegenwart*.

DAR

AUTHOR'S FOREWORD (1949)

To write this German book I had to emigrate in 1933 from a Germany whose stifling atmosphere after Hitler's conquest left me no air to breathe. The most important and pressing task imposed by the catastrophic world situation upon historian and sociologist alike, it seemed to me, was to determine just what had really happened and just what position we really occupy on the historical continuum. Since then I have been engaged in this attempt to fix our bearings in relation to the present, to identify the historic coordinates of our time.

I am deeply indebted to the new Turkey, brought into being and into the orbit of Western culture by Atatürk, for the privilege of having been able to devote myself to scholarly pursuits from that time till today. Along with numerous other refugee colleagues, I was invited to cooperate in this acculturation process under quite ideal conditions.

Now that the manuscript has already assumed dimensions quite beyond its projected size, and after I have twice almost followed the old Horatian admonition, *nonum premere in annum*, I now face the alternative of publishing it in its present form with all its shortcomings, or of postponing publication to an indefinite and unforeseeable future. Inasmuch as thoughts are not private property but a good held in trust, I felt I could no longer justify such a delay. And the longer I hesitated the greater grew my awareness that the task, apart from the added aggravations arising from my situation as a refugee, exceeded by far the powers of one individual, and that it required the broadest possible cooperation on the part of colleagues. What I offer now is but a modest initial contribution to this cooperative work, a contribution that, at best, may have warrant to console itself by recalling Goethe's saying about the creativity of the inadequate.*

I owe thanks to many friends for their tireless, comradely urging, and in the highest measure to Wilhelm Röpke. He repeatedly and

* The allusion appears to be to the closing lines of *Faust*: "Das Unzulängliche / Hier wird's Ereignis, . . . Das Ewig-Weibliche / Zieht uns Hinan." [Editor's note.]

persuasively pointed out that in the current state of affairs time was of the essence. Nevertheless, I still felt I could not be responsible for immediate publication, because of the way my work had been originally planned. Finally, Röpke himself most effectively relieved me of the agonizing pressure of this inner conflict. He did so by making available to international public opinion a consistent critical and political programmatic world view, based upon our shared convictions and findings, in his four interrelated books published since 1942: *Die Gesellschaftskrisis der Gegenwart, Civitas humana, Internationale Ordnung,* and *Die deutsche Frage*—all underpinned by his treatise on political economy, *Lehre von der Wirtschaft.*

Of my book's deficiencies and unevennesses, I am more keenly aware than anyone. The greater part and the most grievous of them result from the fact that my path led straight across the demarcated technical areas of scores of special disciplines. It was neither dilettante rashness nor cavalier arrogance that led me to overlook the perils of such a procedure: "The situation prevailing in historical science today compels us to cross the traditional boundary lines of the special branches of scholarship for the simple reason that the problems that are actual and fruitful today extend right through them. As nobody can be a universal specialist, each one is dependent upon the corrective and complementary cooperation of different specialists. All that can be rightly demanded is that a scholar be a real expert in one area at least, that starting out from there he bring the requisite perceptiveness to the other areas and, finally, that he exercise the requisite self-control and accuracy."[1] Such a necessity typically arises at turning points in the history of ideas. When the situation is, after due filtering, becalmed and stabilized again, and when the new viewpoints and methods are accorded recognition and acceptance, the domains of specialists can again be staked out, fenced in, and left to them for undisturbed and leisurely concentrated revision.

Given the vastness of the area under study, obviously only broad outlines could be sketched here. From time to time, however, I have gone into individual points in some detail in order to provide a precise verification of these general lines. I have also taken issue with the specialist literature in part regarding important passages and in part regarding some that were singled out accidentally. Such a procedure could be defined as a series of exploratory drillings or probes; it is to be hoped that it will not only be considered fitting but enlivening as well.

Every book, as Lichtenberg once wrote, has many authors. In periods of the cult of personality one often saw something derogatory in this fact and therefore suppressed and hid it as much as possible. On the contrary, I view it as highly gratifying and gladdening proof of the eminently social, cooperative, and commutative character of all science, of the belief in the community of thinkers. Accordingly, not only have I cited my coauthors wherever I could identify them, but going beyond the customary practice, I have also let them speak for themselves whether or not I first owed the insight to the author in question, or merely found it confirmed in his writings subsequently: *vivant qui ante nos nostra dixerunt!*

I believe in this community of thinkers to which I feel deeply obligated. It finds an especially beneficent sanction in the experience of convergence, in the often truly astonishing concordance with others who, though starting out from wholly different points of view and procedures and though striking out along wholly different paths, have arrived exactly at the same finding. Of late this experience of convergence has been so frequent that I view it as symptomatic of what is transpiring in the field of the history of ideas. And this is most reassuring, for in a time so out of joint as ours one could sooner have expected the very opposite. Such a development seems to prove that the universal-historical earthquake, along with the multiple calamities it has wrought, has also torn down dividing walls and laid bare fundamental facts now discernible in the accrued terrain. Let us take this time in the history of ideas with the heightened possibility it affords for understanding things to the best of our abilities—nobody knows how long it will last.

Some readers may miss in my text any references to Arnold J. Toynbee. The six volumes of his *Study of History* already published (the complete work as planned is to consist of twelve volumes) represent a truly superb achievement in terms of mastery of the material and of intellectual penetration. Our points of departure and the way we formulate our questions differ so markedly that without a preliminary fundamental discussion, to which I hope to get around soon, the effects of any particularized references would unavoidably have been distorting and misleading.

The very opposite reason explains the absence of any reference to Alfred Weber and his "cultural history as cultural sociology," a work, moreover, whose historical framework is of broader scope than mine. We both stand on the ground of the Vienna school of ethnography and its epoch-making retroactive enlargement of our historic space. We both work with the scientific tools of the sociologist as they have been developed from Karl Marx to Max

Weber for the analysis of historical interconnections. There is no
better formulation of what I consider to be the fundamental question than that found in Alfred Weber's own words: "The core of our
question is: where do we actually find ourselves in the stream of history, not as an individual people, but as mankind borne by this
stream. What is this stream accomplishing with us? We have the
feeling that it is bent upon carrying us into a new existence at an
enormous, nay at a soaring speed." "Ours is the need to clarify the
unprecedentedly muddled present situation, to orient ourselves
with regard to its significance, by surveying the motive force of the
stream of history, its course, its configurations and its dynamics, in
the hope that we can thereby learn something about our own fate."
These words appear on the first page of *Kulturgeschichte als Kultursoziologie*,[2] a work whose impetus laid the foundation of a cultural
sociology from the viewpoint of universal history. We younger
scholars can hope only that our subsequent attempts may not be
unworthy of this admirable model.

"I am ever more convinced with each passing day that theoretical
work accomplishes more in the world than practical work; once the
realm of the idea is revolutionized, reality does not bear up." This
conviction, as formulated by Hegel,[3] also lies at the base of my work.
It is becoming customary to oppose it with the trivial truism that
human nature, as experience teaches, by and large, always and
everywhere, remains the same. All efforts to change it therefore are
utopian and doomed to failure.

The factual core of this objection hits the mark—fortunately. For
without this constant of human nature there would be no unity of
human culture and history, no possibility of understanding and of
agreement. Just as little would there be the possibility of identifying the dimensions of what, anthropologically, is of the human essence, is normal and healthy. But this fact by no means precludes
the possibility of "reforming the world." Though human nature is
indeed immutable, pursuing its innate endowment, the same does
not hold for the enormous range of variation of possible sociological
situations to which the same human nature reacts differently. All
momentous historical changes consist of such a change of sociological situations, and to a great extent they are responsive to deliberately exercised human causation. Such changes of the sociological
situation have been effected by deliberate human causation—in
Germany in 1933, 1945, and 1948, for example, and we are all familiar with their sweeping consequences. Here the mechanism of causation, for instance, did not first require a corresponding change on
the part of each individual so that the total change could be brought

about by a summation of these individual changes. Rather, the very opposite occurred, in that the change of the situation was wrought by the decision of a few over the heads of the many; only subsequently did the thus-altered total situation powerfully and almost irresistibly affect each individual. This typical mechanism of causation as such is completely neutral: it can as easily be applied for positive or negative ends, for bettering or worsening the world. Therein, of course, lies an opportunity as well as a danger. It is incumbent on us to combat the danger and to exploit the opportunity.

It is here too that history's function in human life is determined. That "the present is understood exclusively by elucidation of the past"[4] is absolutely true, but it still leaves open the question as to what is gained by such an understanding of the present.

Our will is directed from the present toward the future, and this future willed by us is obviously the real sphere of the *pros hémas* in the ethical terminology of the Stoics—of that which concerns us and for which we are responsible. Each one of us, more or less consciously, holds some notion of such a future goal. It can oscillate between the conservative wish that everything remain as is, and the revolutionary will to bring about a radical upheaval. It is each time polarizingly coupled with its despised and combatted opposite. But we know now, especially since the historicism of the nineteenth century, that the proposition *ex nihilo nihil*—out of nothing, nothing comes—holds true for history, too. Every historical event has its own prehistory, its historical roots from which it has grown and can be understood as the continuation and consequence of the latter. According to the goal for the future that we espouse and strive for, and toward which we orient our efforts, we now search in the past for the prehistory, flowing into the present, of what we strive for as future goal on the basis of the present: for that historical line whose continuation yields the direction toward the future for which we strive. In other words, the extension backward of the desired forward direction is the espoused basic coordinate of history.

Accordingly, and conversely, the prehistory of what we fight against in the present and on behalf of the future is what we retroactively and negatively appraise in history as harmful and baleful. From the anthropological conviction that what we consider good and worth striving for is ultimately identical with the standards of uncorrupted human nature, it necessarily follows that a pathogenic historico-sociological primal situation is bound to be bared in respect to every corruption that has continuing effects. With Jakob Burckhardt we must approach history "as it were as a pathologist"; with Hölderlin we must ask: "How did it begin? Who brought the curse?" Thus the historian as a culture-critic, in diagnosis and therapy, holds the responsibility-laden office of a *medicus rei publicae*, a physician of the commonwealth. Only by such a truly radical understanding, literally reaching to the roots, can all what is opposed to the "ought" really be uprooted and the entanglement that thus ensued be unraveled: *comprehendendo solvitur*—through understanding it is solved.

We can not treat here the related question: is such a valuation and disvaluation purely subjective and arbitrary, or does an objective measure, a trans-subjective criterion for it exist? As the reader must have gathered, I am convinced that such a universally valid standard exists and that it lies precisely in the immutable nature of man, in those fleshly tables of the heart of which Saint Paul speaks.[5] In the secularizing further development of the scholastic doctrine of *lumen naturale* this anthropological standpoint became almost a common property in the Enlightenment of the eighteenth century, although the difficulties of its realization were underestimated in the flush of youthful enthusiasm. That is one of the points at which a spiral-shaped return to the eighteenth century would be required. On the other hand, because the assertion that "man learns what he is from history" still holds true, and because the validity of this truth has further deepened since the horizon-widening inclusion of ethnology into history, it is not a question of applying the anthropological standard to history ready-made and from the outside. Rather, it is one of developing this standard in a productive reciprocity with historical knowledge and of constantly testing and corroborating it anew.

"Who wants to take correct concepts from the present without knowing the future? The future determines the present, and the latter the past." "We live in the feeling of the future and only therewith do we unseal the past." The historian "is the man to tell his contemporaries the particular location of history on which they stand, the future spaces into which the voices of our history call."[6] When in an ancient Greek proemium the Muses call upon prophetic poets and thinkers to proclaim the present, the future and the past,[7] the triadic solemnity of this archaic-sacred formula expresses a primordial feeling for the deep and the inner connectedness of these three concerns.

Nevertheless, the historian can assume an active or passive, energetic or tolerant, wishful and volitional, or merely expectant, perhaps even fearful, stance toward the future envisaged by him. Nor need he be clearly conscious of his attitude and of its connection with his view of history. But in any transformation, no matter how blurred, the structure shown holds true for every view of history and historiography. Even its lowest level, the bare chronicle, is invisibly shaped by a future direction borne by the wish and the expectation that things remain and continue as heretofore, that the rule and succession to the throne of the dynasty, under which and for which the chronicler writes, continue in the future with the same unshakable monotony with which he records it. Even Ranke's quietistic and allegedly objective historical writing has as background the halcyon Indian summer of the Biedermeier period with its own unspoken feeling of "Verweile doch, du bist so schön": "Tarry a while, thou art so fair!"

On the basis of this fundamental methodological conviction I have resolved to leave no doubt of any kind about what I affirm and reject in the past, present, or future. I affirm freedom and reject domination, I affirm humaneness and reject barbarism, I affirm peace and reject violence. These pairs of opposites are the great poles between which the drama of universal history is enacted. Our present stands in the middle of a crucial, worldwide, battle between freedom and an extreme form of barbarism and violent domination. Our future will depend on the outcome of this battle. This combat situation consciously determines the standpoint of this book and of all my work. As historian and sociologist I inquire into the specific character and the historical origin of every tyranny that threatens us today, and into the origin and changing fates of that tyranny-opposing freedom whose defense has been entrusted to us. That question lies at the base of Parts 1 and 2 of the present work, whereas the concluding Part 3 is devoted to an analysis of the present situation created by this basic conflict.

Those who judge the present situation soberly with the eyes of nonparticipant observers might very well conclude that our cause is none too hopeful and that, all things considered, the chances against it outweigh those in its favor. But for those who know that they are committed to the cause of freedom for good or ill, for those who see in freedom the only meaning of this experiment in anthropogenesis, such a threat will be but one more reason for them to stake their all, to do their bit, and to leave the rest to universal history, pursuant to the courageous utterance of William of Orange: "It is not at all necessary to hope in order to endeavor, nor to succeed in order to persevere."

If Goethe was right when he declared that nobody can judge history save him who has experienced it for himself, then it has been a long time since any generation has been called upon to render historical judgment in such measure as has our own.

FREEDOM
AND
DOMINATION

INTRODUCTION

1. The Widening of Our Historical Horizon

Down to the eighteenth century Genesis and Homer were considered the oldest records of mankind. As recently as 1818 Goethe laid it down as a hallmark of an educated person "to be able to give to himself an account of three thousand years."[1] The decipherment of hieroglyphics and of cuneiform writing and archaeological excavations in the Near East in the nineteenth century extended this range of history backward by another two or three millennia.

Only in the early decades of the twentieth century did there come about that grand synthesis of historical geology, genetics, anthropology, ethnography, archaeology, and history that extended our horizons geographically around the globe and temporally to the first origins of man, the development of the species *homo*; that is, to about a million years.

This implies not only a more than hundredfold deepening of our perspective but also a total redefinition of our mental system of coordinates. The generation of our parents could still assume that the condition of mankind prevailing in the past few thousand years was its normal state of existence. Instead, we shall see that these last millennia are part of a late, very special, and extreme development, that within the newly formed image of human history they come to lie not at the center but at the outer edge.

A culture can be fully understood only by tracing its historic roots. The roots of all contemporary civilization go back beyond the six-thousand-year horizon of written history, since writing itself is a typical product of civilization. And a "radical" critique of civilization and reassessment of our cultural self-consciousness—that is, a critique and reassessment going to the very roots—such as is here intended must take its starting point precisely from this origin of civilization and from the circumstances surrounding it. That is, it must reach back to a period that only since this last great widening of our horizons has come within the historical range. As Goethe said on another occasion, "There can in our days be no doubt that world history must be rewritten from time to time." "Was there ever an epoch which made such rewriting as necessary as does our own?"[2]

2. The Significance of Ethnography for the Science of History

Ethnography until the nineteenth century was chiefly limited to accumulating a vast number of observations in literature and of artifacts in museums, then classifying this material and recording resemblances between various parts of it. In so doing, ethnographers assumed that whatever was more primitive, simpler, even coarser must also be older. This implied that all peoples since the development (or creation) of man had undergone the same progressive development from lower to higher stages in which we ourselves—because of our own admirable qualities, of course—had advanced furthest, whereas primitive peoples—because of the regrettable defects of their endowment—had become arrested at earlier stages of the same course of development, condemned, as it were, forever to sit in preparatory school while we already had graduated from college. In sum, the prevailing view was that all societies had evolved along parallel lines, although the lines were of shorter or longer duration.

To this theory of parallel evolution later research opposed a more complex evolutionary scheme whereby human development, like a family tree, split off into various branches, allowing multiple intersections among the resulting lines of cultural descent. The first impetus to this newer theory came from the geographer Friedrich Ratzel (1844-1904), who assumed that the problem of geographic spread of ethnographic details could be resolved, as could the corresponding problems in the geography of plants and animals, by reconstructing the "migrations" of peoples and cultures. This view was applied to ethnology by several of Ratzel's students, including the imaginative and organizationally talented but undisciplined Leo Frobenius (1873-1938) and the more methodical and exact Fritz Graebner (1877-1934), who had been trained as a historian. The leadership in this school of ethnography soon devolved on Father Wilhelm Schmidt and his disciple Father Wilhelm Koppers, who had at their disposal the vast descriptive material gathered by members of their missionary order, Societas Verbi Divini. This "Vienna school" of ethnography in 1900 began publishing the bimonthly review *Anthropos*. A systematic compendium of its findings is the work by Schmidt and Koppers, *Völker und Kulturen I: Gesellschaft und Wirtschaft der Völker* (Regensburg, 1924; published as part 3 of the collective work *Der Mensch aller Zeiten*). Later findings are contained in Wilhelm Schmidt's major work on religious history, *Der Ursprung der Gottesidee* (vols. 1-7, Münster, 1912-1935).

Some of these works have been criticized for scholastic over-subtlety—and no doubt it is difficult to escape the drawbacks of one's advantages. But—precisely because I personally feel free of any denominational ties—I must consider it inadmissible that the findings of the Vienna school of ethnography should be rejected because many of its leading representatives are Catholic priests.

The most serious obstacles to a general acceptance of the "diffusionist" thesis of the cultural-historical school of ethnography are the connections it draws between cultural phenomena separated by enormous geographic distances. But the geographic spread of the human race itself proves *a fortiori* the possibility of such far-flung migratory connections.

A synthesis of the findings of geology, archaelogy, and ethnography has been undertaken in Oswald Menghin's monumental *Weltgeschichte der Steinzeit* (Vienna, 1931). The corroboration of the research of the Vienna school into cultural genealogy by the findings of archaeologists and historical geologists provided for both sides an important confirmation. An excellent brief summary of these converging findings, enriched by the author's own critical perspective on universal history, will be found in Fritz Kern, *Die Anfänge der Weltgeschichte* (Leipzig, 1933).

3. THE HISTORY OF THE SUPERSTRATIFICATION HYPOTHESIS

The recognition of the fundamental role in world history of the phenomenon of *Überlagerung*, or superstratification, goes back to the great Arab sociologist Ibn Khaldun (1332-1406), who abstracted it from the Arab conquests, a superstratification whose results were before his very eyes.

The Frankish superstratification of Gaul, also still in vivid memory, and with factural repercussions in the social structure of prerevolutionary France, gave rise to the so-called Franco-Gallia controversy, begun by François Hotman (1524-1590), author of *Franco-Gallia* (1574), and Jean Bodin (1530-1598). This controversy reached its climax with the three-volume *Histoire de l'ancien gouvernement de la France* by Comte Henri de Boulainvilliers (1658-1727) who deduced the seignorial rights of the nobility from the fact that they were the heirs in law of the original conquerors. David Hume (1711-1776), too, was clear in his own mind about the role of violence in the origin of the state.

A remarkably generalized formulation of the superstratification thesis is found in Condorcet, who wrote (1794) that "the origins of feudalism . . . can be observed each time when the same territory has been occupied by two peoples between whom victory has established an hereditary inequality."[3] And Augustin Thierry (1796-1856) asserts more generally that "each nation" has been "created by the mixture of several races: the race of the invaders . . . and the race of those invaded."

In contrast, Jules Michelet (1798-1874) in his *Histoire de France* (1833-1862) points back to a view of the French nation as a single historical entity. The truth would seem to lie in a perspective that gave its due to each of these opposing viewpoints.

"The history of all hitherto existing societies is the history of class struggles." This famous thesis, with which Karl Marx opened the *Communist Manifesto* (1848), thus is at bottom nothing but a transposition into generalizing and Hegelian-absolute terms of a view that prevailed in French historiography from the time of the revolution until Michelet.

Superstratification as a general phenomenon was placed at the center of the political sociology of Ludwig Gumplowicz (1838-1909) and of Franz Oppenheimer (1864-1942), through whose work the present author was first introduced to the thesis.[4] In the United States, Lester F. Ward (1841-1913) followed Gumplowicz and Gustav Ratzenhofer (1842-1904) in developing the hypothesis.

The superstratification thesis still encounters a certain amount of squeamishness and irritable denial, even by persons unable to deny the overwhelming evidence on which it rests. This ambivalent reaction may be explained by the fact that, as we shall see, all political organization in higher cultures or civilizations, originating as it does in superstratification, includes two diametrically opposite structures: the confederative or communal structure of leadership and the societal structure of domination. It is only natural to try to suppress the unedifying part of the existing polarity and to treat attempts at exposing it as so many acts of spite or malice. The more so since, on the part of many proponents, and especially the Marxists among them, such a thersitical desire to expose and debunk was indeed often at work.

Marxism has additionally confused the discussion totally by introducing the element of pure domination as one of the defining elements into its very conception of the state—a procedure that amounts to a polemical *petitio principii*. To say that "the state originated in conquest," in any case, gives an excessively narrow formulation to the superstratification thesis. It invites the objection that the confederations of the Iroquois or the founding of the Swiss confederacy give examples of the possibility of the peaceful formation of states. The latter example in particular makes it clear that the fear of being conquered also can prompt political unification. And if we were to restrict the term *state* to those forms originating in conquest, what are we to call the corresponding political structures in classless, single-layered human groups?

The prehistoric conditions in which superstratification could take place have been illuminated for the first time through the researches of the Vienna school; yet prehistoric and ethnographic research into the subject is still in rapid flux. To make my own presentation more concrete, I have often gone into some detail based on my own as yet unpublished studies. But I should like to emphasize at this point that all the further ideas of this book in no way depend on these more or less hypothetical details. The indispensable assertion underlying the remainder is merely the historic fact of *Überlagerung*, or superstratification, as such. And this historic fact is known even from recorded history, in such a large number of examples and in such detail that it cannot be doubted. Even so vehement an opponent of the Vienna school as Richard Thurnwald writes: "Indeed these early agricultural regions of the archaic cultures are time and again overrun by gatherers and herders, and the peasants made to pay tribute."[5] And: "Such occurrences took place at various points on the globe and at different times, starting from similar preconditions and following the same social-psychological scheme, even though the details differed." The fact of superstratification itself thus is conceded on all sides. That elaborations of, and judgments on, that fact are inhibited by squeamishness is another matter.

As Fritz Kern has written, "Under historic conditions we never see a pure peasantry . . . producing an upper stratum with a weapons monopoly above the unarmed masses of laborers. . . . Class divisions are alien to the democratic peasant culture. A lordly culture never appears in history as the result of peaceful accumulation of goods." "Hence the supperincumbency thesis of Schmidt and Oppenheimer is in need of much refinement, but, once so revised, contains a sound core." ". . . Only superincumbency made possible the brilliant archaeological remains of the lords of fortress and land. Pyramids could not be built until the formerly free river peasants had to a very considerable degree been transformed into *fellahs*."[6]

To what extent the consciousness of the importance of such insights is spreading is clearly demonstrated in a lecture titled "Rational and Irrational Elements in Contemporary Society," delivered by Karl Mannheim in London in 1934, which I may here be permitted to quote at some length:

Thanks to the investigation carried out by ethnologists and sociologists we know . . . that all the highly developed cultures in history originated from the forcible conquest of autochthonous communities, mostly peaceful peasantries, by nomadic peoples. This element of coercion penetrated so deeply into the otherwise pacific peasant society that it dominated its whole structure. It is because this contradiction, which underlay the original social situation, has never, from the earliest times until to-day been eradicated, that contemporary society is still so very antithetical in character. . . . The "ultima ratio," both in our external political relations and in our final decisions in international politics, is force.

Psychologists who study only the working of the mind of the individual and pay no attention to its relation to the totality of the social process are apt to forget that the decisive fact is not that the sadistic element is latent in the human psyche, but that the organization of society has, from nomadic times till our own day, given this irrationality an objective function.

. . . Thus it follows that the most urgent task in the immediate future will be to establish a closer cooperation between the psychologist, the historian, the political scientist, and the sociologist.[7]

PART ONE

The Origins of Domination

*For only through elucidation of the
past can we grasp the meaning of the
present.*

Goethe

CHAPTER I

The Rise of High Cultures

1. THE LAW OF THE CULTURE PYRAMID

In its total expanse, the whole particular development that encompasses all the hitherto existing cultures of mankind occurs in the last ten thousand years of human history. If we equate the time elapsed between the emergence of man and the present to one century, the rise and development of all high cultures (or civilizations) would occur exclusively in the last year of that century. We have no indications that the level of culture now exhibited by extant so-called primitive peoples had ever been surpassed previously.

How is it possible that cultures were formed, that the threshold of so-called primitiveness was crossed only in the last ten thousand years of the hundredfold longer period since man's emergence, only in the last year of this "century" of ten millennia?

From a sociological standpoint this question can be answered easily. Any high culture presupposes a very high degree of division of labor and specialization. Whole groups of the population have to be permanently set free for employment in a variety of activities of a higher mental kind, more or less removed from the direct production of food. Obviously a specialization of this type is out of the question for a horde of thirty members. Nor does a tribe of three hundred or three thousand members even remotely provide a sufficient basis for specialization.

Because primitives practice an extensive type of cultivation, the land used for subsistence per person is correspondingly large. When the number of persons belonging to such a coexisting group increases beyond a given and relatively low figure, the area required for effective cultivation becomes so large and the resulting inconveniences so irksome and unproductive that the group inevitably splits up. Thus limits of a purely economic character are imposed upon the numerical size of groups living together under primitive ethnological conditions.

As civilizations, however, are bound up with a highly specialized division of labor presupposing a correspondingly large homogeneous population, an elementary and necessary interconnection ensues that establishes a close proportion between size of population and cultural level. We could call this the law of correlation between the width of the base and the potential height of the apex of the *culture pyramid*.

A sociological base sufficiently broad for the formation of high cultures was first constituted by the occurrence throughout history of the phenomenon of superstratification, by the formation of the first "empires" over an extensive territory by way of conquest. Obviously, this required fulfillment of two preconditions: a settled lower stratum, economically productive enough to create surpluses considerably above its own minimum needs that would make conquest a tempting and lucrative prospect, but capable of little military resistance; and an upper stratum militarily and organizationally qualified to play the conqueror's role and to effect the superstratification. Both prerequisites, as we shall see, are of recent date, and the effect of their conjunction was felt for the first time in the first half of the last ten thousand years.

What I have called the sociological law of the culture pyramid had already been clearly formulated by the French sociologist, social statistician, and social reformer Adolphe Coste (1842-1901):

> This principal phenomenon from which all the others proceed, in my opinion, is the multiplication of persons making up society. This is what I call the demotic condition of progress.
>
> . . . I do not mean simply to speak of absolute development of the population: I mean to speak of the extension of the same political, doctrinal, economic discipline to an ever-increasing grouping of the population. Hence it is more a matter of unification than of numerical growth. If a particular part of the world is peopled with 100 millions of inhabitants and divided into a hundred thousand savage hordes of a thousand persons each, the social state will be rudimentary, barely above that of an animal grouping. If these same 100 million, in the same part of the world, brought together under one state, obeying identical laws, are united by a faith and common hopes and know how to expend their efforts in concert, the result will be a prodigious civilization, such as we have not yet been privileged to know.
> . . .
> The specialization of functions is established only by virtue of the social unification of populations. . . . This is why I contend

that the diversification of functions, the specialization of co-
operators, and the success of the inventors are merely the consequences of the increase of the unified population.[1]

2. The Rise of Nomadism

The last ice age with its aftereffects was the last great change in the
climatic and geographic conditions of our planet, and it had a crucial
impact upon mankind's development. According to the customary
view, as established by Albrecht Penck, the whole ice age, or Di-
luvium, encompasses four glacial epochs and three interglacial periods, after which there begins a new geological period, the Alluvium.

In reality, there is not a single geological or other criterion that
would substantiate the view that the end of the fourth and (up to
now) last thrust of ice brought a whole geological age to a close, after
which it was supposedly succeeded by another. Only a naïve egocen-
trism could see a new geological age beginning expressly for our
present time and the few millennia of *spatium historicum* in the old
sense. Rather, everything supports the view that we are still in the
ice age as much as ever and, consequently, in its fourth interglacial
period.

The division among geological ages is by no means merely a superficial question of definition. Rather, it has a fundamental morphological importance for the structure of our historical consciousness. From this point of view, therefore, it is important to drop the
naïve distinction between Diluvian and Alluvian and set the fourth
interim of the ice age, the Quaternary era, in place of the Alluvium.
The Quaternary era, which began with the first of the (hitherto) four
ice ages about four to six hundred thousand years ago, was experienced by human beings at first hand.

The latest ice age began about forty-five thousand years ago,
reached its peak twenty-five thousand years ago, and its close barely
ten thousand years ago. During this period, the average global
temperature was about eight degrees Celsius lower than at present.
The Alps formed one large glacier, and an ice sheet covered Scan-
dinavia, the Baltic Sea, and Finland, even stretching into Russia.
The central Asian mountain ranges and the Iranian-Armenian-
Anatolian mountain barrier were partially glaciated and yet passable.

Albrecht Penck, doyen of geology, impressively described the
changes: "Amu Darya and Syr Darya were well-watered and filled

Lake Aral. This inland sea flowed through the Uzboi and likewise spilled over into the Caspian Sea, the latter via the Manych into the Black Sea, . . . [holding] the Bosporus around sixty meters above the surface of the Mediterranean. . . . Its drainage area . . . probably extended up to central Asia." Penck further describes a "giant tributary" that ran through the Dardanelles valley and combined with waters from rivers and mountains, so that the meltwater of the entire Caucasus was glaciated. The Dardanelles in this form was not unlike the later Saint Lawrence, traversing inland lakes and probably containing a waterfall similar to Niagara Falls. In effect, this interconnecting body of water, with a multiple mountain barrier, separated the plains to the north from those to the south. Eastwards the same plains were also locked in by the Altaic mountain barrier and the Himalayas. Thus there were obstructions to the south, north, and east; the Urals, in the west, were probably not a barrier. However, Penck says that between the southern edge of the ice and the northern shore of the Caspian Sea there was a gateway to the west about five hundred kilometers wide, with the Volga as a frontier river. This uninviting gateway consisted of subpolar tundra, with ice and snow in the winter, and high, glacial water from the Volga in the summer, Because of more favorable European climatic conditions, there was little inducement to take advantage of this gateway eastward. Asians, subjected to the rigors of the ice age, did not consider escape through the northwest; the primitive culture did not encourage attempts to overcome geography.

The result: During the last ice age a Eurasian lowland region, essentially consisting of western Siberia, was sealed off, absolutely and practically, from the rest of the world. This region had already been populated by primitive hunters who generally fashioned their weapons and tools of bone. These people, however, had been cut off from the rest of humanity for thousands of years, deprived of the possibility of escaping the increasing harshness of the climate and the shrinkage of their living space by migrating southward. They were dependent solely on themselves and the animals that shared this ice-prison with them. But necessity is man's sixth sense. So this calamity, which had pushed the men and animals jointly affected by it into a symbiotic work community, led to a saving and productive solution: stockbreeding and nomadism.

Hunting wild herd animals was originally an activity carried out in natural response to the situation: a horde of hunters simply followed a herd on its seasonally fluctuating grazing paths. Thus the hunters became ever more familiar with the life habits of "their" herd. If the hunters wanted to avoid disaster, they had to learn how to protect pregnant animals, drive away predators—in short, how to manage the herd. The harder the times became, the more the hunters became aware of their dependence on preserving the stocks of animals. Thus evolved a gradual and imperceptible transition from hunting to solicitous care, what remained constant at first being the benefit accruing from the killing of individual animals. Such transitions from hunting to animal husbandry can still be seen today, particularly in regard to the reindeer.

Restrictions, some of them even sanctioned by religion, on the killing of wild animals developed early among the hunters. The attendant deity grows angry with the hunter who kills more than he needs. The bad conscience toward the animal itself, which is expressed in the legend of Saint Hubert and probably forms an essential root of totemism, produces an effect in the same direction. The modern licensed hunter and gamewarden also have a responsible attitude toward their quarry, similarly coupled with a half rational, half irrational justification. Johann Jacob Reinhard (1714-1772) rightly regarded hunting "as a kind of wild stock breeding."

In hunting wild animals that live dispersed, the hunter must lie in wait for the quarry: he catches sight only of individual animals for a brief time and is therefore poised with concentrated energy for the kill; he is keyed to a fever pitch to bring down the quarry for which he is lying in ambush. It is quite otherwise when it is a matter of hunting animal herds; there a solicitous attitude particularly suggests itself because the hunter has the whole population of the herd, hence its increase or decrease, constantly in his purview. Moreover, the hunter group, migrating year after year with the same herd (transhumance) gets to know its herd intimately and develops a kind of kinship feeling with it. Thus the transition from hunting animals to breeding them is continuous and all but inevitable.

The natural herds in which wild gregarious animals of the steppes live and in which they migrate seasonally are quite sizable. Nomads acting as herdsmen acquired an influence over the size and composition of the herd, an influence that grew with their experience as herdsmen; yet the natural size of the herd must usually have been considered the optimum.

The size of the nomad group in question must correspond to that of a large herd if it is to be able to manage the herd successfully. Such management is beyond the capacity of an individual family. Once this group grew considerably beyond the nuclear family, it required, at the same time, a close-knit solidarity, the greatest possible unity, and the strictest leadership authority. The result was the patriarchal extended family as the characteristic life-style of all nomads. It presents, above and beyond the small family, the closest kinship group: genealogical considerations naturally play a special role for stock breeders. It stands under the dictatorial leadership of the patriarch, which is viewed as the extended, broadened, and strengthened authority of the family-father and therefore beyond any discussion. Leadership, moreover, requires not just physical strength (as among hunters) but circumspection, calm, and—above all—experience. The most difficult and dangerous situations that could suddenly arise during nomadic migration were those that occurred most rarely, those for which the chance of having at one time experienced them—and accordingly learned to cope with them—was proportionate to age. On the other hand, the relatively comfortable and hazard-free way of life of the nomad, unlike that of the hunter, fostered longevity. These factors encouraged the absolutist authority of the patriarch and a special reverence for old age with its pondered experience and wisdom.

The herd, for its part, had to have a certain number of head per nomad so that the nomadic group could live from it. If the size of the herd, through an epidemic or other misfortune, dropped below the minimum, or if the herd was destroyed, the herdsman had no alternative but to try to join a luckier and richer group with a large surplus herd. Such persons were indigents and supplicants; all they had to offer was their labor. It is likely that such supplicants came into the family as servants—a role that later and probably under influence from other cultures passed over into that of an actual slave.

Quite unlike the cultivators, the nomads left their dead behind and lost even spatial contact with them. Consequently a distant, detached, and cool idea of the Beyond was formed among them, like that still encountered in the Greek Hades, Semitic Sheol, or Germanic Hel: the dead are powerless, dimly conscious shadows that disappear along with one's remembrance of them.

Because nomads have no sense of attachment to place and only the sky above remained the same, it was very difficult for them to develop a site-bound cult. On earth they constantly had to make instant decisions about migrations, rest stops, and the like. This led to the superior, rational, purposeful overview of the geographer and the strategist and prevented the rise of gloomy and superstitious constraints. Nomads also had to take an ever-active attitude toward nature and the course of the year. There was neither time nor repose for metaphysical speculation and meditation. All this was conducive to a farsighted, soberly rational, purposeful outlook, to "steppe-clarity, steppe-soberness, and steppe-rationality."[2]

The attitude of nomads to their animals was likewise marked by a sober and practical expediency. Uninhibited by superstitious tabus, they used the milk, flesh, bones, horns, skin, and hair of their animals with great technical intelligence and facility. Dogs came into use as animal power, domesticated gradually from wolves and jackals.

3. THE RISE OF THE PEASANTRY

Meanwhile a further development of planting culture had taken place south of the great Asian mountain and ice barrier, presumably on the fertile plains of Indochina and India. In this culture women exercised economic and social leadership: matriarchy was native to the region.

Neolithic planting peoples, through peaceful or warlike means, absorbed traits peculiar to totemic hunting peoples: improvements in handicraft and techniques—i.e., the active, specifically masculine, joy in tinkering and inventiveness. Continuing the arduous toil entailed in dibbling each individual plant hole separately in the ancient customary manner did not suit those who had acquired this technical attitude and who took pleasure in inventiveness. Rather, the obvious idea occurred to them of lumping together a row of discontinuously dug plant holes into a continuous furrow that could be worked like a conveyor belt: this signified the transition from the garden bed to the field, the passage from the hoe, spade, and dibble to the draw-hoe, the draw-spade, and the drawn-dibble with the help of a haft lengthening into a pole and a crossbar drawn by two women.

This newly fledged labor technique of the hand plow was combined with the transition from the vegetative (asexual) reproduction of cultivated plants to the generative (sexual) reproduction of varieties of grain, with transplanting as an intermediate stage.

This newly awakened technical sense also questioned the need for continuing the irksome and exhausting task of dragging something behind by means of a pole with a crossbar pulled by two persons. Thus the ancient, modest pulling apparatus of the sledge and of the primitive sled, with a movable roller underneath it finally developed into the two-wheeled handcart, with fixed massive disk wheels resting on the rotating axle, and pulled by two persons in the same way as the draw-hoe.

Development of a prepeasant, Late Neolithic planting culture must have occurred during the last ice age, with the hermetic sealing off of regions of the North. But now the ice age came to a close, the glaciers melted, the waters dried out, and the barriers between north and south were steadily lowered. At the same time, the possibilities for overcoming them through man's transport techniques increased. The Late Neolithic cultivators from the South and herdsmen from the North may have met probably somewhere in the Northwest (Afghanistan, eastern Tibet, or Turkestan). For the nomads this contact left strong religious traces; the oppressive magic of the cult practiced by the Late Neolithic peasants manifestly exerted a mysterious attraction on the cool rationalism of the nomads. Because herdsmen were already familiar with the primitive use of their oxen as draft animals harnessed to sledges and summer sleds, and because dragging a hand plow and a handcart using manpower was back-breaking, it was not too great a step to use the powerful and docile ox rather than man for drawing.

Owing to this adaptation, the ox first changed from a wild herd animal into a real domestic animal. Two quite different forms of animal keeping, according to origin and character, are in question here, and we should therefore strictly distinguish in concept and terminology between domestic and herd animals. With domestic animals, the animal joins man locally; with herd animals, man joins the animals in their seasonal migrations. The dog, as we saw, appeared as a self-domesticated animal among nomads. The pig and the fowl, born scavengers, seem to have joined settled cultivators as a result of a similar process of self-domestication.

Where this adoption of plow culture occurred on the part of tribes that had lived primarily as cultivators, tending cattle was a job for men; women continued their hoeing and tended the small livestock bred by cultivators, such as pigs and chickens. They were also responsible for running the household and for the storage of provisions; in short, they had the "power of the keys."

This peasant plow culture, uniting the highest developed planting culture with the highest developed stock breeding, combining the two most advanced prepeasant breeding cultures, signified an enormous cultural advance: the domestication of plants (and of small livestock) by the woman and of large livestock by the man were joined here in a productive synthesis, resulting in the most effective reciprocal increase of plants and animals alike.

At the same time this felicitous conjunction produced an important social result. For the first time, in contrast to both the matriarchy of planters and the patriarchy of hunters and nomads, there was achieved a healthy symbiotic equilibrium, in economic and social respects, between the two sexes, based upon the division and the amalgamation of labor. And this equilibrium was maintained on the basis of monogamous family life.

The gloomy, oppressive atmosphere of the Late Neolithic planting culture was also dispelled as the result of a strong infusion of clear and cool nomadic rationalism. This peasant economy and mode of life, economically productive and humanly satisfying, immediately spread eastward and westward to east Asia, North Africa, and western Europe.

This peasant life-style represents the zenith of man's human development up to then. In the more than two hundred generations that have passed since then it has economically and socially preserved itself as much as a human institution can. Here was fully achieved for the first time that equilibrium between the two sexes—lost since the original gathering stage of primordial culture, among cultivators disturbed to the disadvantage of the male, among hunters and nomads to the disadvantage of the female (albeit to a lesser degree)—an equilibrium that forms the surest foundation of monogamy. Here are also united the good features of all hitherto existing cultures, but without their drawbacks. Everything that has been achieved in cultural advances beyond this high point has up to now always been achieved at the cost of the calibrated equilibrium, stability, and health of the life situation that had been achieved in the peasantry. The task of establishing, for the third time in the history of mankind, a vital equilibrium on the level of civilization that has meanwhile been achieved, still lies before us as by far the most important and by far the most difficult of all tasks.

4. EARLY SUPERSTRATIFICATIONS AND EARLY SUPERINCUMBENCIES

a. Hunters over Cultivators

Those planting cultures that have survived independently or as a historically recognizable component in some other culture appear to be instances not of an original pure planting culture but rather of one mixed with traits, mostly totemistic, of a hunting culture. Such a mixture, moreover, seems to have come about usually through warlike rather than peaceful means.

We have to consider the possibility that superstratifications had already occurred during the struggles between hunters and cultivators. For instance, a band of young hunters may have attacked a planter settlement, killed off the males, and installed themselves in their place, forcing the female planters, whose job was to do all the garden work anyway, to work for them. Much in the sociological structure of the "higher" planting culture would most easily lend itself to explanation on this basis. In particular, this might explain the rise of men's societies as well as the fact that woman's monopoly in productive gardening changed from a positive privilege into a negative one, from a dignity into a burden. Even if such a hypothesis were confirmable, we would be dealing with a sociological process quite different from that which occurs with nomadic superstratification. When the difference between conquerors and conquered coincides with the natural difference between the two sexes, and when, therefore, a reproduction is possible only through a continued and ever renewed generative mixture of the two groups, the result cannot be the formation of two population layers, each reproducing itself separately. Such a one-time occurrence, however, can certainly lead to a permanent institutional discrimination against women and to their relegation to an inferior position, and to a more or less pronounced "male domination." Where the corresponding dividing line coincides with the natural line of demarcation between the sexes, the natural equilibrium between the two sexes is disturbed, of course, to a greater or lesser degree; but no new, unnatural social dividing line is created. Community remains, albeit with a more or less disturbed inner equilibrium. The picture changes radically, however, when nomadic stock breeders appear as the bearers of superstratification.

b. Herdsmen over Planters

The original herd-animal nomadism we have been discussing, without wheel, wagon, or the technique of horseback riding, had already fully changed the human situation with respect to techniques of locomotion. If man at first was forced to follow his herds and their seasonally fluctuating grazing routes, often across broad stretches of hundreds of kilometers, he also gradually learned to replace this passive accompaniment with an active "driving" of the herd pursuant to his own wish and will. This required the complicated technique of driving cattle in the normal sense—i.e., the herdsmen's ability to bring the animals to a desired destination. Animal instinct was supplanted by human intellect, with the herdsmen consciously foreseeing and planning the route and its risks, consequences, and requirements: adequate food and drinking water, constant mapping out of the route so that it would not run into an insurmountable impasse, protection against the rigors of the climate, and against animal and human predators. Such a development must have been very gradual and surely not without much trial and error. Although man was closer to his instinctual apparatus at that time, he was most probably the one who first had to learn from animals and their mysterious sureness of instinct. At earlier preherdsman cultural levels every long-range change of abode of whole social groupings, involving the transport of infants and others incapable of independent movement, of household utensils, and, above all, of provisions, would have been a major and almost insoluble problem. Since the men had to be ready for instant defense, the distance traversed daily was forcibly reduced, and the extremely limited amount of provisions that could be taken along remained a major handicap even with the most optimal attempt to adapt the arrangement to the purpose. And without provisions, the migrants were at the mercy of unassessable circumstances and accidents in unknown regions.

All this had now changed completely. The migrants now had at their disposal a provision that, in practically unlimited amounts, moved itself automatically on its own legs. Moreover, they could even have their tents and household utensils, their aged and infirm transported by the animals, sledged or as pack burdens.

Up to then human distribution probably had proceeded with the same unconscious or semiconscious slowness as marked the distribution of animal species. Only now were genuine "migrations" in large groups and over long stretches possible, migrations of whole hordes and tribes "with bag and baggage," "with kith and kin."

This erratically increased freedom of movement in large groups, along with the practically complete solution of the problem of provisions, in itself created the possibility of developing a new and great military superiority in attack, namely, the superiority of numbers. In his classic treatise *On War* (3:8 and 11) Clausewitz describes numerical superiority as follows: "In tactics, as well as in strategy, [numerical superiority] is the general principle of victory," and "The best strategy is always to be very strong, first generally, then at the decisive point." Obviously stock-breeding nomadism, as such, provided unprecedented different opportunities for the exploitation of this timelessly valid principle of all warfare.

Seafaring peoples appear as a superincumbent ruling stratum in exactly the same role as bovid herdsmen, especially in Polynesia. For geographical reasons they had exchanged their original herd animals for the ship, the "horse of the waves."

The net results of this prehistoric early superincumbency of bovid herdsmen (or seafarers) over cultivators are those altogether tropical superincumbent cultures of archaic character in central and eastern Africa, across Southeast Asia and Polynesia up to Central America.

The difference between each of the two components compared with the later superincumbency of equid herdsmen over cattle-breeding peasants (from which our own culture and the genuine high cultures equivalent to it have emerged) explains the fact that the result also turned out differently.

Although peasantry forms a foundation for superincumbency that is economically viable as well as socially hardy and balanced, the mixture of matrilineal planting culture and patrilineal hunting culture (on which the archaic superstratification cultures rest) is far less efficient and viable economically. Culturally, moreover, it is largely eccentric and distorted. Indeed, there often seems to be a reciprocal intensification of the questionable aspects of both components of the mixture. The superstratifying nomadic conquerors seem to have brought to this infelicitous mixture only the element of domination and the multiplier of the intensification process.

In the later superincumbency of herdsmen-warriors over cattle-breeding peasants, the latter—precisely as the result of cattle breeding—already have a marked nomadic trait; and the stock-breeding on both sides, with all its exertions, forms a strong community in work and in mood between the upper and lower strata. Accordingly, the distance between them can never be intensified to such gruesome, grotesque dimensions as in the present context of herdsmen-planter superstratification, where one finds court ceremonials in which a subject was permitted to approach the king only by groveling in the dust with a tuft of grass held in his mouth—truly a "bestial servitude." Human sacrifice, which (with cannibalism) stems from the cultural complex of the planters, sprouted hideously in these cultures in a way at once brutal and refined. The slave trade, with its manhunts, also seems to have had its origin among these societies of herdsmen superstratified over planters.

Here, then, lies the ultimate origin of large-scale slavery as an industrial system, whence it apparently spread to Egypt and Carthage, and from Carthage to Rome. A new diffusion thrust dates from the fifteenth century, when the Portuguese discovered and took possession of the west African coast, immediately organizing a brisk trade in Negro slaves, the "black ivory." Negro slaves were shipped to America, and the slave plantation system that the Spaniards erected in America, a system of large-scale agriculture employing slave labor, also spread to eastern Europe at the same time (see pt. 2, sec. 17).

The contrast between large-scale slavery and the keeping of familial household slaves is vast and somewhat analogous to that between the breeding of herd animals and the raising of domestic animals. In large-scale slavery the human being is the herd animal; in household slavery he is the domestic animal. Household slaves belong to the family; as a rule they have the same legal and social position as the children of the house, except that they never legally come of age. "In the early stages of culture slaves are on the whole leniently treated, and there is little difference between young slaves and free children. But the slave always remains a 'younger brother,' . . . and when the master who educated him dies, he becomes the subject of the master's child, who has been the companion of his childhood."[3] Our present Western institution of domestic service stems from this individual household slavery; by contrast, mass slavery imposed on capitalist large-scale enterprises both in agriculture and in industry left a nefarious sociological imprint that remained particularly evident until it was softened and blurred by the social reform movements of recent centuries.

c. Herdsmen over Peasants

Herdsmen have superimposed themselves not only over planters but also over peasants, who had already adopted the ox from the stock-breeding culture in a highly fruitful way. And precisely because of the close cultural kinship and community between conquering herdsmen and conquered peasants, the result seems to have been as felicitous and satisfactory as the superincumbency of herdsmen over planters was infelicitous and unsatisfactory.

The superincumbency of nomad herdsmen over peasants leads us out of prehistory into early history, for here it is mainly a question of the "Jamdat-Nasr migration," which with a fair degree of certainty can be said to have begun at the end of the fourth millennium B.C. Its point of departure seems to have been in Turkestan; by way of Anatolia it reached the Aegean, Greece and Crete, Egypt, Mesopotamia, and India. And in all these places it led to the formation of the oldest historical high cultures: the pre-Helladic in Greece, the Cycladic high culture in the Aegean, the Minoan on

Crete, the Dynastic in Egypt, that of Sumer and Akkad in Mesopotamia, and the Harappa culture in the Indus Valley. Their bearers, at all events in Egypt and Akkad, were Semites, whose languages, when they mixed with native languages of North Africa, gave rise to the so-called Hamitic languages. Indeed, the Semitic spearhead groups might even have come to North Africa in the last centuries of the fourth millennium—a hypothesis the Egyptian chronology seems to support. The same migration movement probably also brought the Semitic Canaanites to Syria.

Most of these cultures, especially the Old Cretan-Minoan, the Indus culture strikingly related to it, and to a lesser degree also the Old Sumerian culture, offer a most impressive embodiment of peace and heightened joy in life, of the principle "live and let live." They stand in sharp contrast to the aforementioned morose archaic cultures, while the Egyptian culture seems to occupy a certain intermediate position. On Crete, as in the Indus Valley, the cities had neither walls nor other defenses, neither fortresses nor castles: hence, war without and rule through violence within were out of the question. The highly civilized city layouts of the Indus culture, in particular, also give a striking impression of a democratic order of things.

Two nude male torsos dug up in Harappa that belong to the Indus culture of the third millennium B.C. were at first supposed to be Hellenic, and at first sight any unbiased observer would hold them to be precisely that. They show, in fact, a freedom in the conception and representation of the human body which otherwise is nowhere to be found before the Greeks. They constitute one of the greatest riddles of this astonishing high culture, whose solution will never be found so long as we cannot read their writing. The Harappa culture was completely destroyed in the second millennium B.C. as the result of a barbarian invasion that seemingly killed off the possibility of further development. But the closely related Minoan culture was able to transmit its legacy to the Greeks.

5. War Chariot and Riding Horse

Whereas the origin of cattle breeding is still enveloped in almost total obscurity, research conducted in the last decades on the origin of horse breeding has shed much new light on the subject. The practice starts with the Altaic Turkic peoples (Turanians), who also play a leading role in the development of the war chariot and who then emerge as the horsed peoples *par excellence*. It was from them as the primary horse breeders that Semites, as well as Indo-European peoples, adopted secondary horse breeding, vehicular transportation, and horseback riding.

The peasant oxcart, later elaborated to the four-wheeled wagon —still used in its original form by peasants from Spain through Anatolia to East Asia—conveys loads easily and safely. But it has very little speed, and the oxen draw it with a grave and meditative air at a slow pace. The peasant is in no hurry. What matters to him is not saving time but saving labor, his own and his family's.

The situation is quite different with the horse and its related breeds. The rapid trot and gallop are suitable to them, and extraordinary velocities can be attained. The exploitation of this possibility became obvious the moment equid herders came into contact with peasants—another productive synthesis from the fateful post-ice age contact between north and south. The equid herdsmen at first adopted the oxcart as it was, a two-wheeled wagon, and hitched their swiftest and most spirited animals to it. The war chariot was born when the military usefulness of this fast vehicle was perceived. The oldest war chariot, depicted in the famous relief on the ancient Sumerian boundary stone of Ur (end of the fourth millennium B.C.) is essentially an oxcart to which equids are yoked. Equids were also yoked to the subsequent four-wheeled wagon, occasionally used as a war chariot.

The peak of this entire development was attained in the middle of the second millenium B.C. by the extraordinarily high grade, positively elegant and smart-looking Syrian racing chariot. In the two intervening millennia men must have labored with enormous intensity to develop this weapon of war and sporting machine, of pivotal importance to them, and its technique of application.

A new military and historically important stage was reached by the use of equids, especially the horse, for riding. The great migration of around 1200 B.C. was no longer undertaken by war chariot peoples, like that of around 2000 B.C., but by mounted peoples. Before the riding horse completely replaced the war chariot, there was an intermediate stage when "chariot and rider" were mentioned in the same breath, usually with the more traditional and more aristocratic "chariot" in first place. In the leading cultural area of the eastern Mediterranean, however, the war chariot had exhausted its role by the middle of the second millennium B.C. Soon the Sarmatian invention of the stirrup began to spread, the Iranian small iron and lamella plate for horse with rider appeared, and from A.D. 300 on, from the Roman Empire up to China, the mounted phalanx of heavily armored riders acquired a decisive importance in warfare and held its own for more than a millennium until the emergence of firearms. The military importance of the light cavalry, although spasmodic, extended into the nineteenth century. Its obsolescence as a military factor, apart from its peripheral employment, was not exposed until World War I.

This new technique of movement of swift travel and of riding at trot and gallop must have created an intoxication with speed, a wholly novel attitude of self-reliance on the part of man toward space and distance that could mount in intensity to a veritable mania for racing. Just so, my generation has experienced at first hand the ubiquitous spread of the railroad, automobile, and airplane and their effect on one's feeling for life. At that time the impact of this new vitality made itself felt in religious representation. Up to then an individual who desired to petition a deity was obliged first of all to summon or attract the deity in question, a task in which he did not always readily succeed. Now, however, there is no longer any distance that man considers insurmountable, and the ends of the world no longer seem unreachable. Indeed, in daydreams man fancies himself seated in a sun chariot or similar mythical vehicle racing heavenward, as space rockets streak toward the planets today. This feeling begot the idea of the journey to the Beyond, the journey to Heaven and Hell, and not only after death but also for those who were individually blessed or numinously trained already in this life, for instance, by way of a trance or swoon representing death. This, in turn, opened the possibility of making oneself independent of the epiphany of the deity, of its obligingness in making an appearance. Now, when necessary, one could drop in on the god, so to speak, a visitation the nomadic magician-priest, the shaman, is still wont to practice today. Thus arose that widespread revelation literature in poetry and prose which no longer, as formerly, is opened by an epiphanic revelation of the deity, but conversely, by a journey to heaven of the prophet and seer. This literature then worked its way into the loftiest regions of Western philosophy. Parmenides begins his famous didactic poem with a sun chariot streaking heavenward, a racing chariot drawn by mares, which is fully described down to its last technical detail. Later this became the source of the famous metaphors and similes in Plato describing souls setting out for a journey to heaven in horse-yoked racing chariots.

By far the most important effects of this advance in transport techniques, however, were felt in the domain of warfare. The war chariot and riding horse, as revolutionary innovations in the techniques of war, now took their place beside the possibilities for developing military superiority already inherent in horse nomadism as such, the exploitation of which by herdsmen we have already followed. As contemporaries of World War II we can picture this with particular vividness, having experienced how the invention of the automobile and the airplane, with their systematic and ruthless military exploitation, developed into a military and political catastrophe. The tank is to the automobile exactly what the war chariot is to the oxcart. The invention of mechanical means of transport—the railroad and automobile—was the first really decisive advance of transport technology within the last ten thousand years that can be compared to the invention of the oxcart. Thus, technically as well as historically, an exact correspondence exists between the war chariot and the tank.

Indeed the advance from pedestrian to war chariot was so momentous that in comparison to it the still considerable advance from the war chariot to the riding horse recedes into the background so far as universal history is concerned. The war chariot enables the aggressor to storm forth in whole squadrons at overwhelming speed, despite the heaviest armor, to draw near the defenders fighting on foot with fully unexpected physical energies, and to attack them from the vantage point of a higher position.

The very consciousness of this military superiority could have given warrant for raiding expeditions. Population pressure and overpopulation are also conceivable as triggering causes. Moreover, the rise in temperature in the postglacial epoch, which in an oscillating reaction for a short time even went beyond the present-day temperature level, led to desiccation and the formation of deserts in the southern parts of central Asia, as the result of which the climate again put pressure on the nomads living there. This time, however, only after it had opened wide the gateways toward the west, east, and south.

As soon as the melting of the last glaciation freed the routes, three great steppe corridors, cloverleaf in formation, led from the central Asian core region of nomadism in a western, southern, and eastern direction: westward across southern Russia into central Europe, southward and southwestward by way of the Iranian mountain range, bordering the plateau, to the giant Arabic-North African tablelands; eastward across the depressions and passes of the central Asian mountain range and the Tarim basin to the Mongolian tablelands and further toward Manchuria and China. Today uninhabitable and inaccessible deserts have been formed in the center of all these steppe plains; but this is a late phenomenon resulting from increasing dehydration. In the first millennia of the postglacial epoch everything here was still covered with a hardy steppe vegetation and, consequently, passable without hindrance. All these three great steppe corridors, therefore, repeatedly served as the highways of peoples, as the great arterial roads of waves of migrating nomadic peoples.

The first wave of herdsmen at the end of the fourth millennium B.C. was followed by the much more violent and tempestuous wave of the war chariot people of about 2000 B.C., and finally, around 1200 B.C., by that of the first mounted people, which then joined further waves of horsemen up to the last assaults of Mongols and Turks against Christian Europe.

The wave of war chariot peoples since 2000 B.C. brought the first Italics to Italy, the Ionians and Achaeans to Greece, the Hittites to Asia Minor, the Hurrians and Mitannians to northern Mesopotamia, the Kassites to Babylonia, the Hyksos by way of Syria to Egypt (over which they ruled from 1730 to 1580 B.C.) and, finally, the destroyers of the Harappa culture to India. With the exception of the last-named, all were peoples or led by peoples of Indo-European stock.

The first migration of horsed peoples, the so-called Aegean migration beginning around 1200 B.C., brought the Dorians to Greece, the Chaldeans to Mesopotamia, the Medes and Persians to Iran, the Aryans to India, the Phrygians, Mysians, and Bithynians to Asia Minor, the Aramaeans to Syria, the Israelites to Palestine, and the Philistines to the Palestinian coast; it led to the great attack of the "sea-peoples" on Egypt. Egyptian sources describe the terrifying momentum behind this thrust: "Not one stood before their hands, from Kheta, Kode, Carchemish, Arvad, Alasa, they were wasted. They set up a camp in one place in Amor. They desolated its people and its land like that which is not. They came with fire prepared before them, forward to Egypt. . . . They laid their hands upon the land as far as the Circle of the Earth. Their hearts were confident, full of their plans."[4]

6. SUPERSTRATIFICATION OF EQUID HERDSMEN OVER PEASANTS

Ever new masses of peoples were pushed through the central Asian *vagina gentium* in ever repeated contractions. Like a spring tide, wave upon wave, they rolled through steppe regions and passes and spilled over across the three continents of the Old World.

Now, to the terror of the rest of mankind, became manifest the enormous superiority which the possession of animals and their military use had procured for these herdsmen.

The rider appears on the stage of history like a new breed of man, marked by a powerful superiority: he is over two meters in height and moves several times faster than a pedestrian. The enormous impact that the first of such riders must have made on peaceful peasant stockbreeders is depicted in the legendary form of the centaurs.

Added to this enormous military superiority of the individual rider was his capacity to effect concentrated mass formations in concert with his fellow horsemen. Thanks to their mobility, even a small horde of them could appear suddenly at any place with concentrated superiority of numbers. This superiority was enormous and irresistible, and was intensified even further by the panic their coming sowed among those attacked and threatened, so that almost any attempt at resistance was stifled from the start.

The peasantry that had just come into being, as if by act of Providence, now offered itself as an alluring prospect of war spoils to these herdsmen-warriors, these born conquerors. In its capacity for mobilization and movement as infantry, this peasantry was far inferior in military technique to the cavalry of the drivers and riders, for it was attached to widely scattered tilled areas. But it did possess an extraordinary economic viability—thanks to the high productivity of its work force (equally distributed between both sexes) and the use of draft animals and the cultivation of plants. In consequence of structural conditions (to be discussed in detail later) it was also characterized by an astonishing social steadfastness and a capacity to bear burdens, which enabled it to maintain its healthy vital structure without undergoing any essential deformation despite the pressure of a superstratification lasting through millennia.

Thus, from both sides, from above as well as from below, the objective conditions for a genuine superincumbency were established. Accordingly, where conquering drivers or mounted nomads ran into a population of sedentary plow-peasants, they installed themselves as the ruling stratum and thenceforth lived on the labor, dues, and services of the subjugated.

Here was real "exploitation" in the strictest sense of the word; here the "surplus value" created by the peasants as the result of increased productivity was unjustly appropriated by the conquerors. The latter now needed only to devote themselves to ruling, to fighting, and to the knightly way of life, often taking up residence in castles whose turrets rose about the huts of the peasants like the lords "high on the horse" above the peasants themselves. The analogy of the castle as a petrified horse and the horse as an itinerant castle is especially clear in the later stage of development, where horse and rider are enveloped in heavy armor like a wall.

The herdsmen-warriors who thus installed themselves as the ruling stratum were accustomed to a broad overview of things, to deployment in wide open spaces and to giving orders warily, as a result of their experience with their native herds and pasture lands with the boundless horizons of their steppes. They now put into practice the same trait on a large and wide-ranging scale as superstratifying conquerors. And it was strengthened and deepened even more by the special character of their religious representation and feeling. The old nomadic belief in a great heavenly god led easily to the idea of a religiously sanctioned, uniform, all-embracing world rule "as in heaven also on earth"—in accordance with the motto of Genghis Khan, "One God in heaven, one Ruler on earth."

"Nothing recurs so frequently in the speeches and letters of these despots as their invocation to heaven, to the supreme God, who supposedly has assigned to them the mission and the authority to subject the whole world to themselves and even to punish men for their sins against God: Genghis Khan coined the expression 'the scourge of God' in application to himself when he, a pagan, in a formal sermon in the mosque of Buchara reproached the conquered Moslems for their sins against God."[5]

Nomadic conquerors first created the prerequisite for the rise of high cultures through superstratification, or else they only later took the spotlight of the written tradition of high cultures as a result of their irruption on a mission of conquest installing them as the ruling stratum; as a result the events that triggered this irruption, in general, can only be inferred. Only in the case of Islam does the storm in the offing occur in the light of transmitted history. There we can read that the Bedouins and oasis traders of Arabia had for centuries led a localized, circumscribed existence, that what had to supervene upon their latent warlike potential to activate it and to fit them for their universal-historical role as conquerors and bearers of superstratification was the electrifying effect on their minds of a charismatic prophet and his religious doctrine, in particular the doctrine of Holy War, which numinously consecrated this very embarkation upon the path of conquest and domination and made it into a religious duty. What distinguished Omar's irresistible bands of horsemen, which had inundated the eastern part of the inhabited world since 634, from the Arabic tribes that had lived almost historyless up to 622, if not Islam, the religious call of Muhammad the Prophet? We are on the sure ground of documented history when we imagine earlier nomadic irruptions into alien territories as having the same cause: nomads transformed into conquerors by religious enthusiasm. And what we know about them at the moment of their entry into history and thereafter eminently accords with this view. Moreover, the Islamic superstratifications offer the example of an altogether spontaneous and active historical movement, one not forcibly unleashed by a calamity.

Whereas hitherto the formation of political and social units had not gone beyond hordes, tribes, village communities, cantons, and similar small structures of direct personal relationships, here for the first time arose large political structures, veritable "empires," their areas vast as the steppes, and their subject populations numerous as the herds to which the conquering nomads had earlier been accustomed. The speed of their chariots and horses assured them both of military superiority in the initial encounters and of administrative control after the conquest; the development of road building techniques further accentuated the same superiority. The political and social structure of these large empires first made possible the rise of high cultures in accordance with the law of the culture pyramid—through subjects, numbering hundreds of thousands and ruled despotically by a unified governmental authority, and through the concentration of the tributes levied from these subjugated masses in the hands of a thin stratum of conquerors and rulers and its patriarchal-monarchical head.

"From now on superincumbency took the place of the dislodgment practiced formerly. Barbarism laid itself over civilization. And the ruling nomads, once a 'horror' to the civilized plow peasants, were soon refined, assimilated, and finally absorbed. Later—indeed quite often, and all too often—a new swarm of barbarians breaks in from the north." Everywhere "the nomads were the destroyers, but also the organizers. Everywhere, with the primitive Germans, Akkads, Mediterranean peoples, Chinese, and Indians, they set the patriarchy of the stock breeders in the place of the matriarchy of the plow peasants. Where the monarchic nation-state is found, it originated from the patriarchal large family."[6]

As the result of the superincumbency of warrior-nomads over

peasants, a new configuration, a "new natural aggregation of external and internal factors of human life" was created, which furnished the "opening configuration" for the development of all high cultures.[7] And only now "does the real, the full history of mankind begin."[8]

In the course of development, after the first fresh superstratifications of pure herdsmen over pure plow peasants, an increasing profusion of mixed types of superstratifiers and superstratifications ensues. A second superstratification can be effected in such a way that the new superstratifiers dislodge or destroy the old ones and take their place, share rulership with them and intermix, or simply add themselves on top of them as one would add a story to a house. Or a mixture of two peoples originating in superstratification can become a ruling class over a third.

For the reason that this form of high culture with a knightly upper and peasant lower stratum prevailed in Western history until the end of the Middle Ages and is accordingly familiar to us, we shall call it "medieval" or "feudal" in the broadest sense of those terms.

From the remotest to the most recent times, moreover, distinctive utensils of herdsmen, such as whips and shepherd's crooks, have been preserved as insignia of sovereign authority alongside the planter's club and the huntsman's spear, as outer signs of the origin of medieval rulers in stock-breeding herdsmen.

Superincumbencies occurring in widely separated places and eras exhibit remarkable structural similarities that extend from the geopolitical to the religious sphere and merit elaboration. Most superincumbencies are effected not once and for all but in successive waves that often spread over many centuries. Usually this undulation first comes to a standstill at some geographical or political barrier, or it may stop because the first wave of superstratification leads to the formation of an imperial high culture that bars the path to subsequent waves.

Such a typology, once elaborated on the basis of historical material, may then also be applied (with a requisite dose of caution) to the reconstruction of prehistoric happenings.

Certain characteristic traits of social psychology—such as the mutual attitudes of nomads and settled populations toward each other—are also to be observed throughout. The early historical sources of settled peoples are replete with lamentations over the low cultural level, the barbaric crudities, and the rapacious aggressiveness of nomads. Conversely, nomads experience the culture of the settlers, especially that of the city dwellers, both as irresistibly alluring and as dangerous, overrefined, degenerate, dissolute, and morbid.

For the nomads, such mutual and depreciatory awareness of cultural contrasts repeatedly led to warnings against the temptations of a settled life and to vows of abstinence from it and of faithfulness to the innocence and simplicity of their own tradition.

Warning against the temptations of the Canaanite peasants and city culture are found over and over again in the historical and prophetic books of the Old Testament. The famous Old Testament curse on agriculture at the expulsion from Paradise (Genesis 3:17-18) does not prove that work has always and everywhere been viewed as a curse. Rather, it springs quite concretely from such nomadic depreciation of the peasantry and its compulsion to perform arduous physical labor—hateful and contemptible to nomads. And this disdain was combined with the transfiguring remembrance of the carefree feeling of the original gathering of the clan.

Around 842 B.C., in the Book of Kings (2 Kings 10:15-23), we meet a Kenite tribal chieftain, Jehonadab ben Rechab, as a friend of the bloody usurper Jehu, zealous for Yahweh. Two hundred and fifty years later, 597 B.C., we learn the following about him and his family from the prophet Jeremiah (35:6-10). The Rechabites, publicly tempted by Jeremiah to drink wine, reply: "We will drink no wine: for Jonadab the son of Rechab our father commanded us, saying, Ye shall drink no wine, neither ye, nor your sons for ever: Neither shall ye build house, nor sow seed, nor plant vineyard, nor have any: but all your days ye shall dwell in tents; that ye may live many days in the land where ye be strangers. Thus have we obeyed the voice of Jonadab, the son of Rechab our father, in all that he hath charged us, to drink no wine all our days, we, our wives, our sons, nor our daughters; Nor to build houses for us to dwell in; neither have we vineyard, nor field, nor seed: But we have dwelt in tents, and have obeyed, and done according to all that Jonadab our father commanded us."

Again six or eight centuries after Jonadab and Jeremiah respectively, at the same place, it is said of John the Baptist that he eats no bread and drinks no wine—for which many people, of course, consider him crazy.

From the year 312 B.C. there is the following report about the Arab Bedouin tribes of the Nabateans: "It is a law among them to sow no grain, to plant no fruit bearing seed, to drink no wine, to build no house. Whoever is charged with a contravention against this prohibition forfeits his life."[9]

However justified the appraisals of nomadic culture as being close to nature, simple, and uncorrupted may be, the superior civilizational level of settled peoples was obvious: otherwise there would have been no temptation either to conquest or to the assimilation of the conquerors to the culture of the conquered. The catastrophe of the superstratification leads at first to a cultural decline, or even collapse, from which a new culture only gradually rises—but this new culture, according to the law of the pyramid, turns out to be superior even to the previous culture of the conquered.

CHAPTER 2

Structural Elements of High Cultures as Conditioned by Superstratification and Feudalism

1. THE SOCIAL STRUCTURE OF SUPERINCUMBENCY

Superstratification produced, for the first time in history, human social groupings that, in their *inner* structure, were based on bloodshed and violence. This is not to say that the history of mankind up to then had unfolded idyllically and bloodlessly. On the contrary, the irregular wars of the hunters against alien tribes were even bloodier and crueler, since hunters, unlike conquering nomads, had no interest in sparing the enemy as a future economic base. Up to then, however, ruthless brutality and violence had been applied only outwardly against beasts and against alien human beings, the latter being viewed not as humans but as a species of especially repulsive and dangerous monkey. This outlook finds its most significant expression in the fact that many primitive peoples use the word that means "human being" in their language as the distinguishing designation reserved exclusively for their own tribe and its members. Those not belonging to the tribe are not considered human beings. From this springs the sociological difference between inner morality (community morality) and outer morality (the morality of violence).

Among hunters, if a war prisoner was not tortured to death, the only other possibility was to adopt him solemnly as a fully qualified member of the tribe, through a rite of rebirth. For there was no room for a fellow hunter in one's own ranks who did not feel unreserved allegiance to the group. This sheds strong light on the transformation here in question: before, things were so arranged that inner morality dominated the inside of each social structure, and outer morality was applied exclusively outwardly. With superstratification, a distinctive act of outer morality becomes a foundation of society's internal structure and exercises a determining and continuous effect. For the first time outer morality, the morality of violence, penetrates, domineeringly and determiningly, into the interior of a social body.

> We stand at that historical turning point which has raised the antagonistic and parasitic drives, never lacking in the makeup of human nature, to a principle of culture. . . . With the founding of a society calibrated into social estates, we come upon the discovery that a guiding economic policy can subjugate economically productive labor. The management of other human beings was methodically discovered and was practiced on a large scale; on it was built the unearned income of a minority that accordingly segregated itself socially from the strata of the working population as a stratum of proprietors of land and weapons and set itself over them.[1]

The human significance of this beginning of all high cultures and all great states was perceived for the first time and with profound horror by Jacob Burckhardt: "An echo of the terrible convulsions which accompanied the birth of the State, *of what it cost*, can be heard in the enormous and absolute primacy it has at all times enjoyed. . . . Where the convulsion was a conquest, the primordial principle of the state, its outlook, its task and even its emotional significance was the enslavement of the conquered." Later he speaks of "the general habituation to the permanent mistreatment, indeed the leisurely extirpation of the enslaved people, accompanied by an infernal arrogance in the victor, who accustoms himself to utter contempt for human life and who makes this sort of domination over others into an integrating part of his pathos."[2]

The same thesis, following Burckhardt, was restated by Friedrich Nietzsche, although Nietzsche's valuation soon turned to the opposite extreme:

> The State originates in the cruelest way through conquest, through the production of a race of drones. Its lofty destiny now is to make a culture develop from these drones.[3]
>
> . . . That such an alteration was no gradual or voluntary alteration, and that it did not manifest itself as an organic adaptation to new conditions, but as a break, a jump, a necessity, an inevitable fate, against which there was no resistance and never a spark of resentment. Second, that the fitting of a

hitherto unchecked and amorphous population into a fixed form, starting as it had done in an act of violence, could only be accomplished by acts of violence and nothing else—that the oldest "state" appeared consequently as a ghastly tyranny, a grinding, ruthless piece of machinery that went on working till this raw material of a semi-animal populace was not only thoroughly kneaded and elastic, but also *molded*. That fantastic theory that makes it begin with a contract is, I think, disposed of. He who can command, he who is a master by "nature," he who comes on the scene forceful in deed and gesture—what has he to do with contracts? . . . [Such persons'] work is an instinctive creating and impressing of forms, and they are the most involuntary, unconscious artists there are: their appearance produces instantaneously a scheme of sovereignty that is *live*, in which the functions are partitioned and apportioned. . . . They are ignorant of the meaning of guilt, responsibility, consideration, are these born organizers; in them predominates that terrible artist-egoism that gleams like brass and knows itself justified to all eternity in its work. . . . It is not in *them* that there grew the bad conscience, that is elementary—but it would not have grown *without them*, repulsive growth as it was; it would be missing, had not a tremendous quantity of freedom been expelled from the world by the stress of their hammerstrokes, their artist violence. . . .[4]

The fateful psychological effect of this social structure was not fully discernible so long as the wounds inflicted by superstratification still bled, were still unhealed and open, so long as the conquerors and conquered still confronted each other as unintegrated aliens with different languages, customs, religions, and perhaps also divergent racial traits. In Sparta an effort was made artificially to maintain this brutal initial state of the superstratification. One of the official duties of the ephors at the beginning of each year was to declare war against the subject population in a solemn, juridical and magically effectual form. Thus, on the one hand, it was an attempt to prevent healing of the social wounds, on the other, to forestall any fits of bad conscience by continuing to treat the subjugated population according to martial law—i.e., with unchecked arbitrariness and brutality.

However, as wounds healed, masters and slaves intermingled and grew together into a single social body with the same language and the same religion, and the earlier, externally forced obedience of the subject people gradually became a duty of conscience, with all the sanctions of religion and morality. Thus, the bloody deed of superstratification played a role in the real social fall of man: as a hereditary curse and original sin, it burdens, however covertly, everything that has sprung from it.

"One gets the impression," Freud wrote in *The Future of an Illusion*, "that civilization is something which was imposed on a resisting majority by a minority which understood how to obtain possession of the means of power and coercion."[5]

All of us, without exception, carry this inherited poison within us, in the most varied and unexpected places and in the most diverse forms, often defying perception. All of us, collectively and individually, are accessories to this great sin of all time, this real original sin, a hereditary fault that can be excised and erased only with great difficulty and slowly by an insight into pathology, by a will to recover, by the active remorse of all.

In contrast to these realities, there stands as historical justification of superincumbency the creation of high cultures and of all their works, which have constituted the pride and the authentic accomplishment of mankind. There have been few successful efforts to search for energies that might have produced the same result peacefully. A drive strong enough to effect a voluntary cooperative alliance growing out of small societal structures of primitive peoples has not yet come to light.

Superstratification may be likened to a strong toxic substance that, in the course of a chemical production process, is indispensable for the precipitation of important synthetic reactions, but must be completely separated later if the product is not to be burdened with correspondingly poisonous properties.

What comes into being here, moreover, is something uncanny: the power of an accomplished fact, the taking over of the management of others' affairs "for their own good," not only without authorization but even in the face of protest—an extremely dangerous line of reasoning that is "as hard to handle as the blade of a knife."

The conquerors rightly can claim for themselves not only the creation of highly developed social structures and cultures; they can also claim that they are responsible for the maintenance of a highly graduated hierarchical social structure.

Awareness of the positive obligations of leadership in the interest of the whole—therefore indirectly also in the interest of the subjugated strata—is born of the situation itself, for, without this awareness, it is utterly impossible to maintain the new social structures created by superstratification. Hence, successful conquerors are always aware of these obligations and rarely neglect to set off this true accomplishment in the best light. Obviously, they do not distinguish between voluntarily recognized leadership and forced tyranny, between the administration of positions of social command and control in the common interest and the exploitations of them for the selfish advantage of the ruler.

The insignia of the dignity of leadership sacred to each community lie for use or abuse in the bloody hands of the conqueror. Justified indignation against violence and injustice as well as insolent revolts against law and order are beaten down with the knob of the same guilded scepter. It is not for nothing that the purple of the king's mantle shows the color of blood.

The usurped lordly privileges and the self-assumed obligations of leadership are so intertwined as to become indistinguishable, and the overlords themselves have the greatest interest in reinforcing this growing confluence. Yet the more indistinguishable the mixture, the stronger, in the long run, is the toxic effect of the admixed injustice, for then it becomes difficult to prevent justified resistance to force and violence from also striking at the leadership at the same time.

The situation resulting from superstratification shifts its emphasis from the realm of physical force and unbridled lust for power to that of ethical and religious sanctions; but on the rulers' part this is not wily camouflage or the tribute that the vice of dominion pays to the virtue of community. Rather, it is a transition from the original encounter toward what, in fact, is a relatively higher, better, and more equitable situation. We can only blame the rulers for lack of courage and unselfishness in their failure to pursue this path to its end. But such a demand probably goes beyond normal human capabilities. Hence it might more properly be addressed to the subjugated, urging them to expend *their* energies in this direction and to do *their* part, since such a transformation coincides with their selfish interests. As Aristotle writes: "The weaker are always anxious for equality and justice. The strong pay no heed to either."[6] This would mean, in sum, that there is not only a *right* to resist but a *duty* to resist.

The American Indians have provided the most effective proof of this thesis. Because they resisted being pressed into labor-slavery, whole villages and tribes, including women and children, preferred voluntary death when their heroic defense proved hopeless against the superiority of European arms. Christian conquerors, therefore,

had no alternative but to import Negroes from Africa. The latter, living in archaic superstratified empires, had for years been bred and raised to be submissive. Thus, in America the requisite lower stratum had first to be created through importation—a process that we might properly call substratification or subincumbency.

The victory of the conqueror in the struggle of superstratification regularly ends with a truce or armistice dictated and imposed by the upper stratum. Normally only a lower stratum, disadvantaged by it, can possibly have an interest in breaching it. We call such a renewal of the superstratification struggle from below *revolution* when it occurs fundamentally and along the whole front, *revolt* or *uprising* when it remains a sporadic and instinctive counterreaction. And we speak of a *coup d'état* when an upper stratum is violently dislodged from its position by another social minority group within the same governmental body. If improvement in the condition of the lower stratum has occurred, the upper stratum may renew the struggle for superstratification overtly or covertly, suppressing the lower stratum and grinding it down to a lower level. Such action is generally subsumed under the concept of *coup d'état*, but it has nothing to do with revolution. Rather, it is the opposite, since its aim and outcome is not improvement, but destruction of the social condition of the lower stratum. Accordingly, we could speak here of an anticipated counterrevolution.

Every revolution invokes the right to resistance as its legitimation and emotional justification. But often such a claim is only partially warranted. The moment the revolutionary active segments of the lower stratum are successful, they tend to set themselves in the place of the former upper stratum pursuant to the old tune of *"ôte-toi de là que je m'y mette!"* Thus actors have merely changed or exchanged their roles, but the tragedy of superstratification itself continues. At best, such a development slackens the pressure of the superstratification, but it can also substantially intensify it. Revolutions are often nothing more than the violent change of the upper stratum: the violence which they unleash (and perhaps for technical reasons cannot help unleashing) revives the daily remembered brutality of superstratification.

Such is the enormous difficulty of overcoming the superstratification structure once it has established itself. And it is all the more difficult, indeed absolutely hopeless, so long as one does not know what the true situation is and so long as one lacks a clear theoretical notion of what a social structure free of superincumbency and domination would look like—where the optimum synthesis of unity and freedom lies, and by what criteria leadership differs from domination.

Yet, this unavoidable distinction was already fundamentally laid down in a saying of Jesus that appears in the synoptic gospels: Mark 10: 42-44; Matt. 20: 25-27; Luke 22: 25-26: "Ye know that they which are accounted to rule over the Gentiles exercise lordship over them; and their great ones exercise authority upon them. But so shall it not be among you, but whosoever will be great among you, shall be your minister: And whosoever of you will be the chiefest, shall be servant of all." In this superbly realistic passage, it is not the struggle for rank and dignity as such that is condemned; rather, what is exclusively pointed to is the productive path of accomplishments that really are unselfish and on behalf of the community— and the attitude that these require.

Saint Augustine (354-430) also enjoins (*City of God* 19. 19) that "in active life it is not the honors or power of this life we should covet . . . , but we should aim at using our position and influence, if these have been honorably attained, for the welfare of those who are under us." Elsewhere he asserts that "there is no iron and no poison that I fear as much as the passion to rule" (*De consideratione* 2. 6). Frederick the Great's exacting description of the king as "the first servant of the state" also has its roots in this tradition. Our task is to apply it to modern conditions and to spell out its concrete sociological and political implication.

2. ANTINOMIES AND BIPOLARITY OF THE POWER STRUCTURE

High cultures, based on division of labor, could develop only within the framework of the state created by superstratification. And the feudal stigma of this principle of superstratification has remained indelible and unmistakable in the most varied aspects of government, society, and culture. In our days we have witnessed a catastrophic relapse into the most brutal superstratification.

Superstratification is only one end of a pronounced bipolar situation. For the bloody original situation of raw, unbridled superstratification endured almost nowhere, nor could it endure in the long run. Superstratification doubtless offered the conquerors a maximum degree of pleasure, derived from the feeling of lordship, but its security and stability was minimal. Moreover, this situation—even for its beneficiaries—is too unnatural, too eccentric, too remote from social structures consonant with human nature. Hence it is subjected eventually to the natural pull toward community.

Thus a development began that joins two social bodies into a single, uniform body with a structure of community. Since each step in this direction requires the conquerors to limit their arbitrary rule and partially to renounce the pleasure of exercising power, they proceed along this path at first only when they need to stabilize their dominion. The tendency at first is only to replace the maximum of overlordship with its optimum. From this stems that antinomic, tension-charged, and ambivalent type of state and culture that is characteristic of all high culture since then; it reconciles the conflicting features of community with leadership and of dominated noncommunity. Both of these conflicting tendencies are always present, no matter how different their proportions in a given case. Anyone who disputes the existence of leadership and community places himself at variance with the facts as much as the person who denies the existence of domination based upon force and violence. This central antinomy is a constitutive element of all high cultures and their states up to and including the modern democratic state.

Usually the result is that the upper stratum claims all privileges that in the community belong to leadership, but it accepts the strict duties incumbent upon such leadership only pursuant to its inclinations of the moment, using the doctrine that "might makes right." Conversely, all duties incumbent upon the led—but not the corresponding rights—are shifted onto the lower stratum.

There also exists, corresponding to the despotic pressure from above, a latent or open revolutionary counterpressure from below. This counterpressure and resistance, even if temporarily submerged, is never absent and is the "thorn in the flesh" which prevents the system from achieving equilibrium. The "social question," in its covert or overt forms, has constituted the great writing on the wall of all social structures that have originated through conquest. Only since superstratification is "the history of all hitherto existing society the history of class struggles," as the *Communist Manifesto* asserts.

Accordingly, overlordship is always somewhat unsure and threatened. It is threatened from below by the resistance of the subjugated populace, from the outside by the attempt of new conquerors or neighboring empire-builders, and from within by competing counterclaimants or by the desertion of lower-level leaders. Such a many-sided and permanent threat, inherent in the nature of the "medieval" situation, also severely slows down any effort to achieve a measure of pacification. It thus compels the rulers to pursue the opposite course of trying to maintain, renew, and, if possible, intensify the original warlike character of the superstratification.

But any overlordship is more secure and stronger abroad when it better fulfills the duties of leadership required inside. And the more it can base itself upon the voluntary consent of the underlying population, the fewer the energies it will be forced to squander to attenuate internal tensions and frictions. The ideal picture of the "shepherd of peoples," with its singularly nomadic stamp, corresponds to this requirement.

The chronicles of medieval kingdoms have handed down examples of "good princes" who more or less correspond to this ideal. But the very profusion of praise eagerly showered upon them proves the rarity of this felicitous phenomenon—even though, upon closer scrutiny, the standards of judgment of the woe-inured subjects turn out to be extremely mild and lenient.

Historical tradition just as frequently presents the opposite extreme, the "wicked," harsh, and cruel ruler—which is all the more remarkable, since chroniclers were usually directly or indirectly in the service of the princes.

At all events the subjects involved had no other alternative than patiently to endure the domination in its specific type, good or bad, as they endure sunshine or rain. As Tacitus once formulated it (*Hist.* 4. 8), they were "devoutly wishing for virtuous princes, but willing to acquiesce under any sort." Even a successful uprising signified at best a change of masters, not their complete removal.

So long as the distinction between rulers and ruled neatly coincides with the original racial distinction, the result is a highly visible social structure; such a structure is not easy for the far more numerous mass of the ruled to champion, since it openly turns its seamy side to them. If, however, the racial barrier erodes as the result of physical and social mixture, and if the attempt is made to strengthen internal cohesion with community ideologies for the purpose of winning the consent of the ruled, the door is opened to internal confusion, contradiction, and double-dealing. We are still more or less caught in the toils of this development today.

At all events, the division of the social body into two strata, its cleavage into rulers and ruled, is a permanent source of internal tension and unrest. The class barrier itself is latently or openly contested and accordingly gives rise to ever newer shiftings in one direction or the other. Divisions in each of the original classes may lead to the formation of a plurality or multiplicity of strata, an extreme example of which is provided by the Indian caste system.

At first the conquerors were always a tiny minority compared with the conquered—corresponding to the degree of their military and organizational superiority. To exploit the opportunities implicit

in this disproportion was for the conquerors both an emotional challenge to their expansive vitality and their self-confidence and a rational challenge to their calculating self-interest. After all, the
fewer there were among whom the booty had to be apportioned, the
greater the individual's share would be. On the other hand, such a
manifest numerical disproportion often only served to heighten
their racial self-consciousness. Viewed from below, of course, the
same numerical proportion could be observed with the sober eyes of
rationalism without magico-theological timidity, or, conversely, it
could operate as a stimulus to revolution in regard not only to the
arithmetical injustice of the distribution but also the numerical
superiority in the event of a struggle. This was one more reason for
the upper stratum and its theological specialists to prevent the penetration of such rationalistic considerations so far as possible.

3. Society instead of Community

In contrast to community, this antinomic bipolarity between friend-
liness and hostility, between inner morality and outer morality,
between association and separation, between centripetal and centrifugal forces, henceforth constitutes the real sociological nature of
society.

Until the advent of superstratification men had always, or nearly
always, lived in communities. Not, to be sure, in a communist community of goods or in mechanical equality, but in a naturally grown,
voluntary hierarchy based upon reciprocal recognition. The group in
which people lived together had always remained so small that each
one knew everybody else, each one stood in a direct personal relation with everybody else, and each one could depend on everybody
else. The whole life of each individual unfolded within this organic,
narrow, warm, supportive structure of community.

Those fortunate people who unbrokenly and exclusively live in a
natural setting of community are rarely conscious of this state. But
we who have been expelled from this paradise are aware of what we
have lost. For one of the fateful consequences of superstratification
is precisely this transition from *Gemeinschaft* to *Gesellschaft*, from
community to society. Through superstratification and its resulting
despotic power structure many small communities were forced to
submit to alien peoples who, in keeping with the notions of their
earlier way of life, would treat them like criminals or wild beasts.
Furthermore, many small communities, alien to each other, were
forcibly linked together by their new overlords, for good or ill, into a

greater society. This fateful linkage binds together peoples most of whom do not know each other, have never seen each other, who are wholly alien to each other, and who have no personal relationship with each other. In every country today there are hundreds, indeed many thousands of villages and towns whose very names the average citizen does not know and which he will never hear about or see in his lifetime. The denizen of the city for the most part does not know who lives next door, or even on the floor above or below him. Of the man of the high cultures, Adam Smith writes: "In civilised society, he stands at all times in need of the co-operation and assistance of great multitudes, while his whole life is scarce sufficient to gain the friendship of a few persons."[7]

Only as a result of this enlargement of political structure, conditioned by superincumbency, moreover, has it become impossible for the whole people to gather physically in full strength and to be politically active, according to the rules of "direct democracy." Thus arises the difficult problem, organizationally and technically, of popular representation with all its implications—which is far from being satisfactorily resolved today.

Furthermore, an unnatural, coerced societal linkage in the long run also has a distorting, destructive, and disintegrative effect on the natural communities affected by it: the social structure has an inherent tendency slowly to incorporate everything that it lays hold of. On the other hand, society itself, as a substitute for community, produces new, always more or less pathological pseudointegrations tending to progressive degeneration.

The final state toward which the process of societal decay, dissolution, and destruction moves is what we call *atomization*, the division of community into its last, no-longer-divisible components—fully isolated individuals. To be sure, this state of complete atomization in general cannot really be achieved, but only approached. For man, a communal being by nature, in the long run finds absolute isolation psychologically unendurable, even when it does not physically make life impossible. Durkheim has shown that the ultimate cause of the shockingly high suicide figures lies in progressive atomization (*désencadrement*).[8]

In terms of individual psychology the consequence and the correlative of atomization is what Fritz Künkel calls *Ichhaftigkeit* ("self-involvement"), which he points to as the fundamental psychic illness of our time in its variegated manifestations and disguises.[9] The social *désencadrement* throws the individual back upon himself, upon his own ego. It is important to see that this self-involvement does not rest upon innate sinfulness or wickedness but is the consequence of and psychological reaction to a pathologically disturbed social situation within a quite particular period of historical development. The individual who can feel secure and happily embedded in the community feels no need to withdraw into himself, to proclaim that "my self is my castle," and there artificially entrench himself.

The social result of atomization is mass society—a state of underintegration that makes itself noticeable inwardly and outwardly in the most different ways. Outwardly, underintegration is detrimental to the capacity for social action, to efficiency, including specifically the war potential of a society. As a consequence of this, the lords and rulers who are ultimately responsible for this state and brought it about also have a special selfish interest in overcoming it. Since they cannot return to the natural and healthy state of integration that existed before superincumbency, they are forced to look for substitute forms of integration that must have the strongest and swiftest effect possible and yet support and maintain superincumbency and overlordship. No wonder, therefore, that only degenerate, distorted, pathological forms of integration can come into being and that their result is only a *pseudointegration*. Artificially nourished and intensified hatred against outer (or inner) enemies is a favorite means of such pseudointegration, and it is all the more effective the more the enemy can be presented as fearsome, depraved, and contemptible. Human worship of deified rulers, leaders, prophets, unquestioning obedience, blind readiness to sacrifice, are other such means. The unnatural, pathological character of this pseudointegration betrays itself in its hostility to natural forms of integration, which it views as dangerous competition, especially the family. "Whoever loves father or mother more than me is not worthy of me; and whoever loves son and daughter more than me, is not worthy of me"—this is as much the claim of totalitarian states as of any religion of salvation.[10]

However, since man, as a communal being, needs social embodiment as much as bread, underintegration leads to a hunger for integration that can degenerate into an integration mania and can make pseudointegration a social narcotic.

This tendency is not only exploited by rulers (and by would-be rulers) but also expresses itself outwardly and spontaneously in a pathological readiness for social crowding and in those mass psychoses that are the subject matter of Gustave Le Bon's psychology of crowds.

Healthy integration, as in everything that grows naturally, finds its measure from within; it stops when it has attained its optimum. Not so with integration mania: since pseudointegrations cannot really satisfy the insatiable hunger, those addicted to it can never receive enough; as a result, escape into the maximum replaces search for the optimum. This leads to the phenomenon of *superintegration*, which demands the individual's whole being and leaves no room for independence and autonomous responsibility. Needless to say, such overintegration, being pathological, is an unstable state.

Overintegration and underintegration therefore tend to self-destruction and self-dissolution, which under certain circumstances can be explosive. Thus the vicious cycle begins anew, unless it is broken by a conscious return to healthy modes of integration.

4. SADISM AND MASOCHISM

Superincumbency brought victors and vanquished, as upper and lower strata, into opposing social situations that would eventually produce equally diverse effects in selection, breeding, and hereditary character traits. The upper stratum was trained to cultivate lust for power, arrogance, pride, a sense of superiority, toughness, cruelty, and sadism, for the more it possessed and practiced these characteristics, the more solidly it sat in the saddle of superstratification. The corresponding characteristics of the lower stratum were subservience, flexibility, submissiveness, servility, spinelessness, masochism—for the more it possessed and practiced these characteristics the better it adapted itself to the role assigned by fate. The virtues of the ruler stratum were boldness (without which they could not have won mastery), openness (there was no need for them to hide anything from anybody), and physical attractiveness and munificence (after all, they had it made). Against these virtues stood the vices of the subjugated: cowardice (not to knuckle under was to court disaster), deceit and cunning (the defensive weapons of the weak), pettiness (after all, the lords had scarcely left them the bare essentials). And these are exactly the characteristics used repeatedly, in various times and places, to demonstrate the inferior nature of the subjugated, their predestination to their role as slaves. In Greece the upper classes, in noble modesty, called themselves "the beautiful and the good" and those below them simply "the bad." At the same time, we must recognize that there are many true virtues and values—ethical and aesthetic alike—for the unfolding and cultivation of which only the social situation of the upper stratum provided margin and opportunity, so that they are as a rule to be encountered only within the upper stratum. But since it was the upper stratum itself that monopolized these possibilities of development through despotism and exclusion of the lower stratum, this, by the requirements of social justice, should have made its members ashamed rather than proud.

As Herbert Spencer wrote, "The ideas, and sentiments, and modes of behaviour, perpetually repeated, generate on the one side an inherited fitness for command, and on the other side an inherited fitness for obedience; with the result that, in the course of time, there arises on both sides the belief that the established relations of classes are the natural ones."[11] Or, as Rousseau had epigrammatically formulated it earlier: "If there are slaves by nature, it is because there were slaves against nature."[12]

Obviously the traits bred into upper and lower strata are at once polar and complementary; they support and strengthen each other and in the long run lead to a kind of pathological symbiosis. To be sure, the purity of the breeding lines was broken as a consequence of the sexual domination that repeatedly channeled the blood of the upper stratum into the lower. For no matter how the social and legal position of the illegitimate was regulated, the effects were corrosive. Either they brought lordly blood and lordly characteristics into the lower stratum (and we often meet such illegitimate sons of lords as the born leaders of uprisings and rebellions). Or else, if they remained, as in Sparta, within the upper stratum, the racial purity of that stratum, upon which their hereditary claim to rule rested, was compromised.

In the long run the original strict division of the population into an upper and lower layer did not remain intact. Intermediate strata were formed everywhere in all the different ways possible. Nowhere was there a lack of those from the lower class who, in exchange for modest recompense, offered their services as slave-drivers or noncommissioned officers to keep their class-fellows in their place. Here we have that truly amiable combination of masochism and sadism for which the folkwit of the Berliner has invented the apt designation of *Radler* ("cyclist"), where the bent back of the cyclist represents toadying to those above and the pedaling kicks to those below. Fichte writes: "Each one who considers himself a lord of others, is himself a slave. If he is not really one, he nonetheless has the soul of a slave, and will humbly crawl before the first man stronger than himself who subjugates him."[13]

Masochism and sadism can also be divided into different time phases, in that feudal or quasi-feudal upbringing exhorts children to masochism, adults to sadism. Recruits in the old Prussian-German army were mistreated and tormented by the "old fellows," and later, as "old fellows" themselves, could exact compensation from the new recruits for the abuses and humiliations endured during their own training. The same situation prevailed formerly in English boarding schools. And from ancient Rome we read accounts that in every house each newly purchased slave was tormented by the old ones acting in concert.

Truly horrifying and explosive quantities of social sadism and masochism have been accumulated since the original superincumbency and handed down from generation to generation.

Moreover, sadism and masochism are not only polar and complementary in concept; they are also fundamentally dependent upon each other in sociological reality. Superincumbency creates a fateful symbiosis between sadism from above and masochism from below. Without masochism from below, the sadism from above would not be viable or capable of functioning. It is a gross distortion to brand lust for power and brutality as vices but to view submissiveness, blind obedience, and self-sacrifice for alien purposes as virtues.

The true opposite of these destructive and complementary social vices is not any mechanical ideal of equality. Rather, it is a complementary set of virtues: on one side a set of leaders who lead from a sense of responsibility, and on the other a set of followers who follow autonomously for the sake of goals that they have chosen, and affirm, themselves. The sadism of overlords and the masochism of underlings are only pathological and exaggerated caricatures of these complementary social virtues, on which all human coexistence depends for its healthy and natural hierarchical structure.

5. The State Originating in Superincumbency

Government, or the state, was the institutional form in which superstratification became solidified. By this we do not mean that no governmental structure had existed before. If the state is defined as an ideal type by the attribute of sovereignty—i.e., independence on the outside and undisputed competence within—the state can be considered as old as mankind. By the same token the largest community structures in which men lived together exercised governmental functions and possessed a governmental character from time immemorial. Thus viewed, the state, like every grown structure, obviously develops out of embryonic initial forms. Nevertheless, the governments formed by the higher hunting cultures, with their chieftaincy and their strict organization for the chase and for war, already seem to have attained a considerable and imposing degree of development even before superstratification and its effects.

Yet we must not fail to recognize that superstratification also marks the most profound and crucial turning point in the history of the state. If we are to make a subdivision within the broad general concept of the state, it probably would be best to distinguish between a community state and a despotic state, a cooperative state and a class state, or a one-stratum and a two-strata state. The two-strata despotic class state, the typical state form of all high cultures, is a secondary phenomenon originating in superstratification. Changing it back to the classless community and cooperative state is the governmental and political aspect of the great task facing mankind today.

Marxism, by erroneous definition, narrows the concept of state to the class state originating from superstratification. From this, logically if implausibly, it deduces its projection that the state will disappear along with superstratification. But when, in keeping with this definition, Marxism asserts that the only aim and function of the state are suppression and exploitation of the lower stratum, it makes a prevalent into an absolute condition. It thereby overlooks that bipolarity which, as we have seen, constitutes precisely the typical social structure created by superstratification.

If one had ever dared to ask the rulers by what legal right they exercised domination, the answer would have been either the open appeal to the right of the sword or to investiture through God's grace (the theory of the divine right of kings). The latter, obviously, is only a theological simile for the same situation and indicates some participation of priests in the power structure. The platform of power is narrow or broad and graduated in different ways: the conditions for admission to the power structure and the criteria for remaining in it change. The personnel occupying the platform change at an ever faster and more violent pace, a process to which Pareto has given the technical term "circulation of elites."[14] (Here the expression "elite" is no longer wholly objective, but indulges in somewhat attenuated form in the self-praise of "the good and the beautiful.")

These distinctions find expression in the usage of Western languages, where Greek compounds are used for different forms of government, in which the first element is the distinctive one, the second element contains derivations either of *kratos* (-cracy), "power, despotism," or of *arche* (-archy), "rule"—thus monarchy, autocracy, aristocracy, oligarchy, plutocracy, ochlocracy. Now democracy, with an innocent matter-of-factness, places itself in the same series. Should we take it at its word and insinuate that it is a *-cracy*, a despotism like all the others and that it distinguishes itself from them only because it is the "people," the *demos*, who are in the despot's place?

The possibility of conceptualizing such a state-form, a demo-cracy in the fullest sense of the word and of its two component parts, is not in doubt. Indeed, it has been classically proved by Rousseau. In the state-forms of monarchy, oligarchy, or aristocracy, a minority had always held sway over a majority. Obviously this can also be reversed. Given corresponding prerequisites, the hitherto ruled majority can wrest power from others and, through its representatives, exercise it in the same way as before; only now it is directed against the formerly ruling minority or, eventually, against the minority of the moment in general.

Unfortunately, there is no doubt that several of such self-styled democracies espoused wholly different and far more beautiful theories and ideologies. In practice, however, their conduct more or less closely corresponds to the aforementioned construction; therefore, by choosing the designation "demo-cracy," they have unwittingly and involuntarily revealed their true nature. Whoever in such a democracy wanted to bring something about in a democratic way was scrupulously concerned to win a parliamentary majority. By this technical-formal subordination to the principle of majority rule, he believed that he had completely performed his democratic duties. Once, however, he succeeded in garnering the majority of votes, then woe to the vanquished. Unctuously dripping with good democratic conscience, the majority (or its representatives) placed themselves in the seat of constitutional power, and the minority, reduced to the status of underdog by the divine judgment of the ballot, now patiently had to endure a new superstratification with its horrors—in this case mostly budgetary. Such a vulgar-democratic governmental system could, in sum, be defined as superstratification by rotating majorities.

Three progressive steps, nevertheless, have been achieved as a by-product of such democratization.

Formally, the exercise of power in the state, including the majority power acquired by the majority, is subject to definite formal rules and legal procedures. Arbitrary, formless exercise of power is no longer possible.

Definite limits are also set to governmental interference in the individual's private sphere. A minimum of rights, as reserved rights, is guaranteed the individual against the state.

Finally, the majority possessing state power, pursuant to the rules of the game of parliamentarism, alternates so that each one has the chance, as a member of some group, some day to share in its exercise.

So long as these modest practical achievements are compared with the democratic ideals of freedom, equality, and fraternity, we can speak ironically about their inadequacy, and in some circles this is still fashionable as a sign of a "progressive" attitude. However, since we have the opportunity to compare this still most imperfect and incomplete "democratic" process with its pronounced opposite and counterpart, totalitarian collectivist tyranny, we become aware that it is the incomparably lesser evil. But the worst mistake of this vulgar-democracy is not its imperfection as such—no matter how gross—but its altogether insufficient capacity for defense against the ideological and political attacks of totalitarian collectivism.

6. Priesthood and Theology

Initially, production of higher level culture was made possible in the "medieval" social structures when lords used the revenues levied from the subjugated strata for specially gifted groups, whose talents could be exercised in their service and at their command, for the creation of culture. The result of this was the vocation of art to serve the needs and luxuries of the lords, including their representation in sacred painting. Science was supposed to gather and increase all serviceable knowledge, to secure the sovereign power, and to warn and protect the rulers from threatening dangers, whether coming from men or cosmic-magical powers.

The ruler is the first life-molder of this world. He knows the great models of the mythic age, the good rulers; he must know the secrets of nature, and he fathoms ever more deeply the traditions of his people. He gathers in himself not only all the knowledge concerning the world, the past, the positive energies of his people, priestly wisdom and experience, but also the rich treasures of literature which are brought together in his "library," in his "archives," and which transmit to him primordial knowledge. God, world, the preworld, and the energies of the people are condensed in him into an immense force which acts magically on everything and everybody.[15]

When such mental labor was embarked upon earnestly and intensively, it came increasingly under the sway of immanent laws and requirements peculiar to the departments of art or of knowledge involved. Conflicts and tensions ensued because these objective requirements did not always coincide with the services desired, rightly or wrongly, by the rulers; moreover, no one can serve two masters. These conflicts sooner or later had to be decided in accordance with the adage that he who pays the piper calls the tune. The same feudal structure that had created the precondition for the higher development of mental activity also brakes the dynamic of this development and limits to its potential.

The priesthood, organized as a social estate, is the typical feudal form of the specialization of higher intellectual interests. The French language, by its designation of the intellectual as *clerc*, keeps alive the memory of this state, showing that the secularization of this estate in our own culture is itself a recent phenomenon.

The relation between priests and knights is subject to all possible variations, ranging from the assumption by the priesthood of a secular role (hierocracy) to the administration of the priesthood by the secular power (Caesaro-papism), with the most diverse intermediate forms of cooperation, struggle, or compromise. Still, in one way or another, the priests are linked to the ruling class as deputies, as co-incumbents, or as aspirants.

Religion belongs to the most decisive fundamental forces of the human mind and for the formation of human communities. At issue here, however, is the special historical form that religious sentiment assumes when it is administered in a medieval-feudal social structure by a priesthood interested and involved in exercising dominion. The theologies of revelation and salvation are this feudal form of religion. It is very difficult for us to acquire a distance of real objectivity toward it because, for historical reasons, it is the only form in which religion has come down to us in the West. Nonetheless, this theological form of religion unmistakably bears the stigma of feudalism. For just as political feudalism demands submissiveness from the subjugated as the prime virtue, so does theology count it as a fundamental and central virtue of the faithful to show intellectual submissiveness, to render the *sacrificium intellectus*.

Normally we hold as true what strikes us as intelligible, and among contending convictions we choose the more intelligible. The theological fall of man (the fall of man to theology) occurs at the moment when it is considered a duty and merit alike to espouse and hold fast to a particular preestablished belief, and conversely, as soon as it is considered a guilt and sin alike to abjure it and adopt another; then conscience no longer is the lawful judge but becomes the prosecutor, already knowing what is right even before it hears witnesses. Theology declares the most extreme degree of bias, the "will to believe"[16] as a virtue—indeed, an absolute categorical imperative.

In the intellectual sphere what was later systematized as the doctrine of the two truths—i.e., the distinction between a higher and a lower, a divine and a human truth—corresponded to the two-tiered society of rulers and ruled, upper class and lower class. This two-tiered truth finds its sociological embodiment in the class opposition between priest and laity. Revelation is the higher, divine truth, originally and directly reserved to the priests as a theological aristocracy, as an upper stratum of higher beings closer—indeed, akin—to God. The empirical cognition of the objectively true and factual is fundamentally accessible and demonstrable to everybody in the same way; hence it is in the last resort altogether democratic. Revelation, on the other hand, is aristocratic, conferred only upon the elect, the lofty, the blessed, and handed down by them by heredity—later also through co-optation.

Moreover, no matter how different the contents of specific revelations may be, all of them perforce accord with the superior spiritual sovereign dignity they claim for themselves—and the messengers of revelation—against the lower profane truths of laymen. A far-reaching solidification and petrification sets in, however, if as a result of the situation created by superincumbency, the theology of revelation becomes a system administered by priests—a religion on horseback, so to speak—and therefore one of the most important spiritual supports of the existing power structure of "throne and altar." Thenceforth whoever dares strike at the theological tradition strikes at the holiest foundations of the ruling class itself, of the ruling class whose justification is something altogether irrational to the subjugated classes: they may view it as intolerable, but "they must believe in it." In this contrast to the unlimited religious tolerance that up to then had reigned among the "primitive" religions, we can now see the emergence of the notion of orthodoxy, so characteristic of all theology, along with the zealous fanaticism displayed in its defense. Outwardly, the result is theological imperialism, in the form of missionary zeal for conversion of others. The internal result is a theological police—the Inquisition in all its varied forms.

The Indian doctrine of rebirth is an especially pointed and obvious example of the nexus between theology and domination. Here the caste system proliferated to fantastic dimensions and the priesthood arrogantly claimed the highest caste for itself. The doctrine was elaborated to the point where it declared that only the willing individual who had subjected himself to the caste system in this life could count on membership in a higher caste in the next life.

Perhaps the most fateful service that theology rendered the ruling class is the exaggeration and glorification of the position of the ruler himself. As a result, the ruler is actually deified in his lifetime and declared to be God or an incarnation of God, accordingly demanding and receiving reverential homage from his subjects. There are also periods in which the divine kingship represents only the traditional court ceremonial, to which any occupant of the throne, as incompetent or dissolute as he may be, has equal claim. It is this situation that changes the original conception of the charismatic god-king into a counterimage and revolutionary dream-wish: the true, good king will appear and overthrow the false, wicked, arrogant despot and establish an ideal kingdom. Here is the taproot of the idea of the divine king, of the eschatological kingdom of the Messiah, Savior, Redeemer, Mahdi, Messo da Dio, including all its transformations, sublimations, and secularizations. This idea is based upon a theological exaggeration and glorification of superstratification and its overlordship, as well as upon the historically real god-kingship.

Characteristically, salvation religions appear exclusively in superstratification cultures. For it is precisely the hopelessness of trying to escape the pressure of the despotic ruler that transforms the need for salvation and the longing for redemption into a general phenomenon. At the same time, it stamps this longing with the representational forms of its own despotism. At first an immediately imminent liberation from earthly tyranny and despotism was promised through the establishment of the kingdom of God on earth, in which the last will be first. Only the ever-repeated disappointment of this chiliastic expectation compelled its theological displacement into the Beyond and sublimation of the primordial political hope of salvation.

Because theological thinking, with its authoritarian bent, removes itself from the objectifying, controlling and converging effects of rational criticism, the theological character of medieval cultures also fosters the rise and preservation of unbridgeable differences and contradictions of all kinds.

The idea of God itself was influenced in manifold ways by the social structure of domination. As the idea is always acquired through projecting of the highest human authority of the moment upward, God thus is no longer family-father, clan chieftain, or patriarch, but the reigning sultan. This analogy is at times carried into the smallest details of the court ceremonial, with archangels as dignitaries, and with angels as servants, musicians, or bodyguards whose principal duty seems to consist in forming a choir; all reverently cluster around the sultan-deity, hailing him and exuberantly bowing before him on suitable occasions. In Homeric Greece, an oligarchic aristocracy had driven back the primordial head kingship, and this gay, life-loving, chivalric form of domination was projected onto Mount Olympus, where Zeus plays the role of Agamemnon. Nor is this parallelism restricted to antiquity. Luther's God occasionally bears the unmistakable features of a patriarchal German sovereign. The reciprocal relations between absolutism, with its grand and petty sun-kings, and the baroque representation of God are striking.

Religious commandments in regard to human attitudes and behavior are also conditioned in manifold ways by the circumstances of overlordship. The fatalism of oriental religions is a direct consequence of the prevailing despotism in the countries where they arose and spread, with the concomitant incalculable vagaries, arbitrariness, and crushing power of its sultanic decisions.

We encounter two typical forms of intellectual opposition to the priesthood and its theology in the frame of "medieval" intellectual history, one more religious in character, the other more intellectual.

The earliest case of religious opposition known to us is that of the Egyptian king Ikhnaton (1370-1352 B.C.). He wanted to replace the dissolute syncretism of a priestly theology, which had degenerated and congealed into abstruseness, by a naturalistic, monotheistic, and universalistic sun worship, whose testimonials still stir us with their religious vitality and warmth of feeling. But under his stepson and second successor, the dislodged old priestly class soon managed to have "sons of learned people, whose names were known" appointed as priests. "And he paid them handsome salaries" as a triumphant inscription informs us with ingenuous frankness.[17] Nor did the heretical sun priest Eje, whom we must regard as Ikhnaton's real religious inspirer, when he ultimately seized the reins of power, help matters much: the new religion was beyond salvaging, and the reaction engineered by the old priesthood triumphed.

Zoroaster's struggle against the Magi, however, is a classic example of opposition on religious grounds in the name of ethico-religious vitality against a ritualistic-theological rigidity. It ended up in a typical way with a tragic cogency: the conquered Magi incorporated the figure and the teaching of Zoroaster into their own theology, their canon and their activity.

The first recorded rational, antitheological, antiritualistic opposition to the priestly system and doctrine seems to have arisen in India in the seventh and sixth centuries B.C. Its main intention seems to have been toward a "prescientific science," and it appears in the profoundly anti-Brahmin speculations of the Kshatriyas, which find their echo in the Upanishads, a movement joined in their own way by two sixth-century Kshatriyas, Mahavira and Buddha.

Upanishad teachings were later appropriated by the Brahmanism they attacked; they have therefore been handed down to us in the Brahmanic canon of the Vedas and in a Brahmanic revision. More important still, the whole intellectual atmosphere of the time was so pervaded with theology by Brahmanism that even antipriestly and antitheological impulses aiming to abolish priestly claims to exclusiveness could, in the last resort, lead only to a sublimated theology—which, though secularized to a certain degree, was more magical than deistic. Numinous substances reminiscent of manna from heaven were set in the place of numinous persons; it was a theology as it were in the neuter gender rather than in the masculine or feminine—as though only the Holy Spirit were to be left of the Christian Trinity. This highly sublimated, quasi-magical theology in Hellenized form is the origin of what we customarily call metaphysics—which, as we shall see, played a far-reaching, fateful role in all subsequent intellectual history. Its danger ultimately lies in its sublimated character, in the degree of its refinement. Where crude theology finds the doors bolted, metaphysics, as a form of philosophy, still works its way in through the keyhole.

7. FEUDALIZATION OF LIFE AND FEELING

The fundamental structure of dominion of the "medieval" cultures encroaches upon even the most intimate relations of family life, as it does on religion. And in this sphere, as in that of religious development, it is a question of a definition of ideas that have persevered, though weakened and modified in many ways, far beyond the Middle Ages and partly down to our own times.

There is hardly a part of our lives that is free of features conditioned by feudalism and superstratification. All our European social protocol, manners, and forms are dominated by it—as indicated by the following description of German manners at mid-century:

According to the situation one always tries to anticipate the other person, either by an expression of submission or, on the contrary, by showing him on appropriate occasions that the other need not fancy that he is "something better." We let each one who is "less" than ourselves feel that we can demand preference and consideration which we ourselves "need not" show. The curt, condescending, abrupt way of speech likewise has its root here. As in a fencing match we are constantly on guard that the other does not "step too close" to us, that we "yield him nothing," that we not "take anything from him." The striving to outdo the other in refinement, the whole blasé and affected manner of so many people, and also a great deal of envy, bitterness, and hatred originate here.[18]

The modern Western type of housing and household management, insofar as it has not preserved a pure peasant character, is more or less pronouncedly determined by feudal ideal representations; and it squints, so to speak, upward for models to go by. Even the peasant often squints upward at the bourgeois, and the worker squints upward even more. Frequently the petty bourgeois looks up to the high bourgeois, who in turn looks up to the lords of the castle for his cues.

The typical European household, in style and technique, is fully adapted to the presence of servants—servants who have historically evolved from house slaves, serfs, and subjects assigned by command to service in the castle. (The peasant menials who always sat at the family table are on a quite different sociological plane, although reciprocal influences and modulations also are found.) Today, of course, this feudalistic system of domestic service is on the wane because it stridently conflicts with the self-assertion to which socialism and the labor movement have educated the worker: there is a lack of submissiveness below, and a lack of good conscience and self-assurance above. Those in the United States who can keep a black maid, or those in central Europe who can have servants brought in from backward, pious, and (usually) eastern and agrarian-feudal regions are objects of great envy.

Neither in America nor in Europe has the impossibility of keeping servants led to the conclusion that it is time for a resolute rejection of the feudal ideal of a life-style tailored to slaveholding. In Europe the housewife prefers to take over the work hitherto performed by domestics (and by so doing notices for the first time how unpleasant and often superfluous it was). In the United States numerous household appliances, the "iron slaves," have taken over the work of domestic servants to the extent that such work can no longer be done outside the house and industrialized. Up to now the American development seems to lean more toward mechanization and standardization of the traditional feudalistic household using modern technology than toward a fundamental defeudalization. Indeed, a millionaire who can has silver candlesticks with wax candles held by liveried servants, and he strives, not always tastefully, to outdo his feudal models in social pomp and circumstance.

It would be incomparably healthier and more natural to make the best of the circumstances that force us to abandon domestic servants—that is, to become aware how dishonest the feudal character of the whole relation was as it existed hitherto, rather than renounce it and all its consequences once and for all.

The ideal of feudalism evidenced in housing and life-style is most strikingly expressed in the hotel industry. In exchange for his money, the affluent patron wants to feel, and is expected to feel, if not like the lord of a castle at least like a guest in one so that for the duration of his stay his boldest social dream-wish can finally be realized. Hence the attire of the reception personnel, at least of the doorman dressed in chevroned livery like a lord's lackey; hence the manner of greeting the guest deferentially at the entrance and the fawning attention that follows for the duration of the stay. For this purpose swank hotels especially engage an authentic butler with matching mien and moustache. Hence also the pompous high-sounding names: in the Levant the shabbiest sixth-class lodging calls itself the "Palace Hotel."

The same pseudofeudalism characterizing hotels was until recently the hallmark of the big-city apartment house, especially in the "better" neighborhoods. Not even the builders of New York skyscrapers believed they could forego battlements and gothic or Renaissance form. Money was vainly poured out for tasteless ostentation, pompous staircases with imitation marble, while practical features like soundproof walls and ceilings were neglected (nobody could see them!). Ground plan arrangement and interior decor, in the same way, were imitation feudalism.

The criticism that up to now has been leveled against such practices has always been a protest in the name of taste and "authenticity," protesting their bogusness, their sham and their kitsch—that is, from the standpoint of "authentic" feudalism, their feudalism was declared inauthentic because imperfectly imitated. Our protest is against the feudal ideal itself, and against setting it up as a model—not against the greater or lesser degree to which it may have been attained.

At all events these are vital problems that must be tackled earnestly and vigorously. We should make it a point of pride "to learn how little is enough for man"—not for the sake of asceticism, but for the sake of a zestful and joyous frugality. We should work at this task consistently and cheerfully in order to test and to demonstrate how little one needs to live a beautiful and joyous productive life rooted in human dignity. Present conditions in Germany signify an unmistakable inclination in this direction.

8. Feudalization of the Family

From the history of Roman law we know that absolute authority over the lives of all members of the family, especially of children, originally was given to the *paterfamilias*. Far from being something primordial or pristine, this phenomenon is but the highest juridical peak of the family structure, which, since nomadic times, had been strengthened, generalized, and stabilized by superstratification. Obviously, in all times it must have been a rare exception for the *paterfamilias* to make actual use of his right of homicide. But we can and must imagine the autocratic, despotic position of the father and the absolute subservience of the children in the day-to-day aspects of family life, which corresponds to the frame of such a juridical position and which also survived the gradual mitigation of this legal status.

Where household slavery prevailed *de jure* or *de facto*, it set off the tendency to blur the social distinctions between the children and the slaves of the house. For it is as difficult to rule over two kinds of subordinates as it is to serve two masters. The Latin word *puer* designates the child as well as the slave. Conversely the German word *Mädchen*, orginally the diminutive of *Magd* ("woman servant"), has come to mean servant-girl and daughter alike. If this meant a rise in status for the slaves, it naturally meant a degradation for the children. But even if we disregard the special case of household slavery, it is more than obvious that the dictatorial attitude to which the lords had become accustomed in dealing with the subjugated lower stratum was also applied to their own children. The latter after all are defenseless, dependent and need protection. Their position is often on a par with the lower stratum and their daily care is mostly assigned to members of that group. This leads to a dictatorial, authoritarian pedagogy, and the relation between generations acquires the structure of a superincumbency of the older generation over the younger, with incalculable social, psychic, and intellectual consequences.

Feudal theology and asceticism have contributed their share to the elaboration and sanction of such authoritarian pedagogy. "He that spareth his rod hateth his son: but he that loveth him chasteneth him betimes" (Prov. 13:24) was a core aphorism for the pedagogical wisdom of Christian churches. And through the centuries it has strengthened the conscience of millions of cane-wielding fathers and educators, and indeed transformed their pedagogic sadism into a positive religious duty. In the West in the Middle Ages "the rod made its way from monastic cells into the children's room. The morality of asceticism and the punishment pleasing to God conquered the family: original sin was to be cudgeled out of existence."[19]

By contrast, the child rearing among primitive peoples is reported to be exceptionally mild and liberal. Although with hunters very gruesome tortures as tests of courage are customary, the upbringing as a whole is by no means conducted in this brutal-sadistic way, and torture is not decreed a punishment for delinquency. Rather, it is a question of a special branch of study, a type of professional training pertaining to hunting and warfare. This essential difference is often overlooked. On the other hand, compare the systematic sadism in child rearing of the highly superstratified Aztecs, as it is described for us in the Codex Mendoza in word and picture.

Since "adults" in general established themselves feudalistically as a ruling upper stratum over their children, it was natural for the children to strive mightily to be received one day into this privileged estate. "Only adults may do that"; "Once you're grown up, you may do it too"—such locutions repeatedly suggested this view. This led to the quite general superordination and right to command that any adult in many European countries can claim over any child with whom he comes into contact in public—a pronounced class prerogative, and a pronounced transference of the superstratification structure into generational relationships.

9. Feudalization of Self-Consciousness

Superstratification also tends to strike inwardly and to install itself even in man's relation to himself: there is an introverted despotism, a "having power over oneself," an inner self-superstratification or "self-control" that sometimes becomes self-hatred. Arrogance and partial self-contempt often go hand in hand. Just as the boundary between upper and lower strata in the social structure tends to shift and displace itself in many ways, so the social boundary in the personality structure can cut right through one's own ego: one no longer looks down only on others but also on oneself. A part of one's own ego overlays, rules, does violence to, and despises the other part. Thus is formed within man a "superego" bearing pronounced feudal-sadistic features. Obviously this does not mean that the correct thing would be "to let oneself go." On the contrary, such a "letting go of oneself" is one of the lordly prerogatives wrongly claimed by the feudal morality. But, exactly as with children, one can be humane or domineering, kind or cruel, just or unjust, chivalrous or hateful toward oneself. Just as there are punished children, so there are also self-punishing and self-mistreating adults. Naturally this has corresponding consequences in behavior toward others. And in self-rearing as in child rearing, the more humane and chivalrous methods need not be the less effective.

10. Superincumbency and Asceticism

One of the most characteristic and striking phenomena associated with "medieval" cultures is their ascetic deprecation of the sexual drive. This stems in part from a warlike occupational resentment, originating in hunting cultures, directed against the natural erotic element in feminine tenderness, peasant comfort, and the nesting warmth of the family hearth.

But there is a more important point: since wars of aggression by male armies were fought against whole populations, one of the oldest maxims of military law is: "To the victor belongs the bride!" This already held true for the unregulated warfare of hunters; later it was stabilized into a permanent condition by nomadic superincumbency: girls and young women of subjugated peoples are declared fair game for the men of the upper stratum, and this notion has persisted in agrarian-feudal regions of eastern Europe until recent times. The so-called *jus primae noctis* was the attempt (hardly meant to be taken seriously) at legal formalization.

The Greek legends also claim feudal sexual prerogatives for the gods over the wives and daughters of mortals. This is merely a projection onto Mount Olympus of the actual conditions existing on earth between the aristocracy and its lower stratum during Mycenaean times. The lines in Molière's *Amphitryon* declaring that *"un partage avec Jupiter n'a rien du tout qui déshonore"* are just as much a mythic projection of the sexual prerogatives accorded the absolute prince.

Eventually, the result is an extreme social-sadistic attitude toward the erotic, which, in the form of the so-called marriage by abduction, also encroaches upon one's own family relationships. For example, in ancient Sparta compare the highly significant coexistence of sexual domination over female helots and marriage by abduction within the ruling stratum itself. Here, the sadistic component, which lies anatomically and physiologically in male sexuality, develops hypertrophically and achieves absolute sway. The erotic associates itself indissolubly with the social gradient of domination in its most brutal form. This distorted form of male sensuality is irreconcilable with the tenderness, intimacy, warmth, and humaneness inherent in a healthy erotic sensibility. As a result these feelings of *agape*, cut off from those of *eros*, were restricted to the relationship with mother and sister, to whom the incest taboo applied. This fostered a fateful cleavage between sensuality and tenderness, "earthly" and "heavenly" love. The taproot of the so-called "double standard" of morality, in which the same illegitimate sexual intercourse for the female partner is considered defeat and shame but for the male as victory and military glory, lies in this degenerate social structure rather than in the nature of the erotic.

This male-supremacist character finds its clearest institutional expression in the harem, the pen in which captured women were kept, characteristic of a series of superstratification cultures. In contrast, the loftier and tenderer need for erotic exchange between equals is often shunted off into homosexuality.

"The most universal tendency to debasement of love life," of which Freud has written,[20] lies in this complete feudalization of the erotic. Understandably, therefore, the bad conscience and the protest of all the gentler and finer feelings were directed against such brutal distortion of the erotic. But, one often throws the baby out with the bath and seeks the guilt not in the feudal-sadistic attitude as such, but in sexuality itself. Only thus can we explain the way in which the most central and most powerful instinct of man could be belittled and proscribed as impure. For the "Ego is laid hold of by instincts and lives in fantasies which, when the instinct secures its gratification, appear enigmatic and painful to the very same Ego and awaken in it uneasiness and anxiety before this same instinct. Man . . . can no longer, like the animal living in the 'moment,' let the experience of instinct sink back into the sphere of the indifferent and the unconscious after the instinct has been appeased. The subsequent strangeness, however, of his own instinct with its excitations of the fantasy, the anxiety, into which this strangeness easily slides, support the barriers erected by authority, and is in turn again deepened by the outer barrier."[21]

On the other hand, sexual asceticism strengthens warlike attitudes by shunting erotic vitality onto the track of sadistic impulses until the dammed up vitality, cut off from its natural satisfaction, finally finds release in the "ejaculation of the machine gun." Clearly, this reaction is quite welcome and useful to feudalism and its authoritarian-warlike tendencies.

In the system of sexual asceticism, prudery functions as a defensive feminine counterweight to the aggressive sadism to which feudalism deliberately educates the male. Actually, the outcome is a vicious circle rather than a true balance, because prudery provokes sadistic aggressiveness and evokes a counterneed for indecency, a counterjoy in the obscene now felt to have a positively liberating effect. And that provides new grist of moral indignation for the mills of prudery.

All this explains not so much asceticism itself as a widespread readiness for it—but this is precisely what needs to be explained. The impetus toward asceticism seems regularly to have come less from the military caste than from the priesthood. Here certain forms of professional asceticism had developed early, partly conditioned by the fact that pathologically tainted persons exhibit a special bent toward uncommon psychic experiences, partly from their numinous training. And as theology elaborates representations of a better world in the Beyond, it automatically leads to belittlement of this world and its joys, now and then beginning in the naïve form of bidding one to save one's appetite for the better dessert. Thus we read: "Not renunciation for renunciation's sake but as a way to greater pleasure."[22] Hence, an asceticism that outbids rather than belittles. For a priesthood disposed to rule over souls, ethical injunctions contrary to natural human instincts have the further advantage of placing man constantly in the wrong, keeping alive his consciousness of sin and intensifying his need for forgiveness and redemption.

Freud believes that sexual asceticism and renunciation of instinctual gratification is the prerequisite of a high civilization. In truth, the instinctual renunciation still expected from us today by a cultural tradition bearing the impress of Christianity goes far beyond what would really be requisite to culture. Classical Greek culture proves that a considerable degree of individual freedom is reconcilable with the highest civilization. The tragic antinomy posed by Freud, therefore, is not at all inevitable, and it rests rather upon a particular pathologically flawed development of our present-day culture.

Asceticism does not restrict itself to the sexual sphere. It also encroaches upon all other physical pleasures, above all eating and drinking, and upon the general feeling for life. Even the harmless and modest pleasure premiums that a well-attuned and prejudice-free nature has set on the body's excretory functions are despised, deprecated, and tabooed, and this produces a widespread disposition to constipation.

The connection between superincumbency and asceticism dealt with in this section seems to have dominated in this way and to this degree only in Western high cultures. The Islamic, Indian, and Chinese cultures are not strangers to ascetic phenomena and tendencies, but they are on the whole nonascetic and nonprudish to a degree that we find surprising. Indeed this is the main feature of what we in the West view as "oriental" or "Asiatic." This is especially striking in Islam, with its pronounced warlike character, which otherwise is preponderantly Western. In the Koran it is expressly stated: "O ye believers, forbid not such good things as God has permitted you" (Sura 5:89). Of the Prophet himself it is reported that he "never despised a meal and when he craved something he ate it and did not deny it to himself and enjoyed what was available to him and never abstained from a harmless thing."[23] Later in Islam, ascetic influences stemming from Christianity were expressly fought, although with diminishing success. An order like that of the heterodox Bektashi—who eat, drink, and love for the greater glory of God—would be unthinkable in the Christian domain, unless we recall Rabelais' abbey of Thélème. In the Indian Kamasutra, which pedantically systematizes the art of love, specific persons are listed in whose presence sexual intercourse is forbidden. It follows that it is allowed in the presence of all others—an amazing degree of phanerogamy in contrast to our own cryptogamous upbringing—to use the brilliant terminology of Pareto.

11. CHOSEN PEOPLES

The concept of the chosen people is of a historico-theological nature. The priesthood of a successful conquering people can do no better than to ascribe this success to a supreme deity. So long as this divinity is imagined only as the tribal god of the successful tribe, he thereby proves his superiority over the deities of the defeated tribes. If, however, the divinity is imagined as a universal god, a god of the whole world, then the success of this one people presents itself as a special preference, as a selection precisely of this people.

Such a choice, however, is not a unilateral and unconditional act.

The people chosen must prove itself worthy of such grace, by unquestioning obedience to divine commands as proclaimed by the priesthood. This conditional character of the election has pedagogic as well as theological advantages in the hands of an exegetical priesthood. The advantages are theological in that they furnish the possibility of explaining and justifying political failures and reverses as educational measures of the divinity, as punishments and trials.

The history of the chosen people *par excellence*, the Jewish people, furnished abundant occasions for this kind of justification. In hard reality this small people, even at the zenith of its political history under Kings David and Solomon, had never got beyond the status of a Near Eastern petty state of the third or fourth rank. Even this quite modest independence did not last long.

The Assyrians, by far the cruelest of all conquering peoples of ancient history known to us, put an end to this independence with easily imaginable brutality. As a result, the consciousness of being an elect race acquired a penetrating sadomasochistic stamp among the Israelite-Jewish people and developed into an anti-Assyrian countersadism that in the imagination almost matched the brutality of the Assyrian sadism that had set it off. Under the terrible pressure of the cruel Assyrian dominion there developed among the little people of Israel the eschatological revenge dream of its own world rule at the end of time under God's Day of Judgment: "And the house of Israel shall possess them in the land of the Lord for servants and handmaids: and they shall take them captives, whose captives they were; and they shall rule over their oppressors." "They shall bow down to thee with their face toward the earth, and lick up the dust of thy feet." "For thou shalt break forth on the right hand and on the left; and thy seed shall inherit the Gentiles, and make the desolate cities to be inhabited." "And I will tread down the people in mine anger, and make them drunk in my fury, and I will bring down their strength to the earth."[24]

It is only later that the way out of this extremely brutal, still purely nationalistic (Zionist) chiliasm leads to a sublimated conception more appropriate to universalistic religion—the concept of a divine kingdom at the end of time that will unite mankind to itself, not through violent subjection but through voluntary conversion. "And there shall be one fold, and one shepherd."[25]

Meanwhile, however, the foreign domination of the Assyrians in Palestine was followed by that of the Egyptians, Babylonians, Persians, Macedonians, Ptolemaeans, Seleucids, and finally Romans until the eventual disappearance of the autochthonous Jewish state. From a purely political view we cannot imagine a more woeful course of history, a starker contrast to the claimed role of a chosen people. This unfortunate small people held fast to this grotesque claim notwithstanding, and with all the more ardor and passion; and they were driven to sublimate it ever more intensively as a result of the brutal contrast posed by political events—developments that have had consequences for world history to this day.

The Jewish people itself owes its unbroken sense of identity under the most desperate circumstances to the notion of being the chosen people and to the theological and organizational systematization of that notion. And in its extremely sublimated, spiritualized and "ennobled" form, the idea of the chosen people found unsuspecting entry even where its cruder forms might have encountered moral resistance. Thus, as a result of the failure to recognize its poisonous character, it could become an uncontested component of Christian and hence of modern Western culture. At the same time, the reversion to less sublimated, more primordial and brutal forms was open at any time when favorable circumstances arose, with the spiritual grandeur of the sublimated version serving as an ideological cloak, as justification of hypocritical disguise. The concept of election was renewed along these lines notably by Calvinism and served as the religious ideology of Anglo-Saxon imperialism. Fichte's *Addresses to the German Nation* claim it for German nationalism, in which its aftereffects lingered until just yesterday, and it later directed itself especially against the people to whom it owed its origin. In Palestine today it returns to its place of origin and to its original form.

12. RACIAL PRIDE

We have seen what the technical-military reasons were for the superiority of nomads, especially the chariot-driving and horse-riding nomads, over settled peoples. This technique of warfare leading to superstratification derives only from the transport technology of the nomadic economy and life-style and obviously has nothing to do with race. It is peculiar to all riding and chariot-driving nomadic peoples, to Turks as well as Mongols, to Semites as well as Indo-Germans.

A biased appraisal of the pronounced somatic difference between the upper and lower strata automatically occurs in analyzing the social situation created by superstratification. In the beginning the upper stratum sets up its physical type as beautiful and that of the lower stratum as ugly. Soon the lower stratum allows this appraisal to be forced upon it and finally makes this appraisal its own—even though such internalization amounts to moral suicide. The racial ideal of the upper stratum was always sharply elaborated, indeed intensified, by appropriate hereditary selection. Abundant nourishment, favorable and hygienic living conditions, solicitous care, protection against overexertion—all contributed further to its physical improvement. Even a measurable increase in height has occurred as a result of appropriate life-styles. Conversely, negative selection, oppression, poverty, need, undernourishment, inadequate clothing, dirt, endemic diseases, and overexertion shaped the physical type of the lower stratum.

Race theory becomes a characteristic of the feudal world view once power becomes hereditary within the ruling stratum, once the offspring can adduce as claim to this inheritance their mere descent, their blood relationship to that race which, through superstratification, has proven its mysterious and irresistible supremacy—indeed its divinity. According to this notion, mankind by nature and divine will is divided into superior and inferior races predestined to rule or to serve. The highest, unchangeable distinction that can be awarded to a human being, according to this notion, is to be born the scion of a master race: foresight in the choice of parents becomes the highest achievement! Beaumarchais (1777) has Figaro (act 5, scene 3) say to the representative of this "aristocracy of birth": "Nobility, fortune, a rank, offices, all that makes one so proud! What have you done for so many good things? You took the trouble to be born, and naught else."

According to Schiller, only "base natures" are respected on the basis of what they do; "noble" natures on the basis of what they are.[26] Race theory thus serves as the most important justification of the despotic power structure from the second generation onward. It originated from this apologetic function and is really comprehensible only in terms of this function.

The longer superstratification lasted, the more the actual accomplishment of successful superstratification receded into the background as a justifying principle, compared with that of mere descent. In the absence of such a distortion one would expect that the more recent title attained through merit would be more highly valued and that the noninheritable titles of nobility, awarded in many countries as a military distinction, would be more prestigious than those that are merely inherited. As we know, however, the opposite is true. Only in Japan did the newer nobility enjoy greater prestige than the older within the frame of a merit aristocracy, which simply lapses after six generations if not renewed for newly acquired merit.

If, however, it is the blood of the conquering race that legitimizes domination and, correspondingly, the blood of the conquered race that by divine ordinance and by right, or else by "nature," condemns it to servitude, then the conquerors are duty bound to maintain the purity of this precious "blue" blood, of the magic source of their superiority, of their claim to rulership. In keeping with the stock-breeding origins of the conquerors and the feudal character of horse-breeding and equestrian sports, preserved to this day, this demand is stylishly clothed in terms borrowed from the language of stock-breeding: as, for example, in Theognis and Plato—and in the writings of modern racists.[27]

Moreover, this racial pride was transferred to the evaluation of animals. After the superstratification of horse-breeders over cattle-breeding peasants and over keepers of asses, those animals bred by the subjugated peoples were viewed as contemptible compared with the victorious horse. It is amazing to note the tenacity with which this attitude, wholly unjustified on rational grounds, has persisted to this day.

From Württemberg in southern Germany in our own century we have the following report:

> In medium-sized farms, use of the cow as a draft animal would frequently be a crucial factor in terms of profitability; the yoking of horses signifies a greater liability because the utility is restricted to pulling power and eventual dung production, whereas the cow allows possibilities for more versatile uses. The peasants in the Württemberg region, however, do not let this profitability factor play a primary role in their considerations. They reject this changeover because a peasant using a cow enjoys less social esteem than a peasant using a horse. Upon being questioned about this one peasant replied, "If I go around with a cow, I won't get a wife."[28]

In Turkey the donkey was until recently the draft animal used by peasants to bring products to the city and hawk them from street to street and house to house. A horse would be unnecessarily fast, pretentious, and expensive. Furthermore, the draft donkey played a highly characteristic role in all the streets and alleys of Istanbul—not least to the delight of the tourists, who featured it in their snapshots of street scenes. But it was precisely this that offended a sensitive nationalistic self-consciousness. In early 1937 an article appeared in the press, written by the government press chief of that time, under the caption: "The Donkey and Foreign Photographers"; soon thereafter the donkey was forbidden on the streets of Istanbul and Ankara.

Race theory is a typical product of the cleavage of society into two strata or layers, as conditioned by superstratification. Thus it inevitably runs into unresolvable inner contradictions if it is propagated as a "myth" refurbished along the lines of a vulgarized Darwinism, together with the myth of the folk community, which, at least in theory, replaces the notion of multiple societal strata. One pseudo-solution is to exclude from the folk community, as a pariah caste, an easily recognizable minority and then to use it as an example of racial inferiority in contrast to the noble, thoroughbred qualities of one's own racial strain. Although originally the ruling noble race was strongly in the minority and proved its superior valor by overcoming this numerical handicap, the situation is now exactly the opposite. Yet the trampling underfoot of a defenseless minority is not exactly a suitable occasion for heroic feelings, and one attributes to this minority, despite its manifest weakness and defenselessness, a mysterious wickedness connected with danger. An appropriate rationalization is the proclamation of one's own racial superiority over all other peoples beyond one's own borders: here the situation reverts to the superstratification situation in *statu nascendi*. It challenged the self-proclaimed chosen race to prove its superiority in effecting superstratification over those considered racially inferior.

We can approach the race problem with two quite different questions. One is anthropologically static: Can the character and traits, the virtues and vices of different peoples be traced to their race? Generally, those who pose this question are confident that the race to which they belong combines all conceivable virtues in itself in contrast to the many vices, faults, and repellent traits of other races. Further, these racially conditioned virtues have the priceless advantage of being innate and irreplaceable, delivered free of charge and postpaid at birth, and also of being guaranteed to one's descendants without their having to do anything to merit them or incur any risk of their loss. A truly enviable arrangement! Taken seriously and scientifically, of course, this is the most questionable aspect of the race problem, for notions like national character are highly problematical and elude analysis. The correlation of personal character traits with the heredity of particular races up to now has not gone beyond a few quite crude and summary conclusions. Scholarship so far has had no conclusive success in separating biological from cultural heredity; indeed the task has not even been seriously attempted or even recognized as a fundamental problem.

The other question is of a historical, dynamic character. Every easily identified race anywhere today, every single component of a mixed race recognizable today must in some way or other have originated at a particular point in time, in a particular way, and under particular conditions. This is a clear and unambiguous formulation of the question, and in the pursuit of this line of inquiry the findings of recent anthropological research, notably that of Eickstedt, have been impressive and highly promising.[29]

13. Feudal Distribution of Property and Income

The original superstratification, which came upon a lower class of pure peasants, usually began as an "occupation" with a partition of the arable soil among the conquerors. Obviously the resident peasants were distributed along with the land, since the overlords had no intention of working like peasants: land without people would not have been of the slightest use to them. For the people who continued to till the land that had once been theirs, the essential difference was economic; they now had to hand over as much as half of the product of their labor to the conquerors. The latter, with their entourage, thenceforth lived "off the surplus of the land" and gradually could develop this luxury into that very mode of life, that very set of occupations and skills that was to furnish the basis of high cultures. But at first there literally was "exploitation," a seizure by violence or the threat of violence of the "surplus value" that the subject peasant produced over and above his bare minimum of existence. At first the unlimited, direct power of command of the lords over the subjugated insured this appropriation, and any legal structure of rules of landed property would have been an unnecessary detour. The only formality accompanying the original occupation no doubt was no more than a reciprocal demarcation of the districts allotted for exploitation, designed to prevent quarrels among the conquerors.

Later the development of manifold sociological and legalistic constructs kept abreast of changing conditions to ensure the undisturbed collection of revenues due to the overlords. We shall deal in another context with the motive forces that ultimately gave a plutocratic direction to this development. The consequence that interests us here is that the direct control of the lords over the subjugated, viewed from the aspect of the latters' personal bondage, after several interludes, came at last to cease. The manorial system now remained as the overlords' only economic anchor and as the source of ground rent. And since the soil was no longer used for exclusively agricultural purposes, the same principle of particular ownership came to apply to other labor-produced means of production.

The legal successors of the original conquerors, whoever they might be, at all events were still a minority of the population. But, they held in their hands all capital in the way of property ownership and consequently were the recipients of all unearned income and revenues. Meanwhile it became possible, with the advent of the economic principle of free competition, to acquire property also by exercising one's economic ability and conversely to lose it for lack of such ability. But this did not alter the fundamental fact that a minority, now as before, owned through inheritance rather than merit a considerable portion of the landed wealth or that these hereditary proprietors had an incomparably greater chance of coming out ahead in the economic competition.

According to Mirabeau there are "only three ways enabling one to live in society: one must beg, steal, or be paid for a service."[30] There is, however, still a fourth way: to have inherited wealth and to live from the income of it. It is highly revealing that Mirabeau forgot to mention this fourth way. Obviously he repressed it despite—or because of—the fact that it was of the greatest importance to himself. For we can hardly assume that he wished to subsume it under the rubric of stealing, present or past.

The concentration of ownership of all essential capital in the hands of a small minority may thus be traced to the original superstratification during which the conquerors, in the simplest way imaginable, appropriated the property that formerly was divided more or less equally among the whole population and then redistributed it among themselves. The perpetuation of this one-sided distribution of property normally occurred through hereditary succession; or on occasion through the political victory (mostly in war) of one conqueror over another. With the transition from aristocracy to plutocracy it also became possible to become a member of the capital-owning minority by partially or wholly economic means. Inherited capital—and its further accumulation—at all times has maintained its preponderant and dominant position over capital newly acquired by the economic accomplishment of outsiders. The pious legend according to which the original accumulation of capital is the fruit of "industry and thrift" has rightly been ridiculed as a fairy tale from Marx to Oppenheimer and exposed as a self-serving lie.

The only question that might still require clarification in view of this chain of facts is why, under more or less free competition, the once highly concentrated ownership of capital was not more widely dispersed, but apparently concentrated even further. This poses a complex and intriguing problem that urgently invites study. At all events one of the essential causes of this restricted dispersion would seem to lie in the sociological fact that traditional conceptions and customs maintained and strengthened the aristocratic structure created by superstratification even after its plutocratic transformation. Moreover, the human qualities needed to preserve inherited wealth—especially when reinforced by one's upbringing—are found far more commonly than those needed to acquire new wealth—especially if discouraged by one's upbringing. The formation of large-scale enterprises and large-scale industry, partly for technical-economic reasons, partly as a consequence of the traditional accumulation of capital ownership, and partly out of sheer megalomania, reinforces the same tendency.

Be that as it may, the uneven distribution of capital does not for its explanation require us to posit any occult economic forces, whether an invisible monopoly of land operating in a free real estate market or some uncanny quality of capital itself as in the Marxian magic formula that value begets surplus value.

14. Feudal Monopoly of Learning

In the cultures created by superstratification it is not only property and income that are distributed unevenly in favor of the upper stratum but also intellectual goods. Only the upper stratum, along with its dependents, enjoys the freedom needed for a constant concern with the "higher" things—i.e., intellectual matters. Expressed in modern terms, the upper stratum enjoys a monopoly of learning. But this monopoly of learning must be viewed in various contexts and judged differently in each.

The law of the pyramid, as we saw, states that the rise of high cultures first became possible as a result of specialization and of large-scale division of labor, when certain groups of the population were exempted from daily physical labor required for the satisfaction of immediate physical needs. This implies just as clearly that the production of intellectual goods and the full-time professional life are viable only for the members of this minority group, for the leisure classes in the broadest sense.

This connection, moreover, holds true not only within a setting of superstratification but quite generally and fundamentally. Higher intellectual culture presupposes, at all times and places and by its own inner logic, that its devotees can concentrate upon cultural matters as their chief occupation and are freed from the physical labor required for the provision of food and their other physical needs. Reason further dictates that the leading positions in the hierarchy (an inevitable concomitant of every high culture and of every human group of any considerable size) must be entrusted to these practitioners of the higher cultural functions.

All these requirements are given in superstratified cultures, or else these would not have developed or survived—and of course this circumstance is often adduced to justify and defend the persisting stratified structure. Such defenders of privilege, however, tend to overlook the feudal stigma that in superstratification cultures adheres to this logically required social structure by virtue of the specific conditions of admission and selection to the upper reaches of that structure.

In superstratified cultures admission to higher education originally rested upon the principle of heredity. Culture, and the opportunity to acquire it, are inherited like power and wealth, and this is the very foundation upon which the upper stratum's monopoly of learning rests. Originally the monopoly of learning (if we wish to employ the term *learning* in connection with these early times) was a mere adjunct to the feudal monopoly of power and wealth; later it became increasingly central as entry into all the higher occupations and positions, with their added bonuses of influence, prestige, and income, became dependent on formal training. Today the possession of higher education is the most important single prerequisite for membership in the upper stratum. And this indeed is the reason why the Bolsheviks, turning the tables on the old order, have excluded the offspring of the former upper stratum from educational opportunities so as to reserve them for the proletariat, the former lower stratum. In this case only the roles are changed, while the old feudal plot is maintained and even intensified; the old monopoly of education is merely stood on its head.

To abandon or defeudalize this superstratification culture, and yet maintain that hierarchy of learning that is indispensable to all high cultures, is possible only when the crucial selection for admission to all stages of higher education is made exclusively on the basis of talent and ability, of innate endowments of mind, imagination, and motivation.

15. Feudal Authority over Men

In the next chapter we shall discuss the motive forces from which, and the manner in which, the beneficiaries of conquest and unlimited personal dominion came to impose upon themselves certain limitations, regulations, and legal rules. As a result of these limitations, only economic advantages finally remained in the hands of the upper stratum—e.g., as a steady revenue derived from the domination of the lower stratum. Essentially this was due to the fact that, apart from special public and governmental organizations, only small, family enterprises existed within the private economy. This predominant form of enterprise, in agriculture and in handicraft alike, constituted the strongest bulwark protecting the workday of the lower stratum from the despotic pressure of the upper stratum. Even if the legal status of the lower stratum was that of a slave, as long as their work took the form of peasant farming or of handicraft or small-scale industry, that work necessarily retained a measure of independence, a basic character of self-employment. Dependency was limited *de facto* to the obligation of making specified payments in kind from the product of their labor, payments which even in the worst cases left at least the bare minimum required for the physical existence of the worker and his family. At worst this reduced many or all in the lower stratum to marginal producers, which some of them would have been anyway. For the peasant himself the net effect was the same as if the fertility of his soil had correspondingly diminished. Above all, the peasant's bondage was usually limited to the quantitative economic sphere. Consequently, the situation of the peasant simply became that of a hereditary tenant with a lease requiring payment in kind. Peasant family enterprise offered no opportunity for the development of direct feudal dominion within the economic sphere.

Even when the lord did not live exclusively from payments but also managed one or more agricultural enterprises through his agents, nothing very much had changed as long as these remained small-scale enterprises. If the lord managed his manor with house slaves or even with hired help, these were integrated into his family. And even if he managed his manor with tenants who were obli-

gated to perform labor services for him by way of *corvée*, such forms
of service, given the small size and relative rarity of lord-managed
enterprises, did not play a significant role.

Therefore throughout the entire long period from stabilized, legal
superstratification until the advent of large industry, the dependency of the lower stratum, regardless of its legal form, for practical
and economic reasons manifested itself only in a diminution of income because of the enforced payments in kind and in an obligation
to perform occasional labor services. There were thus two sorts of
manorial taxes payable in kind: the bigger part in produce, the
smaller part in labor. This taxation, on the average, must surely
have been moderate; in the long run, it had to leave free a bare
minimum existence.

To use Walter Eucken's classification and terminology, in the
economic order of this period the private, centrally managed
economies of the lower stratum coincided with the smallest and
most intimate natural social unit, the family (enlarged by some auxiliary labor where necessary).[31] Toward the outside, these largely
autarchic family enterprises found themselves partly in voluntary
relations of reciprocal economic exchange and partly in involuntary
and one-sided political relations with the world outside them. The
manors of the upper stratum, which numerically formed a tiny
minority, performed, on the one hand, the functions of a tax collecting office, receiving and administering the politically exacted payments in kind; and, on the other, that of one or more centrally managed industries directly owned by the lord. Here, too, the workers
were forced to labor for their masters, but the extent of this forced
labor at first was so modest, that the example of the surrounding
peasant or artisan enterprises by and large set the sociological and
economic norms for life on these manors as well. All these receiving
or producing structures were subordinated to the purely consumptive great household of the lord and his entourage (occasionally also
to that of the abbot and his monks). This lordly household assumed
enormous dimensions and, of course, was centrally managed. However, in consequence of its consumptive character (including also, of
course, the preliminary stages of consumption) it did not affect the
organizational forms of production of the regular economy. The dependent people incorporated in it are menials, domestic servants,
not workers. Their sociology and their psychology are of a very
different sort. They are accepted into the lord's family but with
lesser rights; they are, as it were, children by morganatic adoption.
The institution of the "ministerial" nobility—that is, the rise of such

servants, or even slaves, to the highest political offices—is significant in this respect. As long as the family enterprise of peasants and artisans was the normal mode of production, the economic sphere could provide a refuge of the lower stratum from the despotic pressure of the upper stratum in all its more direct forms of expression. Since the upper stratum lived from the productivity of the lower stratum, it had compelling interest in the highest possible level of the lower stratum's productivity and therefore in seeing to it that the producers, whether peasants or artisans, could work undisturbed. So long as production was carried on in family enterprises, there was no possibility that members of the upper stratum could take direct command and charge of hundreds or thousands, indeed tens or hundreds of thousands, of independent petty enterprises. The lords could exact from these enterprises certain deliveries according to their particular productive capacities; to the extent that it was a matter of payment in kind, this amounted simply to delivery without payment. But all other aspects of the enterprise had to be left to the personal responsibility and disposition of each entrepreneur. Each peasant and artisan was and remained the independent central manager of his own family enterprise, regardless of his legal status: slave or serf, free tenant, or freeholder and taxpayer. The day's work in his family enterprise was his sanctuary against the arrogance and arbitrariness of the lords. Every disturbance of this sphere signified the danger of diminished productivity and hence of a smaller share for the lord. The interests of the upper and lower strata were identical in regard to the undisturbed independence of the family enterprise. The lord was punished for every disruptive encroachment upon this independence by an automatic diminution of his revenue, whether in money or in kind.

All this holds not only for peasant-managed agriculture, but largely also for artisan-managed industry. Here, too, petty and family enterprises were the general rule. Even the "ergasteries," which are sporadically referred to in Greek antiquity, and in which the workers were slaves, were probably enterprises of modest size consisting of agglomerations of petty artisans working alongside each other, as in post-medieval European "manufactures."

A fundamental change in this economic condition of life of the lower stratum first comes about with the emergence of large-scale enterprise as a new form of social organization. The oldest of these large-scale enterprises were developed to construct great governmental or public buildings. In Exodus 2:5 we have a vivid depiction of the sociological character of such public works in ancient Egypt.

Only very late, and in some areas, did this organizational form encroach upon the domain of the private economy. The links were formed by mines, which were managed mostly by lessees of the state who employed hundreds or thousands of slaves, whose living and working conditions were manifestly inhumane. One report on unsanitary conditions and the resultant mortality rate recalls the conditions of present-day forced labor in the Soviet Union. In agriculture, plantations operated like large-scale enterprises, probably also following the Egyptian model, seem first to have developed in Carthage; from there they were taken to Rome, where this form of large enterprise ran rampant and became one of the main causes of Italy's decline. In all these places, the labor force at first consisted primarily of slaves. In Western economic history the development toward large-scale enterprise begins chiefly at the turn of the sixteenth century on tropical plantations, which were worked first with shanghaied Indians and then with purchased Negro slaves—alongside white, forced laborers. This form of large-scale agriculture, working with slave labor for the market, then spread from the tropical colonies into the whole of non-Islamic Europe east of the Elbe. Here it led to progressive deterioration of the legal status of the originally free peasants—a legal status that in Russia and also in parts of eastern Germany in the middle of the eighteenth century came to resemble slavelike serfdom.

The development of the plantation economy within Western culture plainly signifies a reversion, going far beyond the genuine high cultures, to the barbaric superstratification cultures of the tropical zone, which were the original setting of slavery and the manhunt; and indeed the Negro plantation slaves in America were drawn from the descendants of these very cultures. The trade in soldiers in which the German absolutist potentates of the eighteenth century engaged may properly be viewed as another form of slave trade.

In Europe, unlike the colonies, neither a disenfranchised indigenous population nor Negro slaves were available as an agricultural labor force, but only free or nearly free peasants whose working time was already taken up by the tillage of their own acre of land. Here one had to undermine the status of the peasant to obtain tractable workers for plantationlike, large-scale enterprise. That, however, was a political problem and in the last resort depended on the power and attitude of the state. In some regions, the monarchy was strong enough to be able to force the nobles to live in the capital and to make them subordinate to and dependent on the ruler, and also to keep the peasants in a status of his direct subjects. In such cases the landholdings of the nobles served them only as a source of revenue. The fateful development of noble landholdings into large-scale enterprises could unfold only where a monarch was too weak to prevent the centrifugal rise of local, agrarian-feudal semisovereignties within his realm, or where he preferred to build his power on the newly created ministerial nobility against the rebellious hereditary-landed nobility. This would involve banishing the nobility to their estates where, in compensation and for sport, they were left a free hand in the management of their holdings.

In the sphere of crafts and manufacture, the story of the rise to large-scale enterprise with a legally free labor force is well known. The house of correction or workhouse, especially in Calvinist regions, also played its role in the ascendancy of modern large-scale enterprise, and the Prussian barracks yard was an important preliminary step toward the German factory.

Large-scale enterprise brings the entire workday of the peasant—hitherto self-regulated—under the rigid discipline of command to which he owes absolute and unremitting obedience. Everything is prescribed: the place and the timing of work, the length of the workday, its beginning, its end and its breaks, its tempo, rhythm, and manner—indeed the performance of the work itself including the posture to be assumed and the individual motions to be executed in its performance. The extremely despotic, superstratification character of this situation appears most brutally in Negro slaves, driven to work like a herd of animals and by the pitiless kurbash of the overseer. Yet it is merely a difference in degree when the brutal slave whip is replaced by the elegant riding stick of the manorial lord or the barking command of the factory overseer. The absolute heteronomy of the workday, the fact that the worker is subject to an alien command without let-up, remains unchanged, and in one situation as in the other he is forced to subject himself to this command on pain of death. For whether the rebellious slave who refuses to work is beaten to death or whether the "free" worker who refuses to work is fired and left to die of hunger, the effect is the same. And the prospect of this effect has exactly the same result in the preventive measures which the individual concerned must adopt. (Modern social and socialist counterinfluences will be discussed later in another context.)

West Africa, with its "slave coast," is one of the oldest and most important centers of slavery in the world. Here a nineteenth-century Fula chieftain, an expert in this field, had the following conversation with the French traveler and researcher Hyacinthe Hecquard:

> We often talked about our forms of government and the relations of different classes in European society. He did not attribute the least importance to the equality of citizens before the law and asked me how my fellow countrymen managed without slaves. His conclusion was that among us, the servants and the poor class in general are the slaves of the rich because the latter, as the result of unemployment, could be put in a situation of extreme indigence in a country where nothing is to be had for nothing.[32]

All the social drawbacks of large-scale enterprise are connected exclusively with the form of organization and of production of the large enterprise as such, regardless of the formal legal status of the worker and unquestionably regardless of the property and legal status of large-scale enterprise. A large-scale enterprise can change owners, its legal form, and its management as often as it pleases, or it can even pass over to public ownership. But the individual worker notices nothing of this unless he accidentally reads it in the newspaper or is informed about it by a notice posted on the bulletin board. Conversely, a slave, who lives and works as a small peasant on a plot of land belonging to his lord, is incomparably better off in his everyday living condition; indeed, he is freer than a "free" farm laborer on a Junker's landed estate east of the Elbe in the nineteenth century, or on a Bolshevik kolkhoz in the twentieth. One can be sociologically free though legally bound, and sociologically bound though legally free. The determining factor is autonomy or heteronomy in the organization of the workday. The legal form of slavery, which in the sociological practice of household slavery presented a comparatively harmless partiarchal situation, first developed the phenomena that are so shocking to our sense of humanity. The legalistic form can either adequately express the real situation or successfully conceal it. The reality of the worker in a large-scale enterprise corresponds at best to the legal form of slavery or serfdom.

The emergence of large factories implies the introduction, for the first time, of feudal patterns into the economy at large. With the rise and spread of large-scale industry, feudal command, domination, and superstratification seize control of the workday of the lower stratum, and since the entire waking life of a member of the lower stratum consists exclusively of work, these forces control its whole existence. This is a patent and obvious social fact, not some abstract and arcane economic or legalistic relationship.

Private property—in general or as a means of production—is not to be blamed. On the contrary, private property constitutes the most solid bulwark against feudalism conceivable, so long as it remains appropriately divided as the small property of the peasant or artisan in his work site and in his instruments of labor. And even with the one-sided acquisition of private property by the upper stratum, these negative influences cannot develop, as we have seen, as long as such development is hindered by the institution of petty and family enterprise. The ravaging social effects of property appear first when the mode of production of large-scale enterprise combines with a one-sided distribution and concentration of property.

Whatever the technical and economic advantages of large-scale enterprise may be, we are concerned here exclusively with its social and historical effects. Large scale enterprise—and precisely within a feudally-infected social milieu—is a social catastrophe, extending and intensifying superstratification far beyond anything that has existed to this point. It permeates the whole workday of the lower stratum. For up to then, due to the organizational form of small-scale enterprise, it was precisely the workday that had remained free of this superstratification structure. It is the organizational form of work, the enterprise form, that makes one free or unfree: small-scale enterprise makes one free; large-scale enterprise makes one a slave.

As we shall see later, the superstratification structure earlier had exhibited a tendency toward progressive decline; compared to this trend, the advance of large-scale enterprise signifies a new upsurge of superstratification and its encroachment upon a major and central domain of life in which, up to then, it had been restricted by small-scale industry. Rational considerations of productivity had required new self-limitations and self-restrictions on the part of the master class, particularly in the economy itself. Here, for the first time, there was a convergence and a coincidence between a lust for domination and the requirements of productivity. Here, for the first time too, men could pursue their lust for domination within the economic sphere without suffering any pangs of conscience—indeed, while considering themselves the very embodiment of progress. No wonder this opportunity was seized with enthusiasm and exploited with a vengeance.

Despotism above and bondage below had increased in the agrarian sector of Western culture since the bloody collapse of the German peasant war in 1525, which had been preceded by similar peasant revolts in other countries. This view has finally prevailed as a result of extensive research in agrarian history. It is also generally acknowledged that in Germany the free towns had experienced their greatest flowering at the end of the Middle Ages, and that their subjugation was largely accomplished under the absolutism of the seventeenth century. These historical perceptions, however, still must be supplemented by the further insight that in the industrial, no less than in the agrarian, sector the advance of large-scale enterprise led to significant diminution of the real freedom of the working masses.

At the same time, in the highest intellectual sphere of Western culture, a movement directly opposite set in. Since it is hard to imagine that a culture moves simultaneously forward and backward, as we are proud of the forward movement and ashamed of the backward movement, and as intellectuals were responsible for the intellectually forward movement, they eagerly succumb to the charming delusion that in the last centuries things have gone forward, "thank God." And in the judgment of large-scale enterprise itself, the progress in production and technology, and the divinely willed necessity and benefit from progress were emphasized by all, the socialists in particular, so that nobody seems to have noted that the real seat of social and human evil must be sought precisely in the most visible embodiment of this progress.

Before any practical conclusions can be drawn from such an insight, it is necessary to investigate diverse aspects of the same matter and consider the findings in their overall context. Only then can one ask whether, and how, it might be possible to defeudalize, to detoxify large-scale enterprise where it is manifestly superior in terms of production and technology and to preserve only its technological advantages in production. Yet it is clear from the outset that such a change cannot come about merely by changing legal property relations. At all events, on the basis of evidence accumulated so far, we see ourselves compelled, for sociological reasons, to place great weight on the argument against large-scale enterprise.

16. RURAL AND URBAN NOBILITY:
MANORIAL PROPERTY AND LANDED PROPERTY

For the development of large-scale enterprise in agriculture, as well as for the position of the nobility in medieval society, there is hardly a more important distinction than that between residence in the countryside and residence in the city. Residence in the city, often induced or forced by the central government, not only makes the nobility a more dependent and pliant functionary of the throne, but also promotes urbanization generally. For Greek history it was highly important that the nobility were settled together on the acropolises through *synoikismos* and hence urbanized. The same holds true for the nobility of Provence and of the Italian commercial cities of the Renaissance, which, in part, forced the "incasamento" of the nobility. In Germany, significantly, "connection with merchants and residence in the city was proclaimed since the late Middle Ages as incompatible with nobility."[33] This accounts for the characteristic Italian form of the Renaissance in contrast to the often philistine coarseness of contemporary German urban culture. The real carriers of resentment against the city and the intellectual development it fosters are not the peasants, but the rural nobility.

But the same flowering of the city, city culture, and city ways in western Europe that drew the nobility into its spell caused the old barter economy of the feudal manors to wither away, plutocratizing and reducing the nobles' landed property to a source of revenue. It had an opposite effect on the agrarian structure of those regions from which the cities drew their supplies of grain and wood, since the nearby environs could no longer supply agricultural products when entire districts became urbanized. From time immemorial the thinly populated plains of eastern Europe had been the natural reservoirs of grain and wood for the urbanized regions of Europe. They had supplied (by way of the Black Sea) the Greek cities, especially Athens, since 600 B.C. Since the waning Middle Ages they had taken over the provisioning of the flourishing cities of western and central Europe (by way of the Baltic and the North Sea) with their increasingly dense populations. Naturally only large producers, not individual peasants with their small and variable surpluses, were able to meet this demand for large amounts of grain from distant localities. As a result, in eastern Europe the landed nobility, unlike its counterpart in western Europe, developed not into income-receiving absentee landed proprietors resident in the city but managers of their own landed estates. The feudal grain plantations of early capitalism produced for distant markets and, at the same time, met their requirements for more land and dependent laborers through progressive disenfranchisement and dispossession of the peasants. Even the originally free east German peasant colonists were thus brought down to the level of the Slavic lower stratum of eastern European origin. Moreover, the development of the east

German agrarian relations since the sixteenth century must be placed in the great international context of the development of large-scale agricultural enterprises of early capitalism, of the plantation economy with slave labor, with production for the market for the large-scale long-distance trade that was to supply the city population of the western industrial regions. This plantation economy developed at the same time in tropical and subtropical Africa and America with Negro slaves and in eastern Europe with serfs or dependent peasants. It would be worth investigating more closely whether not just simultaneity but also the influence of example was at work: whether the tropical plantation economy with Negro slaves served, directly or indirectly, as a model for the eastern European development. At the end of this period the abolition of serfdom in Russia in 1861 coincided with the outbreak of the American Civil War (1861-1865), which led to the abolition of slavery in the southern states of the Union. The structural similarities between the tropical and east European, even east German, plantation system are extensive. Thus, for example, it is characteristic of both that the economic management enjoys administrative and police powers either *de jure* through identity of person, or *de facto* through corresponding one-sided access to the organs of state power. The riding whip of the Junker east of the Elbe and the whip of the tropical slaveholder exercised the same function. And even the role of the pastor in the region of the *latifundia* east of the Elbe often was not unlike that of the missionary in a tropical plantation region. Both frequently strove through spiritual means to keep their white or black flock in "fear of the lord."

In Germany and for Europe the Elbe and the Saale formed a dividing line that was to retain its significance throughout subsequent history between that part of the landed nobility that typically settled in the city, and the Junkers who settled on the land east of the Elbe amidst their large-scale agricultural enterprises. In western Europe initially the vassalage that had sprung from the Frankish *trustis* led to domination based on landed property; but soon the general movement of urbanization engulfed the nobility as well, causing a defeudalization and democratization of social relations. East of the Elbe a retrogressive development took place and gave rise to particularly virulent forms of feudal superstratification. This eastern development occurred on the economic basis of an international division of labor, conditioned by the progress of capitalism; in Germany at least, it also fit in the frame of a very modern mercantile and technical form of enterprise. The latter, to be sure, was further favored because agricultural machines, developed for the big farms in North America, could be used only for the large industry of the eastern European plain, and not at first for small peasant holdings in western Europe.

Later, economic conditions made large agrarian enterprises in eastern Germany so unprofitable that they could be kept operating only by protective tariffs and subsidies, for which precedents could be found in the time of Frederick the Great. Whereas these developments thus cast doubt on the economic viability of large-scale agricultural enterprises in European conditions, the tropical plantation continued to be regarded as the most advanced form of enterprise in the sphere of commercial production for the world market. But here, too, where large-scale enterprise seems to be so solidly anchored, recent developments have favored self-owned small-scale indigenous enterprises, the development of which may be expected to go hand in hand with the irresistible struggle for political liberation from Western imperialism.

For example, world cocoa production, in which European-managed plantations enjoyed a near monopoly up to 1914, today is almost three-quarters in the hands of native West African small peasants, particularly in Ghana. In Indonesia in 1938 twice as much native-produced coffee as plantation-produced coffee was exported. In Brazilian rubber production half of the whole cultivable area planted to natural rubber in 1938 fell to the share of native small peasants. Native small peasant enterprises are also beginning to make headway in other domains of tropical agriculture, which were once reserved for the large-scale industry of the plantation, as for example in banana production. The remaining plantation workers will no doubt become the favorite object of Bolshevik propaganda; hence the days of this form of industry, besmirched with blood and tears, may possibly be numbered—but only where such plantations are under private capitalist auspices. For by a cruel irony the great plantation system based upon the Egyptian model and worked with slaves today celebrates its resurrection in the Soviet Union and thus closes the circle of a fateful development stretching over many millennia.

17. FEUDALIZATION OF ECONOMIC IDEOLOGY

It is clear that the "aristocratic" morality of the superstratifying upper class disparaged and despised work—especially manual labor—directly related to earning a living. This aristocratic disparagement and disdain of work has several roots. One of them lies in the negative attitude toward work that the superstratifiers had already brought with them from their former nomadic existence. All reports on nomadic pastoralists from antiquity onward emphasize this character trait. Of the Thracians, Herodotus reports: "To be idle is accounted the most honorable thing, and to be a tiller of the ground the most dishonorable." According to Aristotle, "the most indolent are the pastoral nomads. They acquire a subsistence from domestic animals, at their leisure and withost any trouble."[34] And Wilhelm Schmidt judges that "the indolence of nomads and their aversion to work, their disparagement of it applied as a value judgment was a baleful legacy, however, which from then onward exercised a most harmful influence upon the whole development of human culture."[35] Certainly among all the most primitive forms of economy, pasturing herds required the least physical labor. Riding peoples especially strive as much as possible to be physically active by giving orders rather than by personal participation, leaving the execution of the orders to their menials. Such an attitude corresponds to the physical situation of the horseman and is directly conditioned by it. He is by nature prevented from doing his own work, for he would have to dismount and tether his horse or have another person hold it for him.

But apart from this nomadic legacy, which the superstratifiers brought with them, superstratification naturally produces a negative attitude toward work. The superstratification system distinguishes itself from the primitive nonrecurring raid as a chronic raid: the subjugated people must work without let-up for their masters, produce for them, and deliver to them everything they need and covet, from provisions and artisan products up to and including personal services. Nor does the situation change when it is translated into plutocratic terms. For if the descendants of the superstratifiers have enough unearned income to buy the products and services of the lower stratum, the real result is manifestly the same.

Indeed, the most important economic aim and practical effect of superstratification is to spare its bearers the drudgery of performing any remunerative work and to shift such activity onto the subjugated strata. As a consequence, work becomes a matter for slaves (hence contemptible), and idleness and a parasitic life a matter for lords (hence superior and noble). Subconscious guilt and the defense mechanism it begets raises such negative valuations to further levels of intensity.

In ancient Greece this aristocratic contempt for work, an early feature of every superstratification, was prevalent in a striking and especially harsh form, although there was no lack of influential countercurrents. It is shameful to see how even enlightened and highly placed ancient writers were driven to seek refuge by all possible means, ranging from sophistry to false pathos, to justify this stand as reasonable. And it is even more shameful to see how such reasonings have been reverently and uncritically passed on by our plaster-of-paris philologists in a puerile and toadying manner.

Turkey, the last country in the European sphere to be superstratified by nomadic horsemen, provides an opportunity for interesting observations. In question, of course, are traditions surviving from Ottoman times, to which the movement of radical modernization inaugurated by Atatürk is threatening, but which did not at once disappear. It is still considered the first rule of distinction not to do oneself what one can have others do. It is considered socially degrading to carry a parcel, even a small one, instead of having it carried behind one by a porter. The shopkeeper, if he is a Turk of the old stamp, sits enthroned in sovereign dignity on his chair and signifies to his subordinate what is expected by barely perceptible gestures of the head or hand. Dust-covered shoes are as shaming and degrading as dirty hands are in the West. Those who find the small change for the bootblack beyond their budget sacrifice their clean handkerchiefs for the social ideal of the shined shoe. The exaggerated social depreciation of the dusty shoe has, moreover, a further consequence in the Near East in that bootblacks—like porters—constitute a special pariah caste; usually, servants consider it beneath their dignity to shine their masters' shoes. In Germany it was not shoes but cuffs that play—or played, especially in Wilhelmine Germany and even under the Weimar Republic—this role of social litmus paper.

The conquerors owed their ruling position and the security of their lordly maintenance not to the work of their hands, but to the force of their weapons. A Cretan (or Dorian) marching song under the telling author's name of Hybrias gives classic expression to this state of affairs and to the corresponding attitude:

> A great treasure to me are the spear and the sword
> And the beautiful body-protecting shield;
> With these I plow, with these I reap,
> With these I pluck the sweet wine of the grape,
> Hence I am called the lord of slave peoples.
> But those who dare not bear spear and sword,

And the beautiful body-protecting shield,
All lie at my feet, and kiss my knee,
And call me Lord and great King.[36]

A moral or pseudo-moral high evaluation and an especially high approval of unearned income—originally from war, raids, and violence—corresponds to the contemptuous depreciation of labor. Here it is a question of the contrast between the "political means" and the "economic means" that Franz Oppenheimer quite rightly has always underscored. According to Cicero, "the Gauls [of Asia Minor] think it disgraceful to grow grain by manual labor; and consequently they go forth armed and reap other men's fields."[37]

This attitude finds its epigrammatic expression in the famous passage in Tacitus describing the large train of followers surrounding the German chieftains: "Nor are they so easily persuaded to cultivate the earth, and await the produce of the seasons, as to challenge the foe, and expose themselves to wounds; nay, they think it base and spiritless to earn by sweat what they might purchase with blood."[38] This is typical superstratification morality, that feudal mentality against which Hesiod directs his proclamation of peasant morality.

Aristotle, in a famous passage of the *Politics* (1. 8-10), distinguishes between two polar "economic mentalities": the static, self-sufficient mentality of the "household" and of "subsistence," which he recognizes as natural, and the dynamic, insatiable mentality of "chrematistics" or the "art of acquisition" (pleonexia), which he condemns as contrary to nature. This teaching exercised an extraordinary influence throughout antiquity, the Middle Ages, and modern times; it has been repeated anew with the same valuation and slight variations of its conceptual formulation, most recently by Werner Sombart.[39] For scholasticism, which also espoused this teaching, pleonexia naturally was an outflow of original sin. From a mundane view, the historico-sociological question how the unnatural attitude of pleonexic insatiability originated has not yet been posed.

For us the answer to the question is obvious. The nomadic conquerors and superstratifiers were the ones who were greedy and insatiable in the highest measure, and who irrupted into universal history under the impulsion of this greed. They bequeathed these traits to their feudal successors, who cultivated them further and kept practicing them as long as political and social conditions permitted.

The peasant lower stratum of all high cultures (including peasant handicrafts), by contrast, is orginally in the grip of the natural static economic mentality of "nourishment," if only because the patriarch-managed peasant industry does not allow for much expansion. In a normal two-layered society this disparity in economic mentality between upper and lower strata remains the rule.

Indeed, the static attitude is a built-in element of the very existence of the peasantry to such a degree that a vestige of it has remained characteristic of peasant nature until our own day. But from time to time certain strata inserted themselves between the upper feudal stratum and the lower peasant stratum—the Western bourgeoisie since the Renaissance, the industrial working class since the nineteenth century. And whenever these new intermediate strata were seized by the same dynamic that earlier had been restricted to the feudal upper class, such a change each time marked the advent of a new postmedieval era—a vivid reminder that an attitude of resignation on the part of the lower stratum is an indispensable and fundamental element of the divine order of things in any medieval period.

Every aspiration of the lower stratum signifies a desire to have more. Outwardly and inwardly, social attitudes filter to the bottom from the top. Thus the economic mentality of the upper stratum gradually filtered down to its lower counterpart, and those on the upper (urban) rungs of the lower stratum were the first to be seized by the new appetites.

The feudal drive to expansion is boundless, not only spatially but quantitatively. The "economic ideology" of pleonexia (insatiability), which from Aristotle to Sombart was always treated as an absolute metaphysical category, in reality is a social-psychological legacy of feudalism, and it is here that it has its concrete sociological locus. To be sure, the feudal upper strata espoused and practiced this pleonexia regularly only so long as social and political conditions allowed them to do so. If the connection between aristocracy and conservatism seems natural and inevitable, it is so only because we know little else and because the aristocracy is in retreat and on the defensive. In such a situation it preaches, always out of the deepest philosophical or religious conviction, satisfaction and contentment—the cult of the *status quo* or even better the *status quo ante*. If, however, others put into practice that expansionist mentality of pleonexia, it is considered abominable, offensive, and uncouth beyond measure. New wealth is as hateful and contemptible as the older wealth is beautiful and estimable. It all depends on who has it.

Not only does the pleonexia of the upper stratum filter down to the lower stratum; so, too, does its depreciation of work. As the upper stratum could afford this contempt for work only because the lower stratum had to work, and did work, the adoption of this feudal attitude by precisely this lower stratum is in itself an absurd and grotesque tragicomic event. The feat has been accomplished and, perhaps, more than all else has contributed to the disgust workers feel for work, ruining their natural joy in work and convincing them that salvation lies in shortening the work day as much as possible and that leisure time alone is the only part of life compatible with dignity and a life worth living.

18. IMPERIALISM

By "imperialism" we mean the modern forms of a phenomenon inherent in all superstratifiers and superstratifications from the outset. Superstratification itself was merely the earliest, archaic manifestation of imperialism.

The idea of world conquest, too, as we have seen, stems from these nomadic herdsmen-warriors. And the idea of world conquest, the desire for dominion "over the four quarters of the world" occurs for the first time to the drivers and later to the riders, to whom no distance seems insurmountable, and to the superstratifiers who, without encountering resistance, irrupted as conquerors in all directions. In western Asia-Europe the idea of world rule is documented first for King Sargon I of Akkad (2310-2255 B.C.), the ruler of the Semitic conquerors of northern Mesopotamia. His successor Naram-Sin calls himself "King of the Four Quarters"; and Hammurabi (1728-1686 B.C.) carried over this title to Babylon, where the god Marduk bestowed it.

In Egypt we come for the first time upon geographically limited titles for rulers corresponding to the sharp geopolitical seclusion of the country. But when the conquering and superstratifying nomads, the Hyksos, invaded the country (ca. 1730-1352 B.C.) we immediately find the universal titles of "Embracer of Countries" and "Ruler of Countries." Ikhnaton (1370-1352 B.C.) regarded himself, in connection with a solar universal religion, as king of mankind.

Even Cyrus II (the Great) received from Marduk in Babylon the ancient title of "King of the Four Quarters"; his successors, the Persian kings, call themselves "King of the Countries," "King of the Great Earth to the Furthest Distance," or "Lord of All Men from the Rising to the Setting Sun."[40] But these Persian plans failed, and the empire decayed; it was conquered by Alexander the Great, in whose unbridled genius the will to world conquest was brilliantly embodied with an intensity previously unknown. Nevertheless, because of his early death Alexander did not go far beyond the remotest frontiers of Persia.

Alexander's failure and the subsequent internecine struggle of the Diadochi made it possible for Rome to advance in fits and starts, spreading its rule over the whole Mediterranean world, with northern outposts west and east of the Alps. Caesar's plans of conquest, reaching out still further, remained as unfulfilled as Alexander's and for the same reason—his premature death. The Roman world empire, which came into being accompanied by universal-historical-messianic acclamations for its rulers, felt itself altogether an *imperium mundi*. Vergil has Jupiter promise the Romans an empire without boundaries in space and time,[41] and Claudian, as late as 400 A.D., equates the subjects of the Roman Empire with all mankind.

After a glorious history of a half millennium, the Roman Empire broke up into a western half, which was inundated by Germanic peoples, and an eastern half, which continued the claim to world dominion.

After another thousand years, the eastern empire was finally overrun by Islam, whose thrusts into the heart of Europe from the southwest and southeast came to a halt in Spain and in the central Danubian regions respectively. Nevertheless, for centuries one could speak of an Arabic world empire and of a world hegemony of caliphs, which ultimately included northern India.

After the coronation of Charlemagne, the old ideas of world empire were restored to life even in the domain of the Roman church, but in practice they signified nothing more than a solemn archaic-sacred symbolism, from which mysterious rays of chiliastic consolation occasionally seemed to break forth. Thus in Dante's *Monarchia* it is the emperor who is to bring universal peace as *curator orbis*. The real power of the German emperors, however, was never of a kind that would have allowed the Holy Roman Empire of the German Nation to have claimed more than purely hegemonic rights. And they, too, were as little successful as the hegemonic aspirations of France and of other European states.

Later, however, politically split Christian Europe mounted little resistance to the Mongols or Turks (just as politically split Hellas had yielded to the Persians two millennia earlier), and the idea of world conquest became obsolete. In the vigorous colonial expansion since the age of discovery, several European states competed and carried the political variations of Europe into the sphere of the colonial world.

The brief interlude of Napoleon's attempt at world conquest, precisely because of its catastrophic collapse, seemed once again to prove the utopian character of such an aim. Thus in modern times in the West the conviction grew that the idea of world conquest belonged among the dust-covered museum pieces of historical antiquities, and division among numerous sovereign state structures everywhere became a lasting political theme. Modern imperialism is merely the struggle over the greatest possible share in this distribution. This very fragmented and changing equilibrium was suddenly interrupted by Hitler's advance toward world conquest, the bloody collapse of which left a world divided into two mighty power groups: Soviet Russia and its vassals on the one side, the Anglo-Saxon powers and their democratic retinue on the other. Now we suddenly seem closer to the possibility of world dominion than ever in the course of history.

Soviet Russia, in its pervasively universalist Marxist state religion combines the idea of world revolution with that of Russian imperialism—a Third Rome in Pan-Slavist tonality. This challenge has forced the democratic side, under Anglo-Saxon leadership, to an equally universal counterdefense; thus we suddenly see mankind divided into two great power blocks that in reality have entered the lists in a struggle for world rule—even if one side, at least, understandably shuns this struggle and therefore will not, or will not yet, acknowledge it to itself or to others.

The solution of a lasting, peaceful, and amicable partition of the world into two separate hemispheres is precluded by the highly aggressive nature of world revolutionary Marxism, and by the apocalyptic invention of the atom bomb.

Superstratification empires, created through warlike means, bear a pronounced warlike character, both internally and externally. Externally this warlike character expresses itself as an insatiable drive to expansion, which in part is a direct legacy of the nomadic infatuation with open spaces, and in part serves to foster and test these warlike virtues. Or else it also serves as a means of deflecting inner tensions and difficulties toward the outside, or of waging preventive war in the face of threatening external attacks. We shall see that there are now strong tendencies in the sphere of internal policy which work toward the elimination of militarism and violence and their replacement by a peaceful order and peaceful attitudes. But even when this inner pacification is more or less achieved, external peace does not ensue except under quite rare and unusually favorable conditions. Sometimes inner appeasement and uniformity and harmony even heighten the latent war potential and can therefore operate as a motive for its exploitation. Conversely, external tensions and dangers act as a coercive force to effect inner unity and are at times sought after with this very purpose in view.

The nomadic conquerors had come to play their combative role from a desire to expand, and their success was apt to reinforce this attitude. Members of the upper stratum, freed from any need to earn their livelihood through peaceful means, were thus able to concentrate exclusively on the craft of war and to train their members as military specialists.

Such specialization demands application and testing, the expansionist original character persists, and the striving for power, wealth, and fame has no inherent upper limit. Historical evidence generally confirms this hypothesis.

The postmedieval development toward plutocracy changes this sociological inner structure. Plutocratic upper strata generally have little time or inclination for military exercises. Accordingly, when the same tendency toward warlike expansionism nonetheless reappeared in the plutocratic period of Western capitalism (if anything more strongly) in the form of imperialism and particularly colonialism, it seemed at first natural to search for a new cause for this phenomenon, a cause inherent in the special nature of capitalism. This search was undertaken, with much ingenuity and compilation of data by the neo-Marxist theory of imperialism, founded by Rosa Luxemburg (following the precedent of Heinrich Cunow) and later reasserted with some vehemence by Fritz Sternberg.[42]

Since Sismondi the general opinion has prevailed that the capitalist economic system suffers from crises of overproduction and will destroy itself in line with Marx's somber predictions. Here lies the cardinal point of the neo-Marxist "explanation," stating that colonial imperialism is the desperate attempt of capitalist countries to open new markets to increasing overproduction by the conquest of new colonial territories. As long as this succeeds, the argument goes, capitalism's last respite is prolonged, but as soon as all colonial territory is divided up and further expansion impossible, its hour has struck.

This would indeed be an entirely new, purely economic and specifically capitalist motive for expansion: the desperate search for new markets under the fateful pressure of industrial overproduction.

Markets in this context is a specialized term of a vulgarized economic theory, as is *overproduction*. The individual manufacturer to be sure needs to be concerned about finding a market for his products: he suffers from "overproduction" when he does not dispose of them, and he can be satisfied when he has found a "market" for them. But the matter is different for the scientific economist, who has—or should have—clearly in mind that every market in an overall economic context is only an exchange. This is especially obvious in colonial markets, because these usually begin with quite primitive forms of barter. Since Europeans have little practical use for cowrie shells, nose pegs, or clubs, the objects of exchange in the long run tend to be raw materials. If these are currency metals (gold, or formerly also silver), limited inflation ensues, stimulating precisely the production of commodities; if they are foodstuffs, they compete with native agriculture; if industrial raw materials, they must be processed, thereby directly increasing the production and supply of industrial products. How then is overproduction reduced by such a process? Whatever the situation of so-called overproduction may be, colonial imperialism is by no means a remedy for it. The attribution of imperialism to overproduction is based on a fallacy in economic thought.

Another neo-Marxist, Rudolf Hilferding,[43] attributed imperialism not to capitalism as such, but to its special form of monopolistic, protectionist, and interventionist finance capitalism. This interconnection actually exists—except that monopolism, protectionism, and interventionism are degenerate phenomena of the market economy, produced by the same political motive forces of feudal origin and character upon which imperialism also rests:

If the attempt to explain modern imperialism and its policy of colonial conquest on the basis of specific theories of capitalist economy has miscarried, nothing more remains than to explain it in full agreement with Joseph Schumpeter.[44] He has solved this problem based on the presumed perseverance of the old precapitalist motives of lust for power, greed for booty, and the drive to expansion. Schumpeter, writing in 1918, considered this perseverance as a mere instance of feudal atavism. Still, it can be proven that viewed from inside the capitalist economy, war and imperialism are nothing but bad business and undesired economic disturbances; they are not the logic, but the illogic of capitalism.

From the first superstratifications to the present day there has been perpetual danger of war among states and within each state a more or less warlike spirit—now latent, now overt—that we have identified as the motive force not only behind the original superstratification but behind all subsequent wars of conquest, including those of Western colonial imperialism.

The central and decisive motive force, which sets and keeps in motion the whole universal historical process of superstratification and all its consequences, was that sadistic attitudinal complex that we have described as the warlike drive to expansion, thirst for struggle, or lust for power. Development in subsequent millennia, to be sure, has in general increasingly restrained the possible sphere of action of these impulses so far as domestic policy is concerned.

But foreign policy has been unable to renounce these sadistic motive forces; they have always been its essential and decisive instrument. In foreign policy and its military implementation, from the first superstratifications up to now, all wars of aggression, all conquests, were triggered by the same impulse. And if the first superstratifications were triggered by overwhelming superiority in military technology, the same situation also operated as a triggering agent on Western colonial imperialism.

The unbroken tradition of *libido dominandi* in the domain of foreign policy is one of the lines on which the social original sin has continued since the fall of superstratification.

19. OBSTRUCTION TO EXPANSION AND DECAY OF EXPANSION

As long as the proper medieval, feudal social structure prevailed, it set rather narrow limits to this boundless expansionist drive. For one thing, the state of transportation technology still was not suitable for the organization and domination of regions of more than middling size. Moreover, the economy of the "Middle Ages" is generally a barter economy. An elaborate monetary system belongs to a late stage of cultural development, and fully occurs only in postmedieval periods. In the older barter economy, any empire had to be divided into districts whose boundaries depended on transport technology, and the military and civil administrator of each of these districts depended upon deliveries in kind, upon labor services that he levied and military forces that personally commanded. This typical structure poses sharply the central problem of feudalism: it continually encourages a yearning for independence among its own officials. The threat to imperial unity posed by such yearning grows exponentially with the expansion of the empire. The technical solution of this problem—bureaucratization of the civilian and military administration on the basis of a fully developed money economy within a state with full powers of taxation—has succeeded only beyond the confines of the "Middle Ages."

Thus feudal domination constitutes not only the original foundation of all "medieval" high cultures; it is also a fetter on their development. At the same time it constitutes the decisive barrier to their self-stabilization and self-unification. The grand image embodied in the prophetic saying of one fold and one shepherd shines as the unfulfillable longing on the far horizon of this knightly-priestly world.

CHAPTER 3

Transfeudal Motive Forces
of High Cultures

1. TENDENCY TOWARD COMMUNITY

Man is by nature a communal being. Community is the form of coexistence consonant with human nature, and an ineradicable longing for community lives in every human being. Hence every noncommunity, every disturbed community, has a built-in inclination to return to community; only in community does it find rest. This holds true particularly for that form of society created by superstratification, which initially is so distant from and so adverse to community.

Within our European culture, serfdom in Russia had been preserved as an especially harsh form of rule by superincumbency far into the nineteenth century, and it set its particular stamp—the slave stain of a servile bearing and mentality—on the east European lower stratum. The two greatest masters of the psychological novel, Tolstoi and Dostoevski, have portrayed the social and human atmosphere of this situation with particular penetration: under such conditions, so distorted by despotism, the need for human kindness and community repeatedly breaks through, like an irresistible force of nature.

Similar observations can be made of other European feudal countries, even those that have not suffered the disadvantages of despotism. Among the rulers, too, the need not to be feared but to be loved by those they rule repeatedly appears, and even Machiavelli is of the opinion that it would be best if both goals could be achieved. That "I may boldly lay my head in the lap of any subject"[1] was not only a goal of princely yearning in the ecstasy of late romantic poetry. The well-known fact that one cannot sit on bayonets rests, in the last resort, upon the natural and unalterable anatomy of the human body—as well as of the human soul; as an eternal verity it repeatedly asserts itself in the long run.

Man's innate tendency toward community can express itself in four ways over against the anticommunal social structure created by superincumbency: (1) by peacefully and often half-consciously and instinctively taking advantage of any opportunities left to push in the direction of community; (2) where such opportunities are blocked, by reinterpreting, veiling, or hypocritically covering the anticommunal realities; (3) conversely, by exposing and criticizing such anticommunal elements; and (4) by overt struggle to overcome the power structure opposed to community.

The innate and ineradicable social nature of man must be considered the first and most fundamental transfeudal motive force within all feudal relations of high cultures. Strong deviation from the essential community structure releases hidden springs of counter-forces which in their violent, explosive form we term "revolution."

2. Tendency toward Democratization

Membership in the upper stratum is enviable: it is the desire, acknowledged or not, of every member of the lower stratum. The upper stratum finds such striving immodest, arrogant, or vexatious. Understandably, it adopts at first a posture of rejection, of pushing back, of pointing to the established barriers. Nevertheless, situations can arise which force the upper stratum to revise this attitude.

The most frequent and least questionable case of this kind is the acceptance of individuals into the upper stratum on the basis of outstanding accomplishment and merit. Every such selection signifies a strengthening of the upper stratum and, at the same time, a weakening of the lower stratum. It creates the impression on both sides that membership in the upper stratum, even among its permanent members, rests upon such special outstanding achievement. It diverts the striving of the lower stratum from group opposition to its masters to individual ambition. "The more," writes Marx, "a ruling class is capable of accepting the most important men of the ruled classes into its ranks, the more solid is its rule." This was written in London and naturally holds true for England, where this capacity and the corresponding social mechanism had been highly elaborated.

More serious for the self-interest of the upper stratum is the admission and acceptance of entire groups. Such wholesale admission tends to occur only when such a group can force its acceptance or when the upper stratum seeks to avoid such coercion by timely compliance. Plutocratization, to be dealt with in the next section, is a particular and important instance of this type.

On the other hand, each broadening and extension of the upper stratum has two great advantages. It stabilizes the situation, makes the upper class less assailable from without and within, and gives its members an easier conscience. Such was the case in Athens, where internal democratization was accompanied by increasingly harsher rule over her allies. Such was also the case in Rome, where a powerful progressive expansion of the empire took place simultaneously with the social rise of new groups pushing forward. And such, finally, was also the case in England, where inner democratization went hand in hand with the spread of the empire before this tendency to democracy extended to the empire itself.

Such progressive replacement of internal domination with an external domination in which even the native lower stratum increasingly shared, need not amount to any diminution of despotism and despotic pressure. In the cases referred to, the number of ruled became even greater, and despotic pressure was exercised far more harshly than before. Nevertheless, qualitatively, it signifies essential progress, for domination is shifted outward from within the social body; and, as we have seen, it was precisely the entry of violence and domination into the body of society that was the toxic, dangerous, and destructive element. Alien rule is always clearly recognizable, is much easier to overcome than domestic dominion, and has indeed been overcome in countless historic cases; the total elimination of domestic domination has not yet succeeded in any major case.

It is important then, despite many necessary reservations, to evaluate positively the inner democratizations that occurred in the three above instances. Viewed as an instance of "cunning of history," this is a rather ingenious arrangement: domination is first transferred from within to without, thereby facilitating the otherwise very difficult process of reducing interior domination—and leaving until later the far easier task of abolishing domination in its foreign form as well. Whatever the pros and cons, the fact remains that high cultures have achieved the highest degree of democratization only in this way.

The inherent tendency to democratization, however, does not halt at this point. Once the democratization process is set in motion, it acquires social momentum of its own. For each person to whom a partial right was granted covets the remainder all the more, and each one who hitherto was denied such a rise on the social ladder all the more desires access thereto. Finally, no further halt is possible, and at most such a social movement, once set in motion, can be arrested or reversed only by a new and most brutal superstratification.

A circumstance of intellectual history also works toward this end with every increasing power. In the measure that rational and logical thought develops and spreads, social discussion more and more is also carried on upon this plane. On such a plane no justification of rights or privileges based on domination is tenable any longer. Arguments that a special group uses only for its own advantage can without further ado be generalized. What's sauce for the goose is sauce for the gander. Even attempts by members of the upper stratum to justify themselves in the forum of reason, in the last resort, regularly and inevitably have this final reverse result. All rational and logical discussion in the social domain inevitably leads to isonomy, to absolute equality of laws and rights.

3. TENDENCY TOWARD EXPANSION

The crudest and most elementary prerequisite of any relationship of community (as of any human relationship) is geographic contact, and this depends on the technology of transport. For mankind as a whole this prerequisite of community until recently had not been met, and it was met as a result of an expansionist drive that over many thousands of years involved both crass material and lofty spiritual components.

We have seen that the push into open spaces, the drive to expansion, is a specific nomadic legacy of high cultures. At the same time we saw that this same drive for expansion tends to reach beyond the limited spaces that can still be uniformly controlled by feudal means and methods. It thus becomes necessary to replace these inadequate feudal means and methods of conquering space by other more adequate means—a substitution which, however, is ultimately tantamount to overcoming feudalism itself.

The transfeudal drive to expansion finds its only natural, its first and last absolute limit in the fact that the earth is round—that is, in the limited extension of our planet itself. The exact, or even approximate, determination of this magnitude, of course, was first achieved by modern natural science and its precise measurement systems. Earlier, the size of our earth was usually grossly underestimated, and those engaged in expansionist drives or bent on global conquest were deluded into thinking themselves much nearer their goal. The ancient oriental world conquerors still conceived of the earth as a disk, limited by the horizon, upon which the firmament seemed visibly to rest. Such underestimations of the real size of the "world" to be conquered naturally had the effect of facilitating plans and fantasies of "world conquest." Even Columbus, as we know, drew the courage for his voyage of discovery from a conception of the globe that assumed its extent to be only half as large as it actually is.

But the inherent drive of the high cultures to push forward into the open spaces finally led both to the knowledge of the true size and nature of our planet, as well as to its control by means of the technology of transport.

4. TENDENCY TOWARD MONARCHY

Man's innate social tendency not only is directed negatively against all that is adverse to community, but also fosters positively all formations that correspond to the natural structure of community. This natural community structure, however, is hierarchical, and the natural necessity of hierarchical gradation, with a single authority as its apex, becomes clearer and more imperative as a society becomes enlarged and as additional demands are made upon it by its environment.

The smallest natural unit of all human social structures, the family (or what sociologists call the *nuclear family* as distinguished from the nomadic *extended family*) finds its natural apex and supreme authority in the father (or in the mother, under matriarchal or semimatriarchal conditions). Since early times the social position of the *paterfamilias* has rightly been regarded as the prototype of all natural human authority.

The nomadism of the breeders of herd animals led them to develop the large patriarchal family that accentuated still more strongly the authoritarian position of the patriarch. This power position as head of a large family corresponded in part to the greater number of persons being led, and in part to the difficulties and dangerous situations that arise from the nature of nomadism itself. Power was centered in persons progressively higher on the scale of authority when circumstances led to the concentration of several large families under a head patriarch or sheikh. This must have regularly been the case with the expeditions of nomadic conquerors, and we may imagine the position of the leader as similar to what we know from recorded history about the Mongol, Turkish, and other conquering hordes. The decision to embark upon such an undertaking already presupposed a trusted and charismatic leader. Success was bound to strengthen the leader's position enormously in the period subsequent to the effected superstratification. If the superiority of the conquerors appears as divinely given, such divine grace, magnified to a magical dimension, inevitably was concentrated particularly in their leader.

With the earliest archaic superincumbency, that of herdsmen over a mixture of planters and totemistic hunters, this trend resembled the chieftaincy system of the higher hunting culture, based upon the sun cult. And that, together with other circumstances, had led to the more intense idea of divine kingship, threatened and compensated, of course, by ritual murder, in which the king became an object of religious worship.

The relations between monarchy and monotheism are interesting. First of all, developed monotheism—which sees in God not the father or the patriarch but the ruler, the sultan, the heavenly king—obviously originates as an anthropomorphic (or sociomorphic) projection of the corresponding earthly power relationships deriving from domination; the monarchy of God was originally by grace of the king. Later, however, representation of the monarchic constitution of the world served as strong theological support and justification of every earthly monarchy: the monarch now claimed to rule by the grace of God. But not only earthly power relationships deriving from domination were projected into heaven. Often new ideas, hopes, desires, trends, tendencies of transformation directed at earthly government, which on earth could make way only slowly and against strong and ruthless resistance, could appear in heaven much earlier and more fully as unopposed projections. Thus Luther's absolutist Heavenly Father precedes the fully developed absolute monarch of the German territorial states, and the stringent absolutism of the Calvinist God, who assigns souls to eternal bliss or damnation according to his arbitrary pleasure (*sic volo, sic jubeo, stat pro ratione voluntas*) is fully a century older than his earthly embodiment in Louis XIV.

But even apart from the inherited patriarchal-monarchic tendency, the situation of the superstratification empire itself was likely to nourish such a development.

Political structures, once they become as extensive and are as beset by multiple dangers as those that originated through superstratification, require a high degree of unitary leadership. The best and the only secure means for arriving at this cohesive leadership is monarchy—a truth that found its classic expression in a famous verse in Homer: "Lordship for many is no good thing; let there be one ruler" (*Iliad* 2. 204f.).

The more pointedly all power and responsibility is concentrated in one hand (*L'état c'est moi*), the more all other members of the ruling stratum are stripped of their power. They can no longer exercise their power on the basis of lordly authority and according to their pleasure, but at most as mandataries receiving their instructions from the monarch. In the external struggle for power a state proves its superiority when it is led rigidly and cohesively so that even states that have deviated from the monarchical principle usually have no choice but to return to it or submit to defeat and conquest by a hostile monarchic state. Either way, with or against the will of those involved, the outcome represents a triumph of the monarchical principle. Dangers in the sphere of domestic policy, especially revolutionary movements of the lower stratum, could also force a return to the monarchical principle in one or another form.

In all superstratification empires the power struggle between central authority and the nobility dominates political and constitutional history. The only safe solution to this endemic problem is, as we shall see, the creation of a bureaucracy. But such a solution presupposes a degree of economic and cultural development which, as a rule, lies beyond the bounds of the Middle Ages and feudalism.

Within the superstratification structure absolute monarchy signified merely a concentration of the total authority of superstratification in a single person. It is as if the variable number of members of the nobility had been reduced to its minimum value of $n = 1$. Only thus is the nature of monarchical "sovereignty" to be understood, not from aprioristic-metaphysical deductions; the bald fact of superincumbency is the hidden source of all such profundity. The maxim *princeps legibus solutus est*—the king can do no wrong—originally held true for the entire upper stratum of conquerors, characterizing their relation to the conquered.

Monarchy started out as a specially concentrated form of the power of superstratification that commends itself by virtue of its organizational and technical superiority; yet in its effects upon the subjects it signified a considerable weakening and dilution of the original poison of superstratification. With superstratifcation, a militarily superior minority had triumphed over the indigenous population, and its military superiority was further strengthened by disarming and suppressing the lower stratum. As long as the numerical relationship between the upper and the lower stratum remained more or less the same, the violent suppression of the lower stratum could be repeated at any time, thus condemning any attempt at uprising to failure from the outset. However, once the principle of absolute monarchy was realized—say, by the physical destruction of the former noble families—the power of superstratification was really concentrated in the person of the monarch and thereby reduced. Sheer physical military superiority as the last support and *ultima ratio* of domination now became a thing of the past. As soon as the military retinue of the ruler became merely his executive organs they were no longer, like the ruling nobility, participants in the government in their own right. Hence the extent to which the ruler could rely on them in critical and extreme situations depended on many external and internal circumstances, not all of which he could control. It was generally advisable for him not to push things to an extreme, to avoid any overt test of strength that might give the upper hand to the aristocracy. The monarch, by virtue of his professional specialization and concentration, now perforce becomes the first magistrate, the first servant of his realm. The monarch is, so to speak, the first lifelong and professional civil servant. The psychological cogencies that, as we shall see, characterize professional officialdom already can be observed in him. Before he can think of anything else, the machinery of the government, of domestic and foreign policy, must begin properly to function. The monarch who not only reigns, but really rules, is so involved with these duties of state and so concerned with their performance that little time and energy is left to him for the mere selfish enjoyment of power. On purely technical grounds, therefore, what Faust, puritanically moralizing, says in respect of the emperor also holds true for him: "He who would command must in commanding find his highest blessing."[2]

On this basis we are justified in considering the tendency to monarchy, to concentration of rule, and of leadership in a single person, as an antifeudal and transfeudal tendency. Of all the structural formations that directly arose from superstratification, the monarchical lies closest to the natural social structure of leadership, and leaves the least margin for excessive deviation from this norm.

Directly connected with monarchy is the principle of heredity of the crown, which similarly is a concentrated form of the hereditary membership in the upper stratum. Where heredity applies to a whole class of the population, one may expect that genetic probabilities, selective breeding, purposeful upbringing, and a sharply distinctive social situation will, as a rule, provide in each generation a sufficient number of individuals who meet the requirements of their situation and thus are able to perpetuate it. But with inheritance of the throne, regulated unambiguously and with no room for choice, the corresponding genetic probability approaches zero in the long run, as historical experience has largely confirmed. The same principle of inheritance that seems to preserve itself in aristocratic breadth fails when concentrated pointedly in monarchy, although this concentration of heredity no doubt is a necessary device imperatively imposed by the very structure of monarchy. Here lies a dilemma which no monarchy in history has successfully resolved. For as soon as the principle of hereditary succession is surrendered, so is the unambiguous nature of the change of generations that enables loyal monarchists to exclaim, "The King is dead! Long live the King!" Every change of sovereigns then becomes a struggle for the throne, with all the dangers and fateful consequences.

Different ways of dealing with this dilemma of monarchical succession are conceivable. (1) One can set in the place of automatic succession a testamentary selection of successor by the incumbent, "of the best by the best," as this principle was phrased during the time of its application under the Roman philosopher-emperors. This method certainly assures a higher level of qualification, but it is purchased at the price of a significantly lowered authority inherent in a relatively arbitrary transfer of power. (2) The requirements of the hereditary monarchical office can be reduced so that any successor of a family selectively bred can meet them. (This finally became the solution in England.) (3) The ruler and leader can be elected with lifelong tenure, or if the term of office is limited in duration or subject to regulated recall, a provisional dictatorship can be used as an emergency measure.

At first sight there is something lofty about leaving the monarchic selection process to the eternal powers of birth and death—an enormous advantage in removing this decision, so fundamenal for the state, from all human conflicts of interest, clashing opinions, and judicious doubts. However, inheritance and lifelong tenure signified a feudalization of the monarchy, a carrying over of the super-stratification-conditioned principle of inherited aristocracy, which viewed supreme leadership as a possession and privilege deriving from domination. However, if we view the supreme leadership of the state as an eminently public office, then it stands in logical contradiction with the ancient feudal regulation of inheritance—and this is where the fundamental problem arises.

5. Egalitarian Tendencies

The social structures preceding superstratification exhibit a hierarchical gradation that all concerned accept as natural. In such a system nobody is prevented from rising to the position that is his due through proficiency and individual merit. Where this may give rise to conflicts, these are fought out on a plane of basic human equality, and this gives a communitarian and democratic character to these primitive units of social organization.

An enormous accentuation of inequality is introduced as a result of superstratification; the inequality between the upper and lower strata falls completely out of the frame of natural democratic gradation, for the first time creating a fundamentally insurmountable social barrier. Paradoxically, however, superincumbency also reinforces equality—a mechanical equality that more or less ignores natural gradations—on either side of this barrier: the equality of the subjects and that of the overlords.

This equality of the overlords is an instance of "honor among thieves." When a numerically small minority establishes itself over a great subjugated mass, as a ruling stratum, it must guard itself against disunity in its own ranks. Now, the most thorough means for avoiding such conflicts and for settling all disputes arising from the distribution of booty obviously is absolute equality. Hence the Spartan term *homoioi* ("peers") and similar designations. Hence also the radical demand of community of goods and women among the ruling supreme stratum of "guardians" in Plato's *Republic* (which, significantly, was often misunderstood as communism). This is why the robbers in the Book of Proverbs (1:14) say: "Cast in thy lot among us; let us all have *one* purse." Later this robber equality of the superstratifiers tends to wane, but in the whole medieval constitutional history of Europe it is noticeable in variegated forms and constitutes one of the most difficult obstacles to a tighter political unity. For ultimately it does not even halt before the supreme ruler, the wearer of the crown, and tries to reduce him, at least, to the position of a mere *primus inter pares*.

The struggle taking place within the upper stratum between oligarchy and monarchy plays a typical role in the history of superstratification states; the less cohesive oligarchy can establish and preserve itself only in unthreatened times of peace, whereas any serious threat from the outside—or even from within and from below—may force a return to the monarchical principle, voluntarily or involuntarily, legally or illegally. The establishment of provisional dictatorship in old Rome is the classic form of regularization and institutionalization of this change.

Modern critics have even managed to see in such expressions of robber equality within the upper stratum genuine expressions of democratic spirit—which would be apposite if the mass of the subjugated and plundered, who are excluded from this equality, were no longer regarded as human beings.

The other opposing tendency toward equality is that of the equality of subjects. As soon as superincumbency has stabilized itself, and has led to the establishment of monarchy, the monarch has an interest, dictated by the situation itself, in abolishing all independent rights of the hereditary nobility that compete with his own rights and in uniting all power in his hands. The most radical expression of this tendency, and the one most consonant with aristocratic racial theories, is the physical extermination of the aristocracy.

The theoretical defenders of absolute monarchy repeatedly stress that just as all human beings are equal before God, so are all subjects equal before the monarch. According to them, the true monarch "has none but God above him, none but subjects below him." The officials and dignitaries of the monarch, even those of the highest rank and closest to the throne, are not excluded from the later category: they all exist *ad nutum regis*, for the use of the king, and owe their position exclusively to the commission of the autocrat, which can be taken back at his pleasure.

An especially important and influential form of the doctrine of equality was the equality of all men before God, as taught by Christianity. This leveling of mankind in the sight of God is a transposition into theological language of the equality among superstratified subjects. Considering the transcendence of God, however, the immanent worldly consequences of this doctrine tended toward absolute human equality.

This equality of subjects in relation to the monarch, compared to some forms of feudalism, marks a very perceptible gain—namely liberation from more direct and tangible oppression by the more numerous, nearby feudal lords.

The sharp material and legal inequality that existed at first between upper and lower stratum was a constitutional component of their separation and maintained itself against egalitarian tendencies. At the same time however, this legal inequality was only the juridical expression of a double standard of morality and ethics, of the social-psychological fact that different codes of human behavior and deportment, of ethical duties and rights, were applied to members of the upper and of the lower stratum. The longer this double morality persists, the more difficult it becomes to maintain it. Every advance in rationalization, every advance in habits of logical thought leads to the demand for a uniform and universally valid morality. This tendency can be expressed by preaching the morality of the lower stratum to the upper stratum, as has been done from the days of the Old Testament prophets to the days of Tolstoi, or by letting the morality of the upper stratum filter down to the lower stratum, mostly in attentuated and popularized form. The second procedure, as we have seen, is in practice much more effective than the first.

Politically all these tendencies ultimately lead to the demand for equality, for absolute equality in form as well as in material substance. At the height of the French Enlightenment, shortly before the Revolution, Helvétius radically denied innate inequalities among different individuals and traced all differences back to social situation, milieu, and upbringing—a conception of an extreme consistency that is at once impressive and frightening.

6. TENDENCY TOWARD REGULARITY

The development from hunters to herdsmen went along with a fundamental change in man's relation to animals. The primary purpose of this relation, after as before, was use of the animals for food. But to make best use of them, the former hunter had to develop better care for the animals. Above all he no longer could give free rein to his passion for hunting and the thirst for blood that went with it.

Quite analogously, the main aim of superincumbency is to let the conquered work for the conquerors. To achieve this aim the greatest possible number of them must be kept alive; accordingly, the attack and the conquest from the outset must be so conducted that the losses of the enemy over whom the superincumbency is to be established do not go beyond unavoidable figures. This requires a sharp curbing and disciplining of warlike instinct, and of the thirst for blood. Subjects, to the nomad, are not a hunter's prey but herd animals.

But the demands for rational self-control that superstratification makes on the conquerors were not satisfied by merely allowing the survival of the conquered. Rather, superstratification makes such demands again and again. For participants in the fresh act of conquest leading to superstratification it was certainly more than obvious that they should first thoroughly enjoy the new situation, satisfying their thirst for power at the expense of the subjugated. Very soon, however, the conquerors must have noted that such conduct hardly fostered the productivity of the lower stratum from which they meant to live. This productivity was all the higher the more the subjugated populace was allowed to work undisturbed, the more secure it could feel in its life and work. After all, the lords live on the economic output of the subjugated: the capacity of the peasants to meet feudal exactions had to be preserved. That was the reason their lives had been spared in superstratification in the first place. The more they produce, the more one can take away from them. But even this reckoning is not correct in its primitive-subtractive form: every relative excess in the deliveries exacted from the subjugated leads to an absolute decline of the product of their labor, whereas a progressive development of the economy and of its productivity is possible only with a modest exaction, leaving the producer an appropriate share of his own surplus. Above all, however, every higher economic development requires consistency, security, and predictability of circumstances; guarantees of life and property; an established legal order and orderly administration of law; undisturbed autonomy of peasants and artisans in managing their enterprises; peaceful marketplaces, equitable market regulations, and their enforcement. From the conquerors this required a final renunciation of all arbitrary exercise of their despotic powers, orderly administration according to definite rules and regulations, self-controlled commitment to law and right. Thus a quantitative heightening of the enjoyment of power had as its prerequisite a qualitative limitation. Let us recall how frequently in history the suppression of brigandage and piracy has been the precondition of trade and economic revival; or, conversely, how in the Islamic East the Sultan's arbitrariness constituted a grave obstacle to the development of a modern rational economy.

7. Tendency toward Legal Order

The tendency to exclude despotic rule exercised by individual members of the upper stratum leads finally to the structure that we call rational-legal order. To be sure, initially, this exists in a purely formal sense, namely that of a constant frame of valid legal regulations upon whose uniform observance and execution one may depend. Such legal uniformity does not imply anything about content of these legal dispositions and is far from eliminating the fundamental and far-reaching legal inequality between rulers and ruled. Rather, at first it consists only of a formalization of the previous inequality. The legal order constitutes itself at first only for the future, not also for the past. But, by virtue of this fact alone, much is already won for the ruled. To start with, they now know once and for all where they stand and can guide themselves accordingly, accustoming themselves to their situation. In addition, legal norms are formulated in peaceful times; on the basis of averages, they appeal to the social conscience and are observed because of their agreement with it. The social conscience, of course, can be perverted to a high degree by despotic structures. Nevertheless, all acute expressions of tyranny that momentarily exceed the norm or the average are thereby placed outside the law.

In disputes among members of the lower stratum the judges, naturally, are members of the upper stratum: juridical authority is everywhere one of the most important and effective forms of domination. As long as no solid legal norms are in effect, such arbitrational activity can be exercised according to pleasure and displeasure and, accordingly, serve as an instrument for a policy of "divide and rule" against the lower stratum; he who wants justice must first purchase the favor of the lord and judge. The cessation or even the increasing withdrawal of this possibility thus signifies indirectly a strengthening of the inner solidarity of the lower stratum.

An essential step in regularizing and strengthening the legal order is the process of committing the law to written form; hence, this tends to form the main demand of the lower stratum at the appropriate stage of legal history, a demand against which it is difficult to raise any rational objection. Thus was this demand successfully enforced by the lower stratum both in Athens and in Rome.

Every setting down, every explicit formulation of a law is a rationalization. A formulated legal axiom stands on a logical plane on which it also becomes possible to raise the question concerning the grounds for its validity. And to the extent that the formulation anticipates such questions and includes its own justification, the discussion concerning its validity is already opened. In consequence, although only indirectly and very gradually, formalism and explicit formulation of laws sets off a tendency toward material justice and notions of natural law.

If, for example, political usurpation and any political act of violence is stigmatized as contrary to law, this naturally is meant only for the future. Inevitably, however, due to the rational principle of generalization, it also turns backward, and a condemnation phrased in solemn legal form strikes at political usurpation as such, and therefore also at the usurpation by which the ruling upper stratum once seized the reins. If acts of violence, beatings to death, and robbery henceforth are to be regarded as unjust, how could they have been just in the past? This creates the need to veil or deny the violent origins that once had been a source of pride: hypocrisy is the obeisance paid by vice to virtue. Self-serving myths tend to be formulated at this point—like the myth dear to plutocracy that the original accumulation of wealth was due only to hard work and thrift.

As soon as the central question is posed about the legal ground and the fundamental justification of legal inequality itself—an inequality on which the very cleavage between upper stratum and lower stratum rests—then it becomes difficult, indeed impossible, to provide such justification within the rational framework of the ongoing discussion. The sophistries to which even the cleverest and most adroit protagonists of inherited legal inequality see themselves forced to resort are well known. There are questions to which the answer can be yes only as long as the question is never posed, questions the very posing of which already implies a negative answer. The tendency thus set off, if pursued to the end, results in the demand for not only formal but also material legal equality, for the equality of all individuals before the law, notably in political and constitutional law—a condition for which the Greek language has the felicitous term *isonomy*. Such isonomy, as it was realized (at least until recently) in all states claiming to be part of civilization, still does not mean that the inequality created by superstratification is abolished once and for all. Rather, the result is that condition characterized by Anatole France's well-known saying: "The law in its majestic equality enjoins rich and poor alike from begging their bread or sleeping under bridges." It follows not that the past accomplishments in this direction are worthless but that they need to be complemented. Isoctesy—equality of opportunity—is the necessary complement to isonomy, as will be discussed in a later context.

How much the legal order of the *Rechtsstaat*, with all its gradually developed elements—even those of "merely formal" nature—means for each individual has been driven home to us in our own day when such accomplishments, after long being depreciated or satirized in Anatole France's manner, can no longer be taken for granted in all countries.

8. TENDENCY TOWARD PLUTOCRACY

Originally the economic significance of superstratification was that wealth follows power, that power confers wealth. And this connection applied not only during the act of conquest and superstratification itself, but also thereafter as long as the master class maintained complete possession of the position achieved by these means. For continuation of this position presupposes precisely that the mere fact of inherited membership in the master class secures for each member an income consonant with his social station. However, that is not possible without renewed violent interference in the distribution of goods, so as to replenish the possessions of the upper stratum—that is, without "compensating injustice."

Once, however, the rationalization and legalization of life has reached the stage of formal written rules—proceeded so far, that is to say, that such supplementary violent interference in the economic order becomes not only difficult but impossible—then, inevitably, more and more individual members of the upper class will become impoverished. They will then sink below the life-style appropriate to their status and thus drop out of the ruling stratum, membership in which now rests on *both* descent *and* wealth. In order to legitimize oneself as a rightful member of the ruling upper stratum one must now distinguish oneself "through wealth as well as through descent" as we repeatedly read in the Greek biographies. And, according to Aristotle, government offices in pre-Draconian Athens were filled "according to nobility and wealth."[3] This is the first phase of plutocracy, which we could call aristo-plutocracy: poverty is already a ground for exclusion; wealth is a necessary, but not yet sufficient, condition for inclusion in the upper class.

Soon, in fluid transition, the second stage is also reached: individual members of the lower class become rich, become accustomed to the style and manner of the upper class; improverished members of the upper class save themselves from the threat of losing their class status by marriage with the daughters of the new rich; and the rich *homines novi* demand at first *de facto* and then also *de jure* recognition of their equal status. The causal relation between power and wealth has now reversed itself: the power of wealth replaces the wealth of power. No longer does wealth follow power, but power, alongside the socal prestige due it, follows wealth. Thus Hesiod[4] says, "For with riches go nobility and honors." And it was exactly thus in France at the end of the seventeenth century:

> Si je n'ay point de naissance, j'ay du bien,
> Et à présent, qui est riche, est noble.[5]

It is precisely against this development that Theognis turns his increasingly resentment-laden formulation: "Wealth, the most beautiful and delightful of all the gods, with thee even the wicked man comes to honor."[6] Theognis is replete with hate-filled and angry outbursts of jealousy felt by embattled aristocrats in the face of the upward social mobility of the members of the lower stratum.

In the France of the *ancien régime*, an aristocratic monarchist complained in exactly the same tones: "We have driven our infatuation to the extreme, we let ourselves be so misled by the dazzlement of wealth as to show the rich a reverence that fills me with alarm. Our fathers, who were far more pious, and—without knowing it— more clever, reserved their respect for the nobility. . . . In the highest social estates one no longer knows how one should distinguish between good and bad society. . . . *O étranges moeurs!*"[7] As Sombart put it, "That is now, therefore, the great world-historical change . . . how the power of wealth develops from the wealth of power."[8] Aristocracy, by way of the intermediate stage of aristo-plutocracy, had transformed itself into plutocracy.

The class inequality, of course, remains: a member of the old aristocracy must first lose his inherited wealth in order to be excluded from his class under the new conditions, whereas a *homo novus* must first earn it in order to be admitted to the charmed circle. The sociological two-layer structure as such remains, but now what holds true for it is the principle "To him who has [the necessary money] shall be given." What is to be given includes titles of nobility and the insignia of feudalism—in short, all the social prerogatives of the old, formerly hereditary, aristocracy. This plutocracy, compared to the former aristocracy of birth, signifies initially an additional regulation *pro futuro* of the conditions of admission to and membership in the ruling upper stratum—and also, conversely, to membership in the lower stratum.

Plutocracy, at all events, represents an advance in the direction of democratization and greater social justice, and it is welcomed as such by the new beneficiaries and fought with bitter hatred by those who once were in a monopolistic position. The road is now partially cleared both for the economic and social decline of the incompetent and for the economic and social rise of the competent. And this social rise, through economic competition, now stands fundamentally open to anyone who possesses the requisite ability to enter. Aristocratic property and income, along with the life-style and social position pertaining to it, can now be individually obtained.

This process of social justice has found its solemn glorification in the magnificent proemium to Hesiod's didactic poem. Here the world ruler Zeus, the guardian of justice, is described as follows:

> . . . through whose will
> Mortal men are named in speech or remain unspoken.
> Men are renowned or remain unsung
> For lightly he makes strong,
> And lightly brings strength to confusion,
> Lightly diminished the great man.
> Uplifts the obscure one,
> Lightly the crooked man he straightens,
> Withers the proud man
> He, Zeus, of the towering thunders,
> Whose house is highest.[9]

But the social power position and ruling class position remain, although the conditions of admission and membership are newly regulated. The old feudal coach remains, and it does not exactly say "All aboard!" Rather, a change of passengers takes place only gradually so that others are accepted. And the corresponding mentality and ideology also survive for a while.

A form of insecurity, both in self-consciousness and in world view is one of the many symptoms of the greater insecurity and flexibility of plutocracy as compared with aristocracy. "Noble birth is a favor shown by the gods that cannot be forced, and it demands respect. On the hand, everybody can make claim to property; it is quickly acquired, quickly lost, and the outer superiority that it bestows is no holy order."[10]

Thus, social inequality, objectively and essentially, has decreased in plutocracy; but subjectively it is felt more strongly. Injustice has indeed become smaller, but more palpable and more vulnerable.

Plutocracy—the rule of the rich—is a social and economic system that rests on two principles, or sets of principles, of quite different origin and structure. The new, epoch-making principle it introduces is that of the distribution of income and property on the basis of market economy, according to economic proficiency. This principle, however, was not carried out radically and consistently. Rather, it supplemented three other principles taken over from the preceding aristocratic epoch:

(1) The state or property and income distribution that was already in existence and that had been created by feudalism was left as it was. For example, the demand raised in Athens of 600 B.C. for a new distribution of land (at that time the only form of productive capital) was nowhere carried through.

(2) The unrestricted right of inheritance was preserved. As a result, not only were preexisting feudal properties passed on without restriction, but every property newly acquired through economic means acquired the possibility of being further inherited indefinitely, by many generations of descendants uninvolved in its original acquisition.

As a result of these two feudal principles, property and income distribution included two categories: (a) Those properties and portions of properties that had been acquired by their owners according to the new ground rules, through their own economic proficiency; and (b) those properties and portions of properties that had been inherited by their owners with economic proficiency playing no role and that either (i) still stemmed from the feudal period and had been acquired forcibly or (ii) had been acquired through personal economic proficiency in the first phase of the plutocratic period by the first person to leave behind an inheritance.

The percentage of properties obtained by hard work (a) and inherited properties (b) varies according to the more or less dynamic character of the period involved. It is obvious, however, that the sum of the inherited properties will always be greater than the properties earned by hard work. This fact already deprives the plutocratic system of any claim to justice and rationality that it could assert in contrast to feudalism. In any case, the bearers and beneficiaries of the new plutocratic system, as a rule, had no real intention of removing themselves from feudalism. Rather, they tended to encourage the third principle that developed as plutocracy took over from feudalism: (3) The social prerogative of the upper stratum came to be structured in such a way that as soon as a certain level of income and property was reached, acceptance into the upper stratum could follow with a corresponding increase of feudal privilege and honors.

In this context a merely negative renunciation of this privilege, according to justice, would not have sufficed because the principle of market economy alone does not suffice for a clear determination of the social structure. Rather, this determination requires, in addition to the economic stabilization of a market economy, a social equalization independent of it, but compatible with it. What it required was not the mere negative renunciation of the feudal principle, but its supersession by a new positive principle of social structure as yet to be formulated.

Moreover, the creation of a new, logically consistent social ideology adequate to establish the impartiality of the market economy would have required a renunciation of social privilege that was precisely what the "self-made man" had earned with so much bitter sweat of his brow. We can well understand why the suggestion of an enormous moral effort with the prospect of a lessening of one's own social position did not exactly appear enticing.

Today we tend to view and to judge plutocracy exclusively from the standpoint of social justice. We see, consequently, only the faults it has in common with feudalism, and not the advantages that its rise brought to bear as compared with the latter. Today we take for granted that public offices should be occupied only by persons of proven competence; the sale of public offices appears to us a glaring abuse. We forget that in its time the plutocratic purchase of public offices, as opposed to their feudal inheritance, presented a democratic advance and was experienced as such and fought against by the feudal-minded with deep resentment. Moreover, the purchaser of an office was as a rule more dependent than a feudal heir upon the appointing central authority, and the danger of insubordination and restiveness was reduced. It was particularly in the self-interest of the buyer to acquire, as far as possible, an office that he was competent to administer; he had not only the alternatives of purchasing different offices, but also other opportunities for the investment of his capital. Hence this circumstance to a certain degree worked selectively in a positive direction.

In line with the original aristocratic mentality, objects were acquired forcibly by "political means," whether in the acute and violent form of the raid, or the chronic and violent form of levying tributes. Alongside these, giving was the only peaceful form of property transfer in keeping with the social station of the conquerors. The exchange of gifts among peers in aristocratic societies plays a considerable role and, like primary aristocratic conceptions, it is an honorable proof of social superiority to give more than one receives.

In the monetary realm, the transition from aristocracy to plutocracy implies that precious metals, especially gold, once used exclusively for bodily adornment, household utensils, or to fill the treasure chest, now are weighed and finally minted into standard coins.

The whole development portrayed here in its last stage depends as much on the existence of a formal legal-rational order as it does on an economic structure based wholly or predominantly on the processes of exchange and marketing. This economic structure ensued without problems as long as the peasant-artisan and family industry was the prevailing form of economic enterprise, since the market economy was the natural form of exchange between so many independent petty industries. The market economy automatically rewards economic proficiency positively, and low or inefficient economic performance negatively; hence it creates an autonomous sytem of economic rise and fall, removed from political influence. And it is in precisely this that its antifeudal effect lies.

The picture changes radically under a centrally guided national economy, a governmentally planned or administered economy. In it, of course, the direction of the economy lies in the same hands holding the political and social power, and therefore there no longer exists an independent economic mechanism with a corrective or equalizing effect on the political and social power relations. Compared with plutocracy, that signifies refeudalization.

9. Tendency toward Government by Taxation

The development of plutocracy on the foundation of the rational-legal order naturally leads to an unprecedented development of the economy, which now determines the social fate of each individual and increasingly pushes into the center of social life and consciousness. Such an upsurge of the economy and of its technical means leads, among other things, to the full development of finance and of the monetary and credit economy—which, advancing, pushes the barter economy into the background.

A total transformation of the feudal epoch occurred as soon as a corresponding development of the money economy enabled central authorities to levy monetary taxes and—correspondingly—to pay salaries to those staffing the local organs of power. Previously, payments in kind from the subjects of a district to the local administrator could not possibly travel to the often distant capital; this became possible with the high specific value of money which, moreover, posed no difficulties in the way of transport. As soon, however, as all (or at least the principal) public payments flowed into the central coffer in the hands of the potentate, and the military and civil governmental bodies were paid, the local independence and autonomy of these mandataries was undermined; an enfeoffed vassal now became a salaried official, officer, or soldier who could be throttled economically by the central authority on any payday by stoppage of his stipend if he were imprudent enough to bite the hand that fed him. Consequently, he was placed in full dependency *ad nutum regis*.

In the following sections we shall see what revolutionary consequences these new possibilities of the tax state had in the civil and military domains.

10. Tendency toward Bureaucratization

Where a strong monarchy came into conflict with the pretensions of an aristocracy, it naturally occurred to the occupant of the throne to try entrusting the exercise of sovereign functions (in the name of the monarch) to more devoted and compliant persons, frequently to members of the lower stratum. If the choice fell (as in tenth-century Germany) on the celibate priesthood (as elsewhere on eunuchs), the danger of feudal right of inheritance to the position was excluded; but then the success of the arrangement depended on reducing the supreme head of this priesthood (the pope) to the position of bureau director or chancellor of the monarch. This is one of the cases in which the competing claims to absolute rulership between priests and soldiers, between Brahmans and Kshatriyas, has had a profound historic impact.

Another typical and frequent attempt to resolve this problem is that of delegating the exercise of sovereignty to men wholly without any following or roots of their own and consequently "made" by the monarch and fully dependent on him: prisoners of war, slaves, eunuchs, freedmen, foreigners, outcasts. This was also by degrees how the central European ministerial nobility originated from the first mention of this practice in Tacitus and from the *missi dominici* of the Merovingians and Carolingians, down to the highest officials of the Great Elector of Brandenburg. The "Cherethites and Pelethites" (Cretans and Philistines) who form the foreign royal guard of King David and also the Mamelukes and Janissaries belong in this context. But all these court officials rose to feudal hereditary status, and from France and England to Japan, history is replete with accounts of dynasties that were dethroned by the commander of their bodyguard, their majordomo, chief butler, steward, vizier, or shogun; ordinarily the sergeant had in reality already led the company.

As long as a barter economy prevailed, all this water pressure, no matter how artificially dammed up, flowed at length into the broad riverbed so deeply cut by the hereditary nobility and its aspirations. The feudal superstratification structure repeatedly reasserted itself, regardless of how much "circulation of elites" may have occurred within this framework.

Only when plutocracy led to a money economy and thus made possible the rise of the tax state could the prince replace the rebellious vassals by appointed, salaried "military and civil attendants" who could be dismissed at any time.

In the course of the same development, moreover, the establishment of a permanent residence as administrative center, and therewith the urbanization of the prince, became both possible and necessary; until then rulership, insofar as it had not come into being originally as domination of a single city had, as a rule, been practiced as an itinerant agrarian occupation. From the viewpoint of transport technology it was difficult, if not impossible, to store as much natural produce as the prince and his large retinue required during the whole year. It was far easier and far more convenient to bilk the regions of a succession of castles in turn and to remain just long enough to use up the assembled provisions.

Originally the administration of a fief had been mainly a matter of orally transmitted orders and instructions, which naturally made any exact or stricter control impossible. Meanwhile, an administration with writing and a system of documents had been developed, and this created the possibility of exact and up-to-date control by the central authority.

Salaries and written documents are the two decisive features of bureaucratization. They make possible the development of a professional and lifelong officialdom of experts. That signifies, first of all, an enormous increase of princely power, and its direct result was the sharp rise of territorial absolutism in modern Europe. When, however, even these officials found themselves in the role of an absolute prince's "civil attendants" (the official terminology in eighteenth-century Prussia), the logical development encouraged the elaboration of a collegial *esprit de corps*, an independent professional ethos, and a professional theory of civil service. The civil servant felt himself the counsel of the commonweal, and occasionally dared to appear in such a role to his prince and bread-giver.

When the officials were priests and the priesthood was not subordinated to the secular power, they had sufficient independence at least to establish standards of judgment, and even of conduct, toward the prince. In the West, the development produced the Reformation, which overcame the priestly social estate and set in its place the doctrine of universal priesthood as well as the Christian maxim that one must obey God more than man. This doctrine, to be sure, was deflected in Lutheranism toward a pious passivity; yet even in this atmosphere of patriarchal servility, every official could feel himself a link in a chain of sovereignty ordained by God. Indeed, according to Luther's doctrine of "calling," each individual Christian in his proper place should consider himself a "bailiff of God." And in Calvinism the "lower magistrates" were the appointed organs of moral and theological control and of the possible right of resistance against the prince. By and large, in Europe in the early modern period we could speak almost of a latent theory of the divine right of the professional civil servant, or state servant; the same Prussian king who called his officers civil attendants called himself the first servant of the state. The independent, self-reliant bureaucracy found its classical embodiment in Prussia in the age of reform under Stein and Hardenberg.[11]

We saw earlier that the development of superstratification-feudalism initially led to hopeless confusion between the interests of the master class and the real common interest, and that the potentates were vitally interested in the maintenance and intensification of this confusion. Through the rise of a professional bureaucracy, based upon the division of labor, which for quite different reasons was of paramount interest to the ruler, for the first time an increasing disentanglement and separation of these two interests developed. The common interest and its exigencies were concentrated at the administrative-technical level in the hands of the bureaucracy.

As long as the administration was exercised as a secondary occupation by members of a ruling class, the power interests of this class unavoidably enjoyed priority. But now an individual began to specialize in administrative tasks as a full-time functionary; his daily and lifelong professional destiny, his livelihood, his social prestige, and his self-esteem depended on the adequacy with which he carried out the tasks assigned to him; and hence the inherent exigencies of these tasks began to take possession of him. The task demands solution, and as it cannot be solved in just any way, he must follow the path that leads to the solution if he wants to avoid failure, whether or not he might find this path in itself to his liking.

Consequently a specialized, fulltime civil service, paid by the state, enjoying life tenure, and answerable to itself—as long as its internal structure and its relations with outsiders are subject to appropriate and reasonable regulations—can have no professional concerns except the interests and the welfare of the state itself, and thus will tend to save these interests as a matter of course. Its professional interest to a great extent is spontaneously coordinated with the common interest; indeed, its very existence depends on the welfare of the state.

There are also specific dangers and possibilities of degeneration besetting a bureaucracy—sociological professional diseases, whose systematic investigation would be of theoretical and practical importance. Among these are bribery, which from the viewpoint of historical development often appears as a residue of (or throwback to) a prescriptive right to the arbitrary levying of tribute or to the regulated demand of fees from the subjugated population. The toadyism of officialdom also belongs here, as we already encounter it in ancient Egypt in the "Teachings of Kagemni" (vizier of the Sixth Dynasty, in the third quarter of the third millennium B.C.): "Bend your back before your superior, then will your house have permanency in its possession and your recompense will arrange itself accordingly. Poverty is decreed for him who is rebellious against a superior: one lives only so long as he is mildly disposed."[12]

By far the worst—and today by far the most immediate—danger of the degeneration of bureaucracy, however, lies in the slipping away from responsibility—from conscious and democratically responsible authority to an absolute domination, a slipping away that makes officials not servants of the people but masters, super-stratifiers. This change of function is willed, taken for granted, and official in all totalitarian states, as one of their outstanding peculiarities. But, disturbingly, a development in the same direction has also been set in motion in almost all countries—a highly alarming proof of how much the tendency to totalitarianism today lies in the course of time, and is by no means limited to totalitarian countries. This is the tendency that has made bureaucracy unloved in the whole world; it has given rise to the opinion that bureaucracy as such is an evil in itself, so that even democratic countries resound with complaints about the insolence of office. It would be a fatal mistake, however, to overlook that a sound bureaucracy is one of the most indispensable and most reliable components of a democratic state order: *corruptio optimi pessima*. Accordingly, it is all the more important to set forth clearly the sociological conditions and limits of such soundness.

The most important of these conditions is that the discretionary power of the bureaucracy must be sharply limited, its responsibility clearly and effectively subjected to public control. In this connection every measure that can serve to activate and to actualize the personal, enforceable responsibility of each official is important. This again presupposes a functioning parliamentarism and, above all, a limitation of bureaucracy to the minimum of those functions whose assumption by the state is unavoidable. For only thus can the subordination of the bureaucracy to the state and the commonality be preserved; otherwise, the bureaucratic apparatus acquires ascendancy and becomes the master and ruler of the state and the people.

It is especially harmful when the bureaucracy acquires economic power in addition to its proper political power. The doctrine of the separation of powers, as classically advocated by Montesquieu, has occasionally been applied with exaggerated political rigidity in its political region of origin. It is, however, nowhere more justified and important than when it is a question of the separation of political and economic authority. Bureaucracy works with salutary effect only within sharply defined limits that must be maintained. This, too, is one of the many important reasons why a nationalized economy reaching into every sphere is a "road to serfdom" and why a new attempt to determine the limits of the state is one of the most pressing needs of our time.

11. TENDENCY TOWARD A POPULAR ARMY

What has been said about the civil state administration also holds true for military matters, which originally had been a duty as well as a right, and at all events the prerogative of the nobility. This weapons monopoly of the nobility, corresponding to the superstratification situation, was bound to come into conflict soon with the elementary military principle of the superiority of the greater number (other circumstances being equal). This led at first to the compromise of giving light and inferior arms to a sufficiently reliable and subservient part of the lower stratum that formed the lightly armed entourage of noble military leaders. But the inner logic of military necessity finally impelled the master class progressively to improve the armament of these nonnoble footsoldiers, to increase their number, and to revise military tactics in terms of their deployment. The phalanx of hoplites superseded the knightly chariot-driving individual fighter, and the Swiss infantry at the Battle of Sempach (1386) defeated the noble army of knights. In antiquity, military development went hand in hand with the rise of the plutocratic "hoplite polis" of Solon, then of the sailors' polis of Themistocles; in medieval Europe, with a heightened military and political importance of the cities and their array of burghers, warships, and artillery; in nascent modern times, with the rise of mercenary armies recruited by early capitalist war entrepreneurs and led by territorial principalities. Finally this development also flowed, under the absolutism of modern times, in a direction parallel

to that of the civil administration, into the rationally bureau-
cratized standing army, whereby the sociological position of the professional officer corresponds to a great extent to that of the professional civil servant.

Thus developed, since the beginning of modern times, the standing armies recruited from the subjects of a country just as—significantly—Machiavelli had demanded and predicted. The French
Revolution made Carnot's *levée en masse* possible, and when
Scharnhorst in Prussia imitated the example for compelling military reasons, it was clear to him that sooner or later corresponding
repercussions in a democratic direction would be inevitable. Finally,
World War I (1914-1918) brought the first "total mobilization."

This whole technical-organizational development of military matters had the most direct and crucial importance for power relations
in the sphere of foreign policy and its development. But it also had
general and far-reaching social repercussions, far beyond the individual influences already referred to. It overcame the hegemonic position of the nobility in the area from which it had sprung. It acted
as a coercive influence toward an ever widening democratization in
all other areas also, for one must be able to rely upon the goodwill of
those upon whom one is militarily dependent; with the "people in
arms," no regime can in the long run make short shrift of it at will.
Since, however, strict uniformity of organization and command is
all the more unavoidable the larger the number of soldiers in the
army, this development also contributed decisively to the
strengthening of "monarchic" or dictatorial, centralist tendencies
in the broadest sense.

12. TENDENCY TOWARD URBANIZATION

Geographically, the division of labor made possible by superstratification finds its expression in the early rise of cities.

Formerly every able-bodied person himself produced what he required for his needs, especially in the way of food for himself and his
family. The more extensive the mode of production, the greater was
the area required for this purpose. This had led to a scattered distribution of families over the terrain. The number of those released
from work directly connected with the acquisition of food, and those
not individually bound to a particular area as a food base, was so
small in each community that the concentration of local specialists
could not have been a factor of great significance. Consequently, the
village in general had been the largest possible unit of settlement.

The village produced the food for its inhabitants and was restricted in size by the area that could be tilled without excessive and unproductive loss of time in getting to and from the arable land distant from the settlement. The development of handicraft, especially in totemistic hunting cultures, soon reaches the upper limit of the possible division of labor, conditioned by the narrow pyramidal base. The settlements forming themselves in this culture complex, in which industrial production and market dealings assume a certain importance, constitute a certain preliminary stage to the later towns, but they could not grow appreciably beyond the size of artisan villages and market towns.

All this changes radically as a result of superincumbency. The upper stratum of the conquerors does not live from the fruits of its own labor, but from its forcibly exacted share in the labor product of the lower stratum. Not only does each conqueror with his family live on this tribute, but also his whole clientele and the whole circle of those slaves, semislaves, or freedmen. He keeps them gathered around him as a warlike retinue, centrally led or held together through conditions of their transport economy, and all must work for him and his family.

As supplies for all these persons are provided as tribute or by the services of the lower stratum, and as the peasant delivers his tribute or performs his services only once a year or at great intervals, allowance had to be made for varying distances and long stretches to be traveled. Hence the orbit, the natural product of which can be gathered together and consumed in one place, is incomparably larger than the maximum extent of a village town line. Further, the same holds true when it is not a queston of forced tributes, but of provisions voluntarily offered in exchange for centrally produced industrial products. Indeed, this free trade in durable and transportable provisions (especially grain, but also livestock and industrial products and other specialties as return freight) ultimately overcomes obstacles posed by trafficking in goods over even longer stretches of land and sea.

The development of trade with distant places leads to the rise of settlement centers, which increasingly concentrate on commercial transport and market dealings and on special products for the local market and for distant trade. At the same time, they grow economically and politically strong enough to shake off the traditional agrarian-feudal dependency, whether the bearer thereof was a (clerical or secular) patrician lord by virtue of his own or transferred right, or a group of city-dwelling, noble-landed proprietors. This

self-liberation of the city as the cultural growth apex is, as we shall
see, a decisive factor of the transfeudal development progress, since
all antifeudal and transfeudal progressive forces in general concentrate in the city.

Specialists in various pursuits who were no longer producing for
direct food demands (and released from the soil for this very reason)
flocked to these urban centers. What drew them there, magnetlike
was:

The accumulation of buyers and parties interested in their products (market orientation).

The favorable traffic situation both for sales to distant localities
as well as for the purchase of unfinished products of distant proveni-
ence (transport orientation).

The exciting and stimulating proximity of their fellows, the pervasive atmosphere of rivalry and competition (tendency to agglomeration).

The higher social, economic and intellectual atmosphere of the
city as the location of the ruling stratum and of those closely bound
to it. This was especially true in politically independent or privileged cities in contrast to the lack of freedom of the rural population:
"city air makes free" in the narrower and broader sense alike. Hence
also the city dweller's traditional feeling of superiority toward the
peasant.

The greater security of life and property, which increased in importance as both were increasingly valued by the city dweller.

The given ecological conditions for the city population of second
degree, namely for the producers of the wants of the rest of the city
inhabitants, as well as for the dealers in the products the latter produced and consumed.

13. OBJECTIFICATION, RATIONALIZATION, SECULARIZATION

Superstratification-conditioned specialization creates, as we have
seen, a tendency toward objectification. The instrument of this rising objectification, as of the increasing specializing progress in the
knowledge and mastery of reality, is the human mind, the *ratio*.
This development signifies an increasing rationalization of thought
first of all and, subsequently, also of action.

It is obvious that the development of applied knowledge—
knowledge as power—lies in the interests of the potentates, and that
this applied or practical knowledge, by its very nature, is rational;

accordingly, it is the interest of power that drives rationalization forward along this line.

But even the insight of pure science, of knowledge for its own sake, is also positively related to the interest of the ruling class. This is true not only because of the repeated experience that pure knowledge is the most effective precursor of knowledge as power, or just because it is a sublime form of luxury, whereby the holders of power show the world what they can do; rather, reason can be found in the most basic structural relationship, because in the final analysis, the desire for knowledge is itself the purest form of the drive toward expansion.

A third category of knowledge, the theological or redemptive, is also linked, positively or negatively, to the ruling power elite. But the longer it is operative as theology and metaphysics, the more it has an inhibiting and restricting effect on the pure rational development of science.

However, another tendency of theological and priestly origin indirectly exercises a strong positive influence on rational progress within and outside the domain of science: asceticism and its rule of self-control. It is asceticism, orginally religious (theological), that educated man to the methodical concern with intellectual matters in general and also to science.[13] Among the most impressive passages in Spengler's brilliant book[14] are those where he portrays how the rational division of time arose from early medieval monastic asceticism, in accordance with which all the clocks in the world have been pitilessly ticking away ever since.

Objectification and rationalization signify knowledge as power, knowledge as rulership, and a heightened effectiveness of the means available for the application of power and the exercise of dominion. But they also signify the undermining of the intellectual foundations of power and domination, as the stubborn fact of superincumbency cannot be justified in any way in the forum of reason. It also signifies secularization, destruction, and dissolution of the theological auxiliary supports that the priesthood has created as the most solid spiritual supports of power.

Now, as we have seen, specialization and intensified cultivation of the mind, based on the division of labor, were usually in the hands of the priesthood. The priests, however, lived on revenues deriving from domination, levied by them or siphoned off to them; hence they had a vital interest in maintaining this feudal domination. And the feudal bending of religion to theology acts again as a fetter to further intellectual development, both within the priesthood itself and in the whole remaining sphere over which the priesthood claims intellectual sovereignty.

The rest of the motive forces considered here exhibit an independent tendency to rectilinear development in an antifeudal direction; in this most important and most central domain of the intellect even this antifeudal tendency is braked by the social conditions deriving from superstratification.

A priesthood as creator, bearer, and defender of the theology of domination is historically the most primordial and, as far as ideal types are concerned, the most concrete construct. But it is by no means a necessary one, nor is it the only one possible. Every despotism that seeks to stabilize itself requires the spiritual help of a theology, and when it does not have a priestly social estate at its disposal, it creates, no matter how well or badly, its "myth" and its orthodoxy.

It is also this theological vicious circle that keeps most high cultures, despite forward-thrusting forces, at the level of the "Middle Ages," which creates the "peoples of the eternal Middle Ages." A direct result of the key position that the scientific-intellectual domain assumed was that all other contemplated developments were arrested and prevented from stepping beyond a certain limit—namely, the limit of medievalism.

That is also the reason why progress beyond the Middle Ages cannot simply be effected automatically once the maturity of a certain stage of development has been reached; instead, the productive accomplishment of a one-time intellectual creation is necessary. From the point of view of universal history, therefore, the question as to where and under what conditions this creative accomplishment first and decisively succeeded and thus broke through that vicious circle of theological restriction of thought and research acquires a crucial importance. For only on this foundation has a real overcoming of the Middle Ages in all spheres become possible.

PART TWO

The Path of Freedom

I wish neither to rule nor to be ruled.
Herodotus
3. 83. 2.

CHAPTER 1

Freedom versus Unfreedom

1. Breakthrough to Intellectual Freedom

The fateful step forward from primitive peoples and archaic peasants to high culture had been achieved through superstratification and purchased at the price of domination and subjection. The crucial questions posed by fate, therefore, were if, how, and when on this new ground of high culture, bondage could be overcome, and independence and freedom consonant with human nature once again achieved.

There are indications of beginnings in the direction of intellectual freedom (which sooner or later, however, came to a stop) in China, India, and perhaps also in Ikhnaton's Egypt. Only in one locality was a truly fruitful breakthrough to freedom ventured: ancient Greece. The repercussions of this feat continue to this day, and we are its heirs. The superiority of Western culture over all others and its present world position rest upon this Hellenic act of freedom and upon the persistence of its impact. The corollary following from this historical situation is that the responsibility for the future of human culture falls solely upon the shoulders of the peoples of the free West.

The Greeks are the people who, as the founder-heroes in the realm of Western culture, alone and for the first time effected this breakthrough in a prototypical, exemplary, and classical manner—i.e., with an impact and a relevancy unbrokenly affecting subsequent ages down to our own day. This achievement singles out the Greeks and their history from the history of other peoples, makes their history our concern, and makes their history appear at least as important as our own. Our own, in turn, receives its loftiest mission and its world-historical dignity and importance from the accession to and the administration of this legacy. The Greeks, of course, are no longer models to us; but now, as before, they remain prototypes.

It is not difficult to appreciate the irreplaceable uniqueness and exclusiveness of this Greek act of freedom within the whole realm of

Western culture. The Romans were by nature decidedly authoritarian and dominating, and their slow assimilation of Greek liberality signified for them a degree of self-mastery. Christianity, as an ecclesiastically organized theology of salvation, demanded an exclusive soul-saving orthodoxy up to and including the *sacrificium intellectus*, and initially it took the liberality of Greek culture into the bargain only under protest and despite itself. When the Germanic peoples took over this culture of Christianity and antiquity, they had not yet, in their own intellectual development, arrived at the corresponding fork in the road. As newly converted Christians they exhibited at first a schoolboyish overeagerness. To be sure, they showed a certain spirit of social and political independence, peculiar to them as well as to other Indo-Germans, and a spirit of community and cooperation that repeatedly breaks through when opportunity is offered; yet nothing suggests that they would have found the path to intellectual freedom on their own. Wherever we come upon a stirring in this direction it turns out to have been elicited by the world of antiquity, including the moment of its greatest revitalization in the Renaissance, the Enlightenment, and the modern world of science.

The viewpoint here adopted is certainly the properly and decisively humanistic one. If we forsake it, the history of any randomly chosen people is just as interesting, just as important, and just as "directly of God," and we find ourselves right in the middle of an unstable historical relativism. The only way out, then, would be to leap to a position that is impregnable as being rooted in subjective inclination or aversion. What we shall attempt here instead are the outlines of a humanistic world history of the West. From this it becomes necessary to subordinate all that follows, decisively and suggestively, to the questions: How did what is specific and what serves as a universal standard in Greek culture, how did the Greekness of the Greeks, originate? How was it preserved, transmitted, developed, and passed on to successive generations down to our own? This way of framing the problem implies that everything that has made possible and promoted this development receives a plus, everything that has jeopardized, hindered, adversely affected or impaired it, a minus sign. These are, of course, value judgments, but they by no means rest upon a smuggled-in subjectivity. Rather, they follow objectively from the underlying formulation of the question. Without some kind of interest or other, there is no occasion whatsoever for concerning oneself with history, and it can only be useful to make this standard-setting interest explicit from the outset.

2. Pre-Hellenic Peoples

Our knowledge of the pre-Hellenic neolithic population of Greece in the fourth millennium B.C. is rather scant; this population belongs to those peasant groups Menghin has called the "eastern Mediterranean village culture,"[1] which has been little investigated up to now. The great migration of herdsmen at the end of the fourth millennium B.C., by way of Asia Minor and the Aegean Sea, reached Crete as well as Greece: the bull inseminated Europa. To the west of the Taurus mountains arose the urban culture of Asia Minor, the Cycladic culture of the Aegean, the early Helladic culture of Greece, and the early Minoan culture of Crete—all closely related to each other. This immediate predecessor of Hellenic culture in the third millennium B.C. was developed by peoples whose names have come down to us as Pelasgians, Leleges, and Carians; they were predominantly of Mediterranean and "Aegean" stock—at all events, not traceable linguistically to Indo-Germanic origins. On the coasts they engaged in navigation and trade, and on the land in peasant agriculture with oxen, sheep, goats, pigs, and dogs as domestic animals, and in the cultivation of grain. They practiced a natural religion based on the changing of the seasons and marked by ecstatic festivals for which the disappearance of vegetation with the outbreak of the summer drought and its reappearance after the autumn rains constituted major events pregnant with excitement. Sociologically, they represented a strong tradition of a planter-mother culture, which also finds religious expression in the central role assigned to a fertility goddess, "the great Mother" who later meets us as Demeter. Indeed, we shall be coming upon the traditions of this pre-Hellenic lower stratum when they crop up again in the post-Mycenaean age.

This prehistoric cultural stratum and its matriarchal character was first brilliantly disclosed by Johann Jacob Bachofen (1815-1877), mainly on the basis of scattered (often even incorrectly interpreted) literary information and of archaeological monuments of classical antiquity. To be sure, he took his cue from the then-prevailing monistic evolutionism in generalizing this culture into a primordial, panmatriarchal stage of all culture as a whole; in seeking to bring it to life for his readers he gave free rein to a romantic sexual metaphysic wallowing in gloomy settings. Bachofen's influence continues here and there to this day. The planter culture, of course (a concept later elaborated by Eduard Hahn) really did include such a gloomy, wildly proliferating element. However, the advent of peasant culture (from which Bachofen could not yet separate that of the planters) brought considerable and highly beneficial elucidations and consolations that obviously had been strengthened by admixtures of nomadic rationality. The pre-Hellenic culture of Greece exhibits features that are intimate rather than dismal.

3. Crete

Crete increasingly assumed cultural leadership within this eastern Mediterranean culture complex of the third millennium B.C. It reached its apogee in the middle of the second millennium and gave rise to an urban high culture, the Minoan culture, which gradually extended its sphere of influence. It also possessed a script—or even several scripts—which unfortunately still await deciphering.

In more than one respect the rise of this high culture stood under an especially lucky star. We do not know the identity of the conquerors here, who must have belonged to the great waves of herdsmen who were on the move around 3000 B.C. Since neither ass nor horse appears, and the ox, alone among domestic animals, dominates both their economic and ritual life, it may be assumed that the conquerors could not have been familiar with any herd animal other than the ox. Since the whole of the Near East and southeastern Europe at that time was already populated by peasants, it is unlikely that they were primal, purely nomadic herdsmen. More likely, they were peasant warriors with a strong admixture of the dynamic traits peculiar to nomadic herdsmen. This suggests strong affinity between the upper stratum and the lower stratum, for both of whom the ox was the standard domestic animal. We cannot establish any far-reaching contrast between them either culturally or otherwise.

As compared with the peasant culture forming its base, the urban high culture of Crete, so far as we know, exhibits no single new and alien cultural element—except, of course, the cultural exchange with neighboring high cultures, especially Egypt, which developed from trade relations. Rather, the Minoan culture appears as the further development, unbroken and organic, indeed as the apogee, of its own peasant foundation, whose feminist admixture also remains preserved in the refinements of courtly life. Clearly, such a far-reaching kinship between upper and lower stratam offers the most favorable preconditions for a relatively mild unfolding of super-stratification and for a relatively rapid and fundamental bridging of gaps arising from social conflict.

The cultic veneration of the bull and of vegetal fertility presupposes a peasant life based in the economic domain. Soon, however, the specially favored position of Crete as the largest island in the Aegean made itself felt, offering the possibility of fully exploiting the stratification-conditioned concentration of power. Fishing and navigation along the coast had already been going on for a long time. However, the Cretans were the first to develop, technically and organizationally, the regular middle-distance voyage, for which the prototype was the round trip between Crete and Egypt. On this basis they monopolized the carrying trade in the whole eastern Mediterranean and made Crete a maritime trade center. Moreover, the very location of this England of the Aegean, from the viewpoint of naval strategy, barred any outside threat as long as control of the sea was in its hands.

The Minoan high culture of Crete distinguished itself from the neighboring high cultures of the same period above all by its peaceableness: in the time of its efflorescence it erected no city walls against outer foes or citadels against the enemy from within. Indeed, the ruling class, manifestly, did not even feel the need to impress its own lower stratum with such structures in order to keep it properly awed: "The palaces of the Cretan courts were outwardly oriented, designed to meet the exigencies of everyday life, and were not concerned with creating showy external effects. The castle did not have a facade."[2]

The warlike element recedes into the background even in art. The few representations of military life are connected mostly with garrison and police service: for instance, a dashing lieutenant with three men reports to a superior of impressive bearing, and another officer issues orders to a military police detail composed of blacks. Obviously, such a reliable military force sufficed to police the "lumpenproletariat"—the unavoidable by-product of urbanization. To all the rest the plutocracy offered enough chances for gain and social advancement to make them willing bearers and collaborators in this social order.

Differences in income were considerable; they did not arise from pressure exerted on those below, but from accumulation at the top of the social hierarchy. High incomes for the upper stratum were not extorted from the lower strata, as in agrarian feudalism, but were profits from trade with distant countries at the expense of foreign upper strata. The increased demand for agricultural products, for export and for the nourishment of the growing city populations allowed even the native peasants to share in these gains. That the

rural lower stratum could lead an easy and happy life is concretely
confirmed in the relief of a steatite vase unearthed at Hagia Triada
(ca. 1550 B.C.), which Fritz Kern describes as follows:

> Beating time with their feet in the stomping-dance, the proces-
> sion of happy rustics marches in twos behind the chief of the
> band who is muffled up in the ritual garment of the goddess.
> The chief of the choir, brandishing the primordial sistrum, em-
> phasizes his presence in the procession. He is followed by three
> professional singers, giving voice to the best of their ability, a
> loud and joyous music suitable for marching.[3]

In the second half of the procession the balanced movement of the
masses—now closed, now slackened—creates a dionysian mood.
Each person is rounded and individualized; nevertheless, the mass
symphonically harmonizes, in an *allegro con brio* or *molto vivace*.
This calls to mind Hesiod's rustic, idealized portrayal of the Golden
Age when men shared their tasks voluntarily, leisurely, and in
great and good fellowship. The vase exactly illustrates this Hesiodic
verse (*Erga* 118f.).

The Minoan plutocracy also lacked the clerical feudalism of a ruling priestly social estate and its theology. There were no temples
staffed by professional priests; rather, there were small domestic
chapels, suggesting that the cult played a correspondingly domestic
role and was observed in the setting of royal or feudal families—just
as later in Attica, the city goddess Athena remained the house
goddess of the king. Cultic rites, moreover, took place in the open air
and seemed to revolve around the epiphany of the vegetation goddess.

The development of Crete into a maritime trade center of the
Near East also accelerated its development from primitive agrarian
feudalism to mercantile plutocracy. As with the later development
of the Ionian trading cities, the landed aristocracy evolved into an
oligarchical plutocratic patriciate, and the king into the wealthiest
among the wealthy. Further, this specialized plutocracy also had a
highly developed constitutional state as a foundation. The reputation for legal security that reigned on Crete in the Minoan age
passed over into Greek legend. Such was the fame of King Minos (after whom the archaeologist Evans named Minoan culture) as a wise
legislator and just judge that even later Greek representations of
life beyond the grave entrusted him with the office of judge of the
dead.

A Homeric verse (*Odyssey* 19. 179) that is not easy to understand seems to imply that King Minos of Crete, residing in Knossos, has ruled for nine years and held intimate talks with Zeus, the greatest of the gods. This conversation, according to ancient readings of this verse, took place every ninth year in the famous sacred grotto near Knossos. Symbolically, the conversation in the *Laws*, written in Plato's old age, takes place on the way from Knossos to this sacred grotto. In this grotto, the king had to give an account of the nine years that had gone by and receive instructions for the following nine. The ancient sources tell us nothing more. According to English and French investigators, it lies in the immanent logic of this construct that the renewed confirmation of domination depended upon the outcome of this sacred consultation, and that it originally involved a kind of kingly ordeal. Kingly ordeals are, however, a specific feature of those archaic divine kingships (dealt with preeminently by Frazer) of the oldest superstratification of herdsmen over planters, of what Frobenius calls the Erythraic culture.[4] And although here in Crete it involves superincumbency of herdsmen over *peasants*—the result of which, in the whole structure, stands poles apart from that older superincumbency of herdsmen over *planters*—reciprocal influences between these two related culture complexes are entirely conceivable, especially the influences of the older on the younger. Obviously, here in Crete an extreme democratization of the great Erythraic sacred kingship had materialized. Although we have no idea how the human representatives of the divinity were organized in Crete, this constitutional regulation, especially under the known Cretan social relations, must have exercised a further democratizing influence.

On felicitous political and social foundations there now developed a hedonistic, plutocratic court culture marked by earthiness and sensuousness, openness to the world, refined taste, and elegance—all readily comparable to the Japanese culture or the rococo culture of the *ancien régime* in France but without the feudalism and absolutism and without the overhanging threat of social debacle that characterized the latter—without the baleful sense of *après nous le déluge*. This pleasure-loving court society also danced on top of a volcano, and a real one in the geological sense: the Minoan cities were more than once destroyed by earthquakes, but at first they were rebuilt each time.

The uniqueness of Minoan culture lies in its sensuousness and joy of life, expressed in art as an impressive decorative naturalism. *Naturalism* here signifies that one sees with open eyes, without impediments and prejudices, that one yields to the impression of the moment, that one delights in the rich and colorful world. *Decorativeness* here signifies that one applies the representation of these impressions in order to embellish and enhance life. And religious veneration is also manifested for this same nature and its vital forces, around us and within us, heightened in the dance to the pitch of joyous ecstasy.

The most beautiful, the most joyous, and the most radiant of all representations of the Beyond stems from the Minoan religion, which remains alien to any exaggerated cult of the grave: Elysium, the fields of the blessed, where dwells and reigns the blond Rhadamanthus, brother of King Minos, famed for his justice. Flowers, with their richness of color and their fragrance, adorn the here and now as well as the Beyond of this happy world.

4. MYCENAE

Such was "the world into which the Greeks entered,"[5] a world which for them was at once alien and alluring. "The woman and the bull—the man and the horse" is the formula with which a historian has brilliantly summarized the contrast between the Minoan and the Achaean.[6] For the Greeks were Indo-Germans; the Indo-Germans, as horse breeders, superimposed themselves over herdsmen-peasants, thus creating cultures in which nomadic wanderlust and addiction to conquest predominated. The Greeks, around the beginning of the second millennium B.C., irrupted into the Balkan peninsula in several great waves, and in even more numerous smaller ones, from the north; they established themselves as a ruling stratum over the indigenous semiplanter peasant population.

This migration is connected with the same great migration of war-chariot peoples, set in motion around 2000 B.C., that led to the fall of the Harappa culture in the Indus Valley, bringing the Kassites to southern Mesopotamia, the Hittites to Asia Minor, the Hurrians to Syria, and, as the most extreme and last tidal wave, the Hyksos to Egypt. This has traditionally been called the "Aegean migration"—a term chosen at a time when its full geographic dimensions were not appreciated.

The first great wave of the Greek migration into the Balkan peninsula must have been formed by the Ionians, who, by way of the eastern part of northern and central Greece, pushed forward into the Peloponnesus.

The Achaeans followed as a second and third wave, in their

van, no doubt, the southern Achaeans (usually called simply "Achaeans"), who conquered the Peloponnesus. Directly behind them came the northern Achaeans, or Aeolians, who occupied Thessaly and Boeotia. As a consequence, the bulk of the Ionians were pushed back toward the southeast and east, into central Greece, above all toward Attica and Euboea.

This Achaean (properly Ionian-Achaean-Aeolian) superstratification led finally to the formation of the Mycenaean culture, so called after its main center, Mycenae. It was of a pronounced despotic, but altogether untheological, character. Judging from all appearances, the pre-Hellenes did not have a priestly social estate, nor did the Greeks bring such a specialized group with them. The warlike, knightly lords erected in the conquered land their cyclopean citadels, with walls whose enormous thickness went far beyond the demands of the military technology of the day. In contrast to the Cretan upper stratum, they needed not only to protect themselves against the outer foe, but also to impress the inner foe, the subjugated and superstratified lower stratum. They commissioned splendid tombs for the eternalization of their fame, in which rich treasures were also interred. Happy warriors all, they led a knightly-lordly existence at the expense of the subjugated population, which accepted the language and cult of the conquerors. The Ionian regions, more or less, took part in this Mycenaean development of the Achaean regions—but, as it would appear, in a more diluted and socially mitigated form.

Nomadic or seminomadic peoples of a lower culture level, coming from the north and lastly from the steppe zones radiating from southern Siberia, as conquerors, broke in upon the high culture zone, which stretched from China and India across Persia, Mesopotamia, and the Near East, up to Egypt. The fate of these nomadic groups varied widely, depending on their endowment, their earlier history, the configuration into which they entered, and above all upon the character of the special, established high culture into whose domain they penetrated. For the Greeks it was of decisive importance that this high culture was the Minoan, and that it was protected by Crete and its control of the seas from direct contact with Egypt, as well as with Syria, Mesopotamia, and the Near East. A comparison suggests itself with the Hittites, close relatives and neighbors of the Achaeans, who were on the move at the same time and for the same reason and who, simultaneously with the latter's invasion of the Balkan peninsula, broke into Asia Minor. Here they came directly under the influence of the old Mesopotamian high cultures, through which, far faster than the Achaeans, and after only a few centuries, they grew into a real high culture stage with script and a high political organization—at the price, however, of their cultural independence. The Hittite empire then found its end in the course of the horse-borne migration, around 1200 B.C., although some of the smaller Hittite states into which the empire was fragmented managed to survive for a few centuries.

As we have seen, Ionian-Achaean Greece, through Minoan Crete (and accordingly also through the Hittites) was guarded most beneficently against Egypt with its primordial theological state slavery, as well as against the aging cultures of Mesopotamia—especially Assyria, with its refined brutality. To be sure, the migrating Achaeans themselves brought enough "Nordic" bellicosity with them, but it remained youthful and naïve and did not extend into molded and hardened forms. The more mature, the more cultivated, the more Minoan this cultural atmosphere was, the more peaceful, democratic, and humane it was. This influence is unmistakably still at work up to Homer's time, when the warlike nature is adolescent and the humanity mature.

Earlier, the Balkan peninsula had formed a natural receiving area for the influences radiating from the kindred Minoan culture of Crete, although the cultural superiority of Crete was by no means as great then as it would be later. However, Achaean superstratification led to a serious cultural decline of the mainland, whereas Crete was able to develop itself further, undisturbed, so that its superiority in cultural level grew. This, in turn, exercised an increasingly greater attraction on the feudal lords domiciled in the Achaean citadels. Since from about 1600 B.C. the Achaean lords, whose seigneurial and war-gotten wealth now displayed a strong demand for cultural products of the highest quality, took over the Minoan culture, which meanwhile had come to full florescence. The result was the Mycenaean culture. At the same time it is a question, on the one hand, of a simple adoption of the Minoan culture through importation from Crete, in the form of ready-made products or of their producers, the Cretan artisans. Many Mycenaean products are barely distinguishable from their Cretan counterparts. Soon, however, up to a certain degree, an independent adaptation and elaboration becomes manifest. This especially holds true for architecture, where the Nordic megaron-type of housing brought along by the Greeks was preserved and its hard, monumental quality cultivated and developed in contrast to the soft, painterly Minoan. In contrast to Minoan peaceableness, the content of representations is predominantly warlike.

To what extent the imported goods from Crete were bought and to what extent they were obtained by pillage cannot be determined in individual cases; it goes without saying that the relations were not exclusively peaceful. When Crete, around 1500 B.C., was struck by a major earthquake, as had occurred two centuries earlier, its peaceful culture, now no longer based on absolute control of the seas, became a fatal liability. Around 1400 B.C., Crete was conquered and devastated by the Achaeans, and Achaean domination and settlement extended up to Pamphylia and Cyprus. After this, Crete never again attained the cultural level that had been thus destroyed. How strongly Mycenaean culture had been dependent upon Crete is demonstrated by the fact that this destruction of Crete soon produced a new decline in the level of the dependent Mycenaean culture—as well as in a gradual development of independent styles and forms that already strike us as predominantly Greek. After this successful concentration of power, a political decline must also have set in, without which the noiseless collapse of Mycenaean power two hundred years later would be incomprehensible.

5. DORIAN MIGRATION

Around 1200 B.C. a new, double wave of Greek superstratifiers surged forth from the north under the pressure of the Illyrians, pushing forward from the Danube basin. This time they consisted of Dorians and the so-called northwestern Greeks, who, like earlier Achaeans and Aeolians, distributed themselves across Greece, but with a stronger outreach of the northwestern Greeks in a westerly and southwesterly direction. It would appear that Mycenae and the surrounding citadels, with their cyclopean walls, surrendered without a struggle to the invading Dorians. At all events, the excavations yield no evidence to the contrary, and a minority of pre-Dorian phylae next to the Dorian in Argos and elsewhere suggest that the Achaeans comported themselves pursuant to the not exactly heroic principle of "If you can't lick 'em, join 'em."

Still later it was the Messenians who put up the stoutest and most stubborn resistance. Messenian wars and Messenian uprisings accompany the whole of Sparta's history. Otherwise, only remote and inaccessible mountain areas bordering on plateaus or mountain ranges, like Arcadia, resisted the Dorian-northwestern inundations.

The attitudes of the newcomers, who were militarily strong, were revealed in the poems of the "noble" Tyrtaeus in which he cruelly mocks the defeated Messenians, although they had fought well and bravely. Two especially serious and pathological later phenomena of degeneration are Christian self-hatred and the love of death—often imputed to us Germans. There is no need to stress that both distortions lie as far as possible from typical Hellenism. Nevertheless, it is highly significant that both are found in a verse of Tyrtaeus in a poem that has always been considered a characteristic expression of the Spartan mentality. In incitement to bravery in hand-to-hand fighting it is said here that one should hate his life, but love the black immortals as the rays of the sun.[7]

Even when it has been established that such emotion-laden rhetoric is not to be taken quite literally, that it is merely a paradoxical hyperbole, it nevertheless remains significant that within the whole domain of ancient culture, as far as I know, it occurs and it is possible only here in Sparta. It would be unthinkable even among the Romans, who were in no way inferior to the Spartans in military prowess.

The result of this storm of the Dorian migration was not just the defeat, but rather the full collapse of the Mycenaean culture; a collapse that could not have been so total and catastrophic if the Mycenaean culture had not had such a marked despotic-feudal character at its apex, if as an aristocratic court culture it had not been bound up with the existence of this feudal power structure, without sufficient indigenous social roots in the broad popular masses. In the pottery, which plays a special role in all excavations, the Minoan-Mycenaean tradition of a highly cultivated decorative art vanished without a trace—which proves precisely that it had been only the imported court fashion of a gossamer-thin upper stratum. The level of culture and civilization drops, as the excavations prove, to the paltriest primitiveness. Once again a highly cultivated master-race culture was apparently destroyed by a second superstratification, as so often happened both before and after.

It is precisely in this purely negative effect, in the destruction of the Minoan decadent Mycenaean court culture that the real merit of the Dorian migration lies for Greek history. "After centuries of foreign control by the Cretan civilization now it is as though a veil were removed which, with the magical and iridescent web of its southern court and city art, had hidden from view the old, still extant traditions."[8] The geometric style presents itself as the rise and the emergence of a primal old form, which up to now had been overlaid and suppressed: "It is the language of a new style, which already speaks a pure and clear Grecian idiom in its first sounds."[9] Attica seems to be the center of this new development, the first time that it plays a Pan-Hellenic leading role.

6. IONIAN MIGRATION

The fact that Greek history, despite the devastation wrought by the Dorians, did not prematurely end in such a tragic way is due to those whose thirst for freedom was strong enough not to bend before Dorian-northwestern barbarism and superstratification. These were the Ionian inhabitants of Attica, who put up a successful resistance to the threatening invasion. And there were those Aeolians and Ionians, surely not the worst, who refused to accept the fate of being trampled into the dust by the new kindred barbarians. They fled to the Aegean islands and to the west coast of Asia Minor; there, shortly before and directly after the fall of the Hittite empire, they established individual settlement-outposts.

In Asia Minor during the Mycenaean period the Hittite empire ruled and made interference by the Achaeans impossible. The Hittite empire had arisen in the course of the same movement of peoples and in the same way as had the Mycenaean, by the superincumbency of Indo-Germanic conquerors over the native peasant population. And it, too, found its demise at the hands of new bands of conquerors who had likewise been set in motion by the Illyrians and had inundated Asia Minor. Indeed, it was the Phrygians, above all, who erected their rule on the ruins of the Hittite empire; yet, like the Lydians who succeeded them, they attained neither culturally nor politically a level that was even remotely comparable to that of the Hittites. Consequently, they could not oppose any effective resistance either to Greek colonization or to Greek cultural influences. Even the emigration of the Etruscans, who at that time left the northwestern coast of Asia Minor by sea, was a natural advantage for the Greeks thrusting eastward. By and large, therefore, the political situation that the latter encountered was unusually favorable. From the time of the fall of the Hittite empire (ca. 1190 B.C.) up to the founding of the Persian empire (553 B.C.) a substantial six hundred years, there was no great power in western Asia Minor that could have been a danger to the Greeks; Ionia, "whose happiness was always conditioned by the lack of outstanding political energies within a broad orbit,"[10] derived advantages from this situation. Thus her settlements, which possessed a passable political independence and which were originally agrarian settlements, gradually developed into flourishing trading ports. In the exercise of this function they later also succeeded in pushing out of the Aegean sphere the Phoenicians, whose script they had assimilated and who here at first had appeared as the successors to the Minoan dominion of the seas. And, although the Mycenaean Achaeans still had been without a script, it was only as a result of the Ionian migration that they were brought up to the level of a high, literate culture.

7. From Aristocracy to Plutocracy

Thus the Ionians who carried forward this development gradually changed their social status: heroes turned into traders; landed proprietors into merchants, shipowners, and freight forwarders; knights into patrician and plutocratic captains of commerce. The Aeolian cities of the northwestern coast of Asia Minor and trading cities on the Greek mainland (like Corinth and Argos) also participated in this development, whose center was the Aegean Sea itself. Leadership, however, increasingly passed over to the Ionian cities of the central sector of the west coast of Asia Minor, and it is very significant that in the Middle East from that time to this day "Ionians" has been the collective name for Greeks in general. In Genesis (10:2) the Greeks appear as sons of Javan (bne Javan); the Persians called the Greeks Yauna, the Indians Jonaka; in Assyrian Greece is called Javanu, and in present day Turkish Yunanistan.

The Greek economy of the late-archaic and of the classical age was neither typically primitive nor typically modern. Rather, it combined "primitive" and "modern" features in an essentially different distribution than that to which we are accustomed from our modern economic history. The production workshops, for a remarkably long time, remained small artisan industries, as a rule family industries, and thus preserved a "primitive," "medieval"—at all events a salutary—stamp. Gradually, however, the large-scale overseas trade, along with the monetary and credit system bound up with it, develops into many more advanced, modern forms; the designation "wholesale merchant" refers not only to the size of the turnover according to the amount and worth of commodities, but also to the distance required for transport. According to the number of those employed, such a large-scale trading *enterprise* could only have been a small *industry* or an association of small industries and, as a rule, probably was nothing else. Neither the head office nor the trading stations abroad, nor the individual freight ship make necessary an assumption going beyond that. Nevertheless a large-scale trading enterprise, for its part, could at the same time retail and transport the commodity production of a very considerable number of artisan small industries.

In the Western Middle Ages we also find, initially, a profusion of artisan and family industries; fully independent, each sold its products directly to the ultimate consumer. The further development was carried out here along different lines and according to the following scheme:

1. A great number of artisan industries deliver their products regularly and exclusively to a large-scale merchant who also trades with distant countries and takes over the further distribution. Thus, they are cut off from the market proper; no longer directly connected with the market, they become commercially dependent on the large-scale trafficker. The latter achieves a monopoly as the buyer of the goods produced by the artisans, who can no longer take advantage of market opportunities and thereby come under price pressure.

2. In consequence of their straitened circumstances as debtors they gradually decline into a state of dependency on the large-scale trafficker for credit.

3(a). They can no longer buy raw material themselves. It is furnished to them by the large-scale dealer and remains his property. They are merely paid laborers on alien material.

(b). Their tools, and also their workshop, become the property of the large-scale trafficker.

4. As they are no longer personally interested in good workmanship and in a proper treatment of the means of production, the entrepreneur must have them supervised by his itinerant inspectors.

5. In order to facilitate and to reduce the cost of this supervision and the placing of orders, all those who work for an entrepreneur are assembled under one big house: the factory as an agglomeration of artisan individual workshops.

Compared with this development, which is familiar to us and which for this reason we view as a natural and self-evident prerequisite stage of the development that in its stormy later course led to modern large-scale industry and proletarian masses, the small productive enterprise of antiquity displayed a remarkable resilience. The command economy of a large enterprise, the herdlike labor under someone else's orders, was quite rightly felt to be unworthy of a free man, to be akin to slavery—and hence it was left to slaves. It should be noted, moreover, that there were only isolated instances of such large enterprises, all of them under public ownership, such as the silver mines at Laurium in Attica, the labor force of which consisted exclusively of slaves who were typically in a worse social position than house and family slaves, being outside a family community. Very much later still, Saint Paul (Galatians 4:1) takes it for granted that the status of the son of the house, so long as he is still a minor, in no way differs from that of a slave. Within the sphere of private economy, it was the slave economy of the Hellenistic-Roman age that first led (somewhat more broadly) to large-scale or at least medium-sized industry. In ancient Greece, on the other hand, the corresponding development usually comes to a halt after state 1 in our scheme. So strong, manifestly, were Hellenic independence and love of freedom that the Greeks were able to oppose a successful resistance to this development the moment it threatened their personal independence.

Although the artisans, as a result, came under pressure in respect to their income and their living conditions, they preserved their full freedom; that they did so enabled them to react politically to this pressure, and in this they were joined by impoverished and debt-ridden peasants of similar social situation. Tyranny (in its original, Greek sense) was the result and expression of this reactive social movement.

In the various Greek culture complexes, moreover, the economic development was neither uniform nor even simultaneous. And until 494 B.C. the mainland, even Athens, lagged far behind the Ionian development.

The amazingly dogged adherence to small industry as a form of production with the complete work-process as the prevailing rule was an extraordinarily important element of health and humanity for the Greek economic and social structure of the archaic and the classic age and, later, of the imperial age as well. This interconnection has already been demonstrated in our consideration of the sociological importance of small- and large-scale industry, of the fateful effects of large-scale industry, and of small industry as the most important real and vital guarantee of freedom.

The sphere of production of the ancient world preserved the same healthy capacity for resistance also vis-à-vis that kind of technical progress that has existed with us from the end of the eighteenth century, exogenously and heteronomously, in the application of the exact sciences. In ancient Greece, a person stuck unshakably to the habitual, leisurely, endogenous, and autonomous perfection of artisan techniques in themselves and according to their own needs. The development of the exact sciences from Pythagoras by way of Archimedes to Hero and Philo of Byzantium in its application, exactly as in modern times up to the eighteenth century, usually was limited to military technology, on the one hand, or toy automata on the other.

The naïve self-consciousness of nineteenth-century Europeans consistently viewed their often extremely eccentric and abnormal manner of existence as the natural measure of all things; the "failure" of the otherwise so intelligent and admirable Greeks in a department so central to the nineteenth century seemed shocking. "In the realm of the mind they have left behind many theories and little practice . . . in a material respect not even *one* invention worthy of mention. . . ." They lacked precisely the "systematic mastery and exploitation of nature by man for the increase of his power, his welfare and his enjoyment"—a deplorable "disproportion between technical and aesthetic accomplishment." The Greeks were "the poorest in inventiveness of civilized peoples," "the strong, practical, technical bent of modern times was lacking to the culture and especially to the science of the Greeks." And precisely this was "a fundamental flaw and the real defective point of ancient civilization," "the economic construction of society and of the state and the absence of a realistic-technical sense connected with it, in men."[11]

8. RISE OF THE POLIS

In the post-Mycenaean age, apart from Sparta, everywhere in the Greek cultural area the polis or city-state (the city and its immediately surrounding territory, representing an autonomous, sovereign, independent structure) formed the external social and political frames of development. The polis can be compared with the free imperial city in Germany in the Middle Ages, if we disregard the latter's rather loose subordination to the empire. The polis is even more comparable to the Italian city republic of the Renaissance. But there are no further examples anywhere of a whole people permanently and exclusively organized in this political life form.

Nearly a thousand such sovereign city-states existed in the Greek area. In terms of size and number of inhabitants they are, by our standards, small towns—save late Athens, which, because of the size of its territory and its population, falls outside this frame. Sparta is another exception, not because of the small number of fully qualified citizens, which would be more in keeping with a small town, but because of the size of its territory, the great number of its disenfranchised subjects, and—above all—because of its rustic mode of settlement and its agrarian-feudal, nonurban social structure. That even the organizational form of the polis remained alien to the Spartans fits in with the obvious assumption that the rise of the polis was mainly conditioned by the defense against the stormy advance of the Dorians.

This political life form of the city-state does not stem from the Mycenaean age; rather, we at first find small territorial states whose peasant population is ruled from a feudal citadel in which the ruler and his retinue dwell. Although settlements consisting of members of the lower stratum were gradually formed in the shelter of these citadels, that did not make them cities in the later sense of that term.

The momentous transition from this widespread form of the agrarian-feudal small state to the much rarer form of the city-state could hardly have been effected without the model of the older Mesopotamian and above all Phoenician city-states, even though these maintained a persistent connection with despotic and priestly rule. The transition therefore probably occurred on the Ionian coast at an especially early date—chiefly in the centuries after the Dorian migration. The Mycenaean feudal system, which had provided a somewhat unstable foundation of public security, was smashed. Public security, without which human life is impossible, had to be built up anew by independent small centers. Such new construction from below was pursued quite instinctively. People drew closer together for mutual aid and protection, especially against the invading Dorians and northwestern Greeks; the Acropolis served as a refuge and a center of defense. The walled polis was also formed in its protective shadow.

This joining together in the polis, this *synoikismos*, occurred under the leadership of the old feudal aristocratic clan, whose megarons (houses) then filled the Acropolis, together with the temples of the gods, so that the Greek nobility of the post-Mycenaean age was regularly housed in the city. The more the nobility lost its lordly prerogatives in the course of democratization, the more it was shunted off in the direction of cultural activity. And it carried out this forced sublimation process with drive and brilliance unmatched by any other aristocracy. As a result, classic Greek culture (like the Italian culture of the Renaissance) acquired an aristocratic-idealistic hallmark that signified an honor and a limitation—a limitation and a social one-sidedness that were especially discernible in Plato.

Once a two-layered culture was formed as a result of superstratification, the purely practical and human higher cultural accomplishments unavoidably came to lie in the hands of the upper stratum. The hallmark of Greek culture lies in no small measure in the degree of humanity and practicality of these cultural accomplishments, and of the members of the upper stratum who were its bearers. For such a result to be accomplished, it was crucial that the Greek aristocracy of the post-Mycenaean age, apart from Sparta, reside in the city. Attitudes of mutual exclusion and repulsion between the nobility and the burgher class, such as characterized the German Middle Ages, had no chance to develop. What occurred, rather, as in the Italian Renaissance, was a reciprocal permeation, a productive synthesis between aristocracy and bourgeoisie. An especially fortunate consequence of this social structure was the uniformity and simplicity—to us quite striking—of life-styles throughout most of the poleis.

The geographical setting of this Greek development was that of a mountainous territory seemingly half sunk in the sea, with countless peninsulas and islands rising out of the water; each larger land surface was subdivided into small districts, sharply separated from each other by rocky mountain chains. The topography was eminently suited to division into an immense number of small, independent city-states, sharply divided politically, each one defending its independence to the utmost, yet all united by language, religious rites, custom, culture, literature, art, and trade, as well as by athletic contests.

To be sure, this fragmentation also implied serious political drawbacks, a "dismemberment," and "eternal civil war in which one Greek turns the weapons against another," as Goethe commented.[12] Sociologically and culturally, however, it had the inestimable advantage of surrounding the small, intimate human life sphere of antiquity with a protective wall against the irruption of massification (mass society)—a wall breached only by the imperialistic-hypertrophic development of Athens. The specific humanity of this Greek culture is also conditioned by this same setting. And because this great number of close life-spheres, each visible at a glance and intimate in its social vitality, was embedded in a common, extraordinarily broad commercial and cultural context, there arose that "happy mixture of union and independence,"[13] that combination of

optimal conditions which are fundamental for all human intellectual development but have been realized only very rarely in history.

The feudal constitutional form of Mycenaean monarchic rule was
no longer suited to this political and social structure of the polis.
Rather, the important new social trend that developed within this
newly created political frame of the city-state, and first of all in Asia
Minor, was one toward democracy. "The new colonization region of
Asia Minor . . . was in itself for Greeks free of any historical tradition; for the immigrants themselves, tradition . . . was in part already breached, . . . in part inapplicable on the new terrain. Here the
newly forming political communities had to create new forms of
political life; here then in Asia Minor occurred the earliest development of that formation of a political community . . . which must be
considered as the typical Greek form of a state; it is that of a city-
state or, more correctly, a city republic, the polis."[14] Athens, also of
Ionian stock and having escaped Dorian destruction and superstratification alike, participated in this development from the outset. Other cities sooner or later followed suit. Only Sparta remained
aloof. We have complete records for the detailed course of this development only for Athens. As for the Ionian cities, not only was the
development violently interrupted by the catastrophe of 494 B.C.,
but even the historical record concerning what had transpired up to
then was in great part destroyed.

The Ionian and Aeolian immigrants to Asia Minor had brought
with them the constitutional form of monarchy that had been prevalent on the mainland and had been rooted in the political and social
conditions of the Mycenaean age. As, however, these roots were now
cut off precisely by the Ionian migration, the loosening of all traditions also affected the traditional notion of kingship. With the new
beginning under fully new conditions each individual had to keep
his end up in the same way, and some others, perhaps, did this as
well as the "king" or even better. Thus there were placed alongside
the king, to whom the cultic function as *rex sacrorum* for the most
part remained, at first a number of "kings" and soon, in general, all
heads of noble families: in short, the transition from monarchy to
aristocratic oligarchy was effected. The restriction to the hereditary
nobility was still consonant at first with the social conditions and
conceptions and found its military support in the fact that only it
could provide for the training, arming, and retinue of the knightly
individual fighter.

The rapidly flourishing trade of the port cities of Asia Minor made
it possible for many who were not nobles to become as rich as many

aristocrats, or even richer. Conversely, many old nobles were reduced to poverty. The development from plutocracy to democracy
was set in motion. Now wealth was added to noble descent as a prerequisite for membership in the ruling stratum. This led to the marriage between wealth and aristocracy and, ultimately, to their
equality.

As we have seen, plutocratic upper strata, with their arrogant
nouveaux riches, lack the sureness of bearing and the magical, awe-
inspiring prestige of the inherited nobility. And if wealth begets
rights, need and poverty beget demands. Impoverished and debt-
ridden small peasants, displaced and debt-ridden artisans make
demands on their creditors, displacers, and overlords. An enterpris-
ing and power-hungry member of the upper stratum places himself
at the head of such malcontents; relying on their superior numbers,
he makes himself a temporary usurper of power—that is, he becomes *tyrant* (as the Greeks called it, using a word of pre-Hellenic
provenance).

Recourse to the traditional monarchical form of government, only
recently abolished in the unilateral interest of the nobility, suggested itself as an obvious step, and in substance tyranny is a kind
of monarchy with a social conscience. But the ineradicable curse of
tyranny is its illegitimacy, the illegality of its acquisition of the
mantle of power, which clearly distinguishes it from kingship. The
less one is vested with authority, the more one must employ naked
force. The tyrant's method of acquiring power also becomes his mode
of exercising it; that leads, sooner or later, to his overthrow.

This bloody episode of tyranny, brief as it remained, had revealed
the central weakness of the oligarchy—its small numbers—and that
gave a new impetus to the otherwise existing tendency to broaden
the base of governance. For, in contrast to the aristocracy of blood,
plutocracy lacks a preordained lower limit of membership, so that
the tendency toward broadening the base of governance (which
gives rise to plutocracy in the first place) cannot easily be stopped.

Once the numinous prestige of heredity was dethroned, the
ascending path to full political rights was cleared for everyone; also,
its steepness was decreased by introducing numerous economic gradations, so that ultimately there was no longer any rational ground
for excluding anyone. The growing need of the national army for
light troops with the cheapest armor, and of the navy for oarsmen,
worked in the same direction; and enlightened rationalism provided
ideological support for demands for universal freedom and equality
based on natural rights. The stage of democracy was reached in

which all adult citizens enjoyed equal legal rights, and the sum total of this citizenry formed the only embodiment of the will of the state and of political sovereignty.

This, in broad outline, is the sequence of development, many stages of which found their classical description in Aristotle.[15] The final stage—which, to be sure, is not recognized as such by Aristotle—is democracy or isonomy. In this stage, ideally, law rules and all who enjoy the rights of citizenship are equal before this law and bound into an indissoluble, vital community through concord and friendship.

Needless to say, such a development was possible only within the frame of the polis and its optimum proportions within the visible horizon: for how could a vital community of life exist among people who did not even know each other?

In the isonomic democracy of the Greek polis, for the first time since superstratification and the creation of the high cultures it made possible, *freedom* again exists—and indeed in a measure that has never been realized since then. "Isonomy"—equality before the law, the constitutional equality of all citizens (except slaves, metics, and minors), that is—the same freedom that in the modern age was achieved again only as a result of the bloody battles of the French Revolution—was achieved here for the first time in the history of high cultures. Furthermore, freedom of thought was not restricted by any theological dogmatism, nor freedom of action by the quasi-theological, ascetic social constraints familiar to us.

Jacob Burckhardt, in his brilliant history of Greek culture, has portrayed the ancient polis as a kind of Leviathan, from which there is no escape and which, like an awesome Moloch, swallows the pitiable individual completely:

> Within its own realm, the polis is most fear-inspiring for the individual if he is not willing to lose himself completely in it. . . .
> There is no appeal beyond the polis, and no escape. . . . And this servitude to the state exists in all constitutions, but most oppressively in democracies.[16]

Exactly the opposite picture is transmitted to us by a profusion of witnesses. "To live as one pleases" is designated as the proper palladium of democracy, not only as its ideal, but rather as its essential reality. The only exception is Sparta, where "it was within no one's power to live freely as he wished." The real relation of the polis to the individual was educative in the highest and most vital sense:

"the city teaches the man," as classically formulated by Simonides.[17] "But in deed and in truth," continues Burckhardt, "Greek freedom was modified by the ubiquity of the state. Not even in religion could the individual find refuge from the state. Moreover, he could not be sure that the gods were good and merciful."

Burckhardt reveals an opposite, modern-liberal, almost anarchist standard in the following passage: "In recent times . . . it is essentially the individual who demands a state advantageous for his own purposes. For the most part all he demands really is security, so that he may freely develop his potentialities. To this end he gladly makes well-defined sacrifices, though the less the state bothers him otherwise, the more content he is." These ideals of the night-watchman state and of Christian charity do not perhaps furnish the most adequate points of departure for a congenial understanding and an impartial judgment of the ancient polis.

Furthermore, nineteenth- and twentieth-century observers believed that they could demonstrate their newly awakened sense of social responsibility by establishing that the whole of ancient culture, with all its glory and all its apparent humanity, really—outrageously, tragically, or regrettably—had rested upon slavery, upon the degradation of servants to the status of mere things. Such judgments refer, of course, to the house or family slaves, of whom all but the poorest households possessed one or more. Yet the situation was not too different—in many Western countries, at least—until recently. Peasants had farm laborers and maidservants, artisans had journeymen and apprentices, middle-class households had domestics. There is little doubt that every scholar who professed to be shocked about slavery in antiquity had at least a servant girl, and perhaps also a cook and a nursemaid, in his own household. Whether or not these servants were legally free or bonded makes no essential difference with respect to the social reality of their lives. What we hear from antiquity about the conditions of servants closely resembled our own recent practice. The treatment, as among us, was at times better, at times worse, and the growing consciousness of human rights in classical Athens in particular is revealed "in the fact that since the time of the bas-relief of Hegeso—i.e., since around 420 B.C.—the Attic tomb *stelae* represent the female slave as a human being enjoying almost equal rights alongside the mistress."[18]

Because of the numerical increase of this slave population in Athens of the postclassical age, the slave question became a social problem. The essential difference was that of juridical status; the only really shocking fact was that Greek slaves, as witnesses, were questioned under torture—yet it is certain that only a very small percentage of slaves ever appeared in court.

The social life-style of the polis became decisive for Greek culture. The cultural precondition of the closed life-sphere was fulfilled here in the most perfect and lavish way conceivable. The astonishingly high accomplishment of Greek culture has at times been explained genetically, has been attributed to the special talent of the Greeks as its creators and bearers. Doubtless this talent was present; but if such a biological explanation is to be more than a pure tautology (as, for instance, Molière's *vis dormitiva*), it must mean that others under the same conditions, with limited talent, would have accomplished nothing like it, or at least nothing of equal value. Such an assertion, however, calls for verification. For the social situation of an optimal life-sphere has been replicated a number of times in Western history—in the Gothic late Middle Ages, in the Italian Renaissance, in eighteenth-century Germany—and *each time*, with wholly different and differently endowed peoples, it has led to cultural peak achievements of the highest order. And history even offers a counterproof. The Greeks of the Mycenaean period, in all essential features, biologically and anthropologically, were exactly the same as those of the classic period; still, for several centuries of the Mycenaean age they accomplished little of a special or noteworthy character. Yet immediately after the consolidation of the polis as a social structure and during the whole time of its undisturbed existence the cultural peak accomplishments followed one another rapidly, just as they did later in the Renaissance.

9. The Greek Landscape

We have seen how strongly the very special and extreme geographic configuration of the Aegean area influenced the political, social, and thus cultural configuration of Hellas, although that influence becomes notable only in the post-Mycenaean period. The same seems to hold true for the geo-psychical influence of the climate, which perhaps somehow already made itself felt in the Mycenaean period but which only now appears in palpable fashion.

The Mediterranean climate is probably nowhere developed in such pure form as in the Aegean. Instead of severe winters, there is a cool rainy season, accompanied by frost and snow only occasionally except in the mountains. Summer is a time of scorching drought, with withered, faded vegetation, when most springs dry up and most riverbeds run dry, when the air flickers because of the dry heat. But even in the most scorching heat the air is salubriously dry and thin, free of a dull and oppressive sultriness. In consequence of this dryness of the air the surrounding world appears with astounding clearness, in vivid colors, and in closeness, without any covering veil.

What a contrast between Homer's sun and Ossian's fog! In the raw north, there is the infinite wilderness of dark woods, bold rocks, powerful trunks, hanging wattle, thick bushes, shrubs and ferns, moist moss, the smell of rotting foliage, "dull, and oozing rock,"[19] the freezing body of the earth, coated bearlike by thick fur and hidden under it. The whole landscape is in the thrall of dampness, of moisture and cold: everywhere springs, brooks, rivers, streams, waterfalls, ponds, lakes, swamps, moors, wind, storm, rain, hail, frost, snow, violent thunderstorms, driven clouds, damp fog—wetting, shrouding, soaking everything, a gloomy, intractable nature. And in the intermediate zone between heaven and earth, where storms rage and fogs curl around trees, brooks, and rocks, there stirs and sighs the realm of the soul—so humid, murky, mysterious, unclear, indistinct, and elusive—a realm of unappeasable yearnings, dimly violent, obscurely emotional, wildly raging, impetuously gripping, of infinite sadness and irresistibly flowing tears.

The Greek landscape is altogether lacking in this humid, soulful layer covering the earth. The aromatic dry, low bushes fit the body of the landscape closely and tightly, forests are rare near the inhabited areas, and where they appear, they are bright, transparent, sun-soaked, dry forests; or else there are clumps of trees, like the tufts of hair on the skin of the human body. Except for these, the body of the Greek earth lies naked in the bright sunlight and directly open to the spirit. This landscape is spirited rather than soulful; it is marked by a corporeality ever ready for, ever open and accessible to the spirit—as close to the spirit as the northern European landscape is close to the soul.

The psychic structure of Greek man is in surprising measure consonant with this structure of his landscape. Among the Greeks the morphological element—the sense of structure—borders directly on the rational element, the sense of form directly on the intellect without soul and feeling being inserted between them, as among us northerners. This special psychic structure forms one of the secrets of unshrouded brilliance of the Greeks, both in the artistic and the scientific domains. Hence the astonishing anticipation in their knowledge of nature, often without any trace of a foundation in experiment, such as the atomic theory of the Abdera school or the theory of sublimation in Heraclitus. Hence the unsurpassed unveiled clarity of their sculpture and architecture.

What we find most astonishing in Greek sensuality is indeed its brilliant soullessness—just as in Greek tragedy the corporeality of fate directly counterposes the spirit in a way that often puts us off, with minimum participation of soul and feeling. It is upon these qualities that the brightness and clarity of the Greek spirit ultimately rest, whereas soul always has something of fog and mist about it.

"The spirit," Ludwig Klages has said, "is the antagonist of the soul," yet the soul can no less be the enemy of both the spirit and the body. In such a conflict would it not be far healthier to side with the spirit and body, especially if one is a member of a nation given to pathological excesses of soulfulness?

10. Ionian Religion and Art

The Aeolians and Ionians—the first political refugees of whom we know in world history—in their flight from the Dorian superstratification, had brought their Mycenaean culture with them from the Greek mainland, including their epic (or probably at first still choral-hymnal) traditional legends of gods and heroes. Native cults were retained; those encountered in a new setting accepted. But the relationship to the old gods, whose shrines had to be left behind and whose protection had failed to halt the onrush of the Dorians, was loosened. Loosened, too, was the relationship to the heroized ancestors, whose tombs and tomb cults had also been left behind in the old homeland. Thus gods and heroes alike became grand and inexhaustible material for the bards.

These bards or rhapsodes find their culmination in Homer. Probably nowhere else have materials of religious orign been artistically mastered with such self-assured secular freedom, force, and grace, and so far removed from theology. For example, in the old Homeric hymn to the Delphic Apollo (vv. 525-539) the priests coming from Crete complain about the impossible and barren region their god has led them to: how are they to live? Whereupon the god, smiling archaically, answers: nothing could be easier! Let each of you take a knife in hand and slaughter sheep without letup—then you will have naught else to worry about! The cultic operation of the holiest oracular site of Greece is treated with irony, and in the cultic hymn the impish irreverence is placed in the mouth of the god himself.

For subsequent generations Homer personified not only the epos but also the beginning of all secular and human literature as such—and what a beginning it was! Since then, secularization has progressed much further, so that it has become fashionable to trace and sniff out the comparatively archaic sacred elements in Homer's work. Certainly such elements are present in residues and, accordingly, are a legitimate theme for sympathetic interpretation. Homer's unique importance, however, lies precisely in the fact that he was the first to break out of these sacred limits, that he proclaims the worldly, not the otherworldly, the human, not the divine, and that he sings humanely and humanly of his gods. And that is precisely what his own divinity rests upon, for the Greeks and for us.

The actual religious sensibility of the Homeric age was quite distinct from the structure of Homeric mythology. Homer's mythology was not properly religious; it was a secularization and aesthetic-literary elaboration of cultic representations. The Ionians of Homer's time continue to observe the public cults of their local shrines, but their real piety has been sublimated into a kind of un-theological deism, which released the cultic gods to frolic in the splendid Olympian carnival of the imagination. Yet this release did not prevent the worshippers' taking these official cults seriously both as magical and as political observances.

The essence of the Greek cults is very difficult for us to grasp. Their place in real life is wholly different from, say, that of Christian cults familiar to us. The Greek cult is not, in our sense, purely religious; rather, it combines political and social with strongly magic elements. It is a matter, so to speak, of magical local politics, a fulfillment of one's magical civic duties toward the state—a "*religion municipale*," to use Fustel de Coulanges's striking expression; the Delphic oracle was the central, supreme, and supervisory authority of this domain. "There was no visible indication of religious exaltation or spiritual satisfaction such as found in Christian religious services. . . . There is no evidence that the citizen ever entered the presence of the cult statue for contemplation and worship."[20] In addition, the cult of the Greek state gods lacked any knowledge of redemption—a contrast already noted by Lactantius, who also mentions the claim to an especially high degree of truth to be found in the emerging theological doctrine: "Deorum cultus non habet sapientiam . . . nec habet inquisitionem aliquam veritatis, sed tantummode ritum colendo qui . . . ministerio corporis constat."[21] It is a question, in the end, of the contrast between "natural" religion and religion of salvation, folk religion and confessional religion, a religion received at birth and a religion acquired by choice.

The domain of religion in antiquity thus offers a distinctly three-layered aspect—three layers that must surely have been differentiated over time: (1) mythology—the gods as relegated to legend; (2) cultic rites—a kind of communal magic involving feasts and festive representative buildings and works of art; (3) the real, living sense of piety—a formless deism.

It is easy for us today to misconceive the religion of the Greek polis according to analogies suggested by over a thousand years of Christian (including several centuries of Protestant) education, and thus vastly to overestimate its psychic intensity and relative importance. The religion of the Greek polis was something far more reserved, more relaxed, more "external," more nonindividual, more social. It did not consist wholly of festive representational decorations, but these were its essential parts. The irrational element in it is magical and not mystical—and this is true even of state-approved mystery cults, which offer very little in the way of "mysticism" in our later sense of the word.

These characteristics (and even the examples given earlier of disrespect toward mythical deities that we find so surprising), however, are by no means an indication of impiety. They merely show the degree of intellectual freedom with which the Greek mind confronted its own myths and even its cults. There was no doctrine of redemption, no revelation, no higher truth, no sacred teaching, no articles of faith, no theological dogma, and no coercive powers of the priesthood in matters of faith and conscience. Consequently, there was full and unfettered freedom of development, not only for knowledge and research, but also for a truly living undogmatic and untheological, unbound piety of the individual.

An invisible light from the cult and its gods, of course, shone on profane life. But this consecration, consonant with the essence of a natural religion, bears upon all aspects and compartments of life. A god is in charge of each one of these aspects and compartments, and thus they are all sanctified by a numinous aura, which includes vital energies tabooed and disparaged as sinful by Christianity. For Christianity as a religion of salvation seeks the holy in the transcendent, in the hereafter, in the otherworldly; it deprecates the totality of the "merely mundane" real world, which incurs an ever harsher disparagement as it stands closer to the vital center.

The same secularization and humanization that we meet in Homer now also seizes—under his influence—the plastic arts. By humanizing all gods, they divinize all men. Of some of their excavated works we hardly know whether they depict a mortal or a deity; of others this can be decided only on the basis of external clues.

For the first time man is presented in a purely human configuration without the stiffness of stylization enforced by a feudal theology. This is expressed most movingly, perhaps, in those instances of archaic art where this religiously-imposed stiffness has just been loosened or is in the process of being loosened, where late archaic art frees itself from the coercion of religious restriction as an opening flower frees itself from the compactness of the bud. For sacred stylization, as we meet it in its most impressive and most perfect form in Egyptian art, is ultimately nothing but the visible artistic expression of restriction, of the bondage of man in the face of the theological religious doctrine of a ruling priesthood. Theologically restricted art is always "mannerist." Hellas has freed man from this coercion of heaven and hell also in the world of the visible.

The original release and unveiling of pure nature in the Greek plastic arts has produced the effect of a revelation on all subsequent generations—at least until recently. Nothing of the kind has been created since then that has not had its roots here, directly or indirectly. Greek art, has shown the world once and for all how man, purely as man, appears. And from man, as the first-born, it subsequently carried over this revelation to the rest of nature.

Until the close of the classical age in Greece a part of artistic handicrafts was private and secular, but authentically great art was public and sacred; hence that amazing combination of realism and idealism in representational art. "The Greeks," as Herder said, "dared to show man in the grandeur with which God created him."[22] For all these works were "sacred sculptures" destined to decorate temples or to be an offering to a deity, and "before God everything must stay eternally."

The Greek temple, significantly, is of both secular and aristocratic origin, having developed from the royal palace, the megaron. Public cultic rites, favored by the climate, took place under the open sky in the Minoan as well as in the Mycenaean culture. There were no temples, only chapels or cult niches inside the princely palace, so that the deity was placed in the role of an honorary guest or coinhabitant of this palace along with the prince. There is no evidence, in archaeology or literature, of Greek temples before the eighth century B.C. After the middle of the eighth century, however, the monarchy was being displaced by the aristocratic oligarchy, and the king was restricted to his functions as supreme priest, as *rex sacrorum*. The deity, transformed from family god of the king into the sanctifying and interceding protector of the community, could no longer be relegated to a mere niche or chapel in the royal palace.

Now the deity demanded a palace or megaron of his or her own; the king, conversely, became only the secondary figure and was assigned to the subordinate and ministering role of the priest. The house of the king became the house of god, the megaron became the temple.

Religious services were held outdoors, not in a church as in northern climates. Ordinarily the burnt offering stood at the center of the rite, and if this offering had been made indoors, the room would have been changed into a large kitchen. Just as the king lived in the palace, but conducted his governmental affairs outdoors, the deity represented by the cult image lived in the temple as his or her megaron, but was borne to the festive religious service in a solemn procession outdoors to the cult site. Still, there was a need for a secure sanctuary, protected against inclement weather during interludes between feasts. This was the specific function of the interior of the temple. It did not serve as a center for performance of religious acts or for the reception of festive assemblies, but as a room in which the image of the deity was preserved rather than displayed. Hence, by modern standards, it had more the function and character of a sacristy, tabernacle, or reliquary—indeed, almost of a jewel box. This explains the surprising narrowness and darkness of the interior of the Greek temple.

Megarons and temples both were originally made entirely of wood; round tree trunks, shaped with the chip ax and supporting square beams, have always remained the unmistakable basic elements of the Greek temple. Advancing civilization, growing wealth, and the need of the polis for more durable and representative dignity for its monuments, brought about the transition from wood to stone, a transition made first in the construction of the temple and only later in the shaping of the cult image. We know of no stone images in wooden temples, but wooden images are commonly found in stone temples.

As a result of this petrification first of the temple and then of the images, the Greek temple divinities became the prisoners of their own house. A stone image is no longer portable, nor could it be worshipped in ample, well-lit indoor rooms, since the maximum technical span for stone if considerably less than for wood. In this way the Greek temple, once made of wood, reverted to a massive stone structure of almost megalithic character, to a work that was almost closer to sculpture than architecture; hence the awesome archaic impression of the Doric temple. The porticos stand around the holy sanctuary like a close chain of sentry posts, like silent bodyguards of the god, defensive, forbidding, ensuring security on all four sides.

The facades of Greek temple architecture, resulting from this development of the outer at the expense of the inner effect, its detachment from the practical connection with the architecture of human habitations and its requirements, gave the classical architecture that thrust toward classicism—that tendency to be representative, to be spectacular, to be "rhetorical," which was then to continue in modern architecture from the Renaissance down to the nineteenth century.

11. Ionian World View and Science

Greek commerce in the archaic Ionian period spanned the whole civilized world of the eastern Mediterranean and of the Near East. In its indirect relations, the outreach of Greek commerce extended considerably beyond. Its customers were the ruling strata of all those areas whose domination-derived income flowed into the hands of Greek merchants in the form of commercial profits. The decisive element here, however, was that these Ionian merchants also summoned up the mental energy to dominate this enormously expanded trade horizon intellectually, viewing and conceptualizing it as *one* world, and setting out on their journeys as much for the sake of knowledge as for profit. For this reason the entire region became the base of a single cultural pyramid, its apex formed by Ionian-Greek culture.

Nature had endowed these people with an engaging talent in all spheres of culture, which to this day can only arouse admiration. In addition to a well-grounded self-confidence they possessed untamable ambition, a drive to surpass, a compulsion to compete. This combination of aggressiveness and drive for power, denied gratification in the martial-political sphere, found an outlet in the domain of culture, intellect, and spirit. Ionian culture is the magnificent result of this fortunate sublimation.

Nor was this bold intellectual development fettered by feudal structures or ruling class interests. We have seen that kingship in Ionian cities was replaced by the oligarchic-democratic coexistence of patrician merchants so typical of trading cities. The profits of their trade stemmed, to be sure, from the domination-derived income of the upper strata of the empires that were their customers; yet these profits flowed to them through the neutralizing filter of foreign trade, and consequently no noneconomic restrictions were attached to them. Although the imperial pipers paid, they could not call the Ionians' tune.

Thus the Ionians enjoyed all the advantages offered by integration within their trade sphere, but without being subjected to the distorting and restrictive disadvantages that the structure of domination usually imposes upon its subordinates.

Sparta offers the only contrast to this Ionian pattern. Sparta's cultural accomplishment was mostly derivative and became almost negative when its superstratification structure was tightened up in 546 B.C. It is as though the Muse of History, in the midst of the Hellenic sphere itself, had wanted to conduct a conclusive counterexperiment in order to demonstrate to us what the sociological *sine qua non* of all Hellenic intellectuality was.

The Greeks themselves were quite aware of this structural contrast, above all in comparison with the Persians. Earlier, all masterpieces of high civilization had been based upon the concentration of despotic power and domination-derived income. The Sumerian, Babylonian, and Egyptian cultures were court cultures or courtly priest cultures, and all their great art was court art. Assyrian art, in its reliefs of kings with their hard, precise elegance and naturalist stylization, was a militaristic court art. Its developmental level corresponds to the central concentration of the empire's power and wealth in the hands of its dominant people and through them in its king. In Hellas there were also tyrants friendly to art and culture during brief periods here and there, as later at the court of Alexander and his Diadochi. The secular flowering of Greek culture, however, lies between these two periods. It did not have a despotic, but rather a liberal, aristocratic-democratic character. It sprang not from monarchic monopolization, but from free competition between countless individuals.

Other things being equal, the more skillful the agrarian conquerors are in applying despotic pressure to squeeze the subdued lower stratum, the higher their income will be. Accordingly, every voluntary relaxation or dilution of this pressure threatens to diminish their income, to impair the foundation of their existence as a master race. Hence their egoistic self-interest is initially opposed to any liberalization of their own attitude.

The situation is exactly the opposite with traders, especially a trader trafficking in distant countries. His income does not stem from peons, but from customers. The views and desires of these different customers are a given to him, and may deviate considerably from his own. The more flexibly he adjusts to them, the more amiably he takes them into consideration, the higher his prospects for gain will be: the customer is always right. Quite unlike the feudal lord, therefore, the trader, because of his economic position, exhibits the greatest possible liberalism for the sake of his personal gain and direct self-interest.

Accordingly, Ionian liberalism and intellectual freedom can be understood as the intellectual superstructure to the economic substructure of a plutocratic, patrician way of life based on trade with distant lands. In the trading cities of the Italian Renaissance, two millennia later, the same situation led to similar consequences. The Dutch liberalism of the sixteenth and seventeenth centuries, as well as British liberalism from the seventeenth through the nineteenth century, could be cited as further evidence.

It has long been observed that within the Homeric period, from the *Iliad* to the *Odyssey*, a certain social development takes place: Odysseus is no longer presented to us as an aristocratic war hero like Achilles, but rather as a traderlike, crafty, and inquisitive seafarer; the ideal state of Phaeacia exhibits remarkably progressive features, and one would look in the *Odyssey* in vain for anything like the Thersites scene: it is written not for heroes but for traders (who, of course, also have their heroism); the atmosphere is pronouncedly that of the Ionian port and trade cities and their patriciates of merchant adventures. Despite this, philosophic interests dominate the two Homeric epics, and these are of free-thinking though pronouncedly aristocratic nature.

The Thersites scene in the *Iliad* shows the feudal upper stratum still in possession of its social superiority and, accordingly, of an untroubled conscience. But toward the end of the eighth century B.C. Archilochus appears, daring to declare war against Homeric feudal ethics. Although a tried and tested soldier and an old veteran, he openly boasts of abandoning his shield on the field of battle—among Greeks, the worst military shame conceivable. With a challenging, cynical insolence he parades his plutocratic and purely commercial approach. After all, "he can buy one just as good at any time."[23] When he leaves his native city it is in the manner of Hesiod's father:

Fleeing not considerable belongings, nor wealth and comfort,
But the bitter need that Zeus lays on men.[24]

Archilochus, then, is a dissolute trooper who boasts of his lack of discipline and control as well as of his power of resistance and his indifference; he makes no secret of being a bastard begotten by a slave girl and an aristocrat. Indeed, he cannot do enough by way of a defying, provocative exhibitionism, poles apart from all aristocratic discretion. The reaction on the aristocratic side altogether matches his extremism. That royalist "denouncer of the mob,"[25] Heraclitus, wanted Archilochus driven out of the prize competitions by the lash along with his opposite, Homer. The lofty aristocratic Pindar holds himself elegantly aloof from Archilochus and his odious love of scandal, which merely took him out of one scrape into another.

Scorn and mockery, hate and anger, wild thirst for revenge and retaliation, the dammed-up and seething passions of the oppressed break forth like scorching streams of lava in Archilochus. Such volcanic explosion, however, at the same time freed the poet, who gives unrestricted rein to his most subjective feelings and thus becomes the creator and hero-founder of all Western lyricism. It is a lyricism much like that of the German *Sturm und Drang* movement, a lyricism also of one-sided masculine sensibility, which did not find its correspondingly one-sided feminine counterpart until Sappho. Archilochus' poetic brilliance, exhibited in the unencumbered vitality of the content and in the artisan mastery and sovereign control of strict form, soon created a Panhellenic place of honor for him next to Homer.

Hesiod was the first to take another bold step toward a position fundamentally opposed to traditional feudal culture and to Homer's aristocratic spirit.

Hesiod's father, a patrician citizen of the port city of Kyme in Asia Minor, had lost his fortune in oversea trade. Thereafter he returned to the land, to continental Boeotia; he settled down on a small farm, brought into the marriage by his wife, in a remote mountain village. The farm seems to have been small enough so that the father did not need any help with the farm chores, and the son was able to hire himself out as a herdsman. The mountain solitude of the trees and rocks of Mount Helicon nurtured the boy's poetic calling.

He seems to have been fully trained in the art of epic recital. Yet Homer's aristocratic frivolity and condescension repelled him; they formed an all-too-irritating contrast to the sober, burdensome work ethic of his peasant surroundings.

Hesiod introduces a sense of responsibility and moral earnestness, a rational, historical-genealogical order into the frivolously colorful, irresponsible capers of the Homeric gods.

Hesiod's theological attitude is extremely progressive. We find not only moralizing expurgation of myths, but also the final triumph of

Zeus. Although this triumph is inevitably achieved with the Machiavellian means of the previous era, it is glorified as the victory of superior wisdom and justice. The immanent tendency toward an ethically based monotheism, or simply toward monotheism itself, is unmistakable, and is further strengthened by the transparent personification of natural objects and psychic forces that are admitted as equals into the profuse ranks of the old gods. Indeed, the history of Ionian natural philosophy (and indirectly that of modern natural science) begins with Hesiod, whose cosmogony exalts the primal principles of space, matter, and attractive force; his mythic-epic names of Chaos, Gaea, and Eros are nearly as transparent as the four elements of Empedocles.

If Hesiod turns against Homer's theology in the *Theogony*, he attacks the latter's anthropology even more explicitly and overtly in the *Works and Days*. Here for the first time a protest of the Ionian democratic spirit against the feudal ethics of "medieval" super-stratification still represented by Homer is expressed. The poet champions the free labor of a self-conscious peasantry against parasitic, ruthless, and violent feudalism; in a sharp and classical definition of the peasant ethic, he sets honest and manly toil above the feudal contempt for labor professed by aristocratic drones. Hesiod is also a precursor of Christianity, meriting the honorary title of a Christian before Christ more than Socrates or anyone else.

Next to a classic catechism of antifeudal ethics, the amazing work contains a rational science of husbandry for the small peasant—a guide for the rustic on how to achieve wealth in an honorable, peaceful, nonfeudal way. For the first time in history Hesiod proclaimed the power of wealth against the wealth of power (v. 313)—a doctrine which, twenty-five hundred years later, in an almost literal concordance, served as a slogan for the French Revolution. At that time Antoine Barnave (1761-1793) distinguished between two kinds of property: (peasant-) bourgeois property, based on work and savings, and feudal property, based on conquest and violent appropriation. Hesiod's didactic poem begins with the apotheosis of competition and ends with the apotheosis of public opinion. Hesiod also fought hard to make the peasant's day-to-day life a fit subject for serious literature, an "earnest realism" that we do not reencounter until the synoptic gospels and that later reasserts itself in the realism of the nineteenth century.

It is difficult to imagine just what the illiterate Boeotian small peasants of the eighth and seventh centuries B.C. were supposed to do with the powerful work of their poetic spokesman. But at the court of Euboea he won a prize for his *Theogony,* and in Ionia itself, where leading strata controlled intellectual and social progress, he gained mounting influence. The peak of this influence was reached in the second half of the sixth century A.D., when the truculent Heraclitus expressly and indignantly admitted that Hesiod was "the teacher of most men" (fr. 57).

Accordingly, it must be asked why Hesiod's forceful beginning in the direction of overcoming the aristocratic ethic and mentality did not prevail. Why was he pushed back instead into the innocuously safe role of mere founder of bucolic poetry, a precursor of Theocritus and Vergil? Probably because the Persian wars and the surprising, brilliant victory achieved under Spartan leadership brought the warlike aristocratic mentality to the fore in all Hellas, whereas democratic Ionia had pitifully succumbed to the same Persians in 494 B.C. Thus all democratic phenomena of the fifth century B.C. contain an unmistakable aristocratic infusion, and Greek classicism does not transcend the spirit of aristocracy but rather incorporates it in its synthesis. The positive and negative consequences of this compromise would long endure.

The Ionian intellectual horizon widened along with the geographic horizon of the Ionian trade cities. The striking difference between countries, cultures, customs, and religions challenged comparison and fostered a relativistic detachment that was increasingly carried over to Ionian native traditions. "The Ionian rhapsode had cleared the way for the Ionian natural philosopher; the latter had built where the former had demolished."[26] Hesiod's freedom in creating new gods "provides the measure of all freedom and all thought, including that of the philosopher."[27] The result of such unrestrained, passionately pursued self-development toward unprejudiced intellectual superiority and breadth was Ionian science, which, after Thales, crystallized into the Milesian school. For the first time in Western intellectual history there arose a science that was altogether untheological, free of authority and prejudice, and dedicated exclusively to scientific fact.

Ionian natural philosophy (including its further development by other pre-Socratics) was the heroic age of intoxicating brilliant anticipation for Western science as a whole. Decisive fundamental concepts and modes of thinking of the exact sciences were created here. Created, so to speak, from nothing: for we cannot marvel enough when we consider over and over again how minimal and how inadequate the empirical foundations were from which these grand ventures of thought started out. Yet it was precisely as a result of this minimum dose of stubborn facts (which served, as it were, as minute points of crystallization) that a brilliant and creative intellectual force could develop with absolute freedom and unencumbered boldness.

12. The Catastrophe of 546-545 b.c.

This new Ionian intellectual freedom had not yet achieved self-consciousness—Thales still lived, Anaximander had not yet found time to make known the overwhelmingly profuse findings of his investigations—when suddenly a catastrophic superstratification broke in over Ionia and Ionian culture. The Persians, a fresh "heroic" people of pronouncedly "medieval" conquerors and superstratifiers, swept over the Near East, overran Lydia (the protective power of Ionia) as well as the Ionian cities, and eventually extended their sphere of dominion as far as the lower Indus and the Nile.

Among the Greeks, the citadel of Sardis, capital of Lydia, had the reputation of being absolutely impregnable. "You have conquered the citadel of Sardis" was an Ionian saying applied to whatever was deemed absolutely impossible and incredible. But Cyrus of Persia had done just that.

a. Orpheus

The Ionians would have been less than human if their intellectual self-liberation had proceeded without inner psychological and social resistance, without a residue of bad conscience, or without traces of opposition. This bad conscience now received the most obvious confirmation conceivable through the shattering victory of a pronouncedly "medieval" theologically bound power—the Persian empire. This bad conscience suggested that the impudent turning away from hallowed traditions and bonds had been a sacrilege, that divine powers indeed stood on the opposing side. An insatiable appetite for theology and salvation gained ground. Ancient belief and superstition emerged from the lower depths of society. Religious dregs were gathered from all sides, even from neighboring barbaric primitive peoples. An anxious spirit of strict observance, which cannot do enough by way of self-denial and confessions of sin—as non-Greek a notion as can be imagined—spread.

The oldest transmitted echoes of this exaggerated strict observance and obscurantism are the Orphic interpolations in Hesiod's *Works and Days* (vv. 724-759), examples of the way people who obviously have no talent for creating literary works of their own are wont to worm their way into high literature. The prohibitions enumerated in these interpolated passages go to incredible lengths. The excretory and naturally pleasurable functions of the human body are hedged about with taboos. Later, this anxious ritualism, so coarsely begun here, was refined and further elaborated. We encounter it in the first centuries of our era in the Pythagorean *Carmen Aureum*, with its anxious questions of conscience "Where have I failed? What harm have I wrought? What duty have I not fulfilled?" and the nightly self-examination of conscience advocated by Seneca.[28]

And in the same passage of the *Works and Days* there appears also (v. 731), for the first time in world literature, the notion of the "divine man" that was to acquire fateful importance for religious and intellectual history up to our day—and it appears in direct connection with prohibitions concerning the evacuation of the bladder! We are not used to imagining the typical Hellene suffering from chronic constipation or anuria. At all events these are afflictions that could well make one experience the body as a burden, as prison and grave of the soul—a common image of Orphic literature.

Disappointed, resentful characters who consider their bodies a burden already appear in the authentic parts of Hesiod's *Works and Days*; for example, an impoverished peasant suffering from malnutrition and edema scratches his swollen foot with an emaciated hand and goes about vainly begging from neighbors and relatives (vv. 496-499, 394-395, 451-454). But where once such types were the objects of sharp disapproval, such members of the lumpenproletariat now enjoyed new freedom in the port cities following the Persian conquest. Hence, it is perhaps no accident that the Orphic pseudopoets inserted their bad verses into those of Hesiod, in whose work they felt more nearly at home than in any other poetry. A wave from the East—bringing ideals of asceticism and feelings of resentment, of renunciation and self-denial, of depreciation of man's aging, ailing, plagued body—had loosened the tongues of these anxious ritualists and given them speech.

It is remarkable and significant that quite suddenly and without precedent, specifically Indian doctrines of salvation appear in Greece. One of these, the doctrine of metempsychosis, the migration of souls—which in its fully elaborated form also includes animals (perhaps even plants) in its circle of migration, and which draws the conclusion of vegetarianism from the inclusion of animals—is known to have been held by Pythagoras.

The grand idea that the whole world—the cosmos—has a soul,

just like the individual human being, and that the soul of man is merely a particle of this great world-soul, belongs to the fundamental ideas of Indian metaphysics since the *Upanishads*. It comes in three distinct versions, each of which comes to be reflected in Greek thinking:

1. *The Atman doctrine*, according to which the world soul is the wind, and the human soul is the breath. This is found in Anaximenes (ca. 585-524 B.C.), Diogenes of Apollonia (second half of fifth century B.C.), and some followers of Hippocrates. A number of classical comedies and tragedies allude to it, and it finally recurs in the conception of the Holy Spirit as pneuma in the fourth gospel (3:8): "The wind bloweth where it listeth, and thou hearest the sound thereof, but canst not tell whence it cometh, and whither it goeth: so is every one that is born of the Spirit" (John 3:8).

2. *The Brahman doctrine*, according to which the world soul is the ether, the heaven-fire, and the human soul is body warmth, or soul warmth. A tiny spark of soul flown off from the heavenly ether in death returns to the divine ether. This belief is found in Heraclitus, in the famous grave epitaph to the fallen of Potidaea (432 B.C.), and in Euripides. The conception of the Holy Spirit as fire corresponds to it, and it constitutes a central conception of gnosticism and of mysticism in all its phases.

3. *The doctrine of the world spirit*, which abstracts the concept of soul, whether in the cosmos or in man, from all sensuous-physical phenomena and defines it only psychologically and rationalistically as spirit, reason, or *substantia cogitans*. This version is espoused by Xenophanes (ca. 570-470 B.C.) and Anaxagoras (500-428 B.C.), and it recurs in familiar spiritual interpretations of the Holy Spirit, thus providing the basis for spiritualism.

There can be no serious doubt that India was the point of origin and of diffusion of all these doctrines of metempsychosis and of the world soul. In India these notions are very widespread and deeply rooted in history, so that we can follow their gradual rise and elaboration step by step. On the other hand, in Greece we come upon them suddenly and without any evidence of specific antecedents. In its earliest attestation in Anaximenes and Heraclitus, the world soul teaching is not so much derived or developed, or even expressly proclaimed, but rather already posited and used for drawing cosmological conclusions. The question of the line of communication from India to Greece also presents no difficulties. After the Medes had pushed forward as far as the upper Indus, Cyrus II had incorporated (545 B.C.) the Ionian port cities into his empire, which extended from there to the northwestern borders of India. Due to this enormous expansion of their empire in an east-westerly direction, the Mede-Persian rulers attached great military and administrative importance to lines of communication in that direction. The Persian imperial highway, which led from the borders of India to Ionia was apparently used not only by royal troop units, officials, and couriers, but also by itinerant preachers, mendicant monks, fakirs, and sorcerers—in short, purveyors of a syncretistic religious broth, whom Heraclitus (fr. 14) enumerates as "sleepwalkers, magicians, bacchants, revelers and mystics." Yet Pythagoras and Empedocles appear as the eminently aristocratic top representatives of this otherwise none-too-respectable fraternity.

That ideas of this sort should have been transmitted directly from India to Greece without being recorded in the intervening areas also is understandable. The tribes and peoples in between were either primitive and uncivilized or else they possessed their own, indigenous, highly developed religious systems; hence, they were religiously saturated and were either not in need of such new teachings or not receptive to them. Ionia thus was the first place to the west where all preconditions for their acceptance were fulfilled: the absence of an indigenous religion of salvation; the secularization and depreciation of earlier religious conceptions; and a sense of catastrophe, and hence the need for salvation, resulting from the Persian invasion of 546-545 B.C.

We are dealing with one of the most fateful events in Western intellectual history: the first transmission of Indian metaphysics to the West. For metaphysics properly so-called—that is, metaphysical idealism—contrary to the claim of its exponents, is not a "general human" phenomenon. In reality it arose but one time and under unique conditions of intellectual history, in India in the seventh and sixth centuries B.C., whence it spread eastward and westward in many waves. The Ionian philosophers, to be sure, had made use of this grand but baneful Indian doctrine of salvation, but mainly in the service of their rationalist quest for natural science explanations. By contrast, with Pythagoras and Empedocles—both Greeks from Italy—its original oriental-theological character as a doctrine of salvation again appeared in unveiled form, whereas Plato's theory of ideas is in this respect profoundly ambivalent.

The figure of Pythagoras rises like a towering peak amid the haze of anonymous and interpolating Orphic scribblers. He was divinely worshipped by his faithful as savior, bearer of revelation, and miracle worker. Moreover, he is the only representative of this category who managed to receive a place in the hall of fame of Greek self-consciousness. Pythagoras, by the explicit testimony of known contemporaries, is attested to have held the doctrine of metempsychosis (Xenophanes, fr. 7) and to have possessed a wide range of knowledge (Heraclitus, fr. 40), a characteristic for which he is likened to Hesiod, Xenophanes, and Hecataeus.

In the Pythagorean sect, the pronouncedly plebeian Orphic movement finds an aristocratic leading cadre, structured like a religious order. Conversion to Pythagoreanism thus becomes the instrument by which Greek thinkers of subsequent centuries accomplish their turning away from the Ionian spirit of Greek classicism, their return to theology and to the ideas of the "Middle Ages."

The Ionian spirit of self-liberation, called to bring intellectual freedom to the world, thenceforth not only had to fight against the surrounding intellectual bondage but also to struggle in its own house with theological and feudalistic tendencies. From this time onward Greek classicism was beset with ambivalence, an ambivalence that was to cast its shadow over all its later influence. To be sure the world of Greek antiquity remains the great intellectual arsenal of freedom, and even its theological-metaphysical tendencies—for instance, Platonism and even Neoplatonism—still contain so much of the Ionian spirit in their blend that they always have a relatively liberal and initially liberating effect on unadulterated theologies of salvation and their orthodoxies. Yet these theological and feudal elements of ancient Greek thought have the negative effects that are characteristic of theology and feudalism anywhere and everywhere. Hence the struggle for freedom must at some point be directed against them as well.

b. Lycurgus

A return to the Middle Ages under the impact of the catastrophe of 546-545 B.C. took different forms in other parts of Greece, yet the consequences were equally serious. Earlier even Sparta had not been able to resist the superior charms of Ionian culture and especially of Ionian art. Tyrtaeus, the classic embodiment of the old Spartan spirit, wrote verses not in Dorian but in Homeric-Ionian language. In the Daedalic school Dorian culture, after digesting Ionian influences, even made an essentially productive contribution to the development of the archaic Greek figurative arts. The so-called Doric temple is no doubt a common Greek archaic architectural form, but it found its earliest development in Argolis and its classic improvement in a Dorian-settled region—although not in Sparta itself.

Thus Sparta participated in the cultural development common to all Greece under Ionian leadership, and these common elements were deeply enough embedded not to be uprooted by the reactionary wave breaking in after 546. Rather, the result was a feeling of ambivalence. Sparta's participation in this Ionian-led cultural movement could not have taken place without arousing the opposition of a minority in Sparta itself. And the abject military collapse of the Ionian cities must have been taken as palpable proof of the direst warnings of these opponents. Thus the Ionian defeat led to Sparta's abrupt, harsh, and deliberate renunciation of its earlier allegiance to Ionian culture and intellectual freedom.

The result in Sparta itself was a kind of cultural isolationism. Earlier philological and archaeological research has correctly dated this revolution in the middle of the sixth century. The impact of the catastrophe of 546 explains and pinpoints the timing. This reaction, a kind of Egyptianization of Sparta, revived the early medieval superstratification structure of the Dorian conquest in its unconcealed brutality, and it developed—contrary to the Ionian spirit—the all-dominant barracks system, the drill book, field service regulations, and homosexuality.

In the history of the West this is the first example—and until recently, the only one—of a deliberate reversion to the primitive and brutal forms of the earliest superstratification. There is little doubt that the traditional, basically antihumanistic glorification of Sparta in German secondary schools did its share in paving the way for national socialism.

The Spartans alone might never have achieved fame beyond their time and place; there were hundreds of such small, despotic and piratical states of which world history has taken no note whatever. Rather, the eternal brilliance of the Ionian-Attic spirit also bestowed immortality upon Sparta—simply because of Sparta's proximity to and involvement with it. Sparta's brilliance is the borrowed, reflected light of the Ionian-Attic sun.

The Romans, as we shall see later, advanced incomparably further along the course taken by the Spartans; yet they were more generous and required less sadistic self-control. Therefore, they could remain fully open to the Ionian-Greek legacy while internalizing certain aspects of the Spartan temper. If there has to be Spartanism, the Roman variant is preferable!

c. Anaximander

In the face of defeatism—of this reversion to the "Middle Ages"—the Milesian school, the intellectual headquarters of the Ionian movement toward freedom, held its banner high in the desperate situation. Anaximander (610-545 B.C.) committed his cosmic doctrine to writing as an intellectual testament for posterity, with that famous foreword that asserts an imperturbable desire for knowledge in the face of adversity.

"The beginning of all things is the Boundless." In it all innumerable worlds, including our own, execute cycles of eternal recurrence. And these infinitely recurring cycles fulfill the demands of the highest justice. When one cosmic state of affairs has destroyed the preceding one, it in turn is destroyed and replaced by the next—which, in its turn committing the same injustice, demands equal reparation *ad infinitum*. The wheel of infinite becoming thus is driven by eternal justice, and everything happens according to necessity.

Two centuries earlier, individuals had sought consolation for catastrophic political misfortune in a theory of cycles. In this doctrine, the four ages of the world correspond to the metals gold, silver, bronze, and iron; thus the wretched present becomes the Iron Age, but with the consoling prospect of an early cyclical return of the Golden Age. This myth, first found after 700 B.C. in Hesiod (*Works and Days* 106-201), must stem from the Near East in the eighth century B.C., when that area had been subjugated, brutalized, and enslaved by iron weapons of the unspeakably cruel Assyrian superstratifiers. The myth of the four ages of the world, brought forth by this unendurable situation, not only allowed the catastrophe to be understood as a justified punishment for moral and religious degeneration, but also allowed the present misfortune, as well as the future return of the vanished happiness, to be viewed as necessary links of one and the same universal law.

Anaximander, a natural philosopher, in a grand transposition carried these ideas into the cosmic sphere. Under his hands, the justification of life portrayed by poets and sages was transformed into a justification of the cosmos in terms of natural philosophy. To the cyclical idea Anaximander added other motifs, in which men have sought consolation in the face of overwhelming political misfortune: the ideas of just punishment for injustice committed, of subservience to an appointed decree, an irresistible ordained fatality, and a consequent trust that necessity would once again lead upward. The idea that there were eternal and inexorable laws in obedience to which all worlds must exist enabled him to rise above the terrible political misfortune of the present, to arrive at an understanding of the incomprehensible.

In the extant fragments of the book of Anaximander there is contained pure knowledge for its own sake, explicative knowledge, cognitive knowledge. The foreword, however, dated and written under the impact of the catastrophe of 546, also offers ontological knowledge of salvation. Yet the body of the work illustrates that as soon as Greek thought is raised above the sphere of the pragmatic to comprehensive general concepts, it becomes naturally scientific, focusing upon the permanent.

The cosmic consolation that Anaximander sought was essentially still in the sphere of ehtics and justice. Later, in the work of the truculent aristocrat Heraclitus of Ephesus (ca. 540-499 B.C.) the emphasis shifts to the esthetic realm. In his eyes the world cycle justifies itself not so much through its justice as through its beauty, which Heraclitus demonstrates in Pythagorean fashion, in the kaleidoscopic, mirrorlike symmetry of its reciprocal cyclical harmony (fr. 51). An "elevated view of life which trusts itself to prove the necessity of all exoteric ugliness for the existence of the esoteric beautiful."[29] It is only in human terms that the one appears as just, the other as unjust: before God all is fair, good, and just, and the highest aim of the philosopher is to behold the world with the eyes of God. This already comes close to the Platonic definition, later so celebrated, of the aim of philosophy: to become like God within the limits of the possible.[30] Here, however, it is accompanied by a passionate emphasis on the need for such a way of looking at things, on the ground of the *logos xynos* common to all. Later, the Stoic maxim "Keep the whole ever in view"[31] was to be derived from this general divine view of the world. The intoxicating, pensive metaphysic of Heraclitus, which thus combines within itself the character of knowledge born of revelation and knowledge born of reason, exercised a far-reaching influence up to the eighteenth century and far into the nineteenth, above all in its lighter, more rationalistic-ethical development by the Stoa.

While the need for salvation in Heraclitus, not far from the Pythagorean *theologia mathematica*, thus found its basic gratification in an aesthetic-geometric way, we encounter in his writings the Indian doctrine of the world soul as world fire and the human soul as a tiny spark flown off from it. This is a remarkable physical hypothesis, a cognitive means for arriving at a unitary explanation of the world, while its mystical aspect and its original ethic of salvation remain hidden.

By the time of Anaximenes of Miletus (ca. 585-524 B.C.), the pupil of Anaximander, the historic catastrophe of 546 B.C. had been almost completely overcome. And, while he adopts the Indian doctrine of the world soul as wind and the human soul as breath, his rationalist version emphasizes the epistemological, natural-science aspect and reduces its original theological aspect to a numinous overtone.

Hecataeus of Miletus (ca. 560-490 B.C.), representative of the next generation, leaves nothing to be desired in terms of naïve self-consciousness, ruthless rational criticism, and systematization. Indeed, in this direction he considerably overshoots the mark. We get the impression of a touchy aggressiveness reminiscent of the eighteenth century. In his philosophy we encounter for the first time the phenomenon of rationalism in the narrow, pejorative sense of the word.

He confronts the mythical tradition of the heroic legends, which he assumes to be so many claims to historical truth, with arrogant superiority. But instead of searching for other, empirically assured foundations of historic fact (as, for instance, Thucydides does later) he considers it sufficient to standardize the legends, systematizing them in the most arbitrary way. And in an equally overbearing and childish way he corrects them according to flat probability and bowdlerizes them by sophistic reasoning. If, for instance, a legend reports that a hero fathered fifty sons, Hecataeus opines loftily that at most they probably numbered twelve. The result was a rationalistic fragmentation that not only lacked the aesthetic and emotional qualities of the legend, but even that prelogical indirect and partial relationship to reality characteristic of all bodies of legend.

Myth competed with history writing in the heroic legend; hence a collision of some sort was unavoidable. The relationship of nature legends to natural science was analogous, except that there one could turn to allegorical-physical interpretations. In the realm of the legends of the gods there was no competing empirical-rational knowledge with which an inevitable conflict would arise. Measured against advanced ethical standards, the content of individual myths would be found objectionable, and corrections of legends on such grounds are found as early as Hesiod. Yet this very criticism of legends on ethical grounds presupposes a continuing belief in the gods.

The earliest record of a denial of the knowability of the transcendental is found in the theological skepticism of Xenophanes (ca. 580-480 B.C.): "No man has existed nor will who has a clear knowledge of the gods and of what I say about the universe. For, even if he should succeed to the highest degree in saying what is right, yet he himself has not seen it. All this has led to nothing but opinion."[32] The same theological skepticism is found later in Protagoras; indeed, it is also the central doctrine of the later skeptics, properly so called.

This critical and skeptical stance toward the mythical tradition was often combined with a positive, enthusiastic attitude toward theologico-metaphysical ideas of a rationalist or specifically deistic character. Thus Xenophanes, with the greatest solemnity, champions a spiritual deism of Orphic origin, and Parmenides claims the same numinous dignity for the extreme rationalistic radicalism of his unity doctrine, which, to be sure, characteristically appears in the guise of a poetry of revelation that presents a secularized theology in allegoric form. The numinous aura that Pythagoras bestowed on mathematics was transferred to logic by Parmenides: the *theologia arithmetica* of the Pythagoreans was transformed by the Eleatics into a *theologia logica*.

Parmenides, in the earlier of his two systems, the *Doxa (Way of Opinion)*, had made manifest the latent dualism of Anaximander and other predecessors, and among all pre-Socratics had set forth the first explicitly pluralistic system. In his later system, the *Aletheia (Way of Truth)*, he rebounds all the more radically into a monism of the most absolute kind. The Milesian school, basing itself on the apparent roundness of the celestial sphere, had represented the world in closed spherical form; Parmenides, by the most absolute and ruthless application of rationalist principles, postulatively constructs it as a single giant monad, a single spherical colossal atom, an enormous cosmic billiard ball, as it were, fully homogeneous in itself. And the totality of experience is condemned as "appearance" and sensory deception: a feat of absolute tyranny of the *ratio*, which leaves all human measure behind. The epistemological-theoretical observations scattered throughout the presentation of this construct are nothing short of a catechism of the most extreme and radical rationalism.

The otherwise meager biographical data on the pre-Socratics offer us an invaluable account of the conversion of Parmenides by the Pythagorean Ameinias. Since his own extant writings exhibit a similar sharp break between the empirical *Doxa* (which takes off from the dualism of Anaximander) and the *Aletheia*, it may be readily inferred that this break corresponds to that conversion. If so, the mathematical mysticism of the Pythagoreans gave birth to the sharpest form of materialistic rationalism conceivable.

Empedocles rightly designates the Parmenidian *Aletheia* as sinful madness, as the height of ambitious hybris, as an arrogantly presumed superiority of the *ratio* (fr. 2. 9-3. 9). And, most interestingly, he points to the theological character and the theological roots of this arrogance: it seeks to learn more than "mortal ken may span" and "to perceive more than is permitted to transient beings." Indeed, Parmenides himself had chosen the guise of a heavenly revelation through the goddess of light for the public statement of his inspiration.

But Pythagorean rationalism was to achieve its greatest heights of boldness only after the great victories over the Persians and Carthaginians in the Dorian colonial empire. Unlike later authors, Hecataeus could consider himself a model of realism and moderation. And in fact, as a politician he belonged to the few sober-minded among the citizenry, who had warned against the suicidal folly of the Ionian uprising—an uprising that in 494 resulted in the final collapse of the Ionian cities and the destruction of Miletus, and by 490 in the great Persian punitive expedition against Greece itself that had lent its help, however inadequate, to the Ionians.

13. Athens: Rise, Greatness, and Fall

The events that ensued are perhaps the most marvelous among the rare miracles of world history. Persia, the superpower, was defeated by the hastily mobilized citizens of a handful of Greek city-states that were not even fully united among themselves. The oppressive melancholy that had been set off by the catastrophe of 546 and had reached its nadir in 494 with the fall of Miletus, came to an end in the events of 490 and 480-478 as suddenly as it had started. For shattered Ionia, of course, this unforeseeable radical change came too late. It now fell to Athens, the honorary home city of Ionia, as successor of destroyed Miletus, to assume leadership.

Athens had long been prepared for such a task. Attica had been able to ward off Dorian and northwestern Greek invaders, a circumstance that created a latent cultural community with the kindred Ionian cities of Asia Minor. The fact that Athens had been settled in pre-Dorian times and had remained untouched by the Dorian migration no doubt accounts for the pride Athenians came to take in their "autochthony"—since the Ionian immigration of 2000 B.C. lay well behind the horizon of historical memory.

Thucydides tells us (2. 15) that the individual poleis of Attica had originally been independent; they subordinated themselves to the military leadership of the king of Athens only under pressure of

war. During the Dorian danger this subordination must have occurred frequently and intensively, so that the desirability of permanently and definitively stabilizing this organization must have appeared especially appealing when the royal throne of Athens was
occupied by a person equal to the task.

The transition from hereditary kingship to the elected office of archon was effected early and, it would appear, peacefully. But the development toward aristocracy and plutocracy led to grave social tensions. A considerable portion of the peasant lower stratum had been
beaten down into indebtedness, bondage, and servitude—except for
those who escaped this fate by flight abroad. Cylon's attempt to set
himself up as tyrant in 636-632 B.C. miscarried, but it initiated a
century of social disorders that continued until the advent of
Cleisthenes—a sequence of events that might appropriately be
called the Attic Revolution.

With the liquidation of Cylon's *putsch*, there followed the so-
called "Cylonian sacrilege," which was to be of such fateful importance for the history of Greek democracy. Megacles, the archon of
the period, had Cylon's followers butchered at the altar of the city
goddess, Athena, where they had fled for sanctuary. By this act he
stained himself and his family, the Alcmaeonidae, with a magico-
religious stigma that was to be legally and repeatedly enforced for
two centuries against himself and his descendants. Among these descendants were his grandson Megacles II, the latter's son Cleisthenes, and great-grandson Pericles. But the Alcmaeonidae were an
Attic noble clan, so rich, prestigious, and powerful that they asserted themselves despite the stigma attached to them. They were
by no means socially excluded and still demanded the customary
prerogatives of full-fledged members of the nobility; nevertheless,
the stain of sacrilege separated them from all others. As a result,
they became predestined leaders of a moderate opposition, an opposition that neither excluded itself from the social community, nor
submitted to its dictates; it sought political support not from the nobility, but among the moderate middle strata. All the politically
prominent Alcmaeonidae adopted this same political line—which,
in the further course of time, established the characteristic position
of the Alcmaeonidae between nobility and tyranny, Dorians and
Ionians.

A few years after Cylon's abortive coup, in 624 B.C. during the ar-
chonship of Draco, and surely under pressure from the lower
stratum, the existing penal laws were codified and put into writing.
This, no doubt, restricted the arbitrariness of aristocratic judges but

otherwise did not lead to any effective social reform, let alone redress the increasingly intolerable economic situation of the lower stratum. Solon, the first great figure of Attic literature and politics, was elected as "conciliator" in 594 to effect such redress in the face of the dangerously widening social cleavages. His importance for world history rests upon his association with the greatest representatives of the Ionian spirit—a spirit that he, by his activity as thinker, poet, and statesman, transplanted to Athens. He replaced the mixed plutocratized aristocracy with a pure plutocracy including a gradation of social ranks. His constitution, founded on liberation of the peasants, combined the powerful cooperative-liberal spirit of true democracy with the sense for organic growth and moderate adaptation to the given and the possible.

Only through Solon and his democratization and Ionicization did Attica and Athens awaken to their world-historical vocation. Now for the first time Attica claimed its position of honor as "ancestral soil of Ionia" (Solon, fr. 4. 2). And the importance of this development was heightened by the turn in a sharply opposite direction Sparta was to take after 546.

To the question whether he thought that the constitution he had left to the Athenians was the best Solon is said to have replied: "The best among those possible under prevailing circumstances." Solon's political achievement is memorable as the first known attempt deliberately to dismantle, step by step, the despotic character of the superstratification structure while reducing dominance and violence to the minimum "by conjoining might and right through the force of law." Solon himself declared, "I have thus done and carried out what I promised." As a politician, Solon is the intellectual ancestor of the political tradition for which Aristotle was to become the leading theorist; he also is the first democratic-liberal statesman of the triad that also includes Pericles and Augustus.

Solon's reform was challenged briefly by the tyranny of the Pisistratidae, which represented the opposite alternative—the displacement of the aristocratic-plutocratic upper stratum with an aristocrat acting as self-appointed leader of the lower stratum. One might have expected that Solon's careful reform scheme would have spared Athens such a tumultuous interlude of tyranny, and Solon himself had proclaimed this as his hope. Still, he had surely intended his constitution not as definitive and unalterable for all times, but rather as a foundation that after a decade of stabilization and probation would be followed by further democratizing reforms. This indeed became the characteristic course for the entire subsequent con-

stitutional history of Athens. Perhaps reactionary efforts at undoing
Solon's reforms set off the opposite thrust of Pisistratean tyranny. In
any case, the foundations laid by Solon's constitution proved so per-
tinent, broad, and durable that the Pisistratidae, in an interlude of
only a few decades, did not dare to alter it in form or manage to
change its substance. The net result was little more than an oscillation around the main trend set in motion by Solon—a *de facto* dictatorship that now by legal and now by extralegal means temporarily shifted the center of gravity to the impoverished small peasantry
and the petty bourgeoisie. Specifically Pisistratus continued Solon's
cultural policy of Ionicization in even more extreme form. Under
him Athens became the real nursery of the Ionian epic, and the only
effect here of the spiritual convulsion of 546 was that cults peculiar
to the politically favored peasant lower stratum and "Orphic" tendencies found encouragement. The latent tension of this juxtaposition was not to become manifest until a century later.

The Athenians of the time of the Pisistratidae did not, of course,
add to the body of the Ionian epos; rather, they included it in their
public recitations, the regulations for which have come down to us.
Homer already had been established as a classic (the first such
canonization in Western intellectual history). The confrontation between the new Ionian and the older Homeric epic themes was accomplished not through a further development of the epos itself, but
through the creation of a new art form, tragedy, in the shape that
has remained exemplary up to today. Just as the gods once had
made their exit into epos, epic legend made its exit into tragedy.
This role of tragedy as the successor of the epic is most clearly discernible in Sophocles. The beginnings of tragedy from Thespis in
534 B.C. are for us enshrouded in mist. All the more prodigiously
therefore do the three peaks—Aeschylus, Sophocles and Euripides—rise before our eyes.

The aristocratic world of the epic, which had meanwhile gone
under, composed by Homer for aristocrats and recited before aristocrats, is now viewed as tragic by a democratic public; the despotic
absoluteness, ruthlessness, and inflexibility of the bearing and the
action appear—as later in Shakespeare—as nefarious as blindness,
indeed, as hybris, and seem a vivid commentary on the decline and
fall of the aristocracy. At the same same time, however, the
tragedies offered heroically intensified, universally valid examples
of challenges to that "great mighty fate which exalts man in crushing him to pieces." Whereas in Aeschylus, from *The Suppliants* to
The Eumenides, the chorus is the bearer of archaic-feudal frenzy

and gloominess, in Sophocles it is progressive democratization, a bourgeois chorus that betides "Woe! Woe!" to the fateful feudal trance of the hero. Although in these two dramatists the archaic-aristocratic world of the myth is still viewed with admiration and shyness and presented accordingly, in Euripides the critical rationalism of Athenian enlightenment has already had its destructive impact. It leads to a passionate and ruthless remonstrance against those elements in the old myths which, measured directly and without historical distance by contemporary standards, now appear as the baldest nonsense, as crying injustice and immorality. Greek tragedy also had reached its end, and it was not to be revived until the Renaissance in several different national rebirths.

Why the *kairos*, the real blossoming time, of the Hellenic-Attic tragedy was so brief and encompasses only the two generations of Aeschylus and Sophocles can be explained on the basis of Athenian social history. Tragedy requires two conditions within its social environment: the power of convention, of traditional social constraints, must still be strong; but it must no longer be unshaken or uncontested. Before Aeschylus, it was still unshaken, after Sophocles no longer strong enough.

The Alcmaeonid Megacles II was a leading supporter of Solon; upon Solon's death he became the natural leader of the bourgeois traders of the coast in their bitter struggle against Pisistratus. This struggle brought many reversals for both sides. The Alcmaeonidae were banished about 540 B.C. and took refuge, as usual, in Delphi, where they reconstructed the recently burned temple of Apollo on a magnificent scale; Cleisthenes (ca. 565 to 500 B.C) now was the head of the clan. Of Pisistratus's sons, Hipparchus was assassinated in 514 B.C., upon which his brother Hippias drew the reins of tyranny all the tighter. The renewed defeat of the Alcmaeonidae at Leipsydrium prompted the enemies of Pisistratean tyranny to appeal for outside help to Sparta; when Hippias was finally overthrown, the political refugees were allowed back home.

The victorious alliance between reactionary aristocrats who wished to undo Solon's work, and Solon's followers with Cleisthenes at the head, soon broke down; the excuse of the Cylonian sacrilege was once again invoked to banish the Alcmaeonidae. Yet Cleisthenes ultimately triumphed. Supported by the broad masses of working people, he resumed Solon's tradition in the most radical form, and became a determining force in the further development of Athens. It is precisely this Athens of Cleisthenes that reached its pinnacle under his grandnephew Pericles and collapsed at the end of

the Peloponnesian War. Solon, Cleisthenes, and Pericles are truly
the three greatest political authors of classical Athens.

To avoid the impression that the liberation of Athens from
tyranny was due to the odious pro-oligarchic intervention of the
Spartans, not only was the merit of the Alcmaeonidae stressed, but
also the contribution of the inner resistance was featured and celebrated as much as possible. Harmodius and Aristogiton, the assas-
sins of Hipparchus, were glorified as popular heroes, and Cleisthenes had the first monument erected to them. King Theseus was
chosen as the mythical patron of the newly arisen Attic democracy.
His noble and philanthropic deeds were sung in several epics and
depicted on the treasure house of the Athenians at Delphi in deliberate antithetic parallelism to the exploits of the rough Dorian
champion Hercules. The democratic concentration of art upon official tasks seems to have corresponded to the antifeudal, legal prohibition of luxurious individual tombs.

Our ancient sources have almost nothing to tell us about the personal life of Cleisthenes, who was so decisive for the history of
Athens and, therefore, of ancient culture. We may surmise, however, that in the twenty-five years of his family's exile at Delphi he
traveled widely, as was the custom among aristocrats; perhaps in
this way he came into direct contact with the Ionia of Anaximenes
and Hecataeus. At all events the antifeudal reform of the constitution that Cleisthenes carried out in Athens (507 B.C.), is marked by a
rationalistic radicalism that certainly did not grow on archaic-Attic
native ground.

The device of ostracism, which had already proved its effectiveness in Ionia, seemed to be an adequate preventive against the return of tyranny. Even Pericles, who through the ostracism of
Thucydides (son of Melesias) in 543, and his own yearly reelection to
the post of *strategos* achieved a lifelong position that might be called
a principate, had to exercise his power more on the basis of *auc-
toritas* than *potestas*.

Ostracism and other devices from the poison chest of Ionian democracy produced their intended effect: from Cleisthenes onward,
Athens never slid back into tyranny or oligarchy. Cleisthenes could
not yet know that in his effort to achieve absolute security for democracy, he was administering overdoses and that the healthy substance of governmental cohesion would eventually be corroded and
dissolved. Nevertheless, almost a century passed before these negative effects became distinctly discernible. At all events, Cleisthenes'
reform, along with Solon's before him, is the first instance in world

history of a deliberate and consistently constitutional reform directed against feudalism and dominion.

In order to eradicate the continuing despotic influence of the old native noble families and their feudal particularism, and to prevent the formation of local cliques, Cleisthenes carried out a reverse land reform that resulted in an intricate and confused patchwork of administrative districts. Each of the major political entities (*phylae*) within the Athenian domain was composed of ten distinct areas (*demes*) scattered over three separate regions. The demes, units of actual local administration, were so small and their number so great that there was no need to fear any dangerous political groupings. Cleisthenes thus provided the first recorded case of "electoral geometry," or gerrymandering. His reform by which persons were to be identified by deme rather than by the customary patronymic served a similar purpose.

This decimal constitution "to be counted on the fingers" was stylishly complemented by an administrative year of ten months of equal length without any consideration of the phases of the moon— an extreme rationalist calendar reform such as did not even take hold in the eighteenth or nineteenth century. The greatest possible use was made of the drawing of lots, both in the formation of administrative districts as well as in the assignment of offices. Daily rotation was prescribed for all important offices, even for military posts.

The next aim, neutralization of the traditional feudal despotic structure and prevention of its regeneration thus was effectively achieved. The moderate-aristocratic bearers of this policy did not even dare exploit the alliance with Sparta, necessitated by the Persian Wars and maintained up to 464-462, for a reactionary revision of the Cleisthenian constitution. And after the end of this pro-Spartan foreign policy, further radicalizations in the sphere of domestic policy were immediately resumed in the direction marked out by Cleisthenes.

From the time of the Cleisthenian constitution on, possibilities of social integration no longer existed within the Athenian-Attic city-state beyond the minuscule local administrative districts. This led at first to an extraordinary centralization, a strengthening of the unity of the state, and the cultivation of Athenian nationalism. Everything that existed in the way of communal energies was diverted into this one remaining channel—a situation reinforced further in times of decline or when an exterior military threat exercised a powerful integrative effect.

How essential the principles of birth and of local roots had been for the power of the nobility, and how successfully Cleisthenes' device of ostracism had struck at this feudal principle is best indicated by the fact that it took as much as half a century, and required the talents of an unusually skillful organizer before the Attic aristocracy reconciled itself to the principle—now so natural to us—of political parties based on the mechanical addition of individuals within a vast organization, regardless of rank, condition, or locality. Even the roughest and bitterest party struggles of the next hundred years never again reverted to a localized basis.

Despite this timely new organization, Thucydides was ostracized in 443 by Pericles, who, until his death in 429, exercised a quasi-monarchical leadership for which no formal provision had been made in Cleisthenes' democratic constitution: "For so long as [Pericles] presided over the affairs of the state" owing his influence "to his recognized standing and ability," he "restrained the multitude, while respecting their liberties, and led them rather than was led by them." Thus, "Athens, though in name a democracy, became in fact a government ruled by its foremost citizen." So reads the remarkable appreciation of Pericles by the historian Thucydides, upholding, in a classical way, the ideal of truly democratic leadership.[33]

Under this leadership of Pericles the most perfect self-realization of truly liberal democracy that mankind has ever succeeded in bringing about up to now was achieved in Athens for the brief span of three decades.

What developed was not only isonomy, or equality before the law of all Attic citizens (a formalism for which socialist criticism, not unjustly, reproves the modern bourgeois "constitutional state"). Rather, the exercise of these same rights and duties was made economically possible even for the poorest citizens by daily allowances from public funds used to enable them to attend festive and dramatic representations. Equally important was the simplicity of style in private conduct: the Greeks of the classic age, especially the Athenians, rejected all provocative luxury in life-style—housing, dress, adornment—so that one is ever and again struck by the plainness of the wealthiest that is attested by archaeological evidence. Hence the considerable differences in property and income could only be expressed in accomplishments redounding to the benefit of the community and in learning. The social surplus thus was channeled into the aesthetic and intellectual spheres: ostentation and luxury were considered contemptible and non-Greek. That is probably the main reason why the "envy of the propertyless" plays

so much less a role in Hellas than in the West today, and why anything akin to class hatred is found only among dispossessed aristocrats.

In no other high cultures were the class differences in attitudes
toward life so small as in classical Greece. The influence of this circumstance on the social atmosphere cannot be overestimated, and it
is one of those points in which the antique world should serve as
model. And this far-reaching egalitarian mental attitude was first
made possible within the frame of the polis—for in the Mycenaean
age, as the excavated palaces and the contents of tombs attest, the
situation was altogether different.

The goal which was here achieved within the limits of human imperfection is beautifully expressed in the famous funeral oration for
those who fell in the first years of the Peloponnesian War which
Thucydides attributes to Pericles. Pericles begins with a presentation of ideals for which these men gave their lives:

> We live under a form of government which does not emulate
> the institutions of our neighbors; on the contrary, we are our-
> selves a model which some follow, rather than the imitators of
> other peoples. It is true that our government is called a democ-
> racy, because its administration is in the hands not of the few,
> but of the many; yet while as regards the law all men are on an
> equality for the settlement of their private disputes, as regards
> the value set on them it is as each man is in any way distin-
> guished that he is preferred to public honors; not because he be-
> longs to a particular class, but because of personal merits; nor,
> again, on the ground of poverty is a man barred from a public
> career by obscurity of rank if he but has it in him to do the state
> a service. And not only in our public life are we liberal, but also
> as regards our freedom from suspicion of one another in the
> pursuits of everyday life; for we do not feel resentment at our
> neighbor if he does as he likes, nor yet do we put on sour looks
> which, though harmless, are painful to behold. But while we
> thus avoid giving offence to our private intercourse, in our pub-
> lic life we are restrained from lawlessness, chiefly through rev-
> erent fear, for we render obedience to those in authority and to
> the laws, and especially to those laws which are ordained for the
> succour of the oppressed and those which, though unwritten,
> bring upon the transgressor a disgrace which all men recognize.
> . . . In a word, then, I say that our city as a whole is the school of
> Hellas, and that, as it seems to me, each individual amongst us

could in his own person, with the utmost grace and versatility, prove himself self-sufficient in the most varied forms of activity.[34]

But was it not Pericles, whose rule Thucydides has so movingly proclaimed the liberal ideal of freedom and equality, who put down and suppressed with armed violence and in the most brutal way any attempt of one of the cities belonging to the "alliance" to claim such freedom and equality? Was that not also the case with Samos, in whose siege and conquest (441-439 B.C.) the most famous great men of Attic intellectual life—Pericles, Sophocles, Archelaus, Socrates, and their guest Anaxagoras—personally participated, while the philosopher Melissus led the Samian defense? Does not the whole glory of the Attic empire under Pericles belong in the same category as the splendor of any superstratification despotism from the Pharaohs up to Louis XIV? And is not the liberality displayed merely a facade—or, to put it more bluntly, a mere fraud?

Different arguments can be adduced to counter this objection, which, from the viewpoint of this book, must be taken very seriously.

First of all, Pericles seems to have been fully aware of the grave danger of such a development. He did his best to prevent it and to carry over the liberal structure of his domestic policy as much as possible to his foreign policy; here he also replaced coercive despotism with consensual leadership. Immediately after the conclusion of the Peace of Kallias with Persia in 449, Pericles solemnly invited all Greek cities to a great Panhellenic congress at Athens, which now, after the formal ending of the Persian War, was to deliberate the restoration of the sanctuaries destroyed by the Persians, the performance of the sacrifices promised to the gods, and the pacification of the seas. There has been some doubt expressed whether Pericles was serious in issuing this invitation. Yet the epigraphic researches of Wade-Gery and Merill indicate that payments of tribute, which up to 449 were paid on schedule, were in large part abruptly suspended around 449-448.[35] This may logically be taken as an indication of Pericles' deliberate and systematic preparation for the congress, which was to transform the earlier imposed war contributions of the allies into voluntary Panhellenic contributions.

Athens would have become formally and officially what in fact it already was—the capital of Hellas. The question therefore was whether this irresistible development was to proceed with the consent of the allies or be forced upon them.

The convening of the congress was frustrated by the Spartans; this signified a tragic turning point and decision for the second alternative. The construction of the Parthenon that same year began, not as a Panhellenic project, but as a purely Attic undertaking. What could be still realized along the lines of the old program was the establishment of the Panhellenic colony of Thurri (443 B.C.) in which Herodotus, Protagoras, Empedocles, and Lysias participated in prominent ways.

After the formal end of the Persian War by the Peace of Kallias (499 B.C.), Pericles must have set great store on grounding the fundamental conflict between Hellenic liberality and Persian tyranny on a deeper level and on making it independent of day-to-day politics. It is consonant with this concern that Herodotus, in his history, presents this conflict between West and East as the first real hinge of history since the Trojan War.

As a result of the failure to convene the planned congress, Athens now was fully under the spell of its deadly rivalry with Sparta. Once the Athenian leadership saw itself forced to embark upon this path of imperialistic foreign policy, there was never any lack of weighty reasons to prompt its continuation.

This initially reluctant Attic imperialism also found intellectual support in the intellectual radicalism of the Sophists: the result was unscrupulous Machiavellianism, proud of its own unscrupulousness, of which one reads, with shuddering admiration, in the Melian dialogue in Thucydides.

Athens during this period experienced not only a qualitative change of its social structure—a *massification* or movement toward mass society—but also a qualitative change, of actual overpopulation. Consequently, Athens, in ever increasing measure, became dependent upon the regular import of grain from what today is southern Russia through the Bosporus and the Dardanelles, and from there across the Aegean Sea. Imperialism now appeared as the securest means for control of this vital sea route; there always was the danger that Sparta might attempt to cut Athens off from its vital imports. English naval supremacy, from the sixteenth to the nineteenth centuries, offers a ready analogy.

However negatively this Attic policy must be judged from our basic viewpoint, it is important to recall that it was applied not within the domestic sphere or within Athenian society, but rather in the field of foreign relations alone. The most fateful and noxious aspects of superstratification on the contrary manifest themselves when the despotic elements of foreign policy seep into the domestic policy of society. This connection existed at the time of the original Greek settlements in Attica as elsewhere over the centuries. However, this inner feudal structure had been progressively dismantled and leveled; it was this democratization in the domestic sphere that, after Solon, Cleisthenes, and Themistocles, had been perfected by Pericles. That Attic foreign policy at the same time turned increasingly toward imperialism only makes the contrasting domestic development stand out all the more positively.

After Solon and Cleisthenes, Pericles became the third great assimilator and transplanter of the Ionian spirit to Athens. This third and last transplant was of decisive importance from the viewpoint of world history, for since the collapse of Ionian resistance and the destruction of Miletus (494 B.C.), the Ionian spirit had been displaced, even at home. Its survival and further fate now depended almost exclusively upon the development of Athens.

This simultaneous development of Athens, of the Ionian spirit, and of the Greek world reached its pinnacle in Periclean Athens. The spirit of this age is evident most directly in the imposing architectural monuments of Pericles' reign and in their sculptural adornment by Phidias and his school, with its Panhellenic synthesis of Attic, Ionian, and Dorian motifs. The same spirit is expressed and reflected, in many different ways, in the last trilogy of Aeschylus, in the life work of Sophocles (497-406 B.C.), in Euripides (480-406 B.C.), and in the earlier comedies of Aristophanes. From a literary point of view it is embodied most vividly in Plato's dialogue-plays, all of which were first performed between 455 and 399 and all but one in Athens.

The Greek Enlightenment of the fifth century B.C., generally known as "Sophism," has been as unfairly discredited by the reactionary romanticism of Plato as was the Enlightenment of the eighteenth century by the romanticism of the nineteenth.

In reality, as has been recognized in the meantime, Socrates himself was one of these Sophists, who frequently fought among themselves; and, from the viewpoint of intellectual history, their importance is extraordinary. It was the Sophists who "led philosophy from heaven to earth" (unjustly claimed only for Socrates) and gave scientific thought an anthropological and humanist turn. The Sophists carried over the liberality of Ionian-Attic thought to the humanities and the social sciences, to domains that up to then had been under the sway of naïve tradition. Understandably, it overshot the mark in the verve of the first takeoff, and the exuberance of youthful delight in freedom sometimes led to nihilism and up to the daredevil arts of a kind of tightrope walk across the void.

The Sophists represent the Greek Enlightenment; they are the inaugurators of most of the Western humanistic disciplines; they decisively influenced the development of public instruction to this day; they extended rational criticism to all spheres of thought and life; and they were the first to conceive of logic as a science.

Rhetoric and flowery expression, the cultivation of artistic form and effect in speech—which to this day has remained much more congenial to Latin than to Germanic peoples—plays an integral role in the works of the Sophists, especially the works of Gorgias, whose place indeed is much smaller in the history of philosophy than in that of rhetoric and rhythmic prose. Gorgias himself, for example, expressly characterizes his *Encomium to Helena* as a rhetorical joke that aims to be taken and enjoyed as a brilliant and dazzling piece of linguistic pyrotechnics. But his famous (or infamous) *On Nature or Not Being* on a higher level was nothing but such a literary *jeu d'esprit*: in three successive passages it produces the staggering proof (1) that nothing exists; (2) that if something exists, it is not cognizable; (3) that if something is cognizable, it is not communicable. Gorgias could not divine that Teutonic philologists and philosophers centuries later would not understand a joke and would take even this set of statements with extreme seriousness. Gorgias's own intention was to be an epistemological devil's advocate of the most temerarious type and by way of this daredevil act to show off his absolute intellectual freedom from vertigo in the manner of Parmenides, Zeno, and Melissus. Like Socrates, Gorgias had no "teaching," or earnestly espoused positive philosophic convictions. And the thesis that a committed and self-respecting Sophist would not undertake to prove has not yet been found. If he delivered panegyrics to the gout, indeed to death, they were after all but favorite bravura pieces, to be disputed pro and con with the same force of conviction. Conceivably, the new technique most effectively recommended itself in legal proceedings—where, after all, it is not a question of being in the right but of carrying one's point.

What distinguishes Socrates from all other Sophists within the common frame of the Greek Enlightenment is his rejection of any self-indulgence in mere rhetoric or verbal elegance, and of all intention to achieve a merely aesthetic-artistic effect. He was concerned only with content, and despite the often playful grace of the conversational form, he is most deeply, objectively, and humanly serious in his arguments. His dialectic is of an almost frighteningly rabid, raving radicalism, with an almost diabolical joy in destructive criticism of Attic democracy—which became the next victim of his dialectical radicalism. If Socrates in his innermost recesses was convinced that this path of radical criticism, pursued far enough with an unflinching rectilinearity, would ultimately lead again to positive and then to definite and certain results, we must concede that he was right in the long run. Yet neither he nor Plato ever went so far. Indeed Plato, as we shall see, deviating from the straight path, executed his characteristic somersault from the skepticism of his teacher into the deep waters of orientalizing mysticism and metaphysics. But if we assert the right and the duty of radical criticism against this deviation and the baneful effects it has had down to our day, we can do so by invoking Socrates against Plato and feel ourselves as the legitimate successors of the direction marked out by him.

Sophism not only laid the basis for later rhetoric. Its style of argument, in which Socrates excelled, is the foundation of all later dialectic, and indeed one of the most important roots of modern scientific thinking. Here lies by far the greatest and most positive contribution of Socrates and Plato to the history of science.

"Our oldest evidence for the existence of Sophism" is Aeschylus's *Prometheus Bound*,[36] a truly mighty portal of late archaic style opening the most modern vistas of intellectual history. If we place it, say, in 457 B.C., it shows us how far the beginnings of this movement, based on Attic soil, go back—precisely as far back as Attic democracy under Pericles. Aeschylus's *Persian Women* had been performed in 472 under the *choragia* of Pericles. In *The Eumenides* (458) he glorified the Areopagus—to the boiling indignation of the aristocrats. That this moving exhortation to unity on the basis of the newly created regime was indignantly rejected by the aristocratic opposition, which had vented its feelings with such venomous malice in the assassination of Ephialtes, is understandable.

The recognized professional founder of Sophism was Protagoras of Abdera (ca. 485-415 B.C.), who in Athens took the place of Anaxagoras in Pericles' entourage, following the former's forced departure from the city (ca. 450 B.C.); Plato himself speaks of him with a certain esteem. His most famous doctrine is the so-called *homo mensura* proposition: "Man is the measure of all things, of the existence of things that are, and of the nonexistence of things that are not." Plato's philosophizing contemporaries, who espoused subjectivist relativism, seemed to have leaned upon Protagoras as their ancestor. As Plato, in his dialogue form, was forced to combat contemporary doctrines imputed to personages of the fifth century, it is understandable that he places this contemporary subjectivism and relativism in the mouth of Protagoras and thus interprets his proposition with much distortion. That, however, he was well aware of the real importance of Protagoras emerges from a passage of the *Laws* (4. 716c4-6): "Now God ought to be to us the measure of all things, and not man, as men commonly say." This is in fact the exact opposite of what Protagoras thought, so that Plato here rightly contradicts him. The original meaning of the *homo mensura* proposition was the denial of a double standard of truth: there is not, as the Pythagoreans and the philosophers influenced by Pythagoras taught, a lower human truth and a higher divine truth (indistinct or in need of revelation), but only one human truth. What does not exist for man has no existence whatsoever, and what exists for him is what appears cognitively: the first express and methodologically conscious "positivistic" negation of all theology and metaphysics. The agnosticism of Protagoras's proposition on the gods fits in with this: "Concerning the gods, of course, I know nothing, neither whether they exist or do not exist, nor which form they could have. Many obstacles stand in the way of such knowledge: imperceptibility and the brevity of human life."[37]

Hippocrates of Cos (ca. 460-375 B.C.) provides the most impressive example of earnestness, human dignity, and nontheological piety, a drive for knowledge to serve society. Statements like "Even to myself . . . no thing seems more divine and none more human than the other, but rather all alike and all divine . . . and nothing happens against nature . . . Rather all is divine and all human" attest to his representation of a liberal, solidly established cheerful piety over against widely prevailing superstitions.[38]

A further fundamental accomplishment of the Greek Enlightenment was the elaboration of natural law—already undertaken by Heraclitus. So long as the established law is experienced as correct and natural, no cause exists for a critical-antinomic cleavage of law into ideal and real. This cleavage occurs only when the established law and its administration no longer correspond to the feeling of right, when the reality of the law is experienced as contrary to the ideal.

We meet it for the first time, in extant literature, in 442 B.C., in Sophocles' *Antigone*. There the heroine, protesting the king's command, which she feels to be immoral, appeals to "unwritten" laws. "For their life is not of today or yesterday, but from all time, and no one knows when they were first put forth."[39] The concept of natural law, the law of nature, is here recognized as the ultimate norm. With the establishment of natural law the Greek Enlightenment forged the theoretical weapon with which every legal injustice, every misuse of form of the law for the legitimation of violence and oppression could effectively by countered. Natural law is indeed the legal armory of the struggle for freedom and human rights.

If the development of the polis led to political equality and parity of all citizens, which found its classical realization in the democracy of Periclean Athens, then natural law not only provided the theoretical foundation of this constitution, but also led far beyond it. The Greek Enlightenment of the so-called Sophists rejects the self-serving traditional polarity of Hellenes and Barbarians or freemen and slaves, proclaiming natural equality and parity of all humans—the idea of the unity and community of mankind. Following the precedent of Aeschylus's *Prometheus Bound*, where for the first time we come upon the concept of "philanthropy," —love of mankind—such ideas crop up again in Euripides, "the poet of the Greek Enlightenment."[40]

> The whole aether stands free to the eagle's wing,
> The whole world is fatherland to the noble man.[41]

And similarly in Democritus:

> The whole earth stands open to the wise man,
> For to the upright soul the whole world is fatherland.[42]

Alcidamas, the pupil of Gorgias (end of the fifth and beginning of the fourth century) says in a speech to the Messenians: "God has given everybody his freedom, nature has made no man a slave."[43] And in accordance with this view the Cynic Diogenes of Sinope (ca. 390-310 B.C.), upon being asked what his native city was, replied that he was a "citizen of the world,"[44] a cosmopolite, and emphasized that "the only proper state is the world state."[45]

This idea of world citizenship was the central point of politics for the Stoics. It is they who have transmitted it to posterity, as with the concept of natural law in general. "We should not," writes Zeno of Citium, the founder of the Stoic school, in his *Politeia*, strongly influenced by Cynicism, "live separated according to cities and tribes, each one with a different conception of law. Rather we should consider all men as fellow citizens and brothers, and the way of life and the social order should be uniform as with a herd that is raised on the same pasture in the same way."[46]

This Hellenic idea of the political unity of mankind, which the Stoics continue to espouse, was obscured by the old monarchic idea of world domination. In modern times, however, when the pride in sovereignty of the ascendant territorial state absolutism rejects the idea of a superordinated world monarchy, natural law again assumes democratic form and reaches out even further. Francisco de Vitoria (1482-1546) boldly writes: "All the world is . . . in some way a single commonwealth"; Francesco Suárez (1548-1617) asserts that "mankind, howsoever divided into peoples and realms, always has a certain unity not only as a species but also somewhat as a political and moral body." Hugo Grotius not only superimposed on kings a "general care for human society" beyond their own sphere of sovereignty, but even speaks of the "community which ties the human species and the various peoples among each other" as the *magna universitas.*[47]

The Socratic Antisthenes, fastening onto the legendary idealization of Cyrus, had espoused the ideal of a world monarchy. Under the influence of Alexander the Great, the world state was no longer conceived of merely a universal city-state, a cosmopolis (cosmic polis), but rather a world empire; thus the nomadic aim of world dominion was synthesized with the Greek ideal of humanity. The Roman empire up to Marcus Aurelius is a realization of this ideal. In Dante's *Monarchia*, the *humana civilitas* with its *pax universalis* was to find its apex in the emperor as *curator orbis*, and Baron Christian von Wolff conceptualizes a *rector civitatis maximae.*[48]

The mentality corresponding to this world view is the love of man (*philanthropia*), with its categorical imperative "Love mankind!" as Marcus Aurelius, the crowned Stoic, once formulated it. This concept also originates in the Greek Enlightenment. Aristippus, a follower of Socrates, coined the word *anthropismos*, of which *humanitas* is a literal Latin translation. It is the historic merit of the younger Scipio, the pupil of Polybius and Panaetius, to have raised this *humanitas* to one of the foremost ideals in Roman culture.

The work of the historian Thucydides is the most remarkable embodiment of the spirit of the Greek Enlightenment and the most direct, literary self-attestation of Periclean Athens. Thucydides, great-grandson of Miltiades and of a Thracian princess, grandnephew of Cimon, came from one of the most aristocratic and richest families of the city.

In the face of the catastrophe of 546 B.C., Anaximander of Miletus had sought solace in an understanding of becoming and passing away as a cosmic cycle. After the catastrophe of 404 and the war of almost thirty years that followed it, Thucydides of Athens sought solace in an understanding of becoming and of passing away as historical phenomena, of the nature of political power and its inescapable contingencies, of the eternal laws of its concentration and its decline. Just as the science of natural history developed as an escape upward, as a creative way out from an intolerable situation, so did the science of human history, truly—with a Thucydidean phrase—a *ktēma es aei* ("gain for all time").

Thucydides, with magnificent steadfastness, rejects illusion, self-deception, and any form of underhanded theological or quasi-theological consolation. This implied a complete secularization of historiography, such as was not again achieved—and then only briefly—until Machiavelli and Guicciardini. Yet whereas their cynicism carries them to the opposite extreme, the imperturbable reflective earnestness of Thucydides always preserves an innate dignity. His work has superior political, sociological, and psychological empirical wisdom without a trace of a philosophy of history. Thucydides' scientific mode of thinking is natural-scientific and medical (but in no way biological in our modern sense). He applies the method of Hippocrates to political events with, however, the exclusion of therapy. Thus, Thucydides offers the remarkable spectacle of a complete free spirit who, without requiring any theological or metaphysical support whatsoever, depends exclusively upon himself and whose truly virile *megalopsychia* (largeness of spirit) is equidistant from cynicism, despair, and despondency: *Si fractus inlabatur orbis, impavidum ferient ruinae* (If the vault of heaven crack, the ruins will strike him fearless still).

He handles the language with aristocratic nonchalance in spite of the demands of linguistic social constraint then coming into vogue for Attic prose. It was the most subjective and powerful Greek prose that had ever been written, as well as the most difficult and untranslatable.

Whereas natural science looks with reverent condescension on the conceptions of Anaximander as upon its infantine beginnings, present-day historical science still regards the accomplishment of Thucydides as the highest peak in its scientific-historical development, a convincing proof of the enormous intellectual development in Hellas from the middle of the sixth to the end of the fifth century. Anaximander started at the beginning of this epoch; Thucydides closed it.

Athens succumbed to Sparta and its hostility after decades of resistance. Sparta, after its reactionary self-cramping of 546, no longer fostered—or even tolerated—cultural accomplishments of consequence at a time when even the smallest Greek city-states vied with each other in cultural achievements of the highest order.

The energetic acceptance of the Ionian tradition by Periclean Athens was bound to intensify the jealous struggle with Sparta for political hegemony into a kind of hate-filled religious war. After the end of the Persian Wars and Athens's pro-Spartan policy (which these wars had conditioned), Spartan policy was made up of an incessant series of intrigues against Athens, including an alliance with the national foe, the Persian king. It was to this Persian alliance that Sparta owed its ultimate victory over Athens; the result was an increasingly stronger hegemonic position of Persia in Greece, until the glorious legacy of the Persian wars was depleted and in 387 B.C. the great king, at the suggestion of the Spartans and upon the advice of the Spartan Antalcidas, could dictate his infamous "king's peace" to the Greeks.

It would have been difficult for Athens, however, to succumb to a foe that was so culturally and morally beneath it had Athens itself not been undermined and weakened from within by dissolution and disintegration. In foreign policy Athens could not resist letting principles of ruthless enjoyment of power, based upon *Realpolitik*, as Thucydides unsparingly characterized it in the horrendous Melian dialogue, enter into its relation with the Greek allies (originally conceived as the leadership position of a *primus inter pares* in the frame of an honorable comradeship). The Spartans generally limited themselves to supporting aristocrats and then maintaining an antidemocratic cartel relationship with them; accordingly, Sparta could set itself up as protector of Greek independence and freedom against Athens.

Furthermore, in Athens the reception of the Ionian spirit had not been consistent and definitive. The decisive transmission of the Milesian legacy occurred through Anaxagoras, Pericles' private tutor, who was more estimable and impressive than original and productive, and whom the history of philosophy overrates.

Anaxagoras initially was a loyal pupil of the last Milesian natural philosopher, Anaximenes. He adopted the latter's doctrine in which the stars of the constellations are glowing, whirling masses of rock chipped off from the earth. Because of the challenging conclusion of a monistic materialism, the charge of impiety was formally made against him by the reactionary political opponents of Pericles (ca. 450); but he escaped by timely flight. That his impeachment had set the religious underworld in motion for predominantly political reasons is evident in the trial of the Pythagorean Damonides, another teacher and adviser of Pericles. Damonides returned to Athens after the ten-year term of banishment. But there was no talk of recalling Anaxagoras, who still lived in Lampsacus.

At all events, the intellectual fighting power of the Ionian school against the reactionary, medieval-theological tradition surely must have been gravely impaired by such weak and inconsistent leadership.

Those who wanted to stir up mass psychosis against Pericles and his enlightened circle repeatedly took advantage of the tested device of bringing formal impeachments on charges of impiety, which in most cases were successful. And it goes without saying that the Spartans did not miss a chance to mobilize such sentiments against Pericles. Finally, by means of the Athenian plague of the year 430 (to which Pericles himself fell victim in 429) the divine powers themselves seemed clearly to concur with warnings of their theologically orthodox followers—a frightening and ghastly punishment exactly like that threatened by the apocalyptic prophets of doom since time immemorial. Unfortunately, the still-young science of medicine, which at that time had reached its greatest pinnacle in Hippocrates, was utterly powerless. Thus, Asclepius conquered Hippocrates, and the old god of healing with his miraculous cures (with Sophoclean participation) was accepted in the pantheon of Athenian patron deities. In the cult of Asclepius and other medicinal gods the superstition-based industry of miracle cures began, from which the educated Athenian until then had been altogether distant; it continued without interruption until the Christian Middle Ages.

The longer the Cleisthenean constitutional reform continued, including its consistent further improvements in the fifth century, the more it fatefully overshot the mark. Now, radicalism was combined with the nihilism of the Enlightenment. Its nonorganic social order prevented not only any resurgence of feudalism, but also the growth of any other organic social formation. This already was true in Cleisthenes' own time, when Athens still was small enough for each citizen to be personally acquainted with every other, and thus for a long time some form of direct, total integration remained possible. But in the second half of the fifth century, the population of Athens constantly increased beyond this critical size. Moreover, this population, in rapidly swelling percentages, consisted of metics and slaves. In addition, the Peloponnesian War forced the whole rural population of Attica to seek protection behind the walls of Athens, which contributed to abnormal overcrowding and overpopulation.

The integrative forces of the Cleisthenean constitution could not cope with the demographic situation that developed during the fifth century, and the fateful consequences of its negative aspects, its radical abolition of all organic infrastructures now increasingly made themselves felt. In the course of the fifth century this led, with sociological cogency, to progressive atomization and massification, which detracted from the highest cultural accomplishments and laid the groundwork for the terrible collapse that followed this pinnacle of achievement. This development, at the same time, also forced certain features, bordering upon demagogy, to intrude upon Pericles' policy, which during his lifetime was concealed by his brilliance and outstanding intellectual level.

The development occurring immediately after his death showed that it had been only the power of his genius that had, *praeter legem*, stamped the form of his leadership upon the Athenian people then in the process of becoming a mass society.

That Pericles could find no successor worthy of him was not a mere unfortunate accident, but rather a consequence of circumstances. Aside from his unique personal qualities, Pericles' leadership reflected a unique historic situation—the one-time transition from aristocracy to democracy. By temperament and manner, he was the aristocrat, through and through; yet by belief and conviction he was the very champion of democracy. This combination of seeming opposites in periods of transition has the captivating charm of uniqueness. But this very uniqueness of Pericles also stood in the way of institutionalization of his mode of political leadership. Under normal circumstances this crisis period might possibly have been overcome. The truly moving attempts at democratic regeneration, undertaken since 403 B.C., show the quantity of healthy democratic energies that were still extant. Unfortunately, this grave internal developmental crisis now coincided with the most serious threat conceivable from the outside, which was tragically begun by the foreign policy so fatefully pursued by Pericles. These two threats continuously reinforced each other and thus moved toward the inevitable catastrophe.

After the death of Pericles the desperate defensive war against Sparta dragged on for twenty-five years, marked by convulsive efforts and by triumphs and calamities in such rapid succession as to foreshadow the vicissitudes of a later, Hellenistic era. At last, in 404 B.C., Athens succumbed. The epoch of supreme cultural achievement that had been ushered in by the victory over the Persians ended for Greece.

14. Intellectual Reaction

The catastrophe of 404 B.C.—the collapse of Athens and its democracy—did not come unexpectedly, as had that of 546 B.C. In intellectual history, however, its effects continued and accumulated. The optimism of the Greek Enlightenment was broken, much like that of the French Enlightenment by the upheaval of 1792-1793. Aristippus and Antisthenes, pupils of Socrates, sought the ideal of "inner freedom" in opposite directions, which Epicurus later was to unite in his great synthesis; the influence of Eastern theology and metaphysics reaches its apogee in Plato; all this against the background of the catastrophe and under its impact.

For the aristocrats and reactionaries of all Greek cities, including Athens, Sparta in the fifth and fourth centuries played the same role that Russia has played for the communists of other countries: whoever was antidemocrat and proaristocrat was *ipso facto* a partisan of Sparta. The aristocratic circles, with their inherited wealth, were, however, the traditional bearers of higher culture and of patronage in poetry and literature. Hence the predominantly literary glorification of Sparta.

In contrast, the religious reaction of Orphicism had originally had a pronounced proletarian character; it had been the wretched and the burdened who sought consolation. Only one who had nothing to expect from this world placed such hopes in a better world in the great Beyond. It was only later that Pythagoras created an aristocratic-hierarchic superstructure in his order.

As that despair over the conditions of this world and over the possibility of its improvement gained ground, and as oligarchic-minded members of the aristocratic upper stratum despaired of a return to the good old times, Orphic and quasi-Orphic ideas gradually filtered upward in Athens as well. Euripides, on occasion, already puts Orphic professions of faith in the mouths of his characters, and their solemnity does not create the impression that the poet's stance toward them was one of rejection. And in Plato the same ideas reached the highest social and intellectual stratum.

Sophism, the Greek Enlightenment, was as a rule progressive and democratic-minded. It was only later that individual feudal reactionaries like Critias learned to use this weapon in a counterattack for their purposes. All the more important was it for the oligarchic party to have at its disposal Socrates, a Sophist and one who was particularly ready to fight, who politically was on their side and led the struggle against the majority of democratic Sophists. Socrates thereby performed an invaluable service for the cause of aristocracy. It must be understood, however, that from the viewpoint of the "class struggle," which at that time was in full swing, Socrates was a "renegade" and a "class traitor." Thus, in an oligarchic party pamphlet of the year 432 B.C., there is mention of people who belong to the demos by birth but are not democratic-minded.

To be sure, Socrates did not pursue such a political course for the sake of material gain, but rather out of conviction and inner passion—which, of course, only made him all the more precious to the oligarchs and, correspondingly, more dangerous to the democrats. Plato on this point outdoes himself in contrasting Socrates with other Sophists, whom he repeatedly rebukes for accepting fees for their instruction. In Plato's opinion, only descendants of aristocratic families with independent incomes are properly entitled to decide intellectual matters—or at any rate only persons subsidized by such wealthy people.

Socrates the Sophist was imbued with a passionate drive to truth bordering at times on the manic, but a drive to truth that first of all activated itself in a nihilistic tearing down, not in a positive, constructive way.

Surely the new could have been built on a terrain that had been so radically cleared. Yet Socrates, for his part, did not do so. And in view of Plato's later development toward an oriental kind of metaphysics and mysticism, was such basic clearing necessary, and was that to be the result of an education to incorruptible sober criticism? Such activity on the part of an old native citizen of Athens like Socrates was far more suitable for undermining all ruling authority than the teachings of any alien Sophist or orator.

Those of us who grew up in the German tradition of classical philology were taught long ago to consider Socrates' professions of ignorance an admirable expression of unconditional honesty and self-criticism. We forget that from a socio-psychological viewpoint such dissolution and negation of all transmitted and commonly held values is nihilism. In reality one cannot seriously argue that Athenians of that time had no real knowledge of "the good" or "the just" simply because they could not clothe them in logical definitions according to the demands of this pedantic schoolmaster.

This destructive activity of Socrates set in just when Athens was gravely threatened from without as well as within, at the time of the Peleponnesian War. Integrative community forces were still alive at the end of this period, as one moving incident of 403 B.C. showed after the catastrophe and removal of the "Thirty Tyrants," when restoration of democracy was undertaken. One might have expected Socrates to do an intellectual's duty in fostering and cultivating such beginnings. Instead he continued, like someone possessed, to pursue his petty triumphs in argumentative, pedantic, and even nihilistic disputations—an activity which in times like those marked the very pinnacle of irresponsibility.

Socrates, expressly questioned about his advice, wanted to shift the responsibility to the Delphic oracle (known to be pro-Spartan), but raised no objection when his loyal pupil, the Athenian Xenophon, entered Persian military service. (The same Xenophon, only a few years later, carried overt high treason so far that in the Battle of Coronea, 393 B.C., he fought on the Spartan side against Athens.) Hence the condemnation rightly followed, and the sentence, which may perhaps appear disproportionate, was a reaction provoked by Socrates to the shamelessness of his provocative first answer: that he should be maintained at state expense in the Prytaneum (town hall) and the no less provocative countermotion of a fine, which would have been an appropriate sentence had the court been dealing with an innocuous or trivial matter.

Socrates had punctually and courageously filled his minimum civic obligations. But the most outstanding merits that he had acquired were of an intellectual-historical and philosophico-historical kind that might have earned him a Nobel Prize for his contributions to intellectual history. To forgive such a person was not within the competence of an Athenian criminal court. His highly irritating form of antidemocratic nihilistic activity, pursued as a radical rationalist and individualist, doubtless had only a destructive and disintegrative effect upon the existing Athenian state and its authority. His first and last real great service to the Athenian state was the heroic way in which he accepted the death sentence.

The Socrates figure created by Plato's brilliant literary artistry is one of the most moving and venerable creations of the Western spirit, and the devotions that the greatest minds have performed before this ideal further heighten its attraction. But all this cannot and should not prevent us from according to the historic Socrates (as well as the historic Plato) their proper places, and from judging Socrates in accordance with his clearly delineated philosophic and political tendency and with the convictions and standards of valuation that underlie the present work. At issue here are not only differences between the historical personality and the devotional image, but also differences in value judgment.

It was unavoidable, and it fits in with all rules of social and political experience, that the collapse of Athens in 404 B.C. would release reactive countermovements of corresponding radicalism within the nation and culture concerned. A simple return to any kind of "good old days," of course, for a long time, was no longer in question; the revolutionary development of the fifth century had made too powerful an impact upon its enemies.

The inevitable reaction cropped up in two forms: a cynical individualism that might be described as "I-feudalism" and a theological collectivism of "We-feudalism." Both have influenced intellectual developments to this day.

Radical mass democracy had denied the inherited claims of the individual aristocrat to enjoy power, as well as collective claims to rulership and leadership of the aristocracy as a class, based upon superstratification. Now, after the collapse of democracy, both claims were reasserted in unlimited and radical form.

The right to unlimited enjoyment of power was now raised to the level of theory, in an adjustment to the spirit of the age and in extremely individualistic form. Critias, a highly influential and ruthless Athenian politician, pupil of Socrates, patron and promoter of Alcibiades, a close relative of Plato, who practiced this ideal with a debonair insolence, espoused it with sharpness, spirit, and verve. It was also similarly adopted in a more scholastic way by the "Sophist" Thrasymachus, who, according to Plato's testimony, overtly proclaimed that might was right. These ideas found their classic embodiment in the person of Callicles in the Platonic dialogue *Gorgias*.

Here, for the first time in Western intellectual history, a brutal fact in the situation of unbroken superstratification was raised to philosophic theory and to a principle and ethical ideal. Here a positive theory of tyranny was proclaimed for the first time. In intellectual history, the line of descent here started—titanism, the cult of genius, the "aestheticism of violence,"[49] and the glorification of the superman—runs by way of Machiavelli to Stirner, Nietzsche, Pareto, Sorel, and D'Annunzio, the herald and poet of fascism.

Plato was the creator and bearer of this theological and collectivist reaction. In his political writings he renewed, in Pythagorean thinking, the old aristocratic Dorian-Spartan social ideal by a grim use of Athenian experiences of the fifth century. For the next two millennia he became a prophet for many.

Athens, the citadel of intellectual freedom, ruined by its own lack of moderation—triumphant Sparta, citadel of feudal backwardness, in alliance with Persian despotism—that was a situation that could certainly make a strong impression even upon powerful intellects.

According to Plato's advice, the humane legislator will best begin his work with the execution or expulsion of all undesirables. Aliens who have earned too much will also be expelled later. All physical work and artisan trades are to be disparaged and contemptuously relegated to the slaves and foreigners who have been allowed to stay in the state for a limited period. Autarchy is the ideal, and hence the greatest possible limitation and control of foreign trade. The import of luxury goods is prohibited, an exception being made for imports required for military purposes. Domestic currency is to be enforced against foreign currency. All foreign money is to be surrendered by private persons upon their return from journeys abroad. Aside from government-organized propaganda journeys, natives are allowed to travel abroad only with government permission—accorded only to especially reliable persons over the age of forty, and "when they come home they shall teach the young that the institutions of other states are inferior to their own."[50] Whoever returns from such a journey abroad is subject to a hearing. If it is found that the returning citizen's mind had been corrupted by foreign influence, he shall be forbidden to discuss these matters with third parties under penalty of death. Foreign visitors are to be admitted only when one can be sure that their reports will be sympathetic and enthusiastic. Preventive censorship and "guidelines" are to be laid down for poets. There are to be a commission for the expurgation and improvement of the national literature, and trials for heretics. For those who are atheists by conviction the sentence is five years in the reformatory; if still unreformed, they shall be subject to the death penalty. The citizen is obliged to denounce atheists. Leaders are advised to use lies and deception in the governance of the led; lies in behalf of the government are viewed as a useful means of leadership.[51]

We are familiar with the repulsive totalitarian concept of the "myth" as it was recommended by that old poison-brewer Georges Sorel, with Mephistophelian craftiness, as a consciously pathetic-sentimental propaganda lie; all that matters is its demagogic, mass psychological impact. "Leadership," "folk community," "blood and soil," the worst propagandistic opiates of national socialism were fabricated according to this recipe. Further, Marx's "classless society" to this day has a corresponding effect complemented by the new propaganda lies, such as "people's democracy." The designation of such a modern means of mass poisoning as "myth" at first blush must appear blasphemy to any humanist-minded person. But in reality it is precisely this concept, with all its modern implications and its perfidies, that is already expressed in the divine Plato. In the *Republic*[52] Socrates is made to say: "How then may we devise one of those needful falsehoods of which we lately spoke—just one royal lie which may deceive the rulers, if that be possible, and at any rate the rest of the city?" There follows a clutter of myths that Socrates at first felt embarrassed to utter; their purpose is to strengthen the consciousness of autochthonousness, of folk community and of divinely ordained class differences—exactly the same lines that are so dear to our modern totalitarian demagogues. "Such is the tale; is there any possibility of making our citizens believe in it?" Socrates asks his interlocutor. "Not in the present generation," is the reply, "but their sons may be made to believe in the tale, and their sons' sons, and posterity after them." Thus the intellectual innocence of the young, which totalitarian regimes rely on, is voiced with the greatest cynicism.

The classic model of Plato's state construction is the Spartan cosmos—enriched, however, by totalitarian methods based on anti-aristocratic tendencies. Plato withdraws from this, the only seriously competing phenomenon, with revulsion and special hatred, just as fascism later turned against bolshevism.

I have cited those features of Plato's state construction in the "Laws" which, being typically totalitarian, are common not only to fascism and national socialism—which are wont to invoke Plato—but also to bolshevism, whose exponents would indignantly reject the comparison. Highly moral preambles and justifications are found just as readily in Plato as they are in the programmatic writings of all versions of modern totalitarianism. And of course the second-rate character of modern totalitarian scribblings cannot be compared with the intellectual and literary level of Plato. This high intellectual level, and the fact that Plato's program was not put into practice, has led to our condoning attitude toward Plato's program for the ideal state. We commonly behave like the highly idealistic fellow travelers did toward communism, despite its visible realization under the Bolsheviks. But the real issue is one of sober sociological classification.

What Plato created is neither more nor less than a complete sketch of the totalitarian state, carried out in detail with the superior intellectual force of one of the most brilliant thinkers in the history of philosophy.

Modern enthusiastic Plato-priests and -priestesses demand from us a genuflection, as it were, if not an outright groveling—not only before Plato as herald but even before Plato as practical politician. As such he had undertaken the three Sicilian journeys and inspired Dion's *coup d'état*.

On his first Sicilian journey Plato's sermons got on the nerves of Dionysius I to such a degree that Plato had to return home. And on his way home, he was captured by the Aeginetans and put up for sale on the slave block, where his philosopher friends were able to ransom him. The second Sicilian journey began with poor Dionysius II, in accordance with the strict Pythagorean curriculum of the Academy, being forced to learn mathematics. The floors of his palace were strewn with sand so that the geometric figures could be traced on them. In the outcome, Dion, in whose interest the journey had been undertaken, was banished and deported by Dionisyus II because of a treasonable letter to a Carthaginian foe. Even more embarrassing and undignified was the situation that arose from Plato's altogether fruitless third journey, from which he was finally freed after the Pythagoreans of Tarentum sent a trireme to fetch him.

Dion's *coup d'état*, heralded as a Panhellenic undertaking by the Academy, began when Dion—who characteristically had acquired honorary Spartan citizenship in the meantime—made use of all his treasonable connections so as to land with Carthaginian help on the coast of Sicily. A series of startling initial successes so much went to Dion's head that he began to believe in his own divinity. Even Plato felt obliged to warn him against such megalomania. Dion evidently no longer considered it necessary to take account of real political forces—considering such calculations far beneath him. He refused to dismantle the walls and moats of the tyrant's palace, which had come to be bitterly hated by the populace, leaving that task to his more fortunate successor, Timoleon. Little wonder that Dion himself was suspected of wishing to reestablish a tyranny. He prevented a democratic redistribution of the land, since landed property of considerable size had to be maintained at any price as the natural foundation of the only true aristocratic social order. When, however, his democratic opponent Heracleides was condemned to death, he prevented execution of the sentence only out of academic pride in conscious virtue.

Finally, everything collapsed in a horrendous moral catastrophe. Dion's closest associate from the Academy, Callippus, had him assassinated. The other friends and colleagues in his entourage did not lift a finger for cowardly fear. "An arbitrary temper has solitude for company," as Plato himself had admonished him in a letter.

Later Callippus was also murdered—it is said with the same

sword that felled Dion. Timoleon, summoned from Corinth, showed what a political virtuoso without any theoretical extravagance or pretension to divinity could do even in a desperate situation. He had council halls and palaces of justice built on the cleared sites, proving his great awareness of the contradiction between democratic liberalism and the importunate approach of the totalitarian Platonists.

The superstratificationist and feudal-despotic nature of Plato's state construction is consonant with the idealistic dualism of his metaphysical world construction. The macrocosm, as well as the microcosm, consists of an upper stratum called to rule and a lower stratum called to serve. This dualistic "idealism" is a metaphysical projection of the sociological superincumbency structure.

We have seen that Indian metaphysics was initially taken over by the pre-Socratic natural philosophers only as a form of physics, and that their dualism had an intraphysical character. What with the Indians had been world soul—in the metaphysical-mystical meaning of that word—like air in Anaximenes or fire in Heraclitus, became only the most important and most active of several fundamental substances or states of aggregation. Thus the transcendent had become immanent, the supramundane worldly, the metaphysical detoxified by physicalization.

Only Xenophanes had counterposed a pure intellectual divinity to the whole material world, and Anaxagoras was the first to draw the corresponding conclusion also with respect to the human mind, both without inferring a depreciation of matter or of the body. This depreciation arises first in the *Purifications* of Empedocles, an Orphic undercurrent in the lofty regions of philosophic literature. But the oriental virulence of the Indian legacy first breaks through in Plato; it is first in him that the stage of metaphysics proper, a dualistic idealism with an ascetic polarity of values, is again achieved. This dualistic-Platonic idealism, which forms the foundation of his theory of ideas, this "bifurcation" (as Whitehead called it) has remained the proper primordial and fundamental form of all metaphysics. And the deep enthusiasm with which the Kantian Schopenhauer reverts to Indian philosophy really closes this metaphysical circle.

For Plato, matter and body, as the baser elements, had to justify themselves with respect to the higher divine world of spirit and soul. And this justification lies exclusively in beauty, since they are its bearers, as a splendor or a reflected splendor of the higher world. Everything not ennobled through beauty incurs depreciation. And normal heterosexual love, in particular, also incurs the most vehement depreciation. Indeed, Plato goes so far as to designate it as bestial, with unconcealed abhorrence and disgust and in a grotesque paradox, as positively contrary to nature (*para physin*).

In Plato therefore we find for the first time the fateful cleavage between heavenly and earthly love that has wrought such mischief ever since. This heavenly love has since then, not wholly undeservedly, flattened out into the trivial concept of so-called Platonic love.

The high valuation of an immaterial, divine, spiritual better Beyond corresponds to a depreciation of worldly matter and body. And in anticipation of the Christian *memento mori*, of the *ars moriendi*, the *meletan apotheiskein* ("ceasing to learn") accordingly, in a perverse and pathological way, became the goal of life. The whole philosophical development of the West to this day stands in a fateful way under Platonic influence: all idealists through direct descent, all materialists indirectly through opposition, and Aristotle, the heir of the pre-Socratics and pupil of Plato, by way of compromise and synthesis.

Against Plato—*amicus Plato, magis amica veritas*—in the religious department the charge of Persianism must be raised, in the political department that of Spartanism. In both departments he betrayed the Ionian-Attic spirit, whose greatest expositor he nonetheless remains in his dialogues. Finally, oriental theology and mysticism, approved by Plato, achieved in Neoplatonism a victory over everything Hellenic—with which in Plato himself it still stands in fruitful tension.

Both our charges against Plato refer to the *direction* of his influence. We are forced to raise them, because it is the intellectual and political direction of superstratification.

Plato can be considered one of the greatest artists of world literature and one of the most brilliant thinkers of intellectual history: unfortunately the degree and direction of the accomplishment are not necessarily connected. According to the degree, the accomplishment can be brilliant and positively towering, according to the direction it may be reprehensible and baneful, and this is precisely the case with Plato. To be sure, such a *complexio oppositorum* of judgment is not easy for the one passing judgment—but the facts of the case force such a conclusion.

Although in the course of world history Plato's role was more foreshadowing and symptomatic than causative, he has held sway within the central intellectual realm of philosophy as "the greatest intermediate bridge of corruption"—as Nietzsche called him[53]—and prompted "medieval" development of the subsequent millennia until recently. If by "philosophy" we mean that rare intellectual twofold structure that proposes to satisfy both scientific and religious needs—a metaphysics that starts out from assured facts so as to lead to heights of ecstatic-mystical self-redemption—it is Plato who truly created this strange mixture worthy of the most fabulous creations of the mythical bestiary. This hybrid of Ionian science and oriental theology is embodied in Plato's dramas of ideas with all the captivating and seductive genius of a great artist. Further development oscillates between the poles of theology and rationalism, whose most extreme points are marked, respectively, by Plotinus and Kant.

The most important among Plato's direct pupils, Aristotle (384-322 B.C), son of a physician, Ionian according to his native endowment and productive personal accomplishment, fell under Plato's influence until his death. Only after being called to the Macedonian court as tutor to the heir apparent Alexander (432) did he experience a certain loosening of rigid Platonic apriorism and idealism, a reassessment of empirical experience and exact observation, without ever succeeding, however, in extricating himself from theological-metaphysical entanglement. Because of this intermediate position between theology and science, "because of this profound and previously unrecognized community of problems with the philosophers of religion in medieval Christendom, Jewry, and Islam, he became the intellectual leader of the centuries following Augustine, whose interior world was enlarged far beyond the limits of the Greek soul by this tension between faith and knowledge."[54]

Man's eternal striving to understand the world as a meaningful whole, into which Aristotle fits himself—this ontological striving that had received a thrust from the meaninglessness of the Ionian catastrophe of 546—was never satisfied in a higher measure on the plane of scientific thought than by Aristotle: what had been attempted since Anaximander finds its fulfillment in Aristotle.

The enormous goal that Aristotle set for himself was to penetrate and present this world as a single whole, as something to be understood, as a structure of scientific thought. And in fact, never in the course of intellectual history was this goal achieved by a single person to such a high degree. Aristotle processed the whole legacy of the pre-Socratics, of Ionian natural science as well as that of Panhellenic-Attic Sophism, into a powerful synthesis. This truly encyclopedic character of the *Corpus Aristotelicum*—its quality as a summary of the entire achievement in thought and research of all of

Hellenic antiquity—helped uniquely to predestine it to transmit this achievement to the Middle Ages.

While Plato's high-flying idealism inclines to exaggerations and extremes, Aristotle's realism bears the stamp of an imperturbable, collected, and balanced striving for equilibrium, for measure and mean, and of an unconditional intellectual integrity in the course of this striving. Humaneness in the sphere of scientific thought is what we can learn from Aristotle.

In the last resort, however, Aristotle failed in his attempt to overcome Platonic dualism and its "bifurcation" and to find the way back to the unity of the Ionian world-picture of the pre-Socratics. The effort remained incomplete, the consequence being that unsystematized Platonism lost its vivaciousness and its enthusiasm. Rapturous vision was transformed into a metaphysical-theological system, almost into scholasticism. What subsequently exercised a negative effect in Aristotle's influence was this residue of Platonism, built into the system as theology against which the original Plato could repeatedly be summoned as a liberator bursting the fetters asunder. But it was precisely Aristotle's *Theologia Platonica* that made possible its scholastic reception by Christianity.

The path away from theology and metaphysics to a soberer, tidier, purer empirical science was continued with increasing consistency by Aristotle's pupil and successor Theophrastus (ca. 373-ca. 288 B.C), who had gone over from the Academy to the Peripatetic School. Even here it seems that the death of the authoritative teacher again had a gradual liberating effect. Only in his late works, written after 314, does Theophrastus arrive at a far-reaching rejection of deduction from metaphysical principles and of the rationalistic straitjacket of a closed philosophic system. "The outstanding findings of his research in his later works attest to the fact that he acquired freedom for his investigations by a deliberate rejection of any system-building and deduction, and by the exclusive assessment of observable processes and their accompanying phenomena he in fact found the correct path to the investigation of the organism." "This new method relieved him of the necessity to do violence to the phenomena with his explanations. Moreover, it differs not at all from that which our present-day biology applies in the investigation of organisms in free nature. That is precisely the reason why the expositions of Theophrastus . . . appear altogether modern." "Thus he first of all gave to biology the method of investigation adequate to it, which consists in the exact investigation and observation of organisms as well as of their relations to the whole constellation of outer and inner factors. In addition, he had excluded all deduced magnitudes, as well as deduction in general, and had also rejected the direct investigation of 'forces,' which are effective in the organism. This method is, moreover, nothing else than the investigative method of natural science." "As a result, further, of the fact that Theophrastus avoided any deductively acquired notions in the explanation of natural processes, while, at the same time, assessing only observable facts, he created the method of explanation which alone can stand criticism."[55]

Finally, the successor of Theophrastus, Strato of Lampsacus (ca. 340-ca. 269 B.C.) applied this method, developed by Theophrastus in biology, to physics; by so doing he did justice to the atomic theory of the school of Abdera. He had already given this atomic theory the form that it essentially maintained in its entire postulative-heuristic period up to Newton and beyond.

All in all, the natural sciences during the years 310 to 250 B.C., a time of the heroic competition as sponsors of the arts and sciences of the successors of Alexander the Great, achieved a level not matched again until the Renaissance and the Enlightenment.

This is a highly constructive and thought-provoking example of how much all intellectual achievement is dependent upon its *kairos*, upon a suitable time structure, upon receptivity and acceptance. Theophrastus, Strato, Aristarchus, in their own accomplishments, remained forerunners without successors because the following generations did not join in their rejection of the theologico-metaphysical line, which constituted their most mature accomplishment. Quite the contrary, the growing political distress of the time was more suited to teaching prayer, until the brutal measured tread of Roman legions trampled all independent political foundations of Greek culture into the dust.

In contrast to Athens, the Ionian tradition was preserved in the Abdera school of atomism, in an original and productive elaboration that has remained the foundation of the world picture of natural science and has experienced a phenomenal upswing in our century. This elaboration of the atomistic theory rested upon a highly fruitful and well-considered synthetic incorporation of the impulse that in the *Aletheia* of Parmenides had been radically exaggerated. Although in the *Aletheia* the truth of visual, auditory, and taste impressions had been rejected with passionate vehemence,[56] Democritus developed from it the doctrine of secondary qualities, which, since Galileo and Locke, forms the epistemological foundation of modern physics: "Color and taste are subjective; only the atom and

space are really objective"[57]—as Democritus puts it in a fragment
that has been preserved. Even the timely anthropological-cultural
turn, which in the Sophists and in Socrates had led to a break with
natural philosophy, was accomplished here in the form of an organic
broadening and incorporation whose range is truly amazing.

How different the course of Western intellectual history could
have been if Ionian science had been transplanted to Athens not by
Anaxagoras, but by men of the productiveness and strict adherence
to an adopted epistemological line of a Leucippus and a Democritus!
When atomism, much too late, made its entry into Athens, the intellectual field was already divided in a way that precluded any possibility of fruitful transplantation. A tragedy, from the viewpoint of
intellectual history, experienced and expressed by Democritus himself. "I came to Athens—and nobody knew me."[58] Not until one
century later, in a completely changed world-historical and
intellectual-historical situation, did Epicurus manage to acquire
Attic citizenship for atomism.

A second tragic misfortune of the atomistic school of Leucippus
and Democritus is connected with an intellectual-historical event as
important as it was enigmatic. The Babylonians had created an
abstract astronomy based exclusively upon a combination of observation and highly developed numerical calculation. The findings of
these calculations acquired in centuries of self-sacrificing labor now
suddenly crop up within the Greek culture complex at the end of the
fifth century, triggering a stormy, volatile development of astronomy in the modern sense of an exact science.

Of the different Greek schools only the atomistic was qualified to
take over this material and carry it forward objectively. Indeed, we
have again become conscious of how closely atomistic and astronomical modes of thought belong together. But this was not only denied
to the atomistic school; the new material fell into the lap of the
Pythagoreans, with their "dangerous consecration" (in the words of
Jacob Burckhardt), who, with their mysticism, constituted the
sharpest opposition to atomism. Their theological attitude was more
oriental than Greek, and their doctrine and observancy was suffused with oriental components; thus they maintained contact with
the Orient as the source of mysterious primordial wisdom like their
present-day descendants, the theosophists, anthroposophists, and
"Zen-Buddhists." Such an aura of mysterious mystic oriental
primordial wisdom, for the Pythagoreans, obviously surrounded everything that came from the hands of Babylonian priests, and the
Babylonians themselves must have done nothing to disturb this

flattery. Thus, Babylonian mathematics and astronomy were taken over by the Pythagoreans, despite the extremely sober "calculability" of their real content.

The fundamental accomplishment of the heroic age of modern natural science in the sixteenth century was to overcome this theological dualism, the view that the celestial world above the moon is divine, spiritual, and perfect, relieved of all the serrility and imperfections of this earthly vale of tears. This dualism was overcome by the conviction that there was but one unitary world, that even the most distant star consists of the same matter and is subject to the same natural laws as our sun and earth.

The apperception of world unity that modern times had to achieve in difficult struggles had already been achieved by the Ionians. It lay at the base of their systems from Thales to Anaxagoras, up to the atomists; and Anaxagoras had to stand a religious trial no different than that faced by Giordano Bruno two millennia later, although the outcome was milder. The Pythagoreans (and Plato in their train) were those who balked at this already acquired insight and threw the world back into oriental theologism for two thousand years. All the more astounding and all the more fateful is the fact that now the findings of Babylonian astronomy—which, as it seems, was altogether sober and untheological—were falling precisely in their hands.

The rare metaphysico-mystic halo that for broad circles to this day surrounds the exactest and soberest astronomic research stems from this historical concatenation—the halo that finds its classical expression in Kant's famous utterance about the starry sky above and the moral law within. This aura has for centuries survived the decay of its kernel—namely, Pythagorean dualistic spiritualism.

15. HELLENISM

The catastrophe of the years 546-545 B.C. had already sharply posed the question about the military and political capability of the Ionians for self-defense. The subjugation of the Ionians to Persian rule, while other Greek city-states continued their independence, created an extremely unstable situation that surely was experienced as such both by the Ionians and their fellow Greeks. The rash attempt at liberation made by the Ionians in the uprising of 494 was doomed to fail; it led to the counterblow of the Persian Wars, which in turn brought the danger of complete destruction of Greek freedom and independence. The triumph of Greek freedom in those wars against all external probability and despite the disunity on the Greek side provided for Greek culture an interval of another one and one-half centuries of freedom and independence. This margin was used in intellectual creation, but in political respects the result was negative. No successful unification of Greece occurred under Athenian or Spartan, let alone Theban, leadership. The Greek form of life, which had created the antique culture of the polis, proved incapable of defending and protecting its own culture against outside attacks. Thus only two alternatives remained: that of decline as soon as a sufficiently strong enemy attacked, or unification within the framework of its own culture but imposed from without.

King Philip of Macedonia (b. 383, reigned 359-336 B.C.) and his great son Alexander (b. 356, reigned 336-323 B.C.) had the foresight to recognize this historical situation and to seize it. Their goal was to unite Greece under Macedonian leadership and erect a world empire that would exclude any outside threat and assure Greek cultural mastery. This ideal was also present in Aristotle's mind when he said that the Greeks could govern all other peoples if only they were politically united. Athens was destined to be cultural capital of this world empire. By no means was there a lack of understanding for such plans and necessities here: Isocrates (436-338 B.C.), whose intellectual level is attested by the hopes that Plato had set upon him, had again taken up the great program of Hellenic unity developed by Pericles in 448 B.C. Much later, in 346 B.C., at the age of ninety-one, Isocrates in his address to Philip tried to adjust this program to the changed world situation by the inclusion of Macedonia. But Isocrates was a man of words, not deeds; the only Greek politician of the time with sufficient strength and passion to proceed from words to action was Demosthenes (384-322 B.C.), the greatest orator of all time, who stubbornly opposed the plan. Although he lacked a constuctive counter program, and although the sovereign autonomy of the Greek polis had proved both its cultural productivity and its absolute political incapacity, Demosthenes succeeded in driving Athens and other cities into fateful opposition to Macedonia and to military collapse.

To punish Athens for its resistance, Philip in 338 B.C. made Corinth the capital of the Greek Federation; it was later destroyed by the Romans in 146 B.C., and intellectual leadership went to Alexandria and temporarily to Pergamum. Athens remained the seat of schools of philosophers, until the last was closed by Justinian in A.D. 529, when Athens was no longer a city of the present but of the past.

In 323 B.C. Alexander, age thirty-three, fell victim to his own lack of self-control. As far as we know, his further plans were directed toward ever further expansion, mainly in a westerly direction. The problem of inner consolidation of the newly created giant empire could only become more insoluble. Alexander was too much the hero, too little the statesman, to cope with this fundamental problem. After twenty years of futile struggle for total sovereignty, the partition of Alexander's empire was finally sealed among the Diadochi. Hellenism was split into Macedonian territorial states vying with each other, just as the Hellenistic world had been fragmented into rival city-states. The ineradicable disunity and mutual jealousy remained the legacy of the classical age. Once again, the problem of defense against a strong external foe remained unsolved. On the contrary, any aggression could set the mechanism of "divide and rule" in motion. And once again here the taskmaster enforcing unity could come only from the outside.

As Alexander Hellenized the Orient, at the same time he orientalized Hellenism.[59] The organizational form of Hellenization appeared in the founding of cities after the Greek model. But the formation of monarchically ruled, territorial land states, after the oriental model, was a form of political integration difficult to reconcile with the old spirit of the polis.

This transition from autonomous, free city-states to absolutist, territorial principalities can be compared to the development of Italy in the sixteenth century, when a pompous style of courtly splendor and heightened expression developed, whose kinship with the baroque is manifest.

The fourth century B.C., despite decline, had still brought forth Plato and Aristotle, Isocrates and Demosthenes, Scopas and Praxiteles. After this the age of the Diadochi (the heirs and descendants of Alexander) began in the sphere of cultural productivity as well.

Classical literature from Homer to Demosthenes became the subject of instruction in secondary schools, which were first systematically organized at this very time. A selection thus had to be made, and the philologists of Alexandria and their successors discharged this task well. Three types of Greek literature were selected: (1) the contemporary literature of the day, which we call "Hellenistic"; (2) literature belonging to a unique, exemplary, classical, Homeric-Attic past; and (3) classicist literature modeled on the classical pattern.

The end of classic city sovereignty with its narrow, closed life sphere and the failure of Alexander's plan for world domination led, in the Diadochian states, to the emergence of arbitrary political formations, which continually changed with the fortunes of war. The only fixed points, the real centers of power in this confused and swirling activity, were the personalities of the rulers. This fits in with the Hellenistic cult of the ruler, and Aristotle is aware of this development: "If there is one person . . . so pre-eminently superior in goodness and political capacity . . . a person of this order may very well be like a god among men."[60] The courts of these rulers, especially in Alexandria and Pergamum, developed as culture centers into concentrated, closed life spaces.

The individual—subject to these ever-changing, warring rulers, and no longer finding in the polis his solidly circumscribed and fully satisfying vital sphere—saw himself thrown back onto dependence on himself. And in fact "personality" now—for the first time in history—comes to be considered "the highest happiness of human beings."[61] The first period of real individualism—of an unmistakably decadent character—sets in.

In the art of portraiture it is now the individual as such, with all the natural setting into bold relief of his peculiarities, who is depicted, without idealization or generalization. And with this interest in personality there now arises in literature the genre of biography, which hitherto, in healthier, more immediate, and more objective times, had been wholly lacking.

The classical form of the polis disappeared, and the Greek world became an arena for booty-hungry territorial princes. Hellenic liberality became introverted and entrenched itself in the realm of the mind. The "sage" withdraws into himself, philosophy becomes escapist and world-disdaining, the wisdom of individuals; "the ideal of inner freedom"[62] now appears. New philosophies spring up that are doctrines of individual salvation, paths toward that inner freedom.

The Stoic school was founded in Athens toward the end of the fourth century by the Cypriot Zeno of Citium (ca. 335-263 B.C.)—presumably of Phoenician, hence Semitic, descent. The religious ardor of the Stoics attained its peak in Cleanthes (331-323 B.C.), the poet of the famous hymn to Zeus; their scientific thoroughness in the encyclopedic erudition of Chrysippus (ca. 280-ca. 204), the "second founder" of the school. Stoicism occupied a central position among the great philosophic schools of the ancient world, for it provided a synthesis of Ionian natural science, Pythagorean metaphysics (both in their Heraclitan definition), the ethics of Socrates and the Cynics, and the humanistic science of the Sophists. The Stoics synthesized

knowledge and faith, with the element of knowledge strongly predominant: cool, lucid, strict, and rationalistic. Their metaphysical
point of departure was the system of Heraclitus of Ephesus (before
540-shortly after 500 B.C.), who equated the blazing fire of the day-
time sky and of the constellations with the eternal *logos* of the world
and of human reason. The highest duty of the philosopher is to keep
his own reason in harmony with world reason and to let his own
conduct be ruled by it.

Of the ancient schools, the Stoic is probably the one with the most
all-encompassing range of synthesis—the most catholic, so to speak;
it was marked by an extraordinary, intense effort toward uniformity
and amalgamation of all component parts. That is evident in its
strongly rationalist theology—its deism, as one might appropriately
call it, using the later term—which pervades all parts of the system
and which gave it also the character of an enlightened popular religion. It is the only ancient philosophy that did not limit itself to re-
cruiting small circles of scholars and initiates; and indeed, both
under the Roman emperors of the second century A.D. and again in
the Enlightenment of the eighteenth century, this deism became the
prevailing world view of the educated classes in general.

Anaximander and most of his successors had accepted the existence of a metaphysical world of essences or spirits as a complement
to our real world. The atomists alone mustered the intellectual
courage and integrity to reject such a solution. Their relentless drive
toward the truth had shown up all such hypothetical complements
to the actual world as mere unprovable assertions. They rejected
metaphysics on epistemological grounds. Personally, they were
sufficiently sure of themselves, with a naïve matter-of-factness, not
to feel the need for any kind of consolation or salvation. Nor did they
display any trace of resignation or pessimism.

But times had changed. The sociological structure that for centuries had formed the natural basis for the autonomy of the polis no
longer existed. And, although Aristotle had defined man as by nature an animal intended to live in a polis, for Epicurus there was no
longer any such entity as a natural, innate community. He knew
only society and voluntary association. Society was a contractual relation between a great number of atomized individuals to avoid suffering or harm. Association was a narrow, sympathetic community
of like-minded friends.

Thus it became a question (as the pupil of Epicurus, Metrodorus, once wrote) of enjoying the delights of this life pleasurably and moderately. Epicurus also teaches us how little is sufficient: "The wealth demanded by nature is both limited and easily procured; that demanded by idle imaginings stretches on to infinity."[63] The existential ideal is imperturbable serenity, a disillusioned detachment, a melancholy enjoyment of quiet. Epicurus is fond of calling this mood "stillness of the sea."

The task Epicurus faced was to replace the security that the isolated individual, now thrown back upon himself, had earlier found in the vanished community of the polis.

And when Epicurus now took over the antimetaphysical atomism of the Abderites, it was no longer simply on the basis of intellectual conviction of epistemological principle alone, but rather as a species of antitheology, an oppositional doctrine of salvation.

The old natural philosophers, such as Anaximander and Heraclitus, had attempted to prove that the world was divinely meaningful, just, and beautiful. In the meantime, however, this numinous atmosphere had suddenly broken. To men who had become insecure in this world, even the Beyond no longer seemed a consolation; inexorable fate had turned into a gruesome calamity; life after death began to hold not the lure of Elysium but the terror of hell; superpowerful deities threatened, monstrous specters sowed fright; comets, eclipses, thunder, and lightning were signs of divine wrath.

However, as the true world, according to the doctrine of atomism, consisted only of space and atoms, this whole spookery was exposed and banished as mere fantasy. And for Epicurus this was the proper meaning of all natural science: "If we were not troubled by our suspicions of the phenomena of the sky and about death, fearing that it concerns us, . . . we should have no need of natural science."[64]

Therefore, it was a question of religious (or pseudoreligious) fear in the face of thunderstorms, that form of "fear of God" that, as we shall see, was to drive Luther into the monastery. Epicurus's only intention was to free men from it, as well as from all superstitious and theological anxieties, and to keep them free. Knowledge of nature no longer is pursued for its own sake, but only as a means to reach this end.

Science was thrown back from the expansive offensive of its youth into the great wide world; weary with the burden of age, it was now on the defensive against theology and superstition. Nothing expresses more pointedly the sharp break between Hellenic and Hellenistic intellectuality. On the basis of the same attitude—in order to make as few commitments, even of a negative sort, as possible—

Epicurus also did not contest the existence of the gods as long as they refrained, as *dei otiosi*, from any perceptible intervention in the affairs of the world.

The more securely and solidly man was socially embedded in his lifetime, the more easily he faced the prospect of dying. For the community that sustained him, in which and for which he lived, did not die with him; it lived on. The generations, which followed one upon the other, replaced themselves, like the trees of the woods sprouting new leaves year after year. This holds true for the well-integrated family—hence the saying that children are the only insurance against death. In even greater measure this is also true for the larger community of many families, so long as this community is as integrated and vigorous as was the autonomous polis. We hear very little of the fear of death in the time of the flowering of the polis.

But fear of death becomes rampant with the demise of the polis; for now the isolated human being has nothing but his own life, to which he desperately clings. Death now signifies the end of all that was dear and joyful to him, the individual, and the threatening void that yawns before him soon is filled with fantasy images of anxiety and fear. Fear of hell and the most varied representations of hell now spread widely.

It therefore becomes a chief concern of philosophy to combat this undignified and unmanly fear of death. For Epicurus this was one of the most important functions of his atomism.

Epicurus's struggle against *deisidaimonia* (superstition) was later intensified to a passionate pitch of *écrasez l'infâme* by Lucretius. His doctrine, with its holy sobriety, is an atheistic religion of salvation like Buddhism. And, like Buddhism, the longer it lasted the more need there was for believers to venerate the person of the founder—a veneration expressed in the moving hymn to the savior Epicurus that forms the proem of Lucretius's third book.

Whereas citizens of the polis (*politai*) peopled the stage of Aristophanes and other ancient comedians, now only private persons (*idiōtai*) do so—e.g., in the work of Menander (ca. 342-290), the companion of Epicurus. To the large numbers of ex-citizens, the philosophic ideal of inner freedom was intellectually unattainable, and participation in one of the court societies was socially unattainable. For them, the decline of their former mode of social integration spelled atomization and massification; their reaction to this lack of integration and to the resultant malaise was a widespread feeling of the need for salvation. Oriental salvation cults already had made an intermittent appearance in the plays of Euripides during the hard times of the Peloponnesian War. Now they played an increasing role in the comedies of Menander, famed for their realism—although the playwright himself, philosophically educated and a true humanist, viewed them with cool detachment. And this eastern influence, as part of which Christianity, too, made its appearance in the antique world, has since flowed without interruption.

16. Rome and the Roman Empire

The Hellenistic world of the Diadochi had lasted a whole century while in the West Rome rose as a menacing new power. Rome's history, generally, had unfolded outside the Greek culture complex—in the domain of "barbarism," to use the condescending terminology of the Greeks. The Rome of the old Republic was a state of peasant warriors, with a sizable aristocratic stratum of large landholders. Its political development was propelled by an extreme form of naked will to power, yet power exercised within the frame of an archaic-religious restraint. Power was to be exercised jointly, as a communal trust, and hence without qualms of conscience—quite on the contrary, as a matter of duty—and its exercise was coupled with a strict prohibition of any individualism and private pursuit of pleasure.

Rome, in heroic struggles, had just defeated its most dangerous foe, Carthage. Thus its victorious energies were freed for further expansion, an expansion that directed itself toward the rich and highly cultivated countries of the Hellenistic East, into whose incessant disputes it was soon drawn. After a victory over Macedonia, the Roman Senate, in a resolution proclaimed at the Isthmian Games, declared the Greek cities "free." Exactly fifty years later, however, in 146 B.C., Corinth was conquered, plundered, and destroyed by Roman legions. In the next hundred years almost the entire domain of Hellenism was incorporated under Roman rule: "A Roman intervention, as we now know, meant for her political opponents destruction, humiliation, and demoralization."[65]

This subjugation by a foreign power of alien stock, of alien language, and of an alien, rustically powerful but barbarically gloomy civilization, might have signified the end not only of Greek society in its independent political-social existence, but also the end of the Greek culture created and sustained by this society. The outcome was otherwise, and this was the consequence of an unusual stroke of fate. After the battle of Pydna (168 B.C.) the Romans, with custom-

ary brutality, had demanded that the Achaean League deport to
Italy a thousand hostages from the upper classes. Among them was
the Greek historian Polybius (201-119 B.C.), whose historical work
made him the first worthy successor of Thucydides. He came to
Rome after 166 B.C. and there made contact with the Scipio family,
which had adopted a son of the victor of Pydna. This highly gifted
son, later known as Scipio the Younger (185-129 B.C.), found in
Polybius his Socrates; following the traditions of his father as well
as those of his adoptive family, he later became the greatest and
most successful Roman general of his time, shaping the direction of
Roman policy for decades. This fateful encounter became decisive
when Rome opted for the full acceptance of Greek culture, overcoming the opposition led by Cato (234-149 B.C.). Polybius had transmitted to the young Scipio an indelible impression of the loftiness of the
Greek spirit. The rising statesman, moreover, was instinctively
aware that a world could be ruled only on the basis of its highest
cultural achievements and in a manner altogether different from
sheer external domination.

The acceptance of Greek culture inaugurated by Scipio and his
circle continued for a century and reached its apogee in Lucretius
(98-55 B.C.) and Cicero (106-43 B.C.). The great didactic poem of Lucretius surpasses his Greek sources and models, notably the prose
expositions of the doctrine of Epicurus. Cicero, probably the most
fruitful transmitter in world literature, cast the rich and noble ideas
of Greek popular philosophy into that form in which it continued to
exercise its enlivening influence until the eighteenth century.

Thus unfolded the first and fundamental phase of that amazing
event for which Cicero posed the famous epigrammatic description:
Vincebamur a victa Graecia—Conquered Greece our conqueror, or,
in the fuller formulation of Horace, *Graecia capta ferum victorem
cepit, et artis intulit agresti Latio* (Captive Greece took captive her
crude victor, and brought the arts to rustic Latium).[66] The climactic
closing of Rome's first Hellenistic phase came with Caesar, the admirer of Alexander, the last and the greatest of the Diadochi, the
Roman heir of Alexander the Great. Had he not been assassinated
at the peak of his influence, he would have foreshortened the later
development of the Roman empire into a Hellenistic-Oriental Sul-
tanate. The orientalization of Hellenism, already in progress, would
have gained new momentum. The ultimate result would have been
a Byzantinization of western Rome.

Yet Augustus, after further bloody confusion, stepped into the
breach created by Caesar's assassination. He changed its course, in

deliberate contrast to his deified, adoptive father. He brought a twofold classicism to the increasingly orientalized, Hellenistic direction of Roman development: a return to the highest ideals and values of the Roman past as they had been idealizingly elaborated under Stoic influence, and to Greek classicism. The Augustan Age stands as one of the great and brilliant zeniths of human history alongside its model, Periclean Athens.

Humanism had first been shaped by the Alexandrians, who first shaped the concepts of classicism and Atticism. The second, Augustan, phase of humanism again reverts to this timeless model of classical values. The cultural policy of Augustus, with calm and moderation, created a barrier that stemmed the murky, rising floods from the East until about 180 A.D., thus affording Western intellectual development a breathing spell of two centuries.

Augustus brought the ideals of *clementia* and *pietas* to the Roman revolution, and he proved himself a classical representative of true humanity.

The Romans' reception not only preserved this superior Greek culture with all its unique and inestimable values and passed it on to posterity; in doing so it also gave to posterity a first example and model of such revival and renewal.

The relief with which mankind, tormented for centuries by external and civil wars, greeted the *pax Augusta* is perhaps best expressed in a contemporary inscription: "The world pacified, the state restored—at last peaceful and happy times have been granted to us."[67] But the empire not only brought peace within but also a high measure of social and democratic equalization. The emperors from Augustus to Marcus Aurelius (with a few inglorious exceptions) could at the same time feel themselves executors of the testament of the Gracchi, for, compared with the republic, the principate signified an unquestionable progressive step in the direction of social justice.

The Augustan Age lasted until A.D. 96: all the Julian and Flavian emperors ruled *ex auctoritate Augusti*, including those—particularly those—who squandered that legacy. The Augustan Age cultivated philosophical education, but its humane and humanistic classicism viewed partisanship for a particular philosophic or theological persuasion as out of place. Such things were best left to the disputatious Greeks. If Augustus himself and Vergil inclined to Stoicism, or Maecenas and Horace considered themselves Epicureans, that was private—a matter of personal taste, and a question of no more import than whether an educated Englishman had studied at Oxford or Cambridge. Socially oriented neo-Stoicism made headway in educated circles; among the lower classes, its influence converged with the ethics of Christianity. The radical ethical demands that were here made of every individual, whether slave or emperor, private or official, were often so uncomfortable for the emperor and his officials as to lead to periodic police roundups against these "philosophers," recognizable by their unkempt full beards. The Stoic Seneca (4 B.C. - A.D. 65), distinguished more by his intelligence, culture, and good will than by his strength of character, became Nero's teacher and minister. This signified a first thrust of philosophy toward the throne—a thrust, however, that was to end with Seneca's deposition and forced suicide; Nero was a most unsuitable candidate for the role of philosopher king. A general expulsion of the "philsophers" followed under Vespasian. With Nerva (96-98), however, neo-Stoicism became the recognized and prevailing philosophy in the empire. Emperors, beginning with Hadrian (b. A.D. 76, reigned 117-138), wore the philosopher's beard, and Marcus Aurelius (b. 121, reigned 161-180) even came to occupy an honorable place in the history of philosophy alongside his revered teacher, the freed slave Epictetus (60-140). *Philosophia militans* had, in barely a century, become *philosophia triumphans*, just as later the Christian Church militant was transformed into the Church triumphant.

The emperors, however, were not Hellenizers only in the intellectual realm. The Greek life-style of the polis, or what remained of it under altered conditions, was their concern. Already under Augustus, "the Roman Empire was to become a commonwealth of self-governing cities."[68] This urbanization now reached its zenith during this period of the Stoic emperors.

> Thus the Empire in the second century presented an absolute monarchy modified by some privileges granted to the higher classes of the Roman citizens and by the self-government of the cities. In truth, the self-government of the cities was almost complete. The imperial bureaucracy very seldom interfered with local city officials. . . . The Roman Empire of the second century was thus a curious mixture of self-governing cities and of an absolute monarchy superimposed on this federation.[69]

The far-reaching administrative independence of the cities constituted a very fortunate counterweight to central absolutism. But a permanent solution to the underlying tension was not found. Even the least degree of urban independence can be maintained only so long as the level of taxation does not exceed a readily bearable minimum. Ideologically, moreover, the cities of the empire still depended on the legacy that had come down to them from the time of the real freedom and independence of the Greek city-states. At that time a glorious ideology had been shaped that no longer really suited the provincial cities of an absolute monarchy no matter how liberally they were ruled.

In the economic and social domains the emperors promoted small-scale enterprise and decentralization of property. Hadrian, in particular, promoted the interests of small peasants and raised the status of the tenant-farmer close to that of the proprietor. "It was Hadrian who promoted in the imperial and public mines the system of letting single pits to small employers or occupants instead of working them by slaves or convicts." "He was the real foster father of the policy inaugurated by Nerva and Trajan and adopted by all the emperors of the second century . . . the policy defending the weak against the strong."[70] Security of travel by land and sea, the remarkable network of roads constantly being extended and improved, the absence of prohibitive tariff barriers, led to an unprecedented development of traffic and upswing in trade: "Everything was accessible, everything known, everything open to commerce."[71]

This Roman imperial period, in the view first asserted by Gibbon, was the happiest epoch in human history. And this Indian summer of the antique world, this happiest epoch of the Roman Empire, was also that of its strongest Hellenization.

Rome's Hellenization, after the preparatory Etruscan and Greater Greece periods, unfolded in three great phases: (1) from Scipio up to Mark Antony and Caesar, direct control of contemporary Hellenism; (2) from Augustus to Flavius, classicism and antioriental purism; (3) from Nerva to Marcus Aurelius, neo-Stoic Hellenism.

In the two following phases—(4) from Commodus to Diocletian, orientalization and barbarization; and (5) from the time of Constantine, Christianization—the cultural emphasis of this process shifts further eastward to non-Greek components of Hellenism.

This incorporation of Rome in the culture area of Hellenism, however, was not a mere unilateral, passive event. The result was a synthesis of Roman and Greek culture, a result that posterity has designated wtih the term *antiquity*. But only part of the Roman tradition entered into this synthesis. Numerous brutal, gloomy, or barbaric components were pushed into the background or excluded as incompatible with the new Greek standards of value and taste. The result was elucidation, enrichment, and humanization. Cicero and Vergil are the two great bearers of this synthesis: for almost two millennia they became the prime representatives of the antique world—a position from which they were first dethroned by German romanticism and the school of classical philology based upon it.

Rome's great historical importance consisted of three major accomplishments: (1) It transmitted Greek culture and thereby rescued it and kept it alive; (2) For the first time, it created in the Roman world-empire a powerful political structure capable of self-defense—a task at which Athens, Sparta, Thebes, Macedonia, and the Diadochian empires all had failed; (3) It made important contributions supplementing Greek culture, and these manly and sober Roman elements came to act as an important counterweight both against the excessively nimble and facile elements of Greek culture, and against the oriental tendencies within Hellenism.

This contribution of Rome to ancient culture has found classic expression in Vergil, the great herald of the Augustan polity:

> Some with more grace may mould the breathing brass,
> And draw from stone, I trow, the living form,
> Plead causes better, map the heavenly paths,
> And tell the rising stars. Roman! be thine
> To sway the world with Empire! These shall be
> Thine arts, to govern with the rule of Peace,
> To spare the weak, and subjugate the proud![72]

The empire of freedom and the empire of law were realized in the Roman Empire and in Roman law, which were Rome's two historic accomplishments. Governmentally, Rome had undergone the typical development associated with the Greek polis, a development from archaic kingship by way of aristocratic and then plutocratic oligarchy toward democratization, through a progressive widening of the circle of citizenship. But this development unfolded at a slower pace, marked by bitter, protracted struggles and numerous setbacks. In addition, this internal political development was outpaced by the external growth of the Roman Empire, which engendered a momentum that fed on itself. Consequently, democratization achieved its zenith not under a republican, but under a monarchical form of government. The autonomism of the empire increasingly required monarchic leadership, a demand Caesar set out to fulfill in a Hellenistic-oriental way, whereas Augustus chose a more Western and democratic model.

The zenith in the science and art of democratic governance had been embodied in Pericles. Augustus saw himself as the Pericles of Rome who understood how to adapt the earlier model to the needs of a world empire that had grown far beyond the confines of a city-state.

What was totally absent in this entire antique legacy was any technique of indirect democracy, any notion of popular representation, and electoral franchise. Ancient political thought was acquainted with either direct democracy or absolutism. The absence of any organizational technique of indirect democracy was the crucial structural flaw of the Roman Empire, and it was the reason why democratic elements such as appeared remained precariously dependent on the good will and the personality of the *princeps*. In short, democracy in Rome was without any institutional embodiment or guarantee, so that the way to despotism, by far personally more convenient and enjoyable to the ruler, always stood open. Then only assassination remained (and was applied often enough) as a corrective and moderating device.

The technique of indirect, electoral democracy, alien to the whole antique world, was developed during the Middle Ages, slowly and tortuously. It is no accident that we still today seem far from final, generally recognized, and satisfying results. Consider, for instance, the dispute over proportional representation, where extreme views pro and con are sharply set against each other.[73]

Although the Roman Empire had assimilated and elaborated traditions of numerous civilized peoples and empires of the ancient world, it resisted change in the domain of civil law. Old Roman jurisprudence was the legal expression of social structure and social outlook: a tenacious peasant individualism, maintenance of a limited family sphere, distance between each person protected under the law, combined with unconditional subordination of all to the general interest. No developed body of law in human history has kept a better balance between freedom of the individual and the unity of the whole.

In Western legal development, outside the sphere of Anglo-American common law, Roman law has been accorded a privileged, prototypical position comparable to that enjoyed by Greek philosophy in the development of Western philosophic and scientific thought. And although the English common law may be ranked as an independent accomplishment alongside Roman law, it is, after all, more recent by one or two millennia, shows many direct or indirect influences of Roman law, and hence does not challenge the priority of Rome's achievement.

The most common criticisms leveled at Roman law concern its individualism, formalism, logical abstraction, and coldness. These, however, are characteristics that mostly belong to the further evolution of Roman law by the Byzantines, by commentators and annotators of the Scholastic period, by the German natural law school of the Enlightenment and especially by the German Roman-law scholars of the nineteenth century.

Roman law is one of the most important legacies of the Republic; its cultivation and elaboration constitute one of the greatest titles to fame of the principate, from Augustus to Marcus Aurelius. If Augustus bestowed upon the most outstanding jurisconsults the right to respond by authority of the *princeps*, this did not signify imperial usurpation of an independent right of authority, but rather recognition and confirmation of this right. Although the imperial council (*consilium principis*) under Hadrian already exercised a centralizing influence, it was not until A.D. 180 that the soldier-emperors established absolute sway in this domain; eradication of senatorial families by the Severi also destroyed the social stratum in which traditional jurisprudence had been handed down. As Max Weber has said: "The downfall of the Roman aristocracy under the Severi was correlated with the decline of the role of responding jurisconsults and parallels a rapidly increasing significance of the imperial rescripts in the practice of the courts."[74] Jurisprudence is subject to centralistic bureaucratization, which Augustus had avoided with a corresponding decline of its productivity.

Roman state and Roman law were the great guarantors of the *pax Romana*, of order and security of law, inaugurated by Augustus and spread across the Western civilized world. In terms of range and content it towers above all previous areas in which peace and security had been established, *pax Sumerica, Babylonica, Persica*. From the *pax Romana*, as we shall see, emerged the *pax Christiana*— which, by way of the *pax Britannica* was transformed into the *pax subhumana* of the nineteenth century; its destruction is the sad accomplishment of our generation.

17. "DECLINE OF THE ANCIENT WORLD": BARBARIZATION OF THE WEST, BYZANTINIZATION OF THE EAST

Had Marcus Aurelius continued Nerva's time-tested principle of adoption "of the best by the best" instead of designating his degenerate son as successor, or if the rebellion organized by Avidius Cassius, directed against this unfortunate successor, had not failed, there is no reason why (as Rostovtzeff suggests) "another pair of emperors of the type of Trajan, Hadrian, and M. Aurelius" should not have emerged.[75]

But the continuation of the regime completely depended upon the sheer chance of succession to the throne, and this indicates the fatal lack of any democratic safeguard in the constitutional structure of the Roman Empire. In its absence, it was tempting for any emperor to slide into absolutism on the oriental model. What prevented despotic behavior was only the emperor's strength of character. At the same time, an emperor had to support himself with real power—that is, the army—according to Caligula's maxim, "Oderint dum metuant" (Let them hate me, as long as they fear me).

Caesar already had entertained the notion of Hellenistic autocracy corresponding to this conception of rulership, but such a development had been deferred for two centuries by his assassination and the succession of Augustus. Caesar had also taken the first step in the direction of military monarchy. His rule was based upon a huge army, ready for combat, unconditionally devoted to him; he exploited his power with Machiavellian cynicism and consolidated it by demagogic, plebiscitarian appeals to the masses—the latter his own invention and in sharp contrast to the traditional hierarchical structures of social integration, which were still abundant. Hence no injustice was involved when this governmental system, inaugurated by him, renewed by Napoleon I, and further elaborated in a trivializing way by Napoleon III, became known by the name of Caesarism.

Rome, as the world's capital, developed into a mammoth city of the worst sort; in a greater measure than Paris ever represented France, Rome represented the Roman Empire. Under Pericles, what had been a well-considered, daring policy of making art and elegant entertainment available to the people at large here degenerated into the threatening clamor of the rabble for "bread and circuses." The decadent cruelty of gladiatorial bouts trampled underfoot the divinity of Sophoclean tragedy.

After the death of Marcus Aurelius, the principate slipped into tyranny. In Saint Augustine's later phrase, the empire, in the absence of justice, became nothing more than a *magnum latrocinium*, a giant robbers' den. The emperor himself became the chief robber who, with his army, tyrannized and plundered the empire. At the time of the "soldier-emperors" the army became the decisive power factor and exercised its role increasingly through brute physical strength. The army set up the emperor—*Exercitus facit imperatorem*—and his head and throne were secure only so long as he enjoyed its favor.

Septimius Severus (193-211), the first full-fledged soldier-emperor, formulated the resulting policy frankly in his cynical maxim: "Enrich the soldiers, then you can despise all the rest of your subjects."[76] His successor, "Comrade" Caracalla (b. 176, reigned 211-217) as he liked to call himself, was of the same opinion: "Nobody needs to have any money except me, so that I can divide it among the soldiers."[77] Army pay increased extraordinarily; so did the tax burden on the civil population over and above oppressive exactions in kind. The natural consequence was "the complete demoralization of Caracalla's soldiers, who were accustomed to behave as if the province were a conquered land."[78] It was a far cry from the cult of discipline that Hadrian had introduced into the army. "The high-born master-soldiers" as they now styled themselves, were the masters of the land.

It was a second superstratification from within—and, so to speak, *ex professo*. And it was this same professionally military character of these new superstratifiers that prevented aristocratic pursuits, refinement, and intellectual development, which usually so rapidly attenuate the process of superstratification. This above all explains the barbaric, raw, and brutal character of this whole period.

The privileged social estates, the *honestiores*, the educated bourgeoisie in the cities and the landed proprietors in the countryside, were robbed of their former rights by the army, but not exempted from their public duties. Rather, they were held liable not only for their own tax payments but also for those of the *humiliores*, the lower estates of their region, the liability being enforced by the emperor as paymaster and commander of the army. For this purpose, these *humiliores* were "bound to the soil" (*glebae adscripti*) or enrolled in obligatory guilds. This retrogressive tax system resulted, by the time of Aurelian (270-275), in a corporative or caste state with hereditary state slavery, based "on the compulsory work of the *humiliores* and the compulsory responsibility of the *honestiores*."[79] The subject existed for the state, not the state for the citizen.

As the well-being of the population, and its ability to pay taxes, decreased apace, the state's financial needs conversely increased due to the policy of systematic bribery of the army by way of pay increases and allowances. Under these burdens the economy finally was simply crushed to the ground. Lactantius writes at the beginning of the fourth century: "Then the number of recipients had become larger than that of the contributors so that, the strength of the colonies having been exhausted, fields were being deserted and cultivated lands once again became woods."[80] The condition of the empire thus was one like Rousseau was to describe much later: "The general effort is devoted to maintaining a governmental authority which its many scattered officials are forever trying either to avoid or to impose. Little enough is left over for the fostering of public well-being, and barely sufficient to guarantee national defense when the need arises. Consequently, when a body politic is too large for its constitution, it tends to collapse under the weight of its own superstructure."[81]

Finally, there was recourse to the device of inflation, so familiar to us today, which had to be pursued by way of currency devaluation. Scarcity of provisions necessarily arose, along with laws and threats of punishment decreed by the same government that was responsible for this state of affairs. Hence we see the full development of that combination of stagnation and inflation, so familiar to us today. The prototype is the great price decree of the year A.D. 301, the *edictum de pretiis rerum venalium*, which, characteristic of Diocletian's cast of mind and style of governance, establishes maximum prices for each and every kind of merchandise on pain of death.

A widespread net of informers (*frumentarii, agentes in rebus*) was the indispensable complement in such a mode of government, informers "who move about everywhere and eavesdrop on what one might have to say."[82]

Caracalla's *Constitutio Antoniniana* of the year 212 had extended Roman citizenship to the consolidated population of the whole empire. This mass regulation, however, brought only a formal improvement for the new citizens while lowering the status of the old citizens. It was a grandiose leveling measure that resulted in progressive massification: At the top, the army headed by an absolutist, deified emperor; below, the great mass of *humiliores* reduced to the condition of state slaves; in between, as taskmasters and slaveholders, the *honestiores*. The whole was bureaucratically administered as a corporate police state with all the characteristics of what Wilhelm Röpke has termed a "command economy": a "centrally administered economy" with the "exclusion of the free choice of profession and of the worksite."[83]

Despite all similarities between the late Roman and modern totalitarian regimes, there are some differences that count in favor of the former. The Roman emperors fell into this system by necessity, not choice; hence residues of humaneness from better times were not persecuted but cherished. The system as such was not glorified and propagandized; rather, the whole age was fully aware of its degeneracy and decline, and everyone fully expected the final catastrophe which, at least in the western part of the empire, was in the immediate offing.

A humane and democratic outlook had been widespread in the Roman Empire of the philosopher-emperors. But there were no institutional safeguards to prevent the fateful reversal of 183-193. What remained as the single positive aim of imperial policy was the will to maintain the empire and its unity by any and all means. Imperial policy was increasingly ensnared in the worst sins Juvenal had warned against: to give up everything that makes life meaningful for the sake of mere survival.[84]

At the apex, it was no longer possible to maintain the personal unity of rule. The dyarchy, a prelude to the later definitive sundering of the two halves of the empire, became in 293 a division into four prefectures, each under one of the two Augusti or two Caesars. After 331 no appeals to the emperor against the decisions of these four praetorian prefects were allowed.

Those wishing to escape the general state slavery either had to flee or join together in robber bands and declare war on society. The consequence was a rapid decline of the security of travel by water or land. The transport of goods had to be carried out under heavy military guard, or if that became too expensive, discontinued. Roads, inns, ports, and other installations fell into ruin. The monetary system increasingly decayed, and the economy lapsed into barter. Taxes, too, had to be converted into payments or services in kind.

Famines broke out and decimated the population. The cities, unable to feed themselves with imported provisions, fell into ruin and were depopulated. As installations for irrigation and of drainage broke down, swamps formed, and malaria and other epidemic diseases became rampant.

The discipline of the army and the reliability of officials in both decayed. As outrages perpetrated by the soldiery and civil wars continued, the empire became less capable of external defense. Open cities, even Rome, once more had to surround themselves with walls. The population rapidly shrank.

Individual landed estates and villages made themselves self-sufficient, at least for minimum needs, since any dependence upon outside sources could endanger survival. Palladius, an agrarian writer of the fourth century, expressly recommends autarchy to lords of the manor.

Only by this growing self-sufficiency "was a situation created . . . on the large landed estates, for which the 'autarchy of the household' (*oikos*) is not an inappropriate designation."[85] Medieval feudalism was a product of this regression and disintegration of the Roman Empire.

Thus the so-called "decline and fall of the Roman Empire" in the final analysis is based upon a general and fatal disease of the social structure, a collapse of its integrative system. It was not the parts, but rather the connections between the parts that failed. The parts were then forced to adapt themselves to this new state of disconnectedness (or at least to the insecurity of the connections) and further to demolish everything that could have lived only through connection with all other parts.

The sack of Rome by Alaric's Goths in 410 and later by the Langobards in 508 were landmarks in this ceaseless decline. The catastrophe of A.D. 410, in particular, is comparable in its impact to the Ionian catastrophe of 546-545 B.C. Until then the decline of the western part of the empire had gone at a gradual, imperceptible pace; now a major historic event demolished the entire structure: Rome, eternal Rome, capital of the world, conquered and sacked by barbarian hordes! The end of an era, the collapse of this world could not be dramatized more sharply in the eyes of contemporaries. It was Saint Augustine who claimed to provide the valid interpretation of this apocalyptic sign and who thereby shaped the future character of Christianity as a religion based in history. Augustine's philosophy of history dominated the entire Middle Ages and provided the basis for that of Bossuet. Only in the Enlightenment with its belief in human progress—in Vico as a precursor and in the law of the three historic stages as developed by Turgot, Saint-Simon, and Comte—was this remarkable Augustinian philosophy of history replaced.

The subsequent reintegration of the atomized world empire occurred in an Indo-Germanic, federalistic way, in contrast to developments in the East, where the tradition of oriental-despotic centralism has been preserved or has renewed itself in a totalitarian way until today.

Accordingly, what we see before us is a negative case of the application of our law of the culture pyramid, culture development backwards. The enormous pyramidal base, which the Roman Empire had formed in its unitary integration, decomposed and crumbled into countless small fragments, and so, *pari passu*, did the culture that had rested upon this integration as its foundation, whose height had corresponded to the breadth of that basis.

The decline through dissolution, just analyzed, was that of the *western* Roman Empire; but the eastern Roman Empire of the Byzantines survived for a full millennium. The fundamental question here is: Upon what did this special development and political coherence of the eastern empire rest?

The answer that the empire simply had not been threatened by external foes in the same measure probably applies, but only in a very limited sense. Apart from the fact that its northern borders were exposed at least in the same measure to incursions of barbarian nomads and semi-nomads as was the western empire, the empires of the Sassanids and of the Arabs were even more redoubtable enemies than any Germanic hordes. Byzantine resistance throughout the centuries proves that internal cohesion here was more solid. What made the difference?

Hellenism was a mélange of Greek and oriental components, the proportions of this mixture being different according to time and place. The oriental components were considerably stronger in the East. These were largely embodied in the urban lower strata of the eastern provinces, superstratified by Hellenism, and indigenous to the eastern half of the empire. Accordingly, the eastern half could not be expected to join, and did not in fact join, in a movement like Augustan purism, which originated as a reaction against these very elements. It was this Augustan movement, as we have seen, that marked the beginning of cultural schism between East and West—a schism that had its solid foundation in the difference in language. For, despite some encroachments either way, Greek remained the prevailing language in the East, and Latin in the West.

The prevailing Roman element, which signified a strong "westernization," found no strong resonance in the East. When strong oriental trends developed in the rulership of the whole empire, this signified internal disunity and tension for the West; but for the East it signified inner unification, a return to its past despotism. The Byzantine Caesaropapism of the eastern church was also consonant with the eastern tradition of divine kingship. In the West, the tension between church and state resulted in dyarchy—which, whatever its cultural consequences, had contributed to undermining and weakening rather than strengthening the state and its central authority.

"The new Rome, which is Constantinople," was founded anew by Constantine in the years 326-330, without the tension-ridden and menacing past of old Rome, as an absolutist royal residence on the site of the old Dorian colony and port city of Byzantium.

In the East, Hellenist tradition was orientalized; in the West, the Roman element worked as a strong counterweight against oriental influence. Also, Augustus had followed a deliberate deorientalizing policy. Thus, in the eastern Roman Empire the specifically Hellenic element, which for its full flowering requires that same freedom in which it originated, was suffocated under the predominant weight of its oriental-theological components. Byzantine culture is an arrested form of Hellenism; the eastern church is Platonic, the western church becomes more and more Aristotelian.

The Islamic empire of the Arabs, based on violent new superstratification, was a formation parallel to the Byzantine Empire, but more "oriental" both in the literal and transferred meanings of that term. These three great empires—western Roman, eastern Roman, and Arabian—all inherited Hellenism, and in many ways the Persian element in the Arabian empire corresponds to the Roman element in the western empire. From many points of view, we can consider even the Abbasid caliphs of Baghdad "executors" and successors of Alexander the Great.

Acceptance of the Hellenistic cultural legacy by the Arabs occurred in several phases, each accompanied by a notable cultural upswing. Within a century and a half of Muhammad's death, almost the whole area to which Hellenism had expanded (including Syria and Egypt, but not Greece itself or Asia Minor) had been conquered by Islam. The resulting cultural upswing reached its apogee under Harun al-Rashid (786-809) and his son, the enlightened Hellenophile Mamun (813-833). Islam, through the Arab world empire, arrived much earlier at broad-minded and liberal conditions than did the Christian West; in breadth of base and height of apex, its culture pyramid may be compared with that of the Roman Empire in 200 A.D. Consequently, theological limitations and prejudice, especially in pre-Turkish Islam, were incomparably weaker than in medieval Christianity. In the Christian Middle Ages, Arab scholars were in disrepute as freethinkers, and the sympathy that later Enlightenment thinkers showed toward Islam (as well as Confucianism) was justified on this basis. Receptivity to ancient philosophical legacies was already well developed in the flourishing Baghdad of the ninth century, so that it would be appropriate to speak of an Abbasid humanism. Indeed, important ancient currents of tradition reached the West first by way of Islam, through translations from Arabic with Arabic commentaries. Hence also the Arabs' advanced position in philosophy, mathematics, natural science, and medicine—as well as in economics, as recent research indicates. In the West, Christian economic thought until the eighteenth century was dominated by the notion of a "just price" enforced by secular authority. But Arab thought, at least from the ninth century onward, moved toward advocacy of a free market price based on supply and demand and justified by reference to a *hadith* (a saying attributed to the Prophet himself), which undermined the setting of prices by government authorities.

The intellectual upswing in the Christian West at the end of the eleventh century was conditioned by its adoption of Arabic mathematics, natural science, medicine, and philosophy as well as by adaptation of Aristotle's writings from Arabic translations.

The second phase of Hellenistic reception by Islam came with the conquest of the Byzantine Empire, which was followed by that period of political strength and rich cultural development of Ottoman absolutism that extends from the conquest of Constantinople (1453) to the reign of Suleiman the Magnificent (1520-1566) and antedates the corresponding development of Western absolutism by two centuries. The assumption of the Byzantine cultural legacy was considerably facilitated by the tolerance with which Muhammad II ("the Conqueror") not only confirmed the competence of the orthodox patriarch of Constantinople, but also broadened it to include civil jurisdiction over the faithful, and with which he brought the Armenian patriarch from Bursa to Constantinople.

The Byzantine Empire, in its desperate struggle for the last centuries, had been not just abandoned but actually betrayed by the Latin Christendom of the West. Now, with the Ottoman conquest, the resulting intra-Christian tensions for the first time subsided. To a West which, as a result of the Reformation and Counter Reformation, had fallen back into the medievality of schism, religious wars, and confessional persecution, the Ottomans' consistently rationalistic centralism proved at first clearly superior. The West in turn began to overcome its handicap with the development of rationalism and absolutism in the seventeenth century. In the age of the Enlightenment, the forces of the Renaissance triumphed over those of theology, just as in the French Revolution those of democracy triumphed over those of absolutism; and only at this point was the world of Islam no longer able to keep pace.

The imperial coronation of Charlemagne by Pope Leo III on Christmas Day of the year 800 created a Frankish-Christian *imperium* whose ruler, as the new Constantine, was to protect the Roman church and Catholic Christendom. The new empire considered itself a continuation of the old *imperium romanum*, so that the imperial coronation of 800 was viewed as the *translatio imperii ad francos*, in accord with the verse in Ecclesiasticus 10:8: "Empire passes from nation to nation."

Roman law, revived at the same time, was considered the law of the *imperium romanum* and contributed considerably to strengthening the sense of continuity.

Since Holy Rome remained the seat of the pope, a kind of dyarchy was created by this renewal of Roman imperial power; the pope named the emperor his coregent, so that there were now two Caesars.

This transfer of the imperial title gave to the Roman emperors of the German nation incomparable prestige but also lured them into unrealistic ambitions in their foreign policy. Italy, through its combination of cultural brilliance and political weakness, exercised an irresistible attraction. But repeated attempts at outreach toward Italy failed.

Had the emperors succeeded in making the Holy Roman Empire a political reality, history might have taken a very different course. As it was, much energy was squandered, and Germany and Italy became the only European countries where particularist forces carried the day in the lengthy struggle between crown and estates. As a result, in both Germany and Italy, the development of the centralized nation-state encountered great obstacles, and the drastic measures adopted to remove them have had their baneful effects to this day.

18. CHRISTIANITY, THE CHURCH, AND THE MIDDLE AGES

The religion of the Greeks and Romans, like that of all original human communities, was a "natural" religion: a religion of nature, a religion of acceptance of this world, a religion permeating all of life and thus quietly taken for granted, a religion into which one was born and with which one grew up as one grew up into other aspects of human life. It enhanced community life, was part of festive occasions, and was used in ceremonial art. The notion of individual salvation was alien because no one felt the need for salvation. There were religious legends, but no religious doctrine, no theology, no dogma, no message of salvation; consequently there was neither orthodoxy nor heresy. Neither Greeks nor Romans ever created any religion of salvation of their own; when they finally came to feel a need for salvation, they satisfied it by importations from the East.

This can be observed in the Persian catastrophe of 546-545 B.C., after Plato's Sicilian debacle, and especially after the Peloponnesian War in 404 B.C. After 546 Ionian philosophy had absorbed Eastern influences but had processed and mastered them in such a way that human reason and human self-consciousness retained the upper hand. It was thus with Plato in his old age and with superstitious disciples like Xenocrates. Although Plato did not create a new religion, he and his successors were indeed philosophers of salvation; although understanding and experience remained as sources of knowledge, the purpose of such knowledge now was to serve the individual's need for salvation. Salvation of the individual through his own knowledge and through action consonant with that knowledge, the securing of inner freedom through entrenchment in the realm of the spirit—these philosophic attitudes remained sufficient for the needs of the educated classes until a fateful turning point, marked by the death of Marcus Aurelius, the Stoic philosopher and Roman emperor, in A.D. 180.

By contrast, this highly intellectual and all-too-scientific philosophy of salvation had, for a long time, not met the emotional needs of the poor and downtrodden. Rapid urbanization in the empire of Alexander and the Diadochi created a city proletariat. This proletariat was quite large and uprooted in the bigger cities, especially Alexandria, Rome, and later Constantinople. Most of this proletariat consisted of slaves, the more skillful and intelligent of whom were often freed. But freedmen were often in a worse legal position than slaves: they enjoyed no citizenship and lacked control over their own fate. They became receptive to the passionate fraternity of sects. This was a natural breeding ground for genuine religions of salvation, which poured in from the East in many variations.

After A.D. 180, the situation in the empire grew increasingly worse. "The world has grown old," wrote Cyprian, Bishop of Carthage, to a pagan in 253: "It no longer stands in the plenitude of its power, no longer in the freshness that formerly distinguished it. Do you believe that the force of life can still dwell in an aging thing, from which in time a fresh vigorous youth might flow? The spring which formerly gushed forth from overflowing veins dries up in old age and flows sluggishly only with a few drops."[86]

As atomization and massification increase, the natural structures of integration disintegrate, and the need grows for a kind of pseudo-integration. "In the heavily laden atmosphere of oppression and powerlessness, crushed souls aspire with an ineffable ardor to escape toward the radiant spaces of the sky."[87]

The need for salvation and the longing for salvation became more general and irresistible, finally determining the intellectual signature of the age. Salvation was sought in the fourth dimension of the invisible, the mysterious, the Beyond—a world that does not disclose itself through knowledge accessible to everyone but through revelation and illumination granted only to specially blessed individuals. The Pythagorean maxim "When it is a question of gods or divine doctrines, believe everything, be it ever so amazing" is first recorded in this period,[88] and it was never more generally or more freely followed. Renan speaks of a "public become credulous."[89] As inaccessibility to sense and understanding became a criterion of a loftier revealed wisdom, religion was soon considered all the loftier the more it contradicted sense and understanding, and one finally arrived at the doctrine of *Credo quia absurdum*: I believe it *because it is absurd*.[90]

The new mental attitude found expression in the portrait sculptures of the late imperial age with their ascetic emaciation, tormented features, and staring eyes. In the Vienna marble bust of Eutropius of Ephesus, we see "no longer a man of the antique world, but a servant of God."[91] The literature of the time (ca. 332-400) exhibits distinctly narcissistic features. Architecture, seen through the enormous format of space, seems to ask man to feel the agonizing sense of nothingness; "Man appears paltry in such halls and under such domes with their high vaults."[92]

Emperors increasingly felt the need for religious underpinning of their political positions, to enhance their authority through the claims of salvation religions. Caligula let himself be called *dominus et deus*, and the despotic rulers Nero and Domitian emulated him. After Commodus, self-deification of the emperor became standing custom: Heliogabalus (204-218) gave himself the name of his Syrian sun-god of Emesa, and Aurelian (270-275) established himself as the son of this god and sun-emperor. Constantine had himself represented as Helios on huge columns in Constantinople. The Sassanian empire, with its Mazdean religion, must have suggested to Romans the idea of placing religion also in the service of their state. Thus arose state religion and state theology, structurally different from the nontheological state cults of the Greek cities, of the Roman Republic, or even of the Roman principate. The concept of orthodoxy was now asserted by the state, and as a direct consequence there was government persecution of heretics—first Christian, later pagan.

What made salvation religions superior to "natural" religions was mainly the formers' dynamic character. "Natural" religions, subordinated to natural cycles, are static and repetitive. They tacitly suggest that one feels well and at home in the eternal present. Once the present has become unbearable, once man feels helplessly delivered over to a catastrophic fate, and once all hope is focused on a

better future—in this world or in the next world or, in chiliastic am-
biguity, in both—then a "natural" religion that hallows the here
and now must seem like sheer mockery. What now is needed is a
religion not of the present but of the future, a religion that sanctifies
the longed-for better future and prescribes the path toward it. What
is needed is the assurance not that things will remain but that they
will change totally—in short, a numinous philosophy of religion, a
religion of salvation imbued with extreme historic dynamism.

Vergil's Fourth Eclogue impressively conveys this feeling of a
need for the historic dynamism of a salvation religion; indeed, it
is a compendium of all relevant thought then found in the Roman
Empire. This is not the place to discuss each of the religious cults
that responded to these needs and among which now one and now
the other gained ascendance—Mithras and Serapis, Isis and the
Great Mother, solar monotheism, Persian dualism, Manichaeanism,
Babylonian-Chaldean astrology, Neoplatonism and syncretic Gnosticism—all these surged together in a whirlpool of confusion. But we
know that this religious pluralism ended with the rise of Christianity, which finally emerged the winner in this struggle for souls and
for the state.

Christianity had originated among the people of Israel, to whom
Jesus felt a passionate and exclusive allegiance. Israel is a peculiar,
indeed a singular phenomenon, and it decisively stamped the character of the Christianity that sprang from it. Israel's beginnings, as
far as they are known to us, emerge relatively late, about the second
half of the second millennium B.C., at a time when high cultures had
existed in Mesopotamia and Egypt for almost two millennia. During
the Aramaic migration, wandering clans of small herdsmen trickled
into Palestine; the land, not yet occupied or cultivated, was only of
moderate fertility, but compared with the deserts and steppes it appeared like the promised land, flowing with milk and honey. The
Israelites, living first in tents and primarily engaged in sheep breeding, turned to farming, which required very hard physical labor.
The arable soil seemed cursed: "Cursed is the ground for thy sake; in
sorrow shalt thou eat of it all the days of thy life; thorns also and
thistles shall it bring forth to thee . . . in the sweat of thy face shalt
thou eat bread" (Gen. 3:17-19).

But these migrated clans felt tied to each other through kinship,
language, work habits, customs, and related religious attitudes;
these common bonds were later interpreted as evidence of descent
from a common tribal ancestor.

The Palestinian settlers formed at first not a political but a religious union, subdivided into twelve tribes—a number corresponding to the months of the year according to a very common practice of the time. The central shrine was the "ark," which, being portable, could often change its seat. But aside from subordinate sacred services, in which probably the representatives of each tribe took their monthly turns throughout the year, a permanent priesthood must have belonged to such a central shrine. The concept of the unity of a single god, the consciousness of Israel's unity as a single people, and the notion of the unity of mankind in a single history are the major intellectual accomplishments of this central priesthood—accomplishments the significance of which for all later history can hardly be overrated.

The previous religious and cultic representations of the immigrated clans had not been altogether harmonious and uniform. In his solemn farewell address Joshua (24:14-15) says: "Put away the gods which your fathers served on the other side of the flood [i.e., the Euphrates] and in Egypt; and serve ye the Lord. And if it seem evil unto you to serve the Lord, choose you this day whom ye will serve; whether the gods which your fathers served that were on the other side of the flood, or the gods of the Amorites, in whose land ye dwell." This illustrates transfer of some groups to the Yahweh religion through a change of faith; it was given the form of a contract, and this form of the *berith Yahweh* was then generalized to Israel's relation to its God.

Later passages mention a merciful act by Yahweh in which he chose the people of Israel as his people. Moses states: "For thou art a holy people unto the Lord thy God: the Lord thy God hath chosen thee to be a special people unto himself, above all the people that are upon the face of the earth" (Deut. 7:6-8).

A contractual relationship between a people and its God, repeatedly renewed in solemn form, makes observance of the contract appear as the most important religious concern, and every violation as the gravest of sins. Moral obligations (concerning the behavior of fellow Israelites toward each other) stand next to cultic obligations; as a result, the moral injunction to holiness acquired great importance. Initially, Israel appraised the gods of other peoples as inferior, and then disputed their existence. The end result was an uncompromising and exclusive monotheism, such as is here encountered for the first time in the history of human religion: Yahweh is a jealous god, and he boasts of his exclusiveness and intolerance.

This centralist monotheism had logical consequences, although the contingent historical development does not unfold according to the rules of logic. If this single god existed, he must also be creator and ruler of the whole world, including all other peoples. These other peoples did not believe in him and did not serve him; rather, it was Israel that served him, had a sacred contractual relation with him; in consequence, Israel became the "chosen people" of this single god elevated above all others.

The god of the primordial and archforebears, the god of Abraham, the god of Israel, the god of Jacob, the volcano-god, the god of Sinai, the god of Horeb, the weather god who speaks with a thunderous voice from the clouds, the god who had rescued them from Egyptian bondage as they fled from their pursuers, the god who had laid upon them the cultic, legal, and ethical injunctions and who watched over their contractually sealed observance—all these could be, inasmuch as none other existed, only the one and the same God, Yahweh.

The numinous experiences of the various clans were now sequentially arranged as though they had been a single stream of experience of the single people of Israel. To the extent that these experiences were geographically bound to a definite place, this implied, in zigzag fashion, a corresponding migration of the whole people. No consideration was taken of the fact that migratory herdsmen, for technical reasons of pastoral life, could by no means move in such large formations. Abraham at first was named as the leader of the exodus from Egypt, a position later accorded to Moses: this must have been the most recent of these experiences and therefore the one most deeply etched in memory.

To this temporal serialization of salvation experiences were added legends of creation, paradise, original sin, the flood, etc. A new theme of historical salvation, of pagan origin, is introduced in the Book of Daniel (167-164 B.C.): the doctrine of the four world kingdoms, of the conquest of Jerusalem of Nebuchadnezzar, leading to the eternal kingdom of God shortly to follow upon the latter event.

For a settled people, impressions and experiences are related to the immediate environment: heights, trees, boulders, springs; and, in addition, to self-established cult signs: stone monuments, altars, graves, and chapels. Wandering peoples leave all such things behind, and heaven is the only numinous object that for them always remains the same. The monistic belief in the god of heaven literally imposes itself upon them.

For nomads, the only entity that remains unchanging is the nomadic clan. The members of the clan are dependent upon each other. Outwardly isolated, internally unified, they stand under strong integrative pressures. The clan is one and all to them. For the nomadic clan the change of generations, the death of the aged, the birth of the young repeatedly unfold during migration. The clan sets its hopes on posterity, and this tends to foster dynamic thinking.

Now nomadic herdsmen have existed in many places and many times; everywhere they stand under these conditions of their life situation. But only in one case has that, by transfer from the clan to the people, led to so exemplary a manifestation as with the people of Israel. The final results were monotheism, the notion of a chosen people set apart from all others, and a uniform consciousness of history spanning the past and the future of mankind.

The Israelites, unlike most other nomads, never established themselves as genuine superstratifiers, but remained democratic. There was no superincumbency over the Canaanites, who had inhabited the territory and they were, generally, absorbed in the course of time. There was no social estate or class distinction into an upper stratum and lower stratum. There were, of course, servants in the status of slaves already in the nomadic period, but they belonged to the family and were treated humanely—which explains why a cohesive social lower stratum was not formed.

The religious union of the twelve tribes was for a long time restricted to this loose form of cultic association, with temporary association for war only in emergencies. Outside the common shrine and its priesthood, there was only a charismatic "judge," who if necessary also assumed command of the army. The pressure and the model of surrounding kingdoms finally suggested the need to imitate them. The judge Samuel therefore annointed Saul as king, but this first attempt miscarried. Full success came only under the next king, David. Not only did he unite the northern tribes of Israel with his southern tribes of Judah, between which he placed Jerusalem as common capital and shrine, but he struck out further. With a combination of military and political skill he established a realm that might even be called an empire—although it did not claim world dominion.[93]

Here, in the courts of David and Solomon, in a closed vital sphere of court and city, in a perspective of magnanimity and spaciousness, and with assured peace since the consolidation of David's rule, there now developed a remarkable literary growth, in the narrative prose containing the accounts of David's rise and Solomon's succession in the Second Book of Samuel and the First Book of Kings. Gerhard von Rad has called these events and the atmosphere from which these accomplishments stemmed, a "typical Enlightenment" and "Solomonian and post-Solomonian humanism." "This Solomonian

Age was indeed the age . . . of a wholly new intellectual start, a kind of Enlightenment, i.e. the age of an awakening of human self-consciousness. Man became aware of his intellectual powers, of his ordering understanding; wholly new dimensons of his environment emerged in this field of vision—not least, man himself, his psychic complexity, the enigmatic unfathomable debt of his inner self. All this entered the field of vision as an utter novelty—as did the possibility of capturing all of human life in narrative imagery."[94] Old Testament scholars call these two pieces historiographical works and designate them as the beginning of the written history of ancient Israel. At the same time, however, they are the earliest and highly important works of what we would now call *belles-lettres*— separation into genres not yet having occurred. They can more readily be classified as short novels, since they "present something altogether new and are at once masterworks of their kind. Beyond that they are completely singular in the whole world of the old Orient. . . . Thus, historical expositions in connection with temporal events emerged from Israel in the Davidian-Solomonian age, long before history writing existed in Greece or in the world known to us."[95]

Beginning with Saul, the Israelite kings behave not much differently from other oriental despots. The great difference was that a man of God always emerged to brand their behavior with the condemnation it deserved and to threaten it with divine punishment. In other words, kings are not absolute. Above them stands a higher norm, also represented by an earthly authority.

Every dynasty, in the Near East particularly, hoped for permanent existence and confirmed this solemnly through their high priests. Thus King David is notified of the following prophecy by his court prophet Nathan: "When thy days be fulfilled, and thou shalt sleep with thy fathers, I will set up thy seed after thee, which shall proceed out of thy bowels, and I will establish his kingdom . . . forever. I will be his father, and he shall be my son. If he commit iniquity, I will chasten him with the rod of men. . . . But my mercy shall not depart away from him. . . . And thine house and thy kingdom shall be established for ever . . ." (2 Sam. 7:12-16).

This solemn divine promise was extended backward to the forefather, Abraham. The unshakable faith in it has ever since conditioned the whole history of the people of Israel; indeed, we can even consider the rise of the present state of Israel as the latest link in this chain of fate.

More immediately and without restriction, however, the promise was barely kept for one generation to the end of the reign of David's successor, Solomon. Immediately after the latter's death, Israel separated from Judah, and David's great kingdom collapsed.

The smaller, southern state of Judah was ruled by David's descendants and included as its capital Jerusalem, with the Temple and the ark. The larger, northern state of Israel was convulsed by incessant bloody feuds over succession to the throne. It was clear that neither of these small states could play an independent role between the great powers of Egypt and Mesopotamia.

Israel became an Assyrian province in 722-721 B.C.; its upper stratum was deported and replaced by a newly installed group. Judah could maintain itself only as an Assyrian satellite. The subsequent fall of Assyria was used by Josiah (639-609 B.C.), of David's dynasty, to reunite Judah and Israel, and, beyond that, to attempt to broaden his rule according to David's model. At the same time he continued through the composition of Deuteronomy (in its original form, at least) to consolidate Israel religiously. In 609 B.C., however, he was killed in battle against the Egyptians, whose brief domination was replaced by the neo-Babylonian rule or the Chaldeans under Nebuchadnezzar.

In 587 B.C. Jerusalem and the Temple were destroyed, and the upper stratum was deported to Mesopotamia. The preservation and continuance of intellectual and religious tradition now lay in the hands of exiles. For these Israelites "living in the Diaspora," the greatest danger was one of losing religious traditions and being absorbed by the "pagan" ambience. Differences from other peoples and separation in all departments was stressed: "Therefore God preserves us on all sides with laws of ritual purity in the matter of eating, drinking, touching and seeing."

These misfortunes might have been taken to refute the divine promises to King David and could have led to the abandonment of the hopes based on them—as indeed happened with all other peoples in corresponding situations. And that would have meant the end of Israel. That it turned out otherwise was the intellectual achievement of the great prophets, active already in the middle of the ninth century B.C. They accomplished a revolution of truly Copernican dimensions in human historical consciousness by interpreting all of Israel's misfortunes not as a refutation of divine promises but, on the contrary, as just and educative punishment for the disobedience, the breaches of the covenant, and other sins committed by his chosen people. Previously Yahweh had been seen to be active only within the confines of Israel itself; now, by contrast, the overpowering enemies of Israel—Egypt, Assyria, Babylon—were interpreted as instuments of his omnipotent will, and thereby a devastating liability transformed into a magnificent asset. Besides, there was now no longer any historical event that could not, in one way or another, be fitted into this theological scheme.

And shortly, a historical event occurred that could be interpreted as proof of God's mercy. This was the replacement of the hated neo-Babylonian kingdom by the Persian empire of Cyrus the Great; his typical Indo-European liberality benefited the oppressed Babylonian priesthood of Marduk as much as it did the priesthood of Yahweh and his holy city of Jerusalem. Thus we read in Isaiah (44:28, 45:3-4) that the Lord "saith of Cyrus, he is my shepherd, and shall preform all my pleasure: even saying to Jerusalem, Thou shalt be built; and to the temple, Thy foundation shall be laid . . . that thou mayest know that I, the Lord, . . . am the God of Israel. For Jacob my servant's sake, and Israel mine elect. . . ." The text of the corresponding proclamation by Cyrus has also been handed down to us (2 Chron. 36:23; Ezra 1:1-4): "Thus saith Cyrus king of Persia, All the kingdoms of the earth hath the Lord God of heaven given me; and he hath charged me to build him a house in Jerusalem, which is in Judah. Who is there among you of all his people? . . . His God be with him, and let him go up to Jerusalem, which is in Judah, and build the house of the Lord God of Israel (he is the God), which is in Jerusalem." The new temple was consecrated in 515 B.C., with the "high priests" as the apex of the hierarchy. After the fifth century B.C., one of the deportees, on the grounds of his high position in the court of the Persian king, was appointed governor of the separate province of Judaea (succeeding the kingdom of Judah) and was commissioned to rebuild the walls of Jerusalem. He consolidated the social structure of his province through a remission of debts. Ezra was dispatched as the royal Persian "state commissar for the law of the God of heaven." "What in this period assumed shape and was embarked upon remained of importance for the whole further course of the history of Israel up to its end."[96]

The transfer of rulership from the Persian king to Alexander the Great seems to have brought no radical change even after Alexander's death. Judaea and Jerusalem at first belonged to the Ptolemies, until Antiochus III (198 B.C.) incorporated Phoenicia and Palestine in his Seleucid kingdom. In a gracious decree he confirmed and broadened all the privileges hitherto granted to the temple and its cult.

The gradual Hellenization of the Near East began with Alexander. It took the form of an acceptance of Greek cultural influence and a general reciprocal tolerance. Even Israel was not averse to such Hellenization. In the fourth century B.C. some silver coins in Jerusalem were stamped with the Athenian owl, others with Zeus on his throne. In the third century B.C., the holy texts were translated into heathen Greek (the so-called Septuagint), and around 175 B.C. the ruling high priest had a gymnasium built in Jerusalem. (See 2 Macc. 4:13f.) Even the Maccabees themselves and their followers were Hellenized to such an extent that the idea of fame accruing to an individual for heroic deeds played an essential role for them.

"In those days went there out of Israel wicked men [the assimilationists], who persuaded many, saying, Let us go and make a covenant with the heathen that are round about us . . ." (1 Macc. 1:11). These "wicked men" now "began to put forth their heads in all the coasts of Israel" (ibid., 9:23). For these pro-assimilationists "remained Jews," although "freethinking."[97] They honored "the God of Heaven of their forefathers, without temple and statues under the sky on the altar, which stood on Zion, free from the yoke of the law in reciprocal tolerance at once with the heathens. What can be more human, more natural, than their desire to force this tolerance on their still-deluded coreligionists? This was the persecution of Epiphanes."[98] "King Antiochus [Epiphanes]"—so reports Tacitus later "strove to destroy the nation's superstition, and to introduce Greek civilization, but was prevented by his war with the Parthians from . . . improving this vilest of nations" (*Histor*. 5. 9). This movement of forced assimilation might have been successful if the king had not gone too far. The details of the tumultuous events do not emerge clearly from the sources, but the privileges earlier granted were rescinded, heathen sacrifices ordered, circumcision forbidden, the Temple looted, and an altar to Olympian Zeus erected on Mount Zion. In this precipitate fashion the "zenith of Hellenism" (2 Macc. 4:13) had been reached in 167 B.C. This led to the revolt of the Maccabees (160 B.C.), whose leader was called Maccabaeus ("the Hammerer"). That the Maccabees finally triumphed after much bloodshed and were able to establish the Hasmonaean dynasty was due to the ruthless determination and religious fanaticism of these defenders of the faith.

Describing the Maccabees, a devout and distinguished Jewish historian wrote in 1937: "Had they been defeated, the light of monotheism would have been snuffed out." "For the success of the measures taken by Epiphanes would have signified the end of

Judaism and would thereby have also made the rise of Christianity and Islam impossible."[99] As a statement of historical causality, this assertion is indisputable—regardless of how one may evaluate the phenomenon of monotheism.

In order to put an end to the confusion surrounding succession to the thrones of the Hasmonaeans, the Romans intervened after 65 B.C., and Pompey conquered Jerusalem, capturing the Temple, in 63 B.C. Despite reasonable Roman administrative regulations, the only consequence was to draw Palestine into the turmoil of the Roman civil war. Herod the Great, king of Judaea by the grace of Mark Antony after 37 B.C., knew how to survive the passage of power to Octavian. He came to enjoy the favor of Augustus, sharing in the benefits of the *pax augusta* as "allied king" until his death in 4 B.C. The division of the kingdom between his heirs, as provided for in Herod's will, proved unstable. Judea, along with Jerusalem, was subjected to a Roman procurator with a seat in Caesarea (an office held by Pontius Pilate from A.D. 26 to 36). Herod Antipas ruled Galilee and Peraea from 4 B.C. to A.D. 39 as tetrarch under Roman sovereignty.

The series of "good" emperors from Augustus to Marcus Aurelius had been briefly interrupted by the Caesarean madness of some "wicked" emperors, and these interruptions were more readily evident at court and in Rome than in the empire. The empire enjoyed the blessings of imperial peace. This peace was felt to a lesser degree in Palestine, the reason being the violent, religiously caused, internal disorders. After a chain of smaller incidents between Zealots and Sicarii ("Stabbers") came the revolt of Eleazar, which was put down by Titus in A.D. 70. The remnants of resisters held out as late as A.D. 73. The Temple was looted, went up in flames, and was never rebuilt. From then, Jewry existed only in the Diaspora.

The last sword-wielding Messiah was Simon ben Kosiba, upon whom Rabbi Akiba later bestowed the Messianic name Bar Kochba ("Son of the stars"). He was able to have his own coins minted bearing the inscription "Simon, Prince of Israel," but was killed in battle in A.D. 135. A Roman provincial capital city, Aelia Capitolina, was built on the site of Jerusalem, but entry was forbidden to Jews on penalty of death. The country received the name of Palestine to honor the memory of the Philistines, rather than that of Israel.

But a century before this, in A.D. 28, an ascetic prophet had appeared on the banks of the Jordan proclaiming the imminence of the Kingdom of God. He called those who wanted to escape the threatening Last Judgment to repentance and inner transformation. As a sacrament of this transformation, he baptized those who had confessed and repented their sins by immersion in the Jordan. Of John the Baptist, we are told in Luke 3:15, "The people were in expectation, and all men mused in their hearts of John, whether he were the Christ, or not." The four Evangelists vie with each other to assure us that this is not the case, that John is not the Messiah, but only his precursor. In the Acts of the Apostles (13:25) Paul has John say: "Whom think ye that I am? I am not he." John (1:8) says of him: "He was not that Light, but was sent to bear witness of that Light." And soon thereafter (1:20) with fourfold emphasis it is stated: "And he confessed, and denied not; but confessed, I am not the Christ." This quite vigorous effort would have been superfluous and incomprehensible if there were not followers who still considered the Baptist the Messiah (and who accordingly had to reject Jesus because the Messiah can have a precursor, but not a successor). But such followers exist even today, although only in the last remnants. These are the Mandaeans, who worship John the Baptist, practice "Jordan" baptisms, and reject Christ as a false prophet: i.e., they espouse the very position that the Evangelists combat with such an expenditure of energy.

When John the Baptist was arrested and put to death, his followers, if they were not to fall into despair and hopelessness, had to look for a new point of crystallization for their eschatological hopes.

Jesus, mighty herald and miracle worker, baptized by John, had been repeatedly invoked as Son of God, Son of David, the Anointed (Christ, Messiah). Of his disciples, it would appear that Peter was the first to acknowledge him. If there is nothing historical in this account—a historical kernel to which subsequently the later community legend could attach itself—the recognized preeminence of Peter (of whom otherwise we have accounts only of human failings or rash impetuosity) is difficult to understand. Even secular historians, who personally feel nothing but condescension toward psychological phenomena of this type, will have to accept the fact that Jesus at some point, presumably as a result of a severe inner struggle, must have arrived at the conviction that he had been called to ascend the throne of David as the awaited Messiah, as king in the imminent Kingdom of God. As one who was only designated Messiah for the time being and not yet installed in office by God, he forbade his followers to proclaim him Messiah prematurely: one must defer to God in that.

Finally, however, things had gone so far that at Passover (probably in A.D. 30), when throngs of the faithful poured into Jerusalem, some suggested "that the Kingdom of God should immediately appear" (Luke 19:11). Jesus made his entry into the city riding on an ass, although he usually went on foot. By his doing so, the prophecy of Zechariah (9:9) was supposed to be expressly and literally fulfilled: "Rejoice greatly, O daughter of Zion; shout, O daughter of Jerusalem: behold, thy King cometh unto thee: he is just, and having salvation; lowly, and riding upon an ass, and upon a colt the foal of an ass."

This messianic reference was immediately understood, and thus ensued the triumphal entry into Jerusalem, to the enthusiastic jubilation of the excited crowds of onlookers, who now finally believed to have seen the fulfillment of their messianic hopes: "Hosanna; Blessed is he that cometh in the name of the Lord: Blessed be the kingdom of our father David, that cometh in the name of the Lord: Hosanna in the highest" (Mark 11:9-10). But divine confirmation, passionately awaited with religious ardor by the crowd, was not forthcoming; the night of Gethsemane, the night of the arrest, followed the last paschal meal eaten in common. That was in turn followed by the trial and crucifixion, ending with the desperate cry, "My God, my God, why hast Thou forsaken me?" Finally, there was the entombment and the discovery that the tomb was empty—which opened the way for belief in the resurrection.

The resurrection was a mere first installment for the awaited *parousia*, or coming of the Kingdom of God. Moreover, compared to any actual second coming, resurrection had the disadvantage, first, that it involved only a single person and, second, that it had been seen only by a small number of witnesses.

Subsequently, Christian theology called for a period of waiting for new fulfillment, a belief in the resurrection of Christ as a pledge of what is still awaited through the proclamation of the *faith*.

This proclamation of a crucified and risen messiah might have remained the creed of one among the many tiny and ephemeral Jewish sects, had it not been for Paul. He eliminated the restriction to Israel, prescribed by Jesus, and opened the door to the Greco-Roman ancient world. This synthesis of antiquity and Christianity forms the foundation of Western culture.

What Christianity owes to Paul can be shown by comparing his fate with that of John the Baptist's disciples, the Mandaeans. The Baptist found no Paul; his community was neither Hellenized nor Romanized, but directed toward the East. This community remained in the oriental sphere and was overcome by Iranian-Syrian Gnostic and other oriental tendencies.

By contrast, the fledgling Christian church succeeded in defending itself against inundation by Gnostic mysticism and metaphysics or by the pretentious oriental pseudoscience of astrology. The Church also succeeded in restricting the life-denying asceticism, which also emanated from the East, to the special organization of monasticism.

But the Church did not stop with mere defense against these two threatening dangers of orientalization. In the struggle against Gnosticism that Paul begins, the Church increasingly uses Hellenistic-Roman rationalism. Paul, the last and greatest of the apostles, was a Jew of rabbinical training, but he had grown up in the Diaspora in one of the centers of Hellenistic culture. He spoke Greek, had Roman citizenship rights, and was proud to be a Greek (1 Cor. 9:21). In an important passage of his epistle to the Romans (2:14-18) he expressly states that the heathens, without knowledge of divine revelation, bear the moral laws of nature written in their hearts—that is to say, he applies to the Greeks themselves the Greek natural law doctrine of the Stoics. Here we have the point of departure for later Christian doctrine of *lumen naturale*, for the elaboration of a Christian natural law, and more generally for the absorption of Greek ideas and Greek intellectual culture into Christianity. Thus did it come to pass "that the whole ancient intellectual and societal culture, which was experienced as rational and natural by ancient philosophy itself, was as such sanctioned and authorized by the Church and, as a divine order of creation, rendered positively unassailable."[100]

The martyr Justin (ca. 100-165) espoused the belief that Christianity was a continuation and culmination of Greek philosophy. In the second century, various ideas were appropriated from the later Stoics. The greatest synthesis between Christianity and Greco-Hellenistic culture and science under platonizing idealism was ushered in through the lifework of Clement of Alexandria (ca. 150-216), of Origen (185-255), and of their Alexandrian pupils.

At the same time, a highly successful Romanization was accomplished in Latin-speaking areas, which from a literary and intellectual standpoint reached its first great apogee in Augustine (354-430). The doctrine of predestination, with its horrid pronouncement on the eternal fate of every human soul, had been created by Augustine in view of the despotic period of Roman imperial power, whose motto "*Sic volo, sic iubeo, stat pro ratione voluntas*" he projects in an equally grandiose and frightening way on God as the heavenly emperor. The image of the Heavenly City, the *Civitas Dei* arose as a counterimage and contrasting vision opposed to the despair of the Earthly City, whose seat, "eternal" Rome, had just been conquered and sacked (A.D. 410) by Alaric's Goths. Thence the Diocletian-Constantinian features in Augustine's absolutist representation of God—a representation that was to have an even larger historical impact through Calvin, born a subject of nascent French absolutism.

The same Romanization of the Church, however, led to creation of a model organization that combined democratic foundations in individual communities with a hierarchical construction of the whole Church. The problem of indirect democracy, unresolved in secular life, found its ecclesiastic solution in the councils. There was social solidarity that united those professing the new faith, and its influence became all the greater as political solidarity disintegrated and crumbled.

There are in the conventional New Testament four different accounts of Jesus; no single canonical version ever was established—a fact that would seem more remarkable were it not so familiar. None of the early Christian communities wanted to give up "its" gospel; finally, the result was recognition of the four most esteemed local gospels as equally important. The character of the Gospels and of the Acts of the Apostles as historical documents has considerably strengthened and enriched the historical authenticity of the Bible, already evident in the Old Testament.

Among all the eastern salvation religions that competed for the position as the state religion of the Roman Empire, Christianity finally triumphed. Its characteristics may therefore here once again be comparatively reviewed. Christianity rejected Gnosticism, whereas other religions accepted it. Further, other religions were associated with the oriental pseudoscience of the time, Chaldean astrology; Christianity alone radically rejected it. Other competing religions had, as central content in their revelation, a mythical, metaphysical, and fantastical approach that obstructed development of any objective-scientific attitude toward the world and reality. Christianity had accepted the naïve account of creation in Genesis, but this account was based on the picture of the world as it appears to the naïve observer and included only a minimum of Babylonian cosmology. And Christianity, for the most part, refrained from adding any complex or exaggerated elaborations to this account.

In lieu of cosmogonic mythology, Christianity, as its legacy from Judaism, had a history of a people, a history of the people of God, that is presented as the central line of the history of mankind and expressly passes over into universal human history through the New Testament. The development of scientific historiography in Western culture is firmly anchored in the historical content of the Bible and of Christianity.

All other religions of high cultures postulate God as a world ruler, heavenly king, emperor, or sultan, and this representation is not alien to the Old or even the New Testament. It even received a new impetus through the absolutism of the Roman emperors, and in the Eastern church through the ceremonial of the Byzantine court. But Jesus' central representation of God altogether deviates from this. What he projects upward is not the state, but the family: for him God is the Father in heaven, the beloved Father. This trusting-familial representation of God, on an eternal-human model rather than a historically changing political model, suffuses religious life with the warmth and intimacy of the family atmosphere and the remembrances of earliest childhood; it was to have far-reaching consequences. It was further strengthened and enlarged in its wifely maternal aspect by the emergence of the cult of Mary. Moreover, this familiarization of the divine was the strongest religious guarantee of the earthly family: the Holy Family sanctified every human family. The human family, which Christianity thus sanctified, is pronouncedly the monogamous small family; this sanctioning of monogamy by Christianity belongs among its greatest and most salutary human accomplishments and merits.

In the Sermon on the Mount, Christianity possesses an extremely refined and heightened ethic of love of neighbor, unparalleled in the whole of intellectual history. To be sure, it initially arose as a corollary of the appeal to repentance in view of the imminent arrival of the Kingdom of God. Nonetheless, it has in no way the character of an eschatological interim or a transitional ethic. But in this world—which, after all, did not come to an end—it has had the effect of a continuing admonition to cultivate the loftiest ethical refinement and sublimation.

In its doctrine of immortality and of the infinite worth of each human being as the child of God and the image of God and in placing every individual human soul in direct relation to God, Christianity furnished a strong counterweight to its other components of restraint and conscience. This complex of doctrines, moreover, gave rise to strong antidomination, antifeudal, egalitarian, and democratic tendencies, and forms one of the most important historical roots of individualism and liberalism.

In the West and in the East it was the function of Christianity to replace failing secular integration with spiritual integration. Whereas in the East the emperor succeeded in getting this integrative instrument into his own hands by combining the leadership of church and state, the Church in the West, under the bishop of Rome, knew how to preserve its independence so that the traditional prestige of the world capital clung to the successors of Peter, who as popes became the recognized heads of the Western church. Ambrose, Bishop of Milan (ca. 340-393) "the first man from the highest social class" to assume this office and at the same time an "outstanding personality,"[101] dared to confront the emperor, and in 390 forced Theodosius the Great to do penance for the bloodbath he had carried out in Thessalonica. Somewhat later there followed a series of great, truly imperial popes: Innocent I (401-417), Leo the Great (440-461), and, after a long interval, Gregory the Great (590-604): these were the proper successors of the Caesars. Augustine (354-430), baptized by Ambrose and his great pupil, belongs in the same series as the most powerful intellectual and literary representative of the Church's claim to world dominion, the *Civitas Dei*. From Augustine stems the utterance: "*Remota itaque iustitia quid sunt regna nisi magna latrocinia?*" ("Without justice, what are kingdoms but great bands of robbers?")[102] This mighty statement of principle has resounded through the centuries, and in our own day we have again become aware of its conscience-stirring eternal truth in all its sharpness.

This reciprocal independence of church and state remained a fundamental fact of Western history until the Reformation. To both sides this separation of power was undesirable; church and state each tried to establish total and unrestricted domination, yet neither succeeded. The church remained the conscience of the state, the state the critic of the church—both unquestionably to the benefit of Western mankind. For as Voltaire knew, this dualism was the strongest guarantee of freedom, the only protection against being totally overtaken by one of the two powers.

The Roman church became for the West the exclusive guardian of two great historical accomplishments of the Roman Empire: first, the intellectual unity of Western man and his consciousness of that unity; second, the culture of antiquity—along with Christian religious doctrine itself—as the source and content of that unity.

Not the whole tradition of ancient culture, to be sure, was compatible with Christianity. But even the didactic poem of Lucretius as well as the frivolous verses of Ovid and others, have been handed down to us in numerous copies laboriously penned by Christian

monks—a subcutaneous liberalism for which we can only be thank-
ful. Toward ancient culture and its monuments, there was a general
and fundamental reverence; and fanatical and purist currents,
which naturally were not lacking, made little headway against that
deep-seated respect.

The Church, in Troeltsch's words, accomplished "an embalming of
the ancient intellectual treasures, which later would again rise
slowly, piece by piece," in part with the help of "Jews and Arabs. . . .
Hence ancient culture survived only through the Church and was
born anew from her womb." What Erasmus once said about
Aristotle—"Only through Christ has Aristotle been saved"—holds
true for all of antiquity.[103] Since then the dialectical struggle between these two world powers, antiquity and Christianity, has dominated Western intellectual history in ever changing phases.

Disintegration of the western Roman Empire had led to a decline
of the culture apex, according to the law of the pyramid. The migration of peoples in fits and starts finally came to a close with the consolidation of the Frankish kingdom, whose ruler, Charlemagne, received the imperial crown at the hands of the pope. But the claim
that was established—namely to unite the Holy Roman Empire—
remained a dream, and became at last a mere heraldic archaism,
renounced at last in 1806.

The Church remained the only power that actually ruled the domain claimed by the Holy Roman Empire. Thus the Church was the
integrative factor for religious, ethical, and cultural unity—and
hence was instrumental in reestablishing the pyramid's base and
raising its apex. Through the remarkable work of its missions, the
Church also successfully resumed the policy of northerly expansion
inaugurated by Caesar; all of central and northern Europe was
finally won—a rich gain against the loss of North Africa and, provisionally, of Spain and southern Italy to Islam.

This momentous historical event, the so-called conversion of
Europe to Christianity, is ordinarily viewed as a missionary success
of the Church. Yet it is primarily a question of the spread of ancient
culture, whose legacy the Church had assumed and to which the
Church owed its cultural superiority. Also, in the purely religious
domain, the traditional peasant religions of the Germans and Slavs,
based on the eternal cycle of the seasons, were no match for Christianity.

The intellectual domination of the Roman church over western
Europe, moreover, was also multifaceted. It was, first of all, a superstratification, not only because of the Church's authoritarian form of

organization, but also because of theological domination claimed by the Church. Representatives of ancient science and culture reproached Jews and Christians for clashing with the fundamental demand of intellectual honesty, upon which science rests. This demand requires one to accept and expound as true only that which meets criteria of possibility, probability, and factuality. Jews and Christians accepted assertions that have all these criteria against them, demanded their acceptance from their followers, and indeed made them the central point of their intellectual life. From such a perspective the belief of Jews and Christians in their sacred writings must logically be condemned as superstition. To be sure, Greeks and Romans also had their myths; and as for belief in the Messiah as God's son, Greco-Roman mythology swarms with sons of gods. The crucial difference is that no educated pagan considered these myths "true" or demanded that they be considered true. He viewed them, rather, as products of fantasy to be judged by artistic standards.

The Church, on the other hand, brought religious, intellectual, and cultural unity, including the unity of Latin culture and language, to western Europe. It also brought with it the latent culture of antiquity, ready for rebirth (the Renaissance)—the highest cultural accomplishment in the Eurasian-Mediterranean area.

The Middle Ages have been criticized for restricting their scientific efforts, outside theology, to mere transmittal of ancient texts after they had been scholastically processed in a schoolboyish manner, instead of directly tackling objective problems. The "unbiased objectivity" with which natural science confronts things is in reality the last step in a long intellectual development, which finally led to the empiricism of the nineteenth and twentieth centuries. As Fontenelle (1657-1757) put it, "The art of conducting experiments, brought to a certain degree of proficiency, is by no means common. . . . Nature seems to have hidden from us primitive and elementary facts as carefully as she has concealed the causes. And when one succeeds in beholding them, it is a wholly new and wholly unforeseen spectacle."[104] If our forefathers had not availed themselves of the enormous mental work, performed beforehand, of the ancient world, this progress would have required a much greater expenditure of energy, and would have unfolded much more slowly; indeed, we would still be a long way from where we are today. So long as the scientific level of antiquity had not again been reached, one could do nothing more intelligent and effective, in order to advance as quickly as possible, than to follow along this already beaten path, instead of unnecessarily and senselessly picking one's own path through the primordial forest of reality alongside this highway. Only when investigators had arrived at that point where the ancients had stopped—and that was first the case between the sixteenth and eighteenth centuries—was it time to reach for the ax oneself to hack one's own path through the thick forest. The trail blazing did indeed take place and was crowned with great success—a success owed to a great extent to the training course pursued up to then in the schools of the ancient world.

Even secular habits and attitudes have been conditioned by Christianity. The familiar Protestant emphasis on duty, positive accomplishment, and practicality becomes a value to be appreciated—particularly after one has lived in a non-Christian country of the Orient where this tradition is lacking.

By far the most important foundations of medieval science were the Greek *Corpus Aristotelicum* (in Latin translation) and the Roman *Corpus Iuris*. Revival and elaboration of Roman law by the medieval commentators constitutes one of the most momentous scientific accomplishments of the Middle Ages. The involved form of both *Corpora*, their numerous imbalances and contradictions, forced scholarly concern to greater refinement, complication, and specialization—to that Gothic style that is the hallmark of scholasticism.

The *Corpus Aristotelicum* was the most comprehensive literary-scientific complex of the ancient legacy, with an especially high content of Ionian philosophic patrimony. Its direct tradition in the western half of the empire encompassed, of course, only a part of Aristotle's writings, which came to the West partly by way of the Byzantines, partly by way of the Arabs. This pagan influx, between 1210 and 1218, encountered ecclesiastical prohibitions which, however, remained temporary. The intensive scholarly analysis of these Aristotelian writings formed a considerable part of the accomplishment of medieval scholasticism. In the nineteenth century it was customary to criticize the medieval Church, as had the Renaissance humanists, for its scholastic cultivation of Aristotle and to see this as one of the main reasons for the inferiority of the Middle Ages. But could anyone have proposed something better or more suitable than Aristotle?

A great part of scholastic work involved subtle elaboration of Christian religious doctrine, along with the continuing assessment of Aristotle's ideas. Nontheological departments initially remained constricted by ecclesiastical orthodoxy. But this constriction in content favored the formal development of intellect that is the main characteristic of scholasticism; and this hypertrophy of the *ratio*, this joy in the gymnastic achievements of one's own mind forms an important prerequisite for the later development of rationalism and of the Enlightenment. "In the science of the Middle Ages there is exhibited a test of strength of the urge to think and an energy to subject all that is real and valuable to thought, such as perhaps no other age offers us."[105]

Thomas Aquinas (1225-1274) marks the classical apogee of scholasticism and of the systematic Christianization of Aristotle. Having a master builder's mind, like Aristotle himself, he achieved an admirable equilibrium between systematic synthesis and reflective criticism. As we have seen, the closed sociological life-sphere is one important condition for a human sense of well-being. In the world of appearance, nature deludes us by suggesting a correspondingly closed physical life-space, with the self as center, which is soon disturbed by the progress of scientific knowledge. Reacquisition of such a closed world picture on a scientific level seems to be an unresolved problem, but Aristotle and Aquinas, each favored by his *kairos*, or right historic moment, attained such closure, as far as humanly possible, through patient, orderly integration of the known world. Moreover, it was enriched this time by inclusion of the Christian plan of salvation, which made the history of the world a deeply stirring drama flowing from a meaningful divine purpose.

Breaches were made in the well-ordered, all-encompassing world of later Scholasticism, especially by the Englishman William of Ockham. In the realm of thought, of the *ratio*, nominalism signifies a return to antiquity. Indeed, the Church perceived this threatening paganization. To be sure, the Renaissance rejected Scholasticism in general, and especially nominalism, even though its teaching had been adopted by the most combative humanists. The fact is that the philosophic fathers of the Enlightenment in the seventeenth century went through the school of nominalism and Spanish late Scholasticism, and owe their training to this school.

Moreover, Plato, as a counterpoint to Aristotle, was not unknown in the Middle Ages. Of the dialogues, the *Timaeus* is the most Aristotelian, the most instructive, and the most encyclopedic; it lay closest to Scholasticism. Thus, in the Middle Ages, Plato was represented by the *Timaeus Latinus*, and other dialogues receded into the background. For many Scholastics, the *Timaeus* was to the *Corpus Aristotelicum* what the Old Testament was to the New.

Given these developments, those in the Middle Ages for whom Aristotle was too rationalistic, sober, and Scholastic turned to

Platonism. For the Renaissance, Plato formed the accepted portal of escape from Scholasticism and the confinement of dogma.

19. GOTHIC AND RENAISSANCE

By definition, a city is not autarchic, as is a village, but rather dependent on imports for its vital needs; cities thus can develop only when such regular imports are assured. After the fall of the western Roman Empire this was no longer the case; as a consequence the cities frequently ceased to exist—although as a rule they were not wholly depopulated, and some continuity of the settlement was preserved. As Pirenne puts it: "Diminished, anaemic as they may be, they subsist."[106] In an economic and sociological sense, their diminished size marked a retreat from an urban to a village culture. The lowest point of this retrograde development was reached toward the end of the ninth century. Later, increasing political consolidation and security, and an improved level of social integration were gradually reestablished, so that the village remnant again broadened into a city and the remaining shell filled with urban life. The same broadening, however, also took place in traditional villages under the protection of ecclesiastical or secular powers, and new cities were founded at points especially suitable for commercial exchange. The western Middle Ages are thus characterized by the general blossoming of innumerable cities.

The cities were walled. The need for this form of defense arose because of the wealth they had accumulated and because of their density of settlement. Walls became the emblem of the city; they separated the burgher from the peasant. The city's capacity for defense, mathematically measurable in the number of able-bodied men for each linear meter of wall, became greater as residential density increased and as houses were built higher and closer to one another. Space for architectural development was available only in an upward direction. Gothic architecture conforms to these constraints. Its progressive development was fostered by the combined effect of military pressures on the sides and a religious impulse thrusting heavenward—in contrast to the broad, square, Romanesque style of the previous, still predominantly agrarian epoch based on the perfection of the original peasant house. So greatly had the character of this earlier Romanesque period been stamped by its predominant barter economy that not even capitals or residential cities were formed. The German emperor, for instance, led a nomadic existence, with his "palatinates" scattered all over the empire; and it was customary—and obligatory—to maintain an "emperor's room" in every monastery or abbey directly subject to the empire, in the event that the roving sublime lord might make an appearance.

Traders hawked their wares in a similar way, from the pack-carrying peddler to the wealthy merchant; the trader with distant countries transported his wares by ship, wagon, or pack animal. Because of this peculiar geographic character of all medieval socioeconomic relations, and the consequent lack of permanent domiciles, such traders could not be integrated into a closely meshed system of local dependencies: those who constantly changed habitats could not make habitats of their own. If their status was legalized, this took the form of direct subordination to the highest supralocal, omnipresent authority. Such was the procedure followed by the Merovingians and Carolingians, bent upon fostering trade, who placed such traders directly under the king's law, protection, and peace. They were thus personally free and directly subject to the empire, united in guilds, and provided with living quarters and warehouses.

As the arts of reading, writing, and computing spread from the monastic schools to the laity, the internal structure of trade and commerce was rationalized, and there was a corresponding increase in the security and speed of communications, especially in northern Italy and the area between the Rhine and the Seine. Traveling merchants, from the tenth century on, increasingly adopted an urban style of life, which, originating from the old Orient, spread its influence across the Mediterranean to southern Europe. Such urban settlements naturally formed mainly at major crossroads, which also tended to become episcopal sees. In their internal organization these new forms of settlement emulated the rural peasant community as the only available model of an independent local association. At the same time, great importance was attached to maintaining the physical and organizational separation of these urban settlements. Sharpening conflicts developed between the jurisdictional claims of the episcopal regional lords and the privileges of the merchants, whose guilds, through a *coniuratio pro libertate* (a "common oath for freedom"—a term recorded in Cologne in 1112) involved the population in a struggle for freedom against the episcopal overlord of the city. Victory in this struggle created the free city, directly subject to the empire; the supreme authority of the distant emperor or king was viewed as a guarantee of—rather than an impingement upon—such freedom. Western Europe, at the height of the Middle Ages, was at a stage of urban splendor and supremacy.

The government in these cities was initially an oligarchy of patrician counsellors who believed themselves to be a kind of original nobility as opposed to the artisans, who owed their freedom to them. Soon, however, development in a democratic direction resulted from the struggle of the guilds of artisans against these old families. And this upward movement of the urban burgesses signified a transition from aristocracy to plutocracy; it was bemoaned as a decline and fall by the aristocratic didactic poetry of the late Middle Ages, however, as had been the corresponding development by Theognis in the ancient world.

On the basis of the *pax Christiana* proclaimed by the Church, international trade developed with distant countries, which joined all cities into a network with strong connections with the Near East, and indeed the Far East. A worldwide division of labor resulted. The world trade network not only increased wealth, but also led to a broadening of intellectual and cultural horizons.

The cultural consequences were not long in coming. The city is the typical location for high culture, since it makes close coexistence of specialists possible. There was also a sense of solidarity and a community spirit. Urban population figures for this period are approximately the same as those for the Greek cities of the classical age. Florence is said to have contained a population of 37,225 in 1422 and 40,323 in 1470. More reliable estimates are available for Germany, and these range downward from 30,000 for Cologne (fifteenth century) and 26,672 for Lübeck (late fifteenth century) to 12,000 for Hamburg (1526), 9,000 for Frankfurt am Main (1440), and 4,000 for Leipzig (1479). All these figures remain well within the range recommended by Plato (30,000) and Aristotle (6,000); even the cities of Italy rarely would seem to have exceeded the maximum of 60,000 laid down by Hippodamus.

This, then, was the sociological foundation of the culture of the Renaissance and of the Gothic era, when German medieval cities had splendid churches and cathedrals pointing heavenward, an inexhaustible wealth of sculpture, and radiant treasures of altar images and church windows comparable to the temples, sculptures, and sacred offerings of the Greek cities of antiquity.

The scientific and theological achievements of Scholasticism also belong to this age; their stylistic kinship to the Gothic has been strikingly pointed out. The influence of the ancient world throughout the Middle Ages took the form of a constant spontaneous and unconscious development akin to the naïve Hellenism of the Augustan period. Accordingly, Erich Auerbach has strikingly designated the Middle Ages as the vulgar-antique world. The Middle

Ages and Scholasticism were the last continuations of antiquity, Hellenisms of an extreme form.

Only in Italy did the further development differ markedly. "Whoever," writes Gerhard Ritter, "knows how to explain the far-reaching difference of this Italian city culture from the life of the German cities—likewise flowering, but of course, more slowly, since the twelfth and thirteenth centuries, on the basis of its economic, social, legal, political and, finally, intellectual presuppositions—at the same time makes comprehensible the abysmal difference between the later Italian Renaissance and German culture in the age of the Reformation."[107]

The common medieval city culture of the West was a precondition and foundation for the Renaissance. The late Gothic period and the Renaissance are two phenomena of the medieval city culture of the West, but the Renaissance as a special Italian development later branches off from the earlier common Gothic development elsewhere in the West. Realism, naturalism, and a striving toward monumentality are characteristic tendencies of the whole Western world of the fifteenth century; realism develops more radically in the north than in Italy, where the urban residence of the nobility in the city and idealist thought influenced by antiquity exercised dampening influences. The decisive factor that was to differentiate Italy from the common urban culture of the later Middle Ages was the revival of antiquity. This became the characteristic that finally was to distinguish Renaissance from Gothic, and that was to bestow on Italy its leading role.

The political position of the cities in northern Italy was from the beginning stronger than elsewhere. The city ruled a far greater territory than it did in Germany, and city freedom was achieved sooner. Frederick Barbarossa had expressly recognized the independence of the Lombard communes in 1183 in the Peace of Constance. The emperor was far away, and when he did make an appearance, he depended on the friendship and help of the cities. By contrast, the pope was too close for the ecclesiastical lords to be able to develop an all too feudal autocracy.

That the nobility lived in the city signified not a weakening but rather a strengthening of the city. Like the ancient acropolis, the *incasamento* concentrated all higher energies of the territory in the city, which developed into the "quintessence of the landscape."[108]

In the secular struggle between cities, territorial princes, and central authority in Italy, the victory did not belong—as in Germany—to the territorial princes, or—as in England—to the estates united in Parliament, or—as in France—to the crown, but rather to the cities. The cities were not, as in Germany, absorbed by princely territories but vice versa. Therefore, urban areas were not scattered as enclaves among princely territories, as in Germany, but, as in ancient Greece, city-state bordered on city-state. And where principalities were formed, they were as a rule city-principalities; they signified only an internal governmental change within the city-state.

In Germany, the more important princes were far superior to any city not only in size of the territory they controlled and in political and military power, but also in social status, so that even the smallest and shabbiest hereditary prince felt himself vastly superior to the burgomaster of the largest and richest city. This order of precedence found expression at every common public celebration, and it came to be deeply embedded in the consciousness of the townsmen. The townsman or burgher felt himself of second rank, inferior to the nobleman, and that in a time in which the idea of *ordo*—rank order—played so fundamental a role as in the Christian Middle Ages. If an extraordinarily bold and self-assertive ruler of any city dared to violate this order, public opinion in general, and even the individual himself, would have considered it *hybris*, punishable arrogance. In the age of absolutism, when most German cities were incorporated by surrounding territorial states and stripped of their independence under the emperor, this was felt to be the execution of a divine mandate. This subordination of German cities with respect to the princes and nobility was also the reason why, in their political attitudes, their bearing and their spirit, they could never rise to the free and bold self-consciousness of Italian and ancient city-states. For the Italian city there was no particular authority before which its pride had to bow.

In Italy a synthesis between aristocratic and bourgeois culture developed because the nobles lived in the city; in the north, especially in Germany and the Netherlands, reciprocal animosity prevailed, which endowed bourgeois culture with a partly unpolished and gross, partly narrow and petty "philistine" character that so often expressed itself in a rough or humdrum realism in the arts. On the other hand, northern art also achieved such a peak of unfettered, heightened expression as the Isenheim Altarpiece.

The German nobility after the decline of knighthood could no longer maintain or create its own aristocratic culture, and cultural accomplishments of the German aristocracy after the Middle Ages were meager; the result was a cultural inferiority of Germany as compared with Italy, Spain, France, the Lowlands, or England, that lasted from the Renaissance until the eighteenth century.

The world trade situation was extremely favorable to Italian development. The most important foreign trade routes between East and West ran across the Mediterranean, for the subject cities of the Byzantine and Islamic realms could not compete on equal terms with the free cities of the West. The crusades made possible a highly successful eastward thrust of commercial power of Italian cities. Nevertheless, these were only relative advantages, differences of degree from the cities, say, of Flanders or of the Hanseatic League. Italy's different relationship with the ancient world was the qualitative distinction that was to have far-reaching consequences for future developments.

The Italian cities in their origins were ancient Roman cities, and consciousness of this origin had never been obscured, interrupted, or replaced by other political or national loyalties. The Holy Roman Empire, whose sovereignty in most cases was only formal, was primarily viewed as additional strengthening, legitimation, and recognition of the Roman tradition. Even Roman law was still in use and enjoyed a revival at northern Italian centers, especially Padua and Bologna.

After A.D. 330 Italy had been ruled from Constantinople, and increasingly become a province of the Byzantine Empire. Byzantine culture, which thus exercised a dominant influence in Italy, in the plastic arts and otherwise, was a late manifestation of the Hellenic-Hellenistic ancient world. In the last analysis even Byzantine mosaics and miniatures, which influenced the beginnings of Italian printing, were also of a late-antique character.

Islamic culture and Arab philosophy, medicine, and science had developed a rich cultural legacy. Islamic-Christian trade relations lay in Italian hands, but political control shifted back and forth. Sicily and Sardinia for a time were under Islamic rule, and the crusades brought a host of former Arabic islands, ports, and coasts under the control of Italian cities.

Italy's own broad continuity with antiquity was thus reinforced by legacies of the ancient world transmitted through Byzantine and Islamic influences.

Day in and day out Italians lived in houses amid the ruins of the ancient world. Ancient architecture, ancient statuary stood daily before everyone's eyes. As Georg Voigt rightly notes: "If the ancient spirit could again come to life anywhere, it perforce had to be in Italy."[109] In this setting, where people had never lost their sense of continuity with antiquity, there now developed a sociologic situation which is striking and, into the least details, similar to that we had identified as necessary for the rise of Ionian-Attic intellectual freedom two thousand years earlier.

In both cases we find a string of flourishing trading cities, speaking the same language, following the same religion, imbued with a common culture, yet independent and engaged in keen rivalry with one another. In both cases there is the favorable commercial-political situation of being intermediaries for trade with the Orient.

The Genoese trading posts and colonies on the Black Sea were in the same locations as those of Miletus. The prosperity of Florence (the successor to Pisa), like that of Miletus, was based upon the production of textiles for foreign markets. In both Italian and old Ionian cities, the foreign traders used their position with respect to the artisans producing for them, to become independent entrepreneurs; they soon constituted an urbanized nobility. Plutocratic oligarchy of the great merchant and commercial lords formed the original foundation of government. Increasing wealth rested not upon feudal seigneurial dues, but upon the profits deriving from maritime trade. The nobility lived in the city, and the *inurbamento della nobilità* corresponds to Attic *synoikismos*. The humanist and Florentine state chancellor Poggio Bracciolini (1380-1459) already explicitly opposes the ideal of *humanitas* to that of *nobilitas*. The city-states, free or subject only to a loose sovereignty (that of the German emperor or of the Lydian king), enjoyed a freedom secured by a balance of power created by the rivalries of outside powers, such as prevailed in Italy before 1494 and in the Near East before 546 B.C. In both cases this freedom came to an end as one of the great powers—here Spain, there Persia—gained control, and the victorious oppressor was a military-theological power. Similarly the invasion of Italy by Charles VIII in 1494 can be compared to the invasion of Ionia by Cyrus in 546 B.C.; the further result was the sack of Rome in 1527, just as it had been the capture of Miletus in 494 B.C. The governmental form of the city republic in both cases was originally under the leadership of the aristocratic patrician families; sooner or later, however, aspiring democratic groups under a chief of the people (*capitano del popolo = prostatēs tou dēmou*) contested this right of leadership; and these struggles eventually led to the establishment of tyrants. Here as there we find the appointment of foreign arbiters (*katartistēres*) for the settlement of internal disputes, and the singular institution of the *podestà* or *signore* fetched from abroad in order to assure a nonpartisan leadership, independent of inner cliques.

A passionate, indeed savage ambition to surpass all others by any means, cost what it may, here as there was the driving force propelling artists as well as poets, merchants as well as savants, individual politicians and entire cities. In all of human history there is hardly a period like these two when people were to such an extent spurred by competition to peak accomplishments in all departments of life.

The ideal of *uomo universale* especially espoused by Leon Battista Alberti (1404-1472) had already been embodied by the Sophist Hippias, when Plato, in the *Lesser Hippias*, introduces him wearing a magnificent set of clothes made with his own hands down to the elegant sandals. The literary man of the Renaissance, like the ancient Sophist, is characterized by his "outer and inner unconventionality . . . with the constant roving, the eternal restlessness that does not subside even in solitude, the need for celebrity, the intensified self-consciousness."[110]

No less intoxicating, radiant, and colorful, no less towering above all around them, were the cultural accomplishments both in ancient Greece and in Renaissance Italy, whether in architecture, painting, and sculpture, or in poetry and philosophy. And these accomplishments both times were borne by an amazing, almost inconceivable profusion of talents of all degrees, up to the highest peak of human genius.

Many of the similarities pointed out here apply, on the Greek side of the comparison, not just to the Ionian cities of the sixth century B.C., but also to the classical age of the fifth and fourth centuries B.C. Florence, of course, has always been compared to classical Athens. France, whose army invaded Italy in 1494, was, like Macedonia, a northern neighboring kingdom subject to the cultural influence of its more advanced neighbor.

And if Machiavelli's *Prince* ended up with the despairing plea for a prince who would have the ability to take in hand the political unification of Italy, so did the publicistic career of the aged Isocrates end with the no less despairing challenge to Philip of Macedon to bring about this same accomplishment for Greece.

It is remarkable in what measure the reappearance of a closely similar sociological situation, after an interval of two millennia, ripened into strikingly similar cultural consequences.

Wherever the legacy of antiquity lay before everyone's eyes in architectural or sculptural works of art, or where the archaeologist's spade brought it to light, that legacy was readily accessible and understandable to any receptive person. When it came to ancient literature, which lay buried in the parchments of monastic scribes, revival required linguistic and interpretational proficiency; and this growing proficiency marks the beginning of modern classical philology and archaeology, indeed of all modern humanistic studies. Such studies now for the first time are called by the term *humanism*, and they are a worthy successor to the earlier humanist movements of Alexandria and of the Augustan age.

This reestablishment of ancient traditions and attitudes was accompanied by an intoxicating sense of joy. This pervasive sense of cheerfulness was a natural consequence of the first fundamental break with Christian anxiety about sin, and with Christian depreciation of this world and its beauty, and of the body and of its joys. After a millennium of ascetic prohibition, for the first time man was restored to his natural rights; and man, in his full independence and dignity, once again replaced a supernatural God as the measure of all things. What could be more conducive to enthusiasm and enhanced feeling of human life? The Renaissance opposed its *memento vivere* to the *memento mori* of medieval Christianity.

The new, antiascetic feeling for life of the Renaissance found unrestrained expression in such works as Boccaccio's (1313-1375) *Decameron*, Lorenzo Valla's (1407-1457) dialogue *De voluptate* (1431), the erotic paintings of Correggio (1494-1534) and Giulio Romano (1492-1546), as well as in Aretino's (1492-1556) shameless poems. With the coarse and brilliant Franciscan monk Rabelais (1495-1553), and the courtly school of Fontainebleau, the movement made inroads in France, then withdrew into Montaigne's (1533-1592) humanistic study in the face of the Counter Reformation.

Rabelais glorified "the vitalistic-dynamic triumph of the physical body and its functions. In Rabelais there is no longer any Original Sin or any Last Judgment, and thus no metaphysical fear of death. As a part of nature, man rejoices in his breathing life, his bodily functions, and his intellectual powers and, like nature's other creatures, he suffers natural dissolution. The breathing life of men and nature calls forth all Rabelais' love, his thirst for knowledge and his power of verbal representation. . . . It is triumphant earthly life which calls forth his realistic and superrealistic mimesis, and that is completely anti-Christian."[111]

Man is in any case mired deeply in original sin, and the layman cannot possibly make the struggle against this original sin his principal occupation. Hence the church in practice contents itself with the sacrament of confession as a mild clerical measure of limiting and fencing in the playground left to the exercise of original sin: sin and confess! That original sin, within this assigned arena, began to exercise ever more actively and enthusiastically was not, from the viewpoint of the church, a radical change in the situation—or need not be as long as the church showed itself tolerant and forgiving. There was, to be sure, no lack of radical and intransigent reactions; yet the most famous and unyielding exponent of such reaction, Savonarola, was cast off by the Church—to be sure, the Church of Alexander VI (Rodrigo Borgia)—and buried as a heretic. The Church acted for the time being according to the broad-minded principle: Who is not against me, is for me.

In intellectual spheres Scholasticism had evolved into nominalism. But this position on the intellectual front was not developed further, since the Renaissance fundamentally disliked the schoolroom air of Scholasticism, holding it irreconcilable with its new feeling for life. Development here went off in a quite different direction, toward that of an emotional-pathetic Platonism.

In one important department of scientific thinking, especially important for practical life, political science, opposition to Christianity was carried to an extreme by Niccolò Machiavelli (1469-1527). Political practice had always been more or less "Machiavellian," and what Thucydides described was particularly so. Political theory, however, had never dared to deny the claims of morality. The treatises on statecraft took the ethical stance of a Christain father confessor. In sharp contrast to this tradition, Machiavelli, in his *Prince* (1513), set forth a diabolic treatise on statecraft wholly free of Christian morality. That which politicians in most cases had disavowed, suppressed, and glossed over in bad conscience was here openly espoused. At the same time, Machiavelli was objectively correct with respect to the actual state of foreign affairs, but he is all the more guilty of evading the fundamental challenge of asking how such a state of affairs could be overcome. He thus becomes the first in a lengthy and dubious series of titanic debunkers.

While the Church was very largely tolerant of the Renaissance movement, indeed took pride in participating in the splendor of the new art according to its abilities, the Renaissance for its part was in general even more tolerant of the Church. Because the Renaissance was free of theological dogmatism, it could not but be tolerant. Just as Greco-Roman paganism had been tolerant, at first, toward Christianity, so was the Renaissance; it was ancient paganism reborn. Greek philosophers continued to participate in cults and divine festivals of their cities, whether or not they "believed" in the gods: why shouldn't their enthusiastic pupils and renewers do likewise? Any different conduct would have been out of place and foolish because the triumph of antiquity over Christianity, of the Renaissance over the traditional Chruch, was already in full progress within the Church itself. Had not Rome developed into the radiant center of the Renaissance, and had not at the same time the popes themselves seen the leaders? And were popes like Alexander VI, Julius II, Leo X, still entirely Christian? Or were they neo-pagan Renaissance men? The post-Tridentine Church is at one with Protestantism in its indignant condemnation of these popes and the secularization and paganization of the Church represented by them. No one, for instance, will approve the infamous pleasures of Alexander VI. This sensuality, wild and kicking over the traces, however, must be reckoned against the no-less-extreme asceticism of so many popes and saints of the previous centuries. Certainly it would have been understandable to have excused these violent deflections as phenomena attendant upon going from one extreme to the other, as pathologies, had the development thus begun been accorded the time and possibility to unfold further and eventuate in a proper balance. Nietzsche was to sum it up later:

> The Italian Renaissance contained within itself all the positive forces to which we owe modern culture. Such were the liberation of thought, the disregard of authorities, the triumph of education over the darkness of tradition, enthusiasm for science and the scientific past of mankind, the unfettering of the Individual, an ardour for truthfulness and a dislike of delusion and mere effect. . . . Yes, the Renaissance had positive forces, which have *as yet* never become so mighty again in our modern culture. It was the Golden Age of the last thousand years in spite of all its blemishes and vices. On the other hand, the German Reformation stands out as an energetic protest of antiquated spirits, who were by no means tired of medieval views of life, and who received the signs of its dissolution, the extraordinary flatness and alienation of the religious life, with deep dejection. . . . They threw mankind back again, brought about the counter-reformation, that is, a Catholic Christianity of self-defense, with all the violence of a state of siege, and delayed for two or three centuries the complete awakening and mastery of the sciences. . . . The great task of the Renaissance could not be brought to a termination; this was prevented by the protest of the contemporary backward German spirit. . . . It was the chance of an extraordinary constellation of politics that Luther

was preserved, and that his protest gained strength. . . .
[Otherwise,] Luther would have been burnt like Huss,—and the
morning sun of enlightenment would probably have risen
somewhat earlier, and with a splendor more beauteous than we
can now imagine.[112]

The Church at the onset of the Reformation found itself in a
critical and hence highly vulnerable stage of development, but one
which was also highly promising for the future. This development
might have proceeded further had it not been inhibited by the Reformation and the Counter Reformation and finally perverted into its
very opposite.

The Roman church (and even more the Greek) had in practice developed great tolerance toward the old pagan beliefs and popular
customs. In many localities a dual religion was formed; for the lower
classes a baptized, primitive paganism, a "vulgar antique world" (in
Auerbach's phrase), and for the upper classes a cultured, intellec-
tualized, and enlightened Christianity, likewise blended with very
lively traditions of ancient intellectual culture.

But this age, which had set itself the task of detheologizing the
ancient-Christian culture and which, under Italian leadership, had
made auspicious progress, now fostered one of the greatest and most
vehement theologians of all time, who succeeded in halting the
progress of intellectual history.

20. REFORMATION AND COUNTER REFORMATION

Given the close reciprocal relations between Italy and the rest of the
Western world in the period of the high and late Middle Ages, it is
amazing how long the Renaissance remained restricted to Italy, and
how strong was the resistance it had to overcome elsewhere. This
proves that the Renaissance initially was closely bound up with the
specific Italian conditions of its origin. Yet we should not overlook
the impetus toward independent but concurrent development even
in places like Germany.

One example is the numinous detheologization of religious painting in the Catholic domain, such as the marked heightening of religious landscapes of Joachim Patinir (1480-1524) and of painters of
the Danubian school, which begins with Albrecht Altdorfer (1480-
1538) and rises to its zenith with Wolf Huber (1490-1553). In the development of the theme of the painting "John on Patmos" we can
instructively follow how the theological figures of the legend ini-

tially form the essential pictorial content of the painting, which barely acknowledges that the event occurs in the solitude of open nature. Later, however, the landscape as background and scenery is more richly developed, and the figures recede in relation to it. The peak of this development is the great woodcut of the master known by the initials HWG (probably ca. 1540) on which the tiny human figures are hardly discernible and the Mother of God, appearing in the clouds in a corner of the drawing, has the effect of an expedient churchly seal impressed upon this document of nature. All the more overwhelmingly, however, does the grandiose landscape, in all its numinous splendor, reveal and unfold itself and become the real content of the vision. The next and last step in this direction leads to the purely numinous landscape as developed by Wolf Huber, stripped of any theological or other appurtenances that could only destroy the impact of the mood. But this hopeful development as embodiment of broader trends in intellectual history breaks off abruptly. In the Catholic sphere, there was a counterreformatory return to theological figure painting, and, in the Protestant realm, a transition to a purely secular landscape as represented, in extreme form, by Pieter Brueghel (1525-1569).

The Reformation was even more of such a disturbance, although the fact that the ancient world had first been reborn in Italy meant that it came to Germany under somewhat inauspicious circumstances. It signified control by foreigners, an outside interference much like that which the Hellenization of Rome once had represented for Cato the Elder.

The Christianization of the Germans had already been a form of foreign control at the time of ancient culture. The developing Renaissance shifted this center of gravity in the direction of the original, liberal elements of the ancient world. It signified a rectification of the ancient tradition as earlier transmitted by Christianity. It was first the Renaissance and Enlightenment that indicated what entry into the culture-complex of Christianity and antiquity signified for peoples of the West.

In princely courts, once the Renaissance was absorbed, leadership lay with the artists, then with the jurists. Both met needs of rhetoric and representation. In the city republics, however, the leadership fell to the learned—on the one hand to humanists, and on the other to physicians and natural philosophers. In German culture this new type of worldly, freethinking Renaissance scholar found its mythical embodiment in the figure of Dr. Faustus. Faust is a wandering humanist, physician, and student of nature, but not—in a medieval way—theologian, or—in a courtly way—jurist or artist. He is the typical representative of the secular intelligentsia of that time, a product of the independent cities. This spread of the Renaissance to the cities of central Europe—a trickle at first—became a broad stream by the second decade of the sixteenth century. Johannes von Butzbach, in his work on famous painters (1505), wrote: "As the greatest painter, God has created the world so magnificently in its ineffable beauty; the human form above all proclaims the glory of its creator; as often as a pious Christian glimpses the beautiful appearance of a human being, he should be loud in his praise of the most beautiful God for this comeliness."[113]

This intellectual triumph of humanism and of the Renaissance also awakened that positive approach already evident in Italy. Erasmus writes: "Uprightness and Christian piety will flourish together with the revival of letters and the sciences. We may congratulate the age; it will be a golden one."[114]

The pitiless hailstorm of the Reformation struck; and the same Erasmus, in deep disappointment and discouragement, was forced to note: "Wherever Lutherism is dominant, the study of literature is extinguished." "A most criminal age . . . the most unhappy and most depraved age imaginable."[115]

The deeply stirred age, almost overtense with expectancy, found its national leader, its demagogue, in Martin Luther (1483-1546). He was an Augustinian monk and doctor of theology in Wittenberg, in a German-Slavic border area far from old centers of ancient Western culture and education. He had remained completely unaffected by the Renaissance, even though he had an unusual opportunity to learn about it. As emissary of his order in 1510-11, he had wandered on foot through Italy as far as Rome and back right through the middle of the high Renaissance shortly before its final flowering. Of all that, however, this German monk saw nothing, or if he did, he turned away with the angry look of Savonarola—whom he later expressly recognized as his precursor. He records nothing about his Italian experience, and he used the humanist Melanchthon only as a language teacher of Greek and Hebrew, the languages of the sacred scriptures—a one-sided relationship that Melanchthon, after Luther's death, described as "disgraceful servitude."

Actually, Luther had a late Gothic mind with certain tendencies to the baroque, a typical phenomenon of the "waning of the Middle Ages." As a philosopher he was an Ockhamist-nominalist Scholastic with contempt for that "harlot reason," and with a theology that declared human will inadequate and divine will irrational. As a theologian, Luther was the pupil of his order's founder, Saint Augustine, and adhered to that most absolutist of dogmas, predestination, according to which God from all eternity has determined the fate—the eternal bliss or damnation—of each human being. For no one could this horrendous dogma be more dangerous than for a manic-depressive, who each time he is in the manic stage will believe himself predestined to eternal salvation, in the depressive stage to eternal damnation. Luther was close to suicide more than once; his psychic energy was directed toward escaping this intolerable state of duress. He believed that he had found such a way out in the Pauline idea of justification by faith alone, by the unconditioned trust in the redemptive power of Christ's expiatory death.

Luther first made this leap from the *decretum horribile* of predestination to justification by faith alone in the so-called tower experience, which for him was to remain the most direct experience of salvation and the central event of his life. By this experience Luther undertook a momentous shift of the psychological center of gravity—and this becomes clearest in comparison with Calvinism, which shifted that center back again. The Calvinist, by effectiveness in action, attains certainty of his election; for the Lutheran, not only the means but also the end are psychologically different. With the Calvinist the means is active, outwardly directed practice; with the Lutheran it is passive, inner-directed emotional experience. And with the Calvinist what is achieved is certainty regarding the content of God's long preestablished decision, whereas with the Lutheran what is accomplished is, in reality, that decision itself. The Lutheran does not want to receive certainty regarding what God has unalterably decided; rather, he wants to feel and experience the grace and the fatherly mercy of his God as directly present. The pious Lutheran conducts himself as though his salvation is being decided only here and now in the experience of faith, and not as though it had already been decided long ago.

With this doctrine of justification by faith alone Luther had acquired that Archimedean point from which it is possible to unhinge the world. The opportunity to do so was to offer itself all too soon.

No fewer than three historical turning points coincided to provide Luther with his unique opportunity. Franz Ehrle has presented the history of medieval theology as a great struggle between Augustinianism and Aristotelianism, in which Plato stands behind the Neoplatonist Augustine. Aristotelianism had won the day with Albertus Magnus and Saint Thomas Aquinas, but in the ebb and flow

of human affairs, it found itself, by Luther's time, at a nadir of tor-
por and decline. A counterpush of Augustinianism was due—indeed
almost overdue—and this, in the context of theology, was the historic moment that Luther used—or misused. The old enmity of Augustinianism (and likewise of Scotism and nominalism) against
Aquinas and Aristotle reached a new apogee in Luther.

This theological *kairos* of Augustinianism coincided with a second, ecclesiastic and political *kairos*. The Church was in a critical
and precarious stage, having, as we have seen, become paganized
under the influence of the Renaissance. Between the two poles immanent in the Church, the mundane and the supramundane, the
sensual and the spiritual, that of natural religion and a religion of
salvation, the Church had drawn closer to the first, becoming sensual and external, while at the same time succumbing to southern,
Roman influences. The Papal States had become an Italian Renaissance principality, the pope (Julius II) a *condottiere*. Outside Italy,
but especially in Germany, this was bound to have an incomprehensible and scandalizing effect. It sparked an opposite northerly tendency toward barbarization.

A third *kairos* lay in the political development of absolutism.
Luther conceived God in the image of a German prince, Calvin according to that of a king of France. And just as secular absolutism
subjected each individual directly to the monarch, so the clerical absolutism of the Reformation subjected each individual to the divinity without the mediation of Church, priests, or saints. The fate of
the individual subject depended upon the favor or disfavor of his
prince, who demanded unconditional subjection; the fate of each
soul depended upon the grace of God and His unfathomable decree.
A gracious God and a gracious prince were concurrent concerns, especially for Lutherans. And just as the absolute prince demanded
unconditional trust and faithful submission from his loyal subjects,
so God demanded as much from the believers according to the doctrine of salvation by faith alone.

The autumn storm of the Middle Ages—or was it the spring storm
of a new age?—raged in the second decade of the sixteenth century,
especially in Germany. In all departments old bonds were breaking
down and there was a general longing for their replacement by fresh
ones. The princes, weary of subordination to the empire, aspired to
absolute sovereignty. The knights strove for a status that would
make them directly subject to the empire, and they wanted influence on the imperial diet. The clergy no longer exercised a function
that could justify its existence at the cost of revenues exacted from

the commonality; the authority of the Church was undermined. The intellectual upper stratum in the cities began to turn toward humanism and the Renaissance. Freethinkers proclaimed a pagan, natural piety and boldly asserted, in opposition to Christian asceticism, "that the natural sexual act can proceed in one sense so that it is of the same value as a prayer before God."[116] The peasantry, in the process of slow economic rise, increasingly resented feudal bondage. Involuntary discontent mixed with hopeful expectation. No one was content; each had the feeling that things had to be different. "The Germans are eager for a new age," said a flyer in 1524.[117] It was an unstable state of affairs. One possibility would have been to accept the Renaissance, and a movement in this direction had already started.

As usually occurs in apocalyptic times, the messianic call for a charismatic leader was raised. Dürer's woodcuts of the Apocalypse (1498) appear in retrospect to express this chiliastic longing. As Dürer himself exclaimed in his diary: "O Erasmus, you knight of Christ, ride forth!"[118]

Luther had an advantage over other would-be leaders "who undertake a cause for which they are not man enough" (as Luther once said of Eck), in his religious absolutism. For a monk, concern for his own and others' salvation was a life task—he was supported at community expense and separated from the world by the walls of the monastery. In one sense Luther remained a monk throughout his life; he appeared indifferent to everything except salvation.

The occasion that led to the explosion was the dispute over indulgences (1517). Luther, objectively speaking, was "in the right"; but he carried the dispute to extremes. The traffic in indulgences speculated on the superstition of the masses. But the essential concern should have been whether indulgences were the most important burdens weighing upon the German nation. Whether the occasion was worthy or not, the German people had at last found their longed-for charismatic hero. The question became: Where would Luther lead this elemental mass movement that he had kindled?

"His reaction" in Gilson's words, was "essentially a return to what was most medieval in the Middle Ages, and moreover to the darkest, in that which we call the 'dark ages': the contempt for [human] nature, for secular science, for philosophy and for its intrusion into religion."[119]

In Luther's own drastic metaphor, god had led him into this situation "like a nag whose eyes are blinded." He was not aware of his historical responsibility, but only of his theological responsibility "before God." In our own day, a biographer of Luther still espouses the conviction that "the authentic Protestant would not only be justified, but rather even duty-bound, to place himself [with] Luther and to pay little attention to all the disturbance of human cultural development for the sake of the incomparably higher value of divine truth. . . ."[120]

Luther, in 1521, was tormented by grave conscientious scruples in the quiet solitude of the Wartburg—but these he put aside as "diabolic promptings." He developed an adroitness in ascribing the voices of his conscience by turns to God and the devil.

Luther's real influence was in many essential matters opposite to what he intended. Hence, his despair at the end of his life, from which he escaped only through religious introspection.

The first great and truly tragic example of the contradiction between effect and intention comes from the first years of his activity and shows at the same time how little he was master of the situation.

Luther came from a peasant background, his bearing and his mode of speech were plain and rustic, coarse to the point of obscenity and boorishness. Thus he seemed to be a man after the heart of the German peasant. He preached "Christian freedom," recognized only the Bible as the highest authority, dared to defy the great of this world—"the drunken and crazy princes"—with impudent courage. As late as 1523, in his pamphlet "Temporal Authority: To What Extent It Should Be Obeyed," Luther had written: "God will make an end of them [the secular princes], as he does of the spiritual lords"—wholly in accordance with the war cry of the Bundschuh insurrection of 1524, which declared noblemen and priests its enemies. And further: "God will no longer tolerate it. The world is no longer what it once was, when you drove as if you were hunting wild beasts."[121] The peasants must have thought that they were acting in Luther's spirit when, in 1524, they rose against their feudal lords and refused to recognize dependencies other than those justified according to divine law and from Holy Writ. And as late as April 1525 Luther wrote in the "Admonition to Peace: A Reply to the Twelve Articles of the Peasants in Swabia": "And the people cannot tolerate it very long if their rulers set confiscatory tax rates and tax them out of their very skins. . . . God is doing this [peasant resistance] because this raging of yours [the princes] cannot, will not and ought not to be endured for long. You must become different men and yield to God's word. If you do not do this amicably and willingly, then you will be compelled to do it by force and destruction. If these peasants do not compel you, others will. Even though you were to defeat them all, they would still not be defeated, for God will raise up others. It is his will to defeat you; and you will be defeated. It is not the peasants, dear lords, who are resisting you; it is God himself, to visit your raging upon you."[122]

In spite of these admonitions, and theological reflections addressed to the lords, along with some milder ones addressed to the peasants, the situation grew more acute. And the same Luther, whom the peasants looked up to as their intellectual leader, in May 1525 wrote his "booklet" "Against the Robbing and Murdering Hordes of Peasants." In it—of course profusely citing the Pauline admonition "Let every person be subject to the governing authorities"—he could not do enough to incite a bloodthirsty murderous agitation against the rebellious peasants. Luther himself had not been so naïve as to expect that the lords would change their ways in response to mere exhortations. He had threatened them that they would be compelled to do what was necessary because of "force and destruction," and had told them that they would perish "as your kind have always perished." What did the peasants do but try to bring about Luther's own prophecies? But if in April it was still God himself who had aroused the peasants and who had set himself against the lords, in May it was rather the devil in person: "These are strange times, when a prince can win heaven with bloodshed better than other men with prayer!" "And there is no place here for patience or mercy. This is the time of the sword, not the day of grace." "Therefore let everyone who can, smite, slay, and stab, secretly or openly, remembering that nothing can be more poisonous, hurtful or devilish than a rebel." "Therefore, dear lords, here is a place where you can release, rescue, help. Have mercy on these poor people! Let whoever can, stab, smite, and slay. If you die in doing it, good for you! A more blessed death can never be yours."[123]

The princes did not wait for such advice to be repeated; the uprising was drowned in blood, as Luther had demanded, with pitiless cruelty. And Luther, upon viewing what he had wrought, said: "All their blood is on my head, but I refer it to our Lord God: he commanded me to say that." Here it appears that doubt never came over him, in contrast to his vocation to monkhood, that this voice—as he put it—may not have been God's but the devil's.

Politically the rebellious peasants strove for direct subordination to the empire. Their goal can be considered as the embryonic stage of an evangelical, social, and national empire, such as the early twentieth century Germany political leader Friedrich Naumann had in mind. But the emperor in Luther's time was a Spanish Catholic. Therefore, the rebels could expect nothing from the empire to which they appealed over the heads of their feudal lords; the military situation became unfavorable for them, despite local and provisional successes.

Luther had predicted that the situation "would ultimately result in the destruction of Germany,"[124] and in fact the terrible collapse of the first German revolution, blessed by Luther, overshadows all later German history. It was a prefiguration of the tragic failure of the bourgeois revolution of 1848. In the movement of 1524-1525 early forms of democratic, as well as national, aspirations had been in close alliance. At that time, the resistance of the German people to its own overlords was broken. Luther could not do enough by way of demanding "Let every person be subject to the governing authorities" and by hammering into consciences this "clear and compelling text of Saint Paul Romans 13 (1)," as he grandly calls it.[125] Even in the matter of criminal authority he knew only suffering obedience. The majority of the German people between 1933 and 1945 conducted themselves in accordance with this teaching of Luther's, which had become a deeply ingrained part of their heritage.

Luther's fanatical subservience and submissiveness went so far that in his sermon "On War against the Turk" (1529), he first of all assured his readers that "He who fights against the Turks, fights against God's foe and Christ's tormentors, indeed against the devil himself," for all Turks "are the devil's own and possessed by the devil, as their master Muhammad and the Turkish emperor himself." But he continues: "So note now, where God ordains that you shall be captured, carried away and sold by the Turks, that you must live for their sake and be a servant, think in such a way so that you patiently and willingly accept such suffering and service sent by God, and that you suffer for the sake of God. . . . You must think that you have lost your freedom and have become property, from which condition you cannot escape without the will and knowledge of your master, without sin and disobedience. For by so doing you rob and steal from your master your body, which he has bought or otherwise brought to himself, which from this time on is not your good, but rather his, like a domestic animal or his possessions."[126]

In this Lutheran ethos of submissiveness as preached to subjects, theology again reverted to the original social function that it had had within the superstratification structure—namely, to replace naked violence as a means for keeping the lower stratum in its place, with higher, more spiritual influence exercised upon the soul rather than upon the body.

Luther paved the way for national socialism even as regards anti-Semitism. One of his most loyal present-day defenders calls his pamphlet "Of the Jews and Their Lies" (1543) "a whole flood of folkish hatred and wicked slander concerning alleged hidden atrocities."[127] Luther here demands the destruction of their synagogues and houses, expropriation and heavy forced labor, indeed complete expulsion from the country as measures against nonbaptized Jews. And in this last sermon, only three days before his death, Luther closed with an "Exhortation against the Jews" with whom one should have no "community or patience."

Just as in Italy, the "monkish squabbles," the theological and dogmatic disputes had for some time ceased to play a role in the public life of Germany and neighboring regions; but now a "redogmatization" (Alfred Weber's term) ensued, first in the Protestant, then in response also in the Catholic realm. Soon, thanks to Luther, monkish squabbles resounded throughout central Europe. Theology came to dominate intellectual life to a degree unknown even in the "darkest" Middle Ages. Theological disputation reached down into artisan workshops and up to the palaces of the princes: "The type of the pious prince, who could not do without his court preacher at every courtly occasion, in order to continue to discuss with him the latest disputes over the Eucharist, is no rarity in the Germany of the sixteenth century."[128]

This universalization and socialization of interest in theological refinements and subtleties shows how inappropriate Luther's slogan of "universal priesthood" was even in the theological realm. Hardly any other department of intellectual activity is less suited to democratization, and more in need of hierarchy than is theology. The effects of this socialization of the mind, inaugurated by Luther, were felt throughout the Enlightenment and the nineteenth century, and are still felt in our day.

And in this sense we can call Luther's standpoint democratic, since his doctrine of universal priesthood led to a far-reaching leveling of Church hierarchy. But Luther's conception corresponded to the illiberal and intolerant notion of democracy as later embodied in Rousseau's doctrine of the absolute sovereignty of the general will. If Luther fought the Church's claim to absolute rule, it was only to claim the same absolute rule for the Bible and his interpretation of it.

All this holds true only for the aging Luther; in his younger years (before 1525), he still espoused a liberal standpoint. Thus in 1523 in "Temporal Authority: To What Extent It Should Be Obeyed," he states: "Furthermore, every man runs his own risk in believing as he does, and he must see to it himself that he believes rightly. As nobody else can go to heaven or hell for me, so nobody else can believe or disbelieve for me. . . . How he believes or disbelieves is a matter for the conscience of each individual, and since this takes nothing away from the temporal authority, the latter should be content to attend to its own affairs and let men believe this or that as they are able and willing, and constrain no one by force. For faith is a free act, to which no one can be forced. . . ."[129]

In the letter to the princes of Saxony on the rebellious spirit there is the following splendid passage: "Let minds explode and meet; if some are tempted meanwhile, fine; so is it in the course of war. Where there is quarrel and battle, there some must fall and be wounded. He who, however, fights uprightly, will be crowned." Similarly, in the "Admonition to Peace" (1525): "Indeed, no ruler ought to prevent anyone from teaching or believing what he pleases, whether it is the gospel or lies."[130]

The thrust of that heightened theological interest was antirational. "The new fervor of religious life that Luther had kindled in the world had worked most violently and most momentously against the rationalization of religious thinking," Gerhard Ritter has written. "Indeed, insofar as the powerful intensification of modern state authority vis-à-vis the ecclesiastical system is connected with the general secularization of European culture, the Reformation has even been the greatest obstacle to this rise: it signifies after all an enormous intensification and revival of clerical interests, religious outlook, far beyond the situation of the late Middle Ages, indeed a violent entanglement of all polities in ecclesiastical questions— hence viewed from the standpoint of the Renaissance (in which the basic features of the modern pure secular State are altogether discernible), it was not only a 'relapse' into the Middle Ages, but rather a Christianization of politics in a measure that had no precedent in the Middle Ages."[131]

In Christian religious history Luther's importance can be compared only to that of figures like Saint Paul, Saint Augustine, and Saint Francis. Within German intellectual history and indeed in the history of the German language, too, Luther occupies an even more dominant position through his translation of the Bible. Few German writers have surpassed Luther in basic linguistic power. His Bible has become something like the Old Testament of German literature. Next to his German Bible appeared the German church hymn, likewise founded by Luther, which was not replaced by major secular lyric poetry until the pre-Romantic period. Luther's letters to his wife and children belong to the most lovable documents of the specifically German form of family life. In these many ways, Luther was to become a German religious hero and a major national hero in the series Luther, Frederick II, and Bismarck: all equally German, equally powerful, equally provincial, and equally baneful in their influence on the German national character they shaped and divided.

To be sure, this movement set off by Luther underwent a whole series of far-reaching transformations, which in the liberal Protestantism of the eighteenth and nineteenth centuries finally conduced very closely to that humane rationalism and spiritualism against which Luther himself had most bitterly fought in Erasmus, Zwingli, and Schwenkfeld. Throughout these successive intellectual transformations, Luther remained the founding hero to his grateful followers, so that for a certain liberal school of theologians and historians interpreting the Reformation he finally became the great Renaissance hero, who in the religious realm accomplished the same feat as had been accomplished by the real Renaissance in the secular realm. This image of Luther, which in an almost touching way stands historical truth on its head, has for a long time been refuted and given up by serious scholars. Nevertheless, it prevails in the deeper strata of public opinion, now as before, so that it may not be superfluous to stress that the critique of Luther we have engaged in here is a compelling consequence of the general evaluation lying at the base of this book: it is directed against the historical Luther, and it proceeds from a set of value postulates that are not too far from those held by enlightened liberal Protestants.

The historical product of the movement launched by Luther was the age of religious schism and confessional persecution that reached its apogee in the Saint Bartholomew's Day massacre in 1572—the age of religious wars, which, in the words of Erasmus, "transformed the world into a robbers' den" and reached its high point in the ravages of the Thirty Years' War. Their "confession," or religious denomination, decided the fate of millions of people. Streams of confessional emigrants wandered through all the countries of Europe and crossed the ocean. The various confessions criticized one and another not just for their different beliefs, but also for their different mind-set, different conduct of life, and different activity and thought in all secular matters. No sphere of life was exempt from dispute; religious antagonism discovered or created differences that extended to mode of dress and style in housing. And the development of economic attitudes and economic structures also went along different ways in the regions dominated by Lutheranism, Catholicism, Calvinism, and other Christian denominations.

The complaint of Erasmus, "Wherever Lutheranism is dominant, there the cultivation of letters is extinguished," holds true in even greater measure for the plastic arts: hence the dreary interlude in the history of German art from the mid-sixteenth to the mid-seventeenth century, which in the Protestant realm begins as early as 1520.[132] Lukas Cranach (1472-1553), after his wonderful *Rest on the Flight from Egypt* (1504) and *Venus* (1509), became the burgomaster of Wittenberg and Luther's court portrait painter, almost on an assembly line basis; he also painted frigid allegories. Matthias Grünewald (ca. 1475-1528), the brilliant master of the Isenheim Altarpiece (1511), whose heightened religiosity in form and color anticipated the baroque of the Counter Reformation, ended his life in artistic sterility as supervisor of the waterworks of the city of Halle. Hans Baldung-Grien (1476-1545), the master of the powerful, pious, and intimate Freiburg high altar of 1516, was for Jacob Burckhardt the high point of all Gothic painting; his woodcut of the ascension of Christ hurtling through space head downwards (1514), in its savage boldness, put the most extreme ventures of the baroque in the shade. He became municipal councillor of the Protestant and iconoclastic city of Strasbourg, and, to the extent that his official duties left him time for artistic work, painted competent portraits, stale allegories, and works like those three technically masterful woodcuts of wild horses in the woods (1534), in which the demoniacal dimension of a dedivinized nature is eerily expressed. The last work before his death, an engraving of 1544, is even more profoundly frightening: with the most exact and brilliant application of the scientific art of perspective drawing as developed by the Renaissance, it sketches, with pitiless hardness, a stableboy stretched out on the floor as though struck by lightning; the boy in turn is bewitched by a harridan of furylike appearance—treated in sharply contrasting impressionistic style—who hurls a brand into the stable. God is dead, long live the devil!

If the atmosphere of the age had such a paralyzing and destructive effect on accomplished artistic masters, it offered all the less encouragement to new young talents; indeed it had a downright sterilizing effect on them.

Even as regards human vitality the Reformation by no means signified only a liberation—as one might infer from Luther's abolition of celibacy, the closing of the monasteries, and Luther's own marriage to a former nun. Luther, to be sure, displayed a gross pleasure-mindedness generally, as is shown by his increasing, soon legendary, obesity. But his doctrine approved sensuality in marriage only as a permissible sin in order to protect spouses from worse sins, as a defense against extraconjugal lewdness—in sum, as a lesser evil: "No conjugal duty," he states categorically, "occurs without sin."[133]

Before Luther's time, in Catholic practice—as still today in Latin countries—secular life was fenced in as the game preserve of natural sin, just as monasteries and convents served as reservations for special ascetic performances. The monastery walls, intended originally to protect this asceticism from any irruption of worldly concerns, conversely protected the world at large from any eruption of asceticism. Now, as these walls were torn down and monasteries secularized, there developed what Max Weber has called "innerworldly asceticism." As Sebastian Franck (1499-1542), the humanist, noted with disappointment: "You think you have escaped from the monastery—now each one must be a monk throughout his life."

No one was more keenly sensitive to what he called the "tragedy of Lutheranism"[134] than Erasmus (1467-1536), the recognized leader of the movement of religious humanism north of the Alps, which had recently come into being. He had viewed it as his life's mission to transmit the Renaissance, in the form of a renascent Christianity, to central Europe, aiming at a synthesis between Italian Renaissance humanism, spiritual enlightenment, and north German piety that would maintain and indeed strengthen the unity of Western culture. Luther's remark that "human concerns in him are more prevalent than divine ones"[135] was intended as a devastating critique of Erasmus; in our view it was precisely that quality that marks Erasmus's superiority to Luther.

Erasmus was neither a medieval nor a Renaissance man. Rather, he was modern, in that his own life was not a goal in itself, neither a transcendent nor an immanent goal, but rather a means to larger ends of scholarly, cultural, and political accomplishment.

In the final analysis, Erasmus was indeed a cultural politician. In this capacity he represented a tendency that remained a hopeless minority in his own time, but the profound justification of which should be all the clearer in our own day. His attitude toward Luther and the Reformation is perhaps from all points of view his greatest accomplishment. There is something positively heroic in the way this frail man, who held high the banner of the cause entrusted to him in the hopelessly muddled and desperate situation of his time, doggedly shunned any cheap popularity and opportunities for mass influence.

The tragedy in intellectual history that is connected with the name of Erasmus was heightened by the premature death of Huldreich Zwingli (1484-1531), who, along with Luther and later Calvin, was one of the three major leaders of the Reformation. Of these three reformers, Zwingli was intellectually the clearest, politically the most liberal, and in his vitality the least inhibited. He "embodied a synthesis of Christianity and antiquity"[136] and, among the three reformers, stood closest to the humanism and sense of vitality of the Renaissance. Zwingli gave his life on the battlefield in defense of his native city of Zurich only two years after the conversation of Marburg, where, with tears in his eyes, he had seen his great attempt to achieve internal unity among Protestants come to naught because of Luther's theological obstinacy.

Luther never gave a consistent, systematic presentation of his doctrine. The long series of his works consists of occasional writings, mostly polemical in character, and a chain of smaller or greater intellectual explosions that repeatedly trigger off a contradiction. To anyone trained in clear logic, or exposed to the humanist revival of Roman law, this tumultuous kind of exposition was bound to be an intolerable sight crying out for the strict and solid hand of a superior and passionately cool systematizer. Likewise, the abysmal naïveté in political matters of the German monk cried out for redress from a cosmopolitan statesman and diplomat. Luther, probably in consequence of his violent temperament that tolerated no rival, did not find anyone in Germany to compensate for these deficiencies of his. All the more decisive, therefore, became the fact that the Frenchman Jehan Caulvin (or Chauvin), latinized Johannes Calvinus (1509-1564), combined in himself all the traits that were lacking in Luther. Just as later the carelessly arranged work of the Englishman Adam Smith was to appear to Jean-Baptiste Say as a "vast chaos of right ideas," so must Luther's literary *oeuvre* have struck

Calvin. In both cases their strict systematization promised deep satisfaction and sweeping success; an outstanding logician, didacticist, and stylist, and a born systematizer of the thought of others, Calvin found here his great opportunity, in which he romanized the German Reformation and applied French clarity to its Teutonic fury. The Roman church was hopelessly outdated; the future belonged to Protestantism, especially when a man like Calvin took charge. Calvin owes his historical success to the exploitation of this opportunity, and this unique opportunity also led him to Protestantism. His biographers, with dutiful zeal, have searched for evidence of Calvin's religious "conversion," but cannot discover anything of the sort. Calvin, in sharp contrast to Luther, was no man to oscillate between exaltation and depression, or to undergo abrupt psychic upheavals.

Apart from the deviation in the doctrine of the Eucharist—a matter where Luther insisted on a philologically and historically untenable magical interpretation—there is hardly any essential idea in Calvin's writings that could not be documented in Luther. That his emphasis differs from Luther's is an inevitable consequence of uniform systematization, which requires decisive answers where Luther's fitful occasional writings allowed frequent shifts of emphasis. Other differences stemmed from the different contexts in which Luther and Calvin operated. Calvin's intention was by no means to establish a separate Protestant church, but rather to embrace all Protestantism into a whole.

Calvin was a strong-willed man with a thirst for power intensified to the point of sadism. As a Catholic he could have become a counterreformist pope; as a Protestant he was dependent upon other, more democratic methods of domination. Calvin viewed himself as the counsel and chief legal officer, as the minister and viceroy of a God who in the absoluteness of his sovereignty outdid the Sultan and Louis XIV; as Calvin himself once put it: "Let His will stand for law, for reason, and for the highest rule of justice."[137] This theocentric absolutism was based upon statements of Luther, especially in the anti-Erasmian *De servo arbitrio*. But what in Luther is a passionate extreme in Calvin becomes a dominant, central point of doctrine. In the central polarity between God and man, Calvin's empathy is on the side of God, Luther's on that of man. Calvin was asthenic, small and slender of stature, pale, with a long, thin, black beard, hollow-cheeked, and of stern and penetrating look. "Victim of a tyrannical father, he developed into a neurotic compulsive character in which the sadistic features were furnished with an enormous affect-intensity."[138] "Like other great idealists, he mistreated himself inwardly and therefore had a great need for punishment."[139] Whereas the rustic-coarse and burly-pyknic Luther was surrounded by a swarm of playful children, who have become familiar to us from his charming family letters, and the valiant Zwingli could even boast of an illegitimate child begotten in his youthful years, Calvin, in the performance of his conjugal duties, managed to produce but one child, unfit for survival, which died a few days after its birth. Calvin expressly preached the religious duty of self-hatred—"haine de nous mesmes"—of which the humanist Montaigne (1533-1592) says: "To hate and despise oneself is a particular sickness which is not seen in any other creature."

Calvin achieved in Geneva what Savonarola had failed to achieve in Florence fifty years earlier: he established an ascetic, pious rule of terror that did not find its like until the terror of the Calvinist Robespierre. Wholly in accordance with Plato's prescription, Calvin began with the expulsion of all those not willing to take a loyalty oath; it was forbidden to discuss public matters outside the council. Even the mistrustful and grudging attitude toward the arts corresponds wholly to that of Plato and Savonarola. A close-knit network of spies and informers has power, as in Plato's state, even over the least details of personal and family life. The penalty for atheism is death. In the first five years of Calvin's rule in Geneva (1542-1546), ten persons were beheaded, thirteen hanged, and thirty-five burned—these last on the purely superstitious allegation that they had spread the plague. The most famous victim of Calvin's reign of terror was a Spanish physician, Michael Servetus (1511-1553), discoverer of the circulation of the blood. Calvin had him seized and burned as he was traveling through Geneva, because he dared to deny the doctrine of the Trinity with its assertion that three equals one.

A similar experiment, only on a larger scale, was successfully carried out by those apt pupils of Calvin who understood how to transform merry old England once and for all into that model country of puritan-ascetic strict morality and prudery, whose old vitality, as compensation for the violence to self that had been imposed upon it, now found its sadistic satisfaction in the colonial domination exercised throughout the empire.

Calvinist Protestantism has given proof of the same fanatical and brutal thirst for power wherever, as in Geneva, it achieved autocratic rule: in Presbyterian Scotland, in the Netherlands of the synod of Dordrecht, and in the puritan New England states of North

America. However, these were only a few cases, limited in time and place.

But the more ruthless one is as overlord, the more refractory he is wont to be as subject. Happily for it and us, Calvinism only rarely and briefly came into the role of *ecclesia triumphans*, of absolute overlord, but all the more often and longer in that of *ecclesia militans*, of the congregation "under the cross" of the threatened minority. Whereas otherwise it would have given itself over to the most total oppression, we are indebted to it now for the most courageous struggle for freedom. The struggle of the German "Professing Church" (*Bekennende Kirche*) against national socialism also belongs in great part in this context.

The independent vitality of individual congregations, their primary sphere of religious solidarity, was originally also Luther's ideal; but in the course of subsequent political developments this ideal had been compromised by assigning to the territorial princes the function of being heads of each Protestant church. In Calvinism, this congregational emphasis was not only preserved but even sharpened because Calvinists so often found themselves in opposition to princes of other denominations. Hence the militant-democratic character of Calvinism in contrast to the pious submissiveness toward temporal authority typical of Lutheranism.

This mighty struggle for freedom that Calvinism—wholly against its original intention—has accomplished finds magnificent artistic expression in the Geneva Reformation monument. It has often been deplored that the best intentions can, tragically, lead to the worst effects. Here is an example, of the opposite phenomenon: negative intentions produced highly positive effects. "It is quite despite themselves that the reformers worked for the triumph of free inquiry. They too could have said on the field of battle: 'We didn't want that.' But without wanting to, wanting indeed the opposite, they did just that."[140] And in the same sense Charles Borgeaud has called the modern democracies "daughters of the Reform and not of the reformers."[141]

The Reformation has, above all, served progress through that which it destroyed. Conversely, the Renaissance worked through its positive aspects and failed to destroy what stood in its way—seeking rather to detour around the obstacle wherever possible.

The Renaissance was on the point of peacefully conquering the Church from within. The Church was in the process of incorporating humanistic secularism and entering into a synthesis with it that could have been highly fruitful. From this point of view, the phenomenon of paganization of the Church, commonly viewed as a degeneration, actually was a positive sign. All this was brought to naught by the Reformation. It opened up doctrinal differences with extreme sharpness, and hence produced an atmosphere of mutual hostility that led to extreme forms of absolutist domination no matter which of the warring sides might win the day. The absolutist territorial Church in both its Protestant and Catholic form signified an impairment of ecclesiastical unity; but each of these separate churches now became stronger within its own borders, for, unlike in the Middle Ages, the clerical and secular powers no longer held each other in check.

Luther's initial theological-political attack confronted the Roman church in a period of transition in which it was as defenseless as a bird in the moulting season or a snake while shedding its skin. The reformers were more papal than the pope, more medieval than the Church; they attacked the Church from the rear, so to speak, and most vigorously took it at its word. They reproached the Church for its progressiveness and broadmindedness, its accommodation with the Renaissance.

When the Church became aware of the seriousness of the situation and had to acknowledge the criticism of the Reformation as justified, an attempt at reconciliation was made in the first half of the pontificate of Paul III Farnese (1534-1549). The humanistically educated cardinals who led this attempt hoped to achieve a mutual reconciliation on the basis of moderation, in a direction not too different from that pursued by Erasmus. With Paul IV (1555-1559), who had already won rising influence as Cardinal Caraffa since the last years of the reign of Paul III, the Counter Reformation's sharpest embodiment finally came to the helm. The situation had grown so catastrophic for the Church that it felt forced to surrender all of its most progressive positions and to retreat in the direction of the Middle Ages, indeed behind the Middle Ages. Intense competition with the Reformation in all important departments became a vital question for the Church, a requirement for self-preservation. As an unavoidable consequence, the unwritten peace treaty between the Church and the Renaissance was no longer valid, and an unmistakable tension emerged. Under pressure, the Church became more orthodox and intolerant than before, and more militant in the preservation of theological positions. Further, the Inquisition was installed—a frightful weapon that could be applied against pagan heretics and Protestants alike.

That baleful tendency of the Spanish Grand Inquisitor Ximenez only now won the upper hand in the Church. Ignatius of Loyola (1491-1556) became the Calvin of Catholicism. The Jesuit order, founded in 1534 and recognized in 1540, set for itself the goal of reestablishing the unity of Western culture that had been destroyed by the Reformation. It did not achieve this goal, and in its pursuit did not always apply unobjectionable means—although the desperate situation can be cited as an extenuating circumstance. How serious the Jesuit order was in pursuing this lofty aim, and how little it had only the narrow, selfish, and domineering interests of the Church in view, is best proved by the zeal with which it dedicated itself to the cultivation of humanistic—and indeed cosmopolitan—culture. It gave evidence of the same liberal attitude later also with regard to Confucianism, a policy that was to bring it into conflict with the Church itself.

Religiously, the Counter Reformation was a belated victory of the Reformation within the Catholic church. It is undeniable that the Counter Reformation brought a greater strictness of morals in contrast to the scandalous excesses of the Renaissance popes, as well as an intensification of religious feeling (although often in exaggerated, pathological form) in contrast to the secularizing tendencies of the Renaissance. But the extreme reaction of the Renaissance against the asceticism of the Middle Ages had already been overcome before the Counter Reformation. A new intensification of religious emotional life was in progress, and without the external challenge of the Reformation would probably have grown in more continuous and less exaggerated fashion.

Savonarola had been burned as a heretic in 1498; had he come a hundred years later he might well have been canonized as a saint. He was distinctly a precursor of the Counter Reformation. Although Giordano Bruno was burned in Rome in 1600 by the Inquisition, he would have been treated the same way in Calvin's Geneva, but not in the Rome of the Renaissance. Just as Calvin's stakes in Geneva were kindled by those of the Spanish Grand Inquisitors, so were the stakes of the Counter Reformation kindled by the Genevan Reformation, the stake of Giordano Bruno by that of Servetus. The infamous recantation trial to which Galileo was subjected (1637) lay in the course of a development to which the Church had been forced by the Reformation. Luther himself and Melanchthon, the contemporary exponents of Protestant orthodoxy, fought the heliocentric system no less sharply. As late as 1721 the censorship commission of Zurich prohibited scientific work because it espoused the Copernican theory! In the Renaissance, on the other hand, no one would ever have dreamed or thought of molesting a man like Galileo. So great was the regression within a single century; Luther and Calvin are responsible not only for the Reformation, but also the Counter Reformation.

Reformation and Counter Reformation are hostile twins. From the viewpoint of intellectual history, both stand on the side of theo-logical-despotic bondage, against that great movement of intellec-tual freedom which, originating in antiquity, found embodiment in the Renaissance and the Enlightenment.

The relapse into extreme medieval thinking produced the Refor-mation and the Counter Reformation and brought about the fateful split between Christianity and the Enlightenment. The spiral movement of intellectual history brings us back in our own day and in changed circumstances to the grand task, whose resolution was so fatefully interrupted by the Reformation. For the more critically we judge the Reformation and Counter Reformation, the more we also must realize that hostility to Christianity as such would signify cul-tural suicide for the West.

21. BAROQUE: STATE AND ECONOMY, ART AND SCIENCE OF ABSOLUTISM

a. The Absolutist State

From Constantine to the end of the Middle Ages the polar dualism between church and state in the West became one of the strongest guarantees of freedom. But this presupposed that the Church could confront any given state as an independent power, as a counter-weight, and as a supervisory authority. For any state aspiring to-ward absolutism, however, this situation became uncomfortable be-cause it did not have exclusive domination over its subjects. On the model of the Byzantine emperor and of the sultan, even the pettiest territorial prince now aspired to be *papa in terris suis*, pope in his own lands.

This wish was fulfilled in an unexpected way by the Reformation. The loss of unity so weakened the authority of the Church as op-posed to the state that the latter's efforts to establish independent churches succeeded even in Catholic countries. In the Lutheran sphere, national or state churches arose with the prince as *summus episcopus* (supreme bishop).

This absolutism of territorial princes was anticipated in Calvin's conception of God. In the conditions of *Realpolitik* on earth Calvin faced many obstacles in realizing his absolutist ideal; but in transposing that ideal to the governance of heaven he encountered no resistance whatever. While Saint Augustine had copied the idea of divine absolutism from the despotism of the emperor, Calvin's absolutist conception of God preceded the earthly absolutism of the Sun King by more than a century.

In Catholic countries theology had a newly strengthened claim to sovereignty, and this claim for submissiveness of minds redounded not so much to the benefit of the Church as to secular absolutism: "Un roi, une loi, une foi": One king, one law, one faith.

The totemistic hunters, the archaic divine kingship of the "Erythraic" culture complex, the ancient oriental despotism, the late-Hellenistic cult of kings, and the Roman cult of emperors all had preceded this concept. Roman law, codified in the period of imperial absolutism, contains centralistic and absolutistic features up to Ulpian's famous formulation: *Quidquid principi placuit, legis habet vigorem*—"Whatever pleases the ruler has the force of law."[142] In the great medieval struggle for hegemony between pope and emperor, the emperor was named by his partisans *lex animata*—the living law. The statement *Rex enim adoratur in terris quasi vicarius Dei*—"The King is worshipped in his realm as the vicar of God"[143]—occurs in a medieval writing mistakenly attributed to Saint Augustine.

Jean Bodin, in his *Six livres de la république* (1576), gives the classic definition of sovereignty, or *majestas*, as *summa in cives et subditos legibusque soluta potestas*: "supreme power over citizens and subjects unrestricted by laws." He designates the prince as the "living and breathing image of divinity," a notion later repeated by Fénelon and Frederick the Great. James I of England (b. 1566, reigned 1603-1625) called kings "Gods on earth."[144] Bossuet named the king a "dieu mortel," and of the absolute prince, Louis XIV himself says: "Holding, so to speak, the place of God, he seems to be a participant of His knowledge,"[145] thus ascribing no less than divine omniscience to him.

The royalist emigrant Thomas Hobbes (1588-1679), systematizing the Caesaropapist ideas of James I and renewing the sociological atomism of the Epicurean school, created a doctrine of state absolutism marked by ruthless logic and gloomy rigor, and he drew the most extreme juristic conclusions from this absolutization of the prince by proclaiming the sovereign's pleasure as the exclusive, the sole practically valid source of law: "To the care of the Sovereign belongeth the making of Good Laws. But what is a good law? By a good law, I mean not a Just Law; for *no Law can be Unjust.*" Therefore it is not acceptable "that man shall judge what is lawful and unlawful, not by the Law itself, but by their own conscience."[146] This is, for all practical purposes, legal positivism. And through his influence upon Rousseau—often overlooked—and thereby upon the Jacobins, the morose Hobbes may rightly be considered one of the chief intellectual ancestors of modern totalitarianism.

The doctrine of *glebae adscriptio* (the prohibition of subjects from moving away from their piece of soil) taken over by late Roman despotism from Egyptian models, had served the Teutonic superstratifiers as legal sanction for feudal domination over their subjects. In the course of the Middle Ages these dependencies and forms of bondage were modified and loosened. The development of many cities whose citizens claimed freedom of movement had considerably increased the actual degree of freedom and stimulated the general desire for freedom. And this rise of social and political freedom had accompanied the growth of intellectual liberalism. This growth of intellectual freedom was further strengthened by the development of the *ratio*, by the process of systematization and rationalization which was being accomplished in the theoretical field of theological and scholarly thought and research. Advances also occurred in different departments of practical life; fostered by the reception of Roman law, a far-reaching rationalization of the state and of its administrative technique set in. For the technique of administration in the narrow sense, the Norman states of southern Italy seem to have formed the most important centers of development: for the technique of finance, the papal curia; for the diplomatic technique of foreign policy, the Republic of Venice. Development of the security of communications and of the technique of communication, of the monetary system and of proper legal forms made possible the formation of a central bureaucracy in the civil and, later, in the military domain; the net result was the abolition of the feudal system, long the most difficult obstacle to any development of statehood on a broader and surer foundation. The technique of warfare had not only been revolutionized as a result of firearms. In the words of Otto Hintze, the "power of military organization based upon public spirit and the cooperative union of the peasants of the Swiss confederation," the moral-political factor of a communal form of government combining the feeling of comradely solidarity of neighbors with the recognized authority of the leader, had already prepared "an end to the feudal style of waging war and had made the infantry a decisive, determining factor in modern warfare." The impact of this advance was felt in all continental countries where "the army became the backbone of the new centralist State."[147]

Political centralism is possible only upon this foundation of rational, bureaucratic technique of state administration; it gives the tendency to monarchy its strongest impetus and surest support. In France the crown, supported by the progressive cities, took this superior technique of state administration in hand and with its help established absolutism; in Germany it was the princes, during the struggle against the emperor and the imperial freedom of the cities. Everywhere this development was accelerated by the Reformation and Counter Reformation, which destroyed the counterweight of a single universal church, everywhere tended toward a merger of secular and ecclesiastic authority, and thus led to a new theological subjugation of minds.

The principle of hereditary succession is both absolutism's strength and weakness. Its strength lies in the fact that it resolves the question of succession in the style of sovereign absoluteness and certainty and removes any possible countervailing influences from above or below. Its weakness lies in the minimal probability, on the basis of the Mendelian laws of heredity, that the successor to the throne will be as competent as his predecessor. In practice many absolute dynasties ultimately foundered for this latter reason. The fateful hereditary succession of Commodus to Marcus Aurelius constitutes a classic, but by no means isolated, example.

The principle of absolutism that the king can do no wrong gives an occupant of a throne with talent and love of power the greatest scope and opportunity conceivable for political effectiveness. At the same time, however, it constitutes an irresistible temptation to misuse this unlimited power as a means for personal enjoyment and convenience. Not even Louis XIV was able to resist this temptation. How much less so the swarm of his inefficient successors and imitators!

The attitude of Catholic absolutism toward the Church was ambivalent. In its radical demand for submissiveness, it was in accord with the Catholicism of the Counter Reformation. But its claim to sovereignty was in conflict with the Church's claim to supranational sovereignty and fostered the creation of special churches enjoying maximum independence. These efforts made themselves felt even in a country as clerical and fanatically orthodox as Spain. They reached a peak in Gallicanism and Anglicanism—the latter overstepping the bounds of Catholicism by effecting a formal break. But one could fight the pope over the question of church sovereignty and still be a passionate Catholic. This tension was absent on the Protestant side; and for the rulers in the Lutheran domain the supreme episcopate of the prince was a welcome strengthening of his power position. But in Protestant as well as Catholic countries throne and altar could mutually support each other in their claims to sovereignty—a relationship that obtained for European absolutism prior to the Enlightenment.

Its links to the orthodoxies of Reformation and Counter Reformation had an equally ambivalent effect upon absolutism. On the one hand, Sir Robert Filmer and Bossuet were correct when they justified hereditary absolutism exclusively on a theological basis as divine grace, the hereditary investiture of the dynasty by the almighty will of an absolute God. Absolute sovereignty, as Hobbes and Rousseau demonstrate, can also be justified rationally; indeed, the emphasis on unitary guidance from a central point is an extreme rationalistic construct. What could not be justified by reason was the irrational principle of hereditary succession stemming from superstratification. And renunciation of this principle of hereditary succession was not possible without casting doubt upon the concept of absolutism itself. This antinomy of hereditary succession, as I should like to call it, is the congenital, incurable, and inevitably fatal sickness of absolutism. The prognosis is bleak: absolutism can neither live without hereditary succession, nor, in the long run, live with it.

Theology was the strongest intellectual support of hereditary absolutism, and its reliance on theology was to bring absolutism in conflict with its own rational motive forces and with ascendant Enlightenment.

Monarchy signified progressive abolition of the great number of feudal dominations; and conversely the concentration of superstratified power and authority in the hands of a single person. The tendency toward abolition of superstratification, latent in this ambivalence of monarchy, first appears openly in enlightened absolutism, and above all in its inherent tendency to self-abolition through constitutionalism and democracy.

Without the intervention of the Reformation and the Counter Reformation, absolutism presumably might have developed more quickly and directly toward some form of constitutionalism and democracy. Unenlightened absolutism is a by-product of the Reformation and Counter Reformation.

The inherent contradiction of absolutism is strikingly expressed by the court tutor and archbishop Fénelon (1651-1715) in his *Tele-*

machus (1699), a work intended as a textbook for future rulers, not as a manual of revolution. "Absolute power degrades every subject to a slave; the tyrant is flattered by pretended adoration; . . . but this enormous power perishes of its own excess. It derives no strength from the love of the people, . . . and renders every individual of the state impatient for a change. At the first stroke of opposition the idol is overturned, broken to pieces and trampled underfoot."[148]

The economic and social position of writer and artist in the baroque and rococo periods must be viewed in this context. Absolutism had taken over the patronage of art along with the centralization of the political and financial means of power. The great majority of the artists, musicians, and writers of the seventeenth and eighteenth centuries lived on the liberality of aristocratic patrons and their social position was not always dignified: on occasion it might sink from that of educator, house tutor, or librarian to that of servant or lackey. Mozart was dependent upon his aristocratic bread-givers, and Lessing had endless difficulties finding an emergency shelter as house tutor or librarian.

b. Colonial Superstratification and Slavery

The conquests of the Normans (aside from the German "colonization" of the Slavic east, which for a time unfolded in peaceful or semipeaceful forms) were the last major superstratifications in Europe. The cultural level of both conquerors and subjects was roughly the same; hence the conquests could be carried out mostly in "chivalrous" forms. However, an opportunity for superstratification suddenly developed in the West that was unprecedented in scope and dimension.

Gunpowder, originally a Chinese invention, had been taken over by the Christian West through Byzantium; its use in the development of firearms marked the greatest advance in military technology since the advent of the war chariot and riding horse. Within the Western cultural complex this development exercised a democratizing influence, consigning the medieval, feudal figure of the armored horseman to the museum of antiquities. It gave a decisive advantage to the Christian defenders of Europe against the Ottoman attack from the East and thus doomed the last onslaughts of Asian horse-borne peoples to failure. In relations with the peoples of the Americas, tropical Africa, and southern and eastern Asia, it endowed Europeans with military superiority comparable to that which war chariots and riding horses had given to the original central Asian nomadic warriors.

The character of the discovery and conquest of America by the Europeans has been described by Georg Friederici in a classic three-volume work.[149] It is by far the cruellest and bloodiest chapter of recorded history before 1933. This conquest was not primarily directed against "primitive peoples" or uncivilized "savages." The cultures of the Aztecs, Mayans, and Incas were at a level of high civilization. They had originated through superstratifications and, moreover, were essentially totalitarian and bloodthirsty (especially the Aztecs). Nonetheless, they were—despite their bellicosity—inferior to the Europeans in war technique; above all, they lacked riding animals and firearms. However, the decisive superiority of the Christian *conquistadores* rested upon their determination to commit any crime, whereas the leaders of the opposite side felt bound to loyalty and faith, to certain fundamental moral concepts. Victories were rapaciously exploited, all the more because the natives were not Christian. That the Indians were "really human beings, capable of receiving the Christian faith and the sacraments" first had to be established by a papal bull of 1537, drawn up on the initiative of the Spanish Dominican Bartolomé de Las Casas (1474-1566), who make it his life's mission to fight for humane treatment of the natives. The papal decree had little practical effect. Even the attempts of the Spanish throne to regulate social relations in the colonies along lines of European feudal relations usually remained on paper. Quite the contrary, the situation in the colonies affected conditions in Europe itself, notably European agrarian conditions.

The mild household slavery of infidels, which had existed under Islam from its beginnings, had been taken over toward the end of the Middle Ages by Spaniards and Portuguese, partly in imitation, partly in reprisal. Just as Christians were made slaves by the Arabs, so were Muhammadan Moors by the Christians. Since the Arabs also enslaved blacks from tropical Africa, the Portuguese took over the slave trade from them. To Muhammadans and Christians alike, of course, the blacks were "infidels."

After the Spaniards in the New World had conquered enormous stretches of tropical and subtropical fertile land and after Indian natives proved unsuitable as agricultural workers, the importation of African black slaves was suggested as an alternative. The prevailing form of enterprise, as soon as sufficient black labor forces were available, came to be the large-scale plantation economy, which evolved precisely at this time. "Capitalist large-scale enterprise sprouts in the beginning of the sixteenth century; the plantation economy with black slaves was the first experiment with this form.

Regardless of whether the product was sugar or cotton . . . the accompanying phenomenon of a class of manual workers, who are nothing else but that, appears in the form of Negro slavery. . . . Hence the Negro slave trade, which stamped its feature upon the tropical colonies, must be imputed to the needs of the rising large-scale enterprise. There the Negro question is the labor question with respect to the agrarian-industrial large-scale enterprise of the plantation."[150] Subsequently the form of enterprise thus elaborated and "tested" was transferred to eastern Europe, with the white slaves drawn from the Slavic lower stratum where no indigenous, free peasantry and no high culture consciousness posed a form of resistance. This east European manorial economy, the deliverer of supplementary grain for the growing urban population of western Europe, led to a progressive deterioration of the situation, in fact and in law, of the rural lower stratum working in this form. The result was that they became legally bound to the soil and to the inherited status of serfdom—indeed of real slavery. In the newspaper *Frag- und Anzeige-Nachrichten* of Königsberg, Prussia, 2 May 1744, we read the following advertisement: "Persons, to be sold in Königsberg," followed by an exact description of the individuals and their suitability. This in the city of pure reason in the making, when Kant was already studying there. We are by no means dealing with a medieval institution: east European serfdom dates from modern times, not the Middle Ages, and is much younger than Negro slavery in the colonies (which goes back to the beginning of the sixteenth century). While the Enlightenment was already in full swing in the higher, urban, educated strata, the last influences of the absolutist age of darkness were reaching their apogee in the backward eastern agrarian regions; the development of the lower and upper social strata ran in sharply opposite directions. Similarly, it seems that Negro slavery in the southern United States attained forms of extreme brutality and inhumaneness only in the eighteenth and nineteenth centuries, the portrayal of which in Harriet Beecher Stowe's (1812-1896) *Uncle Tom's Cabin* (1852) aroused the justified indignation of the civilized world.

c. Art during the Age of Absolutism

The new intellectual bondage brought by the Reformation and Counter Reformation found its expression in art. Mannerism is the art of the militant ascendant Counter Reformation, of the counter-reformatory *ecclesia militans*; the pious baroque is the art of the counterreformatory *ecclesia triumphans*. In mannerism, especially in El Greco (1547-1614), we see how the saint, irresistibly seized by the whirl of the divine, is turned around in a spiral lifting itself heavenward.

In order to find something comparable, we must probably revert to the art of the late Roman imperial age, with its yearning for the Beyond—which, as we have seen, shows remarkable similarities to mannerism.

The art of the baroque, ostentatious and representative, devout and restrained, adapted itself to glorification of the heavenly as well as the earthly absolute sovereign; the baroque is just as much the art of the clerical Counter Reformation as it is the art of secular, unenlightened absolutism. On the other hand, in the art of the baroque, preservation of the legacy of the Renaissance by the Church is also visible.

As soon as the Church of the Counter Reformation had assured its dominance in the territories remaining for Catholicism or reconquered by it, it became evident that the Church had been able to incorporate the vital forces of the Renaissance after all. Opulence and sensuousness are celebrated in the art of the baroque, especially its church art. But freedom was lacking. Baroque art recalls the symbiosis of bigotry and immorality in the princely courts of the time. This whole orgiastic scene has something unhealthily stuffy and congested about it; it stands under an invisible pressure, and this pressure seems to have as its consequence an unnatural luxuriance.

The architecture of the baroque exhibited a polar tension— between opulence and classical rationality, between the swelling, twisting, swinging, flamboyant elements of authentic baroque forms and the antique, Renaissance-like mastered transparence of the Doric columns and of the gable end, which often seem to rise victoriously from that counterundulant and spumescent sea of forms. Yet in other cases this magisterial hard and cold rationality seems to be forced and clamped upon the baroque agitation. It was the great accomplishment of the seventeenth-century French to achieve a unique balance within this tension-filled polarity, especially in literature, endowing the French literature of the period with a character and level thereafter to be experienced as classical in France.

The England of Elizabeth (b. 1533, reigned 1558-1603) occupies a special intellectual-sociological position. England's separation from the Catholic church was not undertaken on the grounds of religious conviction but because of a sultanesque whim of Henry VIII. Consequently, that separation had a loosening impact—as also did the bloody struggle for succession up to the execution of Mary, Queen of

Scots (1587). Motive forces of the Renaissance continued their influence longer than elsewhere, without being stifled by either Reformation or Counter Reformation, although they were soon threatened by the beglooming ascendancy of Puritanism. This was the right hour for an equally brief and steep rise of tragedy, reaching its apogee in Shakespeare (1564-1616), the baroque farewell to the "merry old England" of the Renaissance. That this Elizabethan efflorescence was a legacy of the Renaissance is apparent in the fact that Elizabethan architecture and music started in Italy and were brought to other countries by emigrated Italians or under direct Italian influences.

The bloody religious wars and the cruel confessional persecutions of the sixteenth and seventeenth centuries, ending in frightful disorder and exhaustion, sparked in all the countries involved a flight into the innermost recesses of being as a reaction to the surrounding horror. It was a new surfacing of old mystic subterranean currents, combined with a sentimentalization preparing for a new sensibility. Holland, the old homeland of *devotio moderna*, at that time played the role of an international center; but England, France, and Spain also participated. The movement itself was conscious of its international character and cultivated communications between the countries on a literary as well as a personal plane.

Pietism forms an especially important and partially independent German-Protestant phenomenon within this broader movement. There is no lack in Pietism of romantic influences or counterreformatory devotionalism, especially of Spanish mysticism and of French quietism. Pietism forms, at the same time, the ultimate and most far-reaching outgrowth of the tendencies toward psychic intensification apparent in Luther, who, to quote only one passage from many, wrote: "The gospel requires no physical room nor site to dwell; it dwells, and must dwell, in the heart."[151]

The kinship with mysticism is unmistakable and was consciously cultivated by the pietists themselves. But the mystic seeks solitude, the pietist community; the mystic strives for illumination, the pietist for "inner warmth," or "warmth of the soul." With the mystic it is a question of spirit; he does not want to feel, but to behold God; the pietist feels the most intimate well being among his fellows and with his Bible, in the cozy semidarkness of the German winter evening in a room warmed by a porcelain stove.

Among the intellectually important Germans of the eighteenth and early nineteenth centuries many came directly from Pietism. Hamann (1730-1788), the great precursor of the *Sturm und Drang* movement, experienced a formal conversion to Pietism. His pupil Herder (1744-1803) stemmed from the same intellectual milieu. Wieland (1737-1813) was born in a pietistic parsonage. Goethe experienced his pietistic period under the influence of Fräulein von Klettenberg (1723-1774).

The independence of the evangelical congregation, Luther's ideal, yielded a sociological structure of democratic character; the parson had a leading position as the social consequence of the concept of "universal priesthood." But because for Luther this was a consequence solely of religious ideas (and because Luther was not a politician, least of all a democratic one) this tendency was defeated as soon as it came into contact with the rising absolutism of territorial principalities, which determined the structure of political power of that epoch. Luther acceded, and thus arose the territorial or state church with the supreme episcopate of territorial princes and sovereigns.

If we survey the relation of the baroque to the Renaissance, it must be noted that the Renaissance, even without the intervention of the Reformation and the Counter Reformation, would have developed further. Indeed, much of what distinguishes the baroque from the Renaissance is an expression of such endogenous further development. Michelangelo's (1475-1567) artistic development presumably would not have differed if there had been no Reformation or Counter Reformation—except that it might have found less approval and exercised less influence.

d. The Science of Absolutism

In the realm of the mind there is one sphere in which a sharp and ruthless absolutist centralism, a rigid and unconditional systematic super- and subordination is appropriate and indispensable: mathematics and theoretical physics, especially mechanics. These sciences experienced their triumphal upswing and classic formulation, fundamental for all subsequent time, in the century of absolutism.

Among the systems of the seventeenth century, Descartes represents classicism and Leibniz the genuine anticlassical baroque, whereas Spinoza cultivated mathematical rationalism on a broader scale.

Hobbes also belongs in the ranks of continental absolutist thinkers in that he, although an Englishman, stands in political and intellectual opposition to English development. Hobbes's absolutism is inherent in the structure of his own system, and he supported it theoretically as a political sociologist, as well as practically as a politician. At the court of the exiled pretender to the throne, the later King Charles II, he became a mathematics teacher and accepted a pension from him. On the other hand, he was too detached an observer to overlook the personal inadequacy of this penultimate Stuart.

René Descartes is the real founder of modern rationalism, impressive because of his influence on future generations. His whole mode of thought and argument has a pronounced neoscholastic character; but he no longer recognizes the superiority of revealed church dogma from which, however, scholastic nominalists had already half-extricated themselves by means of the doctrine of the twofold truth. The new rationalism concerned itself only with one of the halves, natural truth; Descartes expressly leaves untouched the claims of revelation outside his own field of work. Hence the equally significant and grotesque facts of his pilgrimage to the shrine at Loretto (1624) and of his praise (1619) of the Holy Virgin for the extreme rational solution to his philosophic doubts.

Cartesianism, which immediately started its triumphal procession across the whole continent, then also spread in the form of a new secular-rational dogmatics, of a rationalist competing theology that bears the family features of theology all too distinctly on its brow.

One of the most characteristic features of the rationalism of the absolutist era of the seventeenth century is the almost undisputed sway it gave to the prejudice in favor of mathematics, to the notion that syllogistic proofs derived from preceding definitions and axioms—a method that found classical expression in Euclid's textbook—are the only valid ideals to which any branch of human learning must aspire if it is to make a claim to scientific status.

By descent and education Descartes, of course, was Catholic, Hobbes Protestant, Spinoza Jewish, Leibniz Lutheran. Although none sought an open break with his inherited confession, and Leibniz even zealously pursued a Christian-ecumenical religious policy, as philosophers they all belonged, nonetheless, to that great fourth confession of antique-pagan humanism, without postulating which—as I have pointed out elsewhere[152]—the intellectual history of that century cannot be understood. From late Scholasticism they took over that logico-dialectical training and its conceptual apparatus—i.e., therefore the further development of Aristotle—but by no means any specific Christian tenets of faith. Their representation of God bears Stoic-Platonic features, and they do not take the other building elements of their systems from Christian faith. On the contrary, these derive from the different philosophical systems of the pagan ancient world. If, without prejudice to their originality, we should like to fit them into specific lines of tradition, then Descartes is possibly a Stoic, Hobbes an Epicurean, and Spinoza a thinker who tries to effect a synthesis betzeen these two schools. Leibniz, in whom components of almost all ancient systems are to be found in more or less original application, could perhaps most readily be designated as a syncretic, Pythagoreanizing Platonist. In all of them reason has replaced the Jewish-Christian revelation as the supreme and sole authority, that reason which at the same time strides irresistibly from one victory to another in the exact sciences. The relation of mathematics to the exact sciences—for their part of antique, not Christian origin—is for all the thinkers of this epoch of fundamental importance, and Descartes and Leibniz belong indeed among the great creators of modern mathematics.

All the leading thinkers of the modern age went through an apprenticeship with the school of late Scholasticism; they owe the athletic prowess of their minds to that training. The contempt of the Renaissance for Scholasticism exercises a persistent influence—especially marked in Descartes; but it expressed itself only in his reluctance to acknowledge his alliance with Scholasticism, his determination to conceal any dependency on Scholasticism to the best of his ability, or outright denying it. Of course, Descartes' mania for, and pride in, originality are also legacies of the Renaissance.

The great metaphysical systems of modern philosophy recognize reason as the sole and deciding criterion. In them, *ratio* lays claim to sovereign absolute rights of dominion. The metaphysicians' bent for systematization has exactly the same monarchic-despotic and centralist quality that was so evident in the politics of the period. We could rightly speak of a century of absolutism—or of an enlightened despotism of reason—in the history of philosophy: the dictate of reason "de par la reine" takes the place of royal ordinances. And these different absolutist and centralized kingdoms of the *ratio*, each one sovereign in itself, conduct the same jealous foreign policy against each other as do the political kingdoms—with expansionist aspirations, periodic wars, and shifting alliances. The systems of Descartes, Hobbes, Spinoza, and Leibniz as intellectual powers are not so different from the confrontations of great powers on the plane of politics.

This parallel was already recognized by contemporaries. Pascal once wrote: "Great men of genius have their empire, their splendour, their greatness, their victory."[153] Descartes compares himself in detail with victorious field marshals "whose forces usually grow in proportion to their victories . . ."[154] And Fontenelle says of Descartes that like Newton, he was a "genius of the first order, born to dominate over other minds and to found empires."[155]

We have already seen how closely dogmatic-radical rationalism and the theology of revelation were blended—despite their traditional sworn hostility—in the first Western philosophic system of radical rationalism, that of Parmenides. He actually propounded it as a revelation from the mouth of God, and under such a pretention developed a world picture which, though marked by ruthless internal logic and unity nevertheless was as flatly at variance with common sense as the most high-flown theological dogma. Unbounded rationalism carried to an extreme here demands, like any theology, a *sacrificium intellectus*—not, to be sure, on the altar of revelation but rather on that of systematic logic. The ruthless despotic sway in the realm of thought here in Parmenides had reached a world-historical high point. In the seventeenth century, the clerical claim to sovereignty advanced by theology was taken over by rationalism and, at the same time, sharpened rather than softened. A striking example is the so-called school of Occasionalism, the doctrine concocted step by step by Geulincx (1624-1669), Malebranche (1683-1715), and Leibniz. It was a doctrine of preestablished harmony, and it asserted that we do not perceive the world with our senses, but rather God's omnipotence, wisdom, and goodness, making the two separate clocks—of our perception, on the one hand, and of reality, on the other—arbitrarily run in precise agreement. As an absurdity this goes far beyond what any theology demanded from its faithful.

Elsewhere in Leibniz's work we also find extremely fruitful, indeed brilliant, morphological intuitions that anticipate the central insights of preromanticism and romanticism (for which reason Herder called him a poet of metaphysics). In Leibniz as in Vico the baroque stretches its hand out to romanticism. But these fruitful and realistic ideas in Leibniz are woven into the abstruse structure of the system; at times the very abstruseness of the system facilitates such insights—yet all this is far from a justification of that system. It is quite possible that a particular correct conclusion can be more easily derived from incorrect than correct premises. In the realm of the imaginary the spirit feels itself liberated from the hard resistance of reality, the incorrect as well as the correct is reachable by it with equal ease, and instinctive brilliance expresses itself in the fact that on occasion it unconsciously guides toward the correct conclusion, which is, as it were, arrived at from the rear.

As a consolation for such extravagant confusions there remained only the justified hope that the coexistence of a number of systems reciprocally combatting each other would in the long run have the same loosening effects as the coexistence of a number of religious confessions combatting each other.

By and large Reformation and Counter Reformation, baroque and absolutism signify a severe relapse (compared to the late Middle Ages and the Renaissance) into intellectual and politcal bondage, an age of eclipse. "Posterity will not be able to grasp," wrote a contemporary in 1562, "that we again had to live in such dense darkness after it had already become light."[156]

The degree of this eclipse had hardly ever been reached even in the much maligned "dark Middle Ages." But the Enlightenment, with this political slogan, aimed less at the Middle Ages than it did at the counterreformatory orthodoxy of its time, which it accused of "medievalness."

In the following sections we shall see how the theological bondage of thought was overcome by the Enlightenment, that of metaphysical system building by empiricism, the exaggerated form of art by classicism, the vital unfreedom of feeling by preromanticism, the political unfreedom of absolutism, finally, by the Great Revolution. We shall see further how Enlightenment and revolution failed, not lastly in consequence of the mistakes made in their struggle against theology and absolutism, mistakes which had been imposed upon them by these same foes. For every struggle signifies, in a tragic way, an adaptation, at once cogent and unconscious, to the foe. *Chacun prend à l'adversaire qu'il le veuille ou non.*

22. Against Intellectual Bondage: Enlightenment

It attests to the depth and the inner strength of the Renaissance that the intellectual impulses it released continued unswervingly along their track, despite all obstacles. The task of enlightenment begun by the Renaissance continued under cover of the ruling theologies. It would be possible to write a history of scientific and intellectual progress during these centuries without mentioning the Reformation and Counter Reformation. Only in the biographical notes on the bearers of this development would either movement make itself occasionally embarrassingly noticeable in the form of emigrations, persecutions, trials, jailings, tortures, and executions. How much more rapidly the same development might have run its course under different circumstances!

Confessional pressure and the Inquisition did not hinder the advance of enlightenment, but the admirable nonchalance, naturalness, and self-assurance of the Renaissance was finally transformed by this terroristic pressure into the dragon venom of hate-ridden opposition. This is evident especially in France, where these conflicts assumed their sharpest form. Voltaire's anticlerical battle cry "Écrasez l'infâme!" was the proclamation, at long last, of a counteroffensive of the Renaissance against the Counter Reformation.

At the same time the borderline between faith and knowledge, between "Christian conviction" and the "atmosphere of paganism,"[157] was under heavy pressure from both sides. The pagan rationalism of the Renaissance was most consistently continued by Italian heretics like the Sozzinis, who represent a straight connection between Renaissance and Enlightenment and who also had to immerse themselves in the illegality of an underground movement. There was an atmosphere in the seventeenth century—as one prominent contemporary expressed it—of longing for the "liberty of the ancients," the "ancient liberty to speak and to think"[158] in contrast to the eighteenth century, when the victory of the Enlightenment brought redemptive relaxation.

In fairness it must be admitted that the Roman church did not let itself be dragged backward further than was absolutely necessary; that it remained conscious of its historical responsibility, and did not surrender the great legacy of the ancient world that had been entrusted to it; the Jesuit order cultivated the tradition of antiquity with special intensity. Even under cover of the Counter Reformation, the humanistic tradition of the Renaissance did not die. Troeltsch even speaks of a "remarkable Renaissance culture of the Counter Reformation."[159] The renewal, representation, and further development of ancient culture was carried on particularly in the more specialized branches of scientific knowledge, and here incomparably more was accomplished in the Catholic than in the Protestant sphere. Most of these scholars were priests or monks, including even the great reviver of Epicurus, canon Pierre Gassendi (1592-1655). In the first half of the seventeenth century the Parisian monastic cell of Father Mersenne (1588-1648) was the meeting place for the leading scholars and most progressive minds. The enlightened French and Italian abbés of the eighteenth century continued this tradition.

In the protective shadow of the Church, a kind of preliminary Enlightenment developed, whose bearers often began by volunteering some particular service for their own denomination; but in the

further course of their work they were driven beyond the narrow
bounds of denominationalism.

Philologico-historical criticism and hermeneutics (the art of interpreting and understanding transmitted texts) made great progress. Here is one of the few points at which the Reformation had a
positive influence upon Renaissance humanism. For as a result of
the Reformation's proclamation of the biblical text—the "word of
God"—as the highest and only authority, the exegesis of this text as
"service to the Word" acquired central religious importance.

Protestantism asserts, in the interest of a universal priesthood,
the universal ability to understand the Bible; Catholicism, in the interests of the authority of the Church and its tradition, asserts the
difficulty of understanding it and the need for explication. Both conceptions, starting from opposite ends, work toward the same result
of promoting the progress of interpretation and its technique. For
example, the French Catholic Richard Simon (1638-1712) made
notable advances in the art of interpretation in the service of the
Counter Reformation: in opposing Protestant claims of absolute validity of biblical truth he emphasized the complex problems of
interpretation and the need for clarification.

The methods of source criticism of historical science and its auxiliary sciences developed in a similar way, particularly in the
Catholic domain. The Jesuit Jean de Bolland (1596-1665) believed
that by recourse to the oldest and plainest version of the legends of
saints, it would be possible to strengthen these edifying writings
against Protestant attacks. The Benedictine Dom Jean Mabillon
(1632-1707) was imbued with the childlike pious conviction that objective truth, once securely founded on textual criticism, would always speak in favor of his Church, its transmissions and its privileges. Through the Jansenist Louis Sébastien Le Nain de Tillemont
(1637-1698) and the librarian Lodovico Antonio Muratori (1672-
1750) the new method was applied to history.

Just as the nominalism of the late scholastic period had developed
within the Church and in the service of the Church, but then served
as the most important armor for all attacks against ecclesiastical
orthodoxy, so here developed critical methods of historical investigation that eventually undermined the authority of all dogmatic
tradition.

Advances in the natural sciences, culminating in the work of
Copernicus, Kepler, Galileo, Huygens, and Newton, created for the
ratio a citadel, a strong point and base for future operations. The
construction of natural science into an "impregnable fortress," as

demanded by Hobbes, was accomplished. This development of the
exact sciences, reaching a zenith at the turn of the seventeenth and
the eighteenth centuries, constitutes one of the essential differences
between the Enlightenment and the Renaissance.

The astronomical doctrine of Aristarchus, as revived by Copernicus, had already dealt a fatal blow to the world of appearances.
Now the doctrine of the subjectivity of secondary qualities, derived
from Democritus and elaborated and made universally acceptable
by Locke, led to a process of quantification and mathematicization of
the scientific image of the world. The world became increasingly
more rational and more abstract, ever more simple and above all
more subject to mastery. This possibility of mastering the world, in
accordance with the principle that "knowledge is power," had been
triumphantly proclaimed previously by Francis Bacon (1561-1627),
the baroque projector and herald of the modern victory parade of
progress in natural science and technology.

In the seventeenth century, inanimate nature stood at the center
of scientific interest, along with the sciences of mathematics,
physics, mechanics, and astronomy that are appropriate to it. Now,
as in Greece in the fifth century B.C., interest shifted from inanimate
to animate nature, from the natural sciences to the human sciences,
from matter to man. The basic viewpoint of Protagoras, that "Man is
the measure of all things," had finally been revived after more than
two millennia. If the seventeenth century was the physical century,
the eighteenth century was the anthropological century. We can observe this shift in its embryonic stage in Pascal (1623-1662), who, in
his *Pensées*, writes: "I spent a long time in the study of the abstract
sciences. . . . When I commenced the study of man, I saw that these
abstract sciences are not suited to man and that I was wandering
further from my own state in examining them than others in not
knowing them. . . ." But he sees himself rather alone with this approach: "I thought at least to find many companions in the study of
man and that it was the true study which is suited to him. I have
been deceived, still fewer study it than geometry." But as early as
1601 Pierre Charron (1541-1603), a friend of Montaigne, had proclaimed: "The true science and the true study of man is man." Barbeyrac (1674-1744) and Burlamaqui (1694-1748) see in the nature of
man the real foundation of natural law.[160] Later, in Alexander Pope
(1688-1744), it is a question of a recognized truth: "The proper study
of mankind is man." Likewise, Rousseau begins the foreword of his
Second Discourse on Inequality: "The most useful and the least ad-

vanced of all branches of human knowledge seems to me to be that of man."

What was still lacking in the anthropology of the Enlightenment was the insight that the essence of man cannot simply be abstracted from a given current and present state, that this fundamental task of the study of man requires a more comprehensive historical foundation. As Dilthey was to put it, "What man is, he finds out from history." But even this basic insight was already hinted at in the Enlightenment itself. Saint-Evremond, an early supporter of Enlightenment hedonism, writes: "All times have a character that is proper to them: they have their abilities, their interest, their affairs; they have their morality, in some fashion, having their defects and their virtues. It is always man, but nature varies herself in man."[161] Lichtenberg (1742-1799) affirms in one of his brilliant aphorisms: "We must not conclude what man can be on the basis of what he is now in Europe." "The real man is not the one who lives with us, we must now seek him out from history."

The somber authoritarian pressure of baroque absolutism in all sectors of life was too extreme. It contrasted too strongly with the liberation that had been set in motion by the Renaissance. The longer the incessant quarrels among theologians and the confessional persecutions and religious wars went on, the more people grew weary of them. Intolerance called for broad-mindedness, orthodoxy for tolerance, the mania for system-building for skeptical criticism, rationalism for empiricism. The century of the baroque demanded the century of the Enlightenment as a counterbalance.

The Church was no longer the unitary representative of the whole of Western Christendom, but split into a number of confessions and sects. There were two main Protestant confessions, with whom above all it was still locked in conflict, and in addition a growing number of denominations and sects. Not even the Catholic bloc that had remained was wholly unified, for the territorial-ecclesiastical strivings of absolutism had led to considerable independence, particularly in France. Spiritualism had always espoused a fundamentally tolerant liberalism, but its followers were lucky when they were spared the heretic's fate. However, confessions and sects, where they developed, were equally despotic and intolerant. Pronounced equilibrium arose between a number of confessions, and in the long run this was the only possible *modus vivendi*. With respect to England, the real fortress of tolerance, Voltaire had seen through the situation and coined a brilliant formulation: "If there were only one religion in England its despotism would be something to fear; if there were only two, they would cut each other's throat; but there are thirty of them and they live in peace and happily."[162]

The situation in philosophy was similar. Development had begun with a "catholic" autocracy of Cartesianism. However, there was a growing number of large and small philosophic churches, sects, and schools, fighting one another. And these schools recognized not revelation but *ratio* as the supreme authority; they were lacking supernatural sanction and the patina of venerable age—hence the dissolvent effect of the quarrel among them made itself felt more rapidly and fundamentally than in theology. Pierre Bayle (1647-1706) drew the fundamental conclusion in both departments. In doing so, he renewed the philosophic school of skepticism of ancient Greece, which had likewise arisen as a reaction to the irreconcilable quarrel among opposing philosophical schools. His famous *Dictionnaire historique et critique* (first published in Rotterdam 1695-1697), forerunner of the *Encyclopédie*, was an especially opportune and effective form for propaganda of these antiauthoritarian views. Each objective arrangement of material presupposes an ordering principle of whose correctness one is convinced; since the skeptic questions all such convictions, all that remains to him is the wholly external principle of alphabetical arrangement.

As the seventeenth century drew to an end, public opinion in France and Holland (and somewhat later also among the upper intellectual strata of other European countries) came to be dominated by various philosophic systems, and by the debates among them. In France at the turn of the century (1680-1715) this led to a "crisis of European consciousness" that Paul Hazard portrayed with vividness and scholarship in his book of that title—a crisis in which European minds turned away from Christianity and toward a revival of the thought of antiquity. It was as a result of this fundamental shift that the eighteenth century became truly the century of enlightenment. Of the end of the seventeenth century Leibniz rightly says: *Finis saeculi novam rerum faciem aperuit*—"The end of the century put a new face on things." After fifteen hundred years of intellectual bondage, heteronomy, and hierocracy, of the subordination of thought to the dominance of faith, man and foremost his intellect, were once again liberated, summoned to an autonomy and independent responsibility. The injunction *sapere aude* was awakened in consciences: "Dare to know."

Voltaire (François-Marie Arouet, le jeune, 1694-1778) took his place as the internationally recognized leader of this movement; and the group around the great *Encyclopédie* published by Denis Diderot (1713-1784) and Jean Le Rond d'Alembert (1717-1783), became, as it were, the general staff. Rarely was there so much brilliance and talent, so much dedication to the cause, and such a feeling of responsibility, so much comradeliness and individualism, so much enthusiasm and captivating verve, so much radiant optimism and beguiling good humor combined in a single group of thinkers.

It was Voltaire who finally led the deistic free thought of the Enlightenment to a great counteroffensive against the "triumphant beast"—an anticrusade, a holy war against what he took to be pretended saintliness. This general offensive of free thought, with Voltaire in the lead, culminated in a full victory for the Enlightenment. The Church itself had to acknowledge defeat by dissolving, in 1773, the Jesuit order, which had served as its bodyguard and shock troop during the Counter Reformation. All the devotion and veneration hitherto claimed by the Church now was transferred to Voltaire, the man who had vanquished it, the uncrowned king of intellectual France, the dragon slayer of superstition, the *écraseur de l'infâme*. As a contemporary put it, "Long live the author of *La Henriade*! the defender of Calas! the author of *La Pucelle!*"[163] Thus is explained this position of a man who, as the prototype of the modern critic and journalist, with his hairsplitting brilliance and his sharp-tongued backbiting, seemed least suited for the role of adored saint and revered redeemer.

In contrast to the economic dependency upon feudal patrons in which most bourgeois literati had found themselves from the Renaissance until the eighteenth century, Voltaire was the first thinker since Erasmus and Aretino to succeed in living independently from his pen. Through circumspect administration of property he became lord of a castle who could associate with other feudal lords on an equal footing—a circumstance that further enhanced his prestige and his political influence.

In the German sphere, the newly achieved intellectual freedom as a rule remained constrained within the limits of respectable moderation: "Man has received from God nothing more admirable than his intellect. . . . In such a manner can one all the more be called a man, the more he knows how to use the powers of his intellect." Thus wrote Christian von Wolff in 1712, in the introduction to his *Reasonable Thoughts Concerning the Powers of the Human Intellect*. "To think correctly and to will reasonably"—thus the Swiss Isaak Iselin formulated the maxim of the age in *Thoughts on the Improvement of the Basel High School* (1757).

What is generally referred to as the "individualism" of the Enlightenment has a very special quality and function. Since the literary periods of German preromanticism, classicism, and romanticism, individualism has been commonly defined as the freedom of every person to develop his singular individuality as differently from that of all others—as originally—as he can, in full freedom from social constraints. This concept of the individual corresponds to that dictum of Leibniz that so attracted Goethe: "individuum est ineffabile"; its ideal type is the "original genius." The result of such individualism as later understood is a variegated, richly contrasting, and vastly heterogeneous state of society. This kind of individualism is the very opposite of the ideal of individuality as conceived by the Enlightenment. The Enlightenment made the individual human being, as an *ens rationale* (that is, each separate individual in a state of wakeful common sense) the measure of all things. Only that which was plausible and useful for the normal individual human being, dependent alone and exclusively upon his understanding, was to be considered valid; indeed, to be valid it had to be in concordance with the understanding of each and all, quite apart from all individual differences and particularities. Only that which could be made clear instantly to an average individual was considered true. It was posited that all individuals were essentially the same. Thus, what was true and correct for one individual was bound to be true for every other. Only coercion and deformation, arbitrary convention and fashion assertedly made individuals different; the more everyone is left in full freedom, the more would human nature appear in its original uniformity. Helvetius went so far in drawing this theoretical conclusion that he altogether denied innate differences among human beings, all differences assertedly being secondary and acquired, the result of different external circumstances—that is, of the environment, as we would say today. The Physiocrats were wholly convinced that their single tax must be as correct for China as for Europe. Aesthetics ordained the same ideal of beauty for all mankind. Nothing lay further from the Enlightenment than the recognition of individual particularities and qualities, or even their glorification—that was one of the most violent charges that preromanticism and romanticism leveled against the Enlightenment, and it was against this attitude of the Enlightenment that they raised *their* passionate counterslogan of individualism.

The Church as a divine institution of salvation had set itself above every individual, and the secular absolutism of the baroque had raised a corresponding claim for the state as represented by the princes; the Enlightenment, in the name of the individual, recognized as the sole measure of things, protested against all such pretentions. Social structures, such as church and state, in relation to the individuals composing them, are secondary and accessory; they are nothing but the sum total of single individuals. A social contract grants to such institutions only the rights that these same individuals specifically transfer to them. Their justification for existence lies in promoting the aims of the individuals. This radical, rationalistic, and atomistic sociology is the essence of the individualism of the Enlightenment.

In Germany, the Enlightenment reached its apogee in Gotthold Ephraim Lessing (1729-1781). The German inheritance of dullness and formlessness seems to have been overcome here for the first time in Lessing. Never since Greek antiquity had a mind confronted the world with more manly self-assurance, more unencumbered cheerfulness and clarity, more joy in fighting and in being reconciled; all these qualities, moreover, were combined with an inexhaustible vitality, an intellectual resiliency, and an engaging boyishness. And although we can hardly imagine a more typical, unrestrained exponent of the Enlightenment, he also to a remarkable extent overcame the limitations of that movement. From the viewpoint of intellectual history the modern era (in the broadest sense) begins with the Encyclopedists in France and with Lessing in Germany. Only from that point onward can we still read books without first having to translate them into our own concepts. Only from that point onward are we free from the musty odor of antiquity and the museum feeling of historical distance. We can trace the matter-of-courseness and unbounded continuity of our direct intellectual tradition only as far back as that point. At this particular place, something new was added to the secular warp of the fabric of intellectual history. In terms of living consciousness, the great caesura between the Middle Ages and modern times really lies here.

The struggle for freedom in the Enlightenment was directed first and foremost against absolute theological authority, with its demand for passive obedience as embodied in the orthodoxy of the Christian churches, newly sharpened by the Reformation and the Counter Reformation. Dogma was acceptable only if it was ready to justify itself in the forum of the intellect. Since dogma usually could not pass this test, its influence gradually shrank until a mere residue of deism was left, which will be discussed in a later context.

The next target was the power of tradition—that tradition of thinking and doing something for no other reason than that it had always been thought and done before. Here, too, testing and justification were demanded. That question of justification of tradition—and of the applicable standards of justification was explicitly raised when Rousseau cast doubt on the validity of all inherited culture.

The longer this question about standards and justification was considered, the more it became a matter of self-testing and self-criticism on the part of the Enlightenment. Rationalism, naïve in its positive constructive aspects, in most cases was quickly discarded. Logic was considered as a standard near to hand, but it presented only a formal criterion that was relative and negative in it effects. Experience offered itself as a positive and substantive criterion, but it rested upon the systematic empiricism of science and, ultimately, on sense impressions. In the ethical and social sphere, self-criticism and epistemological reflection led to anthropology, to the empirical study of the nature of man. The latter, with the employment of crude or refined methods, was selected as the decisive standard.

The picture of human history as a unified, comprehensible whole appeared for the first time in the myth of the four cosmic periods as it arose in the Semitic Near East in the eighth century B.C., and was handed down by Hesiod (after 700 B.C.). Mankind, originally destined for a carefree, happy existence by divine goodness and justice, has sunk lower, stage by stage—perhaps as punishment for its own sin. When the depths of derangement are reached, the sin is atoned for, the great cycle of ages will close, and ultimately the Golden Age will return. Against this view, Christianity presented its schema of the history of salvation from Paradise, through Original Sin, to Redemption and Last Judgment. This view of history found its classic exposition in the *Discours sur l'histoire universelle* (1681) a didactic treatise by Bossuet, the greatest preacher at the court of Louis XIV. This was also a connecting link for Voltaire when he wrote his *Essai sur les moeurs et l'esprit des nations et sur les principaux faits de l'histoire depuis Charlemagne jusqu'à Louis XIII*. This treatise was preceded by a *Philosophie de l'histoire* intended as an introduction and substitute for Bossuet's *Discours*.

Previously, autonomous anthropological standards had been applied to historiography by Thucydides and Polybius in antiquity and by Machiavelli and Guicciardini in the Renaissance, but these remained partial human histories, limited in space and time. No one had yet ventured to apply such standards to the universal history of mankind. Universal history had been conceived of only as a heteronomous, hierocratic, theological history, a history of sin and salvation. Once the historical perspective was fundamentally broadened to include the Far East, historiography was secularized, freed from theological heteronomy, and made autonomous, mundane, secular, and humane. The idea of a "universal history of cosmopolitan intent" (as Kant entitled a work in 1784) had become possible, in the words of Meinecke, through the "consciousness of human solidarity, which was perhaps almost the highest achievement of the Enlightenment, and with a sense of humanity's involvement in a destiny that transcends all limitations of nationality and religion." Thus originated "the great plan of a true universal history, which stood clearly before Voltaire's eyes, and which was to encompass all cultures, all epochs, all peoples with the same love."[164]

Ernst Cassirer has observed that when Voltaire "turns to the past, he does so not for the sake of the past but for the sake of the present. History for him is not an end but a means; it is an instrument of self-education of the human mind. Voltaire does not try simply to reflect and investigate; he *demands* and passionately anticipates the substance of his demands."[165] It was the feeling of responsibility for the future of mankind, prevalent in the Enlightenment, that made possible the conception of a pure and human universal history of mankind.

We shall see how little the nineteenth-century successors measured up to this great conception of history and how arrogantly they celebrated their own decline from it, because of their preoccupation with improvements in detail.

Deep as was the weariness that the incessant disputes and wrangles of the denominations had at last engendered, it was only natural that people overfed for two centuries with such disputatious theology could not suddenly live without any theology whatsoever. They needed a countertheology cool enough to provide relief from overheated confessionalism, classically simple in contrast to the baroque involutions of ecclesiastic dogma, rational in contrast to all manner of irrationalism, and generally consonant with the scientific spirit of the age. The theology of the Stoics met each of these requirements; under the name of deism (a "pure" belief in God) it became the faith of all progressive minds of the age. With some oversimplification such a doctrine could also be viewed as common to all civilized religions and therefore as the original and "natural" religion that was in conformity with "natural" law. The religious feeling, which the people of that time carried as a legacy of two confessional centuries, found in this minimal theology a margin for the development of strong emotions. Most of those who professed this religion of reason were quite earnest; even Toland's passionate hatred of Christianity is not that of an unbeliever, but rather of a heretic, and many a deist was, like Rousseau, ready to protect this rational minimal theology through punitive sanctions.

The natural law doctrine of the Stoics was renewed even earlier than its theology. Originally, Christianity had possessed no legal doctrine of its own, and thus it had been able to incorporate the humane legal doctrine of the Stoics. Aristotle's richer, and materially more abundant, legal doctrine—itself in many ways closely akin to that of the Stoics—was received by medieval scholasticism. The Christian doctrine of natural law, which was cultivated throughout the Middle Ages, experienced a last upswing in the Spanish Scholasticism of the sixteenth and seventeenth centuries, where it participated in the general surge of Spanish intellectual life in the "Golden Age"; it received an added impulse from the necessity of working out norms for the position of the Church to Spain's colonial policy in newly discovered America. The doctrines of the most important Spanish late scholastics, especially of Francisco de Vitoria (ca. 1482-1546), Ludovico Molina (1535-1600), and Francisco Suárez (1548-1617) prepared the way for secular natural and international law, as late Scholasticism did for modern natural science. In both cases this origin was more or less veiled by the successors, so that it had to be reestablished by modern research.

The renovation of secular natural law, with simultaneous reversion to ancient sources, was prepared by Johannes Althusius (1557-1638), accomplished by Hugo Grotius (1583-1645), systematized by Samuel von Pufendorf (1623-1694) and Christian Thomasius (1655-1728), and finally encyclopedically popularized by Christian von Wolff (1679-1754).

Jean Barbeyrac (1674-1744), in his inaugural lecture at Lausanne in 1711, espoused ideas which in their anthropological conclusions led far beyond the rationalism of the Enlightenment—namely, that natural law rests upon the knowledge of man and of standards consonant with his nature, and that history must always serve as reason's control and proof. Only a knowledge of history can cure us of a naïve narrow-mindedness that makes us consider what is customary and predominant in our time and environment as self-evident and universally valid. In the works of his Genevan pupil, Jean-Jacques Burlamaqui (1694-1748), we read: "The idea of law, and even more that of natural law, are manifestly ideas relative to the nature of man. It is therefore from this very *nature* of man, from his *constitution* and from his *state*, that we must deduce the principles of this science."[166]

This rebirth of natural law was of practical as well as theoretical importance. The legal life of the baroque stood under the threefold pressure of tradition, the Church's claim to supremacy, and the same claim set forth by absolute monarchy. Now—with the development of natural law—a supreme court of appeal was recognized over and above any of these pretensions, a norm of legislation designed to protect true law against abuse, or legal enchroachment.

Just as it had with religion and law, the Enlightenment felt called upon to retrace economics to its natural foundations, and here its achievements were most remarkable and momentous: the creation of modern economics through the discovery of the invisible automatic laws of the market. The first discoverer of the principle was François Quesnay (1694-1774); its classic elaborator and systematizer was Adam Smith (1723-1790). Both were deists and Stoics, and both drew from the deistic-Stoic belief in divine world harmony the intellectual strength for their accomplishment. In a brilliant synthesis, the sober Scot combined this deistic-Stoic tenet with Mandeville's Epicurean-Hobbesian view of egoism as the motive force of economics. Smith's accomplishment has remained to date the classic foundation of scientific economics; his demand for economic freedom, derived from this theory, made headway in the nineteenth century and led to the kind of unprecedented upswing in world economics he had predicted. The same development, however, contrary to Smith's parallel prediction, did not lead to universal social harmony, but instead to its direct opposite. This was a tragic result (as I have demonstrated elsewhere[167]) of the same deistic belief in harmony that blinded its adherents to the necessary limiting conditions by which beneficent effects of economic freedom must be circumscribed; all efforts to state such conditions thus were paralyzed.

The same striving for the natural, eternal, and simple norm, which one believed to possess for all time, also dominated the aesthetics of the Enlightenment, whose adherents were convinced, in the words of Winckelmann (1717-1768) that "there is but *one* beauty, just as there is but *one* truth."

The two phases of the English Revolution of the seventeenth century were not undertaken by freethinkers or by men of the Enlightenment. Rather, the English Revolution had partly confessional, partly political antecedents, although there also were some spiritualistic and tolerant groups among the contending nonconformist sects. Above all, however, it involved a coalition of a great number of religious currents that had already come together, for the sake of civic peace, on the basis of reciprocal tolerance. The final restitution of a constitutionally limited monarchy had similar effects in the political sphere. At any rate, intellectual freedom, where it was not posed as a goal—as in John Milton's (1608-1674) demand for the rule of law and "public reason"—was the by-product of these revolutions. The Declarations of Indulgence date from 1672 and 1689, the Act of Toleration from 1689. Freedom of the press was formally proclaimed in 1693—a prodigious event in the Europe of baroque confessionalism.

This development even in its incipient phases soon had its impact on the course of intellectual history. As we have seen in an earlier chapter, rationalism had first been embodied in grand metaphysical systems of an absolutist-theological structure as developed in the countries on the Continent still under political and religious bondage, a development to which England had contributed the emigrant Hobbes. England, by contrast, was already beyond this baroque-absolutist stage. John Locke (1632-1704) was not active as a metaphysical system builder, but rather as a critical epistemologist. He founded an empiricism based on sense perception, proceeding with the typical sobriety and practical sense of the English. The royalist Hobbes had contemptuously rejected constitutional monarchy as a "mixarchy," declaring that "in reality it is naught else but pure anarchy."[168] By contrast, Locke in his science of government espoused constitutionalism and the decentralizing distribution of powers, just as in his empiricist thought he surrendered the autocratic centralism of the baroque system builders. In his constitutional philosophy, to be sure, the *ratio*, now as before, retains the monarch's right of confirmation, yet only by authenticating the evidence presented to it by the empiricism of the senses. The inductive attitude of his sensualistic empiricism implied the decisive rejection of the deductive rationalism of the Continental system builders of the seventeenth century. And what Locke had left by way of theology and metaphysics in peripheral concessions was fully eliminated by his more radical successor David Hume (1711-1776). Hume, with incorruptible good judgment and clarity of mind, removed all philosophic justification from any theology and metaphysics. This was effected not with the agnostic-shrug of skepticism, which can easily combine with mysticism of any sort, but rather on the basis of the calm, overt denial of a mind that feels itself fully and safely at home in the world as it lies before our eyes. Hume's attitude was later aptly paraphrased in Goethe's *Faust*.

> The sphere of Earth is known enough to me,
> The view beyond is barred immutably:
> A fool, who there his blinking eyes directeth
> O'er his peers a place expecteth!
> Firm let him stand, and look around him well!
> This World means something to the Capable![169]

The great liberation movement of the Enlightenment had started out from the rational sphere of thought and cognition; in contrast to the Renaissance it penetrated the sphere of vitality, experience, and the immediate values of life only in the end. What had to be overcome was the depreciation of the body and its sensuous joys that had been renewed and sharpened by the Reformation and the Counter Reformation. The Enlightenment declared war upon this perversion of the scale of values, and obfuscation of life by the "inner-worldly asceticism" (in Weber's phrase) of Calvinism and others. Such a declaration of war already is implied in the elaborate treatment (often considered shocking by his critics) which Bayle in his *Dictionnaire critique* accords to erotic themes. For we should not take at face value Bayle's excuse that this was done to accommodate the publisher's wishes—although even this, if true, would have had a symptomatic significance.

The Dutch neurologist Bernard de Mandeville (1670-1733) and the witty French chevalier Charles de Marguetel de Saint-Denis, comte d'Ethalam and seigneur de Saint-Evremond (1610-1703) belonged to the freethinking men of the world who gathered in London from the end of the seventeenth century. The antiascetic morality that each of them practiced probably was not very different, and both gave a fundamental defense of this morality in their writings. The major difference would seem to be that the younger Dutchman, in line with his Calvinist origins, still called what he espoused in theory and practice "vices," and championed the thesis that human well-being depends on the "vilest and most hateful qualities of man." The enlightened Frenchman looked down with a cosmopolitan's superior smile on such gloomy backwardness. "Note," he writes, "that subtle persons call pleasure that which rude and coarse people have called vice."[170] A half century later the new antiascetic morality had become so pervasive that Adam Smith, criticizing

Mandeville in his lectures on ethics, called the puritanical views posited by the latter "some popular ascetic doctrines which had been
current before this time,"[171]—that is to say, as something uncul-
tured and long outdated.

The contemporaries were well aware of the novelty of their attitudes. As early as 1684, Pierre Bayle had written: "Here we are in
a century which from day to day becomes more enlightened, so that
all previous centuries will be but darkness in comparison."[172] That
is one of the earliest testimonies of that intoxicating feeling for life
by which the Enlightenment was winged and borne, that feeling for
life of a peak existence of mankind, "the remarkable expression"—
in Dilthey's words—"of the now achieved majority of the human
spirit in religion, law, and politics."[173] Or, to quote a French writer
of 1700: "By following reason, we depend upon ourselves alone, and
by virtue of that we become in some manner gods."[174] That is that
"sovereign joy in life," which we meet, for instance, in the portraits
of La Tour and in the busts of Houdon with their captivating combination of spirit, amiableness, and charm. That is the magnificent,
intoxicating emotional exuberance, the magnificent pathos that still
rings out to us in the choral finale of Beethoven's Ninth Symphony.

The Enlightenment is one of the few happy periods of fulfillment
in the history of mankind. It was the first period since the Renaissance (and will probably for long remain the last) in which the
Golden Age was experienced as being in the present rather than as a
wish dream projected into the distant past or to be realized in the
future. As Wordsworth sang:

> Europe at that time was thrilled with joy,
> France standing on the top of golden hours,
> And human nature being born again.

Or, in the words of a German document of 1784, "Our days filled the
happiest period of the eighteenth century. Emperor, kings, princes
affably come down from their feared heights; they despise splendor
and glitter, become fathers, friends and familiars of their people.
Religion tears up the clerical gown and emerges in its divinity. Enlightenment makes great strides. Thousands of our brothers and sisters, who lived in sanctified sloth, are given back to the commonwealth. Religious hatred and coercion of conscience diminish. Love
of man and freedom of thought win the upper hand. Arts and sciences flourish, and our gaze pushes deeply into the workshop of na-

ture. Artisans, like the artists, approach perfection, useful knowledge germinates in all social estates."[175]

Here again the contemporaries were fully conscious of the singularity of this turn. As Antoine Saint-Just (1767-1794), the later revolutionary, noted in his youth, "Happiness is a new idea in Europe." Yet "the greatest happiness of the greatest number"[176] did not simply fall into the lap of these eighteenth-century Europeans; it was the successful outcome of the most ardent endeavors of generations.

The lack of freedom during the baroque period, its overpowering despotic pressures expressed themselves in exaggerated form in its architecture and music, to the point where men felt overburdened and positively crushed. It was in this atmosphere of overheavy beauty that Fontenelle could note[177] that "l'ennui du beau produisit le joli"—boredom with beauty produced prettiness. For this reason in architecture and music, the rococo with its light, thin, elegant forms was welcomed with something of a sigh of relief. This was also the reason why "Bach fell into oblivion": the following generation experienced his baroque weightiness as so oppressive that it welcomed the music of a Haydn, with its pellucid grace and the naturalness of its "soft and touching melodies,"[178] as if it were liberation from a nightmare. In literature, the corresponding development led from the stylized lyric of the baroque to the folksong lyric of German preromanticism, which put its stamp on the German conception of the lyric up to Stefan George.

It is no accident that this movement of the liberation of feeling first developed in England, which had also taken the lead in the political and philosophical spheres. The enthusiastic Platonism of the Renaissance, as whose martyr Giordano Bruno in 1600 mounted the stake, grew nowhere outside of Italy itself such deep roots as it did in England. The Cambridge Platonists are the real successors of the Platonic Academy founded in 1459 by Marsilio Ficino at Florence. The tradition of English Platonism reached its apogee on a European scale in the work of the earl of Shaftesbury (1671-1713), *A Letter Concerning Enthusiasm* (1708). The modern conception of "genius" as developed by Addison originates in this same tradition. Similar literary developments produced the tear-drenched novels of Samuel Richardson (1681-1761), Edward Young's (1683-1765) melancholy *Night Thoughts on Life, Death and Immortality*, Thomas Gray's (1716-1771) *Elegy Written in a Country Churchyard,* and finally the pseudo-Ossianic *Fragments of Ancient Poetry, Collected in the Highlands*, by James Macpherson (1736-1796).

The further development of all these tendencies was probably nowhere broader and deeper than in Germany, and not lastly for the reason that here they found a seedbed that had been deeply ploughed by Pietism. Yet the predominantly English-German development of sensibility and world-weariness, diffuse and sentimental as it was with its tear-stained world picture, received its decisive point of crystallization and its theoretical justification through Jean-Jacques Rousseau (1712-1778). If any writer ever did, Rousseau "spoke from the heart" to his time. And for this reason the hearts of his contemporaries beat for him in truly rapturous fashion.

The men of Enlightenment had endeavored to refine and to rationalize traditional customs and life-styles, and among the upper classes this effort succeeded admirably. It had fought everything that it considered coarse or "irrational," everything that smacked of "superstition" within or outside the church, of cruelty, inconsistency, or absurdity—specific details, that is to say, that offended reason. It would never have occurred to them to attack the social style of life of the upper classes *in toto*. For one thing, that style of life over many generations had come to be taken for granted, had sunk its roots in the unconscious beyond the ken of *ratio*. For another, that style of life, as developed under baroque absolutism, had a distinctly courtly character and hence proved congenial to Enlightenment thinkers, who hoped to attain their goals with the aid of enlightened absolute monarchies—that is, by courtly means.

The courtly life-style of the *ancien régime* had a despotic and feudal character. It required obsequiousness in word and gesture not just toward the monarch but, on a fine scale of gradation, to everyone of superior rank. Even parents were to be addressed as "you" rather than "thou" and to be greeted with ceremonial bows and hand kisses. Dress was stiff and uncomfortable. In such a setting natural feelings seemed lacking in style, and their expression was condemned as an embarrassing lapse, a *faux pas*.

This life-style, unsurpassed in unnaturalness, required an unusually high measure of social coercion for its maintenance; but it was taken over, together with its accompanying social constraints, by the Enlightenment. Who can tell how much humanity was stunted, fell apart, under this hideous pressure, how many individual tragedies may have been enacted as a result? Only in one case did such personal tragedy lead to a fundamental revolutionary protest, to profound resentment triggering an explosive chain reaction—in the case of Jean-Jacques Rousseau.

The French nobility controlled the court, to which the salons were attached; etiquette was the structural law of this sphere of existence—courtly, polished, elegant, witty behavior, a social game, refined to the highest degree by people who lived from their independent incomes and who otherwise were burdened with no cares.

On the other hand, the bourgeois who had to work hard to feed himself and his family found his life centered on his family, and for him holidays were festive occasions following periods of hard work. This cultivation of familial feelings, warmth and cordiality formed the real content of bourgeois community life. Rousseau became the first champion of this bourgeois life-style against courtly aristocracy in France. But Rousseau, beyond this, condemned the Enlightenment as a whole, as his pathologically heightened sensitivity revolted against the no-less-heightened social constraint of the *ancien régime*:

> Today . . . a base and deceptive uniformity prevails in our customs, and all minds seem to have been cast in the same mold. Incessantly politeness requires, propriety demands; incessantly usage is followed, never one's own inclinations. One no longer appears as one is; and in this *perpetual constraint*, the men who form this herd called society, placed in the same circumstances will do all the same things . . .[179]

The attack was aimed at the feudal, despotic pressure upon which this courtly, baroque life-style rested. Rousseau therefore called for a strike against tradition: the goal of *Emile* was the interruption of tradition through isolation.

Rousseau's call for a struggle against the despotism of the baroque could have been considered as a welcome and extremely effective broadening of the battlefront of the Enlightenment, and such an interpretation seemed at first natural to leading men of the Enlightenment like Diderot and Condillac, who were linked to Rousseau in close personal friendship. It soon became clear, however, that the successful leader in this new battlefront was not inclined to subordinate himself to the hitherto common supreme command of the *ratio*. Rather, in all cases of conflict he claimed preeminence for himself and his principle of feeling. It was this claim, apart from unfortunate and partly psychopathically conditioned personal exacerbations and dissonances, that led to the fundamental break between Rousseau and the others.

Rousseau's call "Back to nature!" was neither new nor of itself antagonistic to the Enlightenment. Natural law, one of the most important and central accomplishments of the Enlightenment, had raised and pursued the same demand in the sphere of jurisprudence. Deism boasted of itself as of a natural religion; the Physiocrats thought they had found the natural principles of economy. Rousseau had espoused one of the characteristic demands of the Enlightenment and carried it to a new sphere of application. Appeals to the natural, formerly heard in the rational sphere, were now carried into the emotional sphere as well.

Rousseau was the first to embody the new sensibility of preromanticism (including the *Sturm und Drang* movement). The sensibility of the Enlightenment had assigned to feeling a modest place alongside the *ratio*; now a dominant, superior place was demanded for feeling. None of this implies that Rousseau was an irrationalist in the sense of being basically hostile to *ratio* or intent on eliminating it. Quite the contrary: as soon as the *ratio* found itself ready to grant priority to feeling and to take an oath of allegiance to it, so to speak, it was readily and expressly recognized and confirmed in all its previous rights and privileges. There had been other sensitive men of the Enlightenment before Rousseau, and this combination was characteristic of them. Diderot himself, after all, had exuberantly praised Richardson as early as 1761. Rousseau remained a man of Enlightenment sensibilities, except that he shifted the emphasis to the second element in that combination. In the last analysis, Rousseau's "feeling" is the sentimental aspect of the Enlightenment, Rousseau's "nature" the proper, well-ordered nature of rationalism. Rousseau's supreme law is "the law of nature, this holy, imprescriptible law, which speaks to the heart of man *and to his reason*."[180]

His ideal man follows feelings in the same way: "This man of nature, who truly lives the human life, counting for naught the opinion of others, conducts himself solely according to his inclinations *and his reason*, without regard to that which the public approves or censures." "No one is excepted from the first duty of man, no one has a right to depend upon the judgment of others." At the climax of the *Nouvelle Héloïse*, Rousseau's heroine prays to God: "I desire all that is consonant with the natural order that thou hast established, and with the *rules of that reason* with which thou hast endowed me."

Rousseau was basically a rationalist who became a natural ally and confederate of preromanticism. But there was also latent evidence of destructive, totalitarian tendencies, the effects of which were to unfold only later. Rousseau is one of the most complex and contradictory phenomena of Western intellectual history—all the more difficult to unravel for the reason that he himself was quite unaware of his own significance.

Rousseau's emphasis on feeling had its greatest subversive impact in Germany, where Pietism and English irrationalism had prepared the ground; in Germany the movement that he triggered turned very soon against the Enlightenment and its rationalism. Rousseau's preference for sentiment over reason ("le sentiment est plus que la raison") could be labeled sentimentalism or sensitivism. But his youthful and enthusiastic followers in Germany transformed this into actual irrationalism, and gave the movement a rebellious, titanic character totally alien to poor, timid Jean-Jacques, a character that surely would have filled him with the same fear and horror that the Peasant War had aroused in Luther.

Within the century of the Enlightenment (1689-1789) two polar phenomena developed within this broad movement: rationalism under French and empiricism under English leadership. Empiricism, which recognizes experience as a standard criterion also for the *ratio*, already signified a triumph over rationalism. Consequently it was no accident that complementary, emotional-filled countercurrents to the rationalism of the Enlightenment soon found favorable possibilities for development, especially in England.

Pietism had a part in the corresponding German development of sensibility, but its relation to the rationalism of the Enlightenment soon put it in opposition to conscious experience. The rationalism of the Enlightenment had subjected traditional dogmas to sharp criticism; Pietism accepted it while softening it by intensifying the emotional atmosphere. The pietist and mystic Gottfried Arnold (1666-1714) had already turned against "biting reason" (*die spitzige Vernunft*).

Political or social rebelliousness was remote from Pietism, with its Lutheran respect for temporal authority. But its social structure was democratic; it strove for small congregations, based upon equality and fraternity, in contrast to authoritarian and national churches. Thus it was a kind of return to Luther's original ideal congregation. That this democratic opposition to the despotism of the baroque turned inward, rather than outward, was a Lutheran-German phenomenon. It was a kind of sublimated and introverted revolution—which, as we have seen, first found its productive outlet in an

altogether unobjectionable way in music, in the "realm of tones."
Now, however, by encroaching upon the neighboring sphere of
poetry and literature, the hitherto latent, revolutionary character of
the movement suddenly became visible.

No obvious influences can be traced among Vico (1668-1744),
Rousseau (1712-1788), and Hamann (1730-1788); yet all three displayed strong psychopathological traits (culminating in Vico's case
in actual insanity); and they represent the same broad intellectual
trend, albeit in characteristic national variations—Vico reflecting
his Italian and Catholic, Rousseau his French and deistic, and
Hamann his German and Lutheran background.

Johann Georg Hamann, the Königsberg "Magus of the North," is
perhaps the oddest and most characteristically German figure in
German intellectual history. He was an altogether eccentric genius,
pensive and volatile, knotty and freakish, German to excess, comprehensible only to Germans—and hardly to them. "A kind of
Luther in miniature: but with satyr's horns under the musty rococo
wig," a "mystical *coincidentia oppositorum*"; "earthly sensuousness
and passionate drive toward the suprasensual," "religious and sen-
sualist irrationalism in intimate fusion"—thus some of his inner
contradictions are characterized by his leading biographer.[181] In addition to German Pietism, English skepticism, and English sensualism this rare alloy also contained a strong humanistic admixture. And finally, there was a strong emphasis upon sexuality.

Hamann stemmed from the world of German Pietism. But this at
first did not prevent him, as a prodigal son, from leading a frivolous
rococo life and from letting his intellectual development be guided
above all by Enlish sensualism, in particular by Hume. Both the
worldly life and the sensualistic world picture reached their high
point in the journey to the England of George II. Here in London,
however, also ensued the sudden change, a standard pietistic "conversion" with a repentance-struggle and rebirth, exactly according
to the standard schema of Hallean theology. For Hamann, however,
this conversion was at the same time the call to his intellectual-
historical mission, which went far beyond the narrow limits of
pietist theology into the free realm of the mind. The opposition to
the rationalism of the Enlightenment was now carried by Hamann
into the general intellectual domain. He became the prophet of irrationalism, against the German Enlightenment, "a powerful sign"
to intellectual Germany of the subsequent generations.[182] For the
great movement called *Sturm und Drang* ("Storm and Stress")
German preromanticism took its point of departure from Hamann

and was carried forward by Herder, the great awakener of Goethe. To be sure, Rousseau also exercised an influence upon it at the same time as Hamann, and even more broadly and directly. However, the real direction of the attack against rationalism stems from Hamann.

The conventional term *preromanticism* should not mislead us into thinking that its representatives were nothing but romantics before their time. Many of the most characteristic tendencies of preromanticism, indeed, bear a close relationship—whether of continuation, complementarity, self-criticism, or even self-transcendence—to the Enlightenment. The tension that doubtless arose in most cases, rather, was a fruitful polarity between the extreme wings of the one and the same great forward movement. Hamann was a friend of Kant, as Rousseau was of Diderot. Diderot, as has already been mentioned, wrote an exuberant "Praise of Richardson" (1761). Rousseau was at the same time a man of the Enlightenment and a hero-founder of irrationalistic preromanticism. And as a man of the Enlightenment, as we shall see, in his theory of the state and society he was even a spokesman of a rationalism of the German Enlightenment, acquainting German public opinion with Rousseau in a most understanding and sympathetic way. He was one of the earliest German champions of Shakespeare; he glorified irrational, original genius; and in his last writing, the *Education of the Human Race* (1780), he treads an almost Herderian path. As Ernst Cassirer has strikingly observed about Herder:

Much as he outgrows the intellectual world of the Enlightenment, Herder's break with his age was not abrupt. His progress and ascent were possible only by following the trails blazed by the Enlightenment. This age forged the weapons with which it was finally defeated; with its own clarity and consistency, it established the premises on which Herder based his inference. The conquest of the Enlightenment by Herder is therefore a genuine self-conquest. It is one of those defeats which really denote a victory, and Herder's achievement is in fact one of the greatest intellectual triumphs of the philosophy of the Enlightenment.[183]

The most cogent proof of the close bond between the Enlightenment and preromanticism is the synthesis of the two—prepared by Lessing—which German classicism represents. From Goethe's development it is evident that he began in Leipzig as an "enlightened" and elegant rococo poet; in 1720 in Strasbourg, under the powerful influence of Herder, he embraced *Sturm und Drang* in all its breadth and depth; finally, in Weimar he found the classical synthesis of this thesis and antithesis. The development of classical authors and their fellows in all fields unfolded similarly.

The rationalism of the Enlightenment and the irrationalism of *Sturm und Drang* were two opposite poles; despite this, both had in common the postulate of freedom, the freedom that the Enlightenment demanded for thought, and *Sturm und Drang* for feeling and action. Both opposed the baroque and its association with bondage. If the possibility of a synthesis ensued from this basic affinity, so did the necessity of a synthesis ensue from the unmistakable unilateralness of both. It is the imperishable fame of German classicism to have effected this great synthesis.

Totality, equilibrium, harmony are its essential determining features, corresponding to its fundamentally synthetic character. And indeed, an all-encompassing free equilibrium was again achieved here for the first time since classical antiquity; the golden ring of the ages closed, and, as we shall see, there was an accompanying awareness of this happening.

Shaftesbury and the English preromantics had already shifted their enthusiasm for the ancient world from the Romans to the Greeks, giving Homer, the "original genius," the place of Vergil, the classicist. German classicism, after Winckelmann, developed into a revival of the ancient Greek world, whereas the Renaissance in the main had been a Roman revival.

The optimal conditions for the unfolding of culture, the social foundation of this development was formed by a rare mixture between small city and courtly closed life-spheres. Weimar in 1775, at the time of Goethe's arrival, had an estimated population of six thousand. "God in Heaven," wrote Goethe to Frau von Stein, "what a paradise is Weimar!" (22 December 1779). Jena was even smaller, and Frankfurt am Main, one of the big cities during Goethe's lifetime, developed from around thirty thousand to around sixty thousand inhabitants. For Germany, the classic age was the zenith of its intellectual and human development.

The rationalism of the Enlightenment had not been conducive to artistic production. As Democritus and Plato suggest, nothing originates without a breath of divine madness. On the other hand, the irrationalism of *Sturm und Drang* succumbed to such demonic madness, and the restraining counterweight—the power of form— was missing. Thus, the essential areas in which German classicism unfolded were poetic imagination and musical production. Its theory was predominantly aesthetic, and its philosophy was really a philosophy of beauty. "Only through the morning gate of the beautiful dost thou come into the land of knowledge," was its deepest conviction, and it itself had come to a halt before the morning gate of the beautiful on its way to the land of knowledge.

Moreover, this conception at the base of Germen classical poetry was "*a new form of religion*," "but a secular religion in contrast to the clerical religion of Christianity."[184] Its foundation, as we have seen, was further elaboration of ancient Stoicism.

This deism of Stoic origin was Goethe's first and real religion. In his great dispute with Lavater, Goethe had written: "Yes, I confess to you, were I teacher of my religion you would probably have less cause to upbraid me for a lack of tolerance, than I you" (Weimar, 18 September 1782). In a poem of 1815, he expressly states that recognition of the sign of the cross, to which he had been tempted by the tiny cross on the neckchain of his beloved, is repellent to him and a denial of *his own* god, a renegade act like the temptation of Solomon by the women of the harem to honor the animal-headed Egyptian deities. Goethe, who in another letter to Lavater (29 July 1782) had professed himself "a decided non-Christian" evolved by 1790 into an "un-Christian"—indeed, an "anti-Christian." In a *Venetian Epigram* of that year (no. 66) he counts the Christian crucifix among the four things that are intolerable to him and as repellent as poison and serpents, in a series with tobacco smoke, garlic, and bedbugs. The anti-Christian arrogance that is so violently expressed here did not, of course, last for long, although special expressions of aversion to the symbol of the cross from a later date are not lacking. And if alongside them we can also adduce positive judgments on Christianity and its founder, such oscillations of a considerable latitude, without exception, remain within the frame of that religious-universalistic panentheism in the sense of the parable of the three rings, which forms an article of Goethe's deistic credo. From this standpoint, one must on the one hand recognize the historical religions as different expressions of the same deistic natural religion, and on the other, reproach and abominate them for their disfiguring veilings of this core. Which of the two facets of this ambivalent attitude stepped into the foreground might depend on mood and circumstance.

If deism in the Enlightenment, in the German classic period, and for Goethe was of Stoic origin, it was also developed in ways that were to ancient teaching what liberal Protestantism is to Catholicism. In Goethe, it contained a strong mixture of pantheism that he himself on occasion called "hylozoism." This explains why he could also confront Stoicism with criticism, how the *Venetian Epigrams*, long unpublished and still little known today, no doubt represent the climax of Goethe's freethinking and antitheological development: "What holds true for Christianity, also holds true for the Stoics: it is unseemly for a free man to be a Christian or a Stoic."[185]

A new secular ethic stemmed also directly from this new secular religiosity. Christianity's ascetic depreciation of the world was overcome by "pagan love of life." The full unification of sensual happiness and peace of mind had become possible, and Goethe's *Roman Elegies* are proof of this.

An essay on Winckelmann (1804) contains the fullest expression of Goethe's pagan credo: "If the healthy nature of man is operative as a whole, when he feels himself in the world as in a great, beautiful, dignified, and valuable whole, when harmonious well-being grants him a pure, free rapture, then the universe, if it could experience itself, rejoicing and admiring the peak of its own becoming and being, would arrive at its own good. For to what purpose all this display of suns and planets and moons, of stars and milky-ways, if, in the end, a happy human being does not instinctively rejoice in his existence."[186]

23. AGAINST POLITICAL BONDAGE: REVOLUTION

In 1323 peasant disorders broke out in Flanders, spreading widely and resembling a "real" social revolution. The cities joined the peasants, the sovereign was driven out of the country, the nobility was earmarked for extermination; it was not until 1328 that the movement was bloodily crushed by intervention from the king of France. In 1356 this was followed by the *jacquerie* in neighboring France, and in 1381 in southern England by the peasant uprising led by Wat Tyler and John Ball, and then by the Hussite wars spreading from Bohemia in 1419-1426. Finally, after the mid-fifteenth century, disorders erupted in southwest Germany and Salzburg, Steiermark, Carinthia, and Carniola, which finally climaxed in the great German Peasant War of 1524-1525.

Some of the movements followed the teachings of dissident theologians like Wycliffe (1325-1384), Huss (1369-1415), and Luther (1483-1546), without the approval of their originators. All appealed to the "good old law," softened by customary modifications, while the lords went beyond the sharpest and most obsolete statutes. Appeals to "divine law," however, crop up behind those to common law. As Hesiod, the peasant-poet, had done two thousand years earlier, these peasants appealed to divine justice against unjust human judges. John Ball's famous slogan "When Adam delved and Eva span, who was then the gentleman?" was a striking example of such an appeal carried to the point of rejection of all feudal domination. Yet all these movements, which rose up against organized ruling powers and pursued democratic goals, were bloodily suppressed, and a permanent deterioration of the condition of the lower social strata was the result.

The Middle Ages were replete with successful or unsuccessful struggles against feudal lords and sovereigns. The fact that in the course of these struggles lords also fought against lords is not relevant here except insofar as the rebellious party belonged to the lower stratum. This was the case with the Ditmarsh peasants of northern Germany, who obtained recognition of their customary freedoms, forcing the resident nobility to emigrate or renounce its privileges. This was also the case with the peasants of the original members of the Swiss Confederation after the formation of the alliance of the three Forest Cantons in 1291.

Although there were revolutionary elements in these struggles for freedom, they still cannot be considered real revolutions. Revolutions in the narrower sense can be said to occur only where the struggle is directed against the newly sharpened absolutist domination of a modern territorial state. And only where this absolutist regime, in addition, is an indigenous regime are the criteria of a real revolution fulfilled. For there is a whole group of revolutions which were directed against a modern absolutist regime that was alien or felt to be alien, which exercised a foreign or even colonial domination over the population of the country in revolt. In sum, there is a difference between revolutions sparked by discontent and resentment relating to foreign affairs, and genuine internal revolutions as responses to a domestic situation viewed as intolerable.

The first antiabsolutist freedom struggle against foreign domination was the eighty-year struggle (1568-1648) of the Netherlands against the Spanish crown, which was both a religious and a national war. Its successful outcome brought this tiny nation of peasants, fishermen, and shippers into the front rank of Western nations, under the leadership of a self-willed and self-assured class of burghers. The English, in two internal revolutions, overcame absolutism and fought for their consitutional freedom with results universally recognized as exemplary. But this did not prevent England from pursuing an almost equally narrow-minded and brutal policy of oppression toward its North American colonies as Spain had toward the Netherlands. And this was done even though it involved people of the same nationality and religion who had emigrated in search of freedom of worship and to whom legal equality with the motherland had been expressly assured in many charters. The consequence was the North American war of independence (1775-1782) and the founding of the United States of America. At that time the colonists appealed initially to what had been promised in writs: to the "Constitutional Rights and Privileges," to the "ancient and undoubted right," accordingly to the "fundamental rights of British subjects," the "privileges of natural born Englishmen" and only as a last resort to the "natural, essential and unalienable rights of all men," as the constitution of Massachusetts formulated it in 1780.

Western intellectual history of the seventeenth and eighteenth centuries was dominated by advances of the Enlightenment. If absolutism was not to fall hopelessly behind, it had to follow in its train and transform itself into, "enlightened absolutism." Richelieu himself had espoused the conviction "that the Sovereign placed at the supreme height of mankind, must bring reason to rulership." This implied that absolutism had to accept the criteria of the Enlightenment, submit to the critique of the *ratio*, and renounce its alliance with confessional orthodoxy, surrendering the claims to "blind" obedience that such orthodoxy sanctioned. The long-range consequences were bound to be directed against absolutism itself, to lead to a total transformation or self-abrogation of absolutism. But these ultimate consequences still lay in the distant future; for the present, enlightened absolutism aroused boundless enthusiasm among all those who delighted in progress. In the words of an eighteenth-century Italian historian, "It is permissible to hope for everything in a century in which the spirit of science no longer lives in an unresolvable conflict with the spirit of domination, and in which the swift course of thought is no longer held up by obstacles which despotism is otherwise wont to place in its path."[187]

Later historians customarily have assigned to the Enlightenment praise (or blame, as the case may be) for the subsequent revolutionary overthrow of absolutism. Such a judgment is legitimate if one considers the objective consequences of the activities of the Enlightenment thinkers, but it misconstrues their intent. The men of the Enlightenment, far from being hostile to absolutism, felt a conscious affinity with it. They gave it credit for overcoming feudalism and rationalizing the machinery of government. And Tocqueville is right in asserting that the distance between the real advances achieved under the much maligned *ancien régime* and those actually accomplished by the Revolution is not overly great. In addition, the patronage of absolute princes created attractive and influential positions for exponents of the Enlightenment; it seemed obvious to them that it would be far easier to enlighten the one ruler than his many subjects. This enlightenment of the absolute ruler, this progress from a baroque, courtly, confessional absolutism to an enlightened, philosophic, deistic absolutism was the real political goal of the Enlightenment. Such conversion of the one future ruler succeeded notably in the cases of King Frederick II of Prussia and of the German Emperor Joseph II. The goal not of destroying absolutism but of enlightening it here seemed within reach.

The situation of the feudal nobility was bound to have an important impact on these developments. The objective situation arrayed a number of distinct forces against the interests of feudalism: the crown, with which the nobility competed for power, and those strata that were disadvantaged by the privileges held by the nobility. The indirectly disadvantaged stratum was the bourgeoisie, which was excluded from those privileges, those directly disadvantaged were the serfs and peasants, who to a greater or lesser extent were forced to surrender their labor and their personal freedom to the noble landowners. This convergence of opposing interests from above and below put feudalism very effectively under crossfire. But this coincidence of antifeudal interests was bound to dissolve at a time when the crown no longer needed to fear the rivalry of the nobles, whereas the seigneurial rights and privileges of the nobility with respect to the lower strata continued; the nobility ceased to present a political danger to those above long before it ceased to do social harm to those below.

Absolutism, of course, had been established in the struggle against feudalism, but after its victory the temptation to make its peace with feudalism, at the expense of the lower social strata, was close at hand. In exchange for the nobility's renunciation of its upward aspirations, absolutism was prepared to maintain or even strengthen its traditional seigneurial rights and privileges, particularly those of an economic nature. Such a return of the nobility, or refeudalization of absolute monarchy, took place not only in the France of the *ancien régime*, but also in the enlightened Prussia of Frederick II. Public opinion, especially in France, demanded abolition of the residue of feudal privilege, and for the crown there could have been two motives for championing this demand even at a time when it no longer had to fear the rivalry of the nobility: (1) the overwhelming numerical superiority of the "third estate," which came to be felt more strongly with the progressive atomization of society, and which held out the possibility of effective monarchical rule based on the support of most of the population; and (2) the fundamental demand for equality, based on natural law, which formed a core component of the Enlightenment and which could not help but win the sympathy of absolutism with its tendency to establish the legal equality of all its subjects.

The Enlightenment, however, aimed its fire not only at secular feudalism but also at the clerical bondage of orthodoxy, with which baroque absolutism had been closely allied. To dissolve this alliance between crown and clergy for the men of the Enlightenment came to be a prime goal for the sake of which even their antifeudal demands might be dropped. Such a shift of alignment is evident in Frederick the Great, a freethinker whose friendship with Voltaire and other leaders of the French Enlightenment was not impaired by his despotism and support of feudalism in Prussia's internal affairs.

None of the revolutions of the seventeenth and eighteenth centuries were originally directed against absolutism or, even less, against monarchy as a form of government: where the abolition of absolutism was the consequence, this was far from the intention of the revolutionaries. This holds true, in particular, for the great French Revolution.

The freedom struggles of the Dutch and the North Americans, like those of the Swiss before them, were directed against foreign domination, and it was of little relevance that Spain and England happened to be monarchies. The struggle was not against domestic absolutism but foreign imperialism. The internal government of all three areas (Swiss cantons, Dutch provinces, American colonies) had in any case not been monarchical even before their external liberation. Thus the president of the United States stepped into a position analogous to that of a colonial governor—whose office had not been for life, let alone hereditary. Foreign policy—that is, defense against foreign intervention—also played a crucial role in the English and in the later stages of the French Revolution.

A second important factor was religious foreign policy—the struggle of the various denominations against each other. In the case of the Netherlands the foreign oppressor was of a different nationality and denomination. In the English Revolution the denominational factor played a decisive role; it also was important for the North American development.

All the revolutions of the seventeenth and eighteenth centuries increased the political influence of the urban bourgeoisie; yet nothing would be more misleading than the assumption, which so easily suggests itself to a sociological historiography under the spell of vulgar socialist conceptions, that the bourgeoisie undertook these revolutions in order to attain this political influence. These revolutions were directed toward isonomy, toward equality before the law, toward the abolition of legal privilege; achievement of this aim automatically benefited the bourgeoisie, the most numerous among the politically active groups. Moreover, the urban bourgeoisie, being the economically and intellectually most advanced and active stratum of the population, in the free cities of the Middle Ages and of the Renaissance, had once before taken up both intellectual leadership and political self-determination. Now it merely had to reassert them within the larger arena of a centralistic, unified state.

These are features common to most revolutions of modern times. There is within them, however, a polar contrast that is generally overlooked—an omission that has led, and continues to lead, to the most fatal confusions of moral and political judgment.

As has been stated earlier, all high cultures, including our Western culture, rest on an original superstratification and therefore are two-layered in their sociological structure: a thin upper stratum ruling over a broad lower stratum. Modern absolutism overcame the numerous secondary or intermediate upper strata which had been formed in the course of time, reducing the social structure once again to the original two layers and clarifying or frequently sharpening it. These newly sharpened social tensions can find a violent, explosive release—and this is precisely what we call revolution.

Such a violent uprising of oppressed lower classes can pursue two very different aims: either a softening (ideally an abolition) of the pressure of domination, of the two-layered social structure, in short of superstratification as such; or else a simple reversal of the previous situation, a mere exchange of roles. In the latter case, despotism is not mitigated by the violent change in personnel; on the contrary, it tends to be intensified. These are the two opposite phenomena that are labeled with the single term *revolution* but which must be strictly distinguished if we are to arrive at any clear insight or judgment.

Michael Freund has ironically observed that "the distinction be-

tween good and bad revolutions, between liberal and totalitarian
ones, is nowadays no longer accepted so readily."[188] I believe, however, that this distinction should be reestablished and indeed drawn
more sharply. At the same time we must remember that it is a distinction in the realm of ideal types and that the concrete historical
instances do not oblige us by corresponding only to one extreme or
the other. Still I can think of no instance where, in respect to the
problem area here under discussion and on the basis of prevailing
features, the assignment of a revolution to one or the other category
could be doubtful. It must be noted, however, that totalitarian revolutions more easily approximate their extreme than do liberal
ones—because the totalitarian end is entirely consonant with the
means of revolutionary violence whereas a liberal revolution must
pursue its aims by illiberal means. To that extent the concept of
"liberal revolution" is a contradiction in terms, and this implies a
profound historical tragedy not just for the observer but for the historical actor.

Revolutions aiming at the removal of foreign domination probably belong always to the liberal type: it is significant that the Dutch
and the North Americans, like the Swiss, established republics in
place of the monarchic foreign domination they overthrew. Among
the great internal revolutions of modern times the first one, the
English Revolution, in its two phases, furnishes us a model for each
of the two basic types.

In England, agrarian development had taken a very different
course from that in continental Europe. The English peasant rising
of 1381 was crushed, as was the German one a century and a half
later; yet the result in England was not sharpened oppression but
rather displacement of a maximum number of peasants (to make
place for labor-extensive sheep raising) and transformation of the
rest of them into leaseholders; in sum, a combination of liberation
and expulsion of the peasantry. The development of English absolutism was restrained at first by the traditional feudal freedoms
and privileges of various estates, but by the sixteenth century it had
made such rapid advances that the Stuart kings could hope fully to
keep pace with French absolutism. But their pro-Catholic and pro-
French tendencies spelled disaster. In the face of such religious and
national treason, the representatives of feudal estates (by now
mostly plutocratically transformed) joined in opposition with the
obstreperous Calvinist Puritans. The various Protestant denominations thus united in common revolt against the crown in the first

English Revolution. But following victory and the death of the charismatic Cromwell in 1658, restoration of monarchic legitimacy proved indispensable for national unity. Finally in 1688 a suitable occupant was found for the throne, willing and able to assume a neutral role among the non-Catholic denominations. The resulting guarantees of religious peace furnished the basis of English constitutionalism.

The first part of the English Revolution came in 1642 with the execution of Strafford (justified neither legally nor politically), culminated with the beheading of Charles I, and resulted in the dictatorship of Cromwell—which proved neither durable nor inheritable. This revolution hence turned out far from glorious. In 1688, the incumbent Stuart was disposed of in a swift, elegant, and bloodless maneuver, and the regime that was established by this second revolution proved moderate, well balanced, and durable. In sum, in England a liberal revolution followed in less than half a century upon an illiberal one.

As a result of this early abolition of absolutist unfreedom, England became the leader in the political and intellectual development of Europe. The English constitution was recognized (in France as well) as the model of sober progressiveness. In several departments of intellectual life England assumed the lead: in philosophy and epistemology through Locke and Hume, who made the first fundamental break with theological and metaphysical dogmatism; in natural science, through Boyle and above all Newton, who perfected classical physics and astronomy; in political science through Locke, the first theorist of constitutionalism; in economic science through Adam Smith, the father of the theory of political economic theory and herald of the free market. And whereas those named belonged to the Enlightenment and supported rationalism, the struggle against the one-sided rationalism of the Enlightenment also was waged in England much earlier and with much greater circumspection and constancy than later in Germany.

The Netherlands, England, and the United States thus had been freed from absolutism, and all revolutions between 1568 and 1783 had achieved positive results—a chain of successes that seemed to continue as late as 1792. All eyes meanwhile were turned on France, which, despite its intellectual liberalism had remained politically as backward as Spain, Prussia, or even Russia. Optimistic observers hoped that France would follow the moderate example of England, so eloquently expounded by Locke and then Montesquieu. Well-intentioned and clear-sighted reformers like Turgot sought to achieve such hopes in practice. Why, despite so much hope and effort, did French development miscarry?

By the middle of the reign of Louis XIV, France had emerged as the undisputed leader among Western nations, its government still the prototype of baroque absolutism—unenlightened, denominational, courtly. Yet the splendor of its artistic and literary accomplishments was so dazzling as to reconcile even so stern a critic as Voltaire. Had Louis XIV died in, say, 1683, France's development toward enlightened absolutism might readily have caught up with its intellectual progress. The heir presumptive, the duke of Bourgogne, had been brought up, in Voltaire's phrase, as a "Christian philosopher" by Fénelon and Fleury. Even the opposition that formed in the second half of the reign of Louis XIV, like the Club de l'Entresol and Montesquieu, did not go beyond demanding reforms on the pattern of English constitutionalism. But Louis XIV outlived himself—until 1715—and his grandson, the duke of Bourgogne, had died in 1712; his two actual successors were each more incompetent than the last; and as Voltaire rightly said, absolutism is among all governments "the worst under a weak or wicked king."[189]

The accession of Louis XVI in 1774 offered one last chance. He appointed Turgot, who was fully aware of all the urgent problems and fully equipped to resolve them—precisely the "bold and wise minister" Voltaire had hoped for. Condorcet, writing to Voltaire, welcomed Turgot's appointment, saying that "Nothing better could have happened for France and for human reason." But Louis XVI failed to give Turgot the required support. The calling of the *parlements*, against Turgot's advice, was a grave mistake: their suspension in 1770 had been the single notable success under the preceding reign. Turgot energetically coped with the bread riots of 1775, but he could not hold out beyond 1776—and his reforms remained unimplemented or were even rescinded. Louis XVI's queen, Marie Antoinette, with her favoritism and intrigues, hastened Turgot's fall.

In a highly estimable and impressive letter of 30 April 1774, Turgot foretold the future disaster to the king. "Never forget, Sire, that it was weakness which put the head of Charles I on a block. . . . I cannot repeat enough to Your Majesty what I foresee and what everybody foresees in the way of a concatenation of weakness and misfortune if, once plans that have been begun are abandoned and if the Minister who has put them forward succumbs to the effort of the resistances that are united against him. And what will happen, Sire, if to the disorders of the interior are joined the difficulties of a war to which a thousand imprudent demarches can lead or circumstances can force?"[190] Obviously that made no impression upon Louis XVI: Whom God will destroy, He strikes with blindness.

Nothing perhaps more clearly shows the untenability of absolute monarchy than the fact that the stupidity of such a lamentable figure on the throne sufficed to dismiss a secular statesman like Turgot when he had barely begun his greatest political activity, condemning him for the rest of his life to tormenting inactivity.

At issue here is the specific weakness of absolutism, its dependence upon the hereditary ruler and his accidental qualities. From Louis XI to Louis XIV, the French crown was burdened with too much responsibility to be able to sustain a full century of inept, indecisive, and irresolute rulers. And this plenitude of power acted as an additional corrupting force on rulers who did not measure up to it. One result was a financial-political vicious circle of increased luxury consumption by the court and mounting inability to cover it through suitable administrative or fiscal measures.

In 1786 this financial and political mismanagement drove the minister Calonne to the fateful attempt at imposing new taxes, which in turn led to the convocation of the Estates-General—discontinued 174 years earlier—and to the outbreak of the Revolution.

A byproduct of absolutist centralization was the rapid and unhealthy growth of Paris and the proletarianization of its masses. With six hundred thousand inhabitants in the late eighteenth century, Paris was the world's largest city. In this *ville lumière* were concentrated France's social and intellectual elite; but beneath them there was an uprooted mass, a lumpenproletariat augmented by a steady stream of migrants. Whenever the ancient city of Rome had reached a corresponding point, the emperors expended much energy to hold the populace of the capital in check; the eighteenth-century Bourbons were unequal to such a challenge.

As we saw in our earlier systematic discussion of the subject, there inheres in any monarchy an antifeudal tendency—a tendency to subordinate all subjects alike to the monarch and to abolish any autonomous or hereditary exceptions to this principle of equality of subjects. This tendency was manifested successfully by the French kings, the "rois nivelleurs," reaching its climax under Colbert, but ceasing abruptly with his dismissal and death in 1683. Louis XIV's own attitude, which now came to the fore, was ambiguous: part modern, part medieval, part plutocratic, part feudal. His striving for "glory," his wars of conquest waged in the service of this striving, his boundless ostentation had a pronounced feudal character; he believed himself an unsurpassable high aristocrat. He had used Colbert's radical modernism only as a means to achieve aristocratic-feudal goals, and in the second half of his reign these increasingly came to the fore. Hence the grave blunder of ennobling the higher officials and of the compulsory purchase of titles of nobility, instituted to ease the financial crisis. Much as the hereditary nobility opposed this practice, it was bound to lead to an ultimate merger of old and new nobility, in outright contravention of the venerable maxim *divide et impera*.

In the *parlements*, corporate bodies that represented the estates of the realm and were medieval in character, the new *noblesse de la robe* mostly joined with feudal opposition of the high clergy and of the *noblesse de sang*. The result was a unified representation of the privileged as a class. The century from Colbert's dismissal in 1683 to the outbreak of the Revolution is filled with bitter struggles between the crown and the feudal opposition organized in the *parlements*. This opposition, to be sure, soon took to using the opportune and convenient arguments of the Enlightenment and thus enhanced its appeal to public opinion. But on the part of most of the representatives these arguments were quite dishonest and amounted to sheer demagogy in the service of reactionary feudal forces. As a flyer written by a loyalist put it: "Be reasonable, Frenchmen! The *parlements* defend not your rights, but their own!" "It is better to have one lord than two thousand." In reality, a bitter struggle went on between two forms of government, one medieval-feudal and the other modern-absolutist, but the crown, incapable of any consistent, purposive program of action, repeatedly dismissing ministers loyal to its own modernist program, and instead of benefiting from the struggle was crushed between the two fronts.

In this struggle between absolutism and feudalism, absolutism was repeatedly represented by energetic ministers who believed themselves to be the successors of Richelieu and Colbert, although none was as capable as Turgot. But the crown sooner or later dropped these ministers, and the feudal forces advanced step by step. Thus "the open revolution of the privileged beginning with the assembly of notables of 1787 is only the high point of the aristocratic reaction which, by joining with the rising opposition movement astir in the second half of the reign of Louis XIV, pervades the whole eighteenth century." "It was not the bourgeois-liberalist, but rather the feudal-reactionary spirit that celebrated the first triumph. Absolutism had succumbed to it. The elements embodying opposition to it aimed to reestablish the medieval ideal of government in modern dress, to subordinate royal power again to the control of institutions relating to the estates of the realm. Absolutism was overthrown by the powers of the Middle Ages, and it shipwrecked because of its inability to overcome circumstances and conceptions of times past . . . by the creation of a really modern state consonant to the principles of absolutist doctrine."[191] In France the necessary modernization was not only neglected and instead, refeudalization followed, and that is what specifically provoked the Revolution and made it inevitable.

The English Revolution also had been marked by the clash of two rising, opposing movements: the self-assertion of bourgeois puritanism and royal absolutism. In the French Revolution, as everyone knows, one of the rising movements was the Enlightenment, supported by the bourgeoisie. But not everyone is aware that the opposing movement that made the final clash inevitable was not absolutism but feudalism—which precisely through the weakness of absolutism from 1683 to 1788 had won more and more terrain. The tragedy of the French monarchy was that it not only tolerated these advances of its age-old antagonist but in the decisive battle even explicitly joined the side of this doomed antagonist—thereby precipitating its own doom.

The movement from which the French Revolution emerged was neither republican nor radically democratic, neither nationalistic nor imperialistic. Rather, it rejected—expressly and from profound conviction—all such tendencies. The heading of a chapter in Bodin's *Six livres de la république* (1576) reads: "Changes of Republics must not be made suddenly." Montesquieu's *Lettres Persanes* (1721) contains the arresting statement: "Existing laws must be touched only with a trembling hand."

Even a ruthless freethinker like Holbach, in 1773, wrote: "No, not through dangerous convulsions, not through struggle, through murder and useless crime can the wounds of nations be closed. . . . The voice of reason is neither rebellious nor bloodthirsty. The reforms that it proposes are slow, but thereby they are only all the better assured." Rousseau had declared that he would not have wished "to live in a Republic of new institution," and: "No one is ignorant of how dangerous in a large state is the moment of anarchy and of crisis that necessarily precedes a new establishment. Let one consider the danger of once rousing the enormous masses that compose the French monarchy. Who will be able to restrain the resultant agitation or foresee all the effects that it can produce?"[192] And in

THE PATH OF FREEDOM

Rousseau's *Contrat social* (1762), the real catechism of the Revolution, there appears the prophetic warning that an old people can no longer free itself: "For then these disturbances can destroy it without revolutions being able to reestablish it. And, as soon as its chains are broken, it falls scattered and no longer exists: henceforth it will need a master and not a liberator."[193]

The essential political aims of the movement were: (1) The abolition of the "tyrannie féodale," as stated in the Cahiers of 1789, the residues of feudalism against which the crown had fought since the end of the Middle Ages; and (2) the implementation of urgent reforms which the crown had repeatedly attempted, but not carried out: tax and financial reform, modernization of the administration, abolition of internal customs duties and of restrictions on freedom of trade.

Both aims were achieved and maintained. What the third estate demanded from the king and offered its support for was nothing else but resumption and continuation of the best traditions of French kingship. If he had been conscious of and intent on his own paramount interests, the king would have carried out these demands even without outside pressure. Even at the next to the last moment he could have appointed as adviser Mirabeau, a man of commanding genius (but not exactly unblemished character) who knew full well what had to be done. Seldom does history offer a situation so unambiguous and compelling, and a king of even average ability could have drawn the obvious conclusions. It took all the wretchedness, limitedness, and pettiness of Louis XVI, stumbling from one missed opportunity to another, to fumble even this chance, which once more opened up before him as wide as a barn door. But the blind king now rejected Mirabeau's and Lafayette's efforts to rescue him, just as he had dropped Turgot in 1776.

Although the *ancien régime* was a contradictory mixture of absolutism and feudalism, the tendencies in the Revolution were directed exclusively against feudalism. Its intention, as we have seen, was to overcome feudalism with the help of absolutism, of an enlightened or to-be-enlightened absolutism. It was only because the king did not let himself be enlightened and because he sided with feudalism against his own interests that he, quite unnecessarily, came into the direct line of fire. Although Louis XVI did not know how to live or to rule, he—like the queen—at least knew how to die. The day on which Louis XVI mounted the guillotine was, as his executioner Samson attests in his memoirs, "his greatest, his most courageous day." Unfortunately, it was also the only great and the only truly courageous day of his life. And, of course, this dignified exit from the stage of history affords only an aesthetic, not a political consolation.

The Revolution was in the last analysis, an inevitable substitute for the repeated and vain efforts at Enlightening French absolutism. But even the statement that the *ancien régime* was not overthrown by outside force but collapsed of itself does not go far enough. The political structure of the kingdom had been in need of reform for a long time, but it had also been capable of reform. The *ancien régime* was not completely corrupt. The corruption affected only one structural part—the absolutist occupant of the throne; it was his failure that brought the whole structure down. For even the political degeneration of the court nobility was due to the crown's weakness. The night of 4 August 1789, when the nobility renounced its privileges, proved what this nobility still was capable of when appeal was made to its better instincts.

Least conclusive is the thesis, defended by Taine with all his literary brilliance, that the intellectual upper stratum of the *ancien régime*, the class that supported the Enlightenment, was corrupt and ripe for extinction. This upper stratum, in France as elsewhere in Europe, lived on its feudal heritage; yet the efforts of absolutism had modernized, urbanized, centralized, and plutocratized that stratum more in France than in any other country. That it was a "leisure class" living off its income does not suffice to condemn it. No other social group since the days of Homer and Plato has more effectively and more wittily and charmingly met the demands of cultivation of the mind—which, according to Aristotle,[194] is the true function of such a leisure class. Indeed, the level of social and intellectual refinement of the Enlightenment—largely created and practiced by this class—was one of the highest points of human evolution and laid an essential basis for all further development. Intellectual liberality has always preceded political liberality, and it always is developed first by an upper stratum which, by its leisure, alone has the possibility of devotion to intellectual activity.

The share of the different factors in the bringing about of the first, liberal phase of the Revolution was rather fairly balanced in the words with which, in 1791, Rabaut Saint-Etienne concluded his *Précis de l'histoire de la Révolution*: "The French Revolution therefore was the product of the Enlightenment which had penetrated, more than among other peoples, into all classes of citizens. It began from the moment in which men reflected; the faults of three reigns nurtured it, the resistance of the privileged accelerated it, and French impetuosity carried it through."

The intellectual leaders of France had been reformers, not revolutionaries; as Aulard puts it, "They wanted to reform the monarchy, not destroy it."[195] But the object crumbled in their hands—the material was too defective. According to Aulard, the declaration of war of 20 April 1792, was the fatal rupture. After the king, as a result of his incompetence, and the nobility as a result of its limitations, had made the Revolution unavoidable, both invoked the assistance of foreign powers. The Revolution resulted from the failure of the king and nobility; it was poisoned by their high treason.

The aristocratic emigrants appealed, in their host countries, to the worst instincts of corrupt groups. The more the Revolution degenerated, the more legitimate feudalism and absolutism of the interventionist states appeared as a defense of morality, right, and freedom.

In August 1789, with the nobility's solemn renunciation of its privileges and acceptance of the Declaration of the Rights of Man and the Citizen, the Revolution had achieved its basic goal. If the king had placed himself on that side and thereby facilitated a calm and peaceful execution of this program, the French Revolution could have run its course with less bloodshed and hence even more gloriously than the English Revolution of 1688.

In the summary of his great history of the Revolution, Antoine Aulard observes that "no individual steered the events" of the decade from 1789 to 1799, and that therefore "it is the French people who was the real hero of the French Revolution, provided that we view the French people not as in the condition of a multitude but in the condition of organized groups."[196] Still, the overall course of the French Revolution can be understood only as a phenomenon of mass psychology and mass sociology, and Aulard's qualification simply indicates that the masses in this case were composed of social molecules rather than social atoms. The "Grande Peur" that seized the country in September 1789 already had the character of a mass psychosis; the executions of 1792, in a recent comprehensive study, have been established beyond doubt as a series of "crimes de foules" surrounded by a gloomy and sinister aura of "mystère des foules."[197] The political faction that came closest to providing a coordinated and centralized organization of these small crowds, the Jacobins, appealed by their behavior most directly to these elements of mass psychosis.

In such a situation the intellectual lead that once had been exercised by the liberalism of Locke and Montesquieu now was transferred to Hobbes and Rousseau, and particularly to the totalitarianism represented by Rousseau's *Contrat social*. This transition became evident as early as the autumn of 1788, when the most radical publicists for the first time repudiated Montesquieu with his moderation and respect for tradition.

Against this background and on the basis of the theories of the Calvinist Rousseau, the Calvinist Robespierre put into practice, for the first time in history, a totalitarian state and all its accouterments, with which today we have once again become so intimately familiar: demagogy, terror, mass murder, lootings, appeals to man's basest and most bestial instincts, dissolution of all natural and moral bonds, networks of informers, an omnipotent secret police, and a false social integration through overheated nationalism and imperialism. Still, these pathological phenomena were closely conditioned by the immediate situation; for as soon as the desperate foreign situation abated, the French people at once shook off the regime of terror. Jourdan's victory at Fleurus on 20 June 1794 was followed only a month later by the overthrow of Robespierre and his accomplices.

The perversion of the Revolution through foreign intervention was a circumstance of which the contemporaries were well aware. Of its idealistic beginnings in 1789, Madame de Staël wrote: "Heads were overheated but in their hearts was nothing but good." In contrast, Madame Roland on 9 September 1792: "You know my enthusiasm for the Revolution. [Now] I am ashamed of it. It has been desecrated by criminals, it has become an unholy affair." Many believed, as did General Thiébault, "that it was no longer the Revolution that I wanted to serve and to which, full of pride, I had brought my boundless sympathy." "The cause of the human race is desperate" was the verdict pronounced, in view of the terrible distortion of the Revolution, by one of the last survivors of the Enlightenment and the *Encyclopédie*, Baron Melchior von Grimm (1723-1807).

The French Revolution included two phases which in their character and their aims were almost exact opposites, but these two phases were not, as in England a century earlier, neatly separated in time. The years from 1789 to 1792 were those of the liberal revolution for freedom. In 1792 the totalitarian revolution of domination was begun.

That these two phases of the revolution succeeded each other without interval, that this duality came to be viewed as a unity, and that the second, terroristic phase thus could invoke the aura of the first liberal phase—these circumstances have come to have a baneful influence ever since. The conviction thus arose that terror is an indispensable means, an unavoidable phase, even of liberal revolutions—a notion elevated to the status of dogma in Marx's doctrine of revolutionary dictatorship of the proletariat with its obligatory maximum of terrorist brutality as a necessary precondition of an ultraliberal and anarchist classless society.

Napoleon voiced the opinion that the French people had not expected freedom from the Revolution but equality. It would be more correct to say that the people had felt its freedom to be impaired by the feudal privileges of nobility and clergy and by the king's stubborn denial of demands for equality. Napoleon also has been called the great "bridler" of the Revolution; yet those who saw him in that role were not always aware that the excesses that he bridled went far beyond the true aims of the Revolution, so that Napoleon, by suppressing the excesses, reduced the Revolution as far as possible to its original and essential dimensions. In his domestic policy Napoleon was the great executor and temporary stabilizer of the Revolution. The Code Napoléon is nothing but the detailed legal implementation of the Declaration of the Rights of Man and the Citizen, while at the same time "linking up with the time-tested tradition of the *ancien régime*."[198]

Napoleon's fatal flaw, and the reason for his failure, was his usurpation and illegitimacy—a reflection of the second Jacobin phase—accentuated by his pushiness, vulgarity, his *parvenu* and *nouveau riche* manner. Having seized power illegitimately, he frequently saw himself compelled to exercise it illegitimately. And in foreign policy his influence was wholly destructive—the peoples of Europe came to pay the price for his very successes of domestic policy. Whether Napoleon was to remain or to be removed from the throne in 1814 or 1815 depended exclusively on the decision of the allies, and their opinion on this score changed often. The opinion of the French nation itself—which in 1815 was one of benevolent neutrality—mattered little. It was his illegitimacy that drove Napoleon into unfettered imperialism, into the Russian catastrophe and to his fall. In his famous nine-hour discussion with Metternich in Dresden in 1813, Napoleon, with surprising insight, declared that since he was not a legitimate monarch, he could not endure any diminution of his power in the sphere of foreign policy without forfeiting his throne in France. And Emperor Francis II had already perceived the same truth with complete clarity when, after losing the battle of Austerlitz (1805) he was welcomed with jubilation by his loyal Viennese. On this occasion he turned to the French ambassador and said: "Do you believe that your lord could thus go back to Paris, if he had lost a battle as I have?" What happened to Napoleon after Waterloo fully bore him out. Only because of his illegitimacy was Napoleon forced to continue the Jacobin nationalism and imperialism of the second phase; yet in domestic policy his constant concern was to avoid the excesses of the Revolution and to steer a course of moderation. His illegitimacy, too, forced the allies, as champions of legitimacy, to dethrone him and restore the incompetent Bourbons.

Napoleon liked to view himself as successor to Louis XVI, thereby occasionally earning the mockery of royalist courtiers. When a royalist, fascinated by Napoleon's military glory, suddenly sighed: "If only he were a Bourbon!" he was uttering a deep historical insight. Had Napoleon been a Bourbon, France might have been spared most of the misfortune in the century and a half since 1792, and the whole Western world spared the misfortune of the Restoration and the vice of nationalism.

24. Setback: Romanticism and Restoration

Let us imagine for a moment how European intellectual history would have proceeded if it had been possible for French developments to pursue the positive line that had reached its first peak in August 1789.

At the outbreak of the French Revolution the Enlightenment found itself in a critical yet fruitful and promising stage. An opposition movement, later known as preromanticism, had originated in the nature-smitten poetry of England, had found literary expression in France in Rousseau, and had been transformed in Germany, under Pietist influence, into *Sturm und Drang*; with youthful passion this movement in all its forms objected to the one-sided rationalism of the Enlightenment. This protest was profoundly justified and thus, although it in turn was highly one-sided, it made headway, all the more so because the Enlightenment itself had not been lacking in self-criticism. German classicism offered a first synthesis between Enlightenment and *Sturm und Drang*: it was a masterly attempt to give its due to each of the two sides of human nature, to the head as well as the heart, to thought as well as feeling.

This attempt had been crowned by a whole series of literary master-pieces of timeless validity and by the attainment of an intellectual level never again attained.

Why, despite its versatility, balance, fertility, and rich promise, was this phenomenon of German classicism so short-lived? If any movement in intellectual history seemed destined to endure and bear fruit, surely it was German classicism; yet—tragically—it lasted only a few decades, and its impact outside literature is barely perceptible. This early demise was the result not of endogenous causes but, as we shall see, of external historical circumstances.

Although German classicism offered an exemplary range of syn-thesis, the most gifted and sensitive members of the following gen-eration felt that the irrational counterforces which, in the *Sturm und Drang* movement, had entered the lists against the Enlighten-ment were still insufficiently prepared for combat, had not yet rightly come into their own, had not yet attained their full depth and fruitfulness. A still more intimate reciprocal penetration of feel-ing and intellect was declared to be both possible and necessary; major works of poetry, to be sure, had achieved a balance between the two, but philosophy had not yet provided any solid grounding for such balance. The early romantics of Germany felt themselves called to this very task. If this first generation of romantics had been left to their natural development they would have become the sec-ond generation of German classicism—a tendency readily evident in their ardent veneration of Goethe, which later deteriorated into sterile hero worship for the distantly reigning Olympian. Goethe himself had the painful feeling that the younger generation, despite this veneration, had become untrue to him and to German classi-cism. He expressed his regrets in several letters, the first to a friend of his son: "A German does not need to grow old to find himself for-saken by his pupils." "Train a number of pupils and you train almost as many adversaries." "There are very excellent young people, but the tomfools all want to begin from scratch and work inde-pendently—on their own, originally, arbitrarily, for themselves only. . . ."[199]

The fiasco of early romanticism after its hopeful beginnings has been blamed on the personal inadequacies of its leading repre-sentatives—on the face of it a highly unlikely explanation. What should account for this deficiency in talent or weakness of character of an otherwise highly gifted generation? The true explanation lies in the external historical situation in which all members of that generation found themselves.

The longer the victory of French Enlightenment was delayed by the feudal backwardness of the French monarchy, the more all European eyes were impatiently turned toward France. The whole enlightened world greeted the final breakthrough of the forces of progress in the "great" French Revolution with rapture and jubilation. Even Germany, the country of Lutheran obsequiousness and piety, was swept along by the common sense of elation; even here the Revolution found, as the aging Kant wrote solemnly, "a wishful participation in the minds of interested spectators that borders on enthusiasm."[200]

In the English House of Commons, Charles James Fox (1749-1807), the Whig leader and opponent of Pitt, greeted the French Revolution with the words: "How much the greatest event it is that ever happened in the world, and how much the best!"

Representatives of the old order, if they were not seized by the same enthusiasm, were paralyzed by fear and by anxiety for their vested interests. Throughout Europe only isolated voices of opposition were heard, and those found no resonance. Tom Paine, Priestley, and Bentham in England, Schiller and Klopstock in Germany were made honorary citizens of France, and accepted the honor with emotion and gratitude. German poets like Klopstock, Bürger, Voss, and Friedrich Leopold Graf zu Stolberg penned odes to freedom. The historian Schlözer wrote: "One of the greatest nations in the world . . . finally casts off the yoke of tyranny. . . . Doubtless God's angels in heaven intoned a *Te deum laudamus*."[201] Johannes Müller declared the Revolution to be the happiest event since the birth of Christ, and the day when the Bastille was stormed "the most beautiful day . . . since the fall of the Roman Empire." The storming of the Bastille, after all, had been that indispensable measure of symbolic violence from below on which the Revolution could base its claim to world-historic rank, and everyone assumed that this would be the last of it. Herder considered the Revolution the most important movement of mankind since the Reformation, and his wife as late as 1792 exclaimed: "The sun of freedom is rising, that is certain."[202] The aging Kant, surely a strict moralist, as late as 1798, wrote on the French Revolution: "Such a phenomenon in the history of mankind *cannot be forgotten* because it reveals in human nature a disposition and a capacity for improvement."[203] And even Hegel, toward the end of his lectures on the philosophy of history late in his life, breaks into a real hymn, hailing the advent of right and of the reign of the mind—the true reconciliation, so long awaited, "of the Divine with the World."[204]

The thrilling start of 1789-1790, on which the whole world had fixed its gaze with throbbing heart, ended with a shocking descent into horrors of a kind that no one, after a century of light and peak intellectual achievement, would have deemed possible. The ominous prelude of the flight and arrest of Louis XVI in 1791 was followed by the war of intervention, the removal of the king and the September massacres, the execution of the king, and the Jacobin terror of 1793-1794. The failure of the movement, of which Gentz had said that it would signify the greatest catastrophe in human history, was becoming a frightful reality.

Goethe's reaction is recorded in his *Campaign in France*: "Who had not since his youth been appalled at the history of the year 1649, who had not shuddered at the execution of Charles I and for his consolation hoped that such frenzied scenes among contending factions would never recur. Now, however, all this is being repeated, more horribly and hideously, among the most cultured of neighboring peoples, before our very eyes, day by day . . . I have seen among our men some for whose sanity one might fear."[205]

And barely had the Jacobin terror most frightfully drowned in its own blood when already Napoleon, the "Robespierre on horseback," began to turn terror at home into terror abroad, and, like a new world-conquering Attila or Timur, to engulf the whole Western world in blood and fire. In 1814-1815 he himself collapsed in a frightful catastrophe brought on by his total want of measure and the common resistance of oppressed and threatened peoples.

Never in world history had the highest upswing and the deepest fall followed so closely on each other. Even the catastrophe of 546 B.C., aside from its more limited impact, had not been nearly so precipitous. What foundered was not only the French Revolution, with all the hopes that enlightened Europe had set on it, but the whole secular movement of the renewal of the tradition of classical antiquity that had begun with the Renaissance and reached its climax in the Enlightenment. The impact on tender and finely tuned minds among contemporaries was devastating. Shaken to their depths, they recoiled in horror from the spectacle—only to find that all too soon terror had left the stage to spread to the audience itself: the Napoleonic Wars captured and overran their own countries.

A first result of Napoleon's ruthlessness was the wholesale abolition, in 1803 and 1806, of most of the member states of the Holy Roman Empire. It is hard to understand that such an accumulation of flagrant violations of existing constitutional law could have been celebrated by public opinion then and since as a progressive measure of modernization. What remained from the good old days of Germany, after its brief efflorescence in the eighteenth century, was flattened as if by a steamroller; and Napoleon's work of destruction was continued by Bismarck in 1866.

Another and contradictory element in Napoleon's character has puzzled observers to this day. His flag was the banner of freedom and progress of the Revolution, but it was also the emblem of national subjugation. The Corsican was the harbinger both of internal political freedom and external political subjugation.

Those who had been enthusiastic sympathizers of the Revolution could not effect an immediate reversal of their attitudes: in the history of ideas a moment of fright can last for years at a time. By contrast, those who had been foes of the Revolution from the start required no reversal. It was Burke's distinction that he had foreseen and foretold the disaster from the start. The impact on others is illustrated by Wilhelm von Humboldt's essay "Ideas on an Attempt to Determine the Limits of the Activity of the State," a sort of liberal political program for German classicism. Although ready for the printer in May 1792 it was not published until 1851 (posthumously), when it found far greater resonance in France and England than in Germany.

The abrupt shift from optimism to pessimism that was brought about by the events of 1792-1793 can be observed in many fields of specialty; it appears very sharply in demography. In 1793 William Godwin (1756-1836), the ultraliberal anarchist, published an essay that had been many years in the writing, *An Inquiry Concerning Political Justice and Its Influence on General Virtue and Happiness*, in which he fancied to prove that these qualities are the inevitable result of progress and population increase. It was in protest against this exuberant optimism that Robert Malthus (1766-1834) published, at first anonymously, his *Essay on the Principle of Population*, with its contrary demonstration that the unrestricted growth of population must necessarily lead to general pauperization. And this gloomy so-called Malthusian law of population was to dominate the subsequent development of demographic theory. Quite similarly, Simonde de Sismondi (1773-1842), in an abrupt conversion from the liberal free-trade convictions of his youth, developed, along with Malthus, into an early representative of the antiliberal pessimistic opposition to Adam Smith. And in painting Francisco Goya (1746-1828) changed from the charming rococo paintings of his youth to the bitter accusation and cultural criticism of his later work.

Just as the enthusiastic upswing of 1789 had been considered the crowning perfection of the whole Age of Enlightenment, so now the collapse of the Revolution led to the retroactive condemnation of that entire age. Had not the ill-willed reactionaries and obscurantists, in clamoring against the infernal conceit and arrogance of the Enlightenment, always asserted the terrible truth, and had that truth not now been revealed before the eyes of the world?

Earlier the Enlightenment had been given credit for the first, hopeful phase of the Revolution; now it was made responsible for its terrible consequences and excesses. Klopstock solemnly revoked his odes to the Revolution. Schiller, earlier like Klopstock an honorary citizen of revolutionary France, now hurled his curse at the Enlightenment:

> Woe to those who lend to the eternal blind
> The light of the torch of heaven!
> It shines not for them; it can only set fires
> And makes cities and countries into ashes.[206]

Yet the responsibility for the degeneration of the Revolution into Jacobin terror belongs not to "the ideas of 1789," which were the ideas of the eighteenth century. Rather, it belongs to the events of 1792-1793 (and on to 1815), which ran directly counter to those ideas and were the work of their foes. The responsibility lies, as we have seen, with the feudalism of the French nobility—narrow-minded to the point of imbecility and unscrupulous to the point of high treason—and with the stupidity and weakness of the king. Together these factors brought about the foreign intervention that in turn set off the mass psychosis of the terror and transferred the task of military defense and political reconstruction to a usurper whose sense of his own illegitimacy drove him to demagogic absolutism and nationalistic imperialism.

The winds of history that had earlier swelled the sails of the Enlightenment now blew, with even greater force, in the opposite direction. Whatever had stood out against the Enlightenment now received fresh impetus. The Jesuit order, abolished in 1773, was reestablished in 1814. Conversions to Catholicism multiplied. In Catholic France Chateaubriand (1768-1848) glorified *Le Génie du Christianisme* (1802 and 1828) in lyric tones; in Protestant Germany Schleiermacher (1768-1834) composed his *Addresses on Religion to Its Cultured Despisers*, published 1799, at first still anonymously. The repercussions, of course, varied from country to country. The United States was barely affected, because it was farthest away (incomparably farther, given conditions of travel at the time) and because it had just accomplished its own successful revolution. How differently things would have looked in Europe if the great French Revolution had proceeded according to the felicitous pattern of its English and American predecessors!

There also were differences among European countries. England was little affected, both because of its earlier successful revolution and because it was not, in any case, given to extreme swings of the pendulum. France was too deeply identified with its revolution for counterrevolutionary tendencies to take hold in the long run. It was in Germany that these tendencies were to have their fullest triumph, throwing the country back into its baneful separate development and undoing the rapprochement between Germany and other Western countries by which the Enlightenment had nearly succeeded in restoring Europe's cultural unity after the ravages of the Reformation. Germany, indeed, became the center of the new countermovement. "German history takes pride in a movement for which no other people on the vast historical horizon has ever given an example and which no other people is inclined to imitate. Indeed we have participated in the restorations of modern peoples without having ever participated in their revolutions." This spiteful sally by Karl Marx[207] unfortunately expresses a fundamental historic truth.

It has lately become fashionable to defend Talleyrand, Metternich, and Gentz. And indeed, whenever things go steeply downhill, the further one lags behind the higher up one will be. But the activities of such men at most retarded the development of the Revolution and radicalized it by the obstacles they placed in its way— whereas the only constructive policy would have been to foster the positive forces within the forward-thrusting movement. In Germany, such positive forces were embodied above all in Baron vom Stein, whom Metternich and his minions fought and persecuted in blind hatred. Thus on balance the reactionaries did far more harm than good.

The German historian Barthold Georg Niebuhr, in his passionate opposition to the leveling imperialism of the French Revolution, came to prefer "*old* rust and *one's own* deformities" to any newfangled notions of progress. That "proud and headstrong Bern patrician," Carl Ludwig von Haller (1768-1854), saw fit "to praise coarsely and unabashedly the good fortune of the powerholders of the *ancien régime* in freely possessing and freely enjoying their own power and wealth," and to juxtapose his own theory of a "vigorous, comfort-loving, and ruddy aristocracy" as a doctrine of the "natural state of society as against the chimera of the artificial-bourgeois state of nature."[208] Natural law—elaborated over many centuries from the Stoics and the great jurisconsults of Rome down to the late Spanish scholastics and perfected in what is generally acknowledged as one of the proudest accomplishments of the Enlightenment—was thus thrown on the junkheap. Thus Adam (von) Müller (1779-1829), a talented windbag and rhetorician, could write in 1809: "We may confidently [!] deny any natural law outside, or above, or prior to, positive law."[209] He would hardly have made such a statement if the earnest jurists of the historical school, led by Savigny, had not advanced from criticizing natural law to "simply killing it with silence."[210] No one, to be sure, could foresee into what a juridical, logical, and ethical morass such shortsighted legal positivism would eventually lead. Meanwhile, the immediate result was jurisprudence without right (*Rechtswissenschaft ohne Recht*), as Leonard Nelson has strikingly characterized it. Thus historical positivism in jurisprudence discarded the legal weapon that might later have justified resistance to state authority in its descent into totalitarianism—a weapon that even the medieval Church has passed on (albeit well-sheathed) from generation to generation. Hence the legal positivism of the nineteenth century is one of those ominous tendencies, of which more and more were to accumulate, through which the rise of a new despotism was prepared.

Everywhere new insults were now heaped upon the Enlightenment, and the venomous, scolding hatred of the new critics contrasts sharply with the juvenile arrogance and bluster of *Sturm und Drang*. Anyone who dared come to the Enlightenment's defense, such as the aging and admittedly senile Johann Heinrich Voss (1751-1826) only made himself a laughingstock and was mocked as a living fossil.

German early romanticism, as we saw, had originally set itself the promising task of effecting an even better synthesis between Enlightenment and *Sturm und Drang* than had been achieved by German classicism, a synthesis that would accord greater weight to the irrational and historical components. But now the Romantics were driven into ever greater hostility toward the Enlightenment: that capacity for historical empathy and understanding, in which the Romantics took such pride, they found themselves unable to summon up for the age of Enlightenment. Only at this point did there arise that "romantic" attitude in the narrower sense, which Goethe condemned as a sickness; only now did romanticism become a movement of "intellectual counterrevolution,"[211] although the defection of individual romantics to the camp of political and social reaction often bore a heavy tinge of opportunism. Jacob Burckhardt comments on this discontinuity: "Despite all the efforts at restoration" intellectual developments in the West never recovered from "the fact that the nineteenth century began with a *tabula rasa*."[212]

Romanticism bears the responsibility for the falseness and sterility of the subsequent battle lines of irrationalism versus rationalism that dominated the whole nineteenth century and which still have not been superseded in our own day. And this misdefinition of the issue constituted a major setback behind the great and fruitful synthesis achieved by classicism.

The real leader of the intellectual counterrevolution, and hence also a catalyst for the romantic movement, was Edmund Burke (1729-1797). His first and most important book against the Revolution appeared as early as 1790. Yet until 1792 he was little more than a solitary, if important, eccentric; only from 1793 onward did he acquire wide and profound influence. Hence Burke is the exception that confirms the rule that only the events of 1792-1794—which so tellingly confirmed his worst fears—produced the general apostasy of European intellectuals from the Revolution.

Even in the special department of historical understanding Romanticism often signified a notable setback. One of the most brilliant achievements of the Enlightenment, as we have seen, was to have conceived the powerful program of a purely human, earth-spanning, universal history—a program that brought with it a profusion of specific tasks by way of implementation and supplementation for generations to come. The rationalistic onesidedness of viewpoint and judgment, which still prevails with Voltaire, had been overcome by Herder in 1744 in his brilliant sketch *Another Philosophy of History for the Education of Mankind* (whose title explicitly and modestly invites comparison with Voltaire) and in the four volumes (1784-1791) of his *Ideas for the Philosophy of a History of Man*, in the composition of which Goethe participated. In these works Herder displays his empathy and understanding, his ability to enter into and appreciate individual national characters, his grasp of the far-reaching interconnections sketched in Voltaire's outline; yet he at times slides back into the mode of thought and expression of pastoral theology familiar to Herder as a clergyman. Romantic and postromantic historians have further elaborated this sympathetic and empathetic view of history, with due attention to the full authenticity of all stage settings. As a result the feeling for national individuality and folklore, which in Herder had still been kept within bounds, now was distorted in a highly nationalistic fashion.

Another task that had long been awaiting resolution was to make the methodology of collecting, criticizing, and evaluating documentary sources, as developed by Maurist Benedictines and Dutch Jesuits after the seventeenth century, serviceable to the new secular historiography. This was indeed accomplished in the wake of romanticism by the historians of the nineteenth century.

All the elements of a method for carrying out the grand new conception of history developed by the Enlightenment were thus ready at hand. The manner in which the historians of the romantic age and of the nineteenth century set about this task speaks more for their zeal and industry than for their intellectual brilliance; somehow, in the course of their painstaking labors, the grand conception itself broke down. Ranke here represents a borderline phenomenon: the Western culture complex of Romanic and Germanic peoples to him was still a living single entity, and in his old age he even undertook to write a "universal history." Yet Ranke's successors no longer mustered the strength to take an encompassing view of the whole of mankind. Nationalist observers hailed this dissolution of universal history into so many partial, national histories as progress, and from the pinnacle of such progress they looked down with pity on the supposedly unhistorical Enlightenment. The great perspective of universal history, which Voltaire had conceived and Herder developed as a bold secularization and broadening of the Christian history of salvation, was surrendered to a narrow nationalistic conception of history. As Goethe once put it, "Patriotism has ruined history."[213]

The neohumanism of the German classical period from Winckelmann to Wilhelm von Humboldt had achieved a true, live, and comprehensive conception of Greek culture, which, to be sure, was not free from defects and a certain one-sidedness. The early romantics—notably Friedrich Schlegel—had contributed to deepening that conception, as Schleiermacher did through his translation of Plato and his brilliant introductions. Indeed the German classicists had been so blinded by the radiant light of old Greece that they had been oblivious to the dark or negative aspects which it remained for the romantics to discover. Yet instead of touching up the previous picture with a shadow here or there, the romantic philologists began to sketch an entirely new picture of equal and opposite onesidedness—a picture of penumbra, darkness, and gloom from which the grimaces of Egyptian or even Indian idols seemed to spring forth. The Orphics of the sixth century B.C. had similarly begun with a tendentious, archaizing falsification of history by claiming the pre-Homeric age for their legendary Orpheus and the myths attached to him. Later this historic fiction was combined with the allegedly primordial wisdom of oriental priests, and further spun out by neo-Pythagoreans and Neoplatonists. It was this strand that was taken up by German romantics like Görres and Creuzer. Whereas medieval Christianity had tried to present the Greeks of the classic age as deeply unhappy, under the spell of a gloomy pessimism, and hence deeply in need of salvation, so the Orphic interpretation, as revived in the nineteenth century, purported to prove that the Greeks were fully aware of this need for salvation and indeed were actively seeking it in the arcane mysteries of the East.

The changing interpretation of classical Greece was abetted by a puerile and rationalistic view of the distinction between optimism and pessimism whereby an optimist must find all and everything delightful and whereby anyone who perceives anything as disagreeable or sad is therefore a pessimist. The world and human life abound in enjoyable and disagreeable elements, in brightness and in darkness, and the Greeks would have been hopeless blockheads if they had not been aware of the disagreeable or dark elements. They were optimists, however, in the sense that for them the positive elements were preponderant, and this put them in sharpest contrast to the pessimism and consciousness of sin of Christianity. The Greeks championed the body and its joys, the world and its beauty. For them—aside from a small minority—the world was no vale of tears and the body no foul prison: an unbiased observer could have no doubt on this score.

This rejection of the basic conception of Greece as developed by classicism came with remarkable suddenness and abruptness. Friedrich Schlegel, who had felt in his best and most promising years that his mission was to become the successor to "Holy Winckelmann"—to do for Greek poetry what Winckelmann had done for Greek art—only a few years later rejected his earlier Grecomania. And Novalis, who earlier had spoken of "revivifying antiquity," now became the passionate herald of an emotionally charged medievalism. This neo-Orphic aversion from the antique world toward the Middle Ages was one of the most fateful repercussions of the catastrophe of 1792-1793; next to the Reformation it probably constitutes the most serious rupture in German intellectual history.

The Middle Ages, which now replaced antiquity as the ideal age of the past, were in truth the great epoch of common European culture; yet they were now being viewed "peculiarly enough, in special measure, as a time of independent national development."[214] The Gothic style of architecture, unmistakably French in its origins and in its spirited elegance, was now honored as something primordially German. Similarly a retrospective nationalism saw innate German individual and national traits in institutions that can be found in any people of a similar stage of historic development—an unhistoric conception which, however, underlies as important and meritorious a work as Otto von Gierke's *Geschichte des deutschen Genossenschaftsrechts*. The mystically reified notion of *Volksgeist* (folk spirit), from which culture is supposed to have sprung directly in happier times (just how, no one can tell), has no doubt engendered much enthusiastic study of the history of one's own people. Yet it has just as certainly obscured, not clarified, the underlying sociological realities. The same goes for the romantic notion of the *Urzeit* or primordial age.

Giovanni Battista Vico, who continued the Platonist tradition of the Renaissance into the late baroque age, and who might be called the unacknowledged grandfather of romanticism, had elaborated the Sophist and Epicurean conception of the original state, as handed down by Lucretius, with some admixture of Orphic and Neoplatonist elements, into his conception of a coarse and bloodthirsty, yet mysterious and powerfully creative early age. Its language was poetry, which he mistakenly considered to be older than prose—thus anticipating Hamann's and Herder's doctrine of poetry as the mother language of the human race. The allegedly primitive communism of common property in land also is among the attributes ascribed to this mysterious, frightening, and yet alluring primordial age, and this doctrine was to enjoy particularly wide currency in the nineteenth century, when fear of atomization led to phantasies of overintegration.

One important scholarly contribution did indeed result from this intellectual tradition, the reconstruction of matriarchy as a historical phenomenon, undertaken by the Basel jurist Johann Jacob Bachofen (1815-1887), a disciple of Savigny. Thanks to the researches of the Vienna school of ethnography, we now know into what context this phenomenon belongs—that of the planter culture.

This planter culture appears in the early ancestry of all high cultures, and it exhibits, especially in its late variants, such gloomy and bloodthirsty features as human sacrifice and cannibalism—yet these traits are by no means innate or universally human.

Primitive age, primordial revelation, priestly wisdom of the East, Middle Ages, folk spirit, nation—such were the core concepts and the highlights of the romantic view of history.

The romantic passion for revival of the past stemmed, however, not only from a positive motive of loving devotion, but also from the negative motive of flight from an unattractive present and a menacing future. Where this negative motivation prevails one may speak of historicism in the pejorative sense. When the romantic lovingly immerses himself into the deep poetic atmosphere of an ivy-wreathed castle, when before his spiritual eye the people of that time become alive decked out in their original costumes—the proud knight with his page, the beautiful damsel of the castle waving from her balcony, the simple, honest peasants in huts at the foot of the castle—then it never once even remotely occurs to this tender-hearted dreamer that the castle was built by the *corvée* harshly exacted from those peasants, or that the knight and his whole entourage—including the oh-so-beautiful damsel—lived off the dues and services of these very peasants.

That brilliant circle of eternal adolescents and spirited women that was German romanticism lived in what they called the "realm of the spirit," which had experienced so intimate and warm a renewal through the Pietism of the eighteenth century. This "kingdom of God within you," this earthly province of the better Hereafter, is raised so high above mundane reality with its petty miseries and imperfections that no one should mind being subject to a feudal lord who, after all, has power over the body and not the spirit. Thus romanticism, following upon Lutheranism and Pietism, provided a further fateful element in the development of German masochism, quietism, and introversion. After centuries in which human intellectual history had consisted of a laborious, step-by-step advance of logical thought, romanticism constituted a revolt in the name of magical, prescientific, and prelogical thought. It was now asserted in all seriousness that reason and science, man's loftiest accomplishments of the past, are to be despised—a reversal which Ludwig Klages, perhaps the most extreme representative of this view in recent German intellectual history, saw fit to celebrate as "the most remarkable attempt at restoring a contemplative intellectuality."[215] In the meantime it should have become clear that if human life is in danger of vanishing from this earth this will be due not to the intellect but to the dethronement of the intellect in the name of anti-intellectual counterforces.

The nineteenth century brought the victory of the romantic view in all the humanistic fields of study, and nowhere was the victory more complete than in Germany. And here in Germany the social blindness of romanticism came to be characteristic of the leading strata well into the twentieth century, regardless of a person's partisan affiliation.

In the Middle Ages and in the age of the baroque all artistic expression of vigor, vitality, and human power had been dimmed or distorted through countervailing ascetic or sadomasochistic tendencies. In reacting against these distortions, the eighteenth-century Enlightenment gave itself over to a thinness, transparency, and weakness of form as well as to an anemia of content. With romanticism there came a further reaction, an opposite swing of the pendulum. Yet the reaction was not deep and energetic enough to come down to a new foundation, to new soil on bedrock. Only rarely did romanticism find its way back to the authentic or the primeval, for all its self-conscious pretension in that direction.

Rousseau's opposition to the Enlightenment, for instance, still remained enclosed in rationalism; his tearful sentimentality lacked true depth of feeling and emotional power; his enthusiasm for unspoiled nature and solitude are in sharp contrast to his undisciplined, Bohemian life in the big city. And Friedrich Schlegel's *Lucinde*, apart from its sheer artistic insufficiency, is embarrassingly reminiscent, in the weakness of its emphasis on sensuality, of the rococo lasciviousness of Wieland, which the young Goethe had rightly ridiculed.

And because reason, discredited, can no longer assert itself with power or dignity, the belief now spreads that it must be renounced entirely so as to satisfy the demands of the irrational. "O intellect, wretched intellect!" laments Heinrich von Kleist. The romantic, in confronting the infinite, does not secure his footing on finite ground; rather, he succumbs supinely to the siren call of the boundless distance, to the intoxicating beguilements of the depth of the soul; he loses all sense of proportion to plunge headlong into the bubbling chaos of the deep. Even the German love of death, which Clemenceau was not the only one to find so uncanny and frightening, has its roots in this attitude. The less one feels sheltered in light and in consciousness the more one flees into the darkness of the sub-conscious.

All this is not to deny the real merits of romanticism in develop-ing our sense of historical empathy: all our accomplishments in the understanding of primitive and prerational cultures as well as of medieval-theological-feudal cultures stands on its shoulders. The lasting merit of romanticism is to have made the dimension of his-toric depth, of which the preromantics had a mysterious premoni-tion, into an integral component of our world picture. Even this achievement, however, is marred by a flaw mentioned earlier. Romanticism, which could not do enough for olden times and for tradition and never tired of its historic enthusiasms, is the very movement that brought about the final break in that long and living tradition that had continued unbroken from classical antiquity by way of the church fathers and the Middle Ages to the baroque. Even the less numerous yet still vigorous threads that connected the Enlightenment to the baroque were cut off by the frivolous subjec-tivism of the romantics. The sentimental historicism of the roman-tics created an obstacle to serious and objective historical under-standing; it also interrupted the living historical continuity with the past, the survival of the past as a real presence. It mummified the past, placed it on a pedestal or in a glass case, and made it the object of a cult—with the historian relegated to the role of altar boy or museum curator.

In "reviewing on appeal," as Cassirer puts it, "the great lawsuit that romanticism has brought against the Enlightenment,"[216] our motion is to set aside the unjust sentence that romanticism has passed as prosecutor, judge, and jury against the Enlightenment. But beyond that we file a countermotion for the conviction of roman-ticism on some of the very same counts. In doing so we must accept one important plea for extenuation: the sudden change in the histor-ical circumtances in 1792-1793, to which resistance would have been as laborious as it would have been thankless.

In the field of music, which is of course especially close to the cen-ter of feeling, one would expect a very strong flow of energy to result from the romantic hypertrophy of feeling, as well as a powerful change of historic directions. Both effects indeed occurred. The fact that in the music of the romantic period a heightening of emotional life led to a series of peak achievements, particularly in Beethoven and Wagner, and attained an extraordinary level of artistic expressiveness should not make us oblivious to the humanly unhealthy, pernicious, introverted, tormenting, and pathological aspect of this musical development. Goethe once referred to Beethoven's compositions as "that overfilled music. . . . All is now ultra, all transcends irresistibly. . . . No one knows himself anymore, no one understands the elements in which he floats and functions, no one the material that he processes; simple naïveté now is out of the question. . . ."[217] In no other compartment than in music does Goethe's dictum on romanticism as sickness apply with greater force. With regard to Wagner this has become, since Nietzsche and through him, public knowledge; but in retrospect the continuity of this development back to Beethoven appears ever more distinctly.

We thus feel tempted to apply the exclamation "O Freunde, nicht diese Töne!" not just to the immediately preceding passages of Beethoven's Ninth Symphony but to the entire romantic phase of the composer's work. Note that the "more pleasant and more joyful" sounds that the grand choral finale of the symphony then strikes up revert to the still-unbroken optimism of the Enlightenment prior to the Revolution, to which Schiller's *Ode to Joy* (1785) lends exuberant expression. And this commitment to the "rapture of Enlightenment" was stated, with the loftiest pathos achievable, in 1823, when the sway of romanticism and of its hatred for the Enlightenment were at their very peak. The imposing fugal passages of the late sonatas and quartets reach further back to Bach; their style, appropriate to the composer's maturity, offers, as it were, a synthesis reaching directly across from the romantic to the baroque. Beethoven started out from the classicistic late rococo, then increasingly wallowed in the dionysian depths of feeling of the most extreme romanticism, to arrive finally, in the works of his old age, at a new synthesis—which one would be tempted to call classical if it had not remained an individual peak but had become part of a high plateau.

The designation of "genius," as used in common speech, can unhesitatingly be applied to Richard Wagner—not least because the nineteenth-century notion of genius was created largely in his image. He was a person of great ability and even greater willpower whose lapses into bad taste were of such dimensions as would have been impossible, a generation earlier, with anyone of even the most modest talent. The musical rape and murder that Gounod (1818-1893) perpetrated by superimposing his *Ave Maria* on the first prelude of Bach's *Well-Tempered Clavier*—to the frenetic applause of a sensationalist public—strikingly expresses the relationship of nineteenth-century music to that of the eighteenth.

For nineteenth-century Germans, romantic music took the place earlier occupied by the fateful heritage of pietistic inwardness. The kingdom of sounds for them was the kingdom of the spirit, the "kingdom of heaven within you," into which one could withdraw at any time, no admission charged. As Thomas Mann said in a speech of 1924, "Anyone who is concerned to give to German intellectual life form, consciousness, luminosity, and international validity . . . has had to fight against the ambiguous, dark aspects of German music—even though, in doing so, he might be most painfully cutting into his own flesh. If someone dared to call music 'an obstacle to German humanity,' one would have to hate him yet secretly agree with him."[218]

The architecture of the period of baroque absolutism had given expression, as we saw, to violently theocratic, artistically impressive, and humanly exaggerated tendencies. Hence in this field the swing of the pendulum in the opposite direction toward the classicism of the Enlightenment period was particularly pronounced, as the absolutism of the prince and the deity yielded to the domination of the organizing ratio, the literary recipe, and the tyranny of the drawing board. Thus doubly removed from deeply rooted organic growth, the anemic architecture of the classicist period succumbed to the infection of romantic historicism with devastating effect. Hence the history of architecture in the nineteenth century is a catastrophe that would seem to be unparalleled in all of art history. The large cities of the West in the late nineteenth century beat all previous records for architectural impotence and hideousness. Various countermovements since that time have had notable success in mitigating this grave pathology; it remains to be seen whether they can effect a complete cure.[219]

Philosophy, which throughout the eighteenth century had been the illumining and life-giving sun at the center of the intellectual universe, fell victim to a curious degeneracy.

Hume's detached and unruffled skepticism succeeded where earlier skeptics, from Pyrrho to Bayle, had failed despite much polemical sharpness. For Hume furnished complete and final proof of the

impossibility of any theology and metaphysics whatsoever and of
any allegedly supraempirical knowledge; thus he overcame the
superstratification structure of traditional philosophy. Even Kant,
according to his own famous statement, was awakened by Hume
from his dogmatic slumber: "Metaphysics no longer is a tenable
cause" was his verdict. Yet Kant's fate was, as he himself confesses,
to have once been in love with metaphysics,[220] and one's first love is
not soon forgotten. Kant, in his whole philosophic bearing, is and
remains a metaphysician and, in the final analysis, a Pythagorean
and Platonist. The logical exactitude to which he aspired and pretended is often mere appearance, an external facade hiding a sometimes inconsistent inner structure of thought. Once we really abandon all prelogical modes of theological and metaphysical thought,
Kant's work turns out to be replete with paralogisms, fallacies, and
equivocations. Whereas earlier German philosophy had conformed
to general Western development, Kant now founded—as Schelling
once put it—a "specifically German philosophy."[221] Thus Kant the
philosopher plays a role analogous to that of Luther the theologian;
both have been celebrated equally as German national heroes because of their respective feats of intellectual separatism, of having
taken German developments out of the European mainstream of
evolution.

Kant's lifetime accomplishment, carried out with incomparable
philosophic acumen, was to have constructed an ultimate refuge for
his beloved metaphysics. It was something of an emergency shelter:
cramped and uncomfortable, but all the safer for that. The existence
of God, the freedom of the will, and the immortality of the soul—the
three basic theses of deistic theology and of metaphysics from the
Stoics to Christian Wolff—were not proved; indeed, Kant earned the
sobriquet "all-destroyer" (*Alleszertrümmerer*) by explicitly demonstrating their unprovability. But this to Kant implies by no means
that these unprovable notions should be surrendered; on the contrary, one has the right—indeed the duty—to continue accepting
them. Thrown out by the front door of science as theoretical tenets
and cognitions of pure reason, they had yet managed to creep back
by circuitous backstairs as requirements of ethical consciousness, as
postulates of practical reason and indeed with a greater claim to validity than before. It was a new and extremely subtle version of the
doctrine of the twofold truth, but now it was turned upside down
with theology in the defensive position. In this defensive position of
retreat, this residually theological metaphysics maintained itself as
long as the Enlightenment dominated public opinion. Then, with

the collapse of the Enlightenment in the catastrophe of 1792-1793, better days dawned for it.

Kant, despite his veneration for Rousseau, is a thoroughgoing member of the Enlightenment; indeed, he represents its highest philosophic peak. The *Sturm und Drang* movement could do little in opposition: Herder lacked the intellectual power and training to assert his metaphysical intuitions in contradiction to a virtuoso like Kant. This left as the only philosophic antagonist Friedrich Heinrich Jacobi (1743-1819), a man of delicate sensibility, who was to philosophy what Matthias Claudius was to poetry.

Attempts at synthesis between these two poles were offered by Friedrich Schleiermacher (1768-1834) and Jakob Friedrich Fries (1773-1843), both brought up under the influence of the Moravian sect; yet neither attained the intellectual level of the parallel synthesis in German literary classicism. In part their influence was blocked by the advent of the great speculative systems in the period from 1794 to 1831 as represented by Fichte, Schelling, Hegel, and figures of lesser rank like Schopenhauer.

The eighteenth-century Enlightenment had dismantled the grand metaphysical systems of the seventeenth century, and by a patient training in intellectual honesty had fortified men against the narcotic lure of theology and metaphysics. In contrast to the seventeenth-century practice of deduction from arbitrarily posited first principles, the eighteenth century demanded observation, analysis, induction, reasoning from the particular to the general, not the general to the particular. As Voltaire wrote in his *Traité de métaphysique* (1734), "One must never say 'Let us begin by inventing principles with which we shall attempt to explain everything.' Rather, one must say 'Let us make an exact analysis of things, and after that we shall try to see, with much wariness, whether they may relate to some principles.' "[222]

All this difficult and conscientious self-training to rigor, responsibility, neatness, and clarity, begun in Scholasticism and fully accomplished in the eighteenth century, was now frivolously thrown overboard. In a wild intoxication of enthusiasm, students of philosophy hurled themselves into the surging tides of a bottomless sea of speculation. Philosophy relapsed from the level of science and anthropology that it had attained in the eighteenth century to the supposedly "higher" level of faith and theology. A new Gnosticism began to develop.

Contributions to this upsurge of metaphysics came from the earlier revival of Spinoza by Lessing and Friedrich Heinrich Jacobi, and its attitude of esthetic detachment owed something to the revival of Plato through Schleiermacher's superior translations. Last but not least, as Gerhard Ritter puts it, "the philosophy of German idealism" is a "late-fruit of rationalized Christian theology."[223] Or, as Nietzsche put it more emphatically in his *Anti-Christ*, "Among Germans . . . philosophy has been ruined by the blood of theologians. The Protestant parson is the grandfather of German philosophy, Protestantism itself its *peccatum originale*."[224]

It is no coincidence that Fichte, Schelling, and Hegel started out as theologians. Ludwig Feuerbach speaks of Hegel's "rational mysticism," and Hegel's youthful theological writings reveal the depth of that earlier influence. All three systems move on the level of faith rather than knowledge; they are secularized theology, revelations without a revealing deity. Christian theology through the millennia had trained men to accept a "higher truth," to proclaim *"Credo quia absurdum"*—and as far as absurdity goes, these systems present a considerable advance over Christian dogma. But whereas Christianity claimed for its dogmas the sanction of divine revelation—a tradition unbroken over centuries, a universal consensus, and their indispensability for the salvation of the soul—all such elements of earnestness were lacking in these brand-new, frivolous systems that were succeeding each other at a dizzying rate. Schelling, whom Fichte called "the hero of all fiery and yet wild and confused minds,"[225] produced six or seven such systems in succession, all of them important, all of them interesting, and each of them the more profound and poetical the more remote it was from Fichte. Clearly Schelling was a man of overflowing vitality; no wonder that it was with him that Caroline Schlegel, after going astray in so many directions, found fulfillment and quiet at last. And let us recall that it was to Schelling that Goethe turned over the sketches of his great nature poem, and that Schelling remained the only romantic philosopher who retained Goethe's esteem through all transformations.

At length this secularized theology, devoid of conscientious earnestness and a sense of responsibility, at last deteriorated to the dexterous juggling of a kind of intellectual Ping-Pong. Indeed the authors of these systems do not mean to be taken fully seriously: they indulge in an intellectual game, the rules of which the reader is asked to accept; and it would be rewarding to formulate the latent rules of these games. Yet there is not only an epistemological but also a sociological aspect to this theological or quasi-theological character of romantic philosophy. It is almost like a doctrine of an aristocratic priesthood—hence of intellectual superstratification and a sublimated form of the lust for domination. The practitioners of this philosophy claim to dwell in the "higher regions" high above the heads of the vulgar public, and thus to be exempt from the bothersome compulsions of the laws of the "lower," everyday forms of thought. Everything is permitted, and these self-appointed kings in the realm of the spirit hold indeed that "The king can do no wrong."

Kant already discerned this sociological aspect very keenly and fought it in its very beginnings, in an essay of 1796 entitled "On a Recently Raised Superior Tone in Philosophy." "All fancy themselves superior," he writes, "in the measure in which they believe that they need not work. . . . Things have gone so far of late that an alleged philosophy is unabashedly and publicly proclaimed according to which one need not *work* but merely listen to and enjoy the oracle within oneself in order to acquire thoroughly all the wisdom at which philosophy aims." Such a philosophy "can therefore speak in the tones of a superior lord who need not trouble to demonstrate his property title" and "look down with contempt" on other philosophies. All this, says Kant, amounts to "A despotic reign over the reason of the people through shackling to a blind faith."[226]

Similarly, Henrik Steffens (1773-1845) in his *Memoirs* describes Fichte as a "short stocky man with . . . incisive, commanding features. . . . His speech seemed to be commanding, as if he wished, by an order which one unconditionally must obey, to remove any doubts whatsover."[227] And Goethe once quipped that he "rediscovered Fichte's teaching in Napoleon's deeds and proceedings."[228] Fichte's own turn to a doctrine that one might describe as the absolute dictatorship of the ego—the most extreme possible metaphysical expression of the lust for power—significantly came in 1794, when he wrote: "In my thinking I shall proceed from the pure ego [*vom reinen Ich*] and conceive the same as absolutely self-active, not as determined by things but rather as determining things."[229]

Fichte's *Addresses to the German Nation*, a work of undoubted vigor and courage, have so long been considered the very embodiment of German patriotism and nationalism that their pronouncedly totalitarian character is sometimes overlooked even by antitotalitarians. "The new education," as advocated by Fichte, "should precisely consist therein that upon the soil which it proposes to till it would completely destroy the freedom of the will. . . ." For the products of this new education "freedom of will is annihilated and absorbed in necessity."[230]

Hegel, by his stature and intellectual influence doubtless the greatest nineteenth-century philosopher up to Nietzsche, closes the circle of great Western metaphysicians that opened with Heraclitus—of whom Hegel said that none of his propositions escaped incorporation into Hegel's logic. Hegel's conception of the state is pronouncedly totalitarian and teaches us "to consider individuals generally under the category of means." "The particular is in most cases too small compared with the general; individuals are sacrificed and surrendered."[231]

The violent character of this branch of philosophy expresses itself, even in its language and terminology, in the way it forces its concepts upon things; and of course there is something intoxicating and alluring about this godlike claim to intellectual sovereignty. How many later philosophers to this day have succumbed to this terminological intoxication with power! After the thin-blooded probity of the rococo and Biedermeier periods there evidently was a longing for brute force, and this transition probably is the most characteristic feature of the nineteenth century. In German philosophy it is represented above all by Fichte and Hegel, and it is no coincidence that both Stirner and Marx were Hegelians.

One might call this a relapse into the metaphysical absolutism of the seventeenth century and its *esprit de système*. But it was a descent as well: Descartes' "Cogito ergo sum," reminiscent of Saint Augustine, is after all somewhat more tenable as a point of departure than Fichte's puerile discovery that "I am I"—the "humbug" with which, according to Schopenhauer, this "father of sham-philosophy" opened the new dance.

Mere admiration for the virtuosity with which this strange new breed of philosophers performed on their terminological high wire strung straight across the universe would not have secured them the acclaim they found. Other decisive elements were the remarkable sweep of their cosmic lyricism, their "grotesque melody out of a craggy landscape" (as Marx once called it on first encountering Hegelian philosophy), their boldness and vigor, indeed excessive vigor. Receptivity to these qualities was at its height at this very time, after a decade of "esthetic education" by German classicism and in the period of overcharged emotional excitability in the romantic period.

Yet how pathological this whole phenomenon was, how much it was lacking in seriousness and steadfastness, how unstable and fragile it proved is shown both by the uncanny speed at which these thought constructs proliferated and spread and by the even greater speed at which they declined—in both respects uncomfortably reminiscent of cancer cells. Even before Hegel fell victim to cholera in 1831 the previously irresistible victory procession of the movement had passed its climax. The noisy civil war between the right and left wings of the Hegelian school hastened the collapse—the right pandering to the basest forms of political and religious reaction, the left—far richer in talent—dissolving into nihilism, materialism, communism, and anarchism. The result was a universal philosophic hangover, a terrible discreditation ⦁ any form of thinking that went beyond narrowly specialized knowledge or downright utilitarian application.

In 1857, Rudolf Haym noted in his biography of Hegel that "We find ourselves for the moment in a great and almost general shipwreck of the mind and of faith in the mind generally." And at the same time Alexis de Tocqueville noted in France: "The higher and middle classes now despise and fear ideas, of whatever sort they may be, and think only of their interests."[232]

But now that the turbid floods of this speculative inundation subsided it turned out that the reports of the alleged death of the much-maligned Enlightenment were vastly premature. Its achievements were too weighty simply to be cast aside; yet from its early triumph in the eighteenth century it was thrown back into a militant phase in the nineteenth—with combatants and battlefield in worse condition at that. Nineteenth-century liberalism, which in many ways constituted the direct continuation of the Enlightenment, was by no means up to continuing a legacy of such weight.

The period of Restoration in the narrow sense came to a close with the revolutions of 1830 and 1848; but its effects were not overcome for a long time even in countries where these revolutions were victorious. Economic policy in the late nineteenth and early twentieth centuries "with its return to mercantilist protective tariffs, with its demarcation of marketing zones and fixing of production quotas, with the formation of trade unions and employers' associations moved in a direction which," as Ernst Troeltsch predicted in 1913, "will later also come to be considered a period of restoration."[233] Today, three decades later, this perceptive prediction would appear to have come true.

Wilhelm Röpke has rightly emphasized that the nineteenth century, in many of its proudest accomplishments, merely reaped what the Enlightenment of the eighteenth century had sowed.[234] The relationship of the two periods recalls that between Hellenism and the preceding centuries of classical Greek philosophy. An intellectual movement with unity and central direction is split up into many separate themes and specialized disciplines. What was earlier a mighty roaring stream has been divided neatly into countless small channels that turn the wheels of as many busily humming mills.

The rationalism of the Enlightenment was too strong and broad a stream—too strong also in the social, economic, and technical spheres—for romanticism to be able to stem it. Because the romantic opposition was strongest in the upper classes, with their literary, artistic, and philosophic pursuits, the rationalism of the Enlightenment now sank down the social scale into mere pragmatism, go-getting mediocrity, and philistinism.

The high-powered synthesis of German classicism—which all Germans experience as the last and highest pinnacle of their intellectual history—and the high promise of early romanticism had, unknown to themselves, derived their force and drive from the uninterrupted secular movement of progress represented by the Enlightenment. The debacle of the French Revolution, as we saw, took away this dynamic foundation for the entire eighteenth century. With the interruption of this transmission line the high-powered voltage could no longer be maintained. The result was weariness, decline, and pathology. In literature, romanticism sank back to the unassuming level of the *Sturm und Drang* movement and more particularly its sentimental branch. In other compartments, as we saw, there was a relapse all the way into the seventeenth century. Hence the characteristic qualities of deterioration and relapse that mark the intellectual history of the nineteenth century—of which the contemporaries in their smug self-satisfaction and intoxication with technical progress were, however, quite unaware.

If all these developments are taken together, it becomes clear that we have reached here a vantage point from which the contemporary period becomes visible in its full breadth. It therefore may be appropriate to put aside the chronological-historical outline which our presentation has followed up to this point, and to consider the phenomena of the subsequent period that are most important from our viewpoint—not in temporal sequence, but in thematic arrangement. For the period up to the fall of Napoleon (1815) or perhaps to the European revolutions of 1848 historiography has well accomplished its task of intellectual digestion and of penetrating the consciousness of the educated observer, and this existence of a *communis opinio*, a historical consensus, has made it convenient for us to indicate the implications of our own point of view by marking it off from the received picture. For the more recent period there is neither such received opinion nor, therefore, any possibility of easy juxtaposition of it to our differing perspective. The thicket of recent times gets the more impenetrable the closer we approach the present. What Lytton Strachey has said of the Victorian era can be said of the nineteenth century as a whole: "We know too much about it. For ignorance is the first requisite of the historian—ignorance which simplifies and clarifies, which selects and omits. . . . Concerning the Age which has just passed, our fathers and our grandfathers have poured forth and accumulated so vast a quantity of information that the industry of a Ranke would be submerged by it, and the perspicacity of a Gibbon would quail before it."[235]

Our journey through world history has led us all the way to the uncanny nineteenth century, the demonic period of unfettered enthusiasm for progress characteristic of the Victorian and Wilhelminian age. The perspective on our present time from this vantage point is dark, gloomy, and ominous—as attested to by an ever growing number of prophets of doom.

In the sequel of every superstratification, within the high culture resting upon it, the accomplishment of subsequent centuries and millennia has always been to mitigate the original harshness of the superstratification structure, gradually to transform violence into authority, lordship into leadership. In our Western culture this process has undergone many oscillations, but throughout it has been strengthened by the consciousness of freedom which constituted the chief legacy of antiquity, which was continued by Christianity, and which underwent a series of renewals in ever heightened form. Competition between ecclesiastic and internally divided secular authority contributed to the attenuation of unfreedom—a tendency that continued into the late Middle Ages and found in the Renaissance its greatest development and fertility. Reformation and Counter Reformation interrupted this hopeful line of development. The trend of development was reversed. The so-called modern age therefore brought with it numerous retrogressions to new forms of dominion and repressions:

Reformation and Counter Reformation led to a reinforcement of coercion of conscience, according to the adage *cuius regio eius religio*.

The rise of absolutism with the new territorial states took advantage of all the latest advances in the technique of organization and of warfare to impose a sharpened form of state sovereignty. In the wake of democratization nationalism acquires the character of a secular religion territorially delimited.

Colonial imperialism reverted to superstratification in its bloodiest and most brutal form as it applied this superiority in the arts of war against the native populations of the newly discovered territories.

Large-scale enterprise, first in the agrarian and then in the industrial sphere, brought the growing masses of workers into oppressive dependency, slavery, or proletarianization.

To the extent that, in the realm of ideas, a further advance in consciousness of freedom took place, culminating in the Enlightenment of the eighteenth century, the resulting tensions were sharpened further—tensions which exploded in a chain of revolutions. The most important of these, the great French Revolution, changed abruptly from freedom and liberalism into totalitarianism and terror, and this reversal sealed the fate both of the Enlightenment and of German classicism. The failure of this movement of synthesis at the highest intellectual level brought with it a sharpened split between rationalism and irrationalism. Unfettered rationalism, bent on setting new records, hurled itself upon whatever was technical, whatever could be constructed or organized, and allowed blind enthusiasm for technical progress to become a pseudoreligion. Uncontrollable irrationalism began to wallow in murky depths, from which arise unbridled drives—first and foremost the old, imperfectly tamed *libido dominandi* (will to power) with all its sadistic and brutal accompaniments. Thus are readied the ingredients for a truly diabolic union between unbridled technical progress and uninhibited will to power.

Traditional ideologies had at one and the same time strengthened domination and kept it within bounds; but now the urge to freedom degenerates in rationalistic fashion and is radicalized into an attack on all social bonds in general. It tears off the veils and thus destroys the attenuations of the inherited structures of superstratification, it takes away the hypocrisies and also the modifications and mitigations of dominion—and ends up in nihilism. A depletion of the cultural heritage leads to atomization, isolation, and massification.

Growing masses of proletarianized industrial workers are concentrated in large cities and rebel against the newly worsened lot of a superstratified lower class; behind them stand, still hidden by the mists of a distant future, millions of colored people brutalized by colonial imperialism. An uninhibited rationalism appeals to vague instincts of vengefulness in formulating a terrible credo of counter-superstratification. An apocalyptic thunderstorm, flashing, draws near.

PART THREE

Domination versus Freedom

To the Hungarian Freedom Fighters

INTRODUCTION: SEPARATION OF
UNDERSTANDING AND FEELING

The West had not found its equilibrium after the revolutionary events of the Renaissance and Reformation. The last manifestation of this chronic internal conflict had been opposition between the Enlightenment and preromanticism.

Later, the rationalist thesis of the Enlightenment and the antirationalist antithesis of the *Sturm und Drang* and preromantic movements found their unprecedented, promising synthesis, which, but for the catastrophe of 1792-1793, might have become the major theme of the nineteenth century. Since this synthesis was still in its preliminary, mainly artistic phase, its defensive capacity was practically nil. Each of the two components, disconnected from its complementary counterweight, succumbed to one-sidedness and degeneration. Feelingless *ratio* and irrational sentiment became separated in almost schizophrenic fashion, and each, infected with the poisonous urge to domination originating in the initial superstratification, opposed the other with incompatible claims to sovereignty. Unbridled reason overreached itself in a rationalism of the harshest and most brutal imperiousness. And irrationalism was driven to the equally one-sided antirationalist position of romantic reaction, which in part championed and glorified the old superstratification, and in part proclaimed a new superstratification by the irrational powers of ignorance—worst among them the will to power as such. Both sides to the conflict were at the same time radicalized and coarsened. From the viewpoint of intellectual history, that was the fateful starting point of nineteenth-century developments.

Instead of both sides striving, synthetically, for the common and fruitful mean, rationalism and irrationalism alike became ever more eccentric. Rationalism became ever more flat, paltry, snide, wooden, vulgar, and arrogant. Irrationalism wallowed increasingly in the darksome depths of the gloomy, the weird, the inhuman. As, however, in man's natural endowment, reason and feeling are interdependent, interlocked, and intertwined, a truly radical separation of the two is not possible. Hence even the most radical and extreme rationalism or irrationalism amounted only to a one-sided, excessive predominance of the one or of the other, reinforced by a passionate denial of the opposite. Notwithstanding this reservation, we can, in first approximation, divide the intellectual phenomena of the nineteenth century into those rooted in the Enlightenment and those rooted in romanticism, into rationalist and irrationalist tendencies.

CHAPTER 1

Rationalist Tendencies

1. RATIONALISM

Any movement that does not develop independently and must instead make way for itself in a counterattack runs the risk of being subjected to heteronomous influences. Such was the case with the movement of enlightenment that set in with the Renaissance from the moment it had to engage in long and difficult struggles against claims to sovereignty by the Reformation, Counter Reformation, and unenlightened absolutism. The word *rationalism* denotes this characteristic deviancy.

The censure and reproach implicit in the term *rationalism* is often understood superficially, as though it were a quantitative question of an excess of reason and its employment, as though we should turn down the lamp of our understanding low enough for it to emit a mere twilight glow, wan but cozy. But there can never be an absolute excess of reason or understanding: at most there will be only a relative excess, a comparative deficiency in other human powers and faculties. In truth it is not a question of quantity, but a morphological question of structure, of proportion and symmetry, of balance and distribution, of the proper function of reason and its suitable incorporation into the whole of the intellectual-psychic domain.

The legitimate role of reason, consonant with its nature, is arbitration or judgment. As such, reason is a court of last resort; appeals from its judgment can only be brought before itself. However, its decree is by no means dictatorial or arbitrary. Rather, it is bound to wholly definite procedures deriving from the nature of things and from that of reason itself.

Left to itself, reason can decide only on the basis of logical consistency. If two assertions contradict each other, one of them at least must be wrong. The proper competence of reason is adequate to such a formal preliminary decision, as well as to the likewise formal and relative (or axiomatic) determination whether an assertion is contained in another, and whether one assertion is or is not compatible with another. But these obviously are not positive, productive, substantive cognitions. The faculty of understanding, as Kant saw and proved, is, in and of itself, devoid of content: it is a faculty only of mediate cognition. It must receive its content from elsewhere, from more immediate cognitions. And experience is the closest and the most important—if not the only—source of such content of all original cognition. Hence the one right to which reason is entitled with respect to these contents is that of proving their origin, of proving whether the claim to direct cognition is valid. Direct cognition or experience is the conclusive positive means of proof before the tribunal of reason.

A more special, particularly interesting, and important case develops when direct sense perceptions appear inconsistent with each other, as with illusions, hallucinations, and dreams. Then reason must be used (1) to establish inconsistency and (2) to decide, by way of arbitration, between the two sides.

One might assume that this decision would be made democratically, according to the majority principle. And, fortunately for us, the normal perceptions that are unquestionably consistent with each other are in the overwhelming majority. Yet the real decision takes place according to a qualitative and structural-morphological principle that is higher and more plausible than any quantitative one. For as the task of the understanding, in the final analysis, is to attend to the unity of our cognition, free of logical contradiction, it must decide for the side through which such a unity is exclusively attainable. Illusion, hallucinations, dreams as such can be explained within the context of normal sensory cognitions, but not conversely. One's dream—through dream psychology—can be fitted into one's waking hours, but not one's waking hours into the dream. This then becomes the decisive factor.

However it is not enough to establish that "being awake has historical continuity, but dreaming a specific discontinuity";[1] it has been noted that there are also continuation dreams, on occasion in long series. The decisive factor is not the continuity of each of the two worlds in themselves, but rather the overlapping common continuity of both together—which is attainable precisely in the domain of being awake. The question, charmingly posed by Chuang-tzu, drunk with sleep, upon awakening from a dream: "Was I then a man who dreams he is a butterfly, or am I now a butterfly that dreams it is a man?" can be well and clearly answered in the waking state.

Understanding also has at its disposal a further principle of decision, namely, that of the "simplicity" of logical structure: *simplex sigillum veri* (simplicity is the seal of truth). This is an "empty" analytical principle, a principle through which no content can be given or justified, and no established fact can be refuted or dismissed. Parmenides' "truth" alarmingly shows where its absolute application, in disregard of these bounds, leads. The principle of simplicity has its legitimate, exclusively methodological, supplementary, and heuristic-postulative function only when it is a question of deciding among several theories in themselves free of contradiction and consistent in the same way with the same facts—and, by way of comparison giving preference to the simplest among them. However, as soon as the principle presumes to assert itself against solidly established facts, the opposite maxim becomes operative: *error veritate simplicior* (error is simpler than truth).

The most comprehensive conclusion derived from this principle of simplicity is the systematic construction of an ideal model of uniformity, the ideal demand for unification of all cognitions into a homogeneous system free from contradiction.

The acknowledgment of this ideal—altogether justified as a general principle—signifies the definitive overcoming of the prelogical stage of intellectual development. For this stage, after all, is not marked by a total absence of logic. There is no human being, however primitive, who does not already, step by step, here and there, think and combine thoughts logically, especially where they concern practical interconnections of his environment. The distinguishing characteristic of prelogical thought lies precisely in this point-by-point, disconnected nature of thinking, in the fact that the connection between these isolated oases, the filling in of the intermediate spaces and especially of the outer surrounding space, is not accomplished in a logical way. Only gradually are these oases of rational cognition enlarged more until they finally either directly collide with each other or are connected with each other by a set of logical pathways. At this point the prelogical spheres, conversely, become mere islands or oases in a general logical landscape. This ultimately leads to the conviction that continuous correlation, free from contradiction, is fundamentally possible and that elements conflicting with it must be excluded as error.

On the basis of these reflections we can reformulate more precisely the reproach of rationalism. Such a reproach is legitimate whenever the intellect, the *ratio*, posits its two internal and independent principles (absence of contradiction and simplicity with uniformity) as adequate and self-sufficient, ignoring their emptiness and their need for content; whenever the *ratio*, on that assumption, issues decrees in its own name without conscientious research into relevant facts, without readiness to acknowledge or defer to facts, or even in domineering contradiction to established facts; whenever, in sum, *ratio* succumbs to the illusion of infallibility. The consequence is a subversion of the epistemological separation of powers prescribed by the very structure of the human mind: instead of limiting itself to its proper judicative function, the *ratio* arrogates to itself the legislative function, to which it is not entitled and of which it is not capable.

The result of this arrogant self-assurance and megalomania of the *ratio* is a phenomenon that has been described by Taine as *raison raisonnante*, a form of reasoning "which undertakes to think with a minimum of preparation and a maximum of ease, which rests content with its past accomplishments without trying to extend or renew them, which cannot or will not embrace the fulness and complexity of reality."[2] Such an attitude shirks the responsibility of working seriously, modestly, patiently, and incessantly so as to establish facts and their connections ever more completely, more correctly, and more essentially. With the impertinent presumption of youth, one is inclined to overestimate oneself and one's originality, to dismiss all those who disagree as stupid, to fall into a naïve enthusiasm for progress that dismisses all precedent as antiquated and superseded. When such traits appear not only as a pardonable excess of adolescence but as a permanent and dominant attitude of whole trends and epochs, then we may properly characterize these as rationalism.

Rationalism should not simply be equated with individualism. Irrationalists, by and large, tend to be more individualistic. Rather, it is a question of improperly shifting the burden of proof. Is there a presumption of legitimacy in favor of tradition, of practices and thoughts that seem to have proved themselves over the generations? Or does tradition, by the mere fact of its age, come under the suspicion of backwardness, a charge against which it must try to justify itself in the tribunal of an arrogant and ill-disposed *ratio*?

This latter, rationalist attitude was initially a future-oriented, active optimism. To be sure, it combined a vast underestimation of the past with an even vaster overestimation of its own capacities and possibilities, but it was always based on a feeling of moral responsibility for the future and the shaping thereof. Gradually, however, this feeling of responsibility for the future changed into smug glorification of one's own present and to what had been achieved.

The result was that faith in progress—or, rather, that superstitious veneration of progress, especially in technology, which formed the real religion or ersatz religion of the nineteenth century.

Actually there is hardly an age that had less warrant for such an exaggerated self-appraisal than had the nineteenth century— which, in our view, marked a disastrous decline from the heights of the eighteenth ("the only century of which mankind need not be ashamed"), a fall from which we are still now laboriously trying to uplift ourselves.

Rationalism pressed its critique of traditional conceptions of the soul and divinity against the late, theological forms in which it encountered them. This criticism amounted to a pruning of all fantastical elements, a smoothing of all corners and edges, a bleaching of all colors and variegations. What remained was the empty nonconcept of a *substantia nil nisi cogitans*, and the equally empty concept of God expounded by deism—conceptions that preserved the most dubious elements of the theological tradition while scuttling all legitimate emotional elements and thus creating a spurious impression of primordial simplicity. The next step in the same direction perforce led to an impious atheism and an anti-intellectual materialism.

A similar critique may be made of the demythologization of religion, as advocated in our own day by Rudolf Bultmann in the name of intellectual honesty in theology. Myth is the proper language of the numinous, and the virtues of this language are force of expression, depth, power of form, and colorfulness. Therefore it would seem that what is needed is not the demythologizing of theology but rather the detheologizing and dedogmatizing of myth. The remarkable visions of resurrection, found not only in Paul (1 Thess. 4:15-18; 1 Cor. 15:51-52), but also in the sayings of Jesus himself in the synoptic Gospels (Matt. 24:27-35; Mark 13:24-31; Luke 17:24-37, 31:25-33) seem to have incomparably more content and weight than the demythologized dogma of the immortality of the soul. Christ's resurrection seems mythical no matter how much it is stripped of concrete detail. Can theology be completely demythologized, or would a truly radical surgery kill the patient?

Parallel reflections can be made on the concept of soul or mind. It may be that the polar distinction between body and mind, implied by everyday language, misstates the problem and hence has bedeviled the epistemology of psychology. There is no question about the existence of those phenomena that everyday language attributes to the mind, the soul, or the psyche. In that indisputatious sense man has "a mind" just as he has "a body" or "a will." But the metaphysical assertion of the mind as a *substantia cogitans* goes far beyond such statements; instead of clarifying the problem of consciousness, it leads, by way of arbitrary and unverifiable assertions, to a host of unsolvable problems and difficulties. Hence modern science has rejected the notion of soul or mind—words for which one will search in vain in a textbook of psychology or biology.

The concept of mind, or soul, is theological in origin. To be sure, the soul and its immortality are neither biblical nor originally Christian conceptions. Wherever immortality is referred to in the Old Testament it is specifically rejected.[3] None of the prophets of the Old Testament believed in the immortality of the soul—in flat contradiction to a widespread popular opinion in our own day that makes this belief an indispensable component of all religiosity. The original Christian creed does not say a single syllable about the soul or its immortality. Rather, it teaches the resurrection *of the flesh* and the eternal life of this resurrected flesh. And correspondingly it is not Christ's immortal soul but his body that ascends to heaven.

Anyone who can get himself to go back to the original Christian conception of resurrection of the flesh avoids the problems posed by the Gnostic concept of soul, and thus faces perhaps a simple task— although he faces other problems, the discussion of which would require a wider context than the present one. Any important and critical point in the intellectual evolution of humanity represents a crossroads. Whichever of the roads at the fork was taken implied a surrender of other, perhaps fruitful, possibilities. In regard to the so-called body versus soul (or mind) problem it may be that the Aristotelian formula of *anima forma corporis* (the soul is the form of the body) indicates the last unused fork in the road that might have led to a fruitful resolution. Perhaps we are about to reapproach, by many detours, that same spot.

An especially significant magisterial attitude of rationalism is its habit of beginning any exposition with formal definitions, as if to say: "The world did not exist, ere I created it." Only in mathematics is such a procedure, as Euclid classically handles it, appropriate. Yet rationalism derives from this an erroneous and misleading conviction that mathematics is the science *par excellence* and the model of all other sciences, that every proper science must be conducted *more geometrico* and deductively, and that a field of study can claim scientific status only to the extent that it meets this demand.

This erroneous conviction unmistakably stems from the atmosphere of Pythagoreanism, and it is not surprising to encounter it in classical antiquity. The same prejudice in favor of mathematics also appears in the Christian Neoplatonist Boethius (480-524). The explicit mathematicism of Scholastic method is well known. According to Nicholas of Cusa, there is in mathematics more truth than in any other science. According to Kepler, the human mind was created in order to perceive quantities. And for Galileo, mathematics is the script in which God has written the open book of creation.

Toward the end of the sixteenth century, Nikolaus Hemming (1513-1600) requires "that the method of the mathematical sciences be applied to natural law." Francis Bacon (1561-1626) in his *Two Books on the Proficience and Advancement of Learning* recommends "imitating the wisdom of the mathematician in the determination of the meanings of words, namely, by premising the definitions." The second of the *Regulae ad directionem ingenii*, which Descartes composed probably around 1628, reads: "Those who seek the right path of truth should not occupy themselves with anything of which they cannot have a degree of certainty equal to that of a proof in arithmetic or geometry." Erhard Weigel (1625-1699) applied Euclid's method to logic, metaphysics, ethics, and natural law; Weigel's pupil, Leibniz, finally applied the method of mathematical proof in a political pamphlet entitled *Specimen demonstrationum politicarum pro eligendo rege Polonorum*.[4] Spinoza followed with his main work, *Ethica ordine geometrico demonstrata*, published posthumously in 1677, leading applied mathematics to its classical zenith.

Fontenelle (1657-1757), in the foreword of his *Histoire de l'Academie Royale des Sciences*, wrote: "The mathematical mind is not so attached to mathematics that it cannot be drawn away and transported to other fields of knowledge. A work of politics, of morality, of criticism, perhaps even of eloquence, all things being equal, will be more beautiful if fashioned by the hand of a mathematician."[5] Fontenelle here is defending mathematics against the attack of Pascal (1623-1662). In his *Pensées* (posthumously published in 1669), Pascal dealt with the distinction between the rational and the morphological in an essay entitled "Différence entre l'esprit de géométrie et l'esprit de finesse": "Mathematicians try to treat these delicate matters mathematically, and expose themselves to ridicule in their attempts to begin by definitions and go on to axioms, which is not the way to proceed in this kind of reasoning."[6]

In the eighteenth century the Scottish commonsense philosopher Thomas Reid (1710-1796), in his *Essay on Quantity* (1748), stated that mathematical methods are suitable only for the treatment of quantifiable objects. And at the same time in France Condillac (1715-1780) belonged to those who were aware of the limits of rationalism; in his *Traité des systèmes* (1749) he objected to the imperiousness of the mathematical method and to deductive systems. In his treatise on logic he says: "For the reason that mathematics is a science that is called exact, it has been believed that in order to treat of all the other sciences properly, it was but necessary to imitate the mathematician; and the mania to define, pursuant to the manner of the latter, has become the mania of all philosophers or of those who profess to be such." Elsewhere he condemns "the mania of definition, this sinister method which begins always there where it is necessary to end."[7] In 1826 Goethe wrote under the heading "Further remarks on mathematics and mathematicians":

We must realize and admit what mathematics is, in what manner it can essentially serve the investigation of nature and, on the other hand, where it is of no pertinence, and in what a lamentable deviation science and art have lapsed by a wrong application [of mathematics]. . . . Mathematicians are strange people; through the greatness of their accomplishments they have set themselves up as a universal guild. . . . The mathematicians will . . . gradually rid themselves of the pretension to rule over everything as universal monarchs; they will no longer allow themselves to pronounce everything that cannot be subject to calculation as nugatory, inexact, inadequate.

This rejection of mathematicism was espoused with special emphasis by Jakob Friedrich Fries (1773-1843). He declares that outside of mathematics and physics the right procedure is to begin with "discussion" and to relegate definitions to the end: "It is not a question of forming a concept through combination, to which one of these words then would be attached. Rather, I must presuppose each of these concepts as already given in the language. And the skill lies only in proving, through dissection, what each one who knows the language actually intends by these words." And, correspondingly, in another passage he rejects any preliminary definition: "We understand by this exactly that which is thus denoted in common German linguistic usage."[8]

In general, Fries, as a disciple of Kant, had set himself the task of overcoming Kant's rationalism by synthesis with the irrationalism of the *Sturm und Drang* movement, for him embodied in Herder and, above all, in Goethe's emotional and passionate friend Friedrich Heinrich Jacobi (1743-1819). This task was exceedingly important and was posed by the intellectual-historical situation itself. In the professional philosophic sphere it corresponded to that which in the literary and general intellectual sphere had been resolved by German classicism. But a really adequate solution was beyond the means of this amiable-pleasant and clever-circumspect old-fashioned philosopher of Swedish descent and Moravian upbringing. Despite his not inconsiderable accomplishments and merits he simply did not possess the necessary independence, strength, and productivity.

The outcome of Fries's philosophy is characteristic of the retrograde developments in nineteenth-century intellectual history. His pupil and successor, Ernst Friedrich Apelt (1812-1859), presented his teacher's system in an altogether rationalist way. And this also holds true, in still higher measure, for the extreme rationalist revival of the Friesian school by Leonard Nelson (1882-1927),[9] whose logical and ethical radicalism, heightened to elephantine dimensions, and inexorable one-sidedness had a strong pedagogical impact in his time. As cofounder of the "New Friesian school," I myself am considerably indebted to him in logical and dialectical training.

Mathematical prejudice, in its most blatantly Euclidean form, was overcome after the eighteenth century. But the view that one is required to define any concepts used even outside the natural sciences again gained favor during the nineteenth and twentieth centuries and still plays a certain role today.

Scientism (or "physicism") is similar to mathematicism: the similarity appears in the conviction that physics is the foundation of all natural science, that the "scientific" is defined "in the manner of the natural sciences," and that even humanistic studies can claim scientific character only to the extent that they use the methods of the natural sciences. There is an excellent critical history of this reversal by F. A von Hayek.[10]

Finally, the need for systematization, the mania for system building, is also related to mathematicism and scientism. The striving to classify everything under one common denomination, to replace observations with analogies and conclusions, and to arrive as quickly as possible at an all-embracing totality is part of system building.

As against that we are now on the point of breaking off from hasty systematization and immunizing ourselves against its temptations. We wish to speak only when we know and to be silent when we do not know; to set down every insight as it comes to us; to refrain from any subsequent forced harmonization that could only blot out the most characteristic and most valuable quality; to respect contradictions and inconsistencies in the establishment and processing of facts as a stimulus to further investigation; and to have the courage to leave open our knowledge and thinking—the courage of provisionalness and incompleteness, the acceptance of an open world, true to the old motto of the University of Heidelberg: *Semper apertus*.

Goethe confessed that "I have no system and want naught else but truth for its own sake."[11] And in fact, as Hamann declared, every system is "already in itself an obstacle to truth,"[12] for every *system* as a *closed* body of knowledge *must* be wrong. Since the real world is infinite, not only quantitatively but also morphologically (in respect to the possibilities of perspective, to formulations of the question, and to the extraction of the configurative correlations), only open, unlimited, and incomplete knowledge of reality can be adequate.

Whence derives this thirst for power on the part of reason, which is contradictory to and alien to its own nature? It is nothing but the reactive counterblow against its oppression and enslavement of yore, even in the exercise of its proper, legitimate, necessary, and indispensable functions. The nature of the theologico-priestly intellectuality of the medieval-feudal cultures rested, exactly as did their social structure, on domination and obedience, on the "laudable" subordination of reason to the ruling dogma, on a *servitudo arbitrii* that went as far as *sacrificium intellectus: scientia ancilla theologiae* —science became the handmaiden of theology. The liberation of *ratio* from subjugation to the theological claims of sovereignty was the great intellectual-historical accomplishment of rationalism. But "the slave when he breaks his chains" is subject to the temptation to set himself up as master, and pressure fosters counterpressure.

When the French Revolution, in a famous and scurrilous scene, placed the naked goddess of reason on the altar of Christian dogma, it unconsciously represented a deep truth in intellectual history. Rationalism is a form of degenerate Enlightenment resulting from the struggle against theology and feudalism; it is a counter-superstratification in the intellectual sphere.

The influences of the crude rationalism of the nineteenth century are still felt today; it still has, and probably will continue to have, its camp followers, as is the rule in such cases. But of late its secular reign seems to be declining rapidly, and there are already signs of powerful tendencies toward a reversal. Mankind faces the question of whether it will passively succumb to the mechanics of this fateful oscillation from one extreme to the other, or whether this time it will try to remain as close as possible to the correct median and continue it further, deepening it and securing it in the process.

2. PRAGMATISM, BEHAVIORISM, MATERIALISM

The rationalist counterattack on theology and metaphysics also appears in the development of the concept of truth. Theology had posited a higher, divine and revealed truth over against a sense-mediated lower, human and profane knowledge. Such a bifurcation of knowledge logically derives from the question whether human beings see the world as God, its creator, sees it. Does our human knowledge of the world accord with divine knowledge, which self-evidently is perfect and correct, and which is accessible to us more or less through "revelation"? If we eliminate from this formulation the person of God as author of the world, the problem is whether ordinary, empirical cognition discloses the "real," "true" being of things.

Kant's "thing in itself" is nothing but the original "thing for God" as subsequently secularized, in contrast to the "thing for us." Oddly enough, this loss of clarity and comprehensibility to which the secularization of such reasoning leads, constitutes an initial gain in profundity on the metaphysical level. Doubts about reality follow as the ultimate consequence of this theological problem—a situation from which Descartes extricated himself through a narrow back door. The usurped religious-metaphysical dignity of *ontos ōn*—true existence—was claimed by atomism for mere matter and by Parmenides for his cosmic giant atom. But this theologically exaggerated, speculative concept of a "higher" truth finally provoked the counterattack of a "lower," sober, practical concept of truth—pragmatism's paltry equation of theoretical truth with practical utility. Francis Bacon once wrote: "Quod in operando utilissimum, id in scientia verissimum"[13] (What is most useful in action is most true in science)—so that we witness here a throwback to the seventeenth century. At the same time it is an anticipation of the totalitarian mentality of the twentieth century, as proclaimed by its prophet and herald Nietzsche: "Truth is that kind of error without which a certain species of living being cannot exist. The value for life is ultimately decisive." "The criterion of truth lies in the enhancement of the feeling of power."[14]

Positivists, in order to lend dignity to their position, have often invoked a verse by Goethe[15] according to which "only what bears fruit is true." But Goethe never defended the false or the erroneous as fruitful. The full meaning of the verse is that all truth bears fruit; that which does not bear fruit is also not true. As he wrote to Charlotte von Stein on 8 June 1787: "There is nothing as great as the true, and the minutest truth is great. . . . Even a harmful truth is useful, because it can be harmful only momentarily, thereupon leading to other truths, which ever are bound to become useful, nay very useful. Conversely, the useful error is harmful, because it can only be momentary and misleads into other errors, which become ever more harmful." The relation of truth to utility obviously can be established only for assertions whose correctness or incorrectness can be determined. But before a science develops to the extent that such determination is possible and can receive general acceptance, it has a long and laborious path to tread. Even then this determinate core area of any science remains always surrounded by an infinite zone of that which has not yet been clarified and secured. This zone of the still unknown, of that not yet definitively secured and determined, is the only productive and interesting one in which further scientific progress takes place. Only in this outer zone did Goethe mean to apply fruitfulness as a heuristic intention.

When lack of clarity persists only at the outer edges of a solidly constituted science, then the margin for formulating tenable hypotheses is severely circumscribed by the previously secured results, and verification—or refutation—customarily follows shortly upon the formulation of a hypothesis. It is otherwise with a new science—one that is still in a prenatal, embryonic stage. For it does not yet have a sufficient number of solid, generally recognized findings by which decisions on truth or error can clearly be made—a situation, for example, in which depth psychology finds itself today. In such a case subjective truths, which are different for each investigator and each school, stand in the foreground and are summed up in entire systems of such subjective truths. Since all are groping in the dark, each—with subjective justification—considers only his path fruitful and correct, and each one feels disturbed and reacts with indignant and annoyed defensiveness when somebody crosses his path. Hence the embarrassments of internal disputes among psychoanalysts, the personal tensions, frictions, and hostilities— because disputes over subjective truths, among which no objective determination can be made, always and instantly become personal.

That will change when a scientific field such as psychoanalysis becomes objective and arrives at generally recognized findings.

Understanding of other human beings and other organisms in general occurs by way of "empathy" or introjection. An immediate "understanding" of the behavior of fellow individuals of the same species already occurs among animals; in general it increases with the level of organization, and plays an especially important role with gregarious animals. As in man this gregarious mode of life coincides with a high level of organization, and the special importance of empathy and understanding derives from this coincidence. These characteristics form the prerequisite of social and cultural life.

In the daily and hourly practice of human interactions this instant empathetic understanding of human beings by human beings is so highly developed and refined and has so much come to be taken for granted that we are tempted to apply it, in anthropomorphic manner, to animals as well. In contrast, it is the decisive merit of behaviorism, especially in its more recent and considerably modified form of behavioral research on man and animals, to have demanded, first of all, the most exact and objective determination of real behavior, undisturbed by hasty or uncontrolled empathy. When, however, it is demanded that the investigation be arrested forever at this first stage, we are again in the presence of those extravagant counterattacks and counterexaggerations so characteristic of rationalism and materialism.

The Kinsey reports constitute a grotesque example of this attitude as applied to the intimate sphere of human behavior. Alfred C. Kinsey (1894-1956), a distinguished American entomologist, turned his attention to the sexual behavior of the species *homo sapiens*. The results of his investigation, meticulously carried out with the help of a large staff, have been presented in two compendious volumes[16] that give detailed descriptions of the sexual practices of contemporary Americans, with statistical frequencies precisely calculated—but with no mention whatever of love, tenderness, or any of the feelings that provide the foundation for marriage and family. In real life, a brothel is the only setting in which sexual acts are performed without love or other human feelings—and to which such a method of investigation would thus be appropriate.

Kinsey has often been praised for presenting his materials without salaciousness. But where any reference to human emotions is radically excluded, this exclusion obviously covers negative as well as positive, unpleasant as well as pleasant human attitudes. This dehumanization and emotional frigidity is precisely our main objection to Kinsey. Kinsey consistently assumes that sexuality is a normal biological function which is to be accepted regardless of the form in which it may appear. This is nothing less than a surrender of normative judgment to "brute facts." Inhabitants of the Western world currently find themselves in a period of upheaval when most norms, and particularly those applying to sexual life, are being questioned; and an unbiased knowledge of factual conditions is an important prerequisite for any responsible critique and reconstruction of these norms. But to raise existing factual conditions to the status of norms would be nothing short of grotesque.

Kinsey cannot help but note repeatedly the influence of cultural, moral, and religious norms on the facts he describes; yet he seems to view any such influences as repressive and unnatural. He forgets that man, by virtue of his freedom of choice, needs a cultural substitute for the narrower determination which inborn instinct provides for animals. What would give Kinsey's whole undertaking greater justification are two supplementary volumes—or one, since human questions in this department have to do with relations *between* the sexes—in which all factual material would once more be dealt with from the human viewpoint that the original Kinsey volumes systematically excluded.

Just as the utilitarian concept of truth in pragmatism arose as a reaction against the supranatural concept of truth of theology and metaphysics, and just as in general rationalism arose as a reaction against dogmatism, so did materialism arise as a reaction against theologico-metaphysical "idealism." The result was a heretical, negative form of metaphysics that with fanatical intolerance and mocking grimaces placed naked matter on the throne of the absolute erected by theology; materialism thus resembles a trivialized black mass.

That department of our experience that we call "consciousness," "the intellectual," or "the psychic" forms the point of departure of this problem complex. No approach has yet succeeded in determining the nature of these phenomena satisfactorily. Metaphysical idealism tries to explain them by assuming the existence of a "higher," invisible substance distinct from "lower," palpable, visible matter. This hypothesis, regardless of the complicated and sublimated forms it may assume, is false beyond any doubt, as we have seen. To that extent empiricist materialism, which vigorously censures metaphysics for this assumption, is correct. But this rebuke of a false solution is not tantamount to attaining a correct one. Materialism throws the baby of a fundamentally important problem out with the murky bathwater of a false idealistic solution. This in turn gives the idealist the right to feel superior to materialism and to criticize it as flat or limited, and even prompts leading positivists and logicians like Whitehead and Santayana to return once again to the one and only sacred idealism.

In the philosophy and ideology of eighteenth-century materialism had been a phenomenon of the extreme left. As a result of the romantic reaction, however, the Enlightenment as a whole was increasingly pushed in this direction, so that in the nineteenth century it is a brutal, stunted version of materialistic positivism to which enlighteners tend to resort in carrying forward their ideological struggle.

This struggle experienced a dramatic sharpening in Germany in the so-called "Materialism Dispute" of 1854, the coarseness and rudeness of which makes us so painfully aware of the decline in cultural level compared with the charming intellectuality of the eighteenth century. In reply to the lecture of a Protestant physiologist, "On the Creation of Man and the Substance of the Soul," the zoologist Carl Vogt (1817-1895) penned a pamphlet entitled *Superstition* vs. *Science* in which he proclaimed, as the position of science, the view "that thoughts stand in the same relation to the brain as bile to the liver or urine to the kidneys." But this challenging paradox, which caused such a stir at the time, was far from being Vogt's own invention. Voltaire, one hundred and twenty earlier, had expressed the same idea in a far less crude and objectionable formulation: "God has organized the body to think as to eat and to digest."[17] And even the challenging exaggeration stems already from Pierre-Jean-Georges Cabanis (1757-1808), who, in his *Rapports du physique et du moral de l'homme*, wrote: "The brain is designed to think, as the stomach is to digest, and the liver to excrete bile from the blood."[18] Since Cabanis's work (published about 1798 as a Mémoire de l'Institut, in book form in 1802) was very well known in its time and also existed in a two-volume German edition of 1808, Vogt no doubt based his own formulation directly on Cabanis. Hence it was a well-chewed bone of the eighteenth century that begot such loud barking in the middle of the nineteenth.

Another example of the same coarsening phenomenon, and one with repercussions to this day, is provided by Ludwig Feuerbach (1804-1872). Today known mainly because Marx and Engels wrote polemics against him, he was in the middle of the nineteenth century a leading freethinker who set forth as the quintessence of his *Theogony* ("Struggle against God") the proposition that "Man created God in his image." Few commentators seem to have been aware that already in the eighteenth century the brilliant Georg Christoph Lichtenberg (1742-1799) had expressed the same thought in a far more charmingly formulated aphorism: "God created man in his image. That probably means: Man created God in his own."

The coarsened nineteenth-century version of eighteenth-century materialism was popularized in Germany by Ludwig Büchner's *Force and Matter* (1855), which went through many editions, and later by Ernst Haeckel's (1834-1919) *Riddle of the Universe*, in which insipid materialism was seasoned with saccharine pantheism.

Whereas the struggle between idealism and materialism revolves around the objective aspect of the problem of consciousness, the epistemological aspect of the same problem was to become no less controversial, and it would provide a further arena for rationalism.

The epistemological difficulties of the psychic sphere are seemingly resolved by the doctrine of "internal sense," developed *ad hoc*, according to which, by introspection, we perceive psychic events occurring over time, just as, through perception and external sense, we perceive physical objects and processes in time and space.

The notion of a perception of our own acts of perception first is posed as a problem by Plato[19] and discussed is greater detail by Aristotle. Even the phrase *koinon ti aistheterion* is found already in Aristotle, from which the terms *sensus communis* and *common sense* later emerged. Saint Augustine speaks of an "internal sense," and Aquinas reverts to the notion of a "common sense" that "perceives all that is sensed by the senses proper."[20] John Locke, whose originality in this respect is often overrated, is the first major exponent of the doctrine in modern philosophy. In *An Essay Concerning Human Understanding*, the internal sense is introduced as follows: "The other fountain [besides the external sense] . . . is the perception of the operations of our own mind within us . . . which we . . . observing in ourselves, do from these receive into our understanding as distinct ideas, as we do from bodies affecting our senses. This source of ideas every man has wholly in himself: and though it be not sense, as having nothing to do with external objects, yet it is very like it, and might properly enough be called internal sense." "The internal sense through which the mind beholds itself or its internal state" was rationally systematized by Kant in definitive fashion: "Time is nothing else than the form of the internal sense, i.e. of the intuitions of self and of our internal state."[21]

But Condillac, one of the most independent among the critical minds of the eighteenth century, as early as 1754 had contested this notion of "internal sense" in his *Traité des sensations*.

It can be convincingly proved—and important arguments to this effect are already found in Plato and Aristotle—that there is no such thing as the alleged "internal sense" and that the entire doctrine is nothing more than a postulative analogy or construct of rationalism. This discomforting character of a postulative analogy, with which one feels ill at ease, expressed itself in the stylistic qualifications apparent, for example, in the above passage from Locke. Only Kant expresses himself without hesitancy: here the will to system triumphs absolutely.

The doctrine of internal sense, without being expressly or definitively refuted, fell into discredit and disuse during the empiricist nineteenth century.

One contributing factor to the philosophic entanglement just dismissed is the immanent metaphysics of language—those assumptions which unconsciously or half-consciously underlie the concepts handed down by tradition in every spoken language. The logical systematization of such concepts, if adroitly and successfully achieved, provides extraordinary satisfaction: our language is part of ourselves so that such an exercise makes us feel at one with ourselves: what has been "said" from time immemorial now seems to receive glorious and demonstrable justification. The operation much resembles that of pulling ourselves out of the morass by our own forelock—an enterprise giving rise to profound self-satisfaction and self-admiration as long as one is unaware of what is going on. Even when one does, it remains extraordinarily difficult to extricate oneself from the predicament, for the struggle against language must needs be carried out by linguistic means—an arduous and taxing enterprise.

It is a merit of modern logic to have developed a new method of this struggle in that it rigorously excludes any unintended "resonances" or secondary meanings. And even extreme behaviorism has a methodological and heuristic value, limited but incontestable, especially if applied to the individual himself, a procedure that might be called autobehaviorism.

3. MASTERY OF NATURE AND ITS CONSEQUENCES

The nineteenth and twentieth centuries have achieved their greatest successes in natural science and its technical applications. Here they have an incontestable right to feel superior to all other epochs. We have just reproached rationalists for claiming validity for mathematical-physical methods far beyond their proper sphere; yet here, in the sphere of the mathematical and exact sciences and their realm of practical application, the *ratio* seems to be fully at home and legitimately in charge. Even here, however, it is still subject to the accusation of rationalism—that is, of sinful lust for power.

In Roger Bacon, the scholastic, we occasionally find the phrase "nam et ipsa scientia potestas est":[22] knowledge is power. A later Bacon, Sir Francis, demanded that man exercise power over nature. And the passionate striving for the mastery of nature, in theory and practice, fills the whole seventeenth century, which in this department as well appears as the century of absolutism.

The natural scientific thought of the eighteenth century, under the influence of English empiricism and sensualism, became removed from the power-hungry rationalism of the seventeenth century, and preromantics and romantics stood in pronounced "opposition to the attitude of dominion vis-à-vis nature," which "was not tenable for them";[23] in the nineteenth century a brutal throwback occurred in this respect. The attitude of enlightened absolutism and despotism also was applied with respect to nature. Moreover, the atomic research of our century has done what Goethe still had thought to be happily impossible; it has robbed nature of her veil and forced from her, with rack and screw, what she might not want to reveal to us.

That the ultimate aim of natural science is *mastery* of nature, that man's task is not to incorporate himself into nature or subject himself to her laws but rather to become her monarch and autocrat, was in the nineteenth century—and still is—accepted as a matter of course. "Knowledge is power" was probably the favorite and most inspiring slogan of that slogan-rich century. As Renan put it, "The great kingdom of the mind will not begin until the material world is perfectly subject to man."[24]

Mastery of nature is still considered a justified, self-evident good. We are deaf to the sadistic ring in the phrase, for the implication of nature as the quarry for man the hunter, lying in ambush for the opportunity to outwit her. We are no longer conscious that we ourselves are a part of nature, that she is mother of us all, that we should all be fraternally and cooperatively incorporated into what she produces, and accept gratefully the possibilities of development that such cooperation offers.

How distant we are from the brotherly feeling for nature of Saint Francis, or from that piety toward nature expressed in that stirring inspired hymnic fragment by Goethe *Die Natur*, through which even Sigmund Freud became an enthusiast of the natural sciences!

The rationalist-domineering attitude toward nature that won the upper hand in the nineteenth century, had a paradoxical and fateful consequence: the revenge of nature on man. The mastery over nature which man has achieved in the last centuries in many areas, has always proved detrimental first to dominated nature and then to dominating man. Man becomes an unwise and tyrannical ruler. Man encroaches upon nature to further his own ends. Subsequently, unanticipated harmful consequences ensue that often are weightier than the utility and may also turn out to be irreparable.

Mastery over nature, over plants and animals, is already given to man in the creation story in Genesis. This was at a time, of course, when man's powers over nature were still so few that abuse was hardly to be feared. Nevertheless, in the eastern Mediterranean area, there began that irreversible devastation of forests for constructing ships and buildings and for firewood. Western Asia Minor had been famous for its fertility and its climate in the ancient world. Since then the clearing of forests has led to erosion in the upper valleys and to periodic inundation, swamp formation, and malaria infestation in the lower ones. In the Middle West of the United States disturbance of natural plant covering by the plow, which at first seemed to conquer the world market for American wheat, eventually threatened to make large areas uninhabitable and uncultivable. The devastating consequences of the well-meaning introduction of rabbits to Australia are well known, as is the fact that many animal species have fallen victim to senseless extermination, while others are threatened by it.

Man has struggled even against harmful animals without wisdom or foresight. One of many examples: lance snakes, which are especially venomous and dangerous to human life, "were almost wholly exterminated in Jamaica. From the human standpoint one believed to have accomplished a good deed with this act of annihilation. The unforeseen consequence, however, was an intolerable increase in

the number of rats, whose . . . nourishment soon became too scarce
and who therefore pounced upon the sugarcane plantations. Accordingly, steps had to be taken immediately against the rats, and an
East Indian species of . . . mungos were unleashed against them. The
mungos in fact did a marvelous job in getting rid of the rats. But
they reproduced themselves in such measure that soon there were
more mungos than rats. Now the mungos, in their hunger and because of the scarcity of rats, attacked fowl, lambs, ground-nesting
birds, reptiles and similar animals"—whose disappearance, in turn,
led to a vast multiplication of insects. "The whole former ecological
community had been thoroughly muddled! Only when the alien
mungos were systematically fought and the toad *Bufo marinus* was
introduced against the countless small insects was stability slowly
restored in the upset ecological order of things."[25]

Since the discovery of the microscopic agents of disease, steriliza-
tion—that is, the freeing organisms from microbes—has been considered the ultimate ideal of medicine. Now that we are on the point
of approaching this ideal, by way of antibiotics, life-endangering effects occur unexpectedly as a result of destruction of natural and indispensable bacteria in the intestine. Even with respect to bacteria,
man's mastery and interference in the balance of organic nature
may lead to unexpected and baneful consequences.

Man's reign over nature can lead to senseless imperialism; the
most for the least replaces the ideal of "best."

Goethe's brilliant foresight had seen the evil coming: "Men will go
astray themselves and lead others astray if they treat means as end,
for nothing happens from sheer activity save perhaps the disagreeable."[26]

"Technical progress" becomes no longer a means but rather an
end in itself. The machine is no longer a helper, but a master of men.
Or, as Spengler put it, "The creature is rising against its creator. . . .
The lord of the world is becoming the slave of the machine, which is
forcing him—forcing us all, whether we are aware of it or no—to follow its course. The victor, fallen, is dragged to death by the team."[27]

Modern technology, as much as its advocates may assert the contrary, is by no means utilitarian. It does not serve man to his advantage or utility; it does not measure the value of its accomplishments
in the improvement of living conditions. It stands in the service of
the great megalomaniac, orgiastic-ecstatic, restless cult of absolute
progress for its own sake. Beating records becomes the paramount
issue. With the disappearance of qualitative standards, pure quantity, size, and number, remain as the last measure. The "Cult of the

Colossal"[28] celebrates triumphs as senseless in their inhumanity as they are inhuman in their senselessness. Megalomania, the pursuit of new "records," and the addiction to superlatives spread.

The tallest house is the most beautiful, the biggest industrial plant the best. The small or the medium is, as such, already inferior. How one dwells or lives in the house, how one works in the plant or even whether it is profitable—these are faint-hearted questions by those of little faith! And even if the house comes tumbling down or the plant goes bankrupt, the next one will be still taller, the next bigger than ever! And even though the release of atomic energy first brought death to hundreds of thousands and still threatens millions more, technical progress remains the primary goal.

A man dominated by such a mentality must, of course, feel it a special triumph to interfere in the cosmos, not only as an investigator but as an actor. Unfortunately, an artificial earth satellite has importance for various military goals and therefore is being pursued by both rivals in the cold war with enormous expenditure of funds and talents. The idea of a manned space flight surely is the mindless culmination of this mania for setting records—although there is no lack of contemporaries for whom one would gladly reserve a seat in such a conveyance.

This cult of absolute progress receives classic expression in the famous verses of Goethe's *Faust*, which lay down the terms of the life wager with the Devil:

> When thus I hail the Moment flying:
> "Ah, still delay—thou art so fair!"
> Then bind me in thy bonds undying,
> My final ruin then declare!

A sense of well-being, which for any naturally healthy sensibility is a goal worth striving for, is here degraded as contemptible.

Enthusiasm for progress makes virtue of discontent and lack of balance; for those who are content have no desire to progress—away from a situation that is suitable to them and in which they feel quite comfortable.

A static condition, the opposite of dynamic progress, does not after all signify inertia or rigidity. Rather, it suggests natural movement in self-contained spheres close to the cycle of the seasons and the processes of birth, youth, maturity, old age, and death.

At the present time, of course, mankind finds itself in one of those impossible and unendurable situations—into which it has fallen essentially in consequence of the irresistible progress of the last century—so that already the mere idea of a permanent lingering therein indeed would be truly terrible. The pressing concern of each one of us must be to come out of it, the sooner the better. Thus in consequence of past "progress," further advances have become unavoidable. But at least we should be conscious of the altogether pathological quality of this situation, be aware that it is a grievous necessity and anything but a virtue.

4. TECHNOCRACY AND PLANNED ECONOMY

The nineteenth century prided itself on progressing beyond the Enlightenment of the eighteenth century. At the same time, however, it shifted the emphasis from the progress of humanity to the progress of technology, for which it claimed the same dignity and demanded the same enthusiasm. In fact, the sphere of technology, including the exact sciences upon which it is based, is the only one in which a forward movement can be traced, from the ancient world to Hellenism, and then again from the Middle Ages to the present. The release of atomic energy—and the prospect thus opened, the *dernier cri* of a successful mass suicide of mankind—proves that we have not yet attained the highest point of this curve.

This upsurge of technology presents a triumph of a construct or blueprint. It suggested that the principle of exact planning, calculated in advance, could also be applied to other areas. The rationalism of the nineteenth century had lost natural trust in what develops without deliberate interference. Only that which was planned seemed trustworthy and reliable. "The world did not exist, ere I created it." The "unfounded superstition" was formed "that processes which are consciously directed are necessarily superior to any spontaneous process."[29]

But the obsession with blueprints has not only a scientific but also a domineering component. Just as one aims to achieve mastery over nature and its energies with the help of scientific and technical progress, one uses the same methods to arrive at control of the economy and of other areas of social life. And not only at a control of the product of the economy—as the state has done from time immemorial with its right to levy and collect taxes—but rather of the course of the economy, of economic management itself. This is the demand for planned economy set forth by technocracy.

Planned control or management of economic operations takes place within the limits of an individual enterprise. Any individual enterprise thus constitutes a "total centrally administered economy." As long, however, as only family enterprises exist, the control thus exercised is coextensive with that of the authority of the *pater-familias*. Economic management in such a context does not create new, independent authority or spheres of power.

This first changed with the rise of large-scale industry. If we disregard its prehistory in late antiquity, it developed in the Christian West from the Middle Ages onward, first in large-scale agriculture in the form of a plantation system in the tropical colonies and as a manorial agricultural system in eastern Europe; the former worked with slaves, the latter with serfs. From this it is obvious that new competences and new spheres of domination arose, both of an economic kind and for economic purposes, albeit of a feudal character and clothed in feudal-legal form. Initially, agricultural large-scale enterprise affords the only outlet for feudal, power-hungry natures to exercise private and independent domination over men within the economic sphere.

With the rise of large-scale industry during the "industrial revolution" of the eighteenth and nineteenth centuries, a further such outlet opened up in manufacture, which until then had been restricted to artisan and family enterprise. At the same time, an expansionist trend became discernible, suggesting the possibility of transforming the national economy into a single centrally managed enterprise through the continual enlargement of centrally managed industrial sectors of the economy.

It is highly significant that this dream of dominion, so enticing for those given to a feudal hankering after power, was first conceived by a déclassé representative of the French nobility, Claude Henri de Rouvroy, Comte de Saint-Simon (1760-1825), grandnephew of the famous Duc de Saint-Simon of the court of Louis XIV. Ejected from his traditional family situation by the Revolution, and after adventurous attempts to attain wealth by financial speculation, he became impoverished and, after an abortive suicide attempt, dependent upon the financial support of a former valet. He compensated for these misfortunes on the one hand with brilliant, hateful sallies aimed at the king and court nobility, his former peers, and on the other with intoxicating dreams of power of a great capitalistic planned economy—a project in pursuit of which he gathered a band of enthusiastic, devoted, and adoring disciples around him. It was these disciples who, after his death, systematized the "doctrine of Saint-Simon" in a communal work and gave it its distinct socialist twist, thus creating one of the most important anticipations of Marxism.

By simultaneously appealing to the drive for knowledge through its rationalism and the drive to power through the prospect of leadership positions with enormous scope, the planned economy exercises a strong seduction on large numbers of young people. For the latter, even those who are neither communist nor totalitarian in orientation, such a "Copernican revolution with built-in desk space"[30] offers substitute satisfaction that they cannot hope to attain in the more arduous and riskier competitive arena of a free economy.

In fact, planned economy coupled with a totalitarian state signifies the highest degree of domination above and bondage below that has ever been attained.

5. TECHNICAL PROGRESS

Technology is as old as mankind. When at an excavation there is doubt as to whether discoveries are of human origin, technology determines the ultimate decision. When we determine processed tools or traces of the use of fire, hence traces of technology, we are in the presence of human residues. Thus we define man precisely through his technology as *homo faber*—a "tool-making animal," in Benjamin Franklin's phrase.

Technical inventions have been made since time immemorial, and many of these are still in everyday use. Many clever, brilliant inventions and flashes of inspiration were required to advance from the primitive wattle, which itself represents a primitive invention, to the hand-operated loom. Instinctive insight hides in a complicated physical-chemical event like the burning process in the artful construction of the charcoal kiln. Many similar examples could be cited.

But we have misgivings, because of the sharp contrast in pace of change, in applying the concept of technical progress to such prehistoric developments, to the "age of the tool." The tempo of technical progress that we now take for granted is really an exceptional and extreme phenomenon, which had its beginnings no more than two hundred years ago. Earlier, technological progress occurred at a rate that, by our standards, was one of unimaginable slowness.

Here is one personally observed example: the two-wheeled oxcart to this day still is a customary vehicle on the country roads of Anatolia. Unlike European carts, whose spoked wheels revolve on a fixed axle, Turkish carts have disk wheels that turn with the axle under the box. We find the same cart construction, down to the least technical detail, illustrated on a Sumerian boundary stone of the end of the fourth century B.C., and there are grounds to consider it several millennia older. This cart constituted a considerable technical advance in its time; but the tempo of technical development was so slow that its design did not progress beyond the level attained five thousand years earlier. This rate of change (a one-time-only advance that men found satisfactory for many millennia until the next advance came)—this leisurely, almost geological, pace of change was typical of development from the beginning of prehistory well into the eighteenth century.

The explanation for this sharp contrast between the earlier *largo* and the later *prestissimo* of technical development seems obvious. In old, leisurely times there was no specialized natural science, based on elaborate division of labor, to impart ever new impulses to technical progress. At that time, peasants and artisans, fully occupied with their daily labors, had to make their own inventions; the exceptional aptitude and a suitable occasion for an invention thus occurred only rarely.

But if this presented an adequate explanation, a pattern of full simultaneity would have to be traceable, the change in tempo of technical innovation would have to coincide precisely with the emergence of the exact natural sciences or with their technical applicability. Most strikingly, however, that is by no means the case.

The development of the exact sciences can be traced through two great periods in Western intellectual history: in antiquity from Pythagoras by way of Archytas, Archimedes, Hero, and Philo of Byzantium until the middle of the imperial age of Rome (a period of around seven hundred years); the modern period, beginning with the Middle Ages and the Renaissance, extends up to now. Yet during most of these two periods—during the entire ancient period and in the modern period until the middle of the eighteenth century (over a thousand years), the snail's pace of productive technology, despite the existence of exact sciences and their applicability, remained essentially unchanged. It follows that existence of the exact sciences must have been a necessary, but not a sufficient, prerequisite for rapid technological change. Rather, still other changes had to occur—changes which did not effect a breakthrough before the eighteenth century.

In antiquity the very considerable development of the exact sciences—mathematics, physics, mechanics—led to discoveries that no doubt would have been technically applicable in the sphere of production. The Alexandrian physicists already knew the foundations of hydraulics, the principle of the steam turbine, and many other things that have acquired the greatest importance in our modern technology. But nowhere is there a question of application of those discoveries to the production process. The ancient production technique had essentially developed in the old leisurely tempo of traditional artisan labor. Practical application of this theoretical knowledge took place only in two areas: in the technology of war, and in the development of toy automata—highly brilliant constructions that have been handed down to us in descriptions and drawings of ancient authors. But these latter were mere playthings, without technical or productive use; in the words of Vitruvius, they were "things made not for necessity but for delight and enjoyment." And the same combination of technology in war and useless triviality strikingly recurs in the first centuries of the modern age.

The nineteenth century, in its characteristic fashion, could not marvel enough over the fact that the Greeks, otherwise so intelligent and admirable, could have failed so utterly and remained so far behind in a department so central to us as technology. And in an equally characteristic way slavery has regularly been adduced as the cause of this failure: one had so many human slaves at one's disposal in antiquity that one had no need for iron slaves. This explanation will enlighten no economist. Slaves in antiquity were even costlier than at other times because they tended to be more refractory. Purely from an economic point of view it would have been at least as profitable then as it became later to replace slave labor with machine labor; yet no such replacement occurred. The same development strikingly recurs in early modern times. The development of modern exact sciences—prepared by the nominalist scholasticism of the urban mendicant orders, set in motion by the Renaissance and further fostered by absolutism—led to spectacular advances symbolized by such names as Copernicus, Kepler, Galileo, and Newton. Even though this rapid development of the exact sciences very early led to discoveries that would have been fully applicable in technology and in economic production, such practical application occurred as infrequently as in antiquity, and once again with the same exceptions: military technology and the construction of toy automata. The only further exception was industries owned directly by princes, notably mines. Columbus's voyage of discovery, to be sure, was the practical application of a purely theoretical advance in knowledge, the knowledge of the spherical shape of the earth. Yet this knowledge, in its intellectual-historical roots, reaches back as far as the pre-Socratic nature philosophers; and its belated application also occurred in the service of royal rulers and for the sake of directly expanding their power. (The courage for Columbus's feat, incidentally, derived in part from a vast underestimate of the dimensions of the spherical earth.)

The curiosity cabinets of princes contain a profusion of automata constructed in most complicated and ingenious ways, and hiding the most brilliant technical inventions. It would be an interesting and worthwhile project to trace the latent technical progress implicit in this department of purely playful application.

There are a number of other areas where technical progress was displayed already in this early modern period—one being paintings of the inferno. The sadistic-technical fantasy of the hell-painters from Hieronymus Bosch (ca. 1450-1516) to the younger Pieter Brueghel (1564-1637) cannot do enough in portraying on canvas technical inventions that would intensify the torments of the damned in every conceivable way—even acoustically by the anticipation of mechanized musical instruments. It should give us pause to think that for men of that time unbridled technical progress obviously was considered as something demonic, suitable to hell. But even on earth medieval torture chambers, as Marx once grimly observed, "occasioned the most ingenious inventions."

That the natural science discoveries of those centuries were in principle fully applicable in technology is indicated by an independent literary genre of the period, hard now for us to understand—the writings of project makers. Practical application of technical invention was not permitted, yet progress in the exact sciences cried out for just such application; hence there arose a whole category of literature, partly in manuscript and partly in print, which on paper depicted and advocated the practical use of such technical innovation. The appeals usually were directed to the sovereign princes of the time, and the prospects of tremendous financial gain were calculated in detail. Nor were the authors mere confidence men or swindlers.

A precursor of these project makers in the second half of the fourth century A.D. (ca. 366 or 375) was the author of an untitled treatise on military matters that has come down to us.[31] Among other things he proposed a warship with blade-wheel propulsion and a pontoon bridge. Nine hundred years later, Roger Bacon (1214-1294) postulated the invention of the airplane, automobile, and dynamite. And finally there was the founding hero of technology, Leonardo da Vinci, who furnished construction sketches for the airplane, the submarine, and other amazing objects.

What actually were the obstacles and inhibitions that for more than a thousand years stood in the way of the application of natural scientific discoveries to economic practice? As we shall see, these obstacles lay on both sides: science was not ready to give, practice not ready to take.

Western science in its first Ionian beginnings had been purely mundane and objective and had also objectified transcendental influences from the Orient. With Pythagoras (before 500 B.C.), the man of God, savior, and miracle worker, Western science took a great step away from the clear, bright, and solid reality of the visible and the palpable, toward the realm of theology, metaphysics, revelation, and salvation—toward knowledge suffused with a numinous mist. Since then, and especially since Plato's reinforcement of this step, Western natural science acquired an aristocratic and theological character, which was reinforced in the Middle Ages and which in the Renaissance was diluted only in the sense of a reversion to Platonic enthusiasm. The purpose of this Pythagoreanizing, theological, contemplative, and metaphysical natural science, first and foremost, was to extoll and glorify the wisdom of the creator as revealed in his works. As compared with this grand objective, any idea of a practical or even mercenary application and use of such lofty revelations would have been vulgar, indeed sinful—it might even suggest black magic, with its infernal horrors.

The social feudalism of the knight combined with this intellectual feudalism of the cleric. Artisans were looked down upon as lowbrows, and manual labor was depreciated as dirty—except, of course, the glorious artisanship of war. Thus, in antiquity, intellectual contempt for technology was closely linked with social contempt for those who practiced it.

Christianity, to be sure, opposed its principle of Christian humility to such secular feudalism; yet the theological character of the knowledge of nature, its upward-looking stance, and its metaphysical rank consciousness were reinforced all the more strongly. With regard to the question of technology there thus was little change. Science felt itself neither called upon nor justified in adopting a utilitarian approach. An astonishing proof of how long the contempt for all that smacked of the technical and the mechanical persisted is provided by the first dictionary of the French language, the *Dictionnaire françois* of Richelet (1631-1698), which contains the following entry under the word *mécanique*: "This word, in speaking of certain arts, signifies the opposite of liberal and honorable. . . . Its meaning is base, ugly, and little worthy of a respectable and liberal person."[32]

Nor did the members of the lower strata who worked with their hands, for their part, feel any need for these intellectual goods pregnant with technical progress, and where they did catch sight of them, they rejected them. Such an attitude flowered, first of all, from the prevailing economic mentality of sufficiency ("Nahrung," in Sombart's term). The desire to have more (greediness, *pleonexia*) along with the corresponding economic mentality of "chrematistics" was despised by Aristotle and pilloried by the Church as a mortal sin. But people who are intent only on maintaining and continuing traditional ways of life will find traditional methods of production sufficient for their purpose. There is no urgent need to change or improve those methods.

There were more deep-seated inhibitions. A tale of the Taoist Chuang-tzu (beginning of the third century B.C.) is representative of this attitude: An old gardener, after years of arduous labor, had cut steps into a boulder, so that he could fetch water from a spring every day. A Confucian points out to him that he could have accomplished that more practically and conveniently through a draw well. The gardener replies: "I know this invention well, but I would be ashamed to apply it."[33] The detailed Taoistic justification that he gives for this is, to be sure, specifically Chinese, but we may also infer the underlying feeling of instinctive rejection and defensiveness against any disturbance or interference of the natural world sanctified by tradition.

Even in the legends of Greek antiquity, things go badly with all inventors: Hephaestus limps, Icarus crashes, Prometheus is bound to the rock. And in a famous choral lyric of Sophocles' *Antigone*, the chorus calls out its tragic "woe betide!" on man's presumptuous inventiveness.

Indications of the same attitude are found in the beginning of the modern age, notably all in the classical formulation of the guild charter of the city of Torun (Thorn), of 1523: "No artisan should devise or invent or use anything new, but rather each one out of civic and brotherly love should follow his neighbor." A host of similar regulations from this and succeeding centuries have come down to us, along with corresponding injunctions—historic or legendary—against inventions and inventors. The nineteenth century could see in such provisions repulsive examples of sinister obduracy and backwardness; and in fact, the opposition of technological innovations did seem to become every more cramped. But today we can appreciate that a basic attitude, in itself altogether wholesome and natural, can become inflexible and intransigent out of a sense of impotence in the face of an approaching threat.

Western mankind for centuries seems to have defended itself instinctively with many inhibitions and prohibitions against a momentous and potentially disastrous step into the unknown along a path yet untrod—against foolhardy adventure of unpredictable consequence. Only with the approach of the Enlightenment was this entire cluster of inhibitions overcome, one by one. As one might have put it in the allegorical language of the eighteenth century, the rising sun of reason banished the dark prejudices of the past.

Human attitudes toward the scientific study of nature underwent far-reaching structural changes that had already been prepared for in nominalist scholasticism. In the course of progressive secularization, pious humility and admiration before the wisdom of the creator was gradually replaced by an attitude that eventually revealed itself as a self-assertive arrogance and lust for domination. The mysteries of nature were no longer admired but craftily spied upon; in order to bring them into his power, man acted like a cunning hunter—indeed almost like a wily pickpocket. Knowledge is power; and this power, achieved through knowledge wrested from nature, is exercised and proven by technical application. From something relegated to baser levels, technology became triumphant. If God is viewed as the greater constructor, builder, and master of machines, then the technician is his earthly image and he proves his similarity to God precisely through his practical success. Rarely has there been such a thorough revaluation in the course of intellectual history. Francis Bacon led the triumphant procession of technical progress like a baroque trumpeter blaring forth his fanfare. But before him Leonardo, more quietly, had objected against the depreciation of mechanics. Descartes espoused the same outlook; in the *Discourse on Method* he declares that the aim of science is "to make us as masters and possessors of nature"—an ambition by which man all but vaults onto the throne of God.

Similar revolutionary revaluations occurred in the sphere of economic thought. Under the influence of puritanism, the desire for gain, as long as it did not serve hedonistic consumption but rather abstinent accumulation, was not only freed from any former blemish, but positively elevated to a religious virtue. To earn and to invest as much as possible was now pleasing to God and was the best way to be sure of one's status as one of the elect. The venerable mentality of "sufficiency" was now suspiciously viewed as laziness and as lack of readiness for active glorification of God. This enormously dynamic economic mentality, detached from its theological justification, increasingly made headway. And there was no better way of increasing economic profits in the service of such a mentality than to improve the technique of production—that is, promote technical progress.

Interest in the technique of production of various industries down to their least details became highly fasionable in the eighteenth century. The book market was flooded with multivolume works, copiously illustrated, that served this fashion. The great and famous encyclopedia appeared as *Encyclopédie, ou Dictionnaire raisonné des sciences, des arts, et des métiers* (35 folio volumes, 1751-1780). Goethe, in his autobiography, writes: "When we heard the Encyclopedists spoken of, or opened a volume of their enormous works, we felt as though we were amongst the countless bobbins and looms of a great factory. Amid the buzzing and rattling of the machinery, which confused our eyes and mind, and the manifold and incomprehensible intricacies of the whole, in the consideration of all that goes in the making of a piece of cloth, we began to feel disgusted with the coat we were actually wearing."[34] The social rise of the bourgeoisie, which cultivated the new-fangled outlook, made technology presentable.

This astounding spread of technical interest and knowledge in the general culture of the Enlightenment, which went hand in hand with the development of the system of technical education, also accounts for the fact that many of the earliest great inventors of the eighteenth century were neither learned men nor specialists in the industry involved, but rather lay persons of humanitarian interest. Their naïve enthusiasm was least hindered by traditional prejudices, so that they could form a versatile vanguard for this advancing movement.

Nevertheless, late medieval guild prohibitions and regulations, which the absolutist state with its regimented economic policy had increased and sharpened, still held out against growing pressure of these converging intellectual and societal forces. Yet it was precisely against this mercentile economic policy of absolutism that Enlightenment liberalism, led by François Quesnay and Adam Smith, directed its victorious general offensive under the slogan *Laissez-faire! Laissez-passer!*

One obstacle to free trade after the other fell in England, France, Germany, and other countries from the middle of the eighteenth until the beginning of the nineteenth century. Useful discoveries that had been gathered in the course of a thousand-year development in the exact sciences, but excluded from practical application, now poured forth like a flood over the plains of the economy, fertilizing like the muddy inundations of the Nile. Victorious economic liberalism made such technological applications not only possible but even necessary. Under free competition, anyone who did not want to run the danger of becoming noncompetitive was forced to apply knowledge technically. The faster pace of application not surprisingly had a quickening effect upon science itself, first by providing intellectual stimulation and later also material support.

This unique world-historical situation, culminating over more than two thousand years, led to the unique, unprecedented tempo of technical progress. Amazed and admiring at first but subsequently frightened, we have been witnesses to that progress for two hundred years, and since the turn of the last century it has further intensified. That development constitutes the decisive foundation of the "Industrial Revolution" (expressly so named by Friedrich Engels in 1845).

Of all contemporary movements of the same epoch this was the fastest, mightiest, and most direct. Faith in progress, which as a secularized chiliasm within the religious history of the enlightened eighteenth century had been thrust more strongly into the foreground and which provided a man like Condorcet with final consolation on his deathbed, found here its confirmation and fulfillment. Traditional religious faith, which had satisfied innate and ineradicable religious needs of man and given life solid support, showed symptoms of senescence, decay, and dissolution; it no longer corresponded to man's deep need to give himself with his whole soul and enthusiasm to a conviction. Thus during the nineteenth century, technical progress, with its stirring dynamic and its irresistible striving toward the future, took the place up to then occupied by religion. For broad and leading circles technical progress became the real religion—a religion whose church spires are skyscrapers, whose sacrament is the roaring din of the highest speed, and whose martyrs are those hecatombs of inventors and technicians who died while conducting their experiments. And, like any theology, this godless religion of unfettered rationalism ultimately also demands the *sacrificium intellectus*: any question about the meaning of the whole, any doubt whether the expenditure and sacrifice are worth it, is already a sin against the spirit and an unforgivable weakness of faith.

In the forefront of this development were certain groups of technicians so completely convinced of the absolute superiority of their blueprint mentality that they shaped all other departments of life—foremost among them economic policy—according to their method. And they proclaimed this ideal of "technocracy" with the fanaticism of the illumined and of the "called" as the only true path to the redemption of the world.

Related to these men are those enthusiasts who await the advent of a new world for mankind from "cybernetics" (the term is Norbert Wiener's) and its electronic brains. They fancy that triumphant mechanics has crossed into the intellectual realm, but it has shown no more than that some areas hitherto reckoned among the intellectual really belong to the mechanical and the mechanizable.

Earlier improvements in production techniques, separated from each other by intervals of thousands of years, had developed from specific artisan branches and their needs. In consequence of this endogenous origin, such improvements had an altogether obvious and instantly comprehensible character for all concerned. With the age of technical progress, however, the decisive technical advances came exogenously, from the distant and lofty sphere of pure science, whose development followed its own, alien laws; and between them and the worker there now intruded the new social estate, the engineer, as mediating agent. More and more, the nature of technical progress became incomprehensible to the worker who had to apply it, and this incomprehensibility contributed markedly to the alienation of the worker from his work. This growing gulf between technical progress and the sphere of economic production in which it is applied further strengthened the impression of progress as a higher, irresistible, demonic force to which one felt helplessly delivered.

This character of technical progress in the nineteenth century also explains the role assigned to it in the economic, scientific, and ideological system of Karl Marx. Here technical progress is the real first mover, the only independent variable on whose change all others depend. Marx and his followers are convinced that this is so in the nature of things, whereas in reality the autonomy of technology is a wholly remarkable, unique, and exceptional phenomenon. On the basis of this Marxian dogma, moreover, blind faith in technical progress has also become a central tenet of the Communist-Bolshevist world religion.

Despite the enthusiasm for progress dominating the nineteenth century, there was no lack of warning voices. One of the earliest and most impressive is that of Goethe. In *Wilhelm Meisters Wanderjahre* (1829) he places these gloomy-prophetic words in the mouth of the

"good and beautiful" heroine: "What troubles me is an anxiety,
unfortunately not for the moment, nay, for the whole future. The
machine system that is gaining the upper hand frightens me and
makes me anxious. It comes rolling on like a thunderstorm, slowly,
slowly, but it has taken its direction; it will come and strike. . . .
People think about it, talk of it, and neither thinking nor talking
can bring any help. And who would like to see such horrors
realized!"[35]

Such fear of the machine and the threatening unemployment
it would bring in many places led to a desperate outbreak of
Luddism—the destruction of machinery. The dominant enthusiasm
for technical progress, however, completely drowned out such warning voices or desperate movements of opposition.

At the present time there is need for drawing up a balance sheet of
technical progress. What has technical progress brought to mankind? Our standard of measurement here should not be technology
itself, which after all is only a means, not an end. Rather, it will be
man, in whose service technology allegedly stands. This question
customarily is answered in a fashion that is revealing in its naïveté.
Imagine, it may be said, that you live like your forefathers a
thousand years ago: rooms without glass windows, where in winter
one freezes with open shutters or sits in the dark or at best in a room
lit by smoky pine splinters. Neither electricity, gas, nor running water, neither railroad, nor automobile, nor toilet, and, horrible to
imagine, no cinema or radio—and that not only for a few holiday
weeks, but rather summer and winter, year in and year out. Now,
you see what technical progress has brought us?

But it is a fundamental fact of human psychology that man experiences as gain or deprivation only that which deviates from what is
customary and taken for granted. Therefore, it is psychologically erroneous to assert that people of earlier times were as uncomfortable
as we would be if removed from our life and placed back in theirs.
Indeed, in many respects they were even better off. Our urbanization, our distance from nature, the artificiality and multiple dependence of our life situation substantially detract from our feeling
of vitality. And we also experience them as detractions—otherwise
we would not flee from them, at least on holidays, regardless of discomfort.

The current opinion that technical progress has brought new and
extraordinary reduction of work time also rests upon a similar naïve
fallacy. It is generally assumed that any object in common use today
can be produced in a fraction of the time formerly required for its

production by hand. This would signify a shortening of labor time only if we had retained our old modest needs.

Quantitatively, it is very questionable whether the yearly labor time of a modern industrial worker (including the time spent traveling to and from work) is shorter than that of a peasant or artisan of former times. But even where such a quantitative shortening of the labor time can be shown to have taken place, what is the advantage, when the modern big-city proletarian has nothing meaningful to do with this leisure time than to "kill it" through some kind of industrialized self-narcotization, with pleasures and "distractions" that often are no less exhausting, unsatisfying, and de-energizing than is his work?

Medicine is the only sphere of life in which, of course, things have truly changed. Here, the base line of health is the same for *all* men of *all* times, and any deviation from it—sickness, infirmity, and premature death—is always experienced as a misfortune. Men have done their utmost to fight it, and have experienced the success of such efforts as positive, failure as negative. When, therefore, medical success becomes more frequent and failure more rare, we all gain. But, as far as I can see, this is a situation quite unique to medicine.

Even in medicine, progress has had its unanticipated disastrous by-products, notably the rabbitlike increase of world population. Where once ten children were required to perpetuate a family and reproduce the population, now, as the result of vast advances in public health, two or three suffice. Yet religiously sanctioned customs of procreation adjust but slowly to this sharp decrease in mortality. The difficulty is that measures of public health—the struggle against childbed fever, malaria, smallpox, and the rest—can be instituted by the decision of a few persons at the head of a vast bureaucracy whereas a change in customs of procreation must be carried out by many millions of married couples. The demographic explosion, which appears to have tripled the human population of the globe in only two centuries, is a result of this "phase shift" (as Wilhelm Röpke[36] has aptly called it) between decreasing death rate and decreasing birth rate.

Among the peoples of the West the harm of overpopulation predicted by Malthus has taken the form—thanks to technical progress at a rate that Malthus did not anticipate—taken the economic form not of a net loss but of a gain foregone. In south and east Asia and in parts of Latin America, by contrast, a development is in progress that threatens to confirm the gloomiest Malthusian predictions.

Public health measures on the Western pattern have been introduced far more rapidly than any other measures of economic development, and the result has been a widening of the gap between
population and food supply—a combined impact for which some
Westerners naïvely seem to expect gratitude.

The solution evidently lies in planned parenthood and improved
techniques of birth control, for the world's overpopulation results
not from wanted but unwanted children.

Despite the population increase, a simultaneous rise in productivity has led, within the Western culture complex, to a considerable
increase of real income *per capita* and to an improvement of the
life-style of all strata of the population. It could, however, have led
to a quadrupling of this income and general well-being and to strong
and beneficent relaxation of social tension, if during the same period it had not in large part been offset by an unprecedented population increase. Thus mankind has been deprived of most of the rewards that the enormous technical-economic energy expenditure of
the nineteenth century could have brought it.

It is difficult to specify with any precision what would be the optimum population for the earth as a whole on the assumption—
today more utopian than ever before—that this population were
optimally distributed among the regions of the globe. It also should
be noted that there exists not only an economic but also a sociological overpopulation—the former quantitative, measured against the
food supply, the latter qualitative, measured against the human life
situation. The economic population optimum has repeatedly been
raised by technical progress, especially in the sphere of the production of foodstuffs, so that the advent of economic overpopulation has
been avoided so far and perhaps can still be avoided for some time.
But man, after all, does not live by bread alone, and although this
bread ration is not yet reduced as a result of overpopulation, conditions on this earth will increasingly disfigure and spoil his life by its
transformation into a "rabbit hutch." No matter how far economic
overpopulation can be deferred, sociologic overpopulation has for a
long time supervened in many places and constantly grows worse.

This senselessly increased population, in part produced and in
part made possible by technical progress, is exposed moreover to increasing urbanization as well as the growth of the proletariat and of
mass society. From this springs that alienation of man that Hegel
and Marx diagnosed as the central sickness of modern times, as well
as the discontents of civilization that Freud complained of. Techni-

cal progress has made the large factory the leading form of industrial organization, replacing the family farm as the previously dominant form. And while farming integrated the family into an autonomous work community, work in large-scale industry severs them from each other and subjects herds of dependent workers, male and female, to alien command. As a result, one of the most solid foundations of marriage and the family has been destroyed.

The same technical progress has also saddled us with the "social question" with its manifold ominous complications and dilemmas, and in response to these have arisen socialism, communism, and bolshevism in all their varieties. Communism, ever since Marx's original pronouncements on the matter, has been fully conscious of being a response to technical progress, and the assertion of this interconnection has remained one of its basic dogmas.

The technology of war has been the one sphere in which technical progress throughout human history has been pursued without restraint. This progress since the end of the Middle Ages has conferred on the West an irresistible superiority in weaponry over all other peoples of the world; which, since the age of the great discoveries and circumnavigations, has been the main propelling force behind colonial imperialism with its horrendous brutality and acts of inhumanity. Today we are rebounding from this Western colonial policy, pursued for five hundred years, and bolshevism is on the point of providing the West's former colonial and semicolonial peoples with the most modern technology of war and a corresponding ideology designed to recruit them as allies for its own aims. And this militant "countercolonization" (as M. J. Bonn has called it) is one of the most threatening and sinister elements of our present world situation.

Finally, technical progress, which in its time had been jubilantly hailed as liberator, has brought us a technique of totalitarian control, oppression, and enslavement of whole peoples that goes far beyond anything the most brutal conquerors and oppressors of all previous world history ever dreamed of. This technique extends from the most refined nuances of psychology and organization to the most brutal means of mass extermination—and woe unto us if the latest triumph of the technology of extermination, the atom bomb, should some day find unrestricted application in a world war!

Such are the blessings which mankind owes to technical progress—a progress that originated in a peculiar and unique historic situation; was spurred on by applause freely bestowed by contemporaries for the latest record-breaking accomplishments; and, benefiting from extraneous circumstances of intellectual history, has been pushed into the role—for which it is ludicrously ill equipped—of a substitute religion.

On the other hand, it was the development of science and technology from the end of the Middle Ages that enabled Western culture—until then still in the same rank with the other two great high cultures, the Indian and the Chinese—to outdistance these definitively and at an even faster pace, although in a direction the wholesomeness of which may legitimately be questioned.

In this world-historical role, which Western technology assumed not by choice but by the force of temporary circumstances, it accomplished unique and enormous feats. These technical achievements are wholly unprecedented, not only within the whole history of technology itself, but in all of human history. It would be difficult to find a development that could be compared to it in vigor, impetus, intensity, tenacity, intelligence, and level of accomplishment. Considered in terms appropriate to an athletic contest—that is, considered as an attempt to show what *homo ludens* at his best is capable of—modern technology has undoubtedly set records of achievement of which humanity as a whole and each of its members may be justly proud. That the *direction* in which this unique record achievement was pushed was incorrect and that its results thus have been dubious or even nefarious was the fault not of technology as such but of historic forces of the nineteenth century that employed technology to their ends. Is the long-distance runner to be blamed for the construction and the direction of the track? And do the defects of construction or direction diminish his athletic accomplishment?

I agree with Karl Jaspers's thesis of the "neutrality of technology":

Technology is *per se* neither good nor evil, but it can be used for either good or evil. In itself it contains no idea, neither an idea of perfection nor a diabolical idea of destruction. Both of them spring from other origins in man. . . . The limitation of technology consists in the fact that it cannot exist . . . for itself, but is always a means. This renders it equivocal . . . : It can serve the purposes of salvation or calamity. In itself it is neutral toward both of them. This is precisely why it requires direction. . . . The direction of technology cannot be looked for in technology itself, but it must be sought in a conscious ethos. Man himself must find his way back to the guiding reins. He must achieve clarity concerning his needs. He must put them to the test and determine their hierarchy.[37]

How can this be done? What conclusions for the future can we draw from the mistakes of the past? How can we still, at the eleventh hour, prevent such a disastrous development from simply continuing along its catastrophic course? How is control, a bridling of technical progress possible, a testing and a decision as to which directions of application are desirable and useful to man, which undesirable and harmful?

The answer fundamentally depends upon how we picture the economic and social future, the future order of the economy. For the exponent of a planned economy, the advocate of a command economy, the fundamental answer seems simple: Do this, don't do that! From a neoliberal, free-enterprise standpoint the answer is not so simple.

A key demand of our program of "social market economy" based on a competitive order of actual achievement—a demand very far yet from being realized—is the elimination of all monopolies, cartels, and trusts. To such a demand it is commonly objected that technological progress is now financed largely from the monopoly profits of these mammoth organizations and that, conversely, their dismantling would dry up this source of technical progress. The pros and cons of the current condition of dependence of vast areas of research on organized economic interests tend to be judged the more skeptically the closer the observer is to the relevant details— although there undoubtedly are situations where the interests of pure research and of business coincide.

If monopoly profits should be eliminated for reasons of overall economic policy, it becomes necessary to restore scientific research to the position that it largely held in Europe throughout most of the nineteenth century—namely, being financed by government authority. "Government authority" in this context does not mean under direct control of the central organs of the state but autonomous bodies like the research institutes supported by the Rockefeller Foundation in the United States or the Max Planck Society in West Germany. Community research and contract research could also play an important role in this context.

It will be clear to every liberal-minded person that true research cannot be regulated or restricted by any prohibitions: the spirit bloweth where it listeth. But this refers to pure research, that research which Heisenberg intended when, asked what apparatus he used, he replied: pad and pencil.

But today the path from fundamental research to technical application becomes ever longer and costlier. If public funds are employed to meet these costs, the public and society have the right and the duty to interfere and to judge the direction, purpose, and application of their funds in terms of a perspective that seems desirable and commendable. Here are two simple examples:

Technical progress in agriculture has concentrated on the needs of large-scale holdings, the giant "wheat factories" in the United States or the large landed estates east of the Elbe in Germany: for the machine manufacturers this was the greatest and most convenient source of a profitable business. Accordingly, they constructed tractor ploughs, giant combines, etc., that could cover so many square miles in the shortest possible time. Scientifically and technically, of course, it is just as possible to concentrate construction talent on small agricultural machines and implements. Just as formerly business interests determined a direction to be taken, why in the future should not the public interest in a healthy social and economic development decide upon another direction? Private interests would remain free to apply their own resources at their own discretion, whereas the public interest would determine the expenditure of public funds.

Similar considerations apply in the related sphere of fertilizing techniques. Big chemical monopolies were interested only in the fertilizers they manufactured. Accordingly, their own laboratories, as well as professorships and institutes in agricultural schools of higher learning they financed, were concerned exclusively with artificial fertilizing. The sphere of natural fertilizing—so much more important for rural economy as well as for the future of our soils—was totally neglected.

One accomplishment of technical progress is that it has created a global network of transport and communication, thus providing a necessary, though by no means sufficient, condition for the organizational and political unification of mankind. Such a lofty goal, once achieved, would constitute, retroactively, the only conclusive justification of technical progress. Let us hope that en route to such a goal technical progress will be successfully tamed and guided—without compulsory interventions, in a democratic and liberal way—in directions truly salutary for mankind.

The control of atomic technology is by far the most difficult and burning problem of this whole area. That its military application could signify an apocalyptic suicide of mankind is something on which not only all thinking people, but even leading politicians are agreed. It is equally clear that a real exclusion of this horrendous possibility presupposes the political unification of mankind, the overcoming of the present day cleavage into the Western and Communist camps. But even if we optimistically imagine this goal—compelling for a thousand reasons—as achieved, what would it be like to have atomic technology applied to peaceful purposes exclusively?

Let us suppose that its military application is excluded, that production costs have dropped to levels competitive with other energy sources, and that production of atomic energy for industrial purposes is in progress. Would it then be possible to keep all production sites effectively under control so that no would-be dictator, criminal, or madman of any kind secretly could pursue criminal or military aims and thus terrorize all humanity?

But even apart from this possible sword of Damocles, what would be the prospects of radioactive contamination of earth, water, air? Pollution is already growing as a result of nonatomic industry and its waste products. And where, in the long run, are the upper limits of tolerance for radioactive effects on human beings?

Human beings lack many things that lead to happiness. But atomic technology is not a thing we cannot do without. Indeed, it threatens us with dangers of unforeseeable dimensions. If this is the actual state of affairs, would it not be irresponsible folly to embark on an adventure whose possible disadvantages are infinitely greater than its possible advantages? But, it will be objected, technical progress is in full motion, and who can stop it? The simple answer to this question is: human beings. The blind faith in technical progress and the pseudoreligious enthusiasm for it that prevailed in the nineteenth century has for a long time now evaporated. The worm of doubt gnaws in each one of us. Of course, such secular movements as technological change persist even when their original motive forces have become unsure or spent. There then ensues, however, a situation of increasing flexibility—and symptoms of such instability, like internal insecurity, are already unmistakable.

The mixture of fear and hope with which mankind views the advances of atomic technology can turn out to be highly explosive. No great prophetic vision is required to imagine situations under which the people's attitude toward technical progress could suddenly change to hysterical hate. Should we first wait for such a catastrophe, or would it not be wiser to forestall it and place such latent forces in the service of reasonable goals of prevention and transformation before they are released in a mass-hysterical explosion. Of course, such developments need time. For a lesser or greater number of years things will no doubt run their course. There is not even any immediate prospect of overcoming the current division of humanity, and while this division continues, no effective uniform measures are possible. But we must at all costs prevent a situation where the time is ripe but we are unprepared, where history offers us the opportunity and we fail to seize it: readiness is all.

And just because such a development takes time, we cannot begin soon enough to prepare for it and to set it in motion. In view of the ambivalent feelings that are so widespread on the subject it seems to me by no means hopeless to champion arguments like those that have been advanced in these pages. It is in a time like ours that the utopia of today can be the agenda of tomorrow and the reality of the day after. And even if there should not be the least hope for such a change, the role of Cassandra still would seem to me more honorable than that of the jubilant haulers of the Trojan horse.

Working atomic physicists themselves seem more receptive than others to such considerations. Their attainment of all but divine power has for some time given them pause. "God cannot have willed that, after all!" Otto Hahn is supposed to have exclaimed at the beginning of this development. "We have done the devil's work," declared J. Robert Oppenheimer, the "father of the atom bomb," in 1956. Atomic physicists have felt the weight of their burden of responsibility to be almost intolerable. It may be that the "revolt of the atomic scientists" has already failed—not lastly for the reason that it turned and could turn only against its military application in the Western camp. Still, there would seem to be a further opportunity—and this one perhaps the last—of a broad and more fundamental intervention.

Our present fateful situation of a world divided derives, as we all know, from a utopia jointly concocted by Friedrich Engels and Karl Marx in 1847-1848, and realized since 1917. Now if it is to be a question of utopias, then at least let it be one whose realization would be to mankind's benefit. And utopian or not, what goal should be pursued? For the present, a reasonable program should include an absolute prohibition not only of military but also of industrial applications of atomic energy; concentration of atomic research in a few research institutes, which can be effectively supervised.

Yet, it is by no means a question only of negative measures, of mere retarding and braking measures. The long-run aim must be to redirect powerful intellectual energies, previously subordinated to the striving for technical records, economic gain, or military destruction toward fruitful and beneficent goals. But let me stress again that such control and redirection cannot and must not be applied to the first stage of fundamental knowledge and of brilliant theoretical insight. Conversely, control and redirection must be imposed on the further steps of application and on the expenditure of public funds on such application.

In the impatience that marked the mania to establish records and the blind faith in progress up to now, new discoveries and inventions have very often been applied far too soon, before the dangers arising from them were fully understood or protective countermeasures sufficiently developed. The history of all such advances proves that the excessive costs and damages during the first period of application can be traced precisely to this impatience, to this inability to wait and see. Yet no past discoveries have even approached—in terms of forces released and dangers conjured up—the present orders of magnitude: precocity and rashness in atomic matters endangers all of humanity for all time.

6. Egalité

Two motive forces can stand behind the demand for equality: justice and envy. The two are not always easy to distinguish; often both are at work, and envy loves to hide behind justice.

Some differences are readily obvious. If an individual is convinced that he has a good and proper claim to some possession—at least as good and proper as that of the person who has it—this can be a demand for justice. If the person, however, is gratified by the mere fact that another will *not* have it, then we are as a rule dealing with envy. One can demand equality in the beginning (equality at the start of a competitive process) in the name of justice. Equality at the end, however, may be demanded only in the name of envy. Justice demands to each his own, envy to each the same. An especially clear and blatant case of envy is that which is directed at advantages that are innate or based on fate—situations in which a demand for justice does not come into question or would have to be addressed to nature or to the creator—as, for instance, when a girl hurls acid into the face of her more beautiful rival.

But envy can also come into play in cases less blatant and not so generally condemned. For instance, some leading economists are not ashamed, openly and expressly, to espouse the thesis that a

smaller, but equally distributed national income would be better
than a larger one in which some individuals have a larger share—
better all equally poor than all rich, but some still richer. (The suggestion seems to be that the argument would hold even if in the second case the absolute income of the relatively less well-situated
would be higher.) This by no means signifies that such scholars are
personally driven by envy. However, they do take into account the
envy of the lower stratum as a given sociological datum with which
they think they must reckon. Such a concession amounts to a
social-psychological defeatism, which, if generally accepted, would
have catastrophic consequences.

Superincumbency as such does not lead to manifest envy, as long
as the lower stratum is convinced that its situation is proper, inevitable, or divinely ordained, and believes in the actual superiority of
the upper stratum and its natural calling to rulership. Such, for
example, was the situation of the serfs in Russia until well into the
nineteenth century. But when this divinely willed feudal order is
shaken, especially with the transition to plutocracy, envy becomes
manifest in combination with demands for justice. The question becomes: by what right are life situations so unequally distributed? At
the same time a counterenvy from those above toward those below
occurs, a feeling of indignation because those below are envious and
covetous. With envy, the have-nots begrudge the haves; with counterenvy, the haves begrudge the have-nots. We meet this counterenvy openly in Theognis; its projection onto "Mount Olympus,"
the "envy of the gods," is actually counterenvy.

Clearly, the envy of lower strata is intensified when the upper
stratum does not take the advantages of its position for granted but
ostentatiously and tastelessly parades them—as is typical in plutocratic situations of the *nouveaux riches*. Generally it is not the envious but the envied who are to blame; for they have unconsciously or
even consciously provoked envy, and their indignation is no more
than feudal or plutocratic self-righteousness. All this does not
change the fact that envy is an ignoble and odious attitude, with distinctive effects on the envier. It is not for nothing that we say that
someone is "consumed" with envy.

Justice is the best remedy against envy. In a just world, envy
would be no more than an individual vice. But full justice is not possible in social relations. Even in the happiest marriage or the most
intimate friendship there are various areas where now one partner
and now the other takes the lead. In more complex social structures,
from the family upward, the question of gradation, hierarchy, or

leadership can no longer be left in suspense to be decided from case to case; rather it must take solid institutional forms, as already is the case with primitive peoples who have not experienced any superstratification.

Corresponding observations have been made even concerning gregarious higher animals, both birds and mammals. The "pecking order" of our barnyards, with its "grim seriousness" (in David Katz's phrase), is a degenerate form of the same phenomenon produced by domestication and artificial narrowness of space. In every pack of wild gregarious animals each animal knows its place in the hierarchy. At the same time in the animal kingdom higher rank not only brings rights but, above all, duties—duties that in the moment of danger can rise to the pitch of readiness for self-sacrifice for the sake of the herd.

What is characteristic of all this organic, natural super- and subordination is its voluntary recognition and acceptance by all participants, even when the ultimate establishment of rank order has been preceded by struggles for domination. Moreover, such struggles for rank are much more frequent among herd animals than among primitive peoples, among whom preeminence, as a rule, is decided by higher accomplishment for the community—that is, by competition for the common good—rather than by antagonistic rivalry. It also is characteristic of all these naturally grown gradations among human beings that the rank assumed is neither inherited nor acquired for life. Rather, it is purely individual and specific. It depends upon social capability and accomplishment, and it can correspondingly change at any time.

An altogether different kind of social rank order emerges with superstratification. This new super- and subordination is created "by blood and iron," by violence and weaponry, and it is maintained by the continuing threat of military force. Membership in the upper or lower stratum is hereditary: he who is born above belongs to the ruling upper stratum; he who is born below, to the ruled lower stratum, regardless of individual capacities or accomplishments. Relaxations of this rule are exceptional. Individual possibilities for upward and downward social mobility pertain only to a later phase of decline.

The original social structure based on distinction of birth has a mixed character. The upper stratum not only exercises sovereign power to its own advantage at the cost of the subjugated population; at the same time it also becomes aware of the hierarchical social functions of direction and leadership such as are indispensable in the sort of large social organization arising from superstratification. These lie in the general interest, and also in the interest of the members of the lower stratum. Its Achilles' heel is that the selection and distribution of the occupants on the social scale does not derive freely from individual capacities and accomplishments, and that rulership is reserved to members of the upper stratum. This amalgamation of justified and unjustified gradation developed arbitrarily, but was further promoted by the upper stratum, whose members found it convenient to invoke thier genuine accomplishments in rejecting attacks upon their despotic usurpation.

This was also the situation of the *ancien régime* in the age of revolutions and especially of the great French Revolution. This revolution attempted, in its first phase (1789-1792), to purge the traditional social rank order of its unjustified, despotic structural elements. The change in the second, Jacobin phase (1792-1793), however, went to the other extreme, grimly proclaiming absolute "equality": any head that dared to rise above the general level was to be cut off without further ado.

Complete, radical equality is not feasible in practice. Upon its proclamation there must at least be persons who issue precisely this proclamation and, above all, implement it and undertake the important task of cutting off the heads that tower above others. Thus every politically serious attempt at instituting radical equality inevitably leads to terror and dictatorship in their most blatant forms. Equality is feasible, in practice, only in the form of equality among subjects, and the more radically one wants to eradicate any kind of inequality, the more one falls unavoidably into the most violent forms of extreme inequality. The real opposite of tyranny is not tyrannous leveling but voluntary gradation, suitable to the purpose and allocated on the basis of performance.

On the other hand, the demand for equality as isonomy (equality before the law) rightly condemns every constitutionally based, hereditary or feudal inequality; as equality of opportunity it rejects any form of hereditary plutocratic privilege.

Constitutional equality before the law in Prussia was first achieved in October 1918 under the pressure of military defeat. An argument advanced against it at the time was that the political judgment of eligible voters is not equal, so that if one wanted to weigh rather than count votes, a very unequal distribution of weight would ensue. If an infallible, superordinated authority existed, one that could ascertain this inequality of politial capacity and judgment impartially and establish, without fear of contradiction, a corresponding gradation of the right to vote—then this would, no doubt, be the pinnacle of justice. Since such an authority, unfortunately, does not exist, and since unanimity on assessing the voters' capacity for judgment is simply impossible, no other way out remains than unanimous agreement on the elementary equation that one equals one: that is, equal and universal suffrage. There remains the consolation that even with equal franchise, superior political ability has manifold opportunities to assert itself.

As for any extremely radical egalitarianism, moreover, it cannot be stressed often enough that the principle of justice, of true equality of rights, does not state *idem cuique* but *suum cuique*: not "the same to each," but rather "to each his own."

The radical egalitarianism of the Jacobins found its intellectual preparation in the Enlightenment. Helvetius, with the intellectual boldness (or even rashness) peculiar to him, espoused the idea that all men are equal from birth and that later differences are exogenous, environmentally conditioned, and produced by external influences.

Such a view flies so starkly in the face of every reasonable consideration that it could never have been maintained, if its clear and convincing refutation had not been prevented by two fateful circumstances. In the first place, the attempt to purge from the inherited order of social gradations all arbitrary elements has not succeeded in practice. Second, even in theory the problem has barely been tackled, let alone solved. Sociology and political science to this day cannot define what a social rank order free of elements of domination and based solely on the requirements of the matter would look like under conditions of present-day large-scale societies. Hence, despotic realities as well as egalitarian countertendencies have persisted to this day, each paralleling and reinforcing the other.

The great topical importance of this problem-complex can be illustrated by considering a group of demands for equality contained in the Basic Law of the Federal Republic of Germany, whose implementation the competent bodies are making laborious efforts to effect, with scant success up to now.

Article 3 not only ordains, in section 1, the equality of all persons "before the law" but states more generally that "Men and women have equal rights" (section 2). And Article 117, section 1, states that "Laws which conflict with Article 3, section 2, remain in force until adapted to this provision of the Basic Law, but not beyond March 31, 1953." This adaptation of preexisting laws, however, did not take place either before or after the specified date. Now because there is by nature that minor difference between men and women that—fortunately—even a Basic Law cannot abolish, it would require a thorough anthropological investigation to determine what implications flow factually and reasonably from this natural difference. In contrast, the draft of the Basic Law quite properly stated: "The law must treat like alike; it can treat what is diverse according to its peculiarity." A radical, schematic egalitarianism, as is publicly espoused from many quarters, can here occasion only disaster, interfere in very sensitive morphological structures, and in the last analysis only discredit democracy itself.

Traditional inequalities, even those to the disadvantage of the female sex, are no doubt to a considerable extent domination-conditioned, so that their abolition can only be welcomed. But they are also intertwined with natural inequalities, so that the greatest care is called for in separating the two elements unless we wish to commit a new, fatal injustice and thereby invite future counter-attacks.

The Bonn constitution (Article 21.1) also requires political parties to "conform to democratic principles" in their "internal organization"—a provision obviously inspired by the experience with the National Socialist party, which had an antidemocratic internal structure that for twelve and a half years it imposed on all of German government.

The question arises, however, whether the connection between the internal organization and the external aims of a political party is logically compelling and practically necessary; whether a political party with a democratic inner structure can pursue antidemocratic aims and a political party with an authoritarian internal structure, democratic aims—indeed, whether perhaps a political party with democratic aims is not able to pursue its aims more effectively when its own internal structure is not overly democratic.

This important problem-complex received detailed treatment in *Political Parties* (1905), an influential book by an important German sociologist of the Pareto circle, Robert Michels. Using sharp sociological insight, Michels shows that even the parties of the left, with their democratic and egalitarian programs, are far from democratic and egalitarian in the structure of their own party organization. Rather, they are rigidly hierarchic, even downright dictatorial. Instead of questioning the validity of these egalitarian programs, Michels makes them the basis of his critique.

Other provisions of the Bonn Basic Law, such as the weak position of the federal president, are explicable essentially as reactions to national socialism or to elements in the Weimar constitution making possible the Nazi seizure of power, just as egalitarian tendencies of the second phase of the French Revolution were a reaction to the *ancien régime*.

If the constitution of the Federal German Republic—and likewise those of France and of Italy—goes too far in an egalitarian, democratic direction, changes against widespread egalitarian prejudices and moods, easily susceptible to demagogy, can be carried out only with great difficulty. Thus countries on the developmental level of Turkey or Egypt cannot be ruled on the pattern of a subegalitarian democracy based on the western European model. Rather, they require a very strong admixture of authoritarianism—and the danger of excess in this direction is great. But the danger is only heightened because every deviation from western European norms is from the outset viewed as suspicious or even sinful; the result is that reciprocal understanding and trust is made unnecessarily difficult, and we are deprived of the opportunity to test the question impartially and objectively.

Those who oppose arbitrary privilege by espousing not natural hierarchy or voluntarily accepted leadership but rationalist equality, simultaneously rejecting the equal subjection violently established and maintained by totalitarian dictatorship, have nothing to oppose to usurpation and the rule of force other than anarchy. The courage and rashness required for developing such an internally consistent position has been shown only by a small minority of anarchists properly speaking. Most theorists instead are content simply to minimize the functions of government and thus end up with the inspiring ideal of the state as night watchman. Such a demand for extreme *laissez-faire*, as espoused by the Manchester school, represented—as we shall see—a reaction against the earlier regimentation of the economy, in opposing which it was easy to forget the need for a strong government to police the market and guarantee fair competition.

Equality as a demand of the French Revolution was at bottom nothing more than a negation of traditional feudal inequality. Nevertheless, it would be unfair to assert that there were no positive social ideals set against it. This new positive social ideal was expressed in the demand for "fraternity." But this social ideal was inadequate. Not even the smallest human community, the family, could be maintained in fraternity alone. Just as a family, alongside and prior to the fraternal relation of the brothers and sisters, requires the hierarchy of the relation between parents and children, so hierarchy is required all the more by any larger communities.

These revolutionary ideas of the Enlightenment, of which nine-teenth-century liberalism was born, suffered from the same entan-glement of true and false: truth that gave them impetus, falseness that destroyed them. It is proof of the power of theory over reality that the faulty theory of the eighteenth century shaped the faulty reality of the nineteenth century.

Emergence of high cultures from superstratification rests upon the fact that the members or stipendiaries of the upper stratum are afforded the opportunity for concentration upon intellectual mat-ters, on the basis of incomes deriving from domination. This type of intellectual pursuit has undergone transformations in the course of history, among which considerable extenuations are also found. The Church, as the principal bearer of medieval intellectual develop-ment, was lordly in character; its claims, as proven by the demand for orthodoxy, were enforced by violent means. In contrast to this, however, its legacy, at least in regard to all not expressly privileged positions, was very democratic. The poorest peasant lad, if he was gifted, pious, and eager, could become a monk or priest and possibly rise in the hierarchy. This democratic feature of churchly education was enlarged and stressed by the urban mendicant orders; the same holds true for the lay piety of the waning Middle Ages and of the Reformation. Socially, the Lutheran parsonage was an altogether democratic phenomenon, and Pietism stressed this social character more particularly.

In contrast, secular education in the eighteenth century had a pronounced aristocratic-courtly character, especially in France, where in the seventeenth century under Louis XIV classicism had become a court art. In Germany, too, eighteenth-century intellec-tual life centered around many small princely courts. In England, as in Germany, appointment by a prince or an aristocratic family plays a typical and economically decisive role in the biography of many poets, writers, scholars, and composers.

In the social and intellectual history of the German eighteenth century, an important difference between *Sturm und Drang* and classicism lies in the fact that *Sturm und Drang* exhibits pro-nounced social-revolutionary features, whereas classicism con-cluded its special peace with the feudal upper stratum and was pre-sented at court. As Schiller said,

> Hence the poet should go with the prince
> Both dwell on the heights of mankind.

On the whole the period of absolutism exercised an aristocratic influence upon the social structure of Western education.

The rationalism of the Enlightenment, as it was represented in Jacobinism in the second phase of the French Revolution, fundamentally turned against this feudal educational privilege, as it did against all privilege. The emerging egalitarian blindness to rank order—the fateful exaggeration of a countermovement that in moderation would have been altogether justified and salutary—was in keeping with this radical and revolutionary original character.

Thus, democratization and socialization of thought and education, which placed their stamp on the nineteenth century, became one of the most central and far-reaching influences of rationalism in the social sphere. The gloomy Hobbes had already prophesied this development, and Diderot had expressly urged action in this direction with his stirring call: "Let us hasten to make philosophy popular!" Only "that which Adam too could have known" (Malebranche) was to be viewed as true knowledge. In the background stood a religious conviction—the equality of human souls before God—and the Reformation further strengthened this egalitarian tendency in Christianity by leveling institutional and dogmatic rules: by abolishing the church hierarchy through the doctrine of universal priesthood, by closing down the monasteries and abolishing the cult of saints.

If higher education—direct access to science and art—had been a privilege of the upper class and its stipendiaries, its collaborators, and those it had co-opted, now it seemed that the most central inference to be drawn from the new principle of natural equality was to give everyone direct access to the realm of the mind.

The most logical and effective way of accomplishing such an egalitarian educational ideal would have been a fundamental and thorough reform of the school and qualification system. But inertia in this institutional sphere has not yet been overcome; the path of least resistance was selected, and the most productive work was done outside the legally regulated school system. Thus, the modern system of popular instruction took the form of adult education, for those beyond the age of compulsory schooling.

It began with the conviction that fundamentally, and with sufficient good will on the part of teachers and students, everyone could understand everything; and each individual was supposed to decide questions of doubt on the basis of his or her own judgment. To call upon the student repeatedly to exercise his own judgment, his own decision, was considered as the mark of a good popular educator.

This attitude made excessive demands upon human beings. It is simply impossible to form individual judgments about every department of public instruction. Scholars can have independent judgment in a single specialized department at best. Excessive pressure along these lines has contributed to a widespread malaise in our culture. For when man is faced with the void, when he no longer has a living tradition to trust or to lean on, when he is supposed to decide individually all questions of doubt, then he is placed in an intolerable situation which is bound to lead to universal alienation.

At the same time, with the enormous tempo of progress in the intellectual sphere, science grew more complicated and difficult to comprehend; accordingly, there was a need for a correspondingly greater hierarchic gradation. These two developments ran in exactly opposite directions, making the intellectual situation more problematic and precarious.

With further specialization and divison of labor, the more the majority became dependent upon following the highly specialized accomplishments of the productive minorities; as a result, there was a need for implicit faith with the individual's own judgment limited to one's "sense of workmanship" (C. J. Friedrich), the instinctive feeling about whether someone understands and masters his trade. Yet the public as a whole was constantly called upon to make judgments which in most cases the individuals composing it could not begin to understand; hence public opinion came to be swayed by monomaniacal charlatans who knew how to adapt their intellectual products to such popular lack of understanding and who themselves, in most cases, were only half educated.

The problem, as important as it is difficult, of the proper social rank order in the intellectual sphere still has not been resolved; indeed, it has barely been seriously posed. The consequence is that we have not yet really overcome the violent shifts of the pendulum in matters of education, between feudal-plutocratic privilege and anti-feudal collectivist egalitarianism. As a result, demands for popular higher education, especially in the United States but also in Europe, are directed less at spreading its substantive content than the social privileges deriving from it. This implies the danger of the mass production of a white-collar proletariat. A satisfactory solution can be found only in a thorough reform of our whole system of education and of credentials on the basis of the principle of equal opportunity.

The development of the educational curriculum since the nineteenth century implied a further serious danger. The specialist—

"the man who knows more and more about less and less"—was a
specific product of scientific development of that century. Doubtless,
we owe the unprecedented modern advances in science and technology to this extreme specialization; yet, it also brought the educational system into an increasingly untenable situation. The
neohumanistic educational ideal renewed by German classicism
and applied by Wilhelm von Humboldt to public instruction was no
longer realizable. Maintenance of the claim to universality, with its
simultaneous socialization, produced the type of person "who knows
less and less about more and more." Universal, all-round education
can lead only to semi-education, in which the features of authentic
education are lacking. Alexander Pope warned of just this in his
Essay on Criticism: "A little learning is a dangerous thing."

A first step in leveling in the intellectual sphere was the dethronement of Latin as the language of science and scholarship.
Dante (1263-1321) wrote his poems in Italian and his scientific
treatises in Latin; that was a suitable gradation. Only with hesitation did Italian, the *volgare*, encroach upon learned literature; even
Boccaccio (1313-1375), when he wretchedly perished from an infection of the vulgar scabies, saw therein the just punishment of
heaven for his betrayal of Latin. Bishop Berthold of Mainz, in his
censorship edict of 1485, set forth debatable arguments against
translating Greek and Latin texts into German. Humanism led to a
revitalization of Latin as the language of science and scholarship,
and Ambroise Paré (1510-1590) was sharply criticized by the Sor-
bonne for profaning science because he published a medical treatise
in French instead of Latin. Christian Thomasius (1655-1728), who
delivered lectures in German instead of Latin, had to leave Leipzig
to the executioner's knell because of this "terrible crime, unheard of
since the existence of the university." Those who have until recently
uncritically sided with "progress" against the "pedantic" maintenance of Latin as the universal scientific tongue may yet have second thoughts. Boccaccio's itch already is affecting some, and the
executioner's knell of Thomasius is beginning to ring in their own
ears.

7. Isolation of the Individual

All organically developed, natural religions have the function of
transfiguring life, of conferring on it a higher, numinous dignity.
With their customs, rites, and cults, with their consecrations and
feasts these religions celebrate the course of life: the cycle of birth,

maturity, marriage, death; of spring, summer, autumn, and winter; the succession of the generations. This is the pattern, with variations, in all so-called primitive societies, and, at the highest cultural level, among the ancient Greeks. This function of natural religions corresponds to the innate religious needs of human nature so that even religions like Christianity—that is, established confessional and salvation religions—placed themselves in the service of these needs. Yet the essential characteristics that distinguish salvation religions from natural religions are clearly distinct; among these is the depreciation and dissolution of man's natural social bonds, with a resulting tendency toward isolation of the individual and social atomization. This depreciation and dissolution of natural social structures is a direct corollary of the one "supreme need," the transcendental relation of each individual soul to its God in a one-to-one relationship; and this, in turn, intensifies the need for salvation and excludes anything that could compete with the promise of salvation held out by the new dispensation.

The hair-thin bridges to the Beyond in the Near Eastern eschatologies (the Babylonian bridge of Chubur, the Persian bridge of Chinvat, the "Bridge of the Judge" in Islam) all have the function, like a turnstile at a subway station, of allowing individuals to pass only one at a time and thus isolating them from others. The Persian belief in the Beyond, to which the Christian belief directly reverts, stresses that each individual stands alone, detached from natural interconnections, before the Judge of the Beyond. "Man for man, each for his person," as Zarathustra says. In Plato the dead must face their judges, naked and alone, "deprived of all their kindred." Jesus says: "I tell you in that night there shall be two men in one bed; the one shall be taken, and the other shall be left." And similarly Muhammad: "And when the roaring is heard on that day the man flees from his brother and from his mother and from his father and from his companions and from his children: every man on that day has enough to do with himself."[38] In short, a kind of eschatological "each man for himself, and the devil take the hindmost."

In contrast, a historically recorded example shows how a naturally sensitive person who has been brought up in a natural religion would react to such soul-saving isolation:

The Frisian Duke Radbod (d. A.D. 719) was so far carried away by the preaching of the holy bishop Wolfram that, as one about to be baptized, he had already placed one foot in the holy spring.

When, however, he inquired of the holy bishop where the greatest number of the kings and nobles of the Frisian tribes were, in the bliss of heaven or in the damnation of hell, he was told that his ancestors who had died unbaptized were condemned to damnation. Thereupon, he immediately withdrew his foot from the water and said that he could not renounce the society of his ancestors and sit in the kingdom of heaven with a small number of saved.[39]

The radical isolation of the individual in confronting the question of eternal salvation or eternal damnation, naturally has repercussions also upon the rest of life. When Gautama (ca. 560-480 B.C.) prepared to set forth into homelessness and to become the Buddha, his young bride with her infant son laid herself down on the threshold. Gautama rudely pushed her aside with his foot. "Out of my way, you wretch! Hinder me not in my salvation!" How Jesus himself values family bonds is shown by utterances such as the following: "If any man come to me, and hate not his father, and mother, and wife and children, and brethren and sisters, yea, and his own life also, he cannot be my disciple." "He that loveth father or mother more than me is not worthy of me; and he that loveth son or daughter more than me is not worthy of me." When one of his disciples asked for permission to bury his father, Jesus replied: "Follow me and let the dead bury their dead." And to his own mother he said: "Woman, what have I to do with thee?"[40] To those brought up in a Christian tradition, such utterances have been interpreted, from childhood onward, in the idealizing, extenuating way of the traditional exegesis, rendered innocuous and thereby stripped of their harsh eschatological background and historical reality.

The consequence of this religious outlook is expressed with a terrible emphatic concreteness in a passage that Saint Bernard de Clairvaux (1090-1153) ascribes to Saint Jerome (ca. A.D. 330-420), and which also refers back to the aforementioned Buddhist tradition:

If thy father should throw himself over thee on the threshold, if thy mother with bosom bared shows thee the breasts on which she suckled thee, if a tiny child clings to thy neck—trample down thy father! trample down thy mother! and, dry-eyed, hasten to the banner of the Cross! That is the highest kind of compassion, to be cruel in such cases for Christ's sake![41]

Such theological atomization reaches a highpoint in Calvinism, no doubt because of its revival of predestination. As Max Weber puts it:

> In its extreme inhumanity this doctrine must above all have had one consequence for the life of a generation which surrendered to its magnificent consistency. That was a feeling of unprecedented inner loneliness of the single individual: In what was for the man of the age of the Reformation the most important thing in life, his eternal salvation, he was forced to follow his path alone to meet a destiny which had been decreed for him from eternity. No one could help him. No priest . . . no sacrament . . . no church.[42]

The Puritan theologian Richard Baxter (1615-1691) warned against friendship: "It is an irrational act and not fit for a rational creature to love any further than reason will allow us. . . . It very often taketh up men's minds so as to hinder their love of God." Bunyan's Pilgrim conducts himself in conformity to these precepts: "Now, he had not run far from his own door, but his wife and children perceiving it, began to cry after him to return; but the man put his fingers in his ears, and ran on, crying Life! Life! Eternal life! So he looked not behind him, but fled towards the middle of the plain."[43]

This deep inner isolation emerged in exactly the same way among the Jansenists of Port Royal, who were predestinarians and, in general, represented a kind of Catholic Calvinism. Thus Pascal writes: "We must tear ourselves away from those that are nearest and dearest to us in order to imitate Jesus."[44] And, in fact, it was reported that growing coolness marked his relations with those around him in his last years.

Even in Molière's (1623-1703) *School for Wives*, a verse like the following crops up:

> We are all mortal, and each one
> Is for himself.

And it was not accidental that the renewal of Epicurus's atomic philosophy by Pierre Gassendi (1592-1653) occurred at the same time; and so did the equally atomistic social doctrine by Thomas Hobbes (1588-1679), who has been aptly called the "gloomy fellow-traveller of Epicurus."[45]

But even in orthodox Lutheranism such themes are present, and the German romantic poet Novalis (Friedrich von Hardenberg, 1772-1801) writes in a remarkable combination of brilliant analysis and perverted appraisal: "True anarchy is the generative element of religion. As the destruction of all the positive elements she raises her glorious head as the new world-foundress. As by himself, man rises toward heaven, when naught more binds him."[46]

It is hard to believe that these ever recurrent Christian attacks against natural human bonds should not have left their mark on social reality, on human attitudes and social structures, even though Christianity, in its role as a modified natural religion, had done much to sanctify and strengthen natural communities, and the family in particular—one of the many examples of its *complexio oppositorum*. The fact that in Catholicism all those who took it upon themselves to follow these "evangelical counsels" strictly were segregated into special organizations—the hierarchically organized, celibate priesthood, and especially the monastic orders—also tended to limit or neutralize these isolationist tendencies.

The hermits or monks of India, Egypt, or other countries desired to withdraw from the world and its temptations, to protect their ascetic self-mortification against the disturbing interference of the normal life of normal people. The mystics among them particularly sought solitude in order to be alone each with his God so that he could surrender to his numinous experience without profane disturbances. This numinous experience, as in mysticism properly speaking, is purely internal and springs from the depths of the soul. God, however, can also reveal himself in nature, the divine can also speak from nature and through nature to a human being who confronts her in a collected and receptive spirit.

This revelation in the solitude of nature, of the landscape, finds its representation in Christian art in the pictorial theme of John of Patmos, which found its first classic treatment in Wolf Huber (1490-1557). In painting and graphic arts, pure landscape without accessories represents a relatively rare and late development of the modern era; originally it was directly connected with the sociological condition of solitude. The hermit or solitary individual, that is to say, can either be represented in the picture itself, or he can be the viewer who contemplates the picture in solitary concentration.

The development traced here, as so many others, was first interrupted by the Reformation and Counter Reformation, and not resumed again until the nineteenth century, by such painters as Caspar David Friedrich and Vincent van Gogh.

In the literary sphere, however, a gradual transition from theo-logico-religious to emotional-secular flight into the solitude of na-ture begins somewhat earlier. It was already prepared, for instance, by Petrarch in his beloved Vaucluse springs, "procul ab hominibus, non ab humanitate alienus"—far from human beings but not es-tranged from humanity. Poets, like mystics but with less emphasis on churchly or ecclesiastic themes, begin to seek in the contempla-tion of landscape the revelation first of the divine, then of the divine in nature, and then of nature itself.

The role of this prized solitude, with its original religious and later secular sentimental emphasis, began to converge in Europe from the mid-eighteenth century with a new attitude to nature flow-ing from quite different sources.

The first of these converging trends originated in the struggle of salvation religions against natural and organic social bonds, from their effort to separate man from these bonds so as to secure, as it were, a monopoly for their new form of religious integration; yet the very intensity of this struggle testifies to the unimpaired vitality and strength of those natural social bonds. Religion was forced to expend strenuous efforts to tear people away from them and toward itself.

But with the advent of the second trend all this was radically changed: Men now sought solitude because they no longer felt shel-tered, secure, or embedded in the community, because they were faced with tensions and dissonances, from which they sought flight into the solitude of nature.

The result is a totally different feeling for nature. Whereas for-merly man felt at home in nature after it had been tamed and mas-tered by man, now man conversely began to seek out the wildness and grandeur of untamed, untouched nature.

As the traditional community further decays, one no longer needs to fly from it to be alone. One feels oneself alone and forsaken; one carries one's loneliness around like an inescapable fate, and one senses that loneliness all the more keenly when one is among people. This feeling of fated involuntary loneliness, then, is nothing but a consciousness of the decay of those social structures from which men earlier had fled into voluntary solitude. Henceforth vol-untary outward loneliness is only an expression of the inward state of individual isolation, and outward and inward loneliness begin to reinforce each other in a fatal spiral: "He who gives himself to lone-liness, alas, he is soon alone" (Goethe).

The flight from loneliness into isolation has a very peculiar social-psychological structure. To avoid people by whom one feels rejected or misunderstood is a readily understandable instinctive reaction; but it is an essentially negative act. "Voluntary isolation, keeping oneself aloof from other people, is the readiest safeguard against the suffering which may come upon one from human relationships."[47] But since man, as a naturally social animal, cannot endure isolation, he soon turns to nature as a consolation and substitute. From the company of men, untrue and incapable of understanding, he throws himself into the "bosom of nature," certain that here no falseness or disloyalty need be expected.

Our attitude to nature, however, is essentially conditioned by society. Our feelings toward nature are mostly feelings transferred from the human to the natural environment. In ancient mythology, one imagines nature peopled by beings in human form; this projection is evident in expressions like "the bosom of nature"; but some such projection is probably always present. Disappointed by human beings, man turns to nature, projects onto her feelings and expectations originally attached to human beings or aroused by human beings. These feelings, however, can only be sustained by reciprocity, and only human beings are capable of such reciprocity; thus the lonely individual in his flight into nature, who first experiences social feelings in such abundance that he manages to squander them on surrounding nature, sooner or later will have exhausted his store of such feelings and will come up against the sobering realization that "nature is unfeeling." "Heaven and earth have no love of man. For them every organism is but a wisp"—as we read in an ancient Chinese philosopher.[48]

Those human beings who feel lonely in the midst of people still have a way out—the flight into nature. But there is no longer any escape from loneliness in the midst of nature, from loneliness in the cosmos as a whole. The end result is a feeling of absolute, irrevocable, and inescapable isolation.

Of the far-reaching intellectual, social, political, and economic changes that contributed to this novel phenomenon of cosmic loneliness, the most notable change in the intellectual sphere has been the decline of common valuations. This process has been reinforced, from the economic side, by the proletarianization and urbanization that accompanied the Industrial Revolution. It tore people out of the organic context of peasant and artisan life and herded them instead into settings that were as massive and cramped as they were unnatural and unorganic. The English moralist Adam Ferguson (1723-1816) recognized at an early date "that the division of labor in its

most extreme effects threatens to tear apart the bonds of society."[49]
The result was that the decline of all traditional bonds, that atomization, bleak isolation, and loneliness of every individual among his
fellows that so often has been deplored as the most fearful malaise of
the nineteenth century. But we must not forget that even social
proximity has an optimum limit far short of the maximum, an optimum brilliantly defined by Kant as an "unsocial sociability" and
described in Schopenhauer's parable of the porcupine.[50] Once the
traditional sense of this natural optimal distance is lost, it is extraordinarily difficult to restore it. The result is a pathological oscillation between too great a distance and too great a proximity, between underintegration and overintegration.

Rousseau (1712-1778), whose hypersensitivity in this regard
drove him to the brink of paranoia, already perceived the beginnings of this degeneracy and decay in the middle of the eighteenth
century: "All, with a pretty varnish of words, try vainly to put a
false scent on their real aim; nobody deceives himself and nobody is
the dupe of others, although all speak like him. All seek their happiness in appearance. Nobody concerns himself with reality. All
place their being in appearance; all, slaves and dupes of vanity, do
not at all live in order to live, but to beget the belief that they have
lived."[51]

Similarly Goethe's Werther suffers not only from individual un-
happiness in love but also from a more general disturbance of his
social relations: "To be misunderstood is the fate of the likes of me."
"I play along, or rather I am being played like a puppet. And at
times I grab my neighbor's wooden hand and draw back with a
shudder." In 1810, almost four decades after *Werther*, and with the
period of *Sturm und Drang* and Wertherian world-weariness far behind him, Goethe still could write, in a philosophical passage of his
Theory of Colors: "Never perhaps have individuals been more isolated and separated from each other than at present."[52]

Such passages supply vivid descriptions of a general and objective
sociological process perceived through the heightened subjective
sensibility of a Rousseau or a Werther.

Edmund Burke (1729-1797) predicted in 1790 that under the influence of Rousseau and of the French Revolution "the commonwealth itself would, in a few generations, be disconnected into the
dust and powder of individuality, and at length dispersed to all
winds of heaven."[53] And Friedrich Engels (1820-1895), in *The Condition of the Working Class in England* (1845), describes contemporary London as follows: "The dissolution of mankind into monads, of

which each one has a separate principle, the world of atoms, is here carried out to its utmost extreme."[54]

This theme came to be reiterated with increasing frequency, for example by Nietzsche in 1874 in the face of the frantic economic boom of the 1870s: "We live in the period of the atom, of atomistic chaos."[55] And Dostoevski (1821-1881) states that "men are lonely, silence surrounds them: that is the world." Yet he shows awareness of the ephemeral, historically conditioned character of this phenomenon of social pathology. In the recollections of Starets Sossima, which form the philosophic center of *The Brothers Karamazov*, he has the mysterious guest say:

"But first we have to go through the period of isolation."
"What do you mean by isolation?" I asked him.
"Why, the isolation that prevails everywhere, above all in our age—it has not reached its limit yet. For everyone strives to keep his individuality as apart as possible, wishes to secure the greatest possible fullness of life for himself; but meantime all his efforts result not in attaining fullness of life, but self-destruction, for instead of self-realization he ends by arriving at complete solitude. . . . Everywhere in these days men have, in their mockery, ceased to understand that the true security is to be found in social solidarity rather than in isolated individual effort. But his terrible individualism must inevitably have an end, and all will suddenly understand how unnaturally they are separated from one another. It will be the spirit of the time, and people will marvel that they have sat so long in darkness without seeing the light."[56]

The same feeling still is echoed in the neoromantic poetry of Hermann Hesse:

Truly none is wise
Who knows not the darkness,
That inescapably and softly
Separates him from all . . .

Odd, to wander in the fog!
To live is to be alone.
No human knows the other,
Each one is alone.

Toward the middle of the nineteenth century, atomization reached into the family, and the acute suffering caused by this state of affairs became a major theme of the bourgeois realistic novel, especially those of Gustave Flaubert. In *Madame Bovary* (1857) he describes a luncheon scene between the heroine and her husband that Erich Auerbach has analyzed as follows: "Each of them is so immersed in his own world—she in despair and vague wish-dreams, he in his stupid philistine self-complacency—that they are both entirely alone: they have nothing in common, and yet they have nothing of their own, for the sake of which it would be worthwhile to be lonely. For, privately, each of them has a silly, false world, which cannot be reconciled with the reality of his situation, and so they both miss the possibilities life offers them."

This condition of silliness, or as Flaubert calls it, *la bêtise humaine*, consists in the fact that "each of the many mediocre people" appearing in his novels

has his own world of mediocre and silly stupidity, a world of illusions, habits, instincts, and slogans; each is alone, none can understand another, or help another to insight; there is no common world of men, because it could only come into existence if many should find their way to their own proper reality, the reality which is given to the individual—which then would be also the true common reality. Though men come together for business and pleasure, their coming together has no note of united activity; it becomes one-sided, ridiculous, painful, and it is charged with misunderstanding, vanity, futility, falsehood, and stupid hatred. But what the world would really be, the world of the "intelligent," Flaubert never tells us; in his book the world consists of pure stupidity, which completely misses true reality, so that the latter should properly not be discoverable in it at all; yet it is there. . . ."[57]

To the extent that novelists were not intent upon objectivity in the same degree as Flaubert, and, instead, sided with their heroines, the result was the character of the "misunderstood woman," who abounded in novels, short stories, and plays of the nineteenth century. Droves of misunderstood (and not sufficiently busy) women also constituted the principal readership of those novels, which address themselves directly to the personal situation and problems of their audience. Millions of Emma Bovarys imagined themselves to be interesting, demonic, tragic, and pitiable, when they read of their own fate over and over in varying versions.

The "misunderstood genius"—or, in the characteristic German phrase, "das verkannte Genie"—was another common feature of the nineteenth century, based on a corresponding sociological situation. At the beginning of the century Goethe was fully aware of the novelty and ephemeral character of this phenomenon. On 13 July 1802 he wrote to his friend Zelter: "It is very bad *in our day* that every art, which first of all should work only for the living, insofar as it is competent and worthy of eternity is in conflict with the age, and that the genuine artist *often lives alone in despair*: he is convinced that he possesses and could communicate that which men seek" [my italics]. In the prevailing opinion of the late nineteenth century, however, lack of appreciation, lifelong or at least temporary, becomes the very hallmark of true genius. The social pathology and ephemeral nature of this phenomenon by then were so little understood that Albert Schweitzer, in his famous biography, feels compelled to defend Johann Sebastian Bach for *not* being misunderstood: "If it is one of the signs of the great creative artist, born before his time, that he waits for 'his day,' and wears himself out in waiting, then was Bach neither great nor born before his time."[58]

C. G. Jung gives an interesting, introspective portrayal of the underlying ideal type of the modern man in his lecture "Modern Man in Search of a Soul," first published in 1928:

The man whom we can with justice call "modern" is solitary. He is so of necessity and at all times, for every step towards a fuller consciousness of the present removes him further from his original *"participation mystique"* with the mass of men—from submersion in a common unconsciousness. Every step forward means an act of tearing himself loose from that all-embracing, pristine unconsciousness which claims the bulk of mankind almost entirely. Even in our civilizations the people who form, psychologically speaking, the lowest stratum, live almost as unconsciously as primitive races. Those of the succeeding stratum manifest a level of consciousness which corresponds to the beginnings of human culture, while those of the highest stratum have a consciousness capable of keeping step with the life of the last few centuries. Only the man who is modern in our meaning of the term really lives in the present; he alone has a present-day consciousness, and he alone finds that the ways of life which correspond to earlier levels pall upon him. The values and strivings of those past worlds no longer interest him save from the historical standpoint. Thus he has become "unhistorical" in the deepest sense and has estranged himself from the mass of men who live entirely within the bounds of tradition. Indeed, he is completely modern only when he has come to the very edge of the world, leaving behind him all that has been discarded and outgrown, and acknowledging that he stands before a void out of which all things may grow. . . . It cannot be helped; the "modern" man is questionable and suspect, and has always been so, even in the past.[59]

Also characteristic of the nineteenth century is the emergence of vanity in males—a trait of which one might have assumed that they stood least in need. Vanity is an introversion of the need for social recognition, a self-satisfaction of the drive toward self-assertion, a sterile substitute for external success. It can be found in coquettish women, success-greedy diplomats, actors and others in whom beauty or dramatic talent falls short of the individual's exaggerated expectations. The fact, however, that prominent men in serious intellectual vocations have succumbed to it is a peculiarity of the nineteenth century; it can be explained as a disturbance of the social structure by which a permanent qualitative need can no longer be fulfilled by any quantity externally supplied. Here are a few striking examples from the beginning and end of the nineteenth century. The great jurist Friedrich Karl von Savigny (1779-1861) was said not to pass by a puddle without looking at his reflection in it; similar anecdotes are related about August Wilhelm von Schlegel (1767-1845). And Henrik Ibsen (1828-1906) had a built-in mirror at the bottom of his top hat so that he could admire himself at will.

Other exaggerated conceptions of "genius" also belong in the same context. Thus Balzac's spectral professional swindler, the struttingly ostentatious airs assumed by Richard Wagner, Nietzsche's god-roles as Zarathustra, Dionysus, Christ—turning at last into madness—were in the final analysis so many exaggerated compensations for that peaceful, solid, and secure social context for which they thirsted in vain.

It is no coincidence that both Goethe's Werther and Flaubert's Madame Bovary end in suicide. The sociological causes of suicide have been subjected to a thorough scientific investigation by the founder of modern French sociology, Emile Durkheim (1858-1917) and by his pupil Maurice Halbwachs. They have come up with the finding that one of the principal causes behind the alarming suicide rates is the "désencadrement des individus," the same phenomenon that we have called the isolation of the individual. Man, as we have known since Aristotle, is a social animal; he needs community more than he does daily bread, and where this sense of community is lacking or uncertain the most trivial incident suffices to persuade him that life is no longer worth living: "The true cause of suicide is the void that has been created around the person who has committed suicide; if there were no lacunae of this kind, there would be no suicides."[60]

When a human being finds himself in a situation which runs counter to the needs of his nature and which he therefore experiences as barely tolerable, when he sees no way to change or improve this situation by practical action, but rather sees himself reduced to coping with it by purely intellectual, ideological reflection, then the transposition of his situation into an absolute metaphysical realm suggests itself as one possible solution. If I can convince myself that this situation in truth is the common, necessary, and inescapable fate of all human beings; that all men always and everywhere have been in this situation but have only deceived themselves about its true nature; and that the particularity of our own situation is merely that it no longer permits such self-deception—then there is no longer any sense in lamenting our misfortune. At most one can then be grateful to fate for having forced one to face this final truth and feel oneself superior to all those others who lack such courage and fortitude and hence persist in closing their eyes to this tragic reality.

Arthur Schopenhauer (1788-1860) was the first to apply this metaphysical absolutism to the despair felt by men in the nineteenth century at the pathological disturbance of the social environment. As a passionate protest against the optimism of progress which was so close to the nineteenth-century surface, Schopenhauer's pessimism was to remain throughout the nineteenth century the shibboleth of all far-seeing, discontented thinkers who found themselves in fundamental opposition to their intellectual environment. All the more so since Schopenhauer, although addicted to orientalizing Gnosticism and romanticism, cultivated the tradition of German classicism with a great sense of responsibility and with intense love—an attitude that caused him to be revered by minds as far apart as Jacob Burckhardt, Richard Wagner, and Friedrich Nietzsche.

The feeling of atomization that marked the nineteenth century found its most passionate, deepest, and broadest expression in Søren Kierkegaard (1813-1855). By profession, Kierkegaard was a Protestant theologian who was inclined to subjective radicalism. And now the two lines of intellectual development that we have traced separately dramatically meet: on the one hand, the tendency of Christianity, as a religion of salvation, to detach man from all mundane, secular, and natural bonds in order to place him in a direct or "absolute" relation to God; and on the other, that sociological and sociopsychological development which led to destruction of natural social bonds in external social reality. Hence Kierkegaard's anguished question: "Where am I? . . . Who is it that has lured me into the thing; and now leaves me there? Who am I? How did I come into the world? Why was I not consulted, why not made acquainted with its manners and customs but was thrust into the ranks as though I had been bought of a 'soul-seller!' How did I obtain an interest in this enterprise they call reality? Why should I have an interest in it? Is it not a voluntary concern?"[61] Here we encounter the anguish of boredom, fear, despair, from which when every solid ground shakes underfoot, the only escape is the headlong leap into the abyss of the divine, the abyss of grace, as the only salvation. And it is this plunge that Kierkegaard invites us to execute. Luther already used this simile of the leap "into the abyss, where there is no feeling, nor seeing, nor footing, but rather, where one is suspended freely on the strength of God's counsel and support."[62] And similar themes recur in theology from Pascal to Karl Barth.

When Adolph Jülicher declares Barth's theology to be the "hybris of a pneumatic," one must remember that every new theology is thus experienced by every old one. According to Barth's own courageous utterance, theology here reappears, with penetrating spontaneity, as a "misfortune that breaks in over certain men."[63]

Kierkegaard, with his passionate and brilliant formulation of atomization, thus has become the founding hero of existentialist philosophy; for "anxiety about existence may be understood as a concern about salvation." According to Martin Buber, "Kierkegaard's philosophic secularization," which "cut off the relation to the absolute, for the sake of which Kierkegaard's man becomes a solitary individual, . . . signifies the greatest decisive step from Kierkegaard toward the edge, where Nothingness begins."[64] And this step was taken by Martin Heidegger, whose nihilistic metaphysics of *Angst* reveals "Being as Nothingness," and man as the inhabitant of that Nothingness.

The existential kernel of existentialist philosophy is the social atomization of the nineteenth century, although the philosophers of this school show no awareness of the historical limits or conditions of this phenomenon. Seen in its intellectual and historical context, existentialism is metaphysics stood on its head. Instead of simply accepting his existence as he finds it, man proceeds from the arrogant illusion of absolute metaphysical necessity to the disillusionment of bottomless contingency—a somersault from hybris into despair. To the existentialist, as Jaspers has said, there is existence "only in relation to transcendence or not at all."[65]

This profound disillusionment of existentialism—this hangover in the first stage of sobering up from metaphysical intoxication—is most clearly expressed in Heidegger's French disciple, Jean-Paul Sartre, who has entitled one of his books *La Nausée*. Sartre represents the nihilistic sobering up after the overexcitement of the Resistance and the deep disenchantment with final victory, which was achieved with foreign assistance and thereby (oddly) led to a "second German invasion" in the intellectual sphere. In the symbolist play Huis Clos (Paris, 1944), he establishes the dictum that "Hell is other people" as the sociological quintessence of the human condition—a statement that could well have served as the motto for Flaubert's *Madame Bovary*.

Sartre, of course, has quite rightly protested against the misinterpretation of his existentialism as a "quietism of despair." Rather it is a question of an activism of despair, on the ground of excessive indeterminism and voluntarism driven beyond all bounds: "Man is but what he wills," "Man makes himself," "Man is nothing else but what he purposes," and "what he makes of himself," "Man is freedom," indeed "condemned to be free," "What counts is total commitment," "the total freedom of commitment."[66] From this "heroic morality of commitment in which . . . all meaning is placed in the unconditioned character of the effort as such," the way is not too long to that "type who takes orders in the heroic permanent tension of the preparedness for catastrophe"[67] characteristic of national socialism; in the long run, absolute freedom, which can be endured only with great difficulty, all too easily changes into an equally absolute readiness to follow.

Heidegger and Sartre were originally Catholics, and in Sartre existentialism has the flavor of a theology without God. In Sartre's essay "L'Existentialisme est un humanisme" (a highly misleading title), humanism is meant neither in the sense of an association with antiquity nor in the sense of humanity, but rather as a logical opposite to theism. And in that same essay, Sartre writes: "Existentialism is nothing else but an effort to draw the conclusions of a consistent atheist position." "It is existentialism's point of departure. In fact, everything is permitted if God does not exist"—the very standpoint set forth with an amazing naïveté by Dostoevski's freshly escaped seminarian in *The Brothers Karamazov*. Moreover, Sartre, the self-proclaimed humanist, confesses that "there is no human nature upon which I can rely."[68]

On the other hand, one great merit of existentialist philosophy lies in the fact that it posed anew, and with grim seriousness, the central ontological question of all philosophy—that inquiry into the position of man in the world, which before its advent had been nearly forgotten. Should this rediscovery of ontology by existentialism find a fruitful continuation, this achievement may well in historic retrospect come to outweigh all the negative aspects of existentialism.

The atomization and isolation of man is mirrored in the atomization of the outside world: when man as subject no longer feels meaningfully incorporated in the world, he sees the world of objects as no longer meaningfully interconnected. The visual arts are most directly suited to the representation of such a disconnected and meaningless world—as evident in surrealism, cubism, and contemporary abstract art.

Whereas the real world of Western man became ever more decomposed, meaningless, and ugly in the course of the nineteenth century, art conceived its mission as that of providing a counterweight by presenting the world as gaily, beautifully, and pleasurably as possible. As a result it slid into *kitsch*—superficial embellishment and trivialization. For artists of great integrity and honesty, like Beckmann, Kokoschka, Dix, and others the result was that the portrayal of ugliness was the path of honor—much as materialism was a reaction against idealist philosophy. Here, too, exaggeration in a positive direction changed into an understatement in a negative direction. Just as artists had once presented the world as too beautiful, now they presented it as too ugly, in a despairing, angry protest that it was not as beautiful and as meaningful as their imagination desired. Thus when Oskar Kokoschka (b. 1886), after the depth-psychology portraits of his early work, zealously applied his considerable talent and will to present the world as dismembered and meaningless, to portray people as ghostlike and grotesque as they appeared to him, he made no effort to conceal this mood of despair. "Omnia vana"—all is vain—is the inscription clearly legible on a lithograph of 1921, probably depicting the artist's father on his deathbed.

Cubism tried to produce geometric or pseudogeometric construction as a substitute for the arbitrary world and to substitute for it mathematical structures of a primitive form. If, however, art is to be not representative but abstract, there is indeed a sphere of visual art in which abstraction is the rule and has been legitimately established since ancient times: the sphere of ornamentation. Its realm extends from the lower levels of harmless decoration to the heights of numinous intellectuality. The art of ornament, of course, requires subordination to the laws of craftsmanship and technique, respect for traditional forms—in short, humility—and thus of course was dramatically opposed to the anarchist, nihilist, and revolutionary tendencies of the artist of this school.

With some of the imitators of these recent trends in art one might suspect that it was a lack of creative talent that drove them to sterile theorizing, arbitrariness, and violence. But in the work of an artist of undoubted fertility like Pablo Picasso (1881-1973) it is clear that he is under the spell of an overpowering ideological development. His painterly nihilism might appropriately be labeled existentialism on canvas: cosmic hangover in art.

It also would appear that some profound personal catastrophe prompted the abrupt transition from the moving human warmth of Picasso's pink and blue periods to the hatred of the world and contempt for men that dominated his work from the beginning of the so-called black period, when he painted "in order not to jump out of the window." This change of human attitude is far more significant than the change from one medium to another by which his works are commonly catalogued. Even his dionysian orgiastic paintings are gloomy and hostile to life; like Baudelaire in his *Fleurs du mal* he sings the flesh without loving it.

The same kind of despair no doubt drove Picasso into the arms of communism as the one and only salvation-bearing doctrine, in whose service, among other things, he executed the bobby-soxer-like mourning portrait of Stalin.

The aesthetic theorists and planners of German early romanticism had demanded an "ironic art" as something especially sublime, an art which through ironic distance achieves the highest standpoint from which to view the world and one's own ego. This program has been most concretely realized in the plastic arts by surrealism—a circumstance that clearly reveals its destructive, morbid, and decadent character.

Picasso's later art "is one of the most luxuriant blossoms from the flower of nihilism. Who would deny that the charm of these blossoms lies in their luxuriousness? It is, however, the charm of 'Nothingness,' of the *nihil*, nourished by the soil of 'everything is permitted.' . . . Once everything is permissible, freedom changes into anger, hate, sadism, every human quality into something bestial—and the experience of so much hideousness becomes the enjoyment of the same boundless (and therefore illusory) freedom with which this vicious circle began."[69]

When surrealism, like a "schizophrenic dismembering machine"[70] decomposes the constructive unity of the object of painting into a multiplicity of partial projection planes, that can be called "a method which dissolves reality into multiple and multivalent reflections of consciousness."[71] This last statement, by Erich Auerbach, refers however to the modern novel, which could also appropriately be called surrealistic. Since the novel, among all literary forms, possesses the greatest span and also is best suited to the presentation of more comprehensive interconnections, the dissolution of such interconnections expresses itself most strikingly within literature. And what Auerbach states further about this genre of modern novels holds true exactly in the same way also for the corresponding works of modern painting. All these works of art "which employ multiple reflections of consciousness" engender "an impression of hopelessness. There is often something confusing, something hazy about them, something hostile to the reality which they represent. We not infrequently find a turning away from the practical will to live, or delight in portraying it under the most brutal forms. There is hatred of culture and civilization, brought out by means of the subtlest stylistic devices which culture and civilization have developed, and often a radical and fanatical urge to destroy."[72]

Besides the effect of alcohol, there are, in real life, two other phenomena which show a dissolution of otherwise meaningful interconnections—the babbling of a child and the dream. The babbling of a child as he plays with self-formed sounds or with scraps of words has served Dadaism as a model which in its imitation rejects the compulsion of tradition, of our thought and speech, experienced by it as burdensome, in consequence of which it snaps its fingers at it.

The dream, especially the anxiety-dream, transports us into a world whose components are the same as those of our everyday world but in which these individual features of reality are detached from their lawful and meaningful, calculable and comprehensible interconnections and are combined with each other in an unreal way, thus making possible highly suggestive or threatening interconnections. This model has been espoused by one of the earliest and most important representatives of surrealism: what Franz Kafka (1883-1924) presents in the brilliant simplicity of his language and with tormenting vividness is a nightmarish world enveloped in the

aura of a sublime, perverse religiosity. In an autobiographical retrospect to the year 1920, Kafka indicates that it was as his "most
important and most stimulating desire to attain a view of life (and
. . . to be able to convince others of it in writing) in which life of
course would preserve its grievous ups and downs, but which at the
same time could be recognized with no less clearness as a Nothingness, as a dream, as a floating." At the same time he had no illusions
that this desire, in reality, can be "only a defense, a bourgeoisifica-
tion of Nothingness," "a breath of cheerfulness which he wanted to
give to Nothingness . . . which he . . . felt as his element."[73]

A further difference between plastic art and literature rests upon
the special nature of language and linguistic thought. Plastic art, on
its way toward dismemberment, need not (as does surrealism) stop
at representing recognizable fragments—at the molecules as it
were—of connected reality; instead, it can go back to wholly disconnected and purely abstract atoms of mere lines, points, and color-
specks, which no longer represent anything. In contrast, literature
(if it refuses to relapse into the subliterary infantilism of Dada)
must insure that each one of the fragments yields a comprehensible
and somehow interesting meaning. Even the joining of parts, as in
painting, cannot be accomplished mechanically by the mere fact
that a number of pictorial surfaces coexist within the same frame. In
a literary work the assembling must establish some kind of context,
meaning and unity, however disaggregated.

In modern literature, according to Auerbach, a retrogression took
place to "the wealth of reality and the depth of life in every moment
to which we surrender ourselves without prejudice." This retrogression began with Marcel Proust and was continued by James Joyce,
Virginia Woolf, and others. Yet such a "random moment . . . is comparatively independent of the controversial and unstable orders
over which men fight and despair; it passes unaffected by them, as
daily life. The more it is exploited, the more the elementary things
which our lives have in common come to light."[74]

That assertion turns out to be true, but the question is to what
extent we can draw an effective consolation therefrom. Two houses
may be quite different in ground plan, construction, and style, but if
we dismantle both and stack the loose stones in adjoining piles, all
essential differences will disappear. Whether that can be understood as productive and as a promising reciprocal approximation,
seems to be questionable. Or, to remain within our image, at most, if
both houses were to be rebuilt in a uniform style and in architectural forms harmonizing with each other, such harmony of architec-

tural forms would by no means be assured by the sameness of the building stones and would in no way grow out of it. This would require corresponding designs and building plans. There is no intellectual-historical primordial process of generation through which ruins can arrange themselves together by themselves into new form. Only a superordinated will to form can put together anew, and form can arise only from form, new form from the recasting and elaboration of old forms. This applies in general and fundamentally to all the negativistic tendencies under discussion here. The anarchistic motto, pursuant to which the urge to destroy is a creative urge, is a diabolic distortion of truth.

Despite these fundamental objections it would be incorrect and unfair to judge the tendencies dealt with here only negatively. Common to all of them is the central importance which the decline of ethical values and atomization of society hold for them—the fact that they take these phenomena seriously and choose them as a point of departure. Since these phenomena actually dominate the pathological picture of today, and all the more that of yesterday, a clear and unflinching look into this unpleasant state of affairs is the first and foremost requisite for objective honesty, and as such far from being a just cause for reproach. But this point of departure can lead to a variety of very different tendencies.

Social disintegration and the isolation of the individual may shock us, and we may give expression to this sense of shock in stronger or milder terms. We may denounce as cowardly or smug all those superficial attitudes that seek to deny, dilute, or conceal this condition. Such a sense of shock may simply be expressed in a cry of outrage without regard for the consequences—a kind of nihilistic expressionism—and such revelatory and unmasking expressionism can become intoxicated with its own power of expression, thus creating a situation where he who would point out the depth of the abyss to others is himself seized by vertigo and plunges below: in fact, we sometimes get the impression of a spiritual suicide. Not far from it lies the maxim that one should still kick at whatever is fallen or about to fall. And that again, out of hatred for established values or a deep sense of resentment, can be accompanied by a desire for revenge, by a malicious joy in the misfortunes of others, or by mockery, and finally degenerate into a negativistic vandalism, indeed into a hatred of the world and true nihilism, to which, in Mephistophelian fashion, everything that exists is worthy only of destruction.

We can savor the feeling of superiority derived from seeing, like

Ecclesiastes, that all is vanity and hence to be depreciated and looked down upon. And such a feeling of superiority can be heightened further when one manages to carry it off with the superior assurances of the expert floating high above all difficult philosophic or artistic manipulations in a kind of intellectual tightrope walking above the abyss. We can adroitly and successfully chime in with the negativistic mood of the time. We can, disenchanted, wearied, revolted, give up the game and profess defeatism. We can welcome the decline and the self-destruction of this world because we champion another one that is altogether different and opposed to it, whether it be in the Beyond, or in the future (the secularization of the Beyond).

But even those who are altogether free of such negativisms may be convinced, precisely on the basis of their positive orientation, that the evil is already beyond an easy cure; that therefore a complete, exact, and pitiless diagnosis is the most immediate imperative, and that the only treatment still promising success is a radical surgical operation laying bare all the diseased parts and—through negative valuation—morally excising them. When such a negation in the service of positive advocacy takes its standpoint not outside but within this given real world and sets as its goal not its destruction but its restoration to health, it is difficult to raise any fundamental objection to it. Wherever we come upon this attitude we should welcome it.

Once we become fully aware of the historically conditioned character of the phenomenon of individual isolation in all its varieties, and have clearly identified its specific historic antecedents, we can take comfort in the conclusion that conditions that have not always obtained in the past need not always obtain in the future. More specifically we can derive from such a diagnosis and etiology a set of therapeutic prescriptions that will combat what has been laid bare as the causes of this social pathology. A critique of culture that would be radical—that is, would go to the roots—can only be based on the discovery in history of these same roots. And from such a vantage point we can perhaps give a more confident answer to Nietzsche's skeptical question as to the "Nutzen der Historie für das Leben"—the use of historiography in human life.

8. MASS SOCIETY

The same process that in individuals takes the form of isolation and loneliness manifests itself socially as the tendency toward mass society (massification). A large number of isolated and lonely individuals become lonely because they are no longer surrounded by a supportive community and instead stand only within the cold frame of mechanical social relations; in short, they become a mere mass.

Rapid population increase and accelerated technical progress have, since the industrial revolution, led to intensified industrialization and urbanization, and a corresponding aggravation of all social problems. They also have contributed to that intoxication with progress and that mania for setting records that are among the most characteristic intellectual symptoms of the pathology of the nineteenth century, and which like a feverish euphoria mask all other symptoms of the disease.

The modern large city is the huge retort in which ever-increasing isolation of the individual and the transformation from articulated community into structureless mass take place.

Against those communist and socialist worshippers of progress who are ready to dismiss any negative judgment of the phenomena of massification in large cities as reactionary and sentimental romanticism, we can invoke no less an authority than Friedrich Engels, the friend of Karl Marx and coauthor of the *Communist Manifesto*. In *The Condition of the Working Class in England* section titled "The Great Towns" contains the following passage:

A town, such as London, where a man may wander for hours together without reaching the beginning of the end, without meeting the slightest hint which could lead to the inference that there is open country within reach, is a strange thing. This colossal centralization, this heaping together of two and a half millions of human beings at one point, has multiplied the power of this two and a half millions a hundredfold; . . . all this is so vast, so impressive, that a man cannot collect himself. . . .

But the sacrifices which all this has cost become apparent later. After roaming the streets of the capital a day or two . . . one realizes for the first time that these Londoners have been forced to sacrifice the best qualities of their human nature, to bring to pass all the marvels of civilization which crowd their city. . . . The very turmoil of the streets has something repulsive, something against which human nature rebels. The hundreds of thousands of all classes and ranks crowding past each other, are they not all human beings with the same qualities and powers, and with the same interest in being happy? And have they not, in the end, to seek happiness in the same way, by the same means? And still they crowd by one another as though they had nothing in common. . . . And, however much one may be aware that this isolation of the individual, this narrow self-seeking is the fundamental principle of our society everywhere, it is nowhere so shamelessly barefaced, so self-conscious as just here in the crowding of the great city. The dissolution of mankind into monads, of which each has a separate principle, is here carried out to its utmost extreme.

Hence it comes, too, that the social war, the war of each against all, is here openly declared. . . . Each exploits the other, and the end of it all is, that the stronger treads the weaker under foot, and that the powerful few, the capitalists, seize everything for themselves, while to the weak many, the poor, scarcely a bare existence remains.

What is true of London, is true . . . of all great towns. Everywhere barbarous indifference, hard egotism on the one hand, and nameless misery on the other, everywhere social warfare, every man's house in a state of siege, everywhere reciprocal plundering under the protection of the law, and all so shameless, so openly avowed that one shrinks before the consequences of our social state as they manifest themselves here undisguised, and can only wonder that the whole crazy fabric still hangs together.[75]

The very act of migration from the country to the city signifies, as a rule, a detachment from soil and hereditary possession, from the community of the family, clan, village, and region. The migrant's incorporation in the occupational structure of the city is in most cases precarious. Anyone who does not fit into this external and superficial framework falls not on arable soil where he can strike new roots, but on hard asphalt.

Aristotle, in prescribing that a city should never become so large that the inhabitants no longer know each other personally, identifies a minimal condition of human community. Mass society develops as soon as the individual no longer lives his life in such a known compass, as soon as he no longer personally knows the fellow citizens with whom he has to deal.

"The large city is inhabited by many free persons who are always in contact with each other . . . without a community and a communal will emerging among them. . . . Nowhere else," writes Hellpach, "are so many people outwardly so close and inwardly so distant."[76] The perfect symbol of this situation is the crowded streetcar or subway, where complete strangers are pressed into bodily contact of such closeness as would otherwise correspond only to the most intimate erotic relations.

A growing child first experiences mass society at school, where he is suddenly separated from parents, brothers, and sisters to be locked in an alien building with a crowd of strange contemporaries and equally strange teachers.

A symptom of the development of a mass society—a symptom that has come readily to be taken for granted—is the freedom to move about and to settle, the unlimited right to establish one's residence, which normally today any citizen enjoys throughout the territory of his nation-state. In reality, however, this freedom of domicile is a recent historic phenomenon, which in Prussia, for example, was established as recently as 1831-1842.

The failure of the reform of Prussian local government undertaken a generation earlier by Baron vom Stein ultimately was due in some measure to this very circumstance—that as a result of the proclamation of the general freedom of movement and settlement communities no longer could determine their membership. How could a purely residential community whose composition is left to chance assert itself as an organic and truly self-governing entity?

The self-evident and unavoidable prerequisite for any social group with a communal character is that a new member can enter it only with the approval of those already belonging to it. Once this right of co-optation is abolished and a village community must tolerate the immigration of any stranger, its communal character is destroyed and it is transformed into a mere society.

The sociological result toward which all these tendencies and processes converge is that state of atomized leveling which we call *mass*, that enormous "massification" of Western peoples, the consequences of which we now face. The area of all Western nation-states today is covered with a thicker or thinner layer of dust of sandlike sociological consistency—that is, by an accumulation of individuals more or less detached from organic social bonds.

The laws of this pathological social situation of massification and of its pseudointegration have been thoroughly studied by social psychology and sociology for a half century, in most cases with reference to its more acute form, such as the formation of crowds and the behavior of mobs and mass rallies. The topic here under discussion is this same condition of social malaise in its chronic form.

Nowhere has this chronic tendency toward mass society seized an entire population. Rather, it has at first been limited only to urban and metropolitan areas, which geographically account for only a small (if growing) fraction of the territory. But this urban segment dominates the whole of national life, concentrates within itself almost all political activity effective in the short term, and thus imparts this character to the whole. According to Tönnies, "The more general the condition of *Gesellschaft* becomes in the nation or a group of nations, the more this entire 'country' or the entire 'world' begins to resemble one large city."[77]

Scholarly investigations of the phenomenon of the mass began only toward the turn of the century. Significantly, the first entries came from the Latin countries of Europe: a study by the Italian criminologist Scipio Sighele entitled *The Psychology of the Crowd and of Mass Crimes*, and one by Gabriel Tarde on *Les Crimes des foules* (both 1892), followed by Gustave Le Bon's *Psychologie des foules* (1895). The latter work, published in all languages and in many editions, long dominated the literature.

Let it be noted in passing that the French word *foule* ("crowd," "mob") has a more dynamic connotation, whereas the German equivalent *Masse* [here translated "mass"] is a set of more diffuse, latent, or static relationships. To form a mass in the sense here intended, its component individuals must stand in some relationship to each other, must at least be aware of one another's existence. Yet these relationships do not attain the warmth or closeness of family ties, friendship, or erotic relationships. Rather, they are of a loose, cool, abstract and strictly utilitarian character—like those between passengers on a trolley car, the tenants in an apartment house, or the inhabitants of a modern large city or state in general.

At the same time these relations, generally viewed as loose and cool, can become quite heated as the result of extraordinary events—e.g., during a natural disaster, at a political mass rally, at the outbreak of a revolt or of an international conflict. Usually there is minimal and weak connection among the component individuals of the mass—a condition of underintegration; but under such special circumstances the mass can be converted to a state of psychological overintegration. The chronic underintegration and acute overintegration, though opposites in appearance, partake of the same basic social pathology, and it is for this very reason that one condition can so readily and suddenly succeed the other.

It is a special characteristic of totalitarianism that it strives to destroy all social bonds independent of the totalitarian movement, thereby creating an extreme state of underintegration—which, through its claimed monopoly on all processes of social integration it then proceeds to convert into its own pathological version of overintegration.

However, since these violent overintegrations engendered through terror, intimidation, mass suggestion, mass enthusiasm and mass hate actually have transitory character, one of the greatest difficulties besetting totalitarianism is that of artificially preventing a slackening or cooling off of these heated states of mind through ever new and, if possible, intensified incitement.

The conceptual analysis here employed implies that there is an optimum condition between under- and overintegration, between too little and too much integration. Obviously, under different circumstances this optimum condition can assume different configurations and itself covers a sizable spectrum. To identify this optimal range would be one of the most important tasks of the social science—and the anthropology—of the future.

Sociological theories of the mass, as we saw, were first formulated by scholars who took a critical and negative view of their subject. To Sighele, a student of the psychology of crime, mass phenomena were obviously a matter for the penal code. But even Le Bon, whose book was to dominate the field internationally for decades, dealt with revolutionary mass excesses, whose prosecution by the penal code was prevented only by their success; as René König has strikingly observed, Le Bon reflects "the ethos of the counterrevolution."[78] And Ortega y Gasset (1883-1955), who since the publication of his *Revolt of the Masses* (1930) has increasingly replaced Le Bon's influence, is an outspoken aristocratic "reactionary" of the bilious-brilliant sort, not free from literary snobbism.

In the interval between Le Bon and Ortega, Ferdinand Tönnies's closely related conceptualization—namely the polarity "community and society" (*Gemeinschaft* and *Gesellschaft*)—became widely accepted. When it was first published in 1887 Tönnies's *Gemeinschaft und Gesellschaft* was almost totally ignored. "In its ponderous vocabulary and syntax it reads more like a seventeenth-century treatise of the school of Spinoza and Hobbes,"[79] overlaid with cumbrous, archaic style and conceptualization. Tönnies, indeed, has acquired great merit as an interpreter and editor of Hobbes, and he received his philosophic training in the Marburg school of Neo-Kantianism. In politics, he was a member of the German Social Democratic party; and his partisanship in favor of *Gemeinschaft*, though often unacknowledged, is obvious enough to class him as a romantic. Full of such contradictory elements, his book has remained difficult to digest, and it acquired a very restricted influence. But then it got caught in a sudden, unanticipated change.

The German youth movement, in progress after the turn of the century, which felt an ardent need for common and explicit goals, enthusiastically seized upon the phrase "community versus society." Held to be an expression of "enthusiasm for community hostile to society"[80] the phrase became the central and most stirring slogan of the movement. Helmuth Plessner rightly called "the German youth movement of the Wandervogel" an "attempt to break out of society."[81] Many of its members thus felt impelled to buy Tönnies's book—which accounts for its running into eight editions between 1912 and 1935.

These two currents, the romantic criticism of the masses and the youth movement's romantic enthusiasm for community, combined and thus exercised a considerable influence within German sociology: in Gerhard Colm's article "Mass" in the German *Encyclopedia of Sociology* (1931) there is an explicit and well-balanced synthesis between Tönnies's concept of community, expressed in the emotional tonality of the youth movement, and the dynamic concept of the masses. To be sure, Colm, a socialist, felt obliged despite his treatment of the mass as a "so-to-speak 'pathological' structure" to recognize that "the courage, indifferent to any self-consideration, which is often found in the mass, led to the observation that it is also capable of the loftiest moral accomplishments." "The action of the mass appears as a warning signal of history."[82] The observation found confirmation in the events in Hungary in 1956, as elevating as they were tragic, and in a certain degree through their prelude, the uprising in the German Soviet zone of occupation in June 1953.

In view of the strong influence which this combined attitude of criticism of the masses with a championing of community exercised in Germany for a half century, we can only wonder that opposition to it was so long in forming.

Walter Hegemann probably goes farthest in this opposition. His book, although its subtitle announces a very general "contribution to the psychology of public opinion," contained the challenging main title *Of the Myth of the Mass*. Hegemann speaks of "the so-called mass" and counsels that the "last and decisive step to be taken . . . is to do away unhesitatingly with this thoroughly discredited concept."[83]

Helmut Schelsky, in a similar vein, poses the question "Is the big-city dweller really lonesome?"[84] Under this title, as a small sociologic prime example, he gives a highly impressive portrayal of the way the educated and affluent big-city dweller has been able to adjust himself to the pathological life situation of the big city in an elegant way. In "praise of the big city," he observes that "in the life of the big-city dweller work has become increasingly nonpersonal, but leisure time increasingly more personal, and that the ensuing abyss between the two spheres of the large city . . . is overcome not only in clear temporal demarcations but also as a border of spatial life-spheres in the big city. . . . The more impersonal human relations become in the work sphere and the more personal and individual and elective they become in the sphere of leisure time, the more pleasurably does man experience them today. Thus, the big city today increasingly becomes modern man's *optimal setting*, that in which he feels at home and which he prefers to small city or village life, which laid many more burdens upon him. . . . The native big-city dweller has for so long *adapted* . . . to big-city life in the deeper psychological layers of his being that cramped social relations with their intrusive human closeness, where everyone is interested in everything and everyone knows about everyone else down to the most intimate details, go against his 'nature.' " It should be clear that what is referred to here is a secondary "nature," deformed by the long effect of unnatural relations and of degenerated, cramped social relations. In addition, human adaptiveness, however astounding, also has its limits. And if the latter are not antecedent psychological limits, in the final analysis, they surely are biological. The busy executive, that extreme example of the big-city dweller, succumbs, at an alarming and increasing rate, to ailments like ulcers, high blood pressure, and cardiac arrest—symptoms known in contemporary West Germany as "Managerkrankheit" and "Managertod."

On the basis of the same opposition to the concept of mass and massification, René König also launches a serious attack against the conceptual polarity *Gemeinschaft und Gesellschaft* formulated by Tönnies, in an important treatise on "The Concepts Community and Society in Ferdinand Tönnies." After a thorough argument, König comes to the conclusion that, "probably it would be more serviceable to the matter at hand if we decided no longer to apply these concepts at all."[85] Several of the proofs used by König are interesting and valuable in themselves, but in no way do they justify this verdict.

That Sir Henry Sumner Maine (1822-1888), whom Tönnies in his conscientious manner explicitly and repeatedly names as a precursor, had anticipated Tönnies with his polar distinction between "status" and "contract" by no means proves that Tönnies's conceptualization "is devoid," as König asserts, "of any originality." If "no community is possible without societal factors"—a thesis that in any case requires further proof—and if the converse holds true for "communal features in society,"[86] this merely proves that it is a question of two polar ideal types to which reality can more or less be approximated.

In an important passage, cited by König, Tönnies writes: "The concept of *Gesellschaft*, then, signifies the normal and regular process of decline of all *Gemeinschaft*. This is its truth, and the term *Gemeinschaft* is indispensable for the expression of that truth. For this reason it would have to be coined if it had not been formed previously."[87] Here Tönnies lays bare the empirical-historical sources of his concept. We cannot, of course, recognize his nineteenth-century formulation as regards the allegedly "inevitable process of decay." Rather, it is a question of a contingent development and one conditioned by superstratification—which, however, in the last centuries proceeded at an especially rapid pace. Whether this development can be reversed, whether a reapproximation to the pole of community is possible, is a question toward which Tönnies assumed an attitude that was at times hopeful, at times despairing. Yet even such a reverse development would not invalidate the pair of concepts.

Apart, however, from the self-evident order of rank in the community, everything speaks for the proposition that society and mass had not yet existed before superstratification. The unsuperstratified social structures of primitive peoples, not yet disintegrated under European influences, always bore a pronounced communal or *Gemeinschaft* character. But great empires, which arose through conquest and superstratification, were from the outset typical societal or *Gesellschaft* structures, at least as regards the original relation of rulers to ruled and the reciprocal relations of the many, held together only by the newly instituted common domination. For the rest, these empires included a congeries of small structures wholly or almost devoid of relations among themselves; yet the communal character of each single one of these small structures in itself was still preserved for a long time. In Western culture, general dissolution of such small structures and the rise and spatial concentration of underintegrated masses first took place at the end of the Middle Ages; since then it has been strengthened and accelerated by the effects of the Industrial Revolution.

As a rule the degree of integration, the warmth of social relations decreases with the size of the social circle. The state is not a "marriage writ large," and the demand of romantic-sentimental utopians that it be made into one can only serve to arouse overheated national or nationalistic frothings and to impair the normal degree of social integration usually attainable. The norm can be fallen short of in a state of social pathology, which we call underintegration. However, what must be striven for over against it is not the warmth of the closest sphere of intimacy (bound to lead to an unhealthful hothouse atmosphere) but precisely the best temperature for the specific social formation.

That man by nature needs community, just as gregarious animals do, is an incontestable fact: at least familial community, most likely also friendship, and, when possible, close emotional associations beyond this immediate circle of family and friends. Man—and this must be conceded to the glorifiers of community—could live without society, but not without community. In earlier times, man, to the extent that he lived either exclusively in community or in an undestroyed closer and warmer community within a wider society, was happier; modern underintegrated man needs a greater measure of community.

Yet society is also indispensable. The mere praise of the past at the expense of the present, even where it is justified, represents an activity that may be satisfying to those indulging in it but which for the rest is fruitless. Ultimately, the solution to the problem lies in systematic efforts to achieve a desirable measure of community within the framework of any given society.

9. CAPITALIST DEGENERATION OF THE ECONOMY

The baroque political institution of absolutism expressed itself in economic policy as mercantilism, of which "cameralism" was a German-Lutheran, patriarchal variety. In Holland and England, the Enlightenment-based protest of the growing bourgeois economy against endless misgovernment led to the demand for free trade, and in France to the slogan *"Laissez-faire! Laissez-passer!"* The French Physiocrats projected an economic system of a free market economy for the use of enlightened absolutism. And Adam Smith, under the parliamentary-constitutional conditions of Great Britain, gave a liberal-democratic form of classical theory to this new science of economics, which was later systematized by Jean-Baptiste Say in France and further developed and expanded by David Ricardo in England. This liberal theory of the free market economy provided the bourgeoisie, striving for economic elbowroom, with an intellectual weapon of such sharpness and striking power that it in fact succeeded, step by step, in overcoming all mercantilist restrictions on economic freedom. With the abolition of the English Corn Laws (1846), the conclusion of the English-French Cobden Treaty (1860), and the abolition of the last Prussian-German protective tariffs (1876), the state of economic freedom that had been so passionately desired was at last achieved in the sphere of foreign trade.

The economic upswing that followed this unfettering of economic competition was wholly unprecedented; it surpassed the boldest predictions of its most optimistic advocates. Soon, unfortunately, serious evils set in: the social contrast between "proletarians" and "capitalists" sharpened into open class struggle, and free competition was increasingly corrupted by an overgrowth of monopolies and monopolists. The dominant economic order of *laissez-faire, laissez-passer* turned out to be incapable of mastering these pathological phenomena, and its very existence became threatened.

In a separate monograph,[88] I sought to show that the striking failure of economic liberalism, so successful up to then, is to be explained as a problem in the history of religious doctrine. Eighteenth-century deism, which was itself based on a stoic tradition and which stood godfather to economic liberalism, was permeated with the religious belief that the laws of the market are effluences of divine world reason, and that it would be sinful arrogance to interfere in such a divinely given order with mere human measures. This optimistic, absolutist belief in its subtheological rationalism led to what I have termed a "sociologic blindness" for the political and social conditions under which alone the laws of the market operate beneficently. Only so long as the unrelenting market police of a strong and independent state excludes every private formation of monopoly and every obstacle to competition does the market economy produce an automatic harmonization of self-interest and public weal. For only in perfect competition can one seller obtain an advantage over competing sellers by offering the buyer a better or cheaper product.

Actual historical development went in the opposite direction. Monopoly became the generally accepted ideal of entrepreneurs, who pursued the establishment of national and international cartels and trusts by all available means. The state, already subject to pluralistic disintegration, began to foster this development through protective tariffs, foreign trade regulations, diplomatic intervention, subsidies of various sorts, and through one-sided regulation of transportation and taxes. It ended up secretly—or even openly—encouraging the formation of cartels and the growth of monopolies. Even government regulation of monopoly served, in the last

analysis, as a mere fig leaf. Courts and banks were in league with
the monopolists. A great race for the maximum in plant and industrial size, in width of markets, and amounts of production began,
cheered on by the megalomaniac impulses of public opinion.

The more the pluralistic state accommodated monopoly, the more
the working class saw itself dependent upon self-help along the
same lines. The trade union movement grew, and entered the race
for power by striving for a monopoly in the labor market. At length
it, too, demanded state help for this purpose. Above all, however, the
organized working class in the face of employer associations,
achieved the freedom to organize and to strike—no doubt an important social advance under the conditions of that time. Yet the result
was governmentally approved labor struggles—a stark reversion to
the law of the jungle.

Germany took the lead in all these phenomena of social disintegration. England, in theory and practice the leader in economic
freedom, exhibited until recently a far greater capacity for resistance to governmental pluralism; yet in recent decades it seems to
have felt honor-bound to compensate for this laggardness.

The first and most essential sociological and institutional conditions on which the beneficent working of the market depends are
the exclusion of obstacles to competition and the strict limitation of
market freedom to pure competitive performance. These requirements imply that any kind of restriction on competition, any
possibility of securing a competitive advantage outside the market
or through means other than economic efficiency must be excluded
and prohibited. For it is competitive performance alone that places
the self-interest of the producer in the service of the consumer, that
leaves the producer no other choice in surpassing his competitor
than to provide a better or cheaper service. Monopoly and subsidies
are the most important and dangerous forms of the inadmissible
nonmarket devices.

Monopoly hinders the exercise of competitive performance,
whether by law (in the case of compulsory cartels), by legally enforceable contract, or (rarely) by the anticompetitive use of natural
or technical circumstances. Governmental intervention, in round-
about political ways, secures public advantages for one group of
producers as opposed to other producers, the costs being borne by
consumers and other producers. In practice, interventionism and
monopolism are often combined, although the beneficiaries will
strenuously conceal or deny the connection.

All these antimarket phenomena led, in the last quarter of the nineteenth century, to a progressive degeneration of the market economy. The state and public opinion—whose task it should have been to counteract these tendencies for the sake of protecting economic freedom and insuring fair, competitive performance—not only failed to do so but in numerous hidden ways, abetted this development through court decisions, administrative regulations, foreign trade policy, tariffs, freight rates, etc. To the fundamental blindness and errors of theorists (some of whom launched the slogan that "competition kills competition") were now added the ignorance of public opinion concerning the functioning of the market economy as set forth by classical theorists, the mania for setting records, and the covert or overt political influence of financially powerful interests. When, under pressure from other, disadvantaged interests, legislative countermeasures were taken (as, for instance, in the antitrust movement in the United States or in the recent German cartel regulations), they remained essentially ineffective and served principally to silence inconvenient petitioners or to throw sand in the eyes of the grumbling public. In such ways the government's instruments of monopoly control became tacit accomplices of the monopolists. For interested parties are invariably more knowledgeable in their own area than any state officials. This results in an intellectual dependency of government regulators on the very monopolies they are expected to regulate—which must have a corrupting effect in the long run.

The penetration of the market economy by monopoly, subsidies, and governmental regulations in the end reached such proportions that it caused the entire economy to degenerate into a hybrid structure in which no clear discussion of principles was even possible. Since, however, this state of affairs was alleged to be the necessary consequence of liberal economic policy, liberalism itself came to be condemned.

In fact, however, the wholesale degeneration of the market economy was directly and indirectly brought about by a growing series of subventionist, protectionist, and monopoly-fostering measures of the state—i.e., by ever more flagrant violations of the basic maxim of *laissez-faire, laissez-passer*. Liberalism can be reproached for not having prevented this reversion to mercantilism; but that is a sin of omission, no commission. The catastrophic self-destruction of the capitalist economy came about not through execution of a liberal economic program, but rather through a contradiction of this fundamental prescription of the program. Had governments adhered to the liberal maxim of *laissez-faire*, attending to Adam Smith's warnings against the entrepreneurs' greed for subsidy, economic development could not have deteriorated beyond the stage that it had reached by 1878, or at the most 1900 or 1914.

The fateful step beyond this stage came about through a wholesale pluralist deformation of the political system. The excessive concentration of industry, mostly tending to monopoly, reinforced this process. Such concentration, in turn, was stimulated by the widely held belief in its inevitability and by the enthusiastic applause of a public addicted to bigness. Only in a few instances was this tendency justifiable on technical or economic grounds; in most cases the technically or economically optimal size of enterprise had long since been surpassed. And of course, on weighty noneconomic grounds, even a deliberate shortfall from that optimum might be indicated.

This excessive growth of the size of enterprises, stimulated by all manner of obstacles to competition and often deliberately fostered by the government, had two unavoidable consequences: (1) a rapid and excessive decline in the number of independent, economically and socially sound, small and medium-sized industries, which were held in contempt as retrograde by the megalomania of public opinion and which, in their own ethos, came to be marked by a pervasive inferiority complex; (2) a corresponding rise in the numbers of proletarianized workers herded, for no good reason, into the tenements of the sprawling cities—whose arrogant self-consciousness grew in proportion to the number of their inhabitants.

The result was the ever more rapid growth of a proletariat and of mass society, which we have already described, along with the wholesale uprooting and widespread suffering of these same masses—and finally the growth of political mass movements as revolutionary reactions to this inhuman and intolerable state of affairs.

The undeniable genius of Karl Marx lies in the fact that with prophetic intuition he perceived the ultimate tendency of these developments at a very early stage—no matter how inadequate the forms of scientizing and mathematizing with which his insight struggled for a lifetime. Yet he did not derive from this insight the conclusion that the root causes of the evil should be renounced. Marx, too, was caught up in the quasi-theological superstition of inevitability that was characteristic of liberalism itself and that in Marx's case came to be reinforced by influences from the prophetic tradition of the Old Testament. Above all, in the kind of perversion of values characteristic of the nineteenth century, he concluded that these pathological phenomena ought to be brought to their extreme pitch—indeed, that this extreme constituted the very ideal of development.

Marxism and vulgar liberalism were agreed in their view that the tendency of the Western economy in the nineteenth century was the necessary and inevitable consequence of market freedom. That this development, if carried further, would lead to collectivism was one of the theses of Marxism incorrectly disputed by liberals. The real fallacy did not lie in Marx's conclusion but in the premise common to both.

Only by drawing a sharp distinction between the competitive, or predominantly competitive, economy of the free market, such as envisaged by classical liberal theory, on the one hand, and its subventionist, monopolist, pluralist perversion on the other can we bring clarity into this confused controversy. If we call that degenerate form of market economy in the nineteenth and twentieth centuries "capitalism," the controversy may be summed up as follows:

1. Vulgar liberalism and Marxism incorrectly assume that capitalism is the inevitable economic consequence of a competitive economy.

2. Liberalism rightly denies that socialist collectivism is the inevitable, final consequence of a competitive economy.

3. Liberalism wrongly denies the inevitable connection between capitalism and collectivism, as perceived by Marx.

On the other hand, there is no reason to call the market economy of perfect competition "capitalism." The economy of the nineteenth and twentieth centuries, called "capitalist," is a pathological degeneration; indeed, in many respects it represents the opposite of authentic competitive economy. We therefore urgently need an independent term to differentiate this historically degenerate form—so why not call that form "capitalism," a term that has long enjoyed international currency.

We distinguish, therefore, the free-market economy of perfect competition, which constitutes the normal object of liberal economic theory, from the subsidy-ridden, monopolist, protectionist, pluralist economy of the nineteenth and twentieth centuries that resulted from a quasi-theological perversion of *laissez-faire*, and it is this last which we designate as "capitalist" and "capitalism."

As soon as this distinction between the genuine market economy of liberal economic theory and the "capitalist" economy of the nineteenth and twentieth centuries is recognized, we can very largely subscribe to the socialist criticism of this capitalist economy and even to the Marxist thesis that this "capitalist" economy, carried further, must perforce lead to communism and collectivism. Indeed, one might even speak of "late capitalism" as an unconscious and inconsistent form of protocollectivism.

The neo-Marxist thesis (vigorously disputed by liberal critics) that capitalism is the progenitor of modern imperialism seems to me, from the viewpoint of such a rigorous and restricted definition of capitalism, entirely appropriate—though not in the untenable, vulgarized version according to which capitalism requires a constant widening of markets as an outlet for its chronic overinvestment and overproduction. Schumpeter, to be sure, is correct in concluding that modern imperialism is an expression of the old feudal hunger for power and drive for conquest—which is contrary to the spirit of modern market economy. This fully fits in with our own thesis that capitalism—through its subventionist, monopolistic, and pluralistic character—has given new nourishment and expression to these old precapitalist drives.

Of course, it does not follow that the market economy leads inevitably to capitalism, capitalism to imperialism, and imperialism to communism. Rather, the development of the market economy into capitalism is a phenomenon of degeneration. The connection between capitalism and imperialism does not rest on its free-market elements but on those noneconomic components of capitalism that are inimical to the market economy.

The false concept of capitalism that Marxism took over from vulgar liberalism confronts us with a logical choice: either we can dispute the neo-Marxist thesis of the origin of imperialism and Marx's own thesis of the transformation of capitalism into communism; or else we can, by reconsidering and reformulating the concept of capitalism, give these two theses a new and correct foundation. The second procedure would seem to be more fruitful and more just.

Such a position implies full agreement with the Marxists' and socialists' conviction that capitalism cannot endure and must be overcome. The demonstration that capitalism, carried to extremes, must inevitably result in communism, is in my opinion one of Marx's most brilliant accomplishments. But there also are errors that Marx took over from liberalism in its historic rather than pure form. Along with the socialists we reject capitalism, but all the more do we reject collectivism, which is capitalism in its extreme form. Our most telling criticism of capitalism is precisely that—as the collectivists themselves assert—it inevitably leads to collectivism. Two recent variants of the mixture of late capitalism and collectivism, progressive socialization and the welfare state, most clearly show this tendency of sliding into full collectivism, as will be discussed in a later context.

The transformation of labor into a market commodity (as Marx most strikingly called it) as a result of the separation of the worker from his means of production is one of the most pathological social phenomena of nineteenth-century capitalism, with its industrialization and urbanization. The degradation of labor into a commodity not only takes away the worker's security—the very foundation and dignity of his way of life—but this perversion avenges itself on the entrepreneurs themselves in being the structural cause of cyclical economic crises. Although peasants and artisans can adjust their way of life to declining market prices for their products, the capitalist entrepreneur is ground between the millstones of prices as income and wages as costs. The labor market is the most characteristic structure of modern "capitalist" society, which has as little or as much to do with capital as any other economic order at the same technological level. For the capital intensity of an economy depends exclusively upon the state of its productive technology and the consequent duration of its production process.

From a sociological point of view, the following differences in the worker's fundamental life situation may be observed between (a) large enterprise as it developed in the plantation and manorial economies after the sixteenth centuries and in the industrial economy of the nineteenth and twentieth centuries, and (b) the small enterprise of peasants and artisans:

1. The worker who earlier had spent his entire life on his farm or in his workshop—within the closest and most natural community, the family—is now violently torn from this organic environment. For the longest and most significant part of his life—his working time—he is locked up with strangers with whom he shares nothing more than being subject to the cold compulsion of uniform orders and work regulations—an extreme drop in sociological temperatures from the nestlike warmth of *Gemeinschaft* to the extreme chill of *Gesellschaft*. Work is not longer the product of close community but of cold society.

2. The family as a living community is most grievously injured by this change—reduced to minimal, stunted, or residual forms or, as among plantation slaves, abolished altogether. Children no longer grow up in a full family environment.

3. The peasant or artisan, who had been his own master in his farm or workshop, and hence had decided independently on the division of his time between his work and his family, now finds himself, as a laborer, under the command of strangers from morning to night. Whether this control is embodied in the brutal kurbash of the slave driver, in the elegant riding whip of the junker, or in the cool

instruction of the engineer or the foreman—all this makes no more than a difference of degree. The vital sociologic difference is not that between legal slavery or freedom, but rather between family industry and large-scale industry. The dependent peasant was, as a rule, far freer than the legally free modern worker in a plantation or in a large-scale industrial enterprise.

4. Work is no longer meaningful in itself as an organic part of daily life, but merely a means to an end, the only means available to protect oneself either from being clubbed to death like a slave, or from death by hunger and lack of shelter. Work, once a blessing, has become a curse.

5. Labor output no longer is visibly connected with accomplishment and its success, and just as little with the market situation. Instead, the worker, as long as his labor contract runs, is "paid off" with an agreed wage whose level now depends upon the relation of forces between the entrepreneur's interest in profit and hence the lowest possible wage, and the worker's interest in his own life and hence the highest possible wage. Thus, from the worker's point of view, it seems to be only the greed and stinginess of the entrepreneur that opposes his justified striving for the highest possible income level and the best life situation for himself and his family.

6. As large-scale industry tends to an ever sharper division of labor, the labor output of the individual worker becomes more fragmented and is part of a whole which the individual sees, knows, and understands less and less. Formerly, he performed entire tasks—in agriculture from sowing to harvest and the baking of bread, in artisan work from the felling of trees to the making of the finished tool. The industrial worker today does not even see the finished product, which represents the meaning of work. Hence for him, work itself becomes increasingly fragmented and meaningless.

7. With the progressive division of labor the work of every individual becomes more specialized and monotonous, and more undifferentiated.

8. Whereas the peasant produced mostly for himself and his family, and even the artisan for customers he knew, the worker no longer knows either for what or for whom he works.

9. The peasant has no notion of what unemployment is, nor has the slave. At most, the artisan experiences periods of poor sales. The free wage earner, however, can at any time be fired, can suddenly find himself without subsistence; in sickness and old age, before the advent of social insurance, he is forced to look out for himself. The abyss of economic insecurity, the possibility of being out of work at

any moment, of confronting sudden nothingness—these, for the first time in history, came about as the result of free wage labor.

Economic insecurity in the last analysis is only a sharpened variant of that general and chronic sociologic insecurity that results from the disintegration of traditional enviroment of *Gemeinschaft*.

10. Pluralistic Degeneration of the Political Process

Absolutism as the political executive of rationalism takes its name from its essential tendency to adhere to the motto *L'Etat c'est moi* and to abolish all intermediate authorities between the absolute monarch and the mass of subjects. At the earliest, and this was successfully achieved in the Turkish empire with its recent and ever widening superstratification, its Caesaro-papism and the warlike-activist character of its state religion. In the West, it was developed furthest in the realm of Louis XIV, the "Sun King." During the second half of his reign, however, and even more under his weak successors, a feudalistic relapse occurred, which contributed considerably to the outbreak of the French Revolution. Jacobinism, with Napoleon as its heir, completed the process of absolutist leveling and thereby caught up with the model of the Grand Turk, formerly admired as unattainable. Because this absolutist *tabula rasa* forms the basis of modern state development, its creation must be traced, first of all in France.

The medieval government had emerged from a synthesis of the Roman Empire with the fresh superstratifications carried out by barbaric and semibarbaric Teutonic tribes with their system of loyal retainers. Rulership, aging or youthful, flowed into medieval government from both these sources. With the Teutons the peasant element predominated over the nomadic element. They also brought a share of peasant-libertarian cooperation into the mixture. In addition to this, until the Reformation, the Church remained the custodian of the unified cultural tradition that emerged from the blend of classical antiquity and Christianity; it thus provided a counterweight to the secular rulers' claims to exclusive, absolute sovereignty. The frothing mixture of all these components under changing conditions and circumstances formed the constitutional history of the Middle Ages. The outcome was the rise of the absolutism of the territorial state, most radically developed in France. Here the Revolution, while bringing about a repeated change of incumbents also brought about (under the influence of Rousseau's totalitarian theory) a progressive sharpening of the absoluteness of rule itself.

Napoleon's enlightened absolutism was the most absolute form of rule every established since antiquity.

After Napoleon's military collapse, the Restoration did not go beyond ephemeral half measures. Napoleon III followed in the tradition of his great predecessor—with the difference that distinguishes a conniving, clever demagogue from a brilliant and successful strategist.

Between 1689 and 1789 England was recognized as the model of progressive constitutional aspirations, but France regained this leading position all at once with the Revolution of 1789. Despite the inconsistent and erratic character of French development after 1789, France remained the constitutional model for Europe. For no matter how often or abruptly that model changed, it remained at every stage rational, transparent, and informed by French clarity and the *esprit de géometrie*—and hence easier to follow than the opaque English model with its hard-to-grasp *esprit de finesse*.

Like the Cleisthenian constitution of Athens, the French Revolution smashed the established administrative organization in a spirit of purposive rationalism. Thus, it completed the vertical leveling of ranks of absolutism, horizontally, through centralistic pulverization of geographic patterns. Atomization was now complete.

Sieyès, the most radical and most successful champion of these atomizing tendencies, was bent upon "the deliberate and direct destruction of the provinces as organic units,"[89] such as they had grown in the course of the centuries. He was the intellectual progenitor of the laws on the new administrative division of France adopted by the National Assembly in December 1789. "The constitution is conceived as unitary to so doctrinaire a degree that it is thought to be disturbed or threatened by any strong local power." Sieyès's aim was, in his own words, to make "of all parts of France a single body, out of all the peoples into which she is divided, one nation." Local privileges, he was convinced, could be destroyed "only by abolishing local borders." And Sieyès's associate, Thouret, explained the proposal as follows: "France will be carved into 80 equal parts, each of which was to have an extension of about 324 square miles and they are to be formed in such a way that Paris is the radiating center; these are the departments, each of which is divided into 9 large subdivisions. The latter . . . in turn are divided into 9 subdivisions of the same mathematical size . . . each of which is to span an area of 4 square miles."[90] The number of medium-sized districts was fixed at 720, the smallest districts at 6,480. Indeed, it was even proposed that the departments in general not be given names, but numbers only. When this motion failed, efforts were made to come up with names that were purely geographic and rationalistic—as unhistorical as possible. The "geometric precision" of the plan was censured by a feudal delegate as "the departmental chessboard," by others as that modern system of cutting up the provinces, of fragmenting a nation into unrecognizable parts, as "making a *tabula rasa*" that would "prepare the way for invasions of despotism," a "fragmentation of France" that would "sooner or later . . . lead to the successful taking over by the National Assembly of the direction of the whole administration"—as though this had not been precisely the intention! And only an Englishman like Edmund Burke could express surprise "that men could dismember their native country in so barbaric a way."[91] Despite some dilutions and modifications in detail undergone by the Sieyès-Thouret plan in the course of its implementation, its radical, antiorganic, and nontraditional character remained intact. Napoleon later completed the work of the Revolution in this area.

This atomization of the human geography of France was bound to have similar consequences to those registered two millenia earlier by the Cleisthenian constitution in the more limited situation of Attica. The immediate goal, pursued with brutal radicalism, was in both cases completely achieved. Since then, neither in Attica nor in France have domestic political struggles again unfolded on a local basis, or even assumed any kind of separatist character. But France from that time to this has never again found the security of her internal balance; her domestic politics has gone from one crisis to another—and that despite the preservation of an essentially healthy small peasant and artisan substructure—and this remarkable phenomenon, fateful for all Europe, in the final analysis was probably conditioned by this meausre of 1789. Only this explains the deep and ineradicable mistrust that the average Frenchman feels toward his overcentralized government and its policy, which during elections vents itself in favor of radical opposition parties—Communists, Gaullists, Poujadists—a vote that often merely signifies his profound disapproval of the whole drift of things.

As a consequence of Napoleon's fall, the pressure of despotism slackened and "society" took the state in hand along the path of parliamentarism—that plutocratic society caught up in stormy capitalist development which the Calvinist Guizot called into being with his injunction "enrichissez-vous par votre travail." It was no longer a question of an organically articulated structure, but rather of an atomized mass which began to grow into individual vested interests as a result of the formation of cliques and political parties. Since none of these vested interests was large enough to gain a majority in parliament, the formation of a majority was possible only by way of ever changing coalitions, a system of government which today we call pluralism. Its earliest description and critique, remarkable for its perspicacity, comes from the pen of a radical-liberal French economist—who for this very critique was decried by his contemporaries as a tedious blockhead—Frédéric Bastiat (1801-1850). In an article entitled *L'Etat*, which appeared in the *Journal des Débats* of 25 September 1848, he wrote:

> Man struggles against pain and suffering. However, he is condemned by nature to suffering and to privation if he does not take upon himself the effort of work. Hence he has only the choice between two evils. . . . Up to now, however, no remedy has been found for it . . . except for man to avail himself of the work of others . . . so that all work is for the one and all enjoyment is for the other. Hence slavery and robbery under the most different forms, such as that of war, deception, the act of violence, fraud etc. These are wicked abuses, but they are altogether consonant to the idea that brought them into being. We can hate and fight oppressors, but we cannot say that they are senseless and illogical.
>
> Slavery, thank God, is on the wane and the situation in which we find ourselves gives us the possibility to defend ourselves against direct and naïve robbery. . . .
>
> The oppressor no longer directly compels the oppressed through his own strength. . . . There is still a tyrant and a victim, but now the state, i.e., the law itself, is placed as a mediator between the two. What could be better for the purpose of stifling our doubts and . . . vanquishing all resistance? . . . We turn to the state and say to it: I find that between my enjoyment and my work there exists no relation that satisfies me. In order to bring about the desired balance, I would like to take away a little from the others. However, that would be dangerous were I to do it myself. Can you, state, facilitate matters for me? Can you not assign me to a favorable position, or rather, can you not assign a more unfavorable one to my competitor? Can you not grant me a special "protection" and, not without plausible reason, lend me capital which you have taken from its possessors? Or, can you not educate my children at public expense . . . or guarantee me a carefree life from the age of 50 onwards?

Through this means I would be able to achieve my goal with a good conscience, for in this case the *law* would be acting for me, and I would have all the advantages of exploitation without its risks and its onus.

As it is now certain that, on the one hand, we all make this and similar suggestions to the state and that, on the other, the state cannot provide any enjoyment for the one without saddling the other with work, I believe that I am justified, while awaiting a better definition of the state, to submit, provisionally and with reservation, this my own definition which reads as follows: *"The state is the great fiction by means of which each wants to live at the expense of the other."*

[Thus] one class of society after the other comes to it and says: "You, who can legally and honorably make a grab, take so and so much from the public and then we two, you and I, will divide it with each other."

Unfortunately, the state has an all too great inclination to follow this diabolic counsel, as the state machine is composed of ministers, of officials, . . . who, finally, like all human beings, . . . wish to increase their influence and well-being, and eagerly grab at any opportunity to do so. Hence the state all too easily understands its advantage in the role that the public allots to it; it makes the state the arbitrator, the ruler of all fates. It will then grab very much and reserve very much for *its* people, it will increase the number of its officials, extend the radius of its authority until finally it assumes an extent that can only be defined as oppressive.

The most amazing feature of all this is the delusion which has seized the public. When victorious soldiers made slaves of the conquered they were acting barbarously, but not stupidly. Their aim was like ours: to live at the cost of others—but they at least did not fail of their goal and, instead, attained it. But what are we to think of a people that seems unaware of the fact that *reciprocal* robbery is for this reason no less robbery, or no less punishable because it vests itself in the forms of legality and order, that it does not add to public weal, that, on the contrary, it diminishes it and, indeed, to the very amount that it costs to maintain this wasteful mediator called the "state."[92]

As long as "society" still sees itself in opposition to the old absolutist authoritarian state, or to one of its metamorphoses, it is interested in weakening the power of the state. And it does so by attempting to determine the limits of its power as narrowly as possible and by freeing itself from fettering governmental interference, especially in the economy. As soon, however, as society itself has become dominant in the state through parliamentary pluralism, the opposite endeavor begins: the aim now is to extend as far as possible the public power of the groups of interested parties by means of the state, to the extent that the latter serves the interests in question. The German economic historian Adolf Wagner, in the scientistic-absolutizing style of the nineteenth century, called this "the law of growing State tasks." Hence de Tocqueville's paradoxical observation that "history knows no time where the State has appeared so weak and yet so strong."[93] Weak in independent authority against interested groups, strong in independent power as mandatory and counsel of these same interested groups. The "total" state stands at the end of this line of development.

In the United States, within the framework of the Anglo-American two-party system, a similar development in somewhat different form took place. The spoils system, however, the treatment of the government apparatus as war booty by both parties, enjoying majority rule for the time being, developed early. And other interest groups were concerned to make their influence felt within this two-party system. The New Deal signified a notable advance on the way to pluralism, to the "State as benefactor," and to the "nation-hero-benefactor concept."[94]

Germany initially was far behind on this road to pluralism, for various reasons. For one thing, Prussian officialdom, since the time of the Stein-Hardenberg reforms, embodied an unusually high standard of independent political authority. As a consequence parliamentary parties were forced to place in the foreground their philosophical opinions concerning the exercise of state authority, their interpretation of the general will. To the Junkers east of the Elbe and to a cynic of *Realpolitik* like Bismarck, these parties of principle were as hateful and inconvenient as were the loyalties of the officials. Bismarck tried hard to corrupt officialdom and to transform such parties devoted to basic principles into interest groups feeding at the state trough. This was the real meaning and purpose of his transition to a policy of protectionism in 1878-1879; like Guizot before him, he called upon the interest groups to "Enrichissez-vous!"—not through their own work, but through state intervention. As a result, Germany in one leap moved to the head of this fateful international parade. And if Bismarck had believed that he could keep these vested interests compliant by feedings from the state's trough, his successors learned by experience that the state which begins to feed group interests ends up being devoured by them.

The famous German legal scholar Otto von Gierke (1841-1921) sounded an early warning against the dangerous broadening of government interference. In an address of 1882, he stated: "Similar ideas play their dangerous game even in real life and all too easily create in the temporarily empowered majorities the belief that everything which can be ordered in the form of law can also thereby be changed within the living law and that the majesty of the law can be set in motion with impunity in order to satisfy any need whatsoever of practical utility along the shortest path."[95]

Pluralism, however, reached its pinnacle only in the Weimar Republic. The Weimar constitution itself began as a pluralistic compromise, with its second portion serving as crypt for the solemn burial of the irreconcilable and impractical principles of all the parties involved. None of its sponsors, of course, had espoused pluralism deliberately; yet their intuitive powers of imagining the concrete function of a paragraph of the constitution as a sociological reality was, for the most part, poorly developed—and so was the study of political science in the further elaboration of which Germany had by then yielded to the United States. It is not difficult to demonstrate, however, that the relevant provisions of the Weimar constitution under the prevailing conditions were bound to result in an extreme form of pluralism, and with it an expansion of government intervention on behalf of interest groups temporarily exercising power.

"There is an almost universal view," as I have written elsewhere, "that this expansion of government power beyond its former limits, this involvement of all spheres of life in the government's political activity is a sign of the excessive strength of the State, a sort of *hubris*, a matter of the State no longer knowing its limits. In truth it is . . . a sign of the most deplorable weakness of the State . . . which can no longer defend itself against the concerted attack from vested interest. . . . Each interest group appropriates a piece of State power and exploits it for its own ends. . . ."[96]

Under those circumstances governments could be formed only by way of coalition, a government program formulated only by way of compromise—the kind of compromise that enabled each participant to disclaim responsibility for the result. Logrolling became the highest principle of statecraft, and governmental powers were appropriated by the coalition partners like so much booty. Because of the ever changing parliamentary alignments and the kaleidoscopic change in government coalitions, every party had hopes of being in power some day. Rulership by rotation was the result, with every group taking its turn at being the superstratifier. The common national interest, which no one troubled to deny, but which was not the interest of any group in particular, accordingly suffered.

A suggestive conclusion was to condemn the system of government based on political parties for these results. Already Heinrich Grewe had asked the leading question "Parteienstaat oder was sonst?"—if not a state of political parties, what then?[97]

Phrases like "interest groups" or "vested interests" have a deprecatory ring—especially in Germany, where there is a strong tradition of an authoritarian state, and where any rebellion against divinely willed authority is viewed with suspicion. The reforms of Baron vom Stein aimed at an ideal form of this authoritarian state and for a while achieved it. But such a state no longer exists in Germany, and it will never return. Hence it is inappropriate to condemn from the outset, from the perspective of an ideal that no longer corresponds to reality, an inescapable modern development like that of interest groups.

In a society like ours, many persons belong to each direction of interest. Obviously persons with parallel interests tend to join each other to represent these interests more effectively, and to this there cannot be the slightest objection. Now these interests in part overlap, and in part are opposed to each other and thus cancel out. However, a mere compromise between partly opposed and partly concurrent interests by way of logrolling (*Kuhhandel* is the equally expressive German word) offers no guarantee that the total interests will be protected. A classic example is the cooperation between German agrarians and heads of heavy industry in supporting Bismarck's protective tariff.

Nevertheless, some such reciprocal balancing of group interest is necessary. It must first be established what the full range of particular interests is and how they mutually relate to each other, where they intersect, and where now one side now the other must sacrifice some of its interests. Such negotiations at the lowest level may already lead to a certain reconciliation. Yet this is by no means sufficient. There are general interests that do not coincide with any particular interests and which would be sacrificed in such negotiations among particular egotistic group interests. Sacrifices on behalf of these more fundamental group interests overtax individuals and individual groups. It is the government that must perceive and represent, as conscientiously, objectively, and knowledgeably as it can, these common interests, and, on that basis, seek the support of a broad public opinion.

A plurality of interests at the lower levels is inescapable; but so is the formulation of a unified and responsible policy at the higher governmental level if a political system is to remain viable. The art of liberal-democratic statesmanship consists of letting this plurality of interests below flow into a unified policy above—which, though difficult, is fortunately not insoluble. The best electoral system is one that leads to such a responsible formation of policy, that is, the British plurality system of elections.

11. DEPLETION OF THE CULTURAL HERITAGE

The development of mass society takes the form, in intellectual history, of squandering cultural heritage; it is a disintegration, dissolution, decline of inherited bonds. As the German poet Novalis put it, "We still live from the fruit of better times."[98] Because of their origin in superstratification, all high civilizations were integrated on a feudal and theological basis—a basis which, after the antifeudal and antitheological impact of the Enlightenment, no longer is tenable. Secularization, detheologization, and rationalization thus at length lead to complete disintegration. In such a situation, inherited ideas and ideals are no longer kept alive in a continuous process of self-renewal; yet no new ideas arise to replace them.

For example, it is striking to observe the extent to which rationalism has lived off the depletion of the secularized heritage of medieval theology. Christianity as a system of knowledge, such as it was developed in scholasticism, is salvational knowledge: not a mere gratification of curiosity but rather a contemplation, conducive to eternal bliss, of the Divine Wisdom and the goodness of the creator as revealed in his world plan. The exaggerated place assigned by rationalism to intellectual cognition has its basis in this mystical-religious sanctification of knowledge—and hence rationalism is, at bottom, a most irrational affair. With further secularization this quasi-religious halo was bound to wane and with it the respect for the supreme rule of reason. And since the role of reason had not been stabilized at a position adequate to human nature and to the nature of things, an irrationalist reaction led to a highly materialist form of mysticism whose banality is veiled only by its utter confusion.

The rationalistic fanaticism for equality similarly had its deepest roots in the Christian idea of men's equality before God which, upon being secularized and rationalized, was consigned to the same process of squandering of the heritage. The rationalist belief in progress is a secularized version of faith in a divine plan of salvation—which, in a form more akin to Old Testament prophecy, also underlies Marxism. And the "hidden harmony" and "invisible hand" of classical economics, which—behind everyone's back, as it were—combine all individual egoisms into the welfare of the whole are nothing but the invisible divine *logos*, which according to Heraclitus, governed the world—a notion passed on to modern times by way of Stoic philosophy.

The authority accorded to the state in early modern times and later reinforced in the baroque system of absolutism rests to a considerable degree upon the medieval-theological conception of the divine right of kings. "Public opinion," which was to play such a decisive role in the modern state, was a secularized form of the consensus of the Christian community; and the normative ideas of bourgeois respectability which formed the content of this public opinion were in essence the corresponding articles of the Christian catechism in somewhat secularized and much diluted form.

Even the political and commercial relations among states—which give even to the wars of the nineteenth century something of an idyllic quality in retrospect and which, in the years before 1914, made possible an unprecedented upswing of world trade—rested essentially upon a Western-international code of conduct that had secularized the minimal demands of Christianity; that is, upon a secularized depletion of the heritage of the pax Christiana. As late as 1850 the conservative-religious Berlin newspaper *Kreuzzeitung* could revert to this original theological version of liberal economic doctrine: "Free trade is like a religious service by which men find pleasure in the gifts of their Creator and acknowledge the wisdom by which he has distributed fruits and talents among them."

But such notions, resting on a gradual depletion of the cultural heritage, are likely to crumble under the first major blow that tests their remaining strength. World War I (1914-1918) provided precisely such a test.

The relation of peoples and states to one another developed in a way corresponding to the process of massification and the relation of individuals to each other. Their external economic and cultural relations had become ever more intense. The supportive solidarity of outlook, however, which had once been largely provided by Christianity and the Church, was progressively sapped by secularization. The result was a catastrophe that no one intended yet everyone was willing to risk—a result of a policy of shifting coalitions analogous to the pluralism of domestic policy and with the same result of irresponsibility all around.

12. Nihilism and the Revolution of Irrationalism

The squandering of the heritage that has just been discussed proceeded mostly unintentionally and at most semiconsciously. But there is also a harsher and more extreme version of that process: the conscious, intentional destruction and annihilation of that legacy. This is not always to be condemned: where the legacy is malign and rotten, its dismantling can become an ethical imperative. Any critique of culture, no matter how positive in intent—including that offered in the present work—must also seek to combat and eliminate parts of the cultural heritage.

But there is also an approach totally different in its structure and motives that combats the cultural heritage from a fundamentally negative perspective. It destroys not with a responsible sense of regret, but rather with an irresponsible glee and a note of triumph. Indeed, it indulges in destruction for destruction's sake in accord with Bakunin's dictum that "the urge to destroy is a creative urge."

Shared values, especially those of an ethical nature, convergent views on what is good and evil, worthy of praise or blame, estimable or despicable, are the precondition and foundation of any social cohesion and of the formation of any community. Once this community of interests is called into question, or is lost, a serious sickness of the social body sets in. The disintegration of such a community of shared values unfolds in a series of successive stages. At first part of the group involved still recognizes the shared values but no longer acts in conformity with them, trying perhaps to hide such actions from the view of the larger community. Such furtive contravention of custom is accompanied by a sense of shame and bad conscience, indicating that not the ego but at least the superego still accepts the community's traditional values. But once the antitraditional conduct draws the superego itself away from the communal values, these values begin to receive only lip service, are used only in bad faith and for purposes of deception: the result is what we call hypocrisy.

But whereas ordinary hypocrisy is the almost instinctive tribute that vice pays to virtue, hypocrisy can also take the more complex form of a whole system of cover lies, that is, of an "ideology" in the negative sense of the term. And any such systematic dissembling or masquerade invites exposure, disclosure, and unmasking.

Such exposure at first presupposes, both in the person undertaking the task and in the audience he addresses, an unshakable sense of community based upon a condemnation of the behavior thus scrutinized. It can be directed downward, as when the exposer views himself as standing on the level of the recognized ideals and with honest indignation (or possibly out of self-righteous arrogance) hurls down from this ideal level all those who merely pay it lip service. Or it can be directed upward. Here, the exposer acknowledges that he does not measure up to the ideal standard, and his aim is to bring the others who unjustly pretend to be better down to his own level. This kind of exposure sows suspicion, encourages denunciation, and indulges in destruction for its own sake.

If the conduct exposed in individual cases spreads, the recognized social values rigidify into mere convention until finally they give way to disenchantment and resignation. "This is simply the way things are in the world and in life," the critic now is saying; "We may regret it, but it cannot be helped. Such are we all." With such realistic pessimism the original condemned values acquire an all-but-equal status: their ideality is compensated for by their unattainability and unreality, whereas the contrary conduct in violation of the ideal gains stature from its indubitable reality.

In vehement and defiant minds, however—minds not given to such cool, modest self-criticism—defense of the formerly shared values can instead lead to a passionate reversal of partisanship: love of the unattainable ideal changes into hate; although its validity is not denied, the ideal is rejected, and in a desperate rebellion against God, evil is lovingly embraced and championed. Such a wildly challenging satanism, diabolism, immoralism, appears only as a flickering unsteady flame, or as a disquieting omen that the final stage is no longer distant. This is the stage of absolute nihilism, of the dissolution, disintegration, and negation of all values in general. At first a corrosive cynicism develops to which "nothing more is sacred," a need to demolish, a distinctive mania that holds that one must kick what is down. Beyond this there is a stage of "heroic pessimism," which is proud of its total lack of illusion and which considers this arctic climate of absolute negativism as the logical implication of intellectual honesty.

But since no human being can long survive in such icy regions of absolute negation, since the human psyche, too, abhors a vacuum, new kinds of content rush in to fill this void. And following the distinction of all previous higher norms, these new values can only be purely vital impulses, legitimated by their mere vehemence. A mania for establishing records becomes the new standard and lack of inhibition becomes a positive virtue.

At this point, however, excessive quantity changes into quality. For the most vehement motive forces now are those that hitherto were chained, ridiculed, and despised. The circle now closes, and the result is a "transvaluation of all values": the previous good is declared evil, the previous evil good. Bestialism and the predatory morality of the stronger are expressly proclaimed: might goes before right.

The first emergence of this phased phenomenon can be seen in the domain of rationalism. It is apparent in the sneering, stinging criticism that Thersites levels at the hero of the *Iliad*—a forcible expression of long pent-up criticism by the lower stratum of the declining aristocracy. In the subsequent period, when the tables were turned and the democratic lower stratum achieved political dominance, the aristocratic upper stratum was pushed into a rather hopelessly defensive position, and the thersitical technique of tearing down and unmasking was now employed by aristocrats like Theognis in Megara and the Sophists in Athens. Thucydides, as we have seen, took an objective, independent position in the midst of these party struggles. He continued to champion moral ideals, but he depicted the *de facto* detachment of political action from such ideals with incisive objectivity, and the coolness of restrained passion—attitudes probably most evident in his so-called Melos dialogue.

Almost two millennia had to pass before, toward the end of the Renaissance of the antique world, Machiavelli dared once again to expose the essence of politics as pure power struggle, in savage rebellion against the uncompromising moral injunctions of the Church, which hitherto had always been acknowledged even when they had been violated. The reaction to the Renaissance, as represented by the Reformation and the Counter Reformation, could not do away with this "demonic" doctrine. It could, however, veil it with secrecy so that the crypto-Machiavellian policy of absolutism, down to the time of Frederick the Great, was accompanied by a steady outpouring of anti-Machiavellian literature. Only when Machiavellianism cast off all disguises in Napoleon's revolutionary attempt to conquer the world did Fichte (1807) champion the Machiavellianism of thought against him—thereby creating the first break in the dam that throughout the nineteenth and twentieth centuries was to give way to a veritable inundation.

In the further course of the nineteenth century, there developed a specific German form of Machiavellianism, which soon received the cover name of *Realpolitik*. Already in the liberal Frankfurt Parliament of 1849, the historian Dahlmann made the very significant and prophetic confession: "The path of power is the only one that will satisfy and satiate the drive to freedom—since it is not only freedom that the German loves: for the most part it is the power, hitherto denied to him, after which he lusts."[99]

Finally Treitschke, in the intoxication accompanying the founding of the Bismarck empire, with the utmost brutality proclaimed that "the essence of the State is firstly power, secondly power, and thirdly, still, power."[100] Such was that German nationalistic Machiavellianism as it found its full embodiment in the widely publicized image of Iron Chancellor Bismarck, the master of *Realpolitik*. The "Pan German Association," founded in 1891, provided it with an organizational base, and the retired cavalry general Friedrich von Bernardi (in a book published in 1913, entitled *Germany and the Next War*) with an effective platform.

Atomism, we saw, appeared in the history of natural philosophy first in the form of a "revelation" that the esteemed and highly revered *ontos ōn*, with its divine world spirit and universal soul, was in reality nothing more than empty space in which atoms moved mechanically. Parallel to this revelatory physics—a kind of cosmological behaviorism—atomism also developed a revelatory, unmasking sociology, not unlike that which was carried to an extreme by the cynics. The human world, too, within an empty space free of all higher powers, consisted of single isolated individuals, each one pursuing his selfish personal goals; and communal life took place only as an association for the achievement of selfish purposes of each individual. This revelatory unmasking character of the atomistic theory of society is strongly apparent in Hobbes, with his "bitter harshness"—as Wilhelm Roscher called it. It is no coincidence that a revelatory, vivisecting psychology spreads widely—represented before Hobbes in Montaigne and Pascal and later in La Rochefoucauld, La Bruyère, Fontenelle, Vauvenargues, and Chamfort. In this "school of suspicion" each member could learn from his predecessors the "art of mistrust" and of "unmasking human self-delusions," to use the phrases of Nietzsche, the most famous member of this school.

The sociology corresponding to such an unmasking individual psychology was developed in Bacon's doctrine of idols, in Mandeville's *Fable of the Bees*, and in the valiant tendency of the real Enlightenment "to tear away the veil of prejudices," "to unmask the impostures," as Holbach tried to do in his militant tracts *Le Christianisme dévoilé* (1761) and *Les Prêtres démasqués* (1766). These tendencies were summed up by Helvétius, whom Nietzsche later was to honor as his most important precursor: Helvétius had revealed as the true and ultimate motivation of human conduct "the love of power"—although he adds, in a philanthropic rococo mood, "based upon the love of happiness."

Adam Smith and his school of economic liberalism no longer depreciated egoism as "vice"—as had Mandeville in his puritanical asceticism—but rather identified it as the real motive force of the market economy; they viewed it as altogether legitimate, and sanctified it because of its highly beneficent effects—a development that also contributed to the "transvaluation of values" that was to culminate in the nineteenth century. The self-destruction of idealistic romantic metaphysics in the Hegelian Left added a number of potent toxic residues, as evident in Stirner's solipsist egoism and Marx's cynical, demolishing criticism of traditional "bourgeois" values. And from a very different direction Darwin's Malthusian theory of the struggle for existence and of the survival of the fittest added new grist to the same mill.

Schopenhauer's psychology and metaphysics unveiled the "will," the unrestrained and blind life urge, as the real mainspring both of the microcosm and macrocosm. At the same time he waged war upon it and proclaimed the overcoming of the will as his ideal. This trend of thought reached its last stage in Nietzsche, who, in relation to the human world, specified this will as the "will to power." In opposition to Schopenhauer he passionately espoused it in his radical somersault of the "transvaluation of values."

We know that the will to power in its most naked and brutal form—that is, in the process of superstratification—forms the historical foundation of all high cultures. Yet to overcome this birth defect, this original sin of world history has been the major task confronting civilized mankind, a task with which men have wrestled more or less consciously, more or less successfully for many thousands of years. No final victory, to be sure, had as yet been won, often the evil was veiled rather than abolished. Yet here, in Nietzsche, all these partial and incomplete attempts were roundly rejected and cast aside. Here the will to power as motive force of all superstratification was for the first time both fully unveiled and unreservedly espoused.

The tendency we have been tracing was triggered and driven forward by rationalism, by the unfettered *ratio*, which, with its dissolvent criticism, finally dissolved everything and thus ended in absolute nothingness. This self-abolition and self-dissolution of rationalism, however, opens the door to all sorts of irrationalism. Since reason, in the age of rationalism had entered the arena as a partisan, it was now no longer recognized by the opposing irrationalist party as the judge. And with this express rejection of any rational control, there only remain records to be set and there remains crude success as the only measure of value guaranteeing ultimate success to that tendency which diverts the most powerful forces into its own channel.

CHAPTER 2

Irrationalist Countertendencies

The many phenomena of decay which were surveyed in the preceding chapter, and which assumed especially extreme forms in the nineteenth century, were in most cases rationalistic excesses, that is, one-sided exaggerations of one or another aspect of the Enlightenment. A reaction on behalf of the repressed and neglected counterforces of irrationalism was bound to follow after the obvious catastrophe that befell the Enlightenment in 1792-1794. In this chapter we shall be treating the most important of these irrationalist countertendencies. Further, we shall see that even this deflection in the opposite direction, even where it may at first have seemed justifiable, subsequently went well beyond any healthy or balanced middle position and instead attained pathological, distorted dimensions which long-suffering mankind had not witnessed for a long time.

The split between rationalism and irrationalism is something profoundly unnatural; their mutual hostility rests on a false choice of fronts. All that is natural and healthy in human beings partakes of both the rational and the irrational, in an organic blend. Hence there is no such thing as something either purely rational or purely irrational; even within the same historical phenomenon, rational and irrational aspects alternate to such an extent that it is hard to determine which is dominant and where along the rational-irrational spectrum the phenomenon should be classed.

The great war that the French Revolution proclaimed on domination and feudalism was fought, at least after 1792-1793, along no clear front lines. Instead of directing its attack against dominion and claiming for itself freely accepted leadership—a tactic that would have divided the forces of feudalism which falsely laid claim to both—the revolutionary side accepted the front lines as they had been drawn by the opponent and thus found itself engaged in both true and false battles.

For a century or more, neither side in the intellectual battle was ready to correct the false alignment. The Right did not surrender dominion, the Left did not surrender mechanical equality. Thus good and evil were intertwined in a manner that was experienced as downright intolerable by the best minds on each side. Typically, each side was right in its critique of the other but quite wrong in its presentation of its own case. Gradually the lines hardened and became less and less clear. With right and wrong so nearly evenly distributed and the front lines so unclear, the result was a stalled trench warfare of excruciating indecisiveness.

All this time, the development of mass society and the squandering of the cultural heritage relentlessly advanced. The integrative force of the old ideals diminished. The forces conducive to community formation were depleted. The catastrophe began with the outbreak of the First World War in 1914, and is not yet at an end; nor has it perhaps even reached its nadir.

1. CONSERVATIVE REACTION

From the time of the first superstratification history has been replete with new thrusts of superstratification and with wars of conquest by which one superstratified empire would seek to subdue another. The result was partial or total change in the composition of the upper stratum: alien conquerors came and went. The indigenous peasant stratum, however, managed to endure these changes in overlords: they themselves served, but they continued to survive. Consequently, the basic social structure of superstratification remained unchallenged. Each conquering group was repeatedly threatened by other would-be conquerors but not by its own subjects. And the good conscience and sense of security of the superstratifiers corresponded to this secular docility of the lower stratum.

Successful revolts of the lower stratum took place first in ancient Greece, culminating in the Attic revolution of the fifth century B.C., and again in the series of modern revolutions in the West culminating in the great French Revolution. These revolutions for the first time threatened the earlier sense of security of the upper strata, and two sorts of response were possible. Either one could drop all disguise and pretense, and, with a savage fury borne of desperation, assert the right of the stronger, that is, the original superstratification mentality—the very attitude that the lower stratum is challenging; this reaction is embodied by the figure of Callicles in Plato's *Gorgias*. Or one can emphasize the positive accomplishments of the ruling class—a position embodied in Pindar's injunction *genoio hoios essi*: not "become who thou art," as nineteenth-century individualists mistranslated it, but "become such as thou art"—become a true aristocrat with a sense of *noblesse oblige*.

There is no basis for the formation of political parties or distinct philosophic tendencies as long as the position of the superstratifiers is institutionally recognized and gives them a common outlook and sense of solidarity. Only when this constitutional rank order and upper class hegemony is challenged or abolished does there arise the painful necessity of replacing the earlier organic group structure with a voluntary association resting on the free choice and commitment of each individual member.

As Alfred von Martin has observed, "The conscious advocacy of the conservative principle signifies always a countermovement— the reaction to a destructive action: only when the very existence of particular conditions is seriously endangered can interest in their conservation come to life. Hence conservatism, true to its nature, always finds itself in a position of defense, in the struggle over threatened positions."[1] Conservatism, in sum, is the defensive position of the threatened feudal upper stratum.

Accordingly, the first political party in the modern sense was the aristocratic-oligarchic party organized by Thucydides, son of Melesias, after 449 B.C. against the Attic democracy led by Pericles. From one of its followers, an emigrated Athenian aristocrat, also stems the oldest preserved conservative party tract, which amusingly exhibits most of the stylistic and attitudinal features characteristic of conservative journalism to this day: temperamental vehemence and indignation; bilious disposition; sarcasm; cryptic brevity; coarseness; pithiness; nonchalance as to phrasing; an erratic, hate-induced penetration; and disdain for stylistic and rhetorical elegance.[2]

Similarly, the conservatism of modern times originated as a reaction to the French Revolution. Logically enough the first fundamental and philosophical opposition to the French Revolution came from England; it was directed not only against the degeneration of the Revolution after 1792, but already against the rationalism and radicalism, against the *revolutionary* character of its beginnings. England had ended her revolution exactly a hundred years before that of France began. In England and outside England people believed that the felicitous compromise established since that time, recognized and honored by all progressive-minded persons (including, since 1756, those in France), was a model that made further revolutions superfluous both for England herself and for the rest of the world.

In no other country are the old and the new, the past and the future so easily amenable to readjustment as in England. Even her Glorious Revolution led to such an adjustment and in retrospect made the preceding era seem a remote time indeed. Hence Burke could exclaim that "the very idea of the fabrication of a new government is enough to fill us Englishmen with disgust and horror." With his *Reflections on the Revolution in France* (1790) Burke at once emerged as the fundamental defender and glorifier of the historically evolved state, the state as the bearer of supratemporal values and unbroken tradition and continuity. "The State ought not to be considered as nothing better than a partnership agreement . . . to be taken up for a little temporary interest. It is to be looked on with other reverence. . . . It is a partnership in all science, a partnership in all art, a partnership in every virtue, and in all perfection." "As the ends of such a partnership cannot be obtained in many generations, it becomes a partnership not only between those who are living, but between those who are living, those who are dead, and those who are to be born."

Along with such ideas whose truth, depth, cannot be denied and whose mere enunciation, after their complete neglect in the Enlightenment, signified a breakthrough in intellectual history. Burke also, with naïve self-righteousness, takes up the defense of feudal and upper bourgeois vested interests with phrases of the kind of hollow pathos and heavenward glances that make it so hard to endure conservatism. "The known march of the ordinary providence of God," as he expresses himself on one occasion with unctuous smugness, has led to nothing other than precisely the existing beneficent distribution of property and rights.

From his standpoint of polar opposition, Burke, with brilliant instinct, foresaw as early as 1789-1790 the fateful development which was to lead to the unheaval of 1792 ("There must be blood: the want of common judgment manifested . . . in all their kinds of civil and judicial authorities will make it flow") and even predicted Napoleon's rise to power: "Some popular general who understands the art of conciliating the soldiery . . . shall draw the eyes of all men upon himself. The moment in which that event shall happen, the person who really commands the army is your master—the master of your whole Republic."[3]

Burke was too far ahead of his time, so that even in England he was not much applauded. When in May 1791 he broke with his old party, the Whigs, and with its leader Fox, who had been a close friend, he stood almost alone. Only when the upheaval of 1792 confirmed his prophetic fears and when a deterioration in relations between France and England occurred in 1793 did public opinion shift in his favor. During 1791, Burke's *Appeal from the New to the Old Whigs* had fallen on deaf ears; by 1794 the majority of the party stood on his side.

Nowhere did Burke's ideas, however, find more enthusiastic echoes than among the German Romantics, for whom, in the first decade of the nineteenth century, they were important bridges between early romanticism and the intellectual counterrevolution.

In Germany, the "patriot" Justus Möser (1720-1794) had already tenderly interpreted and passionately defended the past even in its superannuated residues. Möser exalted the past from the standpoint of a burgher entitled to a seat in the senate of his hometown, and from the viewpoint of the free peasants, defending their ancient freedoms. Carl Ludwig von Haller, a Bern patrician, defended feudal domination as such with unromantic-rationalistic bluntness. These two defenders of things past were soon surrounded by a swarm of ecstatic romantics, whose political program is anticipated with remarkable clarity by Novalis (Friedrich Baron von Hardenberg, 1772-1801). In 1798, he wrote: "The world must be romanticized. . . . The lower Self identifies itself with a better Self in this operation. . . . This operation is still totally unknown. By giving the common a lofty meaning, the ordinary a mysterious esteem, the known the dignity of the unknown, the finite and infinite appearance, I thus romanticize it." Such "romanticization" was precisely what the old powers, the absolutist governments and the nobility, as they faced the threat of the Revolution and its repercussions, needed for thier ideological defense. And if Novalis as late as 1799 had lamented "O! lonesome and deeply grieved stands he who ardently and piously loves the olden times,"[4] it was not long before these backward-looking souls were relieved of their loneliness and of their grief alike.

A Prussian radical liberal, Friedrich Buchholz (1768-1843), published a pamphlet in French-occupied Berlin in 1807 entitled *Investigations Concerning the Nobility of Birth and the Possibility of Its Continuance in the Nineteenth Century*—which possibility he of course denied in view of the collapse of Prussian feudalism under the blows of Napoleon in 1806. This sharp but none-too-cogent attack frightened aristocratic circles. But since the members of that circle did not feel intellectually adequate to the task of an effective counterattack, they turned to a well-connected political agent, Friedrich Gentz (later *von* Gentz), who on their behalf recruited Adam Müller (later *von* Müller) who was promised "a highly pleasant existence" as his reward for undertaking that task. Müller, sure enough, gave his lectures on the "Elements of Statecraft" in Dresden in the winter of 1808-1809 before an audience of feudal nobles. His ideas rest essentially upon Burke and Novalis; the lectures exhibit Müller's characteristic combination of dialectical adroitness and spirited eloquence—a combination more familiar in France than in Germany.

The ideology of Prussian-German conservatism grew from such roots. The indiscriminate attack of rationalist radicalism against justified and unjustified forms of hierarchy facilitated an equally indiscriminate defense of feudalism. The inescapable nature of tradition and the inevitability of degrees of leadership could be supported by basic arguments, and gave the defensive forces an understandable sense of superiority. But the beneficiaries of inherited feudal status did not dream of sorting out, on their side, what was and was not justified in their position, for it was the untenable parts of their position that were most enjoyable and in practice most precious. This frequent combination of aristocratic hauteur with crass material interests made it difficult, in generations to come, for any unbiased political person to join the parties of the Right even when they espoused wholly justifiable positions and ideals: witness the failure of the "Wochenblatt" party of Moritz August (von) Bethmann-Hollweg (1795-1887) in 1852, which sought to combine liberal nobility, reformist officialdom, and Protestant pietism; and yet Bismarck's cynical protectionist alliance between East Elbian landed proprietors and heavy industry succeeded only too well. Witness also the failure of the attempt, in the last years of the Weimar Republic, to present an honest and upright conservative viewpoint in a "Free Conservative Party"—an attempt on which the idealist Heinrich Brüning had staked his political hopes. All such experiences indicate how closely conservative *Realpolitik* is wedded to quite different concerns and to what degree the "honest, truly conservative" ideologies are mere facades. Once these ideologies were neatly separated from those material interests, all political weight remained on the side of the material interests.

Ideological conservatism, which in recent times has generally emerged in close conjunction with nationalism and denominationalism, is a quasi-religious phenomenon that shares with organized religious denominationalism the practice of transmitting its tenets at the prelogical, uncritical age of early childhood and later surrounding them with protective and watertight ideological taboos. The result is a curious, mysterious twilight of faith (in contrast with the daylight of knowledge), an alliance with theological themes that withdraws matters from the jurisdiction of rational logic to the prelogical emotional laws of thought. From the viewpoint of intellectual history, this is nothing but the original ideology of superstratifiers, which, through however many changes, has always remained true to itself: *plus ça change, plus c'est la même chose.*

The outsider, however, who has not grown up in such a tradition from childhood, can be converted only in exceptional cases, and can easily give its rock-ribbed upholders the impression that the convert is dishonest or a social climber and toady. Subjectively, of course, this is an unfair impression, since good faith (an amazingly cheap commodity, in any case) is as a general rule readily available and even asserted with great vehemence. If conservatives are deeply imbued with the notion that their self-defense coincides with the defense of the divinely willed order entrusted to them and that the situation is so desperate that the noble end justifies any available means, this action for the good cause will be waged with that fierce and indignant tenacity that often is expressed in their facial physiognomy.

Most of the German romanticists were Protestants, and even those who were later converted to Catholicism displayed a frantic emotional intensity that did not make them at home in Catholicism with its pacific self-assurance. As compared to these Protestants of the German culture complex, the conservative theorists of the Catholic Latin countries—particularly France (de Bonald, de Maistre, Chateaubriand) and Spain (Donoso-Cortés)—had the great advantage of being able to build further upon the medieval tradition of a great theological doctrinal structure with a superior philosophic training. Also, the phrase "responsibility before God" had for them a concrete, institutional content, since in Catholic practice it signified control of the rulers by the Church, the clergy, and the confessional. Moreover, the very term *conservatism* goes back to Chateaubriand's periodical *Le Conservateur* (1818); it spread to England and Germany only in the 1830s.

Prussian-German feudalism, by nature scarcely romantic, at first found in political romanticism an ideological defense that far surpassed its own intellectual level. To be sure, a proper East Elbian squire found its ideas repugnant and all manner of ideology uncom-

fortable. The Junkers considered it scandalous that they had to justify themselves, and their alliance with representatives of the realm
of the mind was forged most reluctantly and under duress. However,
with the decline of romanticism, they came to the conclusion, which
Montalembert had earlier expressed in France, that "not the vague
God of this or that system, but the God of the catechism" was the
only reliable guarantor of the existing order. Friedrich Julius Stahl
(1802-1861) arranged for the deromanticization of conservative
theory, for the changeover from the unreliable romantic pantheism
to the reliable theism of the Protestant creed.

Through Stahl's theism, Burke's aforementioned central idea acquired the following variation: "It is unseemly of the present generation to haul before its court what God has allowed and preserved
through the ages and which it has received without its having a
hand in the matter."[5] Hence a legitimation by legal superannua-
tion—prescriptive legitimacy. And, of course, the clever and adroit
Stahl did not overlook anything that could be used for objective justification of the conservative standpoint against the parties of the
Left. When so honorable and learned a personage as Wilhelm Heinrich von Riehl (1823-1897) demanded national traditions as the
principle of a creative conservatism ("Preserve, in order to continue
to build upon an historical foundation until the new itself in turn
becomes the historical foundation for the future"[6]), it was indeed
difficult to raise any valid objection against such well-founded
wisdom—provided that the true intentions did not go beyond such a
statement.

Behind all these changing ideological facades, in Germany above
all, were the economic interests of the large landed proprietors—
and, later, of heavy industry. They knew how to assert their interests, preferably in the form of a demand for direct or indirect government subsidies. This, of course, was at the expense of the other
strata of the population, whereby the old tribute paid by the subjugated to the superstratifiers reappeared in modern garb.

But political romanticism turned its gaze away from this disagreeable present age toward the pious and Christian Middle Ages,
where the position of the feudal upper stratum, internally or externally, had not yet been shaken. However, the extensive investigation of medieval sources which such romanticism stimulated increasingly brought to light many disagreeable details that marred
this idealized picture. The faith of the Middle Ages and its ecclesiastical embodiment, fought and overcome by Luther, was by no means

attractive to Protestants, and public opinion was still under the influence of the Enlightenment's deprecation of that period as the "dark Middle Ages."

Thus, one was forced to choose an epoch even further back in time than the Middle Ages as the object of one's romantic nostalgia—preferably one about which there was no very exact knowledge and which thus offered greater freedom for speculation, fantasy, and wishful thinking. This period was the Germanic "Urzeit," the period before Teutonic tribes were converted to Christianity. Hence a motley procession of devotees of the cult of Wotan, of race fanaticism, of runic interpretation, and of unalleviated alliteration.

2. INDIVIDUALISM

The roots of modern individualism lie deep in the transcendental individualism of the salvation religions, already discussed in detail in connection with the phenomenon of isolation. This tendency was especially strengthened in German Protestantism after the Thirty Years' War. Karl Holl finds in this period a complete "dissolution of the idea of religious community." "The churchly community-feeling was in the process of disappearing" as a result of "the one-sided emphasis on the idea of personality."[7] This religious idea of personality was transmitted by German preromanticism, romanticism, and, above all, Pietism.

The concept of personality and its superlative—the genius—was a central concept for preromanticism and romanticism. In Germany its development was prepared by Pietism, in England by Platonism. Leibniz attributed the difference between each monad and every other to the *identitas indiscernibilium*. Moreover, he had coined a phrase, the profundity of which fired the young Goethe with enthusiasm: *Individuum est ineffabile*. The egalitarian currents in the theory of the Enlightenment and the philistine features in its practice increased the passionate opposition of the poets of *Sturm und Drang* and their enthusiasm for the *Kerl*, the jolly fellow.

Rousseau gave this outlook epigrammatic expression in the famous opening sentences of his *Confessions*, named after those of Saint Augustine: He is assertedly different from other men. Nature, he claims, had broken the mold from which he had been made; therefore the real theme of this confessional book was *Moi seul*.

Rousseau similarly repeats this idea on other occasions too, almost coquettishly in a smug, mannered formula: "I think differently

from other men." "It is not my fault if my ideas are unlike those of
other men, and it was not up to me to organize my head in another
way."

Now, to be sure, the ideal of unrestricted voluntariness in individual decisions and in the character formation of each individual,
as such, is altogether justified. And to the degree that this ideal is
realized we can expect, as a social and esthetic gain, a lively variety,
a rich and full instrumentation of the social symphony. At the same
time we can expect the highest degree of harmony and unison from
the unrestricted and undistorted freedom of growth to be provided
by the context of an organic community enjoying the full assent of
its members. It is a gross distortion of this ideal situation to attribute a value to mere individual differences, and to make the ability to "be a fool on one's own" the very goal of one's life. Indeed,
under the markedly pathological presuppositions with which we
must deal today, freedom often leads to disunity and dissonance.

The classic-romantic enthusiasm for the ideal of "individuality" is
close to becoming alien and incomprehensible to us: if we inquire
about the basis of this ideal, its roots seem to lie in the pattern of
social entertainment of that period. The educated stratum lived in
small social circles that were in turn interconnected in many ways.
The members of each of these circles met regularly, sometimes
weekly. In these social gatherings each member had a "role," an assigned task, defined by the way in which he fitted himself into this
circle, and by the contribution he made to its social and intellectual
life. That corresponds exactly to the etymology of personality (*per-
sona* = mask, role). This extemporized, "lived" role was for each
member the crucial factor determining his social standing, prestige,
and consciousness. As an "actor" he worked to develop and perfect
his "part": the more integrated, the richer, the more impressive the
better. This must have been what Goethe meant when he called "individuality" "the supreme happiness of human beings" ("höchstes
Glück der Erdenkinder sei nur die Persönlichkeit").

Consider, for instance, Goethe's portrayal of his friend of Leipzig
student days, Ernst Wolfgang Behrisch (1738-1809). The main point
is the proof that Behrisch maintained the same (comic) role
throughout his life. When Goethe saw him in 1801, after more than
thirty years, Behrisch was an old man but still "in the best of
spirits," indulging in "the old jokes with which we shamefully
wasted our time." "He was the same as ever," "he kept up his old
character," remarks Goethe with obvious pleasure and not without
an undertone of admiration for the nonstop histrionic performance:

"Behrisch in every respect was a good character for the theater."[8]

In Goethe's *Wilhelm Meisters Lehrjahre* (vol. 3) the hero justifies his decision to become an actor on the ground that at least on stage total personality was achievable, if only as esthetic effect; in real life this was the prerogative of the aristocrat, while the burgher was condemned to unglamorous, fragmentary, one-sided accomplishment. And this far-reaching sociological interconnection, remote for us today, justifies the disproportionate amount of space given to the theater in this educational novel.

"To play a role" in society subsequently becomes a combination of histrionic appearance and aristocratic reality accessible also to the burgher: to affect noble airs and bearing is a social game played by the bourgeois. Sociologically speaking, this is a particularly interesting variant of the aristocratization of the bourgeoisie, of social slippage of aristocratic life forms and modes. And in the example just cited we have seen that often it was a question of comic rank roles—in which members of the lower strata were allowed to appear on the court stages during the age of Louis XIV.

Goethe gives a general portrayal of the sociological structure of this era in his *Campaign in France*:

> Men of talent succeeded in establishing themselves in their acquired possession of the general esteem, and in their social relations assisted and supported each other; the advantage obtained being no longer preserved by simple individuals, but by a unanimous majority. That some degree of circumspection was necessary here was to be expected; like other children of the world, they infused a certain kind of artifice into their relations; the peculiarities of each were excused, the sensitiveness of one counterbalanced that of the other.
>
> By this means many an individual was brought prominently forward, and was more highly valued, from being adopted into this distinguished company. . . . People thought they knew each other better; and thus it happened most curiously, that many an individual's personal character was made public, who had previously been mixed up, without being noticed, in the ordinary everyday life of society. . . .
>
> The effect of this was stronger and greater than may be imagined; every one formed a high opinion of himself as a definite, complete being, and, relying on this, considered himself entitled also to adopt all sorts of peculiarities, absurdities and defects, into the complex of his precious existence. This result ensued

the more easily, as, in the whole proceeding, the particular nature of the individual alone came into question, without reference to reason in general, which must, however, govern all nature. . . . But another remarkable consequence of this was the
consideration in which individuals were held by each other.
Notable men, admired in life, were reverenced, if not personally, at least in their pictures; and a young man had only to distinguish himself in any way, to make his personal acquaintance
sought after everywhere, and if this could not be accomplished,
they contented themselves with his portrait; for which purpose
the profiles drawn by the shade on the wall were found very useful, affording, when carefully and well done, an exact likeness.[9]

In the study of history in the nineteenth century the "personality"
of authors, artists, or historic actors increasingly became a central
theme. Explanation of works on the basis of the personality of the
artist and of his experiences was viewed as the most essential and
loftiest task of literary, artistic, and musical history. The works
were really only a means for exploring as thoroughly as possible the
personality. People became conscious, with a delicious shiver, of the
alleged affinity between *Genius and Insanity*, to cite the title of a
frequently translated work by Cesare Lombroso (1836-1909).

The conventional biographers of poets and others resemble the
inquisitive child which scratches at its doll to see what is inside it,
only to have the stuffing fall out. Nineteenth-century biographers
could not do enough of this soul-scratching, this hunting after personal intimacies. Yet what should concern us in a poet, and what he
himself was concerned with, was his accomplishment, his poetry.
How he accomplished it is his business, what he accomplished is
ours. Thus his work should be analyzed in terms of intellectual history, of history of form and content. Only those aspects of the work
which do not objectively stand on their own two feet require further
recourse to subjective explanations.

The worship of genius began to flower in the Enlightenment.
Even the arch-skeptic Voltaire had been acclaimed as a kind of
savior. Quesnay, the founder of the Physiocratic school of political
economy, enjoyed adoration in his sect, Rousseau appeared as a kind
of suffering Redeemer, and Saint-Simon was made the object of a
cult of salvation by his followers. Later, the public adoration of famous musical virtuosi, conductors, and tenors was glorified as something sublime, even religious. The pathological and contemptible
character of this attitude first began to be felt when it was extended

to prizefighters and movie stars of both sexes. At last the doctrine that everything was permitted to the "genius" was seriously espoused in leading intellectual circles; a highly effective preliminary exercise, as we can see, for the totalitarian masses' submission to their dictators.

Richard Wagner was not only a brilliant musical performer and "original" composer and poet, but was also filled with the ambition to be the "renewer" of culture. Thus he combined the three main lines of the cult of genius in his person; by his family and his followers he was consciously revered as sect leader, "founder of a religion," and a new Messiah. Nietzsche, at first his herald, later became his anti-Christ. Nietzsche's doctrine of the Superman, for which Kierkegaard's doctrine of the Super-Christian had paved the way, was one of the most effective formulations of the new religion of genius. As the Bible of this his *Thus Spoke Zarathustra* was expressly propagated: the nineteenth-century mania for setting records had here attained its sublimest peak. "Education of the personality" also became the ideal of pedagogy. Yet ironically, as long as no one had talked much about personality, strong, self-willed personalities abounded. Since the ideal of personality was consciously promoted, and the cult of personality widely practiced, real personalities have become scarce. What our so-called personality education delivers are products to whom one is tempted to call out, with Shakespeare's Coriolanus, "Get ye home, ye fragments!"

Originally the concept of genius had been restricted to the sphere of intellectual production, in particular art and literature: even Schopenhauer had ridiculed the cult by asserting that there should also be a genius of the deed. The cult of Napoleon, which especially in Germany assumed the form of genius worship, filled this gap.

Later Prussian-German patriots set Frederick II, "Frederick the Great," against the genius Napoleon, until finally in Bismarck they too could finally produce a contemporary genius of the deed.

Liberal Protestantism of the nineteenth century declared Jesus a "religious genius" in order to bring the "personality" of Jesus closer to "modern man," to make it comprehensible and emotionally accessible. For if salvation is still to be offered to an unholy age, it must be through a new "religious genius," a new savior, a kind of supergenius. Among theologians these notions were propagated by Johannes Müller, while a whole library on Jesus as a genius was written by lay authors. Carlyle's *Heroes and Hero Worship* had paved the way for these tendencies, and Nietzsche's doctrine of the Superman gave them a Holy Writ. That "the cry for a genius leader-personality" was "an hysterical cry and a cry of impotence" was recognized only by a few.[10] The cult of personality and the worship of genius developed into a religion of the educated and semieducated in Germany, so that later the "leader" had only to leap with "brilliant" unscrupulousness onto this gilded throne, which had been on display for so long, and before which the public—the German public at any rate—had so long genuflected.

This cult of genius now seems very much a thing of the past. We are, to begin with, human beings, human beings like any other. He who produces, gives, in addition, the product of his rare creative hours in a concentration such as life affords only exceptionally. When strenuous effort is made to raise a human being of flesh and blood to the level of the loftiest literary conception, this cannot be done without much cramping—aside from its being but a short step from the sublime to the ridiculous. The notion of the genius demands that one must constantly in daily life play himself, his own role in intellectual history; as Stefan George once put it in his versified history of literature, Mallarmé was forever "bleeding for his own monument." How much more human, wiser, and more relaxed was Jacob Burckhardt, who every evening drank his pint of beer in the company of Basle artisans without the slightest trace of condescension or the least effort to be incognito.

3. Reverence and Its Exaggeration

The place of reverence in the social and moral scheme is determined by the fact that it defines the natural slope along which the flow of human tradition runs its course. Without this slope, this flow is bound to come to an instant halt. Tradition and culture would be interrupted. Just as water cannot be made to run uphill, so education, teaching, tradition—in short, culture in general—are quite impossible without reverence. Before anyone can critically develop a contribution on his own responsibility, he must already have accepted innumerable other elements of the contribution of others on the responsibility of others—that is, on the basis of trust and reverence. Through the millennia, the social slope of the cultural tradition has rested upon trust, deference, and respect of each generation for the last. This is also why reverence is accorded to parents and old people for preservation as an important human value; whoever surrenders such a position of deference out of weakness, kindness, or false liberalism betrays the first foundation of culture. Education without reverence destroys its own foundation. The natural carriers of this authority and responsibility are the parents—those "human beings who," in the words of C. G. Jung, "for the first time transmit to the mind of the child those sombre and mighty laws which force and form not only families but rather peoples, nay mankind as a whole."[11]

This natural organic form of reverence rests upon the structure of the family and its bonds among the generations. From it also grows that reverence which holds together the pyramid of all higher social structures. A natural leader is not one who controls the means of forcing the masses behind or beneath him but rather one who sees more clearly what others dimly long for, one who expresses what others inarticulately sense, one who carries out what others would dimly like to do.

If we inquire into the origins of reverence in the development of the individual human being, it certainly is lacking in the baby and small child: their trustfulness toward parents, brothers, and sisters is still devoid of any sense of distance, reserve, or shyness; it is a clumsy trustfulness. A detachment, a distancing from the parents sets in for the first time in the first negative stage or age of defiance. Thus, in fact, reverence first seems to develop in the subsequent latency period. We could view it as a new positive relation to the parents' superiority across the distance created by the first detachment. This reverent affirmation can go so far as to consider the father as omnipotent or nearly omnipotent. This overestimation, often boundless as measured by our adult standards, has its biological importance as an expression of willingly affirmed subordination—that is, of the reverence necessary to this age level. The second detachment ensues at puberty, where criticism of culture has its proper place in human development and where it attempts by way of objective criticism to find an affirmative relationship to parents and to the tradition transmitted by them. Puberty is the period of criticism, of revolt against blind faith in authority, of critical testing, and then conscious acceptance of the culture tradition. Thus reverence takes shape only gradually and relatively late in the course of individual development, and until then social rearing and culture tradition must have already exercised an influence.

But this development of reverence, which lies at the base of all cultural tradition, does not remain unaffected by superstratification and its consequences.

Superstratification created a new two-layered social structure with a distance between upper and lower strata, which until then had not yet existed in cooperative relationships among men. And this artificially exaggerated distance between the two strata was pushed to the extreme in situations where the entire collective power of the upper stratum is concentrated in the person of the ruler.

This tendency reached a high point in early superincumbency, with the god-kings of the great Erythraean culture complex. They were gods or sons of gods, and contact with their bodies or with objects in contact with them brought death. Supernatural capacities were attributed to them. Weather and fertility especially depended upon them. Influences of this extend as far as archaic Greek culture. Hellenistic and Roman rulers, partaking of divine veneration in their lifetimes, upon their death were transposed among the constellations. Even the kings of France were ascribed magic healing powers. The numinous "king's touch" operated on all sides. "Travel with Caesar and his good luck." "A king of England drowns not."

Conversely, the subjects were beaten down in order to make this distance from rulers as great as possible. For instance, they were allowed to approach the "shepherds of the people" only on all fours and with a tuft of grass hanging from the mouth. Or, at royal feasts they were forced to let themselves be butchered as public sacrifices. Or upon the death of a king, all members of his retinue were forced to let themselves be buried alive with him.

The king, however, regardless of his exaggerated claims and the size of his kingdom, or degree of his power, also was only a human being, born of woman; hence strenuous attempts were made to veil this embarrassing antinomy. For example, matters could be so arranged that the king was shown to the people only in full robes during the most solemn moments, at the height of his position. On the other hand, his unavoidable humanity—no one is a hero to his valet—was removed from the subjects by a wall of taboos. Thus no subject could see a great Erythraean god-king eat or drink, under pain of death. On the same grounds, however, the king himself was condemned to death immediately upon exhibiting a weakness, illness, or incapacity of any kind.

Strenuous efforts were made to prop up the person, life, and bearing of the king on the level of his position. For example, the successor to the throne of the Polynesian island of Mangareva in the Pacific Ocean is reported to have been trained as follows: "Shortly after his birth he is brought up to a high mountain and takes up residence in a hut, which had already sheltered his forefathers during their period of training. Without contact with parents and brothers and sisters, he grows up here under the care of his nurse and some female servants. No subject may set foot in his dwelling. The little prince is shown the broad expanse of land around him and it is signified to him that it is his own. 'Your people crawls already at your feet,' he is told. 'One day you will rule over them, and they will belong to you. All that which your eyes behold, belongs to you. Your power is boundless as the ocean that surrounds us. Heaven and earth will receive laws from you.' Thus does it come to pass that the rulers of Mangareva believe that they are the first or the only monarchs of the world, and they are particularly of the opinion that the universe ceases on the horizon."[12]

A modern way out, finally, which signifies a nod to "democracy" and is usually received by the loyal subjects with much emotion, is that of studied understatement, of an ostentatious simplicity in dress, manner, and bearing. Frederick II of Prussia, "Der alte Fritz," in his shabby field jacket was the first to adopt it, and he was followed by Hitler and Stalin. Hitler affected the image of the unknown corporal in the First World War, and Stalin, in his tunic devoid of decorations and with a short pipe in his mouth under the long moustache, the image of "good old Joe"—by which mask of *bonhomie* Roosevelt, along with the American public, would be taken in.

The longer the subjects were delivered to a structured domination, the stronger was their "need for salvation"; and in fact the salvation religions, beginning with Mazdaism and Buddhism, had arisen in settings of this kind. As a counterimage to the mighty, wicked sultan, the figure of a still mightier, good, divine ruler was developed, the Messiah, the Redeemer. All these had pronounced positive characteristics opposed to the negative characteristics and vices of the tyrant. However, this figure was placed still higher above the level of humanity—since, after all, he also had to outdo the secular divine king.

In a Caesaropapist way the mundane autocrats, especially when they had the priesthood on their side (and under their thumb), then also tried to unite the titles of their counterpart, of the redeemer, to their person so as to leave no room for competition from this quarter. Messianic titles like "the Lord's Anointed" or "the Messenger of God" become more and more frequent, and soon hardly a ruler is to be found who does not seek a share of such numinous superelevation, be it finally only through the phrase "by the grace of God" before his title.

Such claims, towering heavenward, are of course believed only by the particular subjects or faithful of the claimant—and these must profess a belief in them on pain of bodily death or of eternal damnation. All other people are convinced that he is a mere human being, sometimes even a man of far below average qualities.

For that matter, unfortunately, we no longer need to reconstruct the image of the divine ruler from the oblivion of the grey and gruesome past. The spectacle of the divinization of a tyrant and of the enslavement of his subjects has unfolded before all our eyes. Iosif Vissarionovich Dzhugashvili (1879-1953), son of a drunken Georgian cobbler, had for decades worked himself up to the position of autocrat of the Soviet Russian world empire and, as Joseph Stalin, exercised a tyranny that in bloodthirstiness and inhuman brutality could match that of any divinized king of the past. Indeed, if there the blood sacrifices of the subjects numbered thousands and tens of thousands, here they rose to millions.

Stalin, too, in accordance with the old ritual, was finally "killed by his menials." But that, of course, was kept strictly secret so that the myth of his supermanhood, posthumously heightened still further, could pass on to posterity and serve his successor as a spectacular background—if only his entourage had been able to agree on this successor. As this agreement was never successfully achieved after four years and a collegiate interregnum of pretenders, each one threatening the other's life, something unprecedented came to pass: the enormous and excessive pressure, which the extant forces no longer sufficed to contain, led to an explosion. And as none of the pretenders would grant to any of the others Stalin's throne with his mythic legend as background, both throne and legend were demolished and the myth of Stalin brutally exposed and destroyed by his own accomplices. At the Twentieth Congress of the Bolshevik party of the Soviet Union in 1956, Stalin was exposed for what he had been: the embodiment of insatiable lust for power, a beast in human form, a mass-murderer wallowing in blood, an insidious traitor who had his own comrades-in-arms tortured and executed after wresting forced confessions from them.

And this same Stalin had been glorified as "Father of peoples," "the brilliant architect of communism," "the great field marshall," the "great standard-bearer of peace," "the great thinker of our time," "the great fighter and genius of our time." In 1949 the Moscow Conference of Bolshevist Youth Organizations promulgated a communication that concluded as follows:

Comrade Stalin, all the ends of the earth are illumined by the sun rays of your life!

Stalin: Banner of the great struggle!
Stalin: Hymn of future centuries!
Stalin: Sun of Russian fate!
Stalin: Happiness of the Soviet Union!
Stalin: Happiness of Soviet Man!
Stalin: Splendor and fame of victories!
Stalin: Wisdom of immortal ideas!
Stalin: Lenin of the present!

Occasionally in antiquity deposed rulers were later cursed and their memory obliterated. Such an operation, however, was regularly carried out by the enthroned successor in his own favor: the blackened past of domination was supposed to allow the glorious present to shine all the brighter. But never was the "cult of person" so greatly condemned, the fall so precipitous and deep as in Stalin's case. Nor, up to then, had it ever unfolded in full view of all mankind.

The archaic ideal of a superhuman ruler, after its collapse in Soviet Russia, cannot be restored; never again will it find a ready will to believe. Perhaps a period of mankind's intellectual history encompassing thousands of years has at last come to a close.

In the modern era in the West the schism between Catholicism and Protestantism, with vehement recriminations of each sect against the other, was hardly favorable to reverence, nor was the way in which absolutism tried to enforce exaggerated forms of reverence on command. This made things all the easier for the rationalistic critics of the Enlightenment. The eighteenth-century Western world was bound to experience a decline and depreciation of reverence. This decline was accelerated even further in the nineteenth century, especially in Germany. And the deliberate reaction of romanticism and conservatism, because of their provocative character, were little suited to halt this decline.

At the peak of this development, however, a memorable attempt at restoring the ideal of reverence was undertaken precisely in Germany during the Imperial period (1871-1918), in the circle around the poet Stefan George. Lack of reverence had been a reaction to the feudal abuse of reverence as a means for moral suppression of the subjugated. Arrogance and pride in progress of the nineteenth century rejected and ridiculed reverence of any kind. In the intellectual-historical recoil it was almost inevitable that the countermovement should also make no distinctions and espouse an aesthetically sublimated aristocratism. Leadership and domination were equated, no distinction was made between the forced dominion of superstratification and a natural grown hierarchy, and Plato's *Republic* was unreservedly accepted among the sacred writings.

Shelley had once declared that "poets are the unacknowledged legislators of the world." It became Stefan George's ambition to become the acknowledged legislator of the world. He succeeded in achieving what Nietzsche had longed for—namely, assembling a circle of worshipful young people around him, "an intellectual and artistic society which feels itself united by wholly particular rejections and affirmations, by a special feeling for life."[13]

Robert Boehringer has written of George: "Once when in his presence it was related that Napoleon reportedly had said, 'J'aime le pouvoir comme artiste,' he shot back: 'J'aime l'art comme pouvoir.' " In 1905 in a great confessional letter he wrote: "I cannot live my life, save in complete outer sovereignty."[14] Understandably, this absolute thirst for power was intolerable to many. Hugo von Hofmannsthal's recoil from the very outset was due to this, and sooner or later it also drove away others and even led to a temporary break with his beloved Maximin who, in a letter of renunciation (30 January 1904) undertook to save his own skin.

At the same time the relationship of the poet to his enthusiastic following was expressly viewed and characterized as "domination," and the claim to equal rank with actual rulers like Caesar or Napoleon was entered. Correspondingly George's devotees believed themselves a superaristocracy, since "the families of the mind . . . stand above the families of blood." Friedrich Wolters, in his *Domination and Service*, expressly glorifies this lust for power and its complement "*the pleasure of serving*," "which is placed in the enormous suspense of the world as the eternal balance to *the pleasure of exercising domination*." "Yet in the vault of distress the cry for new domination reverberates more loudly, and when it comes, the despairing spirits again experience the miracle of what was thought impossible," "the highest possibility that the ruler will give birth to himself in One man," the ruler who "himself is the content of his rulership."[15]

On this point Edgar Salin in his adulatory study of George writes: "Wolters's experience of the ruler not only sees George in a new way; rather, in the image of George and of his domination he shows the origin and gives the sign for new world-substance and new world-construction."[16] To us it seems that this shows the very end of all old world-substance and old world-construction.

Salin calls George "the all wise," speaks of the "more than human power of George," and declares that "borne by the knowledge that in this age George was the voice and the herald of God, the devotion of the disciples to the domineering poet was unconditional and complete and transformed the personal following into an impersonal service."[17] This is an allusion to the Centenary Lines in *The Seventh Ring* (1907), of fundamental importance for the theological history of the George circle:

> Each age has only
> One god, and only one proclaims his throne.[18]

In the early phases of the First World War, George's disciples dreamed not only of "a destruction of the hated Prussian empire," but also of "a new confederation of the Rhine at whose head the poet-ruler was to take his place," since he "was born for rulership." And after the collapse of 1918 "the general perplexity was so great that at times the hope could sprout in some that the German people, plunged into the abyss, would now hearken to the voice of its poet and perhaps even lay the reins of spiritual leadership in the hands of the fellow-citizen." The Master himself "hoped still to experience that some day the faultfinders and cheap politicians among the Germans would also understand that it is not a matter of whether one is Catholic or Protestant or Jew, but rather only of whether he belongs to him and his friends."[19] When a small group of two dozen poets, artists, professors, and students in intimate conversation called itself "the Republic," the humanistically educated person understood this Platonic allusion, and the crude sphere of political reality remained untouched. All this occurred in the area of wishful dreams, and thus George, whose fate was more merciful than Plato's, was spared the cruel test of political realization.

In the service of an exaggerated cultivation of reverence, questions of rank came to the foreground for the George circle in an almost Byzantine way. The great men of world history, expressly recognized as such and canonized as it were, were worshipped almost as preincarnations of the last Buddha. What precise degree and kind of adoration was due to each became a crucial problem.

It is difficult to understand how the heightened human and aesthetic sensibilities exhibited by the George circle could overlook the careerist, parvenu qualities of the great destroyer, Napoleon—who let his initial "N" be stamped anywhere: on tables, on walls—even on gilded chamber pots. With brutal coarseness he commanded the ladies of the court to sexual service. Because of his petty suspicion and jealousy he was constantly concerned about his dignity. He could never suppress an (all-too-well founded) suspicion that he was not being taken at face value. In short, the plebeian vulgarity and manner of the "Little Corporal" were in embarrassing contrast to his official rank.

The dogma of one herald of God in each age, upon which George's pretention to uniqueness rested, forced him to choose between Goethe and Napoleon. Significantly, the decision fell against the all-too-humane Goethe, to whom George accordingly (in his poem *Goethe's Last Night in Italy*) attributes the following soliloquy:

> Fate denied you the lot of more fortunate stems
> Who were accorded a seer at the dawn of their era,
> One who was born as a son, not a grandson of Gaia.
>
> . . . .
> You had no helper like this, and I am not he.[20]

Thus Goethe is made to yield first rank to Napoleon—and, by implication, all the more to George, the hero of the age. How disastrous the lack of distinction between leadership and rule of naked force (and the championing of the latter) was bound to be is made clear in certain passages of George's poetry. These, following Nietzsche, glorify inhumanity, brutality, and the most loathsome superstratification mentality; taking them out of context, national socialism could quite logically claim that they referred to itself. For example, in George's last volume of poetry, *The New Reich*, note a passage of a poem entitled "The Poet in Times of Confusion":

> And when the final hope has almost perished
> In sternest grief, his eyes already see
> A coming light. Unstained by venal mobs,
> By threadbare minds and follies steeped in poison,
> A younger generation rises toward him
>
> . . . .
> Begot the only one who can restore.
> He breaks the chains and sweeps aside the rubble,
> He scourges home the last to lasting law,
> Where lord again is lord, the great is great
> Again, where poise again is poise. He fastens
> The true device upon the nation's banner.
> Through tempests and the dread fanfares of dawning,
> He leads his tried and faithful to work
> Of sober day and founds the Kingdom Come.[21]

Is it not comprehensible that some of George's faithful glimpsed in *Der Führer* the fulfillment of the poet's prophecy? Was Hitler not the only one who could restore, the man who was "begot"? Did he not detest the insane years of ignominy, the threadbare cerebral web of the theorists, the venomous frippery of degenerate art? Did he not break the chains of Versailles, did he not sweep aside the rubble with his New Order? Did he not scourge the deviant and those lost on the way home? Did he not fasten the true emblem of the swastika on the national banner?[22] Did he not plant the Kingdom Come, the New Reich?

And whatever, in the reality of the new Reich, may not have corresponded fully to George's lofty pronouncements—was this not the eternal tragedy of the unbridgeable distance between the ideal and the real? Must not the strength of true faith preserve itself precisely in such trials? Is it not a known fact, after all, that one cannot make an omelet without breaking eggs?

The glorification of political murder is found in another George poem, this one addressed to "The Doer," forming part of *The Tapestry of Life*; it is echoed in "A Poem of My Times" in *The Seventh Ring*:

> . . . With this the rebel
> Attacked the foe's domain with torch and dagger,
> Longing for deeds—but not for deeds alone!

Is it not possible that people like the murderers of Rathenau and their ilk saw this as a reference to themselves? And the "Third Centenary Lines" of *The Seventh Ring* reads:

> A Man! a deed! The people and the council plead.
> Look not to one who shared your feasts. For one who kept
> Besides your slayers many years, or one who slept
> Behind your prison bars, may rise and do the deed.[23]

Does this not fit Hitler and his band of convicted criminals like a glove?

Or a verse from the following, *The Seventh Ring* of 1907:

> Chant of revenge,
> Plunder and sing,
> Saviors, destroy and deliver![24]

Could not the SS unhesitatingly have adopted this as its slogan and viewed its bestial activity as the execution in practice of such a demand? Of course, it was "not meant that way"—but cannot any expressed idea be so exculpated from its own actualization?

And even the notion, later so popular, of race pollution and the demand for genocide are not lacking:

> You, who on reeking corpses swing your scourges,
> May you preserve us from too light an ending,
> And from the worst, the blood betrayal. *Races*
> *Committing this will be wholly uprooted*
> Unless their best is used to halt the doom.[25]

In a related context the "priceless blood" of those "with hair as fair as light"(!) is also glorified; here, too, "blood" is probably meant in the "racial" sense and not, as is otherwise mostly the case in George, in the sense of an individual grace. And already purely linguistically the brutal-prosaic *"will be wholly uprooted"* (my emphasis) seems by far better suited to one of Hitler's infamous Führer-orders than to the lofty style of George's poetry.

It was thus no mere coincidence that the Nazis, after their advent to power, claimed to be the fulfillment of George's prophecies—or, as his follower Salin puts it, "the most part of his oldest adherents had to suffer through seeing Satan's hordes invoking their image and their teaching."[26] All the more so, since some members of the George circle who did not, as Jews, happen to be immune to temptation, did succumb to the lure of national socialism. One of this group at the time dedicated his latest work of scholarship to "The Poet and the Führer"—George and Hitler.[27]

Yet from a vantage point of humanist learning and social standing, such as that of the George circle, anyone should have known from the start what to make of Hitler and his accomplices—anyone, that is to say, who was not encumbered by a less-than-average capacity for judgment or whose standards of judgment were not distorted in that very direction. Such a distortion even afflicted a man like Claus Stauffenberg, who belonged to the closest circle around Stefan George. "As a young officer Stauffenberg had welcomed Hitler's rise, he recognized his tactical skill and his initial successes. He had also let his children be educated along national socialist lines."[28] He considered the year 1933 as "a genuine people's rising" and placed himself "in full uniform at the head of a procession of enthusiastic crowds on the streets of Bamberg." "He was stirred by the power field that [Hitler] was able to generate, his transforming vehemence which made the seemingly impossible in a static world suddenly seem possible. . . . Violently or mockingly he rejected the adverse judgments of those who only complained or calumniated without being able to set something over against it, clinging only to an image of the past."[29]

Over against all that, of course, stands the decisive fact that Stefan George himself eluded the crude attempt of the Third Reich and of its clubfooted propaganda minister to enlist him—eluded it through emigration, death, and a grave beyond the Reich borders.

Stefan George set as his highest goal the shaping of his own being, of his own life and life sphere, seeking to shape them even beyond the level of his own achievement by standards of "objective spirit." Someone like myself, who was in no way connected with him, must concede that George succeeded in this to the most improbable degree and with the most impressive completeness. How one judges such deliberate self-stylization and self-enhancement is another matter. But the way in which this effort, in its highest form, became second nature, and could be borne at once with such heightened dignity and such charming freedom—this is both remarkable and admirable.

The example of Stefan George and his followers also has transmitted a doctrine that comes natural to East Asian philosophy but of which Germans stand in particular need: that thought and life are not two separate things running alongside each other at random, but that our most important task—however we may seek to accomplish it—is to think our life and live our thought.

To revere is one thing; to be moved by the power and greatness of artistic expression is another; and the confusion of that ethical with this esthetic category easily leads to a dim atmosphere heavily laden with incense. Although form and content are by no means independent of one another (for it is the content that acquires concreteness in form), still, esthetic greatness and vigor of form by no means warrant the objective truth and validity of the content. The despicable is by no means always ugly, the beautiful by no means always good. I may very well recognize and fight a content although the form in which it is expressed touches and moves me—no matter how uncomfortable it may feel to be forced into such a split attitude by prevailing circumstances. Indeed, this combination of admiration and rejection is something we are likely to have to learn in many contexts. For example, I may experience Plato as the greatest of Greek dramatists, as an artist of rapturous creativity and vigor, and as a philosopher and teacher of surpassing genius—and at the very same time condemn his role in intellectual history as that of a fateful betrayal of his entrusted heritage of Attic intellect and Ionian science to the forces of theology, feudalism, and the Orient.[30] Anyone who cannot bear such tensions of value judgment should have arranged to be born into a simpler and more perfect world. To be sure it would be best to be able to give oneself wholly to both form and content. But where reality vouchsafes us this in only the rarest of instances it will not do to cloud our judgment through solemn, artificially induced intoxication.

Social masochism, the wallowing in servility, the weak-kneed surrender of one's rights, the blind readiness to subject oneself or to be ruled: all these are to be condemned (indeed they are contemptible). They are vices and betrayals of duty—as much as are the opposite vices of the sadistic category for which in fatal and complementary fashion, they pave the way. To be sure, Christianity in this respect has here perverted our sense of values by glorifying masochism, by surrounding the surrender of legitimate claims of the self with a halo of ethical superiority, and by thus discrediting the manly fight for human rights and depriving it of its sense of self-assurance.

Criticism must be cleansed of all envy and gloating, just as reverence must be cleansed of all masochistic submissiveness. What is really needed is a manly, upright reverence on the basis of a sober, incorruptible critique.

These reflections touch on a fundamental problem of ethics. Responsible criticism and unbending standards of value are the foundation of freedom. Reverence, respect, deference, esteem, consideration, and goodwill are the feelings of descending order of intensity on which the unity of social structures in their organic hierarchy are founded. Hence, here more than anywhere, strict and clean distinctions are called for.

4. *Jugendbewegung* (YOUTH MOVEMENT)

The generational protest in Germany at the turn of the last century known as the *Jugendbewegung* or "youth movement" did not, any more than other such movements, spring out of nowhere. It bore a striking similarity to that other protest against tradition that had been proclaimed a century and a half earlier by the preromantics. The central problem of Rousseau's great educational novel *Emile* had been how to exclude all the unnatural influences of tradition and convention and let the pupil's personality develop wholly in accordance with his nature. What Emile was to attain by being subjected to complex pedagogic constructs, hordes of adolescent Emiles, blissfully unaware of his example, fancied themselves capable of doing by themselves. In the mid-eighteenth century, loose, informal associations of German contemporaries, caught up in the *Sturm und Drang* movement, had translated Rousseau's literary rejection of convention into daily life. The *Sturm und Drang* movement was, so far as we know, the first instance of the sociological phenomenon of generational protest, a movement carried forward by young people just entering adult life; it spread to new recruits of the same age. In specific content, too, there were many similarities between the *Sturm und Drang* of the 1770s and *Jugendbewegung* of the 1890s and 1900s. "In everything they strove to return to what was simple and true; stays and high-heeled boots and shoes vanished, hair powder disappeared, and hair fell in natural locks again. The children were taught to swim and run, perhaps to box and wrestle." This portrayal by Goethe of the influence of "Rousseauistic maxims" on a hostess of his, can be applied without change to the *Jugendbewegung* and its pedogogical impact. A broad, soft collar worn open and outside the coat, and named after Goethe's friend Schiller, became the outward badge of the movement. The culture rubble of the nineteenth century was experienced as oppressive by the youth movement in the same way the *Sturm und Drang* movement viewed the courtly despotism of the post-baroque period. And in both cases it generated similar revolts. As Goethe put it, history came to be experienced as "burdensome rather than enjoyable by an aspiring youth because it fain would begin a new, nay a primordial world-epoch by itself"[31]—a statement that holds true for youth in general, and in particular for the German youth movement of the late nineteenth century. This gave not only an antihistorical but an antiliterary character to the movement, for whose members a collection of folk songs to guitar accompaniment, *Der Zupfgeigenhansl*, became the one and only Bible.

Nowhere perhaps had the artificiality, senselessness, and ugliness of the stale tradition of the German upper classes of the nineteenth century been more exaggeratedly and provocatively expressed than in the customs forced on young people between the ages of sixteen and twenty-six. Confirmation signified membership in the established church, a special examination qualified the young male for abbreviated military service as a reserve officer, completion of the course at a *Gymnasium* was considered a prelude to the "academic freedom" of university attendance—where proofs of manliness were expected to be given by smoking, boozing, whoring, telling smutty stories, brawling, and ritualized duelling.

Such were the rigid constraints of "freedom" in the interval between childhood and adult life for German youths of the upper crust—until one day the generation whose turn it was to be next simply refused to play along. It opposed the conventions of student life, the military spirit of barracks discipline, the arrogance of the upper classes, the big cities and the cult of technological progress, prudery (as well as its complementary opposite, coquetry)—in short, all the traditions and conventions of the nineteenth century. Against the rigidity of prevailing conventions every fellow protester was a welcome new ally.

What above all was put in the place of conventions was a feeling of community and as its expression group hikes through the woods and fields, a primitive life-style, close to nature and based on self-help. There were folk dances, folk songs, guitars. Dress was adapted to this life-style; soft open collars were combined with short pants and sandals. Girls shed the corset with whalebone stays. Bareheadedness became the rule—out of the conviction that the part of the human body most thickly covered by nature had the least need for an additional, artificial covering, save in the event of rain. Bathing was done in common and always in the nude; swim shorts or a swim suit would have caused great amusement—after all, that was the detested social constraint! Contrary to the parents' prudish fear about unbridled promiscuity, these youths turned out to be very proper and conscientious in sexual matters, tending to be somewhat frigid or timid in the face of the responsibility erotic activity enjoins.

The movement, sociologically speaking, consisted of small, informal groups, fulfilling the demands for a life-sphere in which each one knew everyone else. Some of these groups, such as "Der Wandervogel," formed by *Gymnasium* students in the Berlin suburb of Steglitz, adopted a formal structure, registering with the authorities as a society under the Civil Code, prescribing standard caps, and according resounding titles to its founder Karl Fischer, who was successively called Bacchant, Super-Bacchant, and Grand Bacchant. But this authoritarian structure, with its attendant internal power struggles, was alien to most of the groups that sprang up spontaneously alongside each other in many parts of Germany. In most of them there was indeed a structure of leaderhip—either crystallizing spontaneously around one of the youthful participants or else around a somewhat older member. Such were the circles around Stefan George (b. 1868), Gustav

Wyneken (b. 1875), or Käthe Kollwitz (b. 1867). The typical structure was not unlike that of a constitutional monarchy, where the
king reigns but does not govern. Informal ties linked many of these
groups with various reform movements, especially in education, and
with innovative artistic circles protesting against the decadent
Jugendstil of the period.

The first attempt at deliberate formal organization, at the meeting on the Hohe Meissner mountain near Kassel in October 1913
was the beginning of the end: it proved conclusively the inability of
the movement to formulate positive goals beyond the simple original one of shaping the leisure time of young people.

The first postwar years brought to this youth movement an erratic
expansion, an adoption by society at large. Earlier it had been restricted in somewhat aristocratic fashion (despite its democratic
ideals) to individual circles among the young bourgeoisie. The
front-line comradeship of the First World War between members of
petty bourgeoisie and proletariat paved the way for this socialization. The war experience had a strong unifying effect; the dissolution and upheaval of the postwar years favored such expansion. For
those born around 1900 or later, this second phase of the youth
movement, which for exponents of the first phase signified a revival,
was an intense and unique experience. But soon the absence of any
real intellectual leadership revealed itself all the more starkly, and
this vacuum was exploited by political parties, which rushed in with
their youth-oriented slogans. The left wing became Communist, the
right *völkisch* ("popular"), and a small Catholic group was also
formed, linked to the left wing of the Center party. Only now and
from this situation did the formal associational structure spread.

The failure of the Weimar Republic to accomplish the task of
bringing about a new integration of the German people drove this
federative (*bündische*) youth movement into the arms of a variety of
utopians or Pied Pipers. The young people lacked the presuppositions to solve what they perceived as an urgent task in a broad compass. It was for this reason that many of them in good faith placed
themselves at the disposal of the Third Reich. Such a step was facilitated by the total lack, within the youth movement, of a sense for
political realities and also by the eagerness with which national
socialism adapted many of its external forms for its own purposes.
Hitler himself was an ascetic, vegetarian, teetotaler, and non-
smoker, thereby fulfilling the only two substantive requirements set
down at the Hohe Meissner meeting. The "dynamic" of the National
Socialist "movement" could fill the vacuum of tangible substantial

goals. The leadership principle also, perhaps already in a degenerate form, was by no means alien to the youth movement.

Thus the youth movement provided national socialism with a reservoir of idealistic youthful energies. Independent federative organizations were dissolved or persecuted and driven into illegality. The Hitler Youth (HJ) and the German Maidens' Organization (BDM), which had taken over many outer trappings from the youth movement, remained as the only youth organizations. That was to be the end of the movement.

We have dealt with atomization as a major social sickness of the nineteenth century. In a first approximation this atomization usually is pictured as a condition in which the intermediate spaces between atom and atom are quite empty, as though it were a question of the purely negative fact of the absence of the bonds that formerly existed undisturbed in healthy communities. Upon closer scrutiny, however, it turns out that these former ties do not disappear; rather the convictions, values, customs, and habits which originally represented solid and secure bonds among persons become calcified and rotten and at last are shattered. Each individual still carries the residues of these views and ties within him, but they no longer harmonize with the views of others and no longer serve to bind people together; instead, they become the cause of constant misunderstandings and frictions. People are now separated from each other by the very debris of their former bonds. The calcified structure of extinct values now becomes a shell, a restraining crust—as was apparent in our earlier analysis of Flaubert's *Madame Bovary*. In particular, social conventions now separate the individual from his natural environment.

The effect of these calcified social bonds now separating people from one another and from nature grew increasingly more acute throughout the nineteenth century. The more profound and tormenting the resultant sense of meaninglessness, the more people became receptive to some forcible reaction. And the *Jugendbewegung* of the turn of the century was a reaction of just that sort. Its accomplishment was to clear away the accumulated rubble of tradition which separated human beings from each other and from nature. Following the precedents of earlier literary opposition movements, it created a new communal life-style by which it recaptured a direct relationship of human beings to nature and to the organic sphere.

Plato boasts that the highest vital accomplishment of the aristocratic youth of his native city was the capacity to share their leisure in beauty, and his own dialogues are attestations and representations of the artistic expression of his time. This capacity gradually waned, and neither Roman earnestness nor Christian asceticism favored it. The Italian Renaissance brought a new blossoming of great splendor, but of brief duration. Later, in the salons of the *ancien régime*, this capacity to shape leisure in beauty found a new, though more anemic and artificial expression; but the grim earnestness of the nineteenth century moved as far away from such ideals as possible. All the greater, therefore, was the accomplishment of the youth movement when it realized a new shaping of leisure time in beauty, and indeed in a way whose naturalness and relaxation surpassed the Renaissance and the age of the rococo alike.

The sociological explanation for the transitory and unique phenomenon of the German youth movement lies in its character as vehement protest against the nineteenth century. Because it was so successful in this struggle against the excesses of the nineteenth century, the movement itself seems less comprehensible and more quixotic in retrospect. This is a recurrent phenomenon in sociologic history: whenever a historical tendency fights against and triumphs over a preceding one, it seals its own decline through this very victory because its militant attitude becomes incomprehensible with the disappearance of the vanquished foe.

The first phase of the youth movement was composed mostly of sons of well-to-do families who attended the *Gymnasium* and then studied from four to five years at a university. During this time until they began to earn their own livelihood, they were supported by their parents without being subject to their supervision and authority. An artificially fashioned, sociologically unnatural freedom—a freedom from personal subordination as well as from the necessity to earn a living by work, a period of family-financed leisure of five to ten years—that was the "sphere of existence" in which the original youth movement unfolded. This was at once the precondition and the fatal weakness of the movement, the circumstance that gave it the character of a mere leisure-time movement. In its organization of leisure-time activity—in contrast to the beer-reeking, tobacco-saturated atmosphere of the preceding period—it was a full success; but it exhausted most of its vitality in the achievement of this one limited task.

Dialogues on God and the world, on ideological, philosophic, ethical, and artistic problems were held tirelessly. But there is no evidence of any group working together objectively on these problems. Where science began, friendships ceased.

Such objective work on the problems of the time in the spirit of the youth movement would have been possible and necessary. The same humane attitude, which the youth movement so impressively embodied in the leisure-time sphere of youthful associative life, cried out for application to the problems of the social, economic, and political life. This, of course, was possible only by way of earnest work. And since the youth movement in its "federative" structure was not to be won for such work, it remained for individuals to take it up.

But what ultimately happened to all those involved in the youth movement, when the academic freedom which they had enjoyed inevitably ended and the serious problems of life began with the exigencies of earning one's livelihood, establishing a family, and incorporating oneself in social and political reality? They could still cultivate past memories and past friendships. But had not these young people wished for infinitely more? Had they not dreamed of a transformation of the world and of life? Had they not sung, and with religious ardor, "The new age marches with us"? In cultivating a new structure and spirit of community, these young people had looked for decisive experiences and insights. In particular, they had perceived the vital necessity of small, closed life-spheres and the natural gradations of leadership that mark the freest human communities. However, they were not clear how this "new era" would look or how it could be brought about. This new vitality in the small and close sphere were not, however, combined with any grasp of the large historical and sociological laws from the workings of which no small human community can in the long run escape. The movement's very striving for communal intimacy and direct spontaneity barred such broader insights—and in the end the movement was perverted and abused by another movement of a far coarser grain.

5. The Intellectual Derivation of Totalitarianism from Absolutism

Government in the Middle Ages in western Europe rested on a "governmental contract" between king and estates that has antecedents as far back as the covenant of the Old Testament. The contract was drawn up in written form and was signed and sealed, so that there was no need laboriously to infer it from the consciousness of "primitive, uncorrupted men." The series of such formal contracts stretches from the English Magna Charta (1215) by way of the *Privilegio general* (1283) and *Privilegio de la Uniòn* (1287) of Aragon, the Brabant charter of liberties ("The Joyous Entry") to the "arrangement" of the Elector Albrecht of Brandenburg (1472) and the Treaty of Tübingen of Duke Ulrich of Württemberg (1514). When absolutism interrupted this development, the Huguenot monarchomachs in their passionate protest against the religious policy of absolutism (as expressed in the horrendous massacre of the night of Saint Bartholomew in 1572) and in their theoretical arguments, reverted to this structure of historical charters and constitutions wrested from monarchs by medieval estates.

Thomas Hobbes (1588-1679), in his natural and social philosophy, was a follower of the materialist, pessimistic atomism of the Epicurean school. As an emigrant in Paris he was for a time tutor to the future Charles II. He set himself the task of founding the absolutist claims of the Stuarts in a political philosophy based on the central doctrine of sovereignty. Given his temperament and his philosophy, it probably had occurred to him simply to invoke the right of the stronger—the doctrine that might makes right—and its recognition through historic prescription. But philosphy in its seventeenth-century, pre-Enlightenment phase was far beyond such a crude line of argument; the theological justification of monarchy given by Sir Robert Filmer (1604-1653) in his *Patriarcha* relied heavily on historic precedent but could appeal only to people of simple, unenlightened faith. The doctrine of modern political philosophy that Hobbes found to be dominant was the antiabsolutist theory of the social contract. If there was to be a modern justification for absolutism, this was the ground on which it must be provided.

The concept of the social contract had served to refute a ruler's claim to absolute power from the time it was invoked by the adherents of the papal side in the eleventh-century controversy over lay investiture of clergy down to that of the monarchomachs of the sixteenth century. Any contract implied the reciprocity of duties as well as of rights of the two contracting parties—and this was the very meaning and purpose of the doctrine of the social contract. Hence, in Hobbes's scheme, the sovereign by no means could be a party to the contract. The problem for Hobbes was to apply the contract theory in such a way that rights alone, not duties, accrue to the sovereign. As soon as he becomes a party to the contract, even a contract of submission, he acquires duties as well as rights. Yet there was in the tradition of the law of contract a form of contract for the benefit of a third party. And Hobbes, with admirable juristic adroitness, assigned the sovereign precisely this role of third party—a move comparable to that of the Sophists in turning the notion of natural law, originally developed with revolutionary intent, to their own reactionary purposes.

The theory of contract, which had pursued the goal of explaining

the relationship between the prince and his subjects as based upon
reciprocity, was now turned around in the hands of its adversaries
and used to demonstrate the absolute one-sidedness of this relationship—the obligations of the subjects but not that of the ruler. It
was a truly brilliant feat, all the more so since the legal form of the
contract in favor of a third party played no essential role either in
seventeenth-century English or French jurisprudence.

This legal form was alien to Roman law, which held that *alteri
stipulari nemo potest* ("no one can commit others"). Later, in imperial and Byzantine times, exceptions were allowed. The legal com-
mentator Martinus (ca. 1158) was the first to generalize these exceptions in the form of a *pactum in favorem tertii* (contract in favor of
a third party) and Bartolus (1314-1353) "treats this institution already in a way that almost sounds modern."[32] Gierke's assertion
that Hugo Grotius energetically espoused the binding character of
contracts in favor of a third party has perhaps justly been questioned. Nineteenth-century German scholars of Roman law were the
first to free it of all restrictions. Thus Joseph Unger (1828-1913)
proposes that "from such a contract the third person acquires directly and immediately the legal advantage intended for him. This
cannot be again withdrawn or weakened by any subsequent agreement of the contracting parties."[33]

At bottom, Rousseau's doctrine of the social contract is nothing
more than Hobbes's absolutist political theory, except that in the
place of the monarch he sets the equally absolute people. Whereas
Rousseau in his *Second Discourse* (on inequality) had still espoused
the doctrine of the *pactum subjectionis* between people and government, in the *Contrat social* the sovereign—namely, the people—is
no longer a contracting party, but only a favored third person, the
party in whose favor the contract among all the individuals was
concluded. The logical consequence of such a construction, exactly
as in Hobbes, is that the sovereign is absolute and has no contractual obligations whatsoever toward the individual subject. Rousseau's contract then might be described as a *pactum unionis per
subjectionem*—a contract of union by subjection. Hobbes, as an alternative to the monarchy, had always mentioned the possibility of
a corporate body of several persons that could possess sovereignty:
the sovereign could be "one Man or one Assembly of Men." Hobbes
himself, under this heading, thought not of democracy but of aristocracy, and in any case he did not favor this collective alternative.
But by placing the sovereign assembly of all men into this position
of Hobbes's assembly his theory of the state is transformed in one
stroke, as it were, into Rousseau's *Contrat social*.

August Comte called Hobbes "the real father of revolutionary philosophy," and Georg Jellinek (1851-1911) as early as 1891 pointed out this dependence of Rousseau on Hobbes. "The all-powerful king has become the ancester of the all-powerful people, and Thomas Hobbes has found his greatest disciple, one surpassing the master, in J. J. Rousseau. . . . The ruler has changed only his name, but significantly increased his absolute and irresistible power. . . . The sovereign nation succeeded the sovereign king."[34]

J. W. Gough in 1936 suggested that Hobbes's fundamental view of the right of force would have been conformable to a state "where the sovereign power is acquired by Force" (*Leviathan*, chap. 20). But in order to reconcile this all-too-brutal construction with the prevailing doctrine of the social contract, Hobbes, "by a clever manipulation, makes it an argument for absolutism instead of for the right of resistance, and turns the tables on his adversaries." "The social contract was [for Hobbes] really no more than a clever device to confound his opponents."[35] This kind of approach also appears in Rousseau in more than one passage.

Or, as Hans Nef remarks, "in the same way as Althusius transferred the concept of sovereignty, coined by Bodin, to the whole people, Rousseau takes over the concept of sovereignty, further heightened by Hobbes in the meantime, and again transfers it to the people. He winds up, from the point of view of the individual, being no less absolutistic than the classical theorists of absolutism. [Rousseau] thus arrives at the 'omnipotence of the majority' which can easily become Tocqueville's 'tyranny of the majority.' "[36]

Milton, Locke, and (later) Montesquieu espoused the "liberal" counterposition to Hobbes. Thus Talmon is mistaken in asserting that "the branching out of the two types of democracy [liberal and totalitarian] from the common stem [of rationalism] took place only after the common beliefs had been tested in the ordeal of the French Revolution."[37]

In a well-known passage of his *Confessions*, Rousseau explains how he arrived at the conclusion "that everything was radically connected with politics, and that, however one proceeded, no people could be other than what the nature of its government made it." Accordingly, a change in the social structure, as he strove for it, could be brought about only by a change in the structure of the state and of the constitution—a change to be brought about by "taking men such as they are, and laws such as they might be."[38]

Since the Greek Enlightenment of the fifth century B.C. it has been disputed whether large associations, especially the association of the state, are natural structures or artificial, conventional ones.

Heraclitus, Aristotle, and the Stoics represented the first view—
that man by nature is a *zoön politikon*, a state-forming being. The
opposite view was espoused by the Sophist Lycophron, the atomists,
and Epicurus, and in modern times, emphatically, by Hobbes. Rousseau follows this latter tendency. In the *Contrat social*, he explicitly
espouses the view that all associations beyond the frame of the
small family have originated not in nature but convention: "The
social order . . . comes not from nature; it is therefore founded on
convention." If the state, however, in its essence is something conventional, something unnatural and arbitrary, its violence is consequently inevitable. Degeneracy sets in not only at the higher cultural stage of the cultivation of the arts and sciences, but rather at
the very foundation of all that follows, with the founding of the state
by the social contract.

When Rousseau, in a radical and fundamentally revolutionary
way, criticizes the despotic courtly life-style of baroque absolutism,
the question immediately arises as to what, by means of the constitutional change, he perceived as necessary or planned to set in its
place. And here we encounter once again those tragic antinomies
between postulate and construction which we first came upon in
Plato's theory of the state, a theory which had its direct influence on
Rousseau.

Rousseau postulates an innate human tendency toward community rather than society, to use recent terminology; indeed, Rousseau plays a decisive role in intellectual history as one of the pro-
genitors of this polar distinction.

However, the constitutional and political ethos that dominated
the book he planned on *Institutions politiques*, and that on the *Contrat social* that he published as a preliminary installment, led, in its
historic effects, to the most ruthless totalitarian tyranny—including
the terror of the Jacobins and Napoleon's autocracy, the centralized
authoritarian governments of the nineteenth century, and, finally,
bolshevism and national socialism—however great the distance between the original point of departure and those ultimate destina-
tions; for the "progressive" character of modern totalitarianism
should by no means be denied.

Rousseau's goal indeed is community, but his motto seems to be
the latter-day German adage *Und willst Du nicht mein Bruder sein,
So schlag ich Dir den Schädel ein* (If you won't my brother be, I'll
bash your brains in—yes sirree!). So long as all members do, think,
and believe willingly as they are told, there is no problem, and all
goes smoothly. And this, indeed, is the ideal of all totalitarian ty-

rants: they all assure us that they would be only too pleased if they did not have to use violence to bring about the conditions they desire. Their very command is willing obedience, willing subjection. But what if those concerned—or those affected—do not will what they ought to will? This is the point at which the problem first arises, and this is where the path divides. Rousseau's answer, like that of all totalitarians, is: Well, then let them be forced; and they alone are to blame because they did not, as was their duty, will what they voluntarily ought to have willed.

The special formulation of the question raised by Rousseau, the "citoyen de Genève," presupposing the order of magnitude of his home canton, takes this form: How can a sovereign national people constitute itself into a community without some kind of compulsion being forced upon any of its members, in the absence of any odious social—let alone legal—constraints? Ideally by the device of the people, assembled in person, adopting all decisions unanimously—*volenti non fit iniuria*—he who consents suffers no injury. That, of course, is as self-evident and trivial as it is utopian. What happens, however, in situations that regularly arise in practice and that alone pose difficulties—situations where unanimity does not exist and cannot be attained, when, as Rousseau puts it, "there is no longer unanimity of opinion," and "the general will is no longer the will of all?"[39] All that Rousseau now can do, as he confesses with some embarrassment, is to content himself—just like the rest of us—with a mere majority; and this indeed is the only possible solution. Rousseau demands absolute unanimity only for the conclusion of the social contract itself. But, otherwise, "in proportion to the degree of concord which reigns in the assembly, that is, the nearer opinion approaches unanimity, the more the general will predominates"[40]—for which reason he proposes a sort of graduated tariff for majorities of diminishing size, with the bare majority as the borderline case. But how, with this unavoidable recourse to a weighted or simple majority, are we to prevent the majority from doing violence to the minority—to prevent the development of a rule by the majority over the minority that would tear the community asunder? It is at this point that the serious issues first arise. Rousseau, in truth, neither formulates nor answers this question; rather he obscures it and shunts it aside in a manner that one can only call at once brutal and sophistic. Even decisions by a bare majority must be imputed to the general will; every decision, even one by a bare majority, must preserve the dignity and the weight of this unanimous general will. Yet Rousseau is quite aware that even unanimity of a decision does not unconditionally prove it to be an expression of the true general will. "There is frequently much difference between the will of all and the general will";[41] or, as expressed more bluntly in a draft version: "The general will is rarely in that of all."[42] The will of all is a purely quantitative concept, the general will an eminently qualitative one; at bottom it is the concept of that will which bears upon the common good, the *intérêt commun*, which corresponds to the "true interest" of each and every individual and which, therefore, each and every individual ought to will—has the duty to will.

It is a question here of a distinction between "true interest" and "real interest," which played so central a role in the thought of Leonard Nelson, the distinguished German philosopher. No problems arise so long as one draws only the pedagogic conclusion of admonishing the individual to a conscientious self-examination of his true interest, of bringing his "real interest" into harmony with this "true interest." If all individuals succeeded completely in living up to their ethical duty, everything would be well in human society, as all "true interests" are, by definition, in accord. But what if the real interests deviate from one another, conflict with one another despite all pedagogic efforts and ethical exertions, despite all education and self-education? This, of course, is the regular point of departure of any constitutional or political philosophy. If a group emerges that is unwaveringly convinced that it alone knows and represents the true interest and that all others, if they will not do so voluntarily, must be forced to subject themselves to that one true interest, then the crucial choice has been made for totalitarian dictatorship. Conversely, if everyone in the face of existing conflicts of opinion, considers that he as well as others may possibly be in error and is ready to discuss the matter honestly, and in the end to abide by the decision of the majority, then we have the constitutional form of liberal democracy.

Rousseau's general will is a postulative, ideal concept: it is the will of all as it really should be, in accord with the interest of each one and all and exclusively bearing upon the common good. However, when this utopian postulate is not fulfilled there exists no logical, psychological, or sociological coupling between the quantitative concept of the will of all and the qualitative one of the general will. How, according to Rousseau, does one recognize whether a mere majority decision (which in any case does not correspond to the will of all) nevertheless expresses the general will and corresponds to the common interest? The only criterion offered, and an extremely tenuous one at that, is that this decision must be general, that it must express itself in a law of universal application, that it may not be a special law referring to specific individuals, named persons, or families. This does not insure equality, let alone freedom. But is the community really threatened only by such incursions of the legislative branch into the domain of the executive? Are there not many other conflicts that are equally, or more, serious? Rousseau not only fails to take up these important questions, he specifically rules them out of order. Instead of warning the majority against any despotic abuse of its constitutional power, instead of appealing to the conscience of the majority, or reminding it of any eternal and universal norms of natural law, he further reinforces the majority in its presumptuousness and obduracy. "The general will . . . is always constant; unalterable and pure." "The general will is always right." "The Sovereign merely by virtue of its being, is always what it should be." "Of themselves the people always will the good." "The people are never corrupted."[43] The possibility of error and deception is admitted in these passages, but no institutional or even pedagogical conclusions are drawn. On the contrary, the conclusions drawn are nakedly totalitarian: "How can an *unenlightened* multitude, which often does not know what it wants, since *it so seldom knows what is good for it*, execute, of itself, so great, so difficult an enterprise as a system of legislation? Of themselves the people always will the good, *but of themselves they do not always see in what it consists*. The general will is always right, but *the judgment that guides it is not always enlightened*." "Individuals see the good they reject; the public wills *the good it does not see*." These are far-reaching admissions, and the exigencies they beget are correctly seen: "It is therefore necessary to make the people see things as they are, and sometimes as they ought to appear [here the cloven hoof already is visible] to point out to them the right path which they are seeking, to guard them from the seducing voices of private wills, and . . . to balance the attraction of immediate and sensible advantage against the apprehension of unknown and distant evil." But how are these exigencies to be met? "All have equal need for guidance. Some must have their wills made conformable to their reason, and others must be taught what it is they will."[44] Now the cat is out of the bag. Guidance is needed, presumably by leaders who are themselves in secure possession of the absolute truth, and these must *make* the wills of the others comformable to what is right, must inculcate in them what they really want or ought to want. Here is the principle of totalitarianism in unadulterated form.

In contrast to this, a liberal and libertarian-democratic set of precepts would impress on all leaders the virtues of modesty and humility—and such precepts have been admirably expressed by Luigi Einaudi, first president of the Italian Republic. "There is only one thing that we know; it is that we do not know. We have but one motto: we do not know truth, but we seek it, we are never sure of possessing it and we shall begin each day all over again to seek it, ever unsatisfied and every curious."[45] The same precepts are implied in the passionate plea in a letter of Cromwell's (who himself stood much in need of such admonition): "I beseech you, in the bowels of Christ, think it possible you may be mistaken." They are contained, above all, in the norms of natural law, which Hobbes and Rousseau so consistently ignore—norms that, like the stars, will remain forever unreachable, but by which we human beings ought ever to set our course to the best of our conscience and ability; norms the systematic exploration of which would constitute the most imperative task of the anthropology of the future.

Rousseau, like Hobbes, is a legal positivist. There is no mention whatever of values superordinated to the general will. The general will is proclaimed autonomous and self sufficient—indeed, it is incited to the *hubris* of self-deification: "As soon as the legislative power speaks . . . its voice is the voice of God on earth."[46]

Rousseau speaks of the "sophism very familiar to royalist political thinkers . . . to give liberally to that magistrate all the virtues he ought to have, and suppose him always the very thing he ought to be." "Those persons must therefore by very willing to deceive themselves who confound royal government with the government of a good king. To know what this government is in itself we must first view it under weak or dissolute princes."[47] But is it not exactly the same sophism of which he is guilty in the aforementioned passages referring to the general will? Has a courtier ever flattered an absolute sovereign more brazenly than Rousseau flatters the sovereign people and its general will?

In contrast, what Carl J. Friedrich has called *The New Belief in the Common Man*[48] can be justified only in the conviction that the common man is *capable* of good, in sociological conditions whose exact and comprehensive establishment for this reason becomes the most important, difficult, and responsible task of any theory of government. For the fact that under many other circumstances the common man is capable of corruption, indeed of extreme evil, has been proved beyond any doubt by abundant experience, especially of the recent past. The old belief of Rousseau and of his followers consisted in the dangerous superstition that the common man is in all conditions capable always of the good and hence *ipso facto* always and everywhere in the right—a neat inversion of the age-old doctrine of the superstratifiers that he is ever contemptible and never capable of any good.

Rousseau explicitly and emphatically rejects any constitutional limitation on the totalitarian omnipotence of the state, any reservation of human rights of the individual. "The sovereign power has no need of guarantees for the subjects."[49] Such sentiments are echoed almost verbatim by the leading National Socialist constitutional lawyer, Ernst Rudolf Huber: "There is no personal, prepolitical, and external political freedom of the individual which the state would have to respect," "no rights of freedom of the individual vis-à-vis state authority."[50] Rather, all that according to Rousseau is necessary is "the *total* alienation of each associate, and all his rights, to the whole community . . . *without* reservation."[51] "The social compact gives to the body politic absolute command over the members of which it is formed."[52] Rousseau accordingly calls the absolute people "le souverain," and it is indeed the people, or rather the majority, whom he installs on the throne of the most absolutist absolutism, and a most unenlightened absolutism, at that.

"It is here that all men return to their primitive equality, because they are no longer of any account";[53] "In perfect legislation the private or individual will should be null."[54] But this nullification of the individual is performed in favor not of any divinity or transcendental value, but rather of the empirical state. That all-powerful state (or the majority representing it, or the spokesmen representing that majority) is placed on the throne not only of the absolute secular ruler, but also of the spiritual ruler, that of the pope, indeed that of Calvin's absolutist God himself.

The *Contrat social* continues as follows: "Those who dare to undertake the institution of a people must feel themselves capable, as it were, of changing human nature, of transforming each individual . . . into a part of a much greater whole, from which he in some measure takes his being and his life; of altering the constitution of a man for the purpose of strengthening it. . . . They must, in a word, remove man from his own proper energies to bestow upon him those which are strange to him. . . . *The more those natural powers are annihilated*, the more permanent and august are those which he acquires, and the more solid and perfect is the institution: so that if each citizen is nothing and can do nothing but when combined with all the other citizens . . . it may be said that legislation is at the highest point of perfection which human talents can attain." Let us consider the phrase "the more those natural powers are annihilated." Is that not the language of Calvin, the salutary self-nullification of the natural man before God's infinite majesty? Immediately thereafter, in fact, follows a glorification of Calvin and of his "genius": "The compilation of our wise edicts . . . does him as much honor as his *Institution*. . . . The memory of that great man will never cease to have the benediction of the Genevans."[55]

In short, Rousseau projects into the worldly sphere the Calvinist notion of orthodoxy, and proceeds to claim for his general will a coercive right of absolute truth—which theological adherents of that same doctrine could only reject as unfair competition. Rousseau's attitude toward the general will has an unmistakably religious, or pseudoreligious, flavor. His individuals merge into, or surrender themselves to, the general will with something of the feeling of mystical merger into the One and Only.

The dignity of the general will is claimed with emphatic solemnity for any majority decision which observes merely the formal criterion of isonomy. And Rousseau even shows awareness of what this implies: "This is indeed supposing that all the characteristics which mark the general will still reside in the most votes." But what if, by mischance, this should not be the case? Well, then there's nothing to be done: "When that ceases to be the case, whatever measures may be adopted, it means the end of liberty."[56]

Rousseau, moreover, informs the outvoted minority that the decision taken against its explicit wishes, as expression of the general will, in truth expresses its own will, whether the minority chooses to recognize this or not; that therefore its own freedom is in no way curtailed by this; and that, indeed, people must be forced into such true freedom. "Whoever refuses to obey the general will must be constrained to do so . . . which only means that he will be forced to be free."[57] Thus insult is added to injury: it is hard to imagine a more shamelessly brutal line of argument.

Just as the authors of any doctrine of predestination see themselves in the role of the elect—the possibility that they might be among the eternally damned never occurs to them—so Rousseau's political theory is constructed from the viewpoint of a member of the majority. Jean-Jacques, that tender soul, is one of those who love freedom—but, alas, only for themselves. Just as in his daydreams his imagination populated an ideal landscape with beings to his liking,[58] so his imagination peoples the ideal state of the *Contrat social* with people no less to his liking—or if they will not conform to that imaginary vision, so much the worse for them!

Rousseau thus presents one more example not of the freeman, but of the "slave who breaks his chains," of whom Schiller tells us to beware and tremble. In his political theory Jean-Jacques subconsciously takes a terrible revenge for all the oppressions and humiliations he ever endured. Whoever defies his majority is not only given up defenseless to any violence; he is not even allowed the privilege of which Rousseau so freely availed himself, of bewailing his ill fortune.

To quote Einaudi once again:

> Such is the message of the citizen of Geneva: The general will expresses not the vote of the citizens but the recognition of the gods.
>
> Rousseau, perhaps, did not foresee that his doctrine would beget such grave consequences. Gods have risen by the dozens and assumed the role of guides of peoples. We have seen such guides—from Robespierre to Babeuf, from Buonarroti to Saint-Simon, from Fourier to Marx, from Mussolini to Hitler, from Lenin to Stalin—succeed each other, each of them called to teach the ignorant peoples what was their truth, what was the general will of which they had no consciousness. . . .
>
> The formula by which the oracle leads men to the discovery of truth matters little. For Rousseau and Robespierre it is "virtue," for Saint-Simon "the religion of science," for Hitler "the supremacy of blood and race," for Marx and Lenin "the dictatorship of the proletariat." The formulas change and pass; the doctrine of the sole truth, which once discovered must be recognized and followed, persists.[59]

In fairness to Rousseau, it must be pointed out that these fateful consequences could develop only in conditions obtained in large states, conditions which Rousseau again and again explicitly rejects. In small cantonal structures, which were the only ones that Rousseau advocated and put at the basis of his theory, the ties of a living community usually form a strong enough counterweight: everything in such an atmosphere acquires another flavor and tone. Yet his theory, considered in the light of these authentic reservations, would not have been applicable anywhere outside of Switzerland or some other miniscule state still existing at that time. Thus, it is more than understandable that his readers left these reservations far behind and that Rousseau's *Contrat social* exercised its strongest influence in settings explicitly excluded by him. Here, as so often in history, the historical impact of ideas has overstepped the limitations and reservations set by their originators, and it is difficult to decide whether and in which sense this circumstance removes them from responsibility. Can the person who has mixed the poison exculpate himself by the warnings that he has recorded on the labels of his bottles?

It is only one step from Rousseau's absolutism of the enthroned majority to Napoleon's self-enthronement as the embodiment of the popular will; or to national socialist claims that "the Will that takes shape in the Führer . . . is the common will of a community," that "the Führer develops into conscious decision, the seed of will contained in the living community." Here the circle (or rather the downward spiral) closes, and we are back to absolute autocracy—not indeed a hereditary autocracy *de lege* but a Bonapartist, "charismatic" autocracy *de facto*, a form of government that might be described as neoabsolutist.

This totalitarian mentality, this spirit of democratic absolutism of Rousseau's *Contrat social*, acquired its first political realization in the Jacobin terror of the French Revolution and in Carnot's mass levying of troops, the first "total mobilization" in history—a temporary measure made permanent by Napoleon, the organizer *par excellence*.

And Hegel, Napoleon's admirer, with characteristic German extremism gave to the totalitarian idolization of the state its modern philosophical formulation: "All the worth which the human being possesses—all spiritual reality, he possesses only through the state." "The state is the divine idea as it exists on earth." "The shape which the perfect embodiment of the Spirit assumes—the state." "The particular is for the most part of too trifling a value as compared with the general: individuals are sacrificed and abandoned . . . and . . . as a general rule, individuals come under the category of means to an ulterior end . . ."—which indeed all totalitarian dictators have expressly done.[60]

"The state is the actuality of the ethical idea . . . [and] is absolutely rational." "Since the state is mind objectified, it is only as one of its members that the individual himself has objectivity, genuine individuality, and an ethical life." "This idea is the absolutely eternal and necessary being of mind." "In considering freedom, the starting point must be not individuality, the single self-consciousness, but only the essence of self-consciousness; for whether man knows it or not, this essence is externally realized as a self-subsistent power in which single individuals are only moments. The march of God in the world, that is what the state is. The basis of the state is the power of reason actualizing itself." "The nation state is mind in its substantive rationality and immediate actuality and is therefore the absolute power on earth."[61]

Thus read some of Hegel's most extreme statements on this subject, each of course limited and qualified in its context. In fairness to Hegel it must also be recalled that from 1818 until his death in 1831 he taught at the University of Berlin. The state that he had before his eyes thus was the Prussian state of the reform officialdom inaugurated by Baron vom Stein, whose limits of competency Wilhelm von Humboldt, the liberal, had drawn narrowly and who therefore stood at the highest level German public administration was ever to attain.

This Prussian reform administration went into a slow decline around the time of Hegel's death, so that the state against which the radicals of the Hegelian left (Marx, Engels, and others) aimed their criticism was no longer the same.

Napoleon's historical impact was to be as profound in domestic as it had been in international politics, and as nefarious in one sphere as in the other. He founded the modern version of that "Bonapartist" or "Caesarist" form of total governmental omnipotence, where a "charismatic" leader, legitimated only by his successes (and hence with limitless ambition for success) rules an atomized mass, in the name of the people but in self-appointed mission, by the fullest use of all methods of demagoguery, of the most up-to-date organizational techniques, and, if necessary, of terror.

Napoleon III, in resuming the Bonapartist tradition, vulgarized and trivialized it in keeping with the rapid cultural decline of his century, freed it of the original quasi-heroic elements associated with his uncle, and, in sum, adapted it for the handy use of the dictators of our own day. Yet even the centralized, governmental authority of nineteenth- and twentieth-century democracies owes its theoretical basis to Rousseau's transformation of the monarchic absolutism of the eighteenth century. All these various lines of development imply the cult of the great Leviathan; thus they tend to that absolutization and idolization of an omnipotent and omnipresent state which was to become the common feature of all forms of twentieth-century totalitarianism.

6. NATIONALISM

Man is by nature a communal being: the association with his family and with the group in which he lives is instinctive. Culture has deepened this association; extended it to broader circles based upon a community of interests; extended family, clan, tribe, people, and nation; and in part focused loyalties on the rulers of such wider structures.

By nature man is sedentary, not only since his "sedentarization" in the narrower sense (which occurred fairly late and depended on the invention of agriculture and the rectangular gabled hut), but from the very beginning. Even the most primitive "roving" clan at the gathering stage does its gathering within the same small territory and feels as familiar with it and as emotionally attached to it as if it were sedentary. This holds true even for nomads with their regularly oscillating seasonal migrations or transhumance. Hence love of home is innate in man. Later this feeling is concentrated on house and farmyard and thereafter extended to those larger communities of interest up to and including the state. At the same time homeland and fatherland form a polarity which Ernst von Aster formulates as follows: "The *maternal* homeland receive the wanderer, accepts him, he reposes in her; the *fatherland* makes demands upon him and lays duties upon him."[62]

All these associations and combinations have persisted from time immemorial. But our present-day concepts of love of country, patriotism, and nationalism have existed for just over a century and a half, if we accept the nationalism of the French Revolution as a preliminary stage of these; otherwise they are not older than the nineteenth century.

Elsewhere I have tried to define the concept of the nation as an ideal type—that is, maximally rather than minimally; the procedure still seems to me appropriate:

> One could be inclined to accept, for instance, unity of blood, language, or culture in order to define the concept of nation in the most concrete way possible. And there are, of course, examples in which such definitions would be more or less appropriate. Unfortunately, however, they are all invalidated by the counterexample of Switzerland. If we want to form a comprehensive concept that would also apply to Switzerland, then we must essentially limit ourselves to the unity of the geographical situation, to the unity of historical experience, and above all to the unity of political will. But again there are examples where [one or the other of these] is absent. . . . Thus on the grounds of comprehensive logic, we see ourselves driven to an increasingly complex and, at the same time, increasingly emptier, highly peripheral definition which lies as far as is conceivable from the

real kernel of the phenomenon intended, and its lack of concrete substance is replaced by a profusion of provisos and qualifications.

It is wholly otherwise when . . . we take in hand the conceptual tool of the ideal type and ask ourselves how the most complete ideal of a nation, of a national people, conceivably must look. Here nothing prevents us from postulating . . . full unity of blood, of language, of culture, of religion, of territory, of political feeling and will. That really corresponds in the fullest measure and in the most intensive way to what each one imagines and wishes for himself as nation. That no single real nation satisfies this ideal is by no means an objection. On the contrary, in each individual case it can be easily proven that each falling short of this ideal is felt and acknowledged by the nation concerned as a disadvantage and that to the best of its abilities it makes an attempt, if possible, to compensate for this lack. A not inconsiderable part of all national policy falls under this rubric, and even dubious means such as falsification of history and acts of violence of all kinds are enlisted in the service of this purpose. And as regards Switzerland, it is generally viewed—even by its own citizens—as a singular, extreme case, as an exception proving the rule. Indeed, its own policy is quite deliberately and with great circumspection concerned to overcompensate for what is lacking in it of otherwise normal national uniformities by an all the more vigorous cultivation of all the common features to which history has made Switzerland heir.[63]

The nineteenth and early twentieth centuries have rightly been called the age of nationalism; they were an age in which nationalism—in singular combination with the belief in progress—assumed the place of a religion. Earlier only Great Britain, despite all its political upheavals, succeeded in transforming its traditional institutions of social and political integration in an uninterrupted process of transformation and modernization; but as time went on, it too could not avoid a sense of isolation. Hence the direct and indirect influence of contrasting developments elsewhere.

Rousseau was the precursor and prophet of modern nationalism, the John the Baptist of this false gospel; and, as we have seen, he also paved the way for institutions and the ethos of the modern totalitarian state.

The internationalism of Western culture attained two pinnacles: an ecclesiastical one in the Middle Ages and a secularized one in the eighteenth-century Enlightenment. Yet Rousseau treated this international ethos of the eighteenth-century West as something worthy only of contempt and called for its overthrow by chauvinistic nationalism. In his *Considerations on the Government of Poland* he writes: "Today, no matter what people may say, there are no longer Frenchmen, Germans, Spaniards, Englishmen; there are only Europeans. [What we would not give today to be once again so far advanced!] All have the same tastes, the same passions, the same manners, for no one has been shaped along national lines by peculiar institutions." And what Rousseau longs for in place of that is precisely "that patriotic intoxication which alone can raise men above themselves," for which purpose he advises the Polish politicians "to begin in any case to give the Poles a great opinion of themselves and of their fatherland"[64]—a counsel which we know the Poles were not the only ones to follow.

In France, the leveling democracy of the Revolution radically completed the work of the leveling kings. By dissolving all traditional bonds, it made each citizen directly and equally subject to the state, wholly in accord with Rousseau's teachings.

The overthrow of the *ancien régime* created an institutional tabula rasa on which the Jacobins could erect a structure based on the totalitarian principles of the *Contrat social*; it also created an emotional vacuum that now could be filled with Rousseauistic patriotism. These two elements of absolutism and patriotism, which until the time of Rousseau had lain inert side by side, now, on the night of 24-25 April 1792 in Strasbourg, as Rouget de Lisle composed his Jacobin battle song *La Marseillaise*, underwent a violent chemical reaction as esthetically splendid and emotionally stirring as it was to prove baneful for all future history. Traditional forms of social integration, after their violent removal, had to be replaced by a massive process of pseudointegration. In the measure in which traditional theological bonds also melted away, nationalism as a substitute religion remained as the only means of integration. And with the massification and underintegration characteristic of it, there was a simultaneous rise in the demand for overintegration and pseudointegration of which nationalism was to be the prime beneficiary.

The chauvinistic nationalism of the Jacobins was a necessary pathological substitute for the old organically evolved integration of French national feeling centered on the person of the king. The replacement of the gold-embroidered *fleur-de-lis* banner of the royal France of the Valois, fashioned individually by laborious and painstaking artisan labor, with the tricolor, mass-produced by the meter from bales of cloth, is symbolic of this change. Jacobin chauvinism became the model of all the nationalisms of the nineteenth and twentieth centuries, as its tricolor did of all the national flags bearing three stripes, including the black-white-red of Bismarck's German empire.

Just as the modern state from the beginning had claimed political supremacy, so now did nationalism claim for itself the highest exclusive position in the scale of values.

The old attachment to the homeland did not exclude the possibility of emigration for pressing reasons. "Every man is born with the natural right to choose a fatherland for himself," as Voltaire once put it.[65] A despotic regime was considered such a pressing reason: "There is no fatherland in despotism," says La Bruyère (1645-1696). Even Rousseau, in a letter of 1765, writes: "If on earth there is a state in which justice and freedom reign, I am a born citizen of that state."[66] And as late as 1804 Fichte exclaims in his pamphlet *On the Present Age*: "Which is then the fatherland of the truly cultured European? . . . May the earth-born . . . remain citizens of the sunken state. . . . The sun-related spirit will irresistibly be drawn and turn there where there is light and right." Not too long ago this passage was cited in Germany only with ironic intent as a horrifying, crass example of the degree to which even a patriot like Fichte originally had succumbed to the unpatriotic internationalism of the Enlightenment. Those of us who chose to leave Hitler's Germany have come to a new and deeper appreciation of this statement and of the consequences and sacrifices of acting on it—though we might have preferred to put the matter a bit less flamboyantly.

Fichte's internationalism, under the impact of Napoleonic superstratification, changed into an unbridled nationalism and chauvinism; Goethe by contrast clung to his sober humanism even in the face of the wave of patriotic sentiment released by the anti-Napoleonic wars of liberation, to the deep disappointment of nationalists of his own and later times.

Goethe indeed perceived the character of modern nationalism as a mass psychosis of pseudointegration. In a letter of 23 February 1814, in which he had rejected a patriotic play by Achim von Arnim, he wrote that he had found "that enthusiasm really is suitable only for the great mass. One must be unknown to one another, and feel a togetherness only when one desires to warm oneself up, nay to inflame oneself."

And with brilliant depth and farsightedness he saw the terrible danger for the German mind that lay in the nationalist reaction to Napoleon's imperialist action, and directed his defensive and exorcising curse against it in advance:

> Curse him who, on bad advice
> And with excess of boldness,
> Does now as a German
> What earlier the French-Corsican did.
> Let him feel early and late
> As a nagging consciousness
> That, whatever his suffering and violence,
> A harsh lot awaits him and his kin.[67]

The curse and prophecy have been frightfully vindicated in Hitler. In 1763, under the catchword *patrie* in his *Philosophical Pocket Dictionary*, Voltaire had written: "The greater this fatherland becomes, the less one loves it. For a shared love is weakened. It is impossible tenderly to love a too numerous family that one hardly knows." The new Jacobin-Napoleonic nationalism of the nineteenth and twentieth centuries had a pronounced expansionist and megalomaniac character. It holds the very opposite of this Voltairean view: the greater the territory to which it refers, the more intense it becomes. However, it was not only the geographical size of the fatherland that became a goal and an object of pride. In every other area of statistics people became intoxicated with national records.

This expansive Jacobin nationalism of 1792-1793 was the main motive force behind Napoleon's imperialism, which inundated Europe; and his New Order seemed to be on the way to founding a world empire. But the millennium of the world empire founded by this parvenu came to a close in 1814, and even the subsequent flare-up in Napoleon's "Hundred Days" could only confirm the final collapse.

This violent episode of less than two decades changed the mentality of all Europe. If the upheavals of 1792-1794 led to a discrediting of the Enlightenment and legitimized irrationalist, romantic countercurrents, Napoleon's superstratification and threats produced the vehement irrational reaction of a nationalism which superseded the Enlightenment as the prevailing religion.

This romantic nationalism found its most intense cultivation in Germany; under German influence it spread to the East, begetting the Slavic nationalisms, which very soon developed messianic-imperialistic tendencies of their own.

German love of fatherland was not only intensified by Napoleon's brutal imperialism; rather, it was perverted and permuted to chauvinistic nationalism—exactly what in its time happened to Jewish nationalism as a result of the brutal imperialism of the Assyrians. All the unattractive, pathological features of German nationalism have their roots here. It would appear that even the development of anti-Semitism belongs in this context; for example, it had already noticeably reared its ugly head at the "National Festival of the Germans" in Hambach in 1819.

Eventually the Jacobin components of nationalism increasingly won out, and in a new intensive expression made possible by the modern development of psychological manipulation. If the Jacobins had developed an intensity of the nationalist *contrainte sociale* unknown until then, it now attained forms and degrees in times of peace which the Jacobins had attained only under the intense pressure of the threat of foreign war in 1792-1793. But for now, the threat of war and war itself were to be the surest devices for keeping public feeling at the boiling point.

An absolute nationalism that does not recognize any value higher than the nation leads with logical and psychological necessity to the revival of old ideas of the chosen people, to the superiority-delusion of master races, and, in the process of putting them into practice, to imperialism. Imperialism, in turn, provokes bellicosity and the glorification of violence.

We wish to designate these specific modern forms of chauvinistic nationalism, known in English-speaking countries as *jingoism*, as the third, totalitarian stage of nationalism—a stage with whose catastrophic effects we are coping to this day.

In the Middle Ages the Church formed the counterweight to all secular powers and thereby secured a certain degree of freedom; after the schism of the Reformation none of the separated churches was strong enough to play such an independent role. The churches therefore were forced essentially to yield to the state ideology of nationalism, issuing occasional clerical admonitions against its excesses; these, however, did not prevent the national flags of all states from being blessed, or prayers for victory from being intoned, by chaplains of all Christian denominations—a truly shattering distortion of the mission of the one and universal Church. And all Christian churches found themselves ready to work out a *modus vivendi* even with the totalitarian state so long as it was ready to tolerate them. Only where the state began a struggle of annihilation against them did they decide, willy-nilly, on resistance.

The religious or pseudoreligious character that marked the nationalism of modern times, its role as a substitue for religion, was made manifest when it succeeded in deflecting the two most essential streams of thought of traditional Christianity into the muddy and turbulent stream of nationalism.

The Holy Writ of Christianity, the Bible, was dominated by two core ideas: that of the chosen people, which forms the center of the Old Testament, and that of the savior or redeemer, which stands at the center of the New Testament. The Old Testament idea of the chosen people was renewed by Calvin and transferred to the congregations of newly converted believers. At first this had had nothing to do with politically demarcated communities; on the contrary, in most cases denominational distinctions cut across political boundaries. However, as soon as Calvinism attained the supremacy in a political community like Geneva or predominance, as in Great Britain, the idea of the chosen people was also transferred to this political structure; and it was to play an important role especially in the formation of the British national consciousness.

In the first phase of nationalism, among anticlericals and Jacobins, who waxed enthusiastic over ancient Rome, and with Napoleon, as the executor of their testament, the idea of the chosen people still played no role. It became more important in the second, romantic phase, and especially in the German and Slavic regions. It stands at the center of Fichte's remarkable but pernicious *Addresses to the German Nation*. And indeed the proof for the election of the Teutonic peoples, and of the German nation as their protagonist, was adduced in a characteristic German-professorial way with an erudite-philological, linguistic-historical argument: in contrast to the peoples of Romance tongue, who took over the language of the Roman superstratifiers, the Teutonic peoples, and in particular the Germans, preserved their inherited language and thereby the originality and purity of their intellectual culture. It was a most "Aryan" argument, which, tragicomically, was first set forth by the baptized Jew Johann Michael Moscherosch (1601-1669). Here it was a question of the ideas of purity of descent which then, with the development of biology and of Darwinism, was carried over from philology to the more tangible sphere of race theory.

Moreover, the chosen people was not called to enjoy its own election—in contrast to the wretchedness of all the other unchosen peoples. Rather, it felt called upon to make the salvation, that initially was its sole privilege, available in equitable doses also to all other peoples. At the same time, should they resist such a blessing, it was ready to help them, if need be, with the sort of violence already practiced by the Jacobins and Napoleon. Through this seemingly altruistic and humane turning, which in the Old Testament had signified a step forward in refinement and humanization of the idea of election, a high-sounding, respectable ideology was now finally offered to nationalistic imperialism.

After the destruction of the supranational bonds of medieval church and empire, the nation remained as the largest available political community—the penultimate station on the way toward humanity—and thus laid claim to the dignity of being the provisional representative of the unity of mankind. Yet the result was a most undignified spectacle of a multiplicity of mankinds in a state of mutual hostility. That nationalism can be no more than a historic transition will become fully clear when the political unity of mankind will have been achieved.

An equally surprising turn, which seems to be unfolding on both sides of the iron curtain, is the alliance between socialism and the chauvinistic nationalism of different countries. So long as patriotism seemed to be reserved for conservative-reactionary circles, Marx and his internationalist followers could not do enough to ridicule and mock nationalism. When those original claimants to nationalism were liquidated or removed from politics, the socialist mass movements no longer saw why they should abstain from those demagogic slogans of nationalism that had proved so useful to others in the past. Structurally, they fit in very well with totalitarianism, as was already evident in their common Rousseauistic origin. Since the Second World War bolshevism has inherited Russian or Pan-Slavic chauvinism in full force. And since then, the imperialism of Moscow has been engaged in a bitter family quarrel with Tito's Yugoslav national bolshevism; at the same time, the French communists outdo all Rightist political parties in outbursts of French nationalism. And the Socialist party of West Germany, whose official internationalism had not withstood the patriotic tide in 1914, after 1948 also began to use nationalistic slogans.

If during the nineteenth and twentieth centuries the nation developed into the dominant form of integration, and finally laid claim to totalitarian and tyrannical supremacy, the catastrophic consequences of this development appear today. The negative features and lack of control had been part of the essence of modern nationalism since its Jacobin-Napoleonic beginnings. Not only in Germany did this new formation lead "from humanity by way of nationality to bestiality"—as the Austrian poet Grillparzer put it. In addition, the nation—at least the large nation of modern mass states—is either too large or too small: even at its smallest it is no substitute for direct, spontaneous community, and at its largest it falls far short of humanity. "It would be very proper to wish," as Lessing already wrote, "that in every state there might be men who would be beyond the prejudices of the people and who would know exactly where patriotism ceases to be a virtue."

It was not just a freakish, extravagant phrase but a profound insight when Ludwig von Gerlach, a pious friend of the young Bismarck, spoke of the "vice of patriotism." And if the historian Leopold von Ranke viewed nation-states as "thoughts of God," today we must sorrowfully wonder whether they may have been thoughts of the devil instead.

By various causes, Germany (along with Italy) was retarded in its development to nation-statehood, and for that very reason Germany subsequently outdid all other states in chauvinistic nationalism. This chauvinism began under William II with puerile saber rattling and was transformed into grim, bloody reality under Hitler. In its recoil from this experience, Germany once again has had a leading position in overcoming nationalism—and this may well be symptomatic of the future development of other countries in the Western culture complex.

To measure how far Germany has been moved from her nationalistic tradition, we need merely recall the expenditure of chauvinistic passions with which the struggle for the territories on the left bank of the Rhine was waged in the nineteenth century. After that we can easily imagine to what patriotic passion, under the conditions of that time, the present loss of the eastern German territories and the Bolshevist superstratification of central Germany would have led. Of passionate tempers of such a kind there is not the least perceptible trace today. Assuredly the loss of these territories is being deplored, and one would eagerly change it as soon as a possibility should offer itself. However, as this has not been the case up to now one accepts the status quo with a certain indifference—which does not exclude a bad conscience. Apparently the German superego has not yet overcome the attitude of the earlier time, whereas the German ego is already quite beyond that. There is no doubt that in due time the superego will follow the ego and that the whole development is moving in this direction. Self-evidently the duty of conscience for Germans at all times remains that of doing whatever is possible to free their brethren from the Bolshevik tyranny. A firm and responsible will, however, is a better means thereto than chauvinistic exuberance.

In the 1950s, at the time of the formation of the European Economic Community, there was much enthusiasm among German youth for a wider European solidarity, which might well have been a suitable transition stage. But this enthusiasm ran up against the demagogic opposition of German Socialists and resistance by the French to the very European idea they had launched. It seems unlikely that Europe's historic opportunity will recur.

Thus, the world situation seems to leave for Germans no other choice or goal than the responsible solidarity of all mankind and, in the enforced struggle for it, the solidarity of free peoples.

Meanwhile nationalism, which seems to have been overcome—or ought to be in the process of being overcome by Westerners—is making headway in underdeveloped former colonial and semicolonial countries. The forms it assumes there, however, require a separate discusison in a later context.

7. MARTIAL ENTHUSIASM

Modern nationalism, as we have seen, became a substitute religion and thus took the place of most of the forces which had promoted and secured social cohesion and integration. But such a consolidation of crumbling social structures through nationalism involves a pronounced pseüdointegration with unmistakable pathological features of mass psychosis—with underintegration, according to a basic law of social psychology, giving rise to overintegration. Nowhere do these intensifying integrative forces of nationalism appear more strongly than in the phenomenon of martial enthusiasm.

Among particularly warlike peoples or tribes, there probably have always occurred exceptional situations when offensive war was popular at times when it seemed to promise easy success. In all other situations war has usually been considered a misfortune for the peoples involved, a harsh fate that must be endured with manly resolve. Even the Romans, in the time of their most vigorous imperialistic expansion, were by no means bellicose. It was reserved only for our time to introduce a fundamental transformation in this area of human development; only of late has the "war experience" undergone a positive valuation. The rural peasant population was not affected by this transformation; instead it seemed to react in the old way, especially since its vital situation has not changed and was as satisfying as before. The opposite is true, however, in cities— especially big cities—where life is affected by atomization and mass society and seems unnatural and unsatisfactory. And because of this deep disillusionment it experienced the violent integration of

mobilization for war, the transition to the compact state of aggregation of the people in arms, positively as a salvation. This phenomenon reached its pinnacle in the European war of 1914.

The First World War erupted senselessly and violently like a natural catastrophe, and all peoples caught in its grip were truly intoxicated by a sense of integration. The war seemed to fill a void, put an
end to indecisiveness, restore a sense of purpose. Every person now
had his fixed place and his assigned function within the giant organism of the people in arms. The battlefield brought a return to
primordial relationships, an absolute dependency on one's own body
and its efficient functioning. The simplest object—a pile of sand, a
stone, a tree stump—acquired intensity and reality, a reality upon
which life or death might depend. Nowhere could one better experience the rapture of spring than in the trenches of western France in
1916, where, amid the stench of corpses, gunpowder, and latrines,
amid the din of firing and shelling, the woods, much destroyed by
bullet and cannonball, suddenly began to exhale their fragrance and
the birds to sing and warble. Some of us came back, two and a half
years later, with the consciousness of what it meant to live and with
the will to achieve a peace worth living—a peace no less real than
the war. Yet those dreams are as unrealized now as then.

Singularly, the most irreconcilable views prevail concerning the
social psychology of war. It is rather generally assumed, as a self-
evident proposition, that sadistic impulses are at its psychological
root and that, correspondingly, war provides an outlet for sadism.
War thus is viewed as the great opportunity for massive abreactions
of pent-up aggressive and sadistic urges.

As long as war, in a primitive way, was a fight at close quarters
between man and man, it did indeed appeal to sadistic impulses on
both sides. Yet for every aggressor there was a person who had to
resist, so that warfare also required the ability to resist and endure
its consequences. As we read in Homer (Iliad 18.309), "fighting is
reciprocal, and who slays is slain"; or, in the Gospel according to
Matthew (26:52): "For all they that take to the sword shall perish
with the sword." Thus even at a primitive stage of warfare both
masochism and sadism were involved.

Since then, however, with the rapid evolution of military technology, the share of masochism has strongly increased. Activity became increasingly more mechanized and abstract, but passivity—
the suffering of the effects of hostile warfare—remained altogether
concrete.

Even the ideal of "living perilously," which is viewed as
activistic-sadistic, in reality has a strong masochistic ingredient.

The greater the peril the more one is "under pressure" and subconsciously longs for this pressure.

This progressive hypertrophy of masochism in modern war is not only an inevitable consequence of technical development. It also converges with the social-psychological development of the modern mass man, it corresponds to his deepest pathological needs. The need for integration in reaction to mass society, atomization, and isolation has a predominantly passive, masochistic character: one longs to be under pressure, incorporated, integrated, harnessed; at the same time, activity plays a far lesser role. Thus, even the war experience beginning with mobilization is essentially masochistic.

The modern city dweller suffers not only from underintegration in that he lacks a solid and beneficent social environment, but also because this vacuum is in most cases filled with burdens, vexation, and irritation. Poor marital and family relationships, unsatisfactory job situations, trouble with superiors, colleagues and underlings, business and financial difficulties, quarrels with the landlord and neighbors—from all these one is released at once through the call to military service. And to that extent, war can be regarded as a grand collective opportunity to "run away from home."

If the government itself is a substantial cause for added discontent among its citizens, it may well deliberately or instinctively use war to deflect from such internal tensions. The process, however, consists not only in the fact that aggressiveness, originally directed against the government or some other internal foe, is now deflected to an outer enemy. What is even more essential is that the sociologic situation which led to discontent is replaced by a different one which is in many respects socially more satisfying.

And, if victorious war brings one into enemy country, satisfactions of superstratification roles are added for good measure—and these are never enjoyed as thoroughly and unbridledly as by the troops of a totalitarian state. Whereas at home every other thing is prohibited or out of reach, here the conquerors can allow themselves almost everything.

Of course, the war can end with a hero's death for the individual, and indeed does in very many cases. But even this life-endangering aspect of war is not, as a rationalistic interpretation might suppose, only a negative element. I am thinking here not only of the attraction of the life-endangering situation for those who survive it, that highly antithetical intensification of the feeling of life and of the will to live for those who have come close to death, but also precisely of people's readiness for death, their will to die.

As every war some day must end, the liberation from the discontents of the peacetime situation for those who return is only temporary. As a rule, the returned soldier finds that his peacetime situation has deteriorated further, even if he does not return as an invalid or cripple. The only ones liberated from their troubles for good are those who do not return.

The high suicide rates prove that in a number of individual cases weariness with life reaches such a degree that it overcomes the difficult obstacles which stand in the path of individual suicide in conditions of peace—its condemnation as sinful, dishonorable, and immoral by religion, public opinion, and individual conscience. All such scruples are overcome in the case of death in war. No positive action is needed—at most some negligence—to bring it about. Moreover, one dies in a community in which it is easiest to die, and, in contrast to civilian suicide, it is a glorious and celebrated form of dying: "Kein schöner Tod ist in der Welt"—as a traditional German song has it—"There is no more beautiful death in the world [than death in battle]." Thus war constitutes an enormous collective opportunity for a respectable and honorable form of suicide.

To be sure this attitude is not evenly spread among all peoples. The French, because of the still predominantly peasant-artisan character of their society and their enjoyment of bodily pleasures, are more immune against this attitude than, say, the Germans, who as a result of urbanization and prudishness are strongly exposed to the malaise of an unsatisfying life situation. For many other reasons the Germans are, in any case, not given to equilibrium and hence do not feel too comfortable in their own skins. This explains Clemenceau's horror of the Germans' readiness to die, indeed their longing for death, which he scented with the keen insight of hatred.

If to all this is added the overintense, quasi-religious integrative character of nationalism, then war is experienced as redemption, death in war as the redeemer. War is the great sacrament of nationalism, springing from the synthesis between nationalism and imperialism or between totalitarianism and imperialism.

Pacifist sermons, appeals to morality and reason, however logical and persuasive, are completely ineffective on such deep-seated urges in the West. If, however, the readiness for warfare and the conscious or unconscious longing for it essentially rest upon unsatisfactory life situations in peacetime, the only effective countermeasure is systematic activity aimed at improving this unsatisfactory life situation. Such a policy aimed at a better life situation should be the prime goal of any reasonable and humane policy. Its effect will be twofold: by making life more worthwhile and secure, it will both dampen enthusiasm for offensive war and increase the readiness for defense. And that, after all, is the only sane and healthy combination of attitudes toward war.

8. KARL MARX AND COMMUNISM

Karl Marx, founder of communism, created a doctrine of a quasi-theological character. The difficulty, arcane attraction, and world-historical importance of Marxism rest upon the fact that structurally and stylistically it consists of several different layers. Marx was simultaneously prophet, historian, sociologist, economist, and power politician. Accordingly, at least four disparate trends of thought are combined in his doctrine in a particularly effective way.

a. Marx as Utopian and Prophet

As a utopian, Marx continues the line which begins with the Near Eastern myth of the Golden Age, first recorded in Hesiod, and the salvation prophecies of the Old Testament prophets, which receives the form familiar to us in the Christian proclamation of the coming of the kingdom of God. In the Middle Ages, this idea is further elaborated by a profusion of sects, and after the Renaissance it emerges again in secularized form. Among the anarchists and "utopian" socialists of the eighteenth and nineteenth centuries, subsequently, it forms a favorite arena for their most ardent wishes, most extravagant daydreams and happiest fantasies.

In its earliest form, the Golden Age of the future had been represented as a happy primordial time, and the kingdom of God on earth as the final goal of world history, as the absolute fulfillment and last point of repose. Basically, therefore, it is something transcendental and stands outside history, as classically formulated by Engels: "It is the leap of mankind from the realm of necessity into the realm of freedom." Its miraculous birth also is appropriate to such an unrealistic state of affairs. Here, we find ourselves in the sphere of religion, not investigation; of faith, not knowledge; of prelogical and nonlogical thought; of May-day oratory, not political, social, and economic reality. "Both orders: 'the kingdom of God' and 'the socialist society,' are to come 'when the time is fulfilled,' both are to release mankind from the heavy curse of (the biblical or capitalist) original sin; as myths, finally, both are in accord in that they project the ideal state of mankind at once into the past and the future."[68] The *Communist Manifesto* proclaims: "In place of the old bourgeois society, with its classes and class antagonisms, we shall have an association in which the free development of each is the condition for the free development of all."

According to Marx's teaching, the final goal is that happy end of world history, culminating in an extremely liberal, almost anarchistic structure: a kingdom of absolute freedom, a society not only classless but also stateless. In short, in Tönnies's later terminology, the final goal is community.

Saint-Simon (or rather his secretary, Auguste Comte) wrote: "The people no longer has need to be governed, that is to say, commanded. It suffices for the maintenance of order that the affairs of a common interest be administered." Similarly Engels: the state is "at best an evil inherited by the proletariat after its victorious struggle for class supremacy, . . . until such time as a new generation, reared in new and free social conditions, will be able to throw the entire lumber of the state on the scrap-heap."[69] "The interference of the state power in social relations becomes superfluous in one sphere after another, and then ceases of itself. The government of persons is replaced by the administration of things and the direction of the processes of production. The state is not 'abolished,' it withers away." "To carry through this world-emancipating act is the historical mission of the proletariat."[70] Here not only the most radical anarchists of all times find their most extreme ideals unreservedly championed, not only do the optimism of the eighteenth century, the emotional exuberance of preromanticism and Rousseau's rapturous love of humanity celebrate their resurrection: even the Renaissance ideal of the universal man is taken over. However, it is not aristocratically limited to rare brilliant and blessed leading personalities, but socially radicalized as the attainment of the average man. The division of labor with all its one-sidedness ceases, and in the place of the individual, once "unilateralized, stunted, determined," now reappears "the universal realization of the individual," "a total human being"; in short there will be a "coming into being of practical humanism."[71] For only "within communist society" is "the original and free development of individuals not a mere phrase"; only communism "produces the human being in this whole richness of his essence, the *rich* human being *deeply endowed with all the senses* as its constant reality." Man will be free "to do this today, that tomorrow"; in a communist society "there are no painters, but rather at best men who among other things also paint."[72] A true futurist orgy of the most unfettered, anarchistic liberalism.

Some of these formulations smack so much of caricature that one must ask whether they are intended seriously. They stem from

Marx's youthful writings of 1844-1846, when he was between his twenty-sixth and twenty-eighth year, and occasionally give indeed the impression of juvenile nonsense. After all, past increases in the productivity of human economy have been the consequence of an ever-increasing division of labor and specialization; hence one wonders just how the pinnacle of such increase in productivity can follow upon the sudden abolition of all such specialization within the division of labor. Marx never disavowed those early statements. In his preliminary draft of the *Communist Manifesto*, in October 1847, Engels goes even further in such a portrayal of the future communist society. And to the very end, Marx and Engels, albeit more implicitly, repeatedly expressed a positive attitude toward this complex of ideas. Consider also the following marginal note of Marx to the Gotha Program of 1875: "In a higher phase of communist society after the enslaving subordination of the individual to the division of labor, and therewith also the antithesis between mental and physical labor, has vanished; . . . after the productive forces have also increased with the all-around development of the individual, and all the springs of cooperative wealth flow more abundantly— only then can the narrow horizon of bourgeois right be crossed in its entirety and society inscribe on its banners: From each according to his ability, to each according to his needs!"

Toward the end of the unfinished third volume of *Das Kapital*, Marx feels responsible enough to mix some realistic water with this foaming wine of communist chiliasm. Here, in the middle of highly theoretical disputations, he inserts:

In fact, the realm of freedom actually begins only where labour which is determined by necessity and mundane considerations ceases; thus in the very nature of things it lies beyond the sphere of actual material production. Just as the savage must wrestle with Nature to satisfy his wants, to maintain and reproduce life, so must civilised man, and *he must do so in all social formations, and under all possible modes of production*. With his development this realm of physical necessity expands as a result of his wants; but, at the same time, the forces of production which satisfy these wants also increase. Freedom in this field can only consist in socialised man, the associated producers, rationally regulating their interchange with nature, bringing it under their total control, instead of being ruled by it as the blind forces of Nature; and achieving this with the least expenditure of energy and under conditions most favorable to, and worthy of, their human nature. But it nonetheless still remains a realm of necessity. Beyond it begins that development of human energy which is an end in itself, the true realm of freedom which, however, can blossom forth only with this realm of necessity as its basis. The shortening of the working-day is its basic prerequisite.[73]

Here, then the leap from the realm of necessity into the realm of freedom is expressly renounced. Necessity remains forever. The legendary realm of freedom suddenly shrinks into a mere realm of leisure time. This disenchantment, however, never gained wide publicity, and Marx surely had not designed it for a broad public. On an even more private occasion, in a letter to F. A. Sorge of 19 October 1877, he rejects "utopianism" (of course, that of others) as "silly, stale, and basically reactionary." And, in a letter to Marx of 28 May 1876, Engels speaks with the same depreciation of Wilhelm Liebknecht's "mania to ease the deficiency of our theory . . . and to have a picture of the future society, because, after all, the philistines are quizzing them about this."

When Marx sets his allegedly "scientific" socialism over against the allegedly "utopian" socialism of his predecessors, he intends science in the English-language sense of "natural science," of formulation of necessary laws. He does not propose to improve on the earlier recipes of how the ideal state is to be attained through exertion of the will; rather he sees himself as having demonstrated that this state must, by the necessary workings of natural laws, come about and the conditions under which it must so come about. All of which makes human efforts for its realization not superfluous but all the more hopeful and promising. As the content of his image of the future, it becomes not a bit more realistic, but, on the contrary, remains as utopian as that of any of the "utopians" whom he dismissed so contemptuously.

b. Marx as Founder of Historical Sociology

The myth of the Golden Age is not only an inspiring wish-dream, which as fantasy satisfies the emotions, it is also the primal form of the history of philosophy. For this myth causes the harsh realities of the present to be felt all the more desperately, and, beyond that offers important consolations: first, in the paradisiacal primordial time, the ideal condition already existed—which *ipso facto* establishes the possibility of such an ideal state; and second, since time goes full circle, the same movement of world history that has removed us so far from the Golden Age will bring us fully back to it. Marx and Engels took over these ideas, which indeed constitute the decisive point, the truly stirring significance of the whole myth. Of course, they did not content themselves with that naïve postulate of self-evidence which merely makes the wish father to the thought. Rather, the entire body of their historical, philosophical, sociological, and economic-scientific ideas were harnessed to prove the inevitability of such development.

The paradisiacal primordial time apparently was imagined from the outset as communistic. Since it was conceived as a contrast to the harsh present, the easiest and most sweeping way that all haggling over mine and thine could be overcome was to dispense with all private property altogether. In particular, it also corresponded to the idea of mankind as one big family and to the Greek adage that "among friends all is common." This ideal notion of primitive communism was renewed in the nineteenth century in the wake of romanticism. People looked for residues of primitive communism in old traditions, institutions, and customs, tried to establish it on philological and ethnographic evidence, and indeed found this primitive communism not only in the economic and agricultural but even in the sexual spheres.

In 1884 Friedrich Engels published *On the Origin of the Family, Private Property and the State, in the Light of the Researches of Lewis H. Morgan*, a task that he felt to be "in a sense the fulfillment of a bequest" of Karl Marx. These theories, in the meanwhile, have to a great extent been refuted by more detailed investigations. They were the projections of repressed infantile longings of the nineteenth century; in consequence of this emotional context, however, they preserve their haunting quality to this day.

If the myth of the Golden Age viewed private property as a phenomenon of degeneracy, Christianity considered it a consequence of original sin. Pascal and Rousseau are one in denouncing property as the root of all social evil. (A straight intellectual line of descent runs from the eighteenth-century Enlightenment, by way of Morelly, Mably, Babeuf, and Buonaroti down to Proudhon's striking formulation of 1840: *La proprieté, c'est le vol*—Property is theft!). Turn the proposition around, and it follows that the abolition of private property is the necessary and sufficient condition for doing away with all social evils. Or, as Marx expresses it with expert precision, the socialization of the means of production becomes the decisive task.

For Marx, this was not just the gratification of an idealistic-utopian wish-dream. He showed that the rapid accumulation of

capital and the concentration and enlargement of industry were already in full motion; hence irresistible technical progress must logically lead to uniform centralization of the whole economy, placing it
thereby, of course, under the control of all of society. Here one may
also note the influence of the addiction to planning of that
megalomaniac, organization-mad project-mongerer and speculator
Saint-Simon, whose fantasies ran to an enormous increase in productivity. But socialization leads not only to utopian opulence and
bliss; behind this demand stands justice, as well as new enthusiasm
for progress: socialization, as "expropriation of the expropriators," is
designed to repair the old injustice of the "expropriation of the mass
of the people by a few usurpers"; of the "expropriation of the immediate producer," of the "laborer working for himself" (that is, of
the independent medieval artisan). This will not occur, however, in
the allegedly reactionary direction of a just new distribution, but
rather in the highly modern, progressive direction of the utmost
concentration. And as the number of propertyless people will increase, and that of capitalists decrease, in the process of advancing
accumulation and concentration, the majority of the former will
finally acquire such an overwhelming advantage that there will be
no effective resistance against their momentum: capitalism digs its
own grave through its own grandiose progress.

These, however, are only the broad and approximate outlines of
Marx's philosophy of history. They are brilliantly filled in by a gra-
dated structure of theories, which reaches from the tangible level of
the technique of production to the highest spheres of intellectual
endeavor.

Reality, the direct point of departure of human experience, is
neither (as it is for idealism) the mind, nor (as it is for materialism)
matter. Rather, it is our daily life, the concrete situation of man as a
communal being, as a socially living animal, as a *zoön politikon*. It is
everyday life as it daily and hourly unfolds before our eyes, the same
social reality that constitutes the subject matter of the realistic
paintings and of the realistic social novels of Marx's own day, but
which earlier had not been considered a worthy theme for objective
treatment by either art or science. Marx, erroneously contrasting it
with idealism, calls this basic attitude "materialism"; Lenin and
Stalin also were misled by this error and elevated materialism into
a Bolshevik dogma. In reality this view has nothing whatever to do
with materialism as that term is used in natural philosophy, and it
would be more apposite to call it sociological realism or the sociological conception of history. "It is not the consciousness of man that
determines their being, but, conversely, rather their social being

that determines their consciousness."[74] In this celebrated statement, the "social being" covers the sphere of sociology; in fact, the task of cultural sociology is here boldly and brilliantly defined for the first time. This sociological concept of history signifies an enormous and fundamental step ahead and places Marx, as the founder of historical sociology, at least on a level with Comte, the founder of systematic sociology. What has been accomplished since then in historical sociology, including the sociology of religion, the sociology of knowledge, etc., is essentially due to Marx and would not have been possible without him. Historical sociologists, in the final analysis, are all his pupils, regardless of how they may judge his political outlook.

Marx conceived the further structural relationships in such a way that the state, with its political and legal relations, rests upon the sociological base of social reality as the next layer, as it were; with art, literature, religion, philosophy, etc., constituting the last layer above that. Marx is inclined to describe this unquestionable sociological conditioning of the intellectual sphere in the vocabulary of nineteenth-century science as a relationship of unidirectional mechanical causation. The intellectual sphere is degraded to a mere "superstructure" of the "economic-social base" (and also, as we shall see, of technical progress; it becomes a mere reflection or "derivative," in Pareto's term): "The mode of production of material life determines the social, political and intellectual life-process in general."[75]

The historical role of the economy and of the technique of production—rapidly growing in the nineteenth century—had been almost wholly neglected by earlier historical thought; hence this point of departure was well chosen, although Marx, here too, elevates a partial truth into a metaphysical absolute.

Nor does Marx take his stand on physical-physiological determinism in the technical philosophical sense; on the contrary, he appeals constantly and in the most vehement and passionate way to the consciously exercised will of his audience. But the freedom of will and decision of the individual are not unlimited. Each one finds himself in a historical situation which he cannot escape. The recognition of this situation and the need to place oneself in its service and to exploit the opportunities it offers, exercise a further determining influence. Thus, it is an anthropological-historical determinism that Marx espouses, not too distant from the old Stoic utterance *fata volentem ducant, nolentem trahunt* (Fate leads him who is willing but drags him who is not).

Marx's theory of ideology goes one step further. It does not accept any world view as the *bona fide* reflection of the social base; rather, it denounces such views as a cover-up, a contrived excuse, and a partisan plea. There is no doubt that instances of this do occur, and that, in such cases, their exposure not only holds its own fascination but also constitutes a step forward and one of scientific merit. But Marx's personality, as we shall see, inclined him all too readily toward such hostile suppositions and hence toward blurring the lines between the varoius patterns of sociological explanation.

However, the sociological structure of society, "of the social being of man," is not a final and independent state of affairs, but rather depends dynamically upon the technique of production and upon the organizational forms of the division of labor, which is determined by the contemporary stage of that technique. Technical progress is the real independent variable of the whole historical process, the true essence and first mover of all historical dynamism. This theory, too, contains a large element of truth. Technical progress, in fact, has an immanent logic that defines *a priori* the sequences of its development. Technical advances, and the insights of natural science on which it is based, form a series in which no one step can be taken before the logically prior one. But this sequential logic by no means implies that any particular step actually needs to be taken. Not only may the sequence be arrested, but an advance already achieved may become lost—and there are indeed historic instances of such retrogression. Where and when progress is realized, however, it is always bound to the immanent logic of that series. Even after a period of standstill or regression it can proceed only in accordance with this sequence.

All this means that a uniform trend of technical progress can be traced through the history of mankind, and this indeed represents the only uniform and continuous line of progress in history. It is also the only one which, running without interruption, takes a steeply upward turn in the nineteenth century and which that century's general enthusiasm for progress can specifically invoke. Whereas in earlier times the realization of any particular technical advance depended largely on perceived human needs, technical progress since the nineteenth century has become more independent and autonomous as a result of a highly intensified division of labor and pattern of specialization. But woe to mankind when technical progress is unleashed to grow without restraint! The demonic forces that today hold us in their grip arise from the breathtaking tempo of technical progress combined with the steady downward slippage, for the last century and a half, of all other aspects of cultural development.

Far less original and far less fruitful is that part of Marx's philosophy of history which is revered by many Marxists as the real central dogma, the "algebra of the Revolution" (as Alexander Herzen called it): the so-called "historical dialectic," the triad of thesis, antithesis, and synthesis that Marx took over from his philosophic teacher Hegel. This triadic notion applies most clearly to the sequence in European, and specifically German, literary intellectual development from Enlightenment to *Sturm und Drang* to classicism, and there are close analogies in other developments in intellectual history that such a dialectic explanation can serve to illuminate. Neither Hegel nor Marx, of course, would have been satisfied with such a modest empirical claim. Rather, both were imbued with the metaphysical conviction that here they had found the magic key that would unlock all the riddles of history, that in formulating their triad they had once and for all traced the dance step of the world mind. And among many Marxists this conviction has degenerated into an *idée fixe*; they are no longer able to think outside this schema, considering it the real hallmark of Marxist illumination and orthodoxy. Armed with the two magic formulas of historical dialectic and historical materialism, the Marxist experiences a sense of superiority that allows him to rise above all the problems of world history.

But even aside from his historical dialectic and its metaphysical claim to absoluteness, Marx is of towering importance as a universal historian. With the brilliance of the historian as prophet he grasped the dynamic unity of content and the constitutive structures of the epoch he called "the capitalist age." That it is a prophet of doom who looks backward here, that the brilliant flash of insight is the perspicacity of hate, or rather of hate-love—all this holds true, but it serves only to clarify, not to invalidate Marx's stature. Although the creative synthesis achieved here came into being only under the high pressure of the most passionate will to destruction, this political pollution of its origin in no way detracts from its scientific brilliance. Just as Jacob Burckhardt created the concept and image of the Renaissance, so did Marx create the historical conception of capitalism, and Werner Sombart, the non-Marxist historiographer of modern capitalism, explicitly concedes that his own work "aims at naught else but the continuation, and in a certain sense, the completion of Marx's work. . . . I admire him unreservedly as the theoretician and historian of capitalism. . . . All that which is possibly good in my work, is owed to the mind of Marx."[76]

Whereas patriotism distorted nearly all other nineteenth-century historiography, and whereas its professional practitioners even boasted of their defection from the grand conception of universal history of the Enlightenment, Marx was the only historian of his age with enough synthetic and creative powers to recreate a great universal historical world picture encompassing all mankind and its entire temporal experience. In this sense we can call him the greatest universal historian of the nineteenth century—but this statement is still far from providing a complete measure of his accomplishment.

c. Marx as Economist

As an economic theorist, Marx can claim by far the most important accomplishment made by any German economist in the second half of the nineteenth century. The four volumes of his *Kapital* (of which only the first was completed to be published in his lifetime) were the result of a comprehensive mastery and grasp of the entire economic literature of all nations—a literature into which he fully immersed himself in the British Museum in the long years of his London exile; it also shows a penetration of insight and an intellectual intensity comparable only to that of Ricardo, who, through his works, became Marx's teacher in economics.

This is not the place to go into the full (in part highly complex) details of Marx's economic theory. The labor theory of value, which Marx took over from Ricardo, had already formed the foundation for the theory of economic ethics of the Scholastics. In Scholasticism already the polemical edge of the labor theory of value was directed against unearned income (although that of the merchant, not that of the entrepreneur). To that extent, Tawney justly writes: "The true descendant of the doctrine of Aquinas is the labor theory of value. The last of the Schoolmen was Karl Marx."[77] That this labor theory of value only took into consideration the most obvious kind of work—physical, manual labor—was only to be expected at that initial stage of theorizing; yet by Ricardo's time it already had become, in view of the capitalist relationships of his time, an all-too-facile simplification. In Marx this seemingly unobjectionable simplification developed into something of a master lie as he deduced from it his theories of surplus value and exploitation. The worker properly should have "the right to the full yield of his labor"; what he produces over and above his wages as surplus value forms the profit of the entrepreneur. In appropriating this surplus value the entrepreneur exploits the worker, since the entrepreneur pays for the "commodity of labor" only the cost of producing it (the bare minimum that will keep the worker alive) but obtains a far higher return from

the use of that labor. This account disregards not only interest payments and amortization of fixed capital but also any reward for the
managerial and organizing labor that the entrepreneur himself con-
tributes to the success of the total enterprise—not to speak of the
risks of loss corresponding to the opportunities for gain. When Marx
tried to overcome the difficulties of defining labor time—especially
with regard to laborers of different skills—through the artificial
concept of "socially necessary time," this theory became so complex
that it no longer could be assured of any practical applicability.

Marx expended the most ingenious effort in order to prove,
through this ever more complicated elaboration of Ricardo's labor
theory of value, that exploitation of the worker by the entrepreneur
was the inherent and necessary outcome of the rules of the free
market economy, and that, therefore, it could be prevented only by
the abolition of that free economy. This proof today is no longer
accepted by any serious scientific economist. Since the renewal of
economic theory by the marginal utility school we know that a
minimum wage determined by the law of the market in free competition is the same as the marginal product of the marginal worker,
and that all advances in economic productivity of the economy
sooner or later also benefit the worker, as the actual development of
the nineteenth and twentieth centuries fully confirms. Despite this
fact the charge of social injustice that socialism levels against
capitalism remains valid, but this critique legitimately strikes at
wholly different places than those that Marx chose for his attack. It
holds true (1) for all monopolistic and interventionist disturbances
of the free operation of the economy in favor of individual interest
groups; (2) for any concentration going beyond the economic optimum that is not unavoidable on technical or economic grounds;
and (3) above all, for the hereditary plutocratic inequality in the initial distribution of property and income, for the inequality and injustice encountered by all participants in the economy at their very
point of entry. Hence, if we distinguish the sociological conditions
under which free competition unfolds as the "outer rim" of the market, from the market itself and the laws governing it, it becomes
clear that Marx's criticism does not—as he vainly tried to prove—
apply to the laws of the market itself but only to the "outer rim," to
the sociological conditions and preconditions that surround the operation of the market. Marx, who elsewhere had an unusually keen
eye for such extra-economic (historic and sociological) determinants,
on this point follows his teacher Ricardo in all his sociological blindness. In his value theory Marx is a rabid Ricardian.

For the rest, Marx was remarkably free of such a limitation of perspective on purely economic phenomena; rather he consistently sought to fit them into the total context of social life and universal history—an aim pursued but never reached by the antitheoretical German "historical" school of economics of his time. And even though he never attained his own goal of a coherent dynamic theory of the capitalist process of production and the business cycle, it must be conceded that this goal, despite all the efforts expended on its since his time, has not been completely attained to this day. Marx, at any rate, was the seminal thinker who first perceived this grand goal and bent his efforts toward it.

The effect of contradictions and imperfections in Marx's system was the fostering of orthodoxy. Since among his disciples and followers no one was found of sufficient intellectual stature and power to comprehend the entire system and resolve its contradictions, there thus remained room for no more than partial elaborations; and these partial elaborations had to take a point of departure narrow enough not to become involved in the inner contradictions and tension of the system as a whole and be accompanied by an implicit faith in the remainder of that system. Goethe once said that the highest fulfillment that could be achieved by the natural scientist was "to have investigated the investigatable and calmly to revere the uninvestigatable"; just this has been the attitude of Marxists toward elaborating the system of the master.

Marxist propaganda has increased rather than lessened the difficulty of understanding the Marxist doctrine as a theory of political economy. The labyrinthine character of Marx's great theoretical main work, *Das Kapital*, served to reinforce the impression of unfathomable profundity, which increased the fascination of the followers. For the communist propagandist, the scientific work of the master towers like an awe-inspiring mountain peak surrounded by mysterious stormclouds, a peak the average Marxist should. distantly admire rather than attempt to scale. And even among the few trained mountain climbers among them, none could claim to have attained the final summit. Thus Marx remained there, lofty and distant, as a sort of Himalaya of economics.

d. Marx as Power Politician

Marx the utopian had longed for the ultimate condition of society; Marx the philospher of history had posited it as a predestined outcome; and Marx the economic and social scientist had sought to prove its historic inevitability. But how was this ultimate condition to be brought about? Marx's answer was the doctrine of the class struggle and of the dictatorship of the proletariat that was to be the result of this struggle. All hitherto existing history, according to this doctrine, is a history of class struggle. And ever since the historic event of superstratification, history has indeed been just that, as the present book has sought to demonstrate.

In one phase of capitalism, the dominated lower stratum (or at least a portion of it that constantly increases in importance and activity) is constituted by the industrial proletariat; the upper stratum (or at least a portion of it constantly increasing in importance and activity) by the capitalist entrepreneurs. Because of the concentration of capital and of enterprises irresistibly driven forward by technical progress, Marx asserts, this upper stratum becomes ever smaller, the lower stratum ever larger. At last this growing and ever more grotesque disproportion, taken together with the other developmental tendencies, must lead to the final catastrophe, the expropriation of the expropriators, and thereby to the dictatorship of the proletariat. The proletariat, predestined to final, dictatorial rule, must not let itself be misled by bourgeois ideologies and lies: it must wage class war cynically, ruthlessly, and brutally.

There is "only one means of shortening, of simplifying, of concentrating the murderous death pangs of the old society, the bloody birth pangs of the new, only one means—revolutionary terrorism." Marx designates "concentrated conscious class hatred" as "the surest guarantee of a social revolution."[78]

Here we come not only to the denouement of Marx's theory but also to the very core of his personality: an unquenchable thirst for power and an insatiable hunger for domination were his deepest motives—a circumstance confirmed by the testimony of many independent observers.

Marx was expelled from Paris in 1845 at the instigation of the Prussian government and took up residence in Brussels for the following three years. There, the Russian Pavel V. Annenkov (1812-1887), who later was to support Marx financially, describes his impression of him on their first encounter as follows:

He himself represented the type of man who is composed of energy, will power, and unshakable conviction, a type who was most remarkable even in his outward appearance. A thick, dark mane on the head, the hirsute hands, his coat buttoned askew, he nevertheless had the look of a man who has the right and the power to demand respect, however odd his appearance and behavior might appear. His movements were angular, but bold and self-confident. His manners ran positively contrary to all social forms of intercourse. But they were proud, with a suggestion of contempt, and his sharp voice, which had a metallic ring, harmonized remarkably with the radical judgments which he pronounced on men and things. He spoke in no other way save the imperative mood, brooking no opposition, and his words were sharpened even further by a tone which touched me almost painfully, and which suffused all his utterances. This tone expressed the solid conviction of his mission, to rule minds and to prescribe laws to them. Before me stood the embodiment of a democratic dictator, as it might present itself in moments of fantasy.[79]

Carl Schurz (1829-1906) in his *Reminiscences* writes:

In the course of the summer [of 1848], Kinkel and I were invited to represent the club at a congress of democratic associations in Cologne. This assembly, in which I remained a shy and silent observer, became remarkable to me in bringing me into personal contact with some of the prominent men of that time, among others, the leader of the communists, Karl Marx. He could not have been much more than thirty years old at that time, but he already was the recognized head of the advanced socialist school. The somewhat thick-set man, with his broad forehead, his very black hair and bear beard and his dark sparkling eyes, at once attracted general attention. He enjoyed the reputation of having acquired great learning, and I knew very little of his discoveries and theories. I was all the more eager to gather words of wisdom from the lips of that famous man. This expectation was disappointed in a peculiar way. Marx's utterances were indeed full of meaning, logical and clear, but I have never seen a man whose bearing was so shocking and intolerable. To no opinion which differed from his did he accord the honor of even a condescending consideration. Everyone who contradicted him he treated with abject contempt; every argument that he did not like he answered either with biting scorn at the unfathomable ignorance that had prompted it, or with opprobrious aspersions upon the motives of him who had advanced it. I remember most distinctly the cutting disdain with which he pronounced the word *bourgeois*; and he denounced as a "bourgeois"—that is, a detestable example of the deepest mental and moral degeneracy—anyone who dared to oppose his opinions. Of course the propositions advanced or advocated by Marx in that meeting were voted down, because everyone whose feelings had been hurt by his conduct was inclined to support everything that Marx did not favor. It was very evident that not only had he not won any adherents, but had repelled many who otherwise might have become his followers.[80]

Marx at first believed that he could gratify his power drive directly in the practice of everyday political struggle as revolutionary agitator and politician. Accordingly, he set his hopes upon the revolution of 1848. Only when these short-term hopes entirely miscarried, and even so brilliant a masterpiece of political agitation as the *Communist Manifesto* had no direct reverberation, did Marx shift to a long-term preparatory work in the domain of ideas. The fury of the failed practical man was transformed into the cynicism of the radical theorist. But the lust for power remained the dominant signature of his personality.

A fellow refugee of the post-1848 years, after a long conversation with Marx over many glasses of wine in London in 1850, formed "the impression that *his* personal dominance was the aim of all his activity." "He laughs at the fools who parrot his proletarian catechism, as well as at communists *à la* Willich, as well as at the bourgeois. The only ones whom he respects are the *aristocrats*, the pure and consciously so. In order to drive them from rulership, he needs a strength which he finds alone in the proletarians, therefore he has tailored his system to them." This portrayal has an altogether true-to-life and credible ring—*in vino veritas*; what Marx produced as refutation after its publication (obviously very embarrassing for him) has all the earmarks of special pleading and sophistry.[81]

Much of what he indignantly rejected before the public he freely admitted in characterizing himself in his closest family circle. In 1850 he played a parlor game with his two eldest daughters in which each participant had to fill out a questionnaire. Marx answered the questions it contained as follows:

> Your favorite virtue in man: Strength.
> Your chief characteristic: Singleness of purpose.
> Your idea of happiness: To fight.

Your idea of misery: Submission.
The vice you detest most: Servility.
Favorite hero: Spartacus, Kepler.
Favorite motto: *De omnibus dubitandum*.[82]

"Denunciation" is an expression which he was fond of applying in his own polemical writing: "Its essential pathos is *indignation*, its essential work is *denunciation*."[83] Arthur Prinz, in an unpublished dissertation on Marx's system viewed psychologically, calls "the will to dominion" the basic feature of Marx's being, next to "hate and revenge towards his enemies, envy and jealousy towards rivals, defiant lordliness towards his followers and deep contempt of men in general."[84]

e. The Theological Character of Marx's Total System

All the heterogeneous components of Marx's thought and doctrine were finally combined and systematized in an impressive theological edifice. It was no more free of contradiction than other theological systems, yet such contradictions and tensions serve if anything to heighten the dogmatic impact. Nor are logically tenable connecting links among the various components lacking.

The connection of the final state of mankind to the proletariat consists in the fact that the proletariat, which "has nothing to lose but its chains," is the one class whose egoistic interests coincide with the interests of mankind: the radical overthrow of the present state of affairs at any price and by any means—a conception akin to that of liberal economic theory according to which (as Adam Smith teaches) in the competitive economy the egoistic interest of the persons involved automatically coincides with the general interest.

According to Marxian doctrine, economic development, especially by virtue of its tendency to maximum concentration, also necessarily tends toward this collapse of capitalist society. The transition to the final state takes place by way of the "dictatorship of the proletariat," admittedly an extreme form of class domination. This, however, occurs only as a transitional stage and serves to make every form of future domination unnecessary and impossible.

This doctrine is a rare mixture of modern-liberal and primordial-feudal authoritarian components. The idea of the final aim and the mode of thought and argument is liberal. Extremely antiliberal, on the other hand, is the concept of dictatorship of the proletariat, the call to ruthless struggle for power, the appeal to instincts of envy, greed, and hate, and finally the theological eschatology—the belief

in the great miracle of "the leap of mankind from the realm of necessity into the realm of freedom"—which, with its Old Testament
prophetic overtones, requires the same *sacrificium intellectus* as
does any true miracle.

This coupling of both polar extremes—the boundless idealism of
brotherhood, and the equally boundless hate and revenge—is a
simultaneous appeal to the angel and the beast in man, to his loftiest and basest instincts.

The eschatological notion of the classless society is anarchistic.
Only if one is convinced of the innate goodness and brotherhood of
man, whose realization is artificially prevented by the coercive organization of the state, does it become sufficient to demand the destruction of that coercive organization so as to bring out that innate
benign structure. Babeuf had preached the arrival of an ideal final
stage through application of violence, in accordance with old eschatologies in which the kingdom of heaven on earth was preceded
by especially terrible ordeals. The postulated transformation must
have struck the mentality of Russian anarchists like Bakunin as especially obvious. For with Russians, typically, the lust to destroy all
that exists is apt to be followed by a humane embrace. These two
extremes, in fact, lie side by side only in the Russian soul; with
Marx, a cold Machiavellian theory of revolution replaces that simple destructive urge.

Arthur Prinz proves that Marx valued goodness and chivalry as
virtues also in private life and suffered from the fact that because of
the contrariety of his character, these traits were denied to him.
Thus, Marx's classless society corresponds to Marx's ideal superego,
the revolution and the dictatorship to his real ego; and both were
gratified by this doctrine.

The lofty ideal of the final classless society, corresponding to the
most ancient and intimate yearnings of mankind, is the crucial asset
that puts communism ahead of all other totalitarian ideologies with
their unconcealed brutality. This fraternal ideal of the classless society has a profound attraction even to those unfamiliar with the
relevant texts in Marx and Engels. And even in those texts, Marx
preserves a certain vagueness and repeatedly guards against spell-
ing the ideal out in more concrete terms. The conviction of fighting
for an ideal goal has inspired not only German social democracy but
also the British Labour movement, which was never crucially influenced by Marx. But this ideal is not only, as it were, a quantitative
asset, it also brings about a qualitative transformation of the
doctrine—imparts to it the theological quality of salvation knowl-

edge in contrast to the knowledge-as-power offered by the totalitarian world views. It also makes the doctrine immune to logical
refutation—since, in the prelogical realm of salvation knowledge, a
lack of logic becomes an added strength. It is this prelogical, quasi-
religious character of their world view that makes any discussion
with convinced Communists such a hopeless undertaking.

In this way communism appeals simultaneously (1) to the deep
longing of every human being for communal happiness; (2) to the
understandable hatred and vengeful instincts of the oppressed, accumulated over thousands of years, promising a change from
masochism to sadism; (3) to the equally understandable bad conscience of the upper stratum. And by establishing itself as a quasi-
religion and advancing to a prelogical, theological form of thought,
communism renders the logical incompatibility of these appeals irrelevant.

Marx took his ultraliberal conception of the final stage from the
anarchists and from the socialists, whom he labeled "utopians." To a
certain extent he also recognizes them as his precursors, with the
exception of Proudhon, whom he obviously viewed as his only serious rival and therefore systematically belittled. Marx sees the decisive advance from "utopian" to "scientific" socialism as being
brought about by his inclusion of theoretical investigations in economics and by his cynical appeal to power politics. Whereas the utopian "men of conviction" in naïve kindness hope to reach their goal
through persuasion, education, and the power of example, Marx,
with scientific exactitude, points to the only real way to this goal:
the ruthless seizure of power by the proletariat, to which the economic development of productive relationships must inevitably
lead.

We have seen, however, that this whole demonstration, successful
or not, refers only to the development from capitalism to the dictatorship of the proletariat and not to that from dictatorship to the
utopian final goal of the classless society. Not surprisingly, this final
decisive step is described by Engels as a "leap"—a mystic transformation to be believed in just because it is illogical: *Credo quia
absurdum.*

At this decisive point in his theory Marx really relies on a con-
jurer's trick. Eager to overtake the "utopians" along his "scientific"
path toward the classless society, Marx chooses a route which, even
if we were to grant all his arguments, leads not to the classless society but to its very opposite. And the further step into the classless
society is far more utopian than any of those proposed by the

utopians—for this final transition is not made in the least comprehensible. The measures advocated by the "utopians"—persuasion, education, good example—unquestionably lead in the right direction. Marx, by contrast, does not even indicate any path in that direction, and all his snide condescension toward the utopians only serves to cover up his own far greater vulnerability. At the same time, as already noted, it is this eschatological idealism with its appeals to human goodness, devotion, and enthusiasm, that marks the decisive superiority of communism over fascism, which is totally devoid of ideal conceptions on the basis of which sacrifices could be expected.

On each side of the watershed of 1792-1793, there had emerged the sharpest contrast between brightest social optimism, as expressed in Godwin's enthusiasm, and darkest social pessimism, as expressed in Malthus's gloomy predictions, taken over and developed by Ricardo. Marx combines both tendencies not through any attenuation or compromise, but by heightening both in the extreme. With regard to the here-and-now of class struggle, he is an utter pessimist; with regard to the hereafter, an utter optimist. There is an analogy here between the Marxian notion of dictatorship of the proletariat and the Islamic doctrine of holy war. The harmful influence of this ingenious doctrine, developed with such infectious enthusiasm and such penetrating insight, lies not so much in its errors in economic analysis, which were perhaps excusable in their time and which could be compensated for by supplying through political agitation what the final class struggle might turn out to lack in economic necessity. Rather, its truly baneful quality lies in the bold assertion that not only in the dictatorship of the proletariat but also in the preceding class struggles the end must justify the means—whereas the very ends *versus* means connection that links the whole process to the final classless society rests on nothing better than crass self-deception.

The sociological and political line of development that leads from class struggle to the dictatorship of the proletariat is straight and unequivocal, yet it leads to the very opposite of community. It is hard to imagine a purer, sharper, and more brutal form of class domination than the dictatorship of the proletariat. The steps toward it thus are so many steps away from the liberty, fraternity, and community of the classless society. Training for the class struggle isolates the proletariat from the existing national community (based itself on many superstratification elements) and cuts the bonds of moral obligation to other positions of that community. This implies an end to all earlier efforts to bridge or attenuate the harshness of superstratification, a revocation of the social armistice, and a reversion to the state of belligerence that came with the initial superstratification. Indeed, the proposed form of superstratification—the conquest of society by one of its parts—begets a far greater hostility than did the original external conquest.

The famous twenty-fourth and penultimate chapter in the first volume of *Das Kapital* (next to the *Communist Manifesto*, undoubtedly the most eloquent piece of writing that ever flowed from Marx's pen) concludes with the call for the "expropriation of the few usurpers by the mass of people," and logically enough begins with the sweeping observation that "in real history, as is well known, conquest, subjugation, murder, and robbery—in short, violence—play the great role." It is dedicated to the demonstration that the last of the previous acts of that great historic drama, the so-called primitive accumulation, that marks the transition from the feudal to the capitalist order of society, unfolded in this way—that capital came into the world "oozing blood and filth from all its pores from head to toe." In order to strengthen the emotional impact Marx deliberately turns to a procedure which is antithetical to the principles of his materialistic conception of history: "We take no account here of the purely economic springs of the agricultural revolution. We inquire about its violent levers." "The expropriation of the immediate producers was accomplished with merciless vandalism, and under the stimulus of the most infamous, the most sordid, the pettiest, the most meanly odious passions." "Along with the constantly diminishing number of magnates of capital, who usurp and monopolize all advantages of this process of transformation, grows the mass of misery, oppression, slavery, degradation, exploitation; but with that, too, grows the revolt of the working class, a class always increasing in numbers, and disciplined, united, organized by the very mechanism of the process of capitalist production itself." When therefore now "the knell of capitalist private property sounds," "the expropriators are expropriated"—the utilitarian application of the principle "as thou unto me, so I unto thee" to this grand final struggle of revenge and retaliation automatically is suggested.[85]

The false diagnosis (common to Stoic natural law, the Christian church fathers, and Rousseau) that private property is the source of inequality among men, in Marx has led to the fateful conclusion that the abolition of this private property by socialization of the means of production will perforce cause inequality to disappear. The exact opposite is the case. Not only can we see this in the practical example of Soviet Russia, but it can also easily be proven sociologically.

Private property is neither a sufficient nor a necessary condition of social inequality. To be sure feudal inequality can be maintained even under the legal form of private property—that constitutes the essence of plutocracy—but only with difficulty and incompletely. The fact is that private property by no means precludes social inequality, but on balance makes it less rather than more likely.

Collectivization of property, in its negative aspect, signifies the expropriation of all individuals. For if, according to the formulation in the *Communist Manifesto*, private property in bourgeois society *de facto* "is already done away with for nine-tenths of the population," in the communist society it is done away with 100 percent. In its positive aspect it is no more than a verbal label, whose real content depends entirely upon the kind of organization by which this property right is exercised. What belongs to everybody belongs to nobody—or rather to the few who exercise the property right in the name of "everybody." As the scale of operation and the need for administrative concentration and uniformity increase, so does the social inequality between the administrators and the mass of nominal owners. Indeed their property title may give them some psychic satisfaction—especially if they are appropriately conditioned by propaganda—but it confers on them no real claims and no concrete advantages whatever. All of which is to say that collective property makes possible far greater degrees of inequality than does private property.

In the transitional phase of class struggle Marxism leads, by its inherent logic, to an extortionist-pluralistic dissolution of the social body, but in contrast to other forms of pluralism there is no interest on the part of Marxists in keeping alive the goose that lays the golden egg. And the final stage of the dictatorship of the proletariat amounts to a new superstratification of an insidious and acute feudal character, except that the superstratifiers come not from outside and above but from inside and below.

Moreover, for communism in its militant phase there is a special charm and an attraction in the coupling of its two opposite elements. The doctrine of absolute community, or the classless society, gives it the religious impetus of apocalyptic prophecy and purity, a glow and inwardness of true idealism; whereas the doctrine of dictatorship of the proletariat provides a realism of the most extreme rational sobriety and the superiority of a cynical Machiavellianism; and both elements are united within a system of economic analysis of high

intellectual rank. Intellectually, communism bestows a sense of
self-confident superiority. Emotionally, through simultaneous gratification of antithetical and otherwise incompatible instincts, it
bestows an extraordinary heightening of vitality. The crusaders
must have felt a similar sense of satisfaction when, with the blessing of the Church and in honor of God and the Holy Virgin, they
were allowed to murder, loot, and steal. And the same feeling, presumably, was shared by the Islamic fighters in their holy wars, and
by the violent bands organized by the Protestant princes, which,
with Luther's blessing, marched in the German Peasant War.

It is psychologically obvious that followers of Marxism instinctively feel themselves on the side of the hammer and not on that of
the anvil, on the winning, not the losing side of the social struggle,
as dictators in the dictatorship of the proletariat, as commanders in
a command economy, and as planners in a planned economy. Naturally, these notions of the future are all the more potent in their effects when the enthusiast reserves for himself a leading and ruling
position. Only totalitarian movements like communism can hold out
to their followers promises of this kind. In a world based upon a liberal or market economy of free competition, there are no comparable
leadership positions or spheres of power. Only totalitarian movements can *grant* and distribute leadership positions, and through
loyal and enthusiastic following one acquires a claim to them. Accordingly, totalitarian movements like communism can promise
their followers far more than any other less authoritarian movement, and to that extent their propaganda wins hands down over
that of its competitors. Therein lies its strongest attraction, especially for the young. In other totalitarian movements, like fascism
and nazism, such prospects were openly flaunted and were stressed
by the propaganda. With communism these matters are concealed
out of consideration for the common good. Subconsciously or semiconsciously, however, they exercise an equally strong influence.

9. Democratic Socialism

The unprecedented development of Western industry in the last two
hundred years, to which Friedrich Engels gave the name Industrial
Revolution, brought a new sharpening of superstratification pressure in the organizational form of large-scale enterprise. In most
European countries it also at times created lamentable living conditions for the working class—although the direct causes of these were
attributable to the situation in agriculture, where foreclosure of
leaseholders and tenants drove masses of people with no means of

support into the cities. The temporary displacement of artisans by machines produced similar effects. The classic portrayals of this destitution and misery visited upon people by early capitalism are Engels's *Condition of the Working Class in England* (1845) and Gerhard Hauptmann's play *The Weavers* (1892), along with the artistically powerful etchings of Käthe Kollwitz (1895-1898).

In the initial stages of their distress, the workers were still much too powerless to adopt positive measures of self-help; hence they indulged in desperate emotional outbreaks, like the senseless destruction of machinery by the Luddites. Only when conditions had gradually improved, through Christian-humanitarian social measures and as a result of the progress of economic development itself, were the workers in a position to organize themselves: economically in the form of trade unions, politically in the form of labor parties. This development took strikingly different forms in the various industrial countries. In the United States, for example, the workers never went so far as to form a large political labor party; yet Germany, in this respect, enjoyed an internationally recognized position of leadership from 1863 to 1914.

Here Ferdinand Lassalle (1825-1864) founded the first socialist party, Der Allgemeine Deutsche Arbeiterverein (The General German Workmen's Association), to which Wilhelm Liebknecht (1826-1900) and August Bebel (1840-1913), as followers of Marx, opposed their Sozialdemokratische Arbeiterpartei (Social Democratic Workers' Party). In 1875 both organizations combined to form the Socialist Workers Party of Germany, which in 1890, after abolition of Bismarck's antisocialist penal laws, was reconstituted as the Social Democratic Party of Germany (SPD). Since Lassalle, the only opponent who was a match for Marx, was killed in a duel as early as 1864, and since August Bebel, an upright, reliable man embodying all the virtues of the German working class, could never have challenged Marx, the latter increasingly became the recognized formulator of the party's program.

Lassalle had expected and demanded social measures on behalf of the workers from the government, a course which would ultimately have led toward a German Labor party, somewhat along British lines. In sharp opposition to this course, Marx, in long and bitter struggles, pushed through his doctrine of revolutionary class struggle as the key point of the party's program and creed. Yet while German Social Democracy clung to its Marxist revolutionary credo, in everyday political life it pursued a reasonable and moderate democratic, socially progressive *Realpolitik*.

When an intellectual like Eduard Bernstein (1850-1932) found this contrast between theory and practice tormenting, and urged his fellow socialists "to will to seem what [their party] is in reality today: a democratic-socialist party of reform," this "revisionism" found little resonance among the mass of his party comrades. They were caught in their well-established dualism of evolutionary, pragmatic practice and radical revolutionary ideology and rhetoric—a dualism the more easily maintained since the pressure of the Prussian police state kept Marx and Engels away in exile in England.

The one dogma of Marxian theology that had most profoundly stirred the German working class was that of the future classless society, a goal in the espousal of which it could rightly consider itself the heir of German idealism. Meanwhile the grim doctrine of the dictatorship of the proletariat received nourishment from the actual conduct of the class struggle by the opponents of the German working class, ranging from the authoritarian attitudes of some entrepreneurs to Bismarck's penitentiary laws and his statement that the "social democratic question is a military one."

As long as the movement was not strong enough to consider mounting a revolution or violent seizure of power, the fork in the road between democratic and totalitarian socialism still lay in the distant future. But when the collapse of the German Empire in 1918 brought such possibilities within reach, the majority of the German working class opted for social democracy and national responsibility for peace and order. These same attitudes had earlier been expressed in the SPD's unanimous vote in favor of war credits in August 1914, and in the sense of patriotic duty with which the German workers went off to war. The working class not only refused to let the German revolution of 1918 veer off in a Soviet direction but proved that it was prepared to fight, if necessary, for the social democracy it practiced: the Kapp *putsch* failed in 1920, in the face not only of solid resistance from government officials and of aloofness of most of the *Reichswehr* units, but also, and crucially, because of the political general strike called by the trade unions.

The tension between Marxist theory and democratic outlook and practice first became perceptible when the "dictatorship of the proletariat" was translated into reality with the Bolshevik seizure of power in Russia, and Communist parties, beholden to the Soviets, were founded in all industrialized countries including Germany. As a result, the struggle between totalitarian Marxism and democratic socialism became injected into the political battles of the day; yet in these struggles those democratic socialists who continued to profess themselves adherents of Marx were in a logically and demagogically vulnerable position. The fact that the German Social Democratic party was not greatly troubled by this weakness is proof of the strength of its traditional attitudes and its internal discipline.

Nevertheless, the need for a counterprogram distinct from totalitarian Communist-Marxist bolshevism was increasingly felt. And it was obvious that the first item to be eliminated as part of such a reformulation would be the highly objectionable and unattractive concept of the dictatorship of the proletariat, with its open call for violence; the demand for a planned economy and for nationalization of the means of production (via the democratic procedure of majority voting) would be retained. A first attempt at sketching out this non-Bolshevik path was a collective work on *Economic Democracy* of which Fritz Naphthali was the main contributor.[86] After the interruption of this development by the Third Reich, the same tendency was resumed in the demand for "codetermination," adopted for West German heavy industry in 1952. Yet since the SPD meanwhile has expressly given up the goal of a planned economy with full nationalization, now viewing the demarcation between the private and public sectors as a pragmatic decision to be made from case to case, it seems likely that demands that were once conceived as first steps toward total nationalization will be recognized to have lost much of their meaning.

Renunciation of the goal of full socialization and planned economy occurred under the impact of the developments in Soviet Russia and of the Soviet occupied zone of Germany, where the close connection between a totally planned economy and a slave system of government, with its systematic destruction of all freedoms and human rights, was fully visible. At the same time, the spectacular upswing of the "social market economy" of the Federal Republic made fully apparent the far higher productivity of which a market economy is capable. The superiority of the market economy in the matter of productivity, as compared with the planned economy, became more evident.

A different economic model was developed by non-Marxist socialists, especially by the English Fabians. This was the welfare state, which was largely realized by the British Labour party in the years of its parliamentary rule (1945-1951) and in Sweden after the advent of the Social Democrats to the government in 1932. In both countries, the program was carried out with much honest enthusiasm and organizational ability; yet the results do not inspire much confidence. Sweden after 1945 soon used up the profits it had accumulated as a neutral during World War II, and Britain, even under five years of Conservative government, did not recover from the austerity that the welfare state had entailed. Nor is the attitude of the Swedish and British labor movements toward socialization at all unambiguous; hence Hayek's warning that these experiments, even against the will of their sponsors, may turn out to be so many "Roads to Serfdom"[87] deserves to be taken seriously. The aims of the welfare state, as far as they are legitimate, can be achieved far better and at far less cost by a *Vitalpolitik*—a policy aimed at improving the life situation—within the framework of a socially conscious market economy.

But Marxism was not only an economic theory: rather, it offered a complete world view. Once the economic theory is surrendered—or developed further into its very antithesis—it becomes imperative to reexamine all of Marxism: Which of the elements of the remarkable doctrinal structure are compatible with a social market economy? And, concurrently, upon what theoretical foundation does one's opposition to bolshevism actually rest? Where on the plane of Marxism does the demarcation line of the iron curtain actually run?

The final goal of the development of mankind, according to Marx, is the classless society, the establishment, in Tönnies's terminology, of a "community" of mankind; this grand goal of a full realization of human potential is as admirable and worthy of full support now as it was in Marx's day. Marx's own youthful writings on this are often richly exuberant and utopian and should be systematically reexamined in the light of the findings of comparative anthropology; that is to say, this part of Marx's program should not only be supported but also elaborated—in particular the demand for classlessness, which precludes any kind of domination and oppression, and of which the demand for class struggle is the very antithesis.

Marx's extraordinary accomplishment in the sphere of economic theory, as the most important successor of Ricardo, also makes him the founder of the modern dynamic theory of economics and of economic crises. But precisely because theory in this area has been so intensively developed, most of Marx's specific economic theses have been superseded and refuted, in particular his theory of surplus value and exploitation—upon which the notions of wage policy of our trade unions still rest today. Here a thorough revision is called for on the basis of the progress in economics achieved in the meantime.

Along with the theory of surplus value falls the proof Marx thought he had furnished: that private property in the means of production must lead to exploitation and proletarianization of the worker. On the contrary, it has been shown that private property, in the means of production especially, and scattered in as many hands as possible, is the best guarantee of economic and political freedom; full socialization on the other hand, begets the highest degree of unfreedom and exploitation of the worker by the totalitarian state and its dictatorial rulers.

Likewise superseded and refuted—by historical reality itself—is the concept of dialectical materialism. Russian developments since 1917, far from being a product of historical necessity, would never have occurred without the stupid-clever trick by the German general staff of giving Lenin safe conduct and without the personalities of Lenin, Trotsky, and Stalin—just as the Third Reich would not have come into being without the pathological personality of Hitler. To be sure, historical facts form men, but only after these very facts have been formed by men. And every man is responsible for his part in the formation of those facts.

Marx's perception of the role of the class struggle in history—that famous first sentence of the *Communist Manifesto* asserting that the previous history of mankind was the history of class struggle—remains untouched by these objections. It is one of the most brilliant insights we owe to Marx, and the first part of the present work was dedicated to demonstrating that very thesis on the basis of more ample historical evidence. Of course, the important limitation is that it holds true not for all of the previous history of mankind, but only for the period since the advent of superstratification. But Marx and Engels, relying on the ethnography of their day, already proposed this limitation by admitting the existence of a previous original or primordial state of mankind, free from class struggle. Here, therefore, we have an altogether correct and tenable component of the Marxian doctrine.

These correct and tenable parts of the Marxian system fit together very closely and consistently. Mankind originally (before superstratification) found itself in a classless, essentially domination-free state. Domination, oppression, and class struggle came into the world through the original sin of superstratification, taking first feudal and then plutocratic-capitalist forms. Our task thus becomes to find our way back to a classless society, on a higher stage of cultural development. In this connection a leading role falls to the working class, which, as proletariat, was for a very long time most strongly disadvantaged by the existing patterns of domination. The democratic constitutional state and the social market economy (to the extent that their ideals have been put into practice) have already brought us a few steps closer toward the goal. Our task remains that of exposing and overcoming lack of freedom, unjust inequalities, and despotism where they still exist—including their concealed forms that have become part of habitual daily life, and above all the urge to domination in ourselves. The traditional "Prussian" emotional attitude of German socialism toward centralization must be carefully reexamined from this point of view. But the militant, manly, and (in the best sense of the word) revolutionary idealism that the German social-democratic working class has preserved in its best times would fully come into its own in such a struggle for freedom and against despotism.

10. Bolshevism

The Christianization of Russia began almost at the same time as political superstratification by the Varangians. The two apostles to the Slavs, the brothers Cyril (ca. 826-869) and Methodius (ca. 815-885) came to Russia from the realm of the Khazars, much as Germany around the same time was Christianized by Irish missionaries. The result was a spiritual or ecclesiastic superstratification of Russia by the Byzantine Empire. Yet, whereas in western Europe Latin was adopted as the universal language of the Church, Greek did not become the church language of the East. If it had, the later cultural relations between Russia and classical antiquity might have become closer than they were to be in western Europe. Instead, Old Slavonic was used as the liturgical language, and this implied a cutting off of the Russian East from the intellectual clarity of the ancient world. Herein lies perhaps the deepest and most fateful difference of developments in eastern and western Europe.

In 989, the ruler of Russia, Saint Vladimir, declared Greek Orthodox Christianity to be the state religion of his empire. The model he followed was that of Byzantine Caesaropapism; within the rank order of Greek bishops, the patriarch of Moscow occupied only the seventy-first place. The movement toward ecclesiastical independence of Moscow from Constantinople, and hence for more complete dependence of the Russian church on the Muscovite state, was delayed through the dispute over unification of the Greek and Roman churches (1441-1448) and then accelerated by the fall of Constantinople in 1453; full independence was achieved only as late as 1589. In the meantime the church and rulers of Russia had come to consider themselves the third Rome, a notion reinforced by the marriage in 1472 of Grand Duke Ivan III to the niece of the last Byzantine emperor. A century later in 1570, the monk Philotheos of Pleskau wrote a famous letter to Ivan the Terrible, in which he said of the czar:

> He is on earth the only ruler over the Christians, the leader of the Apostolic Church, which stands not in Rome or in Constantinople, but in the holy city of Moscow. She alone in the whole world shines brighter than the sun. . . . All Christian empires have come to a close in accordance with biblical prophecy and they have been merged into the empire of our ruler, that is, the Russian Empire. For two Romes have fallen, but the third stands, and there will not be a fourth.

This notion of the transfer of the Roman Empire to the Russians found its expression in the adoption of the Byzantine double eagle as the official coat of arms of the Russian state and later, in 1574, in the coronation of Ivan IV (the Terrible) as emperor and czar. As early as the fifteenth century, the monk Josif Sanin of Volokolamsk, in keeping with the Byzantinism of the orthodox state church, espoused the absolutist doctrine that the ruler of Holy Russia was by nature equal to earthly men, but by power equal to God in heaven. The same doctrine was later codified by the Diet of 1551: "What God is in heaven, that the Czar is on earth"—an almost literal paraphrase of Genghis Khan's motto: "One God in heaven, one Ruler on earth."

Two traditions thus merged in sixteenth-century Russia. The tradition of oriental despotism from the Babylonians, Assyrians, Persians, and Macedonians down to the despotic rulers of the late Roman Empire and the Byzantine emperors flowed into Russian czarism. And this tradition was reinforced by the fresh contribution of the recent superstratification of the nomadic Tatars from central Asia. In this atmosphere the concept of freedom and independence of cities, which was to become so strongly rooted in the West, constituted but a brief and isolated interlude. The great city of Novgorod, with its forty-seven churches and four monasteries, had begun as a trading town; in the centuries of its independence it had adopted the laws of the city of Lübeck. But already in this period, Novgorod and its sister town of Pskov formed something of an oasis in the desert of Russian unfreedom, and eventually Novgorod itself was to be conquered by Ivan III and devastated by Ivan IV.

Already at the time of the conquest of Russia by the Tatars of the

Golden Horde, the Russian church did not hesitate to place itself at the service of the conquerors, who were not even Christian, in exchange for the conferral of valuable privileges. The same process was to be repeated when Russia centuries later was conquered by the internal Bolshevik superstratifiers, who were not Christians either and whose rule proved to be even more brutal. The period of Russian history known as "the Time of Troubles" (1610-1613), which also included considerable unrest among the serfs, ended when a "priest's child," a son of the patriarch of Moscow, Michael Romanov, ascended the throne and founded the dynasty that ruled until 1917.

In contrast to these developments in the official state church, transcendent religious beliefs found their home in the monasteries, "so that there monasticism became the bearer of the real radical-Christian natural law, of love and of communism. And since the monks were in charge of all actual educational and pastoral activities, Slavic Christianity, despite the total merger of church and state, nonetheless preserved in monasticism the instinctive social-revolutionary ideal of absolute brotherhood, and in this fashion the notion of radical brotherliness suddenly enters into the most secular matters and practices of society—a contrast which has so often amazed the Western readers of the great Russian novelists."[88] This ideal of "absolute brotherhood," so often admired and so emotionally stirring, has something of a social-pathological character in its unbridled and unsteady extremism. The mass of downtrodden human beings is suddenly submerged into an indistinct melange of brotherliness. Nowhere have the masochistic tendencies of Christianity been developed in such one-sided and dangerous fashion as within the Russian Orthodox church. Russian mysticism likewise has the character of a desperate flight from reality, just as the magical practices that emerged in the schism of 1506 have something of a character of desperate clinging to tangible forms of the supernatural.

The Eastern church during the last few centuries has rendered to the temporal despotic rulers of Russia two inestimable services: it has made political subservience a religious duty of the faithful, and it has diverted their religious needs into a harmless mystic inwardness. Hence it seems somewhat incongruous that some supposed experts on the Eastern church still assert that even for us western Europeans, Eastern Christianity should serve as the only effective spiritual weapon against bolshevism.

Byzantium had preserved the legacy of antiquity and preserved also the continuous use of the Greek language; yet under the pressure of its quasi-oriental despotism, this heritage was handed down in a much narrower and more lifeless form than it was in the Latin West. This Byzantine tradition also lacked the characteristic Roman ingredient that in western Europe since the time of Augustus provided an important counterweight against the oriental ingredients in Hellenism. Byzantium, after all, had adopted the Roman tradition only in its late, degenerate, and orientalizing form of the Roman despotism of the late imperial age.

Furthermore, the philosophic tradition of the Greek Orthodox church was based on a dogmatic form of late Platonism rather than on the Scholastic tradition of Aristotle, to which the Roman Catholic church owes such a large intellectual debt. The contrast between Eastern and Western Christianity can be traced back to a considerable extent to this ancient and ever recurring antithesis between the influences of Plato and Aristotle. The transition from Greek Orthodox Christianity to Russian Orthodoxy further emphasized the resulting rigidity. This greater rigidity was in part an immediate result of provincial or even colonial character of the Russian exarchate, whose "dual faith" included many heathen as well as Christian elements. Subsequently the rule of the Tatars, first heathen and later Muhammadan, impeded further cultural contact with Byzantium; Constantinople itself was conquered by the Turks in 1453 even before this Tatar rule in Russia was ended (1480). As a result, Byzantine Christian influences in Russia never went beyond the narrow and provincial scope of the patriarchate of Moscow, whose very existence served further to insulate Russia from cultural contact with western Europe. "The isolation in which Russia found itself as a result of Tatar rule, together with the difference in the two versions of the Christian faith, was a determining factor in creating the unbridgeable gap that has separated western and eastern Europe to this day."[89] In this way Russia not only came to lack the Aristotelian influences of Scholasticism, which transmitted to the West so much of the precious legacy of Ionian-Greek scientific thought, but also failed to undergo that further elaboration and radical development of that same tradition in the Renaissance and the Enlightenment.

In western Europe the Roman Catholic church was able to provide an effective counterweight against the claims to supremacy of secular rulers, while the fragmentation of western Europe into a profusion of autonomous political structures during the Middle Ages created room for a tradition of "freedoms" against which even the absolutism of a later age had difficulty asserting itself. In Russia, the Middle Ages implied a twofold loss of freedom: politically through brutal domination by a people of alien race, religion, and culture; intellectually through the Byzantianism and orthodoxy of the state church. In Russia, therefore, the absolutism of the czars could continue the tradition of the Byzantine absolutism of the established church as well as the brutal superstratification of the Tatars—two tendencies that came to a climax in the fifty years of rule by Ivan the Terrible (1533-1584). It is little wonder therefore that Ivan IV has enjoyed considerable admiration under the Bolsheviks.

A number of historic parallels suggest themselves between the absolutism established by Ivan the Terrible in Russia and the absolutism established in Turkey during the same period. In Russia, however, the social and legal position of the peasantry declined far more sharply. The peasant, referred to only by the contemptuous diminutive *muzhik* ("little man") was bound to the soil and deprived of his freedom to move about at discretion—a change effected as early as 1597 by the ruler Boris Godunov, a descendant of a Tatar prince. Soon thereafter the Russian peasant was further reduced to the status of a serf, and in 1789 Catherine II (the Great) made over the Russian peasants into the property of noble landowners. Of all the lasting forms of superstratification that have developed in the past within the context of high civilizations, this treatment of the peasants in Russia would seem to have been by far the most inhumane and brutal—but also that which was borne with the greatest submissiveness.

The closest parallel that suggests itself is that of the treatment of the helots by their masters in Sparta, which deliberately preserved the virulence of the original superstratification; but even in Sparta things did not go as far as they did in Russia. In Sparta there are accounts of organized uprisings by the helots, who conducted themselves with great bravery; in contrast, the uprising of serfs in 1610-1613 has been all but erased from Russian historical records. The Russian landed proprietors had little fear of resistance from their submissive serfs.

But masochism under changed conditions can easily be converted to sadism—the oppressed, under favorable circumstances, now becomes himself the oppressor. And indeed Russian history offers this full range from extreme submissiveness to boundless brutality.

Maksim Gorki (1868-1936), who certainly may be considered an expert witness on the matter, writes in *Lenin and the Russian Peasants*: "It is this Russian cruelty which has astonished and distressed me throughout my life. Where do its roots lie? I have pondered this question at length, but can find no explanation. I believe that an affinity for a special form of cold-blooded cruelty is peculiar to the Russian people, and to it alone."

Serfdom was formally abolished in Russia in 1861, the year in which the Civil War broke out in the United States. Actual social conditions, of course, changed rather more slowly. Thus we must bear in mind that when the Bolsheviks seized power in October 1917, only fifty-six years had elapsed since the Edict of Emancipation: the entire rural population over fifty-six years of age had been born into serfdom, and those over sixty could remember serfdom as a personal experience.

The czar proclaimed the abolition of serfdom under the impact of the serious defeat suffered in the Crimean War (1853-1856) in order to strengthen his absolute rule by freeing it from this increasingly heavy social burden. The proclamation of constitutional government in 1906, effected in the wake of the defeat in the war with Japan (1904-1905) had the same aim of sacrificing part of the facade in order to save the underlying structure. But the constitutional period also led to the agrarian reforms of Stolypin, which aimed at making the peasants full proprietors of their land and encouraged them to develop a system of peasant cooperatives. Finally, in 1917, a third major military defeat forced the czar to abdicate. Less than a year later Lenin seized power. The interlude of democratic constitutional government between the collapse of czarist despotism and the establishment of Bolshevik rule lasted barely eight months.

The collapse of the czarist *ancien régime* provided a first opportunity for the establishment of democracy in Russia. The program of the *narodniki,* who were supported by the overwhelming peasant majority and might easily have effected an alliance with the Menshevik Social Democrats, might have furnished a useful foundation for such a development. Yet the leaders of these groups lacked the political skill and experience to avert the impending catastrophe. If such a democratic Russia had been recognized as a partner in the postwar international system by the victorious Western powers, it could have embarked on a program of postwar reconstruction that could have dramatically raised the standard of living of the population, which now no longer needed to work in war industries. As a partner in a liberal world economy and with a free organization of domestic economic activity, Russia could have experienced an economic upswing far beyond the meager results yielded by the Bolshevik planned economy. When Bolshevik propaganda keeps stressing the economic advances over the situation in 1914, it tries to make us forget that an alternative regime could have carried out such economic development with far less friction and under far more favorable conditions.

That things took a crucially different turn was due to the diabolic and disastrously successful trick by Ludendorff, then in charge of the German military structure and later an ally of the National Socialists. At a time of total paralysis of the Russian armies, on 3 April 1917, Ludendorff allowed Lenin, Trotsky, and their associates to cross Germany in a sealed train on their way to Russia, thus providing the crucial inoculation of the fatal disease that has ravaged Russia since that time.

What brought bolshevism to power was the very antithesis of a revolution, a counterrevolutionary *coup d'état* by a criminal minority which, by a cynical breach of solemn promises, violently dissolved the legally elected revolutionary Duma. The change was comparable to the fateful change of the French Revolution from its libertarian-liberal phase to its subsequent totalitarian-terroristic phase, except that the change in the French case was not as deliberate.

Russian czarism collapsed in February 1917, exactly as the German imperial regime was to collapse in November 1918. Nicholas II and William II were equally inadequate and weak rulers, and the Russian February Revolution suffered equally from a lack of capable political leaders, as did the later revolution in Germany. In Russia, however, the war continued, exposing the inadequacy of the leadership more clearly. A small minority of Bolsheviks under Lenin, whose first attempt at a *coup d'état* in the summer of 1917 had failed, proved to be the only revolutionary group that knew exactly what it wanted, and it set out with savage energy to attain its goal. Kerenski did not muster the courage to resort to drastic measures against this Bolshevik threat. The increasing insecurity and helplessness of the democratic revolutionary government enabled Lenin and Trotsky finally to effect their second, successful *coup d'état* on 6-7 November 1917. Since the subsequent elections to the Constituent National Assembly brought the Bolsheviks only one-fourth of the votes cast, the legally elected parliament was dissolved by Red troops at the meeting of 18 January 1918; this was an overt violation of all democratic legality, and it was to be followed with a rule of terror by a party three-fourths of the electorate had rejected. In sum, it was an antidemocratic and antirevolutionary *coup d'état*.

If the Bolsheviks, since the end of the Second World War, have installed terrorist governments under a democratic facade in all the countries they conquered, we must recall that their initial seizure of power in Russia took place in the same way, and that Russia never produced a democratic majority in favor of the Bolsheviks. Through this seizure of power bolshevism not only assumed the inheritance of czarism but found itself also ruling over a population of remarkable submissiveness. This submissiveness and pliability of the Russian population had been fostered under nearly a thousand years of ascendancy of its Byzantine Orthodox church. The old czarist upper stratum had exploited this submissiveness mainly for its own hedonistic purposes. By contrast, the Bolshevik superstratifiers exploited the enormous opportunity created by this submissiveness of a hundred million docile people as it had never been exploited before. At first the new superstratifiers displayed an asceticism that contrasted starkly with the preceding pattern of hedonism. After a brief but violent struggle for dominion, they killed off or forced into exile the old upper stratum. The broad lower stratum consisted mainly of peasants, so that the old sociological pattern that had prevailed in Russia from the Varangians down to Ivan the Terrible and beyond, which the reforms of the nineteenth and twentieth centuries had merely camouflaged, was essentially reproduced and continued. There thus was a direct continuation of the old Medieval patterns of rule in a new medievalism—and indeed, superstratification reverted to its sharper and more rigid original forms. This basic sociological continuity provides the essential explanation for the events in Russia.

At first the Bolsheviks took over the forms of the workers' and soldiers' councils that had emerged during the February Revolution. Since, however, it proved incompatible with their harsh centralism, the system was soon downgraded to a mere facade, although the term *Soviet* (council) has been consistently applied.

There can be no doubt that Lenin acted as a Marxist during his seizure of power and viewed his mission as one of carrying out the Marxist program under his regime. What followed was a dictatorship of the proletariat without foreseeable end, in which the totalitarian components of Marxism dominated. The ideal of a classless society was maintained as the ultimate aim, although it gradually faded into the background. Despite the deviations to which Lenin increasingly saw himself forced by circumstances, he himself remained a convinced Marxist until his death. Not so with Stalin, who, unlike Lenin, was not an intellectual. As a seeker after power, pure and simple, he let surrounding realities and opportunities rather than programs and ideologies determine his actions. The eschatological promises of Marxism lay beyond his intellectual horizon. Hence the idealistic aura, which in Lenin's time still surrounded the Communist party and its policy, disappeared completely under Stalin, at least for the members of the ruling stratum. Stalin experienced no inner struggles in abandoning the doctrine of abolition of the division of labor as well as the hallowed Marxist dogma of the "withering away of the state." The new Russia placed the orthodox Marxist doctrine in the position of a state religion, or rather of a state theology, in place of the Greek Orthodox doctrine of the Russian church. Orthodoxy has been strictly enforced with the help of heresy trials, excommunications, and executions. The catalog of heresies, the "Left" and "Right" deviations, has been systematically elaborated. The sharpness and persistence that Stalin and his associates applied to smelling out such heresies was fully comparable to that of the Dominicans of the late Middle Ages. The role played by the appeal to written authority—the Bible in one case and the writings of Marx and Engels in the other—is fully comparable, and so is the imputation of wicked, diabolical motives to the heretics. Two English natural scientists, strictly concerned with objectivity, characterized the approach of present-day Russian biologists in a field theoretically as removed from politics as genetics:

> The types of scientific discourse followed in Russian journals are frequently alogical in form; that is, they do not concern themselves so much with stringent argumentation from factual data, but analyze instead the psychological issues involved in accepting or rejecting the scientific concepts under consideration. . . . It must not be supposed that Russian geneticists are antipathetic to logical reasoning, for . . . they have written many long passages of stringently argued discourse. . . . What is characteristic is not an absence of logic, but an intermixture of logical and alogical methods of procedure. It frequently happens that two or three pages of careful argumentation are followed abruptly by a sudden dart into speculation of an extraordinary type, or into a minute analysis of the motives of their critics, or into quotations from some approved authority. Such sudden metamorphoses in the style of discourse will not be unfamiliar to those conversant with Russian literature.[90]

And they continue to cite the following statement by Berdyaev: "All controversies in the sphere of theory, ideas, and philosophy, and all disputes in the practical, political, and economic world in Soviet Russia, are fought out under the banners of orthodoxy and heresy."[91]

But the similarity to the Christian heresy hunts of earlier centuries goes far beyond the mere method of reasoning and of adducing proofs. That political differences of principle must be condemned as high treason and lead to the death sentence is perhaps understandable, although neither humane nor democratic. That even a deviant opinion concerning the construction of a submarine can cost a designer his life is more difficult to understand—but military technology is at least connected with the waging of war, and hence with politics. That differences of opinion in a department of science as specialized and as remote from politics as genetics can have the same lethal consequences is bound to come as a surprise to anyone who has any illusions about the totalitarian-theological character of bolshevism.

The most famous scientist in Soviet Russia, the most brilliant and successful botanist of his generation, was Nikolai Ivanovich Vavilov (1885-1943). Vavilov managed to put the geography of plants on wholly new foundations and is internationally recognized and celebrated as the most important investigator of the botany of cultured plants since de Candolle. Vavilov had a younger rival, the agriculturist Trofim D. Lysenko (b. 1898), who proved as successful as Vavilov himself as a breeder of plants but as a theorist was a confused monomaniac and vastly inferior to the older biologist. An extremely heated scientific controversy developed between the two in which Lysenko charged among other things that Vavilov's genetic views were reactionary, idealistic, bourgeois, and anti-Marxist. The consequence was that Vavilov suddenly disappeared from the scene and Lysenko emerged as the triumphant successor to all his positions and honors. Vavilov was first consigned to the concentration camp at Saratov and from there deported to Magadan, a village on the bay of Okhotsk, in the remotest, coldest northeastern part of Siberia, where he died within a year.

In this fashion Lysenko convinced himself that he had successfully refuted the bourgeois, fascist Mendelian law of heredity, which forms the entire basis of modern genetics, and that he had replaced it with his own dilettantish neo-Lamarckism. At a meeting held in the Lenin Academy of Agricultural Sciences on 31 July 1948, Lysenko's astounding claims at first ran into violent opposition, until Lysenko announced that he had the support of the Central Committee of the party. At this point all further discussion was terminated and Lysenko soon was designated a "hero of the Soviet Union." His opponents now lived in fear of their lives, even though some of them did not hesitate to capitulate as quickly as possibile and to declare themselves guilty of "having misunderstood the only correct tendency and of having served pseudoscientific genetics, and having conducted themselves as enemies of the people under the guise of scientific objectivity."[92]

Meanwhile, after Stalin's death, fate caught up with Lysenko; he was officially exposed as a swindler and a confidence man and relieved of his posts. In the course of the swing back to Stalinism in April 1957, however, Khrushchev once again eulogized Lysenko.

The practice of proclaiming a single Bolshevik orthodoxy and line as the only permissible one was consistently extended to the whole range of intellectual life, including not only music but also the performance of circus clowns. If Russian intellectual life had been entirely self-dependent, this pitiless control of freedom of inquiry would rapidly have led to catastrophic decline and retrogression. But since autonomous intellectual work continues in the democratic countries, and since Russia is able to select from that work, it has been able to escape the dire consequences of its own cultural policy. Thus bolshevism sponges on the results of intellectual freedom in the rest of the world.

The great Moscow treason trials of 1936-1938, in which the oldest and most esteemed Bolsheviks and associates of Lenin were sentenced to death, aroused astonishment in the Western world, not least because of the behavior of the accused. The defendants vied with each other in pronouncing the vilest self-accusations and self-condemnations, which it is hard to explain as the mere result of torture, injection of drugs, and threats against relatives. Rather, the true explanation seems to be suggested by the analogy of the religious trials of the Medieval and baroque periods: the accused, morally broken, admits the charges because he feels that his conduct is not just a crime but a *sin*, and because the enormous psychic pressure of guilt thus produced is released by orgies of self-accusation and self-punishment.

The defendants of the Moscow trials were themselves convinced and active Bolsheviks, guilty of the very same atrocities and criminal acts as their hangmen. The trials thus were partly a matter of an intra-Bolshevik family feud, partly a bitter and relentless struggle for power; and they also showed that there was a difference of opinion concerning the most effective means of reaching the same goal. Whether, from a Bolshevik point of view, Stalin was not really "in the right" is something that it is almost impossible for an outsider to decide, and even the defendants could not be psychologically sure of their own case. Their very failure was a proof that on the basis of their common Bolshevik convictions, Stalin had been in the right. Moreover, if they had been in Stalin's place, they probably would have dealt with him exactly as he did with them.

The distorted theological and orthodox character of the Bolshevik outlook and mentality makes isolation of the Bolshevist regime from the rest of the world an absolute necessity—a phenomenon that we shall analyze in greater detail in the parallel case of national socialism. The "iron curtain," as Churchill impressively called it, implies a striking confession of bad conscience. It indicates not only how much must be hidden from the rest of the world, but also how necessary it is for bolshevism to hide the rest of the world, its life-style, and its views from Russia's own population. It is thus an obvious confession of how much the Russian leaders, after almost four decades of the most intensive manipulation, fear that a view beyond that iron curtain could have an alluring effect, how much it could appeal to indestructible tendencies in human nature. The pervasive fear of a throwback to humaneness is the clearest proof of how much one is instinctively aware of one's own inhumaneness.

A test of the receptivity of the Russian people to the amenities of capitalism was provided by the reintroduction of these amenities, although in diluted form, in Lenin's brief experiment with the New Economic Policy (NEP) in 1924. On this subject a sympathetic observer of bolshevism writes:

We can indeed say that the time of the NEP . . . was perceived by every inhabitant of the Soviet Union as the happiest period of his life. It lasted only until 1926 and it ended abruptly with the ruthless persecution of those who had become newly enriched. It was the time of free trade and free production in which independent entrepreneurs sprang up like mushrooms from the earth, during which prices dropped to ridiculously low levels as a result of intensely growing competition and of an oversupply of commodities, whereas wages in relation to those prices were higher than they had ever been in czarist times—a time in which people who had earlier lived through the period of "war communism" seemed to have gotten a glimpse of heaven on earth.[93]

Nonetheless it is still somewhat surprising when totalitarian vice finds it necessary to perform its ceremonial bow before democratic virtue, as for example in the Soviet constitution of December 1936 with its almost compulsively democratic attitudes. This so-called "constitution" was promulgated in the interval between the end of the Moscow trials and the execution of its defendants. In speaking of the trials, Stalin is supposed to have said that "Europe will swallow anything"; this constitution obviously was the sugar coating with which the pill was to be sweetened.

The "abolition of the death penalty," which was decreed on 26 May 1947, belongs in this same context. For the Soviet authorities, in dealing with persons who have incurred the displeasure of the regime, it is much easier and more convenient to make them disappear without ceremony than to go through the complex, expensive, and protracted procedure of a formal trial resulting in a death sentence. Hence, formal death penalties could be dispensed with along with formal trials, and at the same time this change of procedure could be advertised to credulous admirers abroad as an impressive proof of the humaneness of the Soviet regime. However, this "great act of socialist humanism," as chief prosecutor Vishinsky called it, had only been in effect for two and one-half years when the death penalty was once again reintroduced for "traitors to the fatherland, spies, and saboteurs"—and obviously a major proportion of those who run afoul of the regime fall into one or another of these categories.

The Bolshevik pattern of domination is historically unique in one respect. All previous superstratification throughout world history had left untouched the superstratified peasantry's attachment to the soil, which was essential as an economic base for the superstratifiers; frequently, indeed, they had strengthened that attachment further by imposing some kind of compulsory bond that tied the peasant to his soil. The Bolsheviks, however, made a concerted effort to reduce the peasantry to the status of proletarian agricultural workers, to destroy the organic traditions of a people of over 100 million such as those traditions had persisted for over a thousand years, and to impose a process of nomadic massification in consonance with Bolshevik ideology. The ruthlessness of the procedure applied can be appreciated if we recall what has been pointed out in earlier sections of this work about the powers of resistance of small peasant family enterprises against the pressures of despotism and a mass society. The peasantry to this day remains the strongest protective force against totalitarianism. In view of the unwavering attachment to the soil of the Russian peasantry, especially in a predominantly peasant region like the Ukraine, the depersonalization imposed by the Bolsheviks cost millions of human victims and led to widespread and devastating famine. The operation began with the proscription of the well-to-do peasants, denounced as "kulaks" and class enemies; and subsequently the upper limit of peasant land-ownership was gradually lowered. The surviving peasants were then forced to enter *kolkhozes*, and the remaining private portion of their own property was gradually reduced. Alongside the *kolkhozes*, highly mechanized government wheat farms were set up. Finally, Khrushchev decided to take away from the *kolkhoz* peasants their last remaining personal holdings, to which they had clung over the years. His plan was to build up mammoth *kolkhozes* and to settle the peasants affiliated with them in large agro-cities, thereby trans-forming them into a proletariat wholly dependent on the govern-ment.

One characteristic which bolshevism shares with all other to-talitarian regimes, and particularly with national socialism, is the cult of the informer. "Nothing is considered nobler within a Kom-somol cell than to discover the *faux pas* of some kind or other by any member and to broadcast the offense. . . . If one inquires into the motives which induce people to lend themselves to act as informers, it is found that ideology plays only a minor role. What is decisive is the general pleasure taken in denunciation—an attitude that is sys-tematically fostered by the government."[94]

The brief duration and provisional character of the dictatorship of the proletariat as a necessary and momentary emergency measure, exceptional and transitional in nature as part of the decisive final phase of the class struggle, is explained by Marx with the assurance of victory of the proletariat and the prospect that, once the opposing class is liquidated, any necessity for such a dictatorship will disap-pear—the dictatorship of the proletariat will come to an end for lack of opponents. On this very basis, Marx demanded that the dictator-ship be as unrestrained and ruthless as possible, because this is al-legedly the most effective way to shorten its duration and to put a stop to its unavoidable horrors. The criterion indicated by Marx for the termination of the dictatorship of the proletariat—that is, the final destruction of the opposing class against which class struggle and revolutionary terrorism were directed—has long since been fully met in Soviet Russia. But what has followed has not been an end to dictatorship but rather its utmost technical refinement and its extension to such remote intellectual spheres as the science of genetics. This prolongation of the dictatorship is justified by the de-vice of creating new class enemies as soon as the old ones have been liquidated: kulaks, Trotskyites, counterrevolutionaries, saboteurs,

and many other groups have successively thus been branded as class
enemies, and any such group momentarily selected naturally finds
itself defenseless against such charges. This procedure has three
advantages for the regime: first, any group which one day conceivably might become inconvenient to the regime is annihilated through
preventive and forcible liquidation; a salutary fear is instilled in all
other groups, as nobody can tell in advance whether it might not be
his turn next; and in this fashion millions of forced laborers are
created for jobs which are too distasteful or too risky for ordinary
workers and therefore would involve excessively high wage costs.
Above all, however, the regime thus furnishes periodic and irrefutable proof that the class struggle is not yet at an end, that its task
has not yet been accomplished, and that it therefore must be maintained at all costs into the future. It turns out that the more the dictators gain the power to make themselves superfluous and thus to
end their dictatorship—as Marx had anticipated—the more they
also gain the power to prolong the class struggle and to establish
their own indispensability. The dictatorship of the proletariat thus
ever anew creates the preconditions of its own existence.

Compared to these sociological and human realities of the establishment of a rule by terror of indefinite duration, the economic aspects that take first place in Bolshevik propaganda and usually are
in the foreground of scholarly discussion on Soviet Russia, are in
fact quite secondary. Even if the productivity of the Russian economy and the living standards of the population had in fact reached
the extreme heights that bolshevism for forty years has repeatedly
promised, this could not alter the cardinal rule of judgment that the
economy is there for man's sake, not man for the economy's sake. In
reality, however, the facts indicate that the economic performance
over the last forty years has been distinctly mediocre and unsatisfactory, particularly when we consider the disproportionate expenditures and the enormous sacrifices that have been made. And to the
extent that bolshevism can indeed claim economic triumphs, these
have been in large measure due to international capitalism, which
repeatedly has furnished the credits, the machinery, blueprints, and
patents, the engineers and mechanics on which the Russian productive apparatus has depended.

This continual transfer of technology from Western countries is
possible because the technical, organizational, and other advances
of the West are regularly published in technical journals and books
and because capitalist patents also are at the disposal of the Soviet
economy at no cost. To the extent that this technical information is

indeed kept secret, in private industry or in Western military establishments, the Soviet Union has expended great effort to extract these secrets through treason, espionage, kidnapping, and the use of defectors from the West. Trade between the West and the Soviet Union also plays a crucial role. Not only does it allow the Soviet economy to make use of some of the most modern machines and other means of production that originate in advanced Western countries, and thus to overcome the shortages and bottlenecks so characteristic of the Soviet planned economy; beyond this, Western imports also serve as an essential source of technical information.

When it is asserted that the Soviet Union's singleminded concentration of all energies on preparations for war are a requirement of self-preservation in an international situation where Russia is surrounded by potential enemies on all sides, two observations are in order. First, this international situation itself is but a consequence of Bolshevik policies. Second, the results of this single-minded concentration on a military effort have had distinctly meager results. When Stalin launched his surprise attack on Finland in November 1939, the Red Army proved to be no match for the diminutive Finnish forces. And when Hitler, who had earlier condoned the Soviet attack on Finland, launched his own attack on the Soviet Union on July 1941, the glorious Red Army suffered disastrous initial losses and took months before it was able to regroup its forces. Only the severity of the Russian winter and the enormous Russian distances, in combination with Hitler's own strategic dilettantism, eventually turned the tide of battle. Even so, Russia presumably would have lost the war if Germany had had to fight on that front alone—all of which is not to be interpreted as a belittlement of the tenacious courage of the ordinary Russian soldier in defense of his own soil. A planned economy is far more suitable for war and for preparation for war than it is for peace; yet the free economy of the United States within a few years managed to build up an incomparably more effective armament industry than the spasmodic Russian planned economy had been able to build over the decades.

The international impact of the Bolshevik dictatorship as a first modern political and sociological example of self-superstratification has been enormous. All dictatorships since that time have taken Russia as their model for overall organizational details, although none of them so far has succeeded in approaching the Russian model in its brutality, cynicism, and unscrupulousness. National socialism, to be sure, through its propaganda of hate, tried to deny this dependency and instead to create the impression of being a profound

and fundamental antithesis of bolshevism. But this negative propaganda only was directed against the Soviet Union to the extent
that it still functioned as the center of management and hegemonic
power of the international Communist movement. In reality there
was no question whatever of a fundamental antithesis between bolshevism and national socialism. Even in the foreign policy of the
Soviet Union, Russian nationalism increasingly replaced the earlier
international policy of world revolution. Far from itself following
the policy of the Comintern or Cominform, Russia increasingly
forced the Communist parties of other countries to make themselves
into the tools of Soviet foreign policy—a pattern of coercion which at
first only Tito dared to oppose. And the internal situation in the
Soviet Union reached a point where international revolutionary
communism, denounced as Trotskyism, is persecuted nowhere as
ruthlessly as it is in the Soviet Union. Presumably Lenin himself
would have suffered a similar fate a generation later. The emotional
focus of this new Soviet Russian nationalism turned out to be the
personal cult of Stalin as a sort of red czar. Thus bolshevism, after
providing fascism with its crucial organizational model, became itself increasingly assimilated to its fascist pupils in matters of ideology.

As time passes, the worship of technical progress, which already
in the West in the nineteenth century had developed into something
of a substitute religion, seems to be developing into the real religion
of the Soviet Union. Already Marx had considered technical progress as the prime mover of world history. This pseudoreligious worship of technical progress, in which bolshevism agrees with other
forms of totalitarianism, combines easily with the political thirst for
power of the leadership since it is also a prime requisite for the aspiration to military superiority. Soviet Russia's turn from international communism to an overheated Russian and Pan-Slavic nationalism became increasingly apparent and eventually led to a
puerile self-adulation and boastfulness. There was no sphere of cultural accomplishment in which the Russians or Stalin himself did
not claim international leadership. Even penicillin was alleged to
have first been discovered by a Russian.

The emigré Russian religious philosopher Nikolai A. Berdyaev
(1874-1948), had originally denounced communism as a "satanoc-
racy" based upon a process of "demonic hypnosis." However, after
the successful defense effort of the Second World War and the con-
cordat hypocritically concluded with the Russian church, Berdyaev
joined this new ideological front of Pan-Slavic messianism: "The

Russian communist revolution did not originate in humanism," he now proclaimed, "but it ended up in humanism and was bound to end up there." And as proof for this statement Berdyaev adduces the circumstance "that even Stalin in his speeches speaks of humanism and its special significance, and that it is also mentioned in Russian newspapers and journals."[95]

The path which Stalin traversed in the three decades of his rule was essentially the path from the still semi-idealistic, Marxist position of Lenin, Trotsky, and others, to the exclusively "realistic" position of a totalitarian Russian national socialism and Pan-Slavist imperialism. The nationalistic and imperialist character of Russian policy found expression in the resumption of the Russian expansionist policy of czarist days as it had been formulated in the alleged testament of Peter the Great and in the programmatic writings of the Slavophiles. Whereas Lenin, on the basis of the nationality principle and the right to self-determination, had given up Finland and the Baltic States, the reannexation of these and other lost territories of the czarist regime became the goal of Bolshevik foreign policy under Stalin. Thus the negotiations which Stalin in 1939 conducted secretly and simultaneously both with Great Britain and with Hitler's Germany resulted in the Soviet-Nazi Nonaggression Pact in 1939 because Germany but not Britain was prepared to grant these territorial concessions. But not content with the annexation of the Baltic States, Stalin soon registered new demands to Finland, Romania, Bulgaria, and the Turkish Straits. But in the negotiations with Nazi Germany of November 1940, Molotov returned empty-handed.

Stalin had hoped that he could watch Nazi Germany and the democracies mutually destroy each other and thus bid for the role of world dictator with his own undiminished military forces. But Hitler's surprise attack changed all this and turned the strategic advantage to the Western powers. The next opportunity for Russian expansionism came upon the defeat of Hitler's Germany.

Stalin's authority, confirmed by an almost unbroken series of successes, had been exaggerated to almost divine dimensions by utterly unrestrained propaganda. His death therefore signified for Moscow a corresponding loss which cannot be fully compensated in the foreseeable future. Stalin's disappearance brought about major changes within the Soviet ruling elite. Malenkov, who first seemed to stand in the foreground, was later displaced by Khrushchev. Contrary to previous precedent, however, by which one might have expected Malenkov to be given a choice of execution or suicide,

Malenkov survived, and there are indications that he may have been protected by the top command of the Red Army, which had an interest in playing out the two civilians, Khrushchev and Malenkov, against each other. Subsequently the principle of one-man rule, as practiced by Stalin, was subjected to widespread fundamental criticism, and the principle of collegiality was proclaimed in its place. This was a clear indication that all those who aspired to Stalin's succession felt themselves too weak to assume it.

The most startling and unprecedented event of this period, however, was the pitiless moral exposure of Stalin in Khrushchev's speech at the twentieth party congress. This posthumous dethroning of Stalin, his doctrines, and his books resulted in an unprecedented weakening of the Soviet totalitarian orthodoxy. The speech presumably was intended for the benefit of the elite of Bolshevik officialdom, and an attempt was made at first to keep it secret. But this attempt failed as a result of a masterstroke by the American intelligence service under Allen W. Dulles.

This second, moral murder of Stalin is an example of a well-known sociological phenomenon in the history of superstratification: the recurrent tension between the ruler and his retinue of vassals, knights, officials, and other accessories of domination. It reminds us that no basic alleviation of the tension inherent in superstratification has ever been achieved in world history, and hence is least likely to be achieved where—as in the Bolshevik case—superstratification has recurred in its very sharpest form. Herein lies the basic weakness of the Bolshevik structure of domination, and the implications of this are worth pursuing.

Stalin's death, and the difficulty the regime experienced in finding a successor to his one-man rule, led to a sharp drop in social pressures, a general loosening of discipline, and a sense of insecurity in all those sharing in the exercise of rule. Nobody knew any longer what was expected of him or to what extent he could count upon immunity for his actions.

The repercussions were felt most strongly among the peoples of eastern Europe, who had become the victims of superstratification by Bolshevist colonial imperialism: East Germans, Poles, Czechs, Slovaks, Hungarians, Yugoslavs, Albanians, Bulgarians, and Romanians. In contrast to the Russian tradition of submissiveness, some of these had a long tradition of being militant in their love of freedom. For them, bolshevism meant alien domination, and to the extent that they do not themselves belong to the orthodox Communist minority, national, philosophic, and religious resistance reinforced one another.

Tito's Yugoslavia had been the first satellite where this line of development came to a head. Yugoslavia did not border directly on Russia, and its tenacity and adroitness in exploiting the changing international constellation enabled Tito, with American help, to assert his independence. At the same time, Tito remained a convinced Communist of the Trotskyite persuasion. His model was a noncentralistic, federalist structure of world communism, with each country left to practice its own particular brand of communism. If this Trotskyite federalism had prevailed over Stalin's centralism, the danger for the West probably would have been even greater, since the explosive separatist counterforces to Russian imperialism would then not have been set off. Yet Stalin's successors obviously did not feel themselves strong enough to live under the tension of Tito's vehement denunciations. Thus Tito, only three years after Stalin's death, enjoyed the triumph of seeing the whole Moscow government travel to Belgrade and of seeing his bitterest Stalinist foes in the neighboring satellite states replaced. In the other satellite states, Stalin's death and the continuing succession struggle led to major political explosions. The first in the series was the uprising of 17 June 1953 in the Soviet occupied zone of Germany, and minor or major disturbances or uprisings subsequently occurred in almost all the other satellite countries.

The most successful rebellion was that in Poland; there, after the Poznan disorders of 28 June 1956, Gomulka succeeded in bringing the oppositional forces under his control on the basis of general confidence in his unflinching courage and his Polish patriotism.

The Hungarian revolution was to be the most violent phenomenon triggered by these developments. Of all the revolutions in world history, none has had the same elemental character of a passionate outbreak of a people's solidarity and desire for freedom, without any advance organization or conspiracy. The Hungarian people showed the world that there were still men and women to whom freedom was more precious than life. At the same time they tore from the face of bolshevism the honorable mask of coexistence, and showed that Soviet imperialism even after Stalin does not shy away from any sort of brutality and betrayal in asserting its domination.

An appeal which I formulated in 1953, shortly after Stalin's murder, and which at that time found no hearing whatever, seems to have lost none of its topicality today, four years later:

An open outbreak of disorders and uprisings, such as not a few of us seem to have hoped for, could—indeed must—lead to a situation where we in the West would be explicitly asked to intervene. But in our present condition, would we be prepared militarily, politically, morally for such a test of our readiness if it were to be offered by the events of world history? But if we are not ready, if we were to fail in the face of such a situation, this revelation of our weakness would be tantamount to the gravest defeat conceivable. We cannot know in advance whether and when world history will put us to such a test; hence there is for us no task more pressing than that of making use of the reprieve which fate seems to be granting us, so as to work daily and hourly with all our energies, each of us in his place, toward the strengthening of our inner and outer defenses. Readiness is all.[96]

The end of the Bolshevik rule of terror would be a liberation for the entire world including the Russian people—although the most difficult task for world peace would remain that of habituating the Russian people to freedom and weaning it from its tradition of masochism. But perhaps such an event would bring the fulfillment of that prophecy, as utopian as it is moving, which Herder made one and a half centuries ago in the spirit of German philosophic idealism:

> The wheel of changing Time turns relentlessly; and as these nations for the most part inhabit the most beautiful land in Europe (if only it were opened to external trade); as it cannot well be imagined otherwise than that in Europe legislation and policy will and must increasingly foster not the spirit of bellicosity, but quiet industriousness and tranquil commerce among peoples—thus also ye deeply sunk, once so industrious and happy peoples will finally be awakened from your torpid slumber, liberated from your chains of slavery and thus be allowed to use your beautiful regions as your property and to celebrate the triumphs of quiet industry and commerce.[97]

11. FASCISM

Developments in Italy, as later in Germany, were profoundly influenced by the Russian model. Yet the ideologies applied were structurally different, which had the advantage that this factual dependency could be hidden behind an exaggerated emphasis on the ideological contrasts and that the artificially fostered fear of the "spectre of communism" could be used as an effective means of propaganda for inducing an atmosphere of mass psychosis.

The situation after the First World War that made possible a totalitarian seizure of power exhibited many similarities in Russia, Germany, and Italy, stemming from the weakness of democratic institutions. Even though Italy, unlike Germany, had fought on the victorious side and was spared a dictated peace, she felt nevertheless that she had not been suitably rewarded by her allies; this provided a specific focus for feelings of dissatisfaction and an insecure national self-image—and hence for underintegration. For a nationalist-totalitarian movement arising in this situation, syndicalism offered itself as the only available revolutionary and collectivist ideology that could compete with communism. And this in fact was the doctrine espoused by Benito Mussolini (1883-1945) after his expulsion from the Italian Socialist party. He is said to have carried Georges Sorel's *Reflections on Violence* with him for years, and in his crucial speech of 24 March 1924 he called Pareto his outstanding teacher. These antecedents account for a vitalistic exuberance, of allegedly Nietzschean origin, for the glorification of violence, for the hankering after "activity for activity's sake,"[98] all of which remained characteristic of Mussolini's personality and of the movement that he led. Mussolini spoke of the "tragedy of violence" and vigorously advocated "the necessity for an uprising that would open up the masses of workers to a feeling for tragedy." And in his speech at the party congress of 21 June 1925 Mussolini described the new fascist way of "living dangerously" as follows: "Courage first and foremost, imperturbability, love for daring, disgust for idleness and any adulation of peace, constant readiness to face dangers whether in the life of an individual or of the community. Detestation of quietude, complete frankness in all relationships, the pride of feeling oneself an Italian at every hour of the day, discipline in work, respect for authority." And similarly in his speech of 6 February 1928: "The dagger between the teeth, bombs in hand, and a sovereign contempt for danger in the heart."[99] Aside from the fact that this Italian type, here portrayed with such amusing concreteness, could hardly be recommended for universal application, it also remains true that such excessive dynamism can only provide the means to some end, the path to some goal, but leaves undefined the state of affairs that constitutes that goal.

It is easy to see that war with the ultimate imperialist goal of world conquest, such as it was espoused by Corradini, would be the goal most consonant with this attitude. Yet such a goal clearly is out of reach for a people as amiable and artistic as the Italians. Therefore weak, defenseless, and conveniently located countries like Ethiopia and Albania alone offered themselves as likely objects for conquest. And even Greece, surely not a modern military power, turned out to be an unconquerable foe for the fascist legions. The attack on Ethiopia was waged with bombers and other modern weapons against African natives armed often only with spears; and the "beauties" of this struggle, with its extreme lack of chivalry, were portrayed by fascist writers with a nauseating estheticism. The League of Nations and the Western powers could not make up their minds to intervene effectively for the defense of either Ethiopia or Albania, and thus gave a preview of their later attitude toward Hitler, who carefully drew the relevant lesson.

Gabriele D'Annunzio (1863-1938), the poet of fascism, on one occasion expressed himself rather vividly with respect to concrete life goals:

> Do you want to fight? To kill? See rivers of blood?
> Great heaps of gold?
> Herds of female prisioners?
> Slaves?

Yet D'Annunzio himself decidedly preferred the great heaps of gold and especially the herds of females to the rivers of blood.

D'Annunzio's esthetic subjectivism, a mixture of Nietzsche, Russian mysticism and French decadence, painted for young people and in resplendent colors, a heroic ideal full of struggle and danger as well as the enjoyment of a cruel voluptuousness and overbearing rage for life as the aristocratic-mystic superiority over the slave-revolt of morality. But such a morality could only be practiced, of course, by individual "supermen" and hence had more of a destructive rather than integrative social effect. Thus only nationalism remained as an integrating ideology as Mussolini put it: "Our myth is the nation, our faith is the greatness of the nation."[100] And in peacetime this ideal was filled in with the attempt at Prussianization of Italian life and Americanization of the Italian economy: punctuality, hard work, dedication to sports, and pursuit of rationality and megalomania.

These admittedly were extremely un-Italian, and, by Italian standards, exceedingly sober and strenuous goals. But a rich tradition was available for aesthetic and decorative trimming—above all, the inexhaustible legacy and ideological tradition of the Roman Empire with its glorious profusion of memories, formulations, ideas, feelings, and symbols, beginning with the *fasces* of the Roman *lictor*, from which fascism derived its name. Such ideological elements had the advantage of making possible an honorable alliance with the Roman church and, on that basis, of strengthening the hegemony of the state and stabilizing the monarchy. In contrast, the so-called corporativism that was supposed to provide the economic element in fascist ideology, turned out to be a mere organization of economic interest groups for the purpose of receiving governmental directions and assuming responsibility for carrying them out.

By and large, since fascism was less distant from Italian traditions, it could also accept more of their legacy, so that fascism caused much less of a break in continuity than did German national socialism.

The profound and long-lasting outcry that followed upon the murder of Matteotti, the general secretary of the Italian Socialist party, indicates how far fascism remained behind bolshevism and national socialism in terms of brutality. If people in Soviet Russia and Nazi Germany had been as excited over a murder of this kind, they would have had a busy life of excitement indeed. The Italian people, moreover, had the good fortune of being able to cooperate in their own liberation by fighting on the side of the allies at the end of World War II and thus were spared a prolonged foreign occupation. When they once again became masters of their own fate, they returned after a brief transition crisis to their traditional ideals— although the goal of domestic political stability has so far eluded them. One major difficulty in this connection has been the prestige that accrued to Italian communists as leading members of the resistance movement. The conduct of Luigi Einaudi as the first elected postwar president, which combined his background as a distinguished economist with extreme modesty and simplicity, provided an extreme and refreshing contrast to the inflated theatrics of fascism.

12. National Socialism

(I) the antecedents

a. From Charlemagne to William II

Aside from the original sin of superstratification, which is the common heritage of all civilized peoples, German history has carried a number of burdens, accumulated far back in time, which had the effect of preparing Germany for national socialism or were used or abused by national socialists for such purposes of preparation. As Hermann Jahrreiss testified before the Nürnberg trials of 1946:

"Wholly special circumstances must exist when a modern people lets itself be ruled despotically, even if it is a people as eagerly submissive as the German people."[101] The following pages will attempt to trace the roots of the most important of these "special circumstances." Naturally it would, in the nature of the case, be impossible to give a complete "explanation," which in any case is possible only with physical and chemical occurrences, the conditions of which we ourselves have created by experimental arrangements. Yet the unexplained element in the disaster of national socialism that struck the German people need not in principle be any greater than it is with other historical events, if only historiography does its duty. Although well-intentioned and serious German observers disagree with such an estimate, this is merely an indication of the extent to which the picture that Germans have formed of their own history is inaccurate and inadequate, to what extent superficial or pseudo-profound elements of self-deception have entered into that picture, how much has been glossed over, and how much it has lost touch with reality.

The present intention, of course, is not to give a complete outline of German history, for which in any case the author is not professionally qualified. Rather the question that we will seek to address is: how could such an event as Hitler's rise to power come to pass in Germany? What is it in German history that has contributed to making the Nazi seizure of power possible? What antecedents was Hitler able to use (or misuse) for his purposes?

We also should keep in mind that there are two very different types of causal explanation. The first is summed up by the phrase "the time was ripe." In such situations all lines of development converge upon a particular event that somehow seems to be "in the air," which must come to pass in one fashion or another, and which is widely expected. We need not debate in this context whether such a *kairos*, such an obvious historic opportunity, cannot also be missed. At any rate, whether it is seized or ignored will not depend upon a single personality. For example, by the beginning of the sixteenth century, a religious renewal was widely felt to be due or overdue. If it had not been Luther who had launched the Reformation, someone else would have effected it, such as Zwingli, who, independent of Luther, had already embarked upon a similar path. Similarly, the formation of the German nation-state in the nineteenth century was clearly due to come about; perhaps it would have come about more honorably and proved more durable under the leadership of someone other than Bismarck.

The event here to be explained, in contrast, belongs in the opposite category. Without Hitler's unique and extremely pathological personality the Third Reich would not have been founded. The Great Depression was already on the wane by the winter of 1932-1933, but the situation cried out for a program of national integration. Such a program could also have been drawn up in an honorable way, so that we can here perhaps speak of a *kairos* that was not missed but rather was scandalously abused by Hitler.

The Holy Roman Empire of the German nation, which was never actually realized, filled the political consciousness of the German people with extensive claims without the counterweight of responsibilities, and it prevented the formation of a centralized nation-state at a time when a rich store of energies could have been made available for this task of national integration. The misfortune was not that these far-reaching claims were made; they were, after all, in keeping with the great traditions of the ancient world transmitted to the West by the Roman Empire and the Roman church, and they had lent grandeur to the crown of Otto the Great and to the age of the Hohenstaufens. Rather, it lay in the fact that the Germans lacked an adequate power base to realize these claims and in the consequent ever-repeated failures to which they gave rise. And while Germans unsuccessfully pursued this lofty aim, they were overtaken by other peoples pursuing the lesser goal of a centralized nation-state, a political form that was to dominate the next epoch of European history. By this statement we do not mean to imply that we follow the outdated nationalism of the nineteenth century in considering such a centralized nation-state an absolute and universally valid aim of historical evolution. Nevertheless, under the conditions obtaining in the modern West, it was an inevitable phase upon whose rapid and smooth attainment much in the history of each people was to depend.

This universalist impulse of the German imperial tradition was to continue intermittently for seven centuries. Subsequently the successes at the periphery that the Hapsburgs registered in Burgundy, Spain, Italy, and Hungary were, from a national point of view, no less fateful than the earlier failures of the Hohenstaufens had been in Italy. The last emperor who took the universal mission seriously was Charles V (1500-1558, reigned 1519-1556), although he pursued it with a distinct Counter Reformation bias—one might call his dream that of a Holy Roman Empire of the Spanish Nation. The failure of this universal aspiration was, of course, also the compelling reason for Charles's abdication.

What it might have meant for the future course of world history if this grand task of a Holy Roman Empire of the German Nation had indeed been accomplished the present generation of Europeans can well appreciate, since under wholly different conditions we are facing the same unfulfilled task of continental integration—and, it would seem, with equally little prospect of success. In the German historical context it is clear, however, that all the strength and idealistic impetus that had been vainly expended upon this unachievable goal was lost to other, more manageable, endeavors.

The successive Teutonic waves of the great migration spilled across Spain to North Africa. This migration had hardly ebbed when the tidal wave of Islamic expansion, originating in the Semitic population centers of the Arab peninsula, began its opposite course, reaching as far as Spain, where for centuries both currents opposed each other. As the Teutonic expansionist drive was blocked from further advance toward the southwest it recoiled in a northeasterly direction. This backward impulse of migration was passed on from people to people and led to a new superstratification of each group by the last—a common occurrence in the history of migrations and stratifications. Thus, Charlemagne's Saxon wars are explicable as superstratifications in a recoiling direction, and the same applies to the deflection of Hapsburg policy toward the Balkans and above all to the German colonization in east-central Europe.

During the great migration the Slavs, moving behind the Teutons, had reached as far as the Elbe and Saale rivers; now the recoiling Teutons took control of Slavic territories east of the Elbe, some of their spearheads eventually reaching as far as the Baltic countries, the Volga and Transylvania. Meanwhile, however, German colonization of the east, glorified in the usual way by nationalist historians as a great national feat, had very nefarious implications for German history, creating a fresh and particularly unattractive instance of superstratification.

This set Germany sharply apart from social and political developments elsewhere in Europe. In northern Italy, where the nobility had taken up urban residence, the proud city-states tolerated no overlordship. In France, the crown allied itself with the bourgeoisie in preparing the conditions for the later nation-state. In England, nobles and townsmen joined in opposition to, and in extracting concessions from, the crown. Only in Germany, where the inferiority of towns to princes had never been effectively challenged, did princely territorial states encroach ever further on the rights of the townspeople. Luther not only rent the previous religious and cultural unity of the West asunder, but also preached passivity and submissiveness to his German audiences. As an Austrian Jesuit was to complain later, "What is most lacking among Germans is joyful courage and a stout heart—there is no lack, though, of colorful dress or of plumed helmets."[102] The European confessional wars of the sixteenth and seventeenth centuries were nowhere fought with such bitterness as in Germany. A German scholar in 1946, looking back at the Third Reich, wrote: "It is as though the Germans were still living in the time of the religious wars, as though the political figure of Adolf Hitler had been the incarnation of the need of the German factional spirit to consign the opponent to the very fires of hell."[103]

As a result of the conversion of the Elector of Brandenburg, John Sigismund, to the Reformed church in 1613, Prussianism developed as an ominously efficient symbiosis between Calvinist sadism among the rulers and Lutheran masochism among the subjects. With Frederick William I and Frederick the Great, Luther's passive obedience was militarized into the mentality that Thomas Mann could trenchantly describe as the "militant slavishness" of the German people. Earlier, Hölderlin had complained that "slavishness grows, and with it a crude courage" among these "barbarians from time immemorial who have become more barbarous through industry and science and even through religion."

The Brandenburg nobility lost its feudal independence, a legacy from the Middle Ages, in the electorate of Brandenburg under the reign of the Great Elector, Frederick William (1640-1688) and, finally, in the kingdom of Prussia under Frederick William I (1713-1740) who carried out the task of subjugating the nobility to royal absolutism. Thus East Elbian nobility, deprived of the right to independent political activity, was confined to the management of its landed properties. The definitive renunciation of political independence with respect to the throne was compensated for by increasing rights of the noble lord concerning the peasants on his manorial domain. At the end of the Middle Ages these peasants still had personal freedom, but their status deteriorated considerably after the Thirty Years' War, declining at last to serfdom. Thus developed the prototype of the East Elbian Junker as gentleman farmer, mindful of any advantage that might be seized, resentful of those above, lordly toward those below, and combining peasant shrewdness and feudal arrogance. The Junker knew how to turn the so-called liberation of the peasants in the early nineteenth century to his own advantage and to wrest massive economic advantages from them; parallel events had reverse effects upon the land-owning nobility of south and west Germany and frequently led to impoverishment of whole families. The result, in the increasingly plutocratic atmosphere of the nineteenth century, was the uninterrupted ascendancy of East Elbian Junkers.

A great rationalization and commercialization of agriculture had been carried out in the second half of the eighteenth century, in part on the Chinese model, chiefly in England; in the intention of its philanthropic propagators, it was supposed to benefit the peasantry. In Germany, however, this rationalization was carried out mainly by the titled owners of the northeastern manorial estates; thus it transformed East Elbian Junkers into modern capitalist, large-scale entrepreneurs in the sphere of agricultural production. As in the plantation economy of the tropics and subtropics, this new rational agricultural technology on German colonial soil was carried out with slave labor. The slave-holding plantation owners of the American southern states in the nineteenth century played a political role in the United States not unlike that of the Junkers in Prussia and Germany except that in the latter case there was no war of secession ending with defeat.

Under the Great Elector (Frederick William, 1640-1688) and his successor, who accepted the Prussian royal crown, mercenaries had always been recruited among the native population. Significantly, the civil administration developed at the same time out of the army commissariat; the entire country was little more than a military supply center. Frederick William I (1713-1740), however, was the first to carry out the "canton" system, which made younger sons of peasants liable for military service. Further, he solidly established the sovereignty of the crown in relation to the nobility; consequently, he could proceed to recruit his officer corps almost exclusively from this class, both cheaply and without fear of disloyalty. That such recruitment was not viewed as an honor by those affected can be inferred from the fact that the king had to send out armed patrols to carry the sons of his nobles out of their castles and herd them into the barracks—which, for the remainder of Prussian history were never to lose their penitentiary flavor.

Despite his rejection of the doctrine of predestination and his sympathy for a socially minded pietism, Frederick William I was to remain a Calvinist; thus, there are references to his "Calvinist stamp," his "advocacy of a Calvinist vocational asceticism, his association with the political energy of Calvinism."[104] Probably no one contributed more strongly to creating the image of real Prussianism than this pitiless top sergeant of his kingdom.

In his son, Frederick the Great (1740-1786), Prussianism found a leading personality, endowed with genius, who became the first integrating symbol of a new German nationalism, as no less a person than Goethe has testified.

Highly gifted, sensitive, rather feminine in his endowments, spoiled by a gentle and loving mother who reared him along the lines of French Enlightenment culture, Crown Prince Frederick was systematically bullied by his competent yet violent East Elbian father. The details are well known and in most accounts they are presented in a patriotically moralizing, even sentimental way. In fact, the crown prince, continually disobedient and systematically deceptive toward the king, prepared, in concert with a group of young noblemen, for the return of the antiroyalist nobility, accepted secret sums of money from the French ambassador and planned an escape first to England and then to France—a series of acts that very properly could be viewed as attempted high treason. But the father's extreme severity was to have dramatic consequences. There remains much doubt whether Frederick's submission to his father's overpowering will and his pleas for reconciliation were sincere. The court physician, Supperville, reported at this very time to his sister, Margravine Wilhelmina of Bayreuth, as follows:

I have had time to study his character only too exactly. The Prince has a great mind, but an evil heart and a bad character; he is a dissembler, mistrustful, obsessed with peculiarities, ungrateful, much given to vice, and unless I greatly deceive myself, he will be even stingier than the King, his father, is now. He has no religion at all and fashions his morality at his pleasure; his whole effort is designed to dazzle the public, and he is an exploiter and despiser of men to boot.[105]

Most of these traits, observed so early and perceptively, remained. While Frederick's relationship with his father was to remain ambivalent during the father's lifetime, a complete change occurred with his death in 1740 and Frederick's succession to the throne. With the disappearance of his paternal opposite his protest was superseded by guilt feelings. As late as the Seven Years' War (1756-1763) the father appeared to him in terrible nightmares. Frederick seemed to have fully internalized and internally sub-

jected himself to the father image of the superego. Frederick's own
nature had been the very antithesis of his father's; yet the father
had smashed that nature and thus prevented any personality development or individuation in line with it. As a result, Frederick's
actual conduct became patterned ever more on that of the father—a
suppression of and terror against the self that was bound to produce
pathological side effects, particularly in the sexual sphere.

Under the impact of this violent reshaping at the hands of the
father, Frederick now developed into a personality of outstanding
genius and of demonic contradictions. He was a brilliant representative of the rococo and the spirit of the Enlightenment (in which he
had been brought up by his cultured mother), yet devoid of humane
or optimistic traits, and he was given to cutting irony and mordant
criticism. Like a Mephistophelian misanthrope he was ever aveng-
ing himself on humanity for the earlier mistreatment he had undergone. Although ascetic in personal habits, he thirsted after glory
and was given to the naked enjoyment of power. Among the many
Machiavellian politicians of his period he was the most successful,
the most heroic, and had the most irresistible momentum. Yet—
well practiced as he had been in taking paternal blows—he was admirable in the fortitude with which he bore the harshest blows of
fate. "A brilliant but arrogant and at bottom lonely, loveless spirit,"
in the words of one of his admiring biographers.[106] His contempt for
the *race maudite*, the cursed human race, to which he had the dubious pleasure of belonging, was expressed also in neglect and a be-
draggled appearance of his body and attire. The longer he lived, the
gloomier grew his cast of mind. When he died people felt no sorrow,
but rather a dull sense of relief.

The frederican (*fritzisch*) ideology that Germans outside Prussia
adopted taught that the genius-hero and leader, proving his
charisma through victory and success, is above any claim or measure of moral and religious tradition. At the same time, Frederick's
own attitude toward German nationalism, which had chosen him as
its idol, was as noncommittal and skeptical as it was toward all
other ideals; he shrank neither as crown prince from taking bribes
from the French court, nor as king from supporting France against
the emperor. He pursued a power policy on behalf of a purely Prussian territorial state without being able to foresee that a century
later it would lead to the founding of Bismarck's empire.

Frederick the Great, by his victories and renown, had made the
Prussian military profession a high honor. The officer corps thus became a privileged social estate, sharply distinct from all other

classes, so that the youngest lieutenant could claim precedence over the highest ranking civilian. Under Frederick the Great, who as crown prince had been the leader of a conspiracy of young noblemen and who ever since felt a special tie to the Junker class, the nobility made a full political comeback. He preferred the nobility in all ways: "It is the sons of the nobility who defend the country, wherefore this race is so good that it merits being preserved in all ways." One of the ways in which the king tried to preserve this race was the practice of financial subsidies to noble landed proprietors, in sharp contrast to his otherwise close-fisted frugality. Hence, the "help to the East" (*Osthilfe*), which was to play such a fateful role in undermining the Weimar Republic, goes back as far as Frederick the Great.

In line with Frederick's view, expressed in his will, that "it would be the first step toward the decline and fall of the army, if we should be forced to make burghers instead of noblemen officers," all officer positions—especially in the "good" regiments of the army—remained reserved for the nobility. Yet, the high rate of casualties among officers in the Seven Years' War had forced the promotion of bourgeois soldiers who had distinguished themselves for bravery. In the parades after the victorious end of the war the grateful king had the officers to whom he owed his victory presented to him individually. If the name of the officer betrayed bourgeois origin, he pummeled him with the famous crutched stick in front of the assembled enlisted men and drove him out of the royal presence. Variations on this model of procedure were often repeated in the history of the Prussian army. The aristocratic officer corps of Frederick the Great was, so to speak, the bodyguard of the absolute ruler, the instrument of his enlightened despotism. Toward the ruler himself, of course, the officers had no rights whatever, no more than did the civilian population, or, for that matter, the enlisted ranks toward the officers.

In 1769 Frederick the Great implored his successor "with all the love of which I am capable" not to dismiss any "of the brave officers who participated in the war under my orders"—a plea meant to extend, as we just saw, only to those of the nobility. His incompetent successors followed this advice so literally that the Prussian army entered the Napoleonic wars with a senile and utterly incapable officer corps of vainglorious Junkers who had been resting on the laurels bestowed on them by Frederick the Great. The consequence was ignominious collapse.

The disastrous collapse of 1806 cleared the way for democratic reform in the army. The military successes of the German war of liberation (1813-1814) were achieved as a result of these democratic reforms introduced by Scharnhorst. After the return of the victorious troops, however, in milder form and without Frederick's crutched stick, the procedure of 1763 was repeated. The bourgeois who had enthusiastically volunteered and whose valor in battle had earned them their commissions were viewed as an alien element; they were discharged at the first opportunity. In 1819, the minister of war, Hermann von Boyen, custodian of Scharnhorst's democratic tendencies, was also dismissed.

In the following three decades a quiet but bitter struggle developed within the Prussian army between the heirs of Scharnhorst and Boyen and those in favor of a feudal-militarist approach. The latter tendency, supported by Frederick William III, steadily advanced. Thus there is a straight line of political continuity from Frederick William I to Frederick William III and down to William I.

The decisive victory of the Prussian troops over the bourgeois revolution of 1848-1849 further sharpened antidemocratic tendencies, which subsequently were entrenched in the army reform of 1862, sponsored by Albrecht von Roon. This military reform of 1862, by expanding the size of the army, led to the victories of 1864, 1866, and 1870, and, by refeudalizing its ethos, to the defeat of 1918. At the outbreak of the First World War the technical superiority of German as compared with French industry, was not reflected in the technical competence of the military. Rather, except for the heavy artillery (viewed as alien and held in contempt), the Germany army, technically, was disastrously inferior to the French, especially in the equipment and training of the field artillery. This, in turn, was a direct consequence of the condescension and contempt with which technical matters were viewed by the officer corps, in contrast to the prestige lavished on the quasifeudal and technically obsolete cavalry.

Here once again we meet a tradition dating back to Frederick the Great. As Brinton has said, "Perhaps in general the criticism, made so often of the Germans in the late [First] World War, holds true of the Prussian army of 1792: . . . Though the cavalry was the best in the world, Prussian artillery was not at all good. Frederick himself had neglected it, and this branch of the army was not sufficiently 'ritterlich' to attract ambitious young noblemen."[107] The defeat of 1918, as well as that of 1806, each in its very different way, is thus attributable to the feudal tradition of the Prussian army.

Bismarck, who financed Roon's army "reform" with his unconstitutional budget and himself seemed a larger-than-life embodiment of the East Elbian Junker, became the victorious champion of a Greater Prussia and conqueror of a Lesser Germany and was to conduct an economic and social policy inspired time and again by covert Junker attitudes. Thus junkerdom and Prussian reaction won through Bismarck their decisive posthumous victory over the reforms of Baron vom Stein. In Bismarck's Prussian-German empire, the junkers dominated Prussian politics by virtue of the three-class franchise, and even the coal barons of west German industry, riddled with the inferiority feelings of the *nouveaux riches*, looked up to them.

In the Rhineland and Westphalia, which later developed into focal points of social conflict in Germany, the prevailing relationship between master and journeyman, owner and workman in the many small enterprises and in the few middle-sized ones retained, well into the nineteenth century, a peasant-artisan-patriarchal character. The arrogance of the East Elbian lord of the manor was totally unknown. The first opportunity for its adoption and application came with development of large-scale industry in the second half of the nineteenth century—the large-scale industry that in its original form unavoidably has something of the barracks and of the slave plantation about it. Large-scale industry thus offered a first opportunity of treating the urban population like east European serfs or migrant workers, thus promoting an unconcealed superstratification structure. And the corresponding ethos was now imported from east of the Elbe, from the noble friends on whom the industrial parvenus came to pattern their behavior.

When an industrialist like Emil von Kirdorf told his workers that it was he who was "master in the house," he merely projected attitudes of the east German manor and of the Prussian barracks to the factories of western Germany. The support that even the German manufacturing industry, altogether against its own economic interests, lent to the policy of subsidies for heavy industry and large agriculture, to social repression, and to a high-strung nationalism—this support derived exclusively from this social ascendancy of East Elbian feudalism. Whoever dared to break rules was faced not only with social ostracism but with inner pangs of guilt.

In line with the same antirevolutionary and antidemocratic tendency, parallel to militant feudalizing tendencies, which extended the social preeminence of the reserve officer to the civil sphere, there developed after 1850 that characteristically German form of fraternity student, or *Corpsstudent*, whom we have already encountered through the eyes of his critics in the German youth movement a generation later.

A general and uniform public school system in a society still not free from superstratification can educate its pupils only along lines that ensure internalization of lower-class attitudes according to their fine hierarchical gradations. That leads to characteristic difficulties, which we have already encountered several times, for the growing children of the upper stratum. Accordingly, in the eighteenth century, separate boarding schools for young noblemen were founded so that the children of aristocratic families would not grow up to be "cringers"—i.e., adopt or internalize the attitude of the lower stratum. In the nineteenth century these boarding schools were incorporated into the public school system; the laws governing compulsory education subsequently made it more difficult for parents to resort to the evasive device of private instruction. After the defeat of the bourgeois revolution of 1848, however, the need for a feudal education for the progeny of the upper stratum once again made itself felt. As it could no longer be met within a uniformly standardized public school system, it became all the more pressing to inject a feudal element into university studies—lest the last such opportunity should be lost. Herein lies the sociological importance of the development taken by the student "corps" from 1850 onwards, and of the other uniformed student associations that imitated their practices. The aim of these student societies was to educate their members to an upper-class consciousness and attitude. It is striking that in doing so they relied on some of the oldest devices of superstratification: riding on horseback—an inefficient mode of urban transport but one permitting the rider to look down on the shuffling philistines; bearing arms, or more specifically, sabers—a privilege denied to other civilians but likely to leave the proud students in lifetime possession of visible duelling scars; seducing daughters of citizens of the lower stratum with impunity; freely disregarding police regulations or other rules of public etiquette; levying tribute on the lower orders by contracting debts without repayment; and, most of all, indulging in alcohol so as to drown out any of one's remaining inhibitions.

The primary difference between the typical Prussian military barrack of the period before 1914 and subsequent Nazi concentration camps was that in the former—in view of the governmental importance of the army—the health and life of those involved had to be protected. Hence mistreatment that might lead to provable cases of death or suicide was forbidden. Within the limits of this major restriction, there is probably no single typical concentration camp practice for which we cannot find analogies and beginnings, in a milder form, in the Prussian barracks. The much-celebrated educational effect of universal compulsory military service in Prussia consisted fundamentally in breaking the backbone of the recruit's self-respect and human dignity and chaining him to the polarity between sadism and masochism. The Prussian sergeant major as disciplinarian was Hitler's direct forerunner. Once again one is reminded of Mirabeau's famous and brilliant formulation: "Prussia is not a country which has an army, it is an army which has a country."

Frederick the Great in his will of 1752 had demanded that one "speak of the military only with reverence, as the priests do of Holy Scripture." This impious wish was to be fully granted in Prussia and later in all Germany. No people in the world has been trained as rigidly as the Germans to revere their army; nowhere has the social position of the officer corps been so exaggerated. After the Roon army reform, even the social precedence of a civilian in the upper classes depended upon the rank he held as an officer in the reserve.

Paradoxically, this Prussian-German militarism had nothing directly to do with war. Nothing could be more erroneous than the conclusion—seemingly obvious and so prevalent outside Germany—that the German soldier, the German officer corps, or even the German general staff had been thirsting for war and hence active in preparing for it. On the contrary, the social prestige of the army was much better deployed in the mess hall, in the barracks yard, or on the parade ground, than on the battlefield. The proper officer considered war a minor interruption—undesirable and dangerous to life at that—of his lifetime professional activity.

Scharnhorst and Boyen (and their successors as war ministers, to the extent that their weaker positions permitted) were by no means opposed to the realities, the objective necessities, of war. Gerhard Ritter strays far from the mark when he speaks of a "natural opposition between bourgeois and military thinking, between a spirit of peace and a fighting spirit" and when he therefore implies that the bourgeois is alien to the spirit "of the army, which is purely a fighting association fully dedicated to one limited purpose, that of destroying the enemy's will."[108] For this was precisely the view of the democratizing Prussian reformers of 1807. The same broad democratizing tendency of the nineteenth century restricted more and more the sphere of influence of the East Elbian Junkers and their bourgeois fellow travelers—except in the sphere of heavy industry. Thus the only remaining refuge for this superstratification mentality was the Prussian army barracks. Such, since the days of Scharnhorst, were the stakes in the struggle of the democratizing reformers against feudal reactionaries, and in this struggle Roon's reform marked the final victory of reaction. And of course Roon was serving a king who as crown prince had distinguished himself by mowing down the revolutionaries of 1848-1849. Bismarck's reactionary domestic policy served to reinforce the archconservative tendencies of the king and his entourage.

The real battle for which the peacetime militarists were yearning was not that against the foreign enemy but the perennial battle of the barracks yard waged against the self-respect and dignity of their subordinates. The further transmission of this superstratification pressure downward was left to the noncommissioned officers, just as in early capitalist industry it was left to the foremen.

Those who deny this case have ever and again revived the notion that being blindly obedient (*Kadavergehorsam*) is indispensable for military efficiency. But this argument applies at most to the antiquated line tactics of infantry with its platoon volleys—and even here it remains questionable whether courage under fire had anything to do with social class origin. But with the subsequent loosening of infantry tactics this argument became irrelevant—surviving as an atavism and self-seeking myth.

After Frederick the Great, the next in the series of great shapers of German nationalism was "heroic Napoleon," as Goethe once called him. Among the militant nationalisms that his brutal imperialism called forth as a reaction, the German stood at the top of the list.

So lamentably and ignominiously had the *ancien régime* of Frederick II collapsed under Napoleon's blows in 1806 that Baron vom Stein, unlike Turgot before him, did not have to open the eyes of a blind king to a future disaster. Disaster had already occurred, plain and for all to see; the old order was dead. There could be no doubt that a thorough reorganization was needed, and Stein and his progressive collaborators set about to make full use of this favorable situation in which history had placed them. Although his ministry stayed in office for only fourteen months, within that brief span and with truly superhuman energy, he set about effecting all those long overdue reforms which were to place Prussia on par with France and England in progressive governmental structure and administration.

This Prussian revolution of 1807 might have been fully as glorious as that in England in 1688 but was from the start a revolution conceived and executed by royal privy councillors. It remains probably the last great positive self-expression in Prussian and German history, a history otherwise so full of tragic failures and abortive developments. The revolution combined the best of a Prussian sense of duty, of Kantian enlightenment, of French reformist verve in the style of Turgot, of English common sense, and of the spirit of independence of the estates of the old Holy Roman Empire of the German Nation. Its chief product was the Prussian-German bureaucracy, which comes closer than any other to the ideal type of modern civil service. It constitutes the basis of the traditional German respect for officialdom, which other Western peoples, especially the Anglo-Saxons, find so hard to comprehend. Hegel observed the best aspects of this reform bureaucracy during his teaching activity at the University of Berlin (1818-1832), which plausibly accounts for his overvaluation of the state. (The greatest practical accomplishment of this Prussian reformist bureaucracy, the founding of the Customs Union or *Zollverein*, took place shortly before Hegel's death.) A by no means uncritical observer, the painter Wilhelm von Kügelgen, in looking back on this period a decade later was to write:

In what a blossom time stood Prussia! Never, as long as history has existed, had one heard of such a state which had attained such a height. An altogether humane government, the most intelligent class of civil servants which had ever existed; a great army, ever battle-ready, so courageous and honorable through and through which, despite all the perfidies of the time, is still to be viewed as inviolate; the best schools in Germany; trade and industry in an unprecedented upswing; a state credit without its like, etc. But at its head a gossipy, brilliant, listless child [i.e., Frederick William IV, who succeeded to the throne in 1840].[109]

But even at the time of the original reforms the "empty, slothful, and insipid king" (Stein's estimate of Frederick William III) and the reactionary East Elbian nobility, which had performed disgracefully on the battlefields of 1806, endured the reformers only as long as the desperate situation and its repercussions required. But after Napoleon's defeat, they once again felt surer of themselves, and further reforms were halted. The solemn promise of a liberal constitution, made in a moment of distress, was betrayed, and, following Metternich's lead, a dogged battle was waged against all progressive tendencies in public opinion, the administration, and the army.

Louis XVI dropped Turgot after two years; the equally short-sighted Frederick William III not only dismissed Stein after fourteen months but, in 1819, also removed Stein's closest associates, Wilhelm von Humboldt and General von Boyen. Nevertheless, in the eleven years since 1808 Prussian reform had time to develop so that, despite the unfortunate course of the revolution of 1848 and despite the blows administered to it by Bismarck and Roon, it set its stamp on the course of events up to 1878-1879.

The Customs Union—in truth a union for the abolition of customs barriers and celebrated as a model of free trade by Cobden and his followers in the English House of Commons—was the last great creation in which Prussian bureaucracy still maintained a free hand; yet meanwhile, in the three decades from 1819 to 1848, progressive tendencies in the bureaucracy and in the officers corps were constantly pushed into the background. This latent contrast in Prussia between progressive bureaucracy and reactionary army had much to do with the failure of the revolution of 1848 throughout Germany, since the revolutionaries could neither wholly rely on Prussia (because of its army) nor wholly reject it (because of its civil service). The army and bureaucracy, on their side, at first watched the advance of the revolution passively and with mixed feelings; at last, as the reactionaries gained control in Prussia, they allowed themselves to be used against the revolution. Of the two aims that Stein and his supporters hoped to reach in the war of liberation—national unity and constitutional-democratic freedom—neither was achieved.

In the struggles between feudal estates and the crown in the late Middle Ages, France and England had preserved the unity of their realms. In France this was done through the alliance of crown and bourgeoisie, which restrained the nobility, in England through the alliance of nobility and the towns, which jointly asserted their corporate rights against the crown. Hence the continuous line that runs from the Magna Charta (1215), by way of the Petition of Rights (1628) and Habeas Corpus Act (1679), to the Bill of Rights (1688), the Act of Settlement (1701), and further. Only in Germany was national unity destroyed because the nobility, while asserting its privileges against the crown, also managed to subjugate the cities. Consequently, the social struggle could no longer unfold in the frame of national unity, nor could the bourgeoisie fight for its political and social rights (as in France and England) within a single national arena. Rather, the bourgeoisie, blighted in its hopes for independence and self-consciousness by the subjugation of the cities to the princes, was forced to pursue two different aims simultaneously: that of national unity and that of its own political freedom. In 1848, it achieved neither: *qui trop embrasse, mal étreint*. This overambitious attempt turned out to be the last stand of a bourgeoisie already inordinately weakened by its historic heritage.

The failure of the economic, social, and, finally political leadership in Germany fell to a bourgeoisie that could not develop self-confidence and independence corresponding to this role.

The failure of the German revolution of 1848—the great misfortune of nineteenth-century German history—"had as a consequence the relapse of the German bourgeoisie into the attitude of obsequious loyal subjects, a change the repercussions of which we still perceive to this day," as Gerhard Ritter himself puts it.[110] It discredited the demand for internal freedom, whereas the demand for national unity now played into the hands of the Junker and *Realpolitiker* Bismarck, who harnessed the apparent fulfillment of both demands to his power play in a service of a Greater Prussia. Thereby he raised himself to the status both of a Napoleon of the German revolution and of a mythical German national hero like Luther or Frederick II. He became, in Jacob Burckhardt's words, "for Germany the very prop and symbol of the mystery of authority."

The struggle of East Elbian reactionary feudalism against bourgeois liberalism, over whose victory Bismarck was to preside, had earlier been fought out within Bismarck's inner self.

Bismarck's father, the Brandenburg estate owner Ferdinand von Bismarck (1771-1845), obviously prized his comfort and red wine more highly than heroism. As a captain in the Prussian army, he petitioned for his separation from the service; the king took such great offense that he ungraciously accorded him a "simple discharge," without the right to wear the uniform or to claim the precedence of his rank. Neither in 1806 nor in 1813—when "the king called and all came"—did he feel any urge to take up arms and to renounce his rural comforts. Instead, the threatening storm of 1806 induced him to take a step in the opposite direction.

With his older brother he traveled to Potsdam in 1806; there both frequented the house of the widow Anna Elisabeth Mencken. Both brothers courted the pretty young daughter of the house, Wilhelmina Mencken (1790-1839), who at last decided in favor of the younger one, although even he was twice her age. That the two feudal middle-aged brothers, in view of the threatening general col-

lapse, should feel an urgent longing for marriage, is quite understandable. The lady whom Ferdinand von Bismarck took for his
bride was, to be sure, *une bourgeoise*, but as Goethe says in *Elective
Affinities*, "disparities of status were easily reconciled by the spirit
of the times."[111]

Bismarck was born on the parental estate in 1815. His clever and
energetic young mother, who with the acquiescence of her good-
natured husband seems to have been running things, raised Otto
along decidedly bourgeois-liberal lines. He was sent to Berlin to the
best modern schools, in which an urban, enlightened, and humanistic
spirit prevailed. He was confirmed by Schleiermacher, so that, according to his own testimony, he left the *Gymnasium* "as a Pan-
theist and if not as a republican, at any rate in the belief that a
republic was the most reasonable form of state." In 1832, when he
entered the university as a law student, he was repelled by the
bourgeois student associations, which impressed him as "combining
utopianism with a lack of breeding." Upon joining an aristocratic
student corps he came to realize that his young feudal peers, who set
the tone there, were ready to despise and fight all those bourgeois-
liberal ideals with which his mother had reared him. He underwent
a radical change of character and set his ambition on wine, women,
gambling debts, affairs of honor, hunting, and riding; he earned the
sobriquet "Mad Bismarck" and proved that despite his semi-
bourgeois origin, he was not to be outdone by anyone in his feudal
deportment. For the next fifteen years, until his engagement to a
pious East Elbian girl, he moved partly in a fasionable, partly in
rural-aristocratic circles, where all bourgeois ways were held in contempt. And if these years went by chaotically and without success, it
was because it had taken him that long to repress the liberalism inherited from and implanted by his bourgeois mother.

After history pronounced its judgment against the German
bourgeois revolution of 1848, Bismarck, now inwardly prepared,
took on the special role of an executor who both executes and in-
herits. As Jacob Burckhardt, with characteristic perspicacity, noted
in a letter of 1872:

> Bismarck only took in his own hand what would have happened
> anyway in the course of time, but without him and against him.
> He saw that the mounting democratic wave sooner or later
> would lead to an unrestrained state of violence, set off either by
> the democrats themselves or by the governments, and spake:
> *ipse faciam*, and waged the three wars of 1864, 1866, 1871.

A German unification brought about by the patriots of 1848 would hardly have been more moderate than Bismarck's; but it would have been the result of honest, democratic methods and hence in the eyes of Western observers, perhaps not more appealing but more understandable and less suspicious. Too much the East Elbian Junker and thoroughbred Prussian to be an enthusiastic German patriot, Bismarck nevertheless needed German nationalism for his Prussian power politics. He saw his first and most important task as that of taking control of German nationalism—which in 1848 he had slandered as a "German swindle"—from the liberals. Such cynicism had its uses: it gave him a distance from which he could ponder national questions, thus saving him from pan-German excesses and blind considerations of political prestige. Bismarck's policy after 1871 was undeniably moderate—but this was because he regarded himself a Prussian, not a German politician. Germany to him was merely the proving ground for Prussian policies, and Prussia in all these years was busy subjugating the remaining German states within Bismarck's lesser-German greater-Prussian *Reich*. If superior wisdom, farsightedness, a sense of responsibility, and a desire for moderation had really been at the core of Bismarck's political personality (as Gerhard Ritter and others would have us believe) such sterling virtues would have had to manifest themselves first and foremost in his German domestic policy. Yet the very opposite was true. With the conquest of the remainder of Germany, Greater Prussia had achieved its immediate foreign policy aim, and her most urgent need was a sufficiently long period of consolidation, obtainable only within a peaceful Europe. Bismarck's fall signified the end of this Greater Prussian policy. Yet no beginning had been made toward a truly German policy—a fact which in no small measure conditioned the fatal insecurity of foreign policy under William II. Nonetheless, Bismarck's dishonest and cynical use of other people's nationalist enthusiasms for his own tactical and power-political ends inevitably led to the abasement and corruption of those feelings—to depriving them of the moral backbone of honest conviction.

As the Napoleon of the German revolution, with his "Prussian Bonapartism on a semifeudal foundation" (as Friedrich Engels once put it), Bismarck appropriated the legacy of the 1848 revolutionaries, whom he so passionately detested. His cynicism and crass tactical calculation is particularly evident with regard to the second major program point that he stole from the 1848 liberals, the democratic demand of universal suffrage. Bismarck never left any doubt that the highly reactionary Prussian three-class system of voting was eminently to his liking and that he had "thrown into the stew" the repellent idea that the Reichstag be elected by universal franchise only because it was "the most potent of all liberal tricks." He meant to divert the stream of democratic feelings into the riverbed of his own Machiavellian policy. Somewhat naïvely, he assumed that universal suffrage, once the guiding influence of the liberal bourgeoisie was overcome, would yield monarchist majorities. No wonder that German parliamentarism, so maculately conceived, never came to an internally healthy and vigorous development.

Since the traditional parties of principle refused to sanction Bismarck's systematic breach of the constitution of 1862-1866 and his cynical power politics, Bismarck used the carrot and the stick to transform them into parties of discrete material interests. This origin of German pluralism in Bismarck's policy of government subsidies was to prove fatal in a subsequent period. At the time, the protective tarriffs of 1878-1879 and the antisocialist laws were used as the carrot; the anti-Catholic struggle (*Kulturkampf*) and sharpened penal laws as the stick—all tactics Hitler could later invoke as precedents. Bismarck was so imbued with the primacy of foreign policy that domestic policy to him became its mere extension, and he was prone to treat the German opposition parties as so many foreign enemies. Generally, as already noted, he often showed less moderation in domestic than foreign policy.

Bismarck, in a parliamentary committee debate of 1862, arrogantly expressed the view that "the great questions of the day will not be settled by speeches and majority decisions—that was the great mistake of 1848 and 1849—but by blood and iron." Later this quotation from the "Iron Chancellor" was to become the political creed of broad segments of the German population. The annexation of Hanover, Electoral Hesse, Nassau, and Schleswig-Holstein, as well as the brutal tribute of 25 million gulden exacted from the free city of Frankfurt am Main in 1866 (in which resentment stemming from his days as Prussian ambassador in Frankfurt most likely played a role) educated the German people to accept the bullying of fellow citizens and to close its eyes to such modes of action. Above all, however, the continuous breach of the constitution, from 1862 to 1866, habituated public opinion to put might before right, and to acclaim triumphant injustice. All that contributed to educating the Germans into what has been aptly described as "a nation of noncommissioned officers and lackeys in privy council."[112]

As early as 1870 the famous physiologist Emil Du Bois-Reymond

(1818-1896), rector of the University of Berlin and president of the Prussian Academy of Sciences, was to pronounce solemnly: "We, the University of Berlin, who have our seat opposite the royal palace are, by virtue of the founding document of this institution, the intellectual bodyguard of the House of Hohenzollern."

Even Gerhard Ritter, in defending Bismarck, feels obliged to point to his

> highly one-sided view of domestic policy as a constant struggle for power against the parties; to the key role of personal hate and personal ambition in this struggle; to his ruthless, at times really brutal, contempt for individuals and for questions of law (not only during the Prussian constitutional conflict, but also during the time of his chancellorship); to his attachment to Junker caste prejudices and to the certain features of class egotism; to certain limitations of his understanding of domestic policy, stemming from the outlook dominant east of the Elbe. . . . What appears most grievous of all to us today—because of its lasting effect—is the deliberate abuse of political ideas and principles for purely tactical purposes, leading to the internal sapping of the great liberal movement, which initially he had fought and then tried to press into his service, to the point of unprincipled opportunism. By treating the political idealism of the parties as mere ideology and by trying to change the parties of ideology into mere pressure groups, by inciting them against each other in order to assert the power and mastery of his monarchical government over them, he destroyed a great store of good will and a readiness for responsible collaboration. . . . The upshot was a stagnation of party life, which increasingly fell prey to economic pressure groups, an apolitical philistinism and uncritical loyalty of the petty bourgeois masses, a blind devotion to the state that could easily conduce to a blunting of the sense of justice. . . . He is . . . the last great cabinet politician of European history—a belated Richelieu, or better still, a spiritual descendant of Frederick the Great in an altogether altered world. In sum he is a deeply lonely figure estranged from his time.[113]

Nevertheless, we are altogether justified in speaking of "Bismarck's ethos"—since Adolf Hitler would fortunately seem to be the only example of a leading political figure wholly destitute of ethos.

Hence, as ethos signifies subordination to higher values, we must ask what these ruling values were for Bismarck—a question that must be answered separately for his foreign and his domestic policy.

As regards foreign policy the answer is clear, confirmed both by Bismarck's own detailed testimony in the famous correspondence of 1857 with Ludwig von Gerlach and by the evidence of his later actual policy. The aggrandizement of Prussian power was Bismarck's highest aim, and indeed he brought Prussian power to its highest and final peak. In doing so he acted as *Realpolitiker*: that is, he refused on the one hand (as he emphasizes in his letters to Gerlach) to recognize any abstract philosophic principles as being above this one concrete aim; and he was able, on the other hand, to concede to any other state the right to complete self-determination in its domestic affairs—and thus, for example, to show remarkable understanding for the problems of the quasi-totalitarian government of Napoleon III.

Quite otherwise in regard to his Prussian-German domestic policy. The Prussia whose power he wanted to enhance and to the service of which he had dedicated his life was a monarchical-feudal Prussia with a well-developed superstratification structure. However, since the internal development of the Western world (including Prussia-Germany) tended in an opposite direction, he blocked this development and turned against its German proponents with hostility, and indeed mortal hatred. For them he showed not a trace of the understanding that he extended even to French Bonapartism. If Bismarck, after his dismissal as chancellor, referred to the "social-democratic question" as a "military one," he was merely echoing what his sovereign, the former "grapeshot prince," had put into practice against the democrats of 1848. Hence the policy of destruction of German liberalism, which Bismarck pursued by stages; hence the *Kulturkampf* and the sharpened penal laws—in short a systematic, if abortive, war of extermination against all democratic tendencies on the Prussian and German domestic political scene. The fateful consequences of this domestic policy—as unsuitable as it was abortive—have not been overcome to this day.

We thus come to the paradoxical finding that Bismarck conducted his foreign policy as a European domestic policy and, on the contrary, his German domestic policy as an antidemocratic foreign policy. Accordingly, as already noted, he treated oppositional German parties in Machiavellian fashion as if they were enemy foreign states. In the sphere of foreign policy he exhibited tolerance and understanding, was able to live and let live. In the sphere of domestic policy, however, he was intransigent and intolerant and felt a radical urge to exterminate ideological tendencies that he considered detestable. Such polar structural contradictions between foreign and domestic policy are, of course, a frequent historical phenomenon, but usually the location of the poles is reversed: thus, for instance, in Periclean Athens as in Victorian England we encounter a liberal, tolerant domestic policy alongside a brutal, imperialistic foreign policy.

Hitler's favorite reference to the personages of Frederick the Great and Bismarck was surely that of a pygmy invoking the name of giants, a vulgar proletarian appealing to two aristocrats. The difference in stature and level is so enormous that we could easily forget that Frederick the Great and Bismarck both took decisive steps along the same path Hitler would take to lead the German people to the abyss. At any rate, these two great despisers of humanity, Frederick the Great and Bismarck, were brilliant and impressive incarnations of a sublimated superstratification approach. The old and venerable German empire had withstood all the storms of fate for more than a thousand years (800-1803). The new German empire, founded by Bismarck, lasted only from 18 January 1871 to 9 November 1918, not even forty-eight years.

Bismarck was dismissed by Emperor William, second and last of the rulers of that name bestowed on Germany by the grace—or wrath—of God. Since birth, William II had been afflicted with feelings of inferiority for which he overcompensated throughout his life. In the quarter century of his reign he accustomed the German people to the leadership of a foppishly vain, hysterically tasteless, saber-rattling braggart. Even the high-sounding references to God Almighty and Providence in his endless, self-intoxicating speeches could readily serve as models for Hitler. His obsession with uniforms recalls medal-happy Hermann Göring, his tirades against "pessimists" Goebbels's campaigns against "grumblers."

The so-called Schlieffen plan was one of the most characteristic products of the reign of this monarch. "Viewed from the standpoint of later events," writes Gerhard Ritter, "the Schlieffen plan appears unmistakably as the beginning of Germany's and Europe's misfortune."[114]

Count Alfred von Schlieffen (1833-1913), chief of the German general staff from 1891 to 1905, left as his major legacy the so-called Schlieffen plan, which, in the event that Germany were to be involved in a two-front war, called, as the first step, for a crushing attack on France delivered through violation of the neutrality of

Belgium and Luxembourg (an earlier version also included the Netherlands on the list).

In the event of a German-French war it was no doubt an extraordinary geopolitical disadvantage for Germany that France's western border was covered in the south by Italy, Switzerland, and the belt of fortifications from Belfort to Verdun, and in the north by Luxembourg, Belgium, and Holland. In between there lay only a narrow corridor which would serve as a trap for any army pushing forward, a geographic fact which, according to the classical concepts of strategy, virtually precluded a German attack on France. If a student of the War Academy, assigned the task of drawing up a campaign plan against France, had avoided this difficulty by positing the nonexistence of Luxembourg, Belgium, and Holland, he would have failed the course on grounds of intellectual immaturity. The political immaturity of the Schlieffen plan was no less, and it was for this reason that Germany failed in the historical test of the First World War.

Because the German strategic situation in a two-front war was so desperate, the idea of a bold *tour de force* along the lines of the Schlieffen plan might well occur to a strategic planner as a measure of last resort—but only if Germany was indeed forced into such a desperate strategy.

For the general staff and its chief, the only responsible course in peacetime would have been to impress this desperate military situation of a two-front war on the emperor, the chancellor, and the foreign office and to draw the political and diplomatic conclusion that an outbreak of such a war must be prevented at all cost. And if such an attitude had been adopted, the outbreak of the war of 1914 would indeed have been prevented. But in contrast, German policy, frivolously and foolishly, did not indeed consciously aim at such a war but risked it and allowed itself and others to stumble into it. But (to quote Ritter once again) a degree of overconfidence that "borders closely on arrogance" was, "after all, a stylistic ingredient of the epoch of William II."[115]

The mischief of the Schlieffen plan, as Ritter shows, was not only that by violating the neutrality of Belgium and Luxembourg it envisaged a most severe breach of international law; above all, it induced a blind trust in the outcome of this "go-for-broke" strategy, and also overrated Austria's strategic prospects. In apportioning the guilt of all the parties for the outbreak of World War I, Germany's share surely consists in its arrogance and overconfidence—a particularly unglamorous sort of *hubris* that is a degenerate form of superstratification mentality. The mere existence of the Schlieffen plan as Germany's only war plan was a scandal from the point of view of politics or international law. In this instance "Prussian-German militarism . . . totally reversed . . . the normal and salutory relationship between policy and warfare."[116] Only this reversal created the "bitter necessity" of which Chancellor Bethmann-Hollweg, an honest but subaltern figure, spoke in announcing the violation of Belgium's neutrality to the Reichstag.

Incredible as it seems, "no formal consultation between the political and military authorities on the campaign plans of the general staff" were ever held. Schlieffen thought of himself as a political layman and considered it up to the statesmen to put forward any objection. The statesmen, in turn, considered themselves incompetent in matters of strategy and felt their social inferiority to the military. As a ranking foreign office official put it: "When the great Chief of Staff and an authority on strategy like Schlieffen considers such a measure necessary, then it is the duty of diplomacy to adapt to this necessity and prepare for it in all possible ways."[117] Bethmann-Hollweg confirms that "during my whole period of office no kind of war council was held in which politics intruded into military matters, either for or against."[118]

The ordeal of the First World War called for strong leadership, of which the kaiser was quite incapable. His hasty flight in 1918 put an end not only to the monarchy but to the entire tradition that had begun with the Great Elector of Brandenburg and Frederick II of Prussia and of which Bismarck had said that "German patriotism needs a prince as a focus for its attachment." "Suppose," Bismarck had written, "that all the German dynasties were suddenly deposed; there would then be no likelihood that German national sentiment would suffice to hold all Germans together from the viewpoint of international law amid the friction of European politics." Although the disappearance of the dynasties became a reality only twenty-five years after Bismarck wrote, the disappearance of national sentiment he had hypothesized did in no way occur.

Just as the path of history that led from Frederick II to Bismarck led many Germans further on to Hitler, so the process of intellectual retreat is now under way by reverse stages. Since the last stage of the road obviously led to disaster, prudence prompts a first withdrawal to the previous, Bismarckian, stage, when, after all, everything went so splendidly. This prudential retreat is characteristic of all those anti-Nazis—altogether too numerous—who would have liked to see Hitler apply greater caution, notably to stop with what he achieved by 1938, in short those who condemn Hitler ultimately only for his failure. After a visit to Germany in 1948, the Basel theologian Karl Barth wrote:

> It is altogether wrong if one now seeks to cure the Germans of *national socialism*, in a great effort of reeducation. This has already been done for some time by the events themselves: there is not one among hundreds with whom in a minute one would not be in agreement that Hitler combined in one person buffoon and devil. . . . The neuralgic point is first reached when one presses forward in the discussion to Bismarck. For most Germans, even for people who have engaged in active resistance, once the national socialist plaster falls off, the German nationalist masonry comes into view. . . . They do not understand that national socialism was nothing but the ultimate outcome of Bismarck's policy, which violently unified Germany with blood and iron into a nationalist, capitalist, and imperialist empire and thereby became the gravedigger of the living freedom of 1848.[119]

Even Friedrich Meinecke, in his confession of faith *The German Catastrophe*, does not attribute blame to Bismarck, let alone Frederick the Great. The evil in German development for him first begins with William II in the 1880s. On the other hand, he recalls the world of Treitschke and his other teachers, which he erroneously identifies as that of "classical liberalism," as a "wondrously rich world." Further, he considers "the desire for national unity and a powerful German state" "altogether healthy." "The founding of the empire by Bismarck remains an accomplishment of historical greatness, and the enthusiastic devotion which we, growing up with it, dedicated to it subsists as a precious treasure in the storehouse of our reminiscences." Thus did the "fundamental revision of our traditional view of history," which he himself had demanded, appear to the most important and most liberal German historian of the older generation who had never sided with the national socialists![120]

More commendable is the attitude of Hans Bernd Gisevius, originally a stalwart nationalist and a pronounced conservative to this day, who was converted to a "supranational outlook . . . that administers a sharp rebuke not only to national socialism but which, going beyond that, is ready courageously to draw the lesson from the collapse of all three political realities: Hitler's dictatorship, Bismarck's empire, and Frederick's Prussia."[121]

b. The Treaty of Versailles and Foreign Policy

On 18 July 1918 Marshal Foch's masterful counterattack near Compiègne routed the right flank of the German forces, whose earlier offensive on the Marne had bogged down some time before. The exhausted German front never recovered and was forced into steady, though orderly, retreat. No one aware of the basic military facts—including those who, like this author, were themselves assigned to the Marne sector in 1918—will credit the propagandistic slogan that German imperial troops were "undefeated in the field," or the infamous legend later spread by German nationalists that the collapse of 1918 had been due to a "stab in the back"—that is, rebellion at home. Revolutionary sentiment first spread when the military situation had already become desperate; it was not a cause but a consequence of the sensational strategic defeat. That the collapse, long overdue, of the Wilhelminian regime was not greeted as liberation by the majority of the German people was an ominous indication of the same "militant servility" that fourteen years later made possible the seizure of power by national socialism.

A crushing military defeat after years of exhausting struggle is always a big misfortune for the people involved. Few events since the days of the Old Testament prophets lent themselves so clearly to the concept of redemptive disaster of learning from misfortune. And if the disaster of 1918 had been taken in this spirit, it could have been a salutary experience for the German people. Instead, a stubborn refusal to accept the plain facts led to a repetition of the catastrophe on a scale a hundred times larger.

The First World War was essentially a war of the old kind, a traditional war like many others before. In moral terms it might be ranked somewhat above the wars of Louis XIV, Frederick the Great, Napoleon I, or Bismarck. Even with the irresponsible violation of Belgian neutrality, committed ineptly rather than deliberately, there was nothing in the antecedents or conduct of this war that distinguished it fundamentally from the wars of past centuries. Having lost the war, Germany naturally had to bear the consequences. (Germany itself had set a bad example of peacemaking in the Treaty of Brest-Litovsk—which, however, was universally condemned even in Germany.) But nothing justified the long-term denial to Germany of international state equality and the treatment of the German people as pariahs. That was a violation of international law and justice, and of principles of human equality. No part of the Treaty of Versailles rankled so much, even among Germans whose sense of self-esteem did not suffer from nationalistic exaggeration. And it gave the German nationalists a welcome opportunity to spread their hate propaganda against the "ignominious peace" of Versailles as a peace "diktat."

That the victors had something of a bad conscience about these particular terms is indicated by their eagerness to force Germany into a unilateral confession of guilt for the outbreak of the war—a confession contrary to knowledge and belief. That same bad conscience was expressed later when the Western powers accepted Hitler's successive violations of the treaty.

A clear case of unilateral war guilt is provided by the Second World War—and any comparison of the circumstances leading to war in 1914 and 1939 shows how unjust was the confession of sole guilt exacted from Germany at Versailles. If war guilt had been justly allotted among the belligerents, the German government's share would have turned out smaller than that of the Austrian and Russian governments, though surely greater than that of all the other belligerents. And a qualitative analysis of this indisputable German share of guilt would have shown it as composed more of stupidity, insecurity, and arrogance than of malevolence or evil intent.

The just and conciliatory peace with which, according to Wilson's original proposals, the First World War should have been ended was poisoned by the tigerlike hatred of Clemenceau, and the demagoguery of Lloyd George. The treaty thus became a hybrid document whose vindictive provisions of power politics took precedent over the impotent League of Nations. Unilateral disarmament, demilitarization of the Rhineland, and the prohibition of German unification with Austria flatly contradicted the right to self-determination. The arbitrarily drawn frontier with Poland and the treatment of Danzig were not objectively justifiable and precluded any German-Polish rapprochement. The reparations were clearly excessive, and the trade provisions of the peace made it impossible for Germany to earn the foreign exchange with which to pay them. And the reparations poisoned Franco-German relations as surely as the eastern frontier poisoned those with Poland. For a necessary reduction in the amount of reparations, Germany could, in the nature of the case, offer nothing but some vague goodwill for the future—and as Briand discovered, this was not to be enough to induce the French parliament to surrender tangible and legally stipulated benefits.

The unjust and shortsighted provisions of the Versailles treaty were to make a major contribution to the developments that precipitated the Second World War. The harsh treaty provisions gave Hitler the chance to make a whole series of demands whose justice neither nonnationalist German nor fairminded foreigners could deny. The same provisions provoked German nationalists into a consistent pattern of sabotage, and their violation, for Hitler, served as a convenient preparatory move from which he plunged without letup into measures for which there was no plausible justification whatever—still pretending that it was only a matter of setting aside the legal obstacles imposed by the victors of World War I.

Since denunciation of the Versailles treaty became part of Hitler's stock in trade, it is easy to overlook the actual injustices contained in it—or even to conclude that, in view of the atrocities committed later by the Nazis, the Versailles provisions were mild. But obviously no logic can justify a punishment as deserved by crimes committed only decades later. On the contrary, it was Clemenceau who passed the ball to Hitler and thus allowed him to score.

The brutalities accompanying the Ruhr occupation of 1923 played further into the hands of the German nationalists and undermined the efforts of German democrats and pacifists at building a new order that would look beyond Versailles.

When Julius Curtius (1877-1948), Stresemann's successor as foreign minister, made the attempt to create a peaceable customs union with Austria with full observance of democratic and parliamentary form, this was prevented by France with irrelevant arguments from the Versailles treaty. Eight years later, however, the French government tolerated the unlawful and military occupation of Austria. If the allied powers had voluntarily and in time made a mere fraction of the concessions to Stresemann or even to Brüning that later were brutally extorted from them by Hitler, history would have taken a different course.

Acquiescence in Hitler's violent *faits accomplis* was part of a long standing pattern that had sanctioned D'Annunzio's attack on Fiume (1919) and Poland's annexation of Vilna (1922) and had tolerated Japan's aggression in Manchuria and China (1931, 1937) as well as Italy's attacks on Ethiopia and Albania (1935, 1939). The halfhearted and ineffective sanctions invoked against Italy in 1936 only served to reveal clearly the impotence of the League of Nations; and so did the deplorable Western policy of "nonintervention" in the Spanish civil war after 1936, while German, Italian, and Russian intervention went on shamelessly and without restraint. The con-cordat concluded between Germany and the Vatican in July 1933 was the first of a long series of diplomatic recognitions gained by Hitler. The naval agreement with England followed in 1935. No government dared refuse Hitler's invitation to the Olympic Games of 1936.

After fifteen years of unsuccessful German policies of conciliation, Hitler had learned a lesson that was to be confirmed by an unbroken chain of spectacular successes: in 1933 the abrogation of the disarmament provisions of the treaty and the introduction of universal military service; in 1936, the occupation of the Rhineland; in 1937, the formal renunciation of the Versailles treaty; in 1938, the invasion of Austria and occupation of the Sudetenland; and in 1939, the occupation of the remainder of Czechoslovakia. All these shameless breaches of the treaty and of international law were accepted by the Western powers.

Chamberlain and Daladier humbled themselves before a raving Hitler, and the democratic peoples of the world hailed Chamberlains' umbrella as the real defensive weapon against the threatening storm of national socialism. Chamberlain, who fancied that he had brought back "peace in our time" from Munich, was celebrated as a savior. In France, the Munich Pact of 30 September 1938, implying the ignominious betrayal of Czechoslovakia in disregard of a solemn treaty of alliance, was greeted with frenetic joy. The approval in the French Chamber of Deputies was almost unanimous: there were 535 *yea* votes, and the *nay* votes, outside those of the 73 Communist deputies, came from 2 deputies with no party affiliation. Such was the extent to which Western opinion had been taken in by Hitler's propaganda.

As a German air force general was to exclaim later: "How cheap would have been a war for Europe at that time, if the Western powers had resolved upon intervention!"[122] But this intervention, awaited with eagerness by all detached and sober observers, failed to materialize, and the German opposition and the skeptics among the German generals, who had opposed these irresponsible adventures to the end, were again and again terribly discredited. In 1939 a *coup d'état* by generals and high officials against Hitler had been in preparation; its execution was prevented by the impact of Chamberlain's ignominious appeasement.

From 1919 to 1939, for a full two decades, the policy of Western nations, the interplay between English-French appeasement and American isolationism, did all in its power to prepare and support the Third Reich, to weaken and discredit internal German opposition. Had the Western powers been so obliging to the Weimar Republic, rather than to Hitler, had they acted firmly against Hitler rather than Weimar, the world catastrophe would not have come to pass.

One might have expected that those critics who later severely reproached Germans for the fact that the German opposition to Hitler was weak and abortive would have used every opportunity to support and strengthen this opposition; but overwhelmingly they did the very opposite. "For more than twelve years, the German antinational socialist emigration had besought a hearing in their host countries. They were not heeded. Their references to the existence of a non-national socialist Germany were impatiently pushed aside. . . . No resistance movement in Europe remained without help from the Allies. None of them would have been able to accomplish even a fragment of what they did without the help of the warring great powers. Only the *German* underground movement (which by far would have been most needful of it) remained without any help, whether material or psychological."[123]

The seemingly inexhaustible patience of the democracies ran out with the attack on Poland—although better reasons (or pretexts) could have been cited for that than for the attack on Czechoslovakia. The forced secession of Danzig, an old German city, was a flagrant violation of the nationality principle and the right to self-determination; and the corridor was a technically intolerable solution, so that here German demands for change could be objectively justified, whereas with respect to Czechoslovakia it had been a question of naked imperialism. Moreover, Poland at that time was itself under a semitotalitarian regime that had flirted with national socialism and participated in the rape of Czechoslovakia. And Czechoslovakia, strategically, had been a strong bastion, capable of a modern military defense, whereas Poland militarily was a hopeless burden. Thus, logic was on Hitler's side when he calculated that those who had just sacrificed Czechoslovakia would even more readily sacrifice Poland.

Despite their declaration of war, delayed by three days, the two Western democracies did not in fact support Poland. This gave Hitler time, after Poland was crushed, to turn against the West with concentrated force and to determine the time and place of attack. To allow him these advantages was a grotesque disregard of the most elemental rules of strategy. Only then, when no further choice remained between suicide and self-defense, did the Western powers brace themselves; only then did they find, in Churchill, a man of steely determination able to cope with a desperate situation.

Without the uninterrupted political failures of England, France, and the League of Nations from 1919 to 1933 and from 1933 to 1939-1940, Hitler's seizure of power and his triumphant rise could have never occurred. The cowardice of the democracies paved the way for national socialism. This does not decrease the guilt of national socialism, nor the guilt of those Germans who enthusiastically or reluctantly marched in its train. But alongside the monstrous burden of German guilt, there stands the guilt of the democracies, their sins of weakness and surrender of their own interests. And Germans who, like myself, chose political exile are honor-bound to raise this twofold accusation. Germans will not be able to explain to themselves either the arrogance of the totalitarian regimes, or the weakness of the democracies, without understanding them as polar, interdependent symptoms of the same international pathological condition.

c. The Weimar Constitution and Domestic Policy

The Weimar constitution, in its application to German domestic policy, was no less fateful than the Versailles treaty in the sphere of foreign policy.

The German transition from monarchy to republic in 1918 was accomplished without any consciousness of its significance. Neither the kaiser nor the gifted but undisciplined crown prince could be seriously considered as candidates for rulership after 1918; perhaps Churchill's idea of a regency for the kaiser's underaged grandson might have been the best solution. It would have rallied the parties of the Right without restricting the freedom of action of the parties of the Left: in Germany in 1918, convinced republicans were as few as they had been in France in 1789. But instead, the leaders of 1918 under Allied pressure sacrificed the integrative symbol of monarchy without any consciousness of the need to replace it with alternative symbols of integration.

Germany paid a heavy penalty for the fact that political science, which had flourished at its universities in the mid-nineteenth century and from there been transplanted to the United States, had withered under the pressure of Bismarckian-Wilhelminian authoritarianism. Consequently, Germans were unprepared, as each article of the constitution was committed to paper, to visualize its sociological implications. If Hugo Preuss (1860-1924), an academic authority on constitutional law, in the tradition of Baron vom Stein, had not already, in strict privacy, prepared a democratic-republican draft of a constitution, the embarrassment in Weimar would have been greater. Generally it was the right-wing politicians, who were neither democrats nor republicans, who commanded the greater expertise and better practical judgment in constitutional matters.

Adherents of that form of rationalism which sees the goddess of justice wielding not a pair of scales but a pocket calculator tend to consider suffrage based on proportional representation the pinnacle of justice. But this conclusion overlooks the fundamental difference between factual research into political opinions and the taking of decisions as a matter of political will. The essential political purpose of the act of voting is to confront the citizen with a clear choice, and the clearest and best choice is, of course, a simple alternative. The plurality system that is the traditional system of voting in English-speaking countries is the most effective system in meeting this demand for clear-cut alternatives. The constituent assembly at Weimar, in a complete misconception of these basic realities, viewed proportional representation as especially democratic, progressive, and just, and through its adoption of proportional representation did what it could to precipitate a fateful splintering of political parties.

As a further consequence, the Weimar assembly inaugurated an era of shifting coalitions, based on pluralist compromises, logrolling, and collective irresponsibility; and the subjects of the Weimar Republic thus became inured to a system that treated governmental power as a species of war booty, and where parties in temporary victorious alliance could treat the minority parties as so many conquered foes. Instead of strengthening the traditional neutrality and loyalty of the Prussian-German bureaucracy, by defining more clearly those activities that were or were not compatible with a civil service position, the republic on the contrary turned many civil service positions into patronage appointments for the victorious coalition—another practice that the men of Weimar considered a particularly democratic trait of their new order.

To be sure the rights of the citizens were violated at first only by way of disastrous economic and fiscal policies rather than through outright attacks on their freedoms. Since partisan coalitions had long since set aside the central and indivisible needs of the state in favor of selfish partisan interests, there even was a certain relief felt when a single-party egotism was substituted for that of the pluralism of shifting coalitions. The state, in becoming the booty of a single party, did of course all the more obviously become an instrument of domination and exploitation; yet for the party in sole control the objective necessities of the political situation now coincided with its own partisan interest. And this was nowhere as true as in Germany, where pluralism had had a full fifteen years to work its mischief but where the objective necessities of policy were far more compelling than usual.

For a country in Germany's situation after the Versailles treaty the necessities of foreign policy were clear-cut: every forcibly imposed condition of peace was resented as unjust and gave rise to demands for its abrogation. The question became merely one of technique, of sequence, of exploitation of circumstances. The grand goal of this revisionism should have been the integration of these tactical measures into a single grand conception in the service of the ideal of a pan-European and ultimately pan-human community of peace. There is no doubt that Stresemann, however limited by the armchair view of the German foreign office, conceived of his task in these very terms, and did so with true dedication and even fanaticism. But he could not even get the backing of the party he himself had created as his political instrument: its very representatives attacked him from the rear and opposed to him the egotistic, pluralistic interests of the party. The attempts at unification with Austria in 1918 and 1930; the role of Wilhelm Cuno, who moved from the post of general manager of a major shipping line to chancellor at the time of the fight against the occupation of the Ruhr; the nationalist demeanor of Social Democratic chancellor Hermann Müller on the occasion of his last appearance before the League of Nations in Geneva in 1930: all these occasions proved the impossibly of appealing to the common national interest over the heads of partisan positions. Such total inability to mobilize a common national will may rightly be called disgraceful—although the policies that followed upon the fall of the republic infinitely added to the disgrace. A constitution properly should provde the mechanism of integration for the expression of the national will, and by such a criterion the inadequacy of the Weimar constitution had been amply demonstrated. It was the defects of the constitution, not the personal inadequacy of the officeholders that brought things to such a pass—although these very defects also had an indirect and negative effect on the selection of the incumbents.

The postwar economic crisis of 1919-1923 was, for Germany, inevitable. But the leaders' ignorance of the principles of public finance and their inability to stand up to blackmailing profiteers converted it into a galloping inflation, which in turn led to the *de facto* expropriation of the savings of the entire middle class—that is, of that stratum who for centuries had been the very bearers of the German cultural tradition. The result was widespread resentment against the Weimar Republic, which had been responsible for the disaster, a crowding of the universities with sons of impoverished middle-class families eager to recoup their fortunes, massive academic unemployment, and hence a vast reservoir of new converts to Nazi propaganda.

The psychological atmosphere of German politics was the worst aspect of all. Bismarck's empire had been supported by a militarist nationalism, mixed with traditionalist sentimentality, to which under William II was added a further element of boastfulness and arrogance. Understandably this entire mentality was thoroughly discredited, among all those of progressive inclinations, by the collapse of the Second Reich and the flight of William II. But since the political integration of Germany, for better or worse, had rested on this ideology and its symbols, the awesome task confronted those who rightly rejected it to discover new forces of integration, to develop new social ties, and create new symbols. The only new ideology readily available was communism, and when this had been rejected by the sound instinct of the overwhelming majority of the German people it became apparent that there was no other available substitute for the old discredited nationalism. Already the embarrassing dispute over a choice of national colors showed that a return to the honorable but long extinct tradition of 1848 could provide no more than a makeshift solution.

The politicians of Weimar were fully prepared to carry out creditably and honorably the normal duties of a politician in an ongoing democratic regime. Even the unusual and more difficult task of taking on the receivership of a collapsed regime they tackled cheerfully and honestly. Having gone thus far, however, they believed that they had fully done their duty. The whole meaning of the collapse of 1918 to them was that democratic politics now could, at long last, proceed as usual. The suggestion that the circumstances of Germany's nascent democracy were very far from usual they rejected with righteous indignation as the product of a morbid imagination, as the ranting of troublemakers determined to deprive them of their well-earned fruits of normalcy. As early as 1916 the sociologist Alfred Vierkandt wrote with remarkable prescience: "Boundless strivings are alive in the nation today which demand

from the state understanding and encouragement, boundless energies which demand to be taken up in its service and to be united
with its might. Only of such a state will one be able to say that the
idea of a civic commonwealth has truly taken root in it."[124] The
Weimar Republic did not perceive this fundamental task and
chance; representatives who demanded encouragement were in
most cases angrily turned away as inconvenient grumblers.

Perhaps the most important and liveliest of these forces was the
youth movement. It had its first heroic period behind it; but its
socialization with the "front experience" of the First World War
made it the more suitable as an additional factor in the political social structure. "The inability of the Weimar State to let the energies
of the youth movement make a genuine contribution to its public
life promoted the rise of national socialism more than any other
single factor. The few attempts at political integration of the youth
movement, as for example were made in the 1920s in the Prussian
reform of teacher training for elementary schools, have proven their
durability beyond the storms of the Third Reich. But these attempts
remained exceptions."[125]

The requirements for social reintegration of the German people as
imposed by the historic situation were indeed abnormal. Only the
radical extremists of the left and right were alert to the situation,
and they used their insight for destructive purposes. Only the nationalist extremists, who soon found their activist leading groups in
the Nazi party, and the Communist extremists, had an ideology
leading to social integration on however pathological a basis.
Caught between these two was the Weimar Republic, lacking any
integrative ideology of its own. This was the primary and deepest
cause for its weakness, for its lack of authority and dignity.

The Weimar Republic's failure is shown in the desperate convul-
siveness with which in 1925 and once more in 1932 it clung to the
presidential candidacy of Hindenburg, the surviving symbol of the
tattered imperial tradition. But for this candidacy, Hitler would
have been elected to the presidency as early as 1932; but even it offered only a brief respite.

The fourteen years of the Weimar Republic stand under the
shadow of this central failure. These years are not devoid of accomplishments by honest men of good will—Stresemann in his
foreign policy, Rathenau, Ebert, Luther, Brüning, even Hermann
Müller with his boyish élan. But the deep shadow of doom hung over
them all. The usual remedies of normal democratic politics were

bound to prove unequal to the task at hand, and the politicians, in any case, preferred to look the other way.

All this contributed to an atmosphere of mediocrity and philistinism. The career politicians clung to their ministerial seats as the well-earned resting places for harassed public servants. And those of the younger generation who were waiting, indeed yearning, to be inspired turned away in bitterness and disappointment. Here was the ultimate source of the listlessness, the dispiritedness—and yet the craving for excitement—that in the end drove the German people into the arms of national socialism. Hitler for his part knew full well why he emphasized the revival of nationalist tradition, the cult of Frederick the Great, the relationship to Hindenburg as the embodiment of this tradition: here lay the very roots of his strength.

The Reich government, formed on 30 January 1933, with Hindenburg as president, Hitler as chancellor, and von Papen as vice-chancellor, once again pressed into service those forces of nationalist integration which had secured the cohesiveness of the empire before 1918 and which the Weimar Republic had renounced—for good reason but without adequate replacement. After fourteen years of marking time and of underintegration, the German people were allowed once again to indulge their nationalistic feelings in the old way and without restraint. In this nationalistic sense Germany now had a truly legitimate government—a legitimacy exceeding that of all the twenty-one cabinets of the Weimar Republic taken together.

Only in this way can one account for the shameful spectacle which took place in 1933 and which Gisevius described as follows:

Everything at this time is in headlong dissolution. Much, to be sure, is conquered, but even much more is surrendered. The number of turncoats is greater than the number of fighters. Perhaps a great deal could have been prevented; definitely things would have turned out better if so many positions had not been voluntarily surrendered in such fashion. Customs, habits, community of interests, ideologies, dogmas, everything is rejected as if it had never possessed any life value. Those storming forward find only fugitive ghosts. The hollowness of the existing orders, the anachronism of dozens of parties, the fragility of groups and associations is strikingly revealed by the fact that there is hardly anyone who rises in their defense. Who fights still? The so-called bourgeoisie took to its heels in the face

of the terror, the remnants of Marxism showed themselves no
less devoid of courage. Whichever way the brown shock troops
advance, they find no serious concerted resistance. It pushes
forward into a void.[126]

d. Final Steps in the Seizure of Power
and the Debit Account of Feudalism

In view of the serious defects of the two foundations of the Weimar
Republic—the Treaty of Versailles and the Weimar constitution—it
is no wonder that despite proficiency and goodwill, the German
people did not in any sphere of life attain any sense of security and,
conversely, that a feeling of hopelessness spread more and more.
The world economic crisis added to the difficulties; its effects were
particularly serious in Germany and led to the social pathology of
mass unemployment; and the result was a pervasive insecurity in
which anything—and nothing—seemed possible. This uncanny feeling that seized Germans after the autumn of 1932 is expressed
nowhere better than in a passage from H. G. Wells's *Mr. Britling*:
"Now everything becomes fluid. The world is plastic for men to do
what they will with it." That is a situation which offers the
maximum opportunity for individual intervention, for good or for
evil. In this atmosphere an aristocratic horse racing fan named von
Papen managed, through a series of clever manipulations, to lift
Hitler into the saddle. This von Papen did in the frivolous belief that
he could harness national socialism to the purposes both of domestic
political reaction and of a nationalist foreign policy.

Hindenburg, originally a Prussian officer of the old stamp, and
even as president of the republic bent upon serving the general welfare in a nonpartisan way, initially was not so unworthy of the trust
granted by the German people. But as the bearer of this trust he became involved with an East Elbian clique under the leadership of
the shrewd old Junker Oldenburg-Januschau and thus was dragged
into the sphere of the East Elbian *contrainte sociale*. The masterstroke in this direction was the bequest of the old family estate at
Neudeck, surrounded by sturdy East Elbian manor lords, the costs
of which with peasant cunning were passed on to industry. In order
to deprive the state treasury of the inheritance tax, the donated estate was registered in the name of Hindenburg's son, Oscar. Thus by
corrupting the old gentleman through his family feeling and by
making him an accomplice, they chained him all the more firmly to
the corrupt East Elbian Junker morality and its bearers. Every
political plot of the subsequent years was hatched at Neudeck and

imposed upon the increasingly senile old man—notably the ouster of the socialist Prussian government, as executed by von Papen on 20 July 1932. It was an authentically East Elbian *coup de main* in which the legendary "lieutenant and ten privates," in Oldenburg-Januschau's contemptuous phrase, though with some numerical reinforcements, were called into action. Without this East Elbian corruption of that wooden giant, the president and ex-field marshall, the fateful continuity and legality of the transition to the National Socialist regime would not have been possible.

Even otherwise was East Elbian feudalism the evil spirit of the Weimar Republic. The *Osthilfe*, or subsidies to East Elbian estates, were, as we have seen, merely a modern enlarged repetition of the subventions already paid by Frederick the Great to noble landed proprietors managing their own estates, and it contributed directly to the circumstances of the Nazi rise to power. The attempt to clean up the corrupt *Osthilfe* prompted the dismissal of Brüning as chancellor in May 1932, and fear of exposure of the scandal the dismissal of Chancellor Kurt von Schleicher immediately before Hitler's accession.

The Social Democratic party posed no immediate threat to these developments, since its Marxist theoreticians treated feudalism as a medieval phenomenon of the distant past, so that the party neglected to take up the fight against this in truth still dangerous enemy; this obliviousness was even mixed, as earlier in Marx, with secret admiration for these aristocrats whose callous self-assurance might well one day be placed in the service of the dictatorship of the proletariat. Even the most intelligent and knowledgable agrarian expert of the SPD, Fritz Baade, let himself be persuaded that the financial rescue of the East Elbian large estates was essential for the maintenance of German food supplies, and basked in the eulogies that were now showered upon him for his objectivity and technical expertise. The Social Democratic trade union secretary, Otto Braun, representative of the interests of East Prussian agricultural workers, as Prussian prime minister liked to ape the hunting manners of the East Elbian manorial lords.

Despite its shrewd and successful tactics, the feudal East German clique felt a growing uneasiness about the numerically rising labor movement which might not be susceptible to such schemes and tricks and would therefore have to be dealt with in more decisive fashion. But for such a last-minute masterstroke there was need for an ally with an equally numerous mass following—a role for which national socialism was the only available candidate. The Nazis were

evidently ruthless enough to wish to administer a deathblow to its
archrival, the socialist trade unions; and would prove, it was hoped,
naïve enough to be outmaneuvered by the cunning of feudal diplomats.

Hopes like these had already prompted a leading industrialist,
Fritz Thyssen, to throw his support to the Nazis, and similar hopes
were inspiring von Papen at his fateful interview with Hitler at the
house of the Cologne banker von Schröder. The alliance thus forged
brought together the direct heirs of feudal superstratification, facing the bankruptcy of their estates and the advance of the socialist
masses; the parvenu industrialists with feudal pretensions who felt
the pressure of the socialist trade unions even more directly; and the
ruthlessly brutal and voracious Nazi superstratifiers of the future.
Old superstratifiers as sponsors and stirrup holders of the new
superstratifiers—it is only on this basis that the deep inner connections and the frightening inexorability of these events become
apparent. The ring of superstratification had again come to a full
close.

The way in which later, in 1945-1946, the German manorial system was "liquidated" in the Polish- and Russian-superstratified regions of eastern and central Germany sets itself on a par with National Socialist atrocities. The feudal East Elbians as a group, who
without regard to person fell victim to this brutal proceeding,
thereby merely reaped what their class-brothers and mind-mates
had sowed. It was a cruel settlement of the debt which they and
their forebears had laid upon themselves in centuries of Prussian-
German history. Here, not for the first time in history, the overcoming of an old superstratification was effected by the imposition of a
new one.

(II) THE DRIVING FORCES

Fatal lines of development of Western social and intellectual history
in general and of German history in particular converged from
many sides to make possible the rise of national socialism. Only by
tracing these major converging lines can one account for this success
story, a success that for a time seemed to reach to the very threshold
of world dominion and whose repercussions, years after its awesome
collapse, remain incalculable.

a. Hunger for Social Integration and
Longing for New Loyalties

The growth of mass society and atomization in the nineteenth century led to a barely endurable degree of underintegration. A people

as capable of—and as much in need of—integration as the Germans was bound to sense the Weimar regime's lack of integrative capacity particularly keenly. This feeling of starvation led to a voracious appetite for integration; thus people's eagerness for submission—their desire to feel themselves parts of a firmly integrated totality—knew no bounds. The corresponding political ideal was that of the totalitarian state, whose demands on the individual tended toward the maximum. Thus the underintegration of the Weimar Republic and the overintegration of the Third Reich complemented each other. The fit was all the more perfect because National Socialist theory could carry its totalitarian deification to the extreme, free of the inhibitions that the anarchist components of Marxism impose on the rival Communist ideology.

The German philistine, who always did have a weakness for nationalism, after 1918 developed a further weakness for social causes. National socialism, whose very label combined the nationalist with the socialist slogan, appealed to these two weaknesses.

To quote Gisevius once again:

> The inflammatory slogans, the new rhythm, the populist vocabulary, the youthful joyousness of the songs, that stirring verve and these passionate promises—how deeply they seized an aroused people! After all they had been through, they simply could no longer resist. . . .
>
> Suddenly people were transformed. . . . Banners, garlands, honorary citizen citations, congratulatory telegrams, changed street names, proclamations of loyalty became everyday doings as much as marches and mass rallies. One victory celebration, one appeal to communal sacrifice succeeds another with breathless speed. A glorious, new feeling of brotherhood overcomes all strata and classes. The professor next to the waitress, the worker with the big industrialist, the housemaid and the merchant, employees, peasants, soldiers and officials, but above all youth, youth and once again youth, all feel themselves as though they had just made the greatest discovery of their century—as *Volksgenossen*, as equal members of one people. The gloomy past is forgotten, the oppressive present sinks behind the transfigured future of the finally realized Third Reich. Nothing remains but a heap of human beings welded together into a mass and acting only as a mass.[127]

However far mass society had developed, national socialism pushed it further. It abolished and prohibited rival ideological structures—though in the case of Catholicism it had to move cautiously at first; it also did its best to undermine the family by all possible means and from all sides; and thus it secured a monopoly position for its own brand of hectic pseudointegration. Nihilism had done a welcome preliminary service by weakening all traditional systems of value that might have opposed nazism.

The decay of traditional values and natural bonds and the new pseudointegration between them produced a new human type which has aptly been described as "the recipient of orders who lives in the constant tension of preparing for catastrophe," whose "deepest happiness consists in being sacrificed by others," and who thus invites "commanders whose art of leadership consists in pointing out goals that are"—or seem to be—"worthy of such sacrifice."[128]

Before 1933 "military subordination" and "military obedience" tended to be used as pejorative terms describing something done to excess. In the traditional Prussian army there was a constant effort, in the training of officers, to balance obedience and initiative. It remained for national socialism to replace this balance with a brutally enforced blind obedience of the subordinate and thus to demonstrate that in the military sphere, too, the most is not the best. An officer in Hitler's army vividly describes the change:

> Earlier the German soldier had been accustomed to act independently, but this spirit of independence was broken by Hitler's system of regulating everything to the minutest detail and enforcing these regulations on pain of death or court martial. . . . "Führer's orders" became a call inspiring terror, and every command post which put those words at the beginning of its telegraphic message thus put into the record that it claimed no responsibility for the content of the message. No one expected a "Führer's order" to have rhyme or reason. It was passed down the line because of the threat of court-martial or execution— often made explicit in the final paragraph of the message. . . . The list of general and regimental officers who because of their conduct during retreats were shot, demoted, or sentenced to hard labor or to jail comprised thirty-six typewritten pages.[129]

The final result, according to Schlabrendorff's concurrent testimony, was that "all tactical considerations ceased: to be surrounded by the enemy became the pinnacle of military wisdom."[130]

In its economic policy, national socialism was not at first dedicated solely to nationalization and central planning; yet the necessities of preparation for, and conduct of, war pushed it in the direction of wartime autarchy and of a wartime plan and command economy—and thus into an unintended imitation of Soviet economic policy. Here, too, the tendency was to maximum—and hence more than optimum—integration.

The German youth movement, as we saw, had ardently espoused "community" over "society." At first this remained an aristocratically tinged ideal limited to small elite circles, but in the post-World War I period it had acquired a more democratic flavor as it descended the social scale. These tendencies, with which the Weimar Republic had been unable to cope, were now abused and harnessed by the Nazis, and the slogan of *Volksgemeinschaft* ("folk community") attracted swarms of dedicated followers from the youth movement to nazism.

The original youth movement had been federative in its structure; but in their aversion toward the surrounding disintegrating society, its members could easily forget that its own federations (*Bünde*) were unnatural formations midway between society and community; their temporary nature was indicated by their atmosphere of forced intimacy, just as the federative, voluntary structure of an engagement is a natural transition to the community of marriage. Even the "grand marriage" of nationhood—to use the metaphor once coined by Novalis—cannot retain permanently the federative structure of an engagement, and any actual marriage which is concluded in such an unhealthy and exaggerated atmosphere of expectancy tends to break up in bitter disappointment. But the brutal and cynical instigators of nazism made good use of such exaggerated social concepts so as to camouflage the true relations of demagogue and mass (or gang leader and gang) behind a pretentious poetic aura of leadership and followership.

We saw earlier that under the spell of a false ideal of egalitarianism, popular education from the eighteenth to the twentieth century had demanded of every "common man" that he inform himself of any conceivable problem between heaven and earth, through lectures, courses, discussion groups, or pamphlets, that he ponder it and pronounce his own judgment. This excessive demand on human rationality led to a growth of irrationalism which constituted an important undercurrent of nazism—and which is equally apparent in the mass media and mass entertainment of the Western world in the mid-twentieth century.

Just as egalitarianism in education and democratic procedures in decision making make excessive demands on individual judgment, so liberalism, with its condemnation of all social structures as vehicles of domination, corroded organic patterns of leadership and made excessive demands on everyone to be his own leader. The natural reaction, at length, was a thirst for leadership, a readiness to follow anyone who claimed a leadership position on some plausible basis. The same longing for loyalty and leadership led, as we saw, to a cult of genius and messianic (if secular) sectarianism, each sect with its own patent medicine of fanciful diet, breathing exercises, sexual gymnastics, or what not, as the vehicle for the world's salvation.

b. Sadomasochism

The conversion of the elector of Brandenburg to Calvinism in 1613 produced a potent social constellation of an activist, sadistic upper class ruling over a quiescent, masochistic, Lutheran lower class. Bismarck's conquests spread and enforced throughout the remainder of Germany this earlier Prussian ideal of lower class obedience. During the same period this traditional attitude was secularized, freed from traditional religious restraints, and transformed in part into military or technical pride—pride in the efficient and precise functioning of the social machine in which the individual was a mere cog. The ultimate result was an enormously strengthened state apparatus in the hands of any leader who, like Hitler, combined ruthlessness with a fine ear for the silent cry for new loyalties and new hyperintegration.

But Germany also had experienced—although later and less than did the countries of northern and western Europe—a tendency toward blurring and leveling of the traditional superstratification structures. Large parts of the upper class had been converted to more or less democratic and liberal ideals, and major portions of the lower class had gained in self-respect and self-reliance. Arrogance continued to be practiced in some circles and submissiveness in others, although prevailing opinion frowned on both. But with the advent of Hitler there now was a deliberate policy of "training one-half of the German people to arrogance and the other half to cowardice."[131] The most extreme expression of this dissociation between, and intensification of, sadism and masochism were the Nazi concentration camps.

c. Nationalism

Modern nationalism is by far the most important of the lines of development culminating in national socialism. We have already followed its intellectual history and the role played by Germany, where romantic-conservative patriotism prevailed, but where gradually Jacobin-radical imperialist nationalism found ever increasing advocacy. National socialism contributed nothing new to these varied currents of thought: intellectual productivity was not its hallmark in this or other spheres.

Luther's religious schism affected Germany more profoundly than other countries. In most other countries, either Catholicism or Protestantism predominated, providing some basis for integration; Germany was split almost evenly into two parts locked in mutual suspicion and warfare. Later, political partisanship, characteristic of all countries, also proved more divisive and intense. Hence in Germany, patriotism and nationalism, more than anywhere else, had to function as the integrative force of last resort, and with the weakening of religious bonds patriotism increasingly became an ersatz or quasi-religion. Ludwig Feuerbach's idealistically intended demand that "Our religion must be politics" became grim reality, and in the new religion of nationalism doubt became sin and criticism heresy.

These developments long antedate national socialism. Bismarck, not without demagogy, had harnessed nationalism to his *Realpolitik*, and the strong grip of nationalism was later evidenced by the alacrity with which the parliamentary delegation of the supposedly internationalist and pacifist Social Democratic party voted for war credits in 1914. The particular arrogance of German nationalism, too, had its roots in the conservatism of East Elbian Junkers. The decisive novelty was that national socialism instinctively recognized and fully unleashed and exploited the latent energies and social dynamism of nationalism, which ever since the French Revolution had only found intermittent and superficial expression.

What we call conscience is by no means something innate, implanted in each individual by God or nature—only the potential for it is. It is neither individual, transcendent, nor absolute, but rather a social phenomenon. Man, by nature a social animal, takes on the prevailing values of the group into which he is born and which raises and surrounds him. In agreement with these valuations, and accordingly accepted by his fellow human beings, he thrives; in conflict with them, in the face of the disapproval, contempt, or indignation of his fellows, he feels acute discomfort to a degree which, as is well known, can push him into suicide. This influence that the values of his social environment have on him is what Durkheim, with a felicitous expression, called *contrainte sociale*. But this *con-*

trainte sociale is not just external. Rather, each individual shares the prevailing values, which he has already accepted preconsciously or unconsciously, so that each individual carries within him an internal representation of the social constraint which influences him much more effectively than any external compulsion; indeed it is the convergence of internal and external forces which first lends full effect to the external constraint. This internal representation of the *contrainte sociale*—its internal commissioner or delegate, as it were—is the conscience or superego.

National socialism, with its extremely cunning system of propaganda and mass suggestion set out deliberately to heighten to the extreme the internal and external forces of nationalist *contrainte sociale*. To accomplish this and make full use of it, nazism of course first had to establish beyond doubt its claim to be the sole spokesman of and the sole object of all these feelings of nationalist *contrainte*.

Luther had inculcated in Germans the saying of Saint Paul: "Let every one be subject to the higher powers [or, in Luther's characteristic translation, "subject to the authority that has power over him"]. For there is no authority but that of God; wherever there is authority, it is ordained by God. Whosoever therefore resisteth authority resisteth the ordinance of God." To establish itself as the beneficiary of this religious command—a step of inestimable value and a precondition for all further successes—national socialism had thus to fulfill two conditions: it must establish itself beyond doubt as the legal and legitimate authority, and it must exercise *de facto* power over the German people. The second condition nazism overfulfilled: never before in German history did any authority exercise physical power over every single German to anything like this extent. But prevailing circumstances made it all the harder for the Nazis to fulfill the first condition—and hence nazism was ready to pay almost any price to do so. Here we are up against the very core of the *arcana dominationis*, the secret of the art of domination, as it applies to the specific German case; here we have the explanation of the seeming contradictions and absurdities in the Nazis' rise to power.

One of these contradictions, apparent from the moment of accession to office in January 1933, was that nazism, in its competition with communism, boasted before its own followers of its revolutionary character, but at the same time did everyting to convince the rest of the German people at every turn of its strict respect for legality. Thus every one of its misdeeds, no matter how infamous, was cloaked in some legal form, before or after the event. Herein lies the importance of the sentimental melodrama, prepared by von Papen, whereby President von Hindenburg and Chancellor Hitler on 21 March 1933 appeared at the sarcophagus of Frederick II in Potsdam; and of the legislation of 1933 that was largely devoted to establishing formal legitimacy and legal continuity for the new regime. Herein lies the importance of the *Ermächtigungsgesetz* (Enabling Act, or more literally, Empowering Law) of 23 March 1933, for the passage of which by the prescribed two-thirds majority of the Reichstag not only Hugenberg's German Nationalists but even the Catholic Center and the Democratic party lent themselves.

The investigation of the Reichstag fire was assigned to the regular police, its adjudication to a regular court—the first could easily have backfired, the second one actually did—all this again to give proof of legality before the German people. The murders committed on 30 June 1934 and during the following days[132] were subsequently formally "legalized" by a decree of the German Nationalist minister of justice, Gürtrer.

Every woman in the occupied countries under Nazi occupation in World War II who was forcibly sent to a German military brothel had a number neatly and distinctly tattooed on her arm. In the concentration camps, records were kept with German bureaucratic thoroughness—no death candidate without a number, no murder however infamous without the requisite filling out of a printed form. One of the sensations at the Nürnberg trials was the testimony that SS judges were particularly bent upon punishment for any violations of such rules by concentration camp personnel, and that some concentration camp commanders were actually sentenced to death and executed for such violations. *Hier herrscht Ordnung*: everything, you see, is strictly legal and according to the rules!

The thread of formal legality and legitimacy was, of course, stretched almost beyond belief, but it was never allowed to snap. It was essential for this purpose that the great majority of bureaucrats retained their offices, and the new regime did—or refrained from doing—the minimum that was necessary to ensure such continuity. All those German Nationalists and other hangers-on who justified their remaining on the job to themselves and to others by claiming that they did so "to prevent greater evil" were able, in fact, to avoid evil in many individual cases. But they did not see and did not wish to see that by so doing they were making ever greater evil possible by rendering national socialism the vitally important service of preserving its semblance of legality. In individual cases the Nazis had to pay the price for such legal compunctions. Thus, a number of declared enemies of the regime, like Bishop Count Galen, a man of exemplary courage, remained unmolested in office and on occasion could with impunity make courageous utterances that must have caused gasps of surprise in their audiences. But this very state of affairs could be invoked by Nazi sympathizers abroad to claim that things could not be as bad as alleged and that contrary reports were mere malevolent exaggeration and atrocity propaganda.

Concessions such as these had the effect that the thread of formal legality did not in fact snap; that an aura of legitimacy was preserved; that power appeared to be invested with authority; and that the German people did not come to doubt that despite the peculiar, incomprehensible, and almost intolerable goings on, they still lived under a legal, and hence divinely ordained, authority, which could not be resisted without disobeying God's ordinance. After all, God's ways and the trials visited by Him upon man were often beyond human comprehension, and this only increases the merit of the faithful who do not waver in their faith. And as a powerful counterweight to all that might be charged against the regime, the Nazi government and its Führer had registered a steeply ascending series of foreign policy successes and thus had overwhelmingly legitimated and confirmed their claim to be bearers of the national mission.

Did not Hitler, as the representative of the Reich, in 1938 in Munich stand at a political pinnacle not even attained by Bismarck at the Berlin Congress of 1878? Did not the prime ministers of England and France appear trembling before Hitler, to beg for peace? Had not Germany, as world power, now reached the very zenith of her history? Could there be a more powerful and more irrefutable national and international legitimation and confirmation?

Even today in Germany there still are many who continue to view the year 1938 as the highest tide of German history, who hold that Hitler is to be criticized only for his subsequent failures, for the insatiability that did not allow him to consolidate what he had achieved by 1938. Many German Nationalists were more or less in agreement with the general direction of the aims of national socialism, objecting only to its vulgarity, its rashness and occasionally its choice of means. Many persons of this persuasion first turned away from the regime when the catastrophe of Stalingrad signalled the inevitability of German defeat. While nazism thus appealed to the nobler instincts of the German citizen—his love of country, his patriotism, his devotion, sense of authority and discipline—it also brought forth, as is well known, their baser instincts through the organization and systematization of terror on an incredible scale. But it would not have been possible to control the Germans by terror alone—as many well-intentioned observers have assumed. Rather, they were controlled by this truly diabolic combination, which appealed at once to their loftiest and basest feelings, which exploited both their respect for authority and their fear of death. And the effectiveness of Nazi terror itself depended on this cloak of legitimacy, on the notion that terror could not be resisted because, incontestably if incomprehensibly, it emanated from the supreme legally constituted authority. Those arrested by the Gestapo were not manacled merely by actual handcuffs; long before, invisible chains had prevented them from resisting what they thought of as divinely ordained authority. This nationalistic readiness for obedience was the strongest political weapon of national socialism. Through it, national socialism had a fifth column in the mind of any individual, even one who was consciously in opposition.

When non-Germans, like the English or French during the Second World War, heard of atrocities committed by a hostile government like that of Germany, they were quite prepared to credit the accounts. There was no need for any inner struggle: patriotism itself required that these criminal deeds of the enemy government be condemned without restraint. But it would be psychologically naïve to expect those same attitudes in the average German, for such an expectation overlooks that in his case the conscientious demands of patriotism run in the very opposite direction—not to sharpen his judgment but cloud it in the extreme. Those, who, like this author, emigrated from Hitler's Germany did so not least because the stifling pressure of this patriotic *contrainte sociale* gave us the feeling of suffocating.

This paralyzing effect of the patriotic *contrainte sociale*, however, extended further and could assume more subtle forms. Anyone who reads the increasingly numerous accounts of the conspiracies against Hitler—all failures—with the eyes of the sociologist is repeatedly struck by the grave inner inhibitions that prevented even individuals who, according to background and philosophic outlook, were wholly removed from national socialism, from taking effective action against Hitler. It was the aura of legality and of nationalism that protected Hitler more effectively than all his elaborate security measures. The same inhibition played an invisible, fateful role in German attempts to make contact with Allied governments so as to shorten the senseless, desperate war. It was these inhibitions that condemned the anti-Nazi conspirators to failure and ultimately to death.

More recently, the traditional Pauline-Lutheran-Kantian morality of passive obedience has been espoused with all earnestness by Julius Ebbinghaus, professor at Marburg, the first rector of his university after the liberation. Ebbinghaus's conduct throughout the period of the Hitler regime was beyond reproach, and his book, *Zu Deutschlands Schicksalswende*, belongs among the most impressive moral documents of a new Germany. But, this same author denies the right of a revolution against a tyrant like Hitler "because a revolution, in accordance with its nature, signifies legal insecurity and consequently suffering for people"—as though the tyrannical regime did not itself bring much greater legal insecurity, and deeper suffering, and as though its permanent legal insecurity were not infinitely worse than any transitional period of legal insecurity—and because "the alleged right of revolution destroys the state as a legal institution." In his opinion, men "must learn that any revolution, even that against an unjust state authority, is contrary to law."[133] In the eyes of this Kantian, William Tell was obviously guilty of high treason and murder.

The issue here is the very core of natural law, which only in extreme situations can supersede positive written law. But this unwritten supreme law is incontestable: to deny it would deliver us helplessly into the hands of any tyrant. And indeed the issue is not one of the *right* but of the *duty* to resist, a duty which provides the only effective form of implementation for the basic human rights and which alone can make a living reality of these. As long as a functioning democratic order provides the possibility through majority decision to effect a legal change of government, there can of course be no doubt that any violent action against the government in office is to be condemned. But as soon as a tyrannical government closes off this safety valve it leaves as the only alternative an explosion of the popular will. Every democratic revolution is an appeal to the popular will, for the expression of which the revolution itself creates the possibility. And the confirmation after the event of this popular will in democratic and liberal elections provides the justification for such a revolution. He who overthrows the tyrant is the executor of the popular will, and the tyrant alone is guilty for having left the popular will with no other avenue, for having created a situation where a change of government can be effected not by legal means but can only be ratified *ex post facto*.

All this indicates the acute need for reviving, in full detail and intensity, the sixteenth- and seventeenth-century debate of the monarchomachs and debates on tyrannicide.

The evident Kantian, and beyond that Lutheran, influences on Ebbinghaus make one realize with a shudder how deeply rooted in German intellectual history are those inhibitions that were responsible for the failure of all attempts to assassinate Hitler, and how deeply entangled with the best and most estimable strands in that same history.

The amazing frankness displayed by Dr. Carl Goerdeler, the mayor of Leipzig and civilian head of the resistance movement of 1944,[134] at a time when utter secrecy was imperative for the success of the conspiracy further attests to the conscientious patriotic scruples of the resistance movement, for good conscience requires openness. A good German, after all, does not conspire, least of all a military officer or high civilian official.

Outside observers could not help the impression that the German opposition to Hitler was dogged by bad luck and many small but crucial mishaps. But behind these external mishaps there was the basic inner hesitation. The great advantage of the French resistance, and that in other countries occupied by Germany, is that they could harness the nationalist *contrainte sociale* for their cause—whereas the German anti-Nazis were fighting against their own people.

That Germans, too, can mount a widespread resistance against *foreign* tyranny was proved by the events of 17 June 1953 in East Germany.

d. Specialization

National socialism benefited not only from passive obedience as preached by Luther but also from Luther's concept of "calling" or "vocation"—that each profession was an office conferred on the individual by God. Increasing specialization—the tendency to know more and more about less and less—is of course an integral aspect of all technical progress, as is amply evident in the country like the United States. But in Germany this tendency has taken a unique and extreme form, where each person passionately clings to a particular profession, closes himself off from all other spheres of life, and wears blinders—all the while indulging the feeling that he is thereby doing his human, his divinely ordained duty. As Hölderlin put it,

Craftsmen you see, not men,
Thinkers, but no men,
Priests, but no men,
Lords and lackeys . . . but no men.

Here is one important explanation of the behavior of German generals and officers. Politics was none of their concern; they knew nothing about it; they were soldiers eager to do their military duty and nothing but their military duty. The Schlieffen plan was an early example of this lack of political concern or sense of responsibility.

e. Militarism

Originating after the First World War, all European fascist parties made fullest use of the wartime, frontline experience, and although there can be no permanent war, it is quite possible to keep an entire populace for long periods of time at the emotional pitch of mobilization. A whole system of staged mass events can keep the popular soul simmering without actually allowing it to boil over. For this there is, of course, need for an enemy as the target of such mobilization. The handiest is an internal enemy, a vest-pocket enemy so to speak, who can be vanquished any time at no risk. Equally desirable is a weaker and ill-armed external enemy who can be overwhelmingly defeated in a colonial war. But at any rate there is no shortage of possible external foes—indeed, in applying fascist principles of foreign policy, a state of tension that can be pictured as a threat to one's own population is nearly inevitable. The wartime experience, whose tremendous integrative power the founders of fascism knew at first hand, can thus be replaced by a permanent synthetic substitute. How long this ersatz formula will serve with constant application is of course another question. And there remains the drawback that in case of actual war, no major increase in dosage is possible.

The fatalism with which the outbreak of the Second World War was accepted by the German people contrasted most sharply with the spontaneous enthusiasm for the war in August 1914; no further raising of temperature was attainable with the real outbreak of the war of 1939-1940. On the contrary, disappointment and the sobering thought that the chain of easy successes, attained without war, had come to an end, predominated. Yet, after all these measureless excesses of pseudo-integration and overintegration within, all that remained was violence toward the outside. As Gisevius puts it:

"Something like a perverted mass psychology almost inevitably results from this incursion into the psychic sphere of a people's life hitherto tended by the school, church, and parental home. It can end in no other way save that one day the proletarianized masses will hit upon war as a way out, upon naked conquest—and booty expeditions and beyond that upon economic and psychic nihilism. . . . The whole system of terror can only truly be explained against this background. . . . Terror is the pathbreaker of a revolution elevated to the status of a goal in itself."[135]

f. Imperialism

Sovereign nationalism, which recognizes no values above the nation, of necessity leads to national megalomania and imperialism.

The popularization of imperialism, aiming at world conquest, was considerably facilitated by the new science of geopolitics. The latter was a specialized offshoot of the field of human geography created by leading German geographers such as Karl Ritter and Friedrich Ratzel; it followed the lead of the Swedish author Rudolf Kjellén and was elaborated by Karl Haushofer, a retired German major general. Geopolitics is, first of all, a legitimate continuation and intensification of political geography. But its abuse under national socialism was a great didactic and propaganda success; imperialism, which otherwise would be lost to the common man because of the remoteness of its goals, acquired a concrete and tangible form through geopolitical maps. The childish gratification over being able to mark ever greater surfaces of the atlas with the color of one's own country played a role in the nationalist enthusiasm propaganda of the Third Reich that is not to be underestimated.

This bent toward expansionism had already been inherent in Prussian nationalism. Its two great heroes, Frederick the Great and Bismarck, were both conquerors—although Frederick's conquests were limited by the small resources of his Prussian state and Bismarck's Prussian conquest of Germany (minus Austria) was camouflaged behind a nationalist facade. The Versailles treaty allowed national socialism initially to continue this Bismarckian policy of conquest disguised as national unification with the annexation of Austria and the German-populated Sudetenland, but later this mask was dropped entirely.

Therewith the fateful ring came to a close, and the state of open and unconcealed superstratification was again attained. This had been the central aim of national socialism from its very beginnings, though it was prompted by tactical reasons to protest its peaceableness—a charade that distorted the face of its initiates into an occasional wry, diabolic smile.

g. Anti-Semitism

Meanwhile, from the seizure of power in 1933 to the unmasking of its imperialism in 1939, nazism needed to find a substitute tactic to prepare the German people for its intended role as superstratifiers. This substitute and preparation were found in anti-Semitism, with its state of permanent pogroms of ever heightened intensity. And the same anti-Semitism also had to serve as an official party world view, almost as a religion. For its essential sterility of ideas made national socialism, with respect to ideology, the poor relation among totalitarian movements. In consequence of the unfortunate national course of German history no ready historic antecedents for such an ideology offered themselves. The Holy Roman Empire of the German nation would not have rightly suited the world situation, even if it had not already been preempted by the earlier Hapsburg emperors, and the cult of Prussia's Frederick II, whatever its attraction, was too divisive and too much linked up with Prussia and Bismarck's Lesser Germany.

Anti-Semitism thus filled the void and became the German state religion and ideology of the Third Reich—the truly heroic notion that the national purpose of a great people of eighty million was to struggle, by all available means, against a diminutive and defenseless minority. Even the simultaneously espoused myth of the "Aryan" race was merely the converse of this anti-Semitism.

The glorification of race, however untenable its specific assumptions, has the effect of renewing the old superstratification mentality from which race consciousness originally had sprung. And this superstratification mentality expresses itself in the sphere of domestic policy in contempt for and brutalization of the Semitic pariah caste invented for this very purpose, and in the "master race" feeling of the party and its functionaries. In the sphere of foreign policy it is expressed in an imperialistic heightening of national self-consciousness.

The unstructured "we" feeling instilled in the populace, the so-called folk community, by a demagogic nationalism stands in conflict with the aspirations to superstratification and conquest fostered by the same nationalism—unless these aspirations can be directed abroad through imperialism. Hence the search for objects on which to vent one's thrust for power and one's sadism. (In the feudalist southern parts of the United States, a lower stratum had to be created through the importation of African slaves.) Most suitable for this role of victim is a minority that displays some deviant physical trait and hence cannot readily escape its intended role. The smaller the size of the minority the less dangerous this game becomes for the majority players and the higher the pitch of sadism it will attain.

These sociological considerations still leave unresolved the question how Hitler came to be imbued with the savage, diabolic hatred of Jews that he no doubt felt and that constitutes the ultimate source of the crimes and atrocities committed against millions of Jews.

A plausible but trivial assumption would be that Hitler imbibed anti-Semitism in the atmosphere of Vienna with its anti-Semitic mayor Karl Lueger (1840-1921). This, however, is contradicted by his own explicit assurance that in his Vienna years he was "hostile to both" Lueger and his Christian Social party, considering them reactionary. Further, "the tone, particularly of the Viennese anti-Semitic press, seemed to me unworthy of the cultural tradition of a great nation." There is no reason to doubt the sincerity of these astonishing assertions since there is no imaginable motive for his inventing these sentiments. Equally believable, on the same grounds and all the more so, is the portrayal of his subsequent conversion to anti-Semitism, to which he refers as "my greatest inner soul struggles," from which "only after months of battle between my reason and my sentiments did my reason begin to emerge victorious. Two years later, my sentiment had followed my reason, and from then on became its most loyal guardian and sentinel."[136]

What subsequent to these assertions is adduced by way of casual, alleged, or real observations could explain an already existing emotional anti-Semitism, but it does not suffice to account for any "bitter struggle" lasting two years. Rather, internal upheavals of such a kind normally arise from an experience of an intimate character. Hermann Rauschning, in his *Talks with Hitler*, also records the impression that Hitler's anti-Semitism must have had reasons of a wholly personal character.[137]

Hitler's origins and early manhood are described in Professor Franz Jetzinger's book *Hitlers Jugend*.[138] The author, a native of the same region as Hitler—the Waldviertel district in lower Austria— and an Austrian official with an intimate knowledge of Austrian law and administrative practice, brought together all the relevant documents, and on this basis provides for the first time a truly reliable account of the subject matter. The following summary is based on this book.

Hitler's paternal grandmother, Maria Anna Schicklgruber (1796-1847), bore an illegitimate child, Alois Schicklgruber (1837-1905), who would be Hitler's father. Almost five years later, in 1842, Maria Anna married an unemployed miller's apprentice, Johann Georg Hiedler (1792-1857). If Alois had been Hiedler's own child it may be assumed that, in keeping with peasant customs, he would have legitimized the child on marrying the mother or soon after. He did neither; yet young Alois was raised in the home of Johann Nepomuk Hiedler, a younger brother of Johann Georg.

This foster father of Alois Schicklgruber, in 1876, accompanied by three witnesses (all of whom were illiterate and therefore could sign only with crosses) appeared before the parish priest of the village where Alois had been born in 1837 and deposed for the record that "Georg Hitler, who was well known to the witnesses present, acknowledged that he was the father of the child Alois, mentioned by its mother, Anna Schicklgruber, and petitioned that his name be entered accordingly in the local parish register." Through this entry in the parish register, Alois, by now thirty-nine years old, was legitimized as the son of the Johann Georg Hiedler, who had been dead for nineteen years; henceforth he called himself Alois Hitler. Jetzinger convincingly shows that this legitimization was invalid under Austrian law and that the statement of the witnesses were false; he reconstructs the motives for this pious fraud on the part of the foster father.

Jetzinger's next bit of evidence comes from the Bavarian lawyer Hans Frank (1900-1948), a minister in the Third Reich and governor-general of Poland, later condemned as a major war criminal at the Nürnberg trials and executed. In prison he converted to Catholicism and "in the face of death" committed to writing his life story. He reports that Hitler in 1930 showed him a letter received from his nephew, William Patrick Hitler, which contained a reference to an illegitimate grandfather of Hitler, and which Hitler understood as an attempt at blackmail.

The investigation that Frank conducted, at Hitler's request, produced the following: "This cook Schicklgruber, Hitler's grandmother, had worked in Graz in the household of a Jewish family named Frankenberger, and this Frankenberger on behalf of his son, who was nineteen at that time, had paid alimony to Miss Schicklgruber from the time of the child's birth to his fourteenth year, the child being Hitler's future father. There also was an exchange of letters over several years between Frankenberger and Hitler's grandmother, the general tenor of which was the common knowledge of the correspondents that Schicklgruber's baby had been raised amid circumstances making the Frankenbergers liable to alimony payments. This correspondence for years was in the possession of a lady related to Hitler through the Raubals."[139] Angela, a sister of Patrick's father, Alois Hitler, had married a Raubal.

Hitler himself did not deny that his grandmother had sexual relations with the Jewish young man of Graz, but maintained that his father was the offspring of another premarital relationship, between his grandmother and his grandfather. Still Frank concludes that "Hitler may have been one quarter Jewish. Then his hatred of Jewry would have been conditioned in part by indignation about his descent, a hate psychosis as among relations."

This, of course, would supply a ready explanation, from the intimate sphere, of Hitler's "years" of inner "soul struggle"—assuming that Hitler knew of these facts as early as 1908. Jetzinger, to be sure, concludes that Hitler first learned them in 1931[140]—or else why order Frank to investigate? But Frank, for one, assumes that Hitler knew or suspected these facts earlier—early enough to account for his "psychotic" hatred of Jews. So the inference that the suspicion first came to him at the start of the "inner struggles" around 1908 strongly suggests itself.

h. Glorification of Violence

In the absence of ideological foundations, like those bolshevism derives from Marxism, German national socialism was driven to espouse in its most radical and naked form the glorification and idolatry of violence, which forms the core of all varieties of fascism, whatever the particular local disguise.

Naked violence, as we saw, in the form of the original superstratification formed the basis of all large states and high civilizations, and most of these have experienced at various times in their histories a reversion to these origins, a rebirth through renewed superstratification.

But nowhere was such naked, brutal violence maintained for long. Instead a moral religious veiling of naked violence set in which culminated in medieval theocracy. Yet this theocratic disguise of domination was gradually undermined through the rise of rationalism, a process that typically goes through the following stages: (1) Theocratic domination succumbs to *secularization* as the protective religious layers are removed. (2) Domination, thus unprotected, is subjected to rationalistic *criticism*, and this criticism becomes increasingly distinctive. (3) This destructive criticism delights in the *exposure* of the feudal, violent elements in all traditional relationships of domination, and of the corresponding hypocrisy of traditional ideologies. (4) This exposure of the violent elements of domination is used to justify *retaliation* in kind—that is, the open use of violence against any domination. (5) The result of this uneven fight between disguised (traditional) and open violence is a general *disillusionment*, a spreading feeling that violence is inevitable. (6) This unveiling of violence, its liberation from all forms of deceit and self-deception is now experienced and promoted as a *higher, heroic* stage. (7) The final result is the open, unveiled, and shameless proclamation of *violence as such*. Thus the circle closes and we come again to the point of departure: violent superstratification without concealment or apology.

Such new outbreaks of superstratification mentality are represented by Plato's *Gorgias* and, in emphatic form, by Nietzsche. In other cases, the same attitude has been vulgarized and trivialized, at times through use of a pseudoscientific social Darwinism. Hitler's *Mein Kampf* is part of this murky undercurrent.

i. "Socialism"

In the beerhall brawls and street fights of the Weimar Republic, National Socialists gradually gained the upper hand over Communists. But it was an intimate struggle with many conversions to and fro and evident family resemblances: national socialism adopted the negative, brutal, and cynically subversive tendencies of communism and also its technocratic-totalitarian enthusiasm for a centrally planned economy. This last similarity lent some justification to the claim that the Nazis were a National "Socialist" movement. But to the street brawler, this bit of Marxian economic doctrine meant little, and he readily replaced Marxian internationalism with nationalism.

The basic similarity between communism and nazism in the Weimar setting is statistically demonstrable: from 1928 through 1932, each party's vote oscillated sharply, while their combined total grew with remarkable steadiness and in turn paralleled almost exactly the growth of unemployment.[141]

j. Thought Police and Ideological Protectionism

Why is it that democracies see no reason to protect themselves against totalitarian propaganda, whereas totalitarian countries institute an elaborate apparatus to insulate themselves from democratic intellectual influences beyond their borders? (In the Third Reich, merely listening to foreign broadcasts was a capital offense.) The reason is no less than the tacit admission that democracy, whatever its defects in detail, by and large is the form of government natural to man—that the vast majority of mankind, if given the freedom to choose, will see no reason to abandon it. Whereas totalitarian attitudes are appropriate only to a small minority of extremely deviant and pathological types, are voluntarily embraced only by them, and have to be foisted on the great mass of human beings artificially and by force. This exactly is what happened in Soviet Russia.

To maintain the pressure of the extreme nationalist *contrainte sociale* produced by totalitarian propaganda, there is need for airtight insulation against outside influences. To give free rein to Nazi propaganda lies, all contact with truth had to be avoided. Only if contact with the relative sanity of surrounding countries was eliminated could the pathological Nazi mentality be made to appear natural. Despite the enormous organizational and technical efforts expended to this end, the Nazi leaders were quite aware that their design of moral corruption of the German people had by no means fully succeeded.

The strenuous efforts of the Nazi regime to keep secret from the German people the full extent of their worst atrocities indicates clearly what popular reaction the leaders expected if the truth had become known, and this provides an unintended tribute to the moral character of the majority of Germans. Thus the Nazis succeeded to restrict the full knowledge of these events to the very small circle of those Nazis directly involved. The average German had no more to go by than occasional unconfirmed rumors which the regime tried to discredit systematically as so much "atrocity propaganda." Furthermore, since any awareness of such matters brought with it the possibility of death or at least the certainty of grave conflicts of conscience, many Germans preferred to learn as little as possible. The net result of this complex interplay of political and psychological factors was that the Nazi regime was able to achieve a maximum of brutality with a minimum of incriminatory repercussion.

Leaders of fanatical religious sects have always tried to shield their followers from the contrasting opinions of the surrounding unbelievers. On a grander scale, the efforts at monopolizing public opinion constitute one of the main bases of totalitarian government. One result is an inevitable tension between public opinion at home as fabricated by the regime, and public opinion abroad where the regime holds no sway. Despite their largely successful efforts at insulating the country from foreign influences, totalitarian regimes respond to such outside criticism with a vehement polemical tone that bespeaks a remarkable nervousness and an awareness of the risks of their attempts at coercing domestic opinion. Above all, it indicates the affinity of modern totalitarianism to the older theological systems—which did not yet need to punish those listening to foreign broadcasts but took equally elaborate and drastic precautions against the reading of heretical tracts. And all religious movements, of course, are most intolerant in their infancy.

k. Demagogy

In the past, democratic mass movements tended to rationalism, whereas emotionalist movements were limited to small elites. Now, at last, emotion and mass were joined. All the various hitherto aristocratic antiliberal tendencies now found their lowest common denominator.

It may seem surprising that a person who himself is marked by vulgarity, who hardly rises above the cultural level of the mass, still may have the ability to become a mass leader. In a social pyramid with natural slope, the height of the apex and hence its distance from the base can be considerable. In mass society, by contrast, the pyramid is flattened, so that a person of the highest cultural level would be floating in midair. He who would lead the masses must stand on the same ground as they: to share in the low cultural level of the masses, to feel no inhibiting obligations toward higher cultural traditions—these are among the very conditions for his effectiveness. This provides his mass following with the opportunity to adulate someone who shares their own lack of culture and taste and not to defer to any "higher" values that seem strange and uncanny to them.

This attitude is, to be sure, ambivalent, like so much in social and political psychology. On the one hand, people want to look up to their leaders as somehow "above" them, whether from a natural sense of hierarchy or from a masochistic education; and they thus will react negatively when this desire goes unfulfilled—as indicated in the Weimar Republic by many jokes about the valiant President Friedrich Ebert, a former harness maker's apprentice, or the charming Chancellor Hermann Müller, who once had been a traveling salesman of toilet seats. On the other hand, any "higher" character will be felt to be alien and incomprehensible, will arouse in the masses a resentful desire to tear it down and drag it down to their own level. Hitler fully satisfied this second, destructive and abasing wish: there was no trait about him that was not common and vulgar.

Moreover, traditional intellectual culture in Germany was particularly stilted and inhibited, and freedom from such deep-rooted inhibitions was one of the essential conditions of his success. Hitler spoke with unconcealed hatred and contempt of the representatives of this culture that he so notably lacked. Generally he was remarkably clear about the negative preconditions of his own effectiveness.

As he wrote in *Mein Kampf*, "Precisely the members of our so-called intelligentsia . . . are not only burdened with a dead weight of the most senseless conceptions and prejudices, but what makes matters completely intolerable is that they have lost and abandoned all healthy instinct of self-preservation." "Even more seldom, however, is a theoretician, a great leader. . . . For leading means: being able to move masses. The gift of shaping ideas has nothing to do with ability as a leader."[142]

From the psychopathology of mobs (the object of long and careful research) it is known that even highly educated individuals, when they accidentally stumble into such a seething mass, will be carried away by it and feel, think, and act exactly as all the rest. From this comes a lesson for the treatment of the mass about which Hitler was equally clear. "All propaganda must be popular and its intellectual level must be adjusted to the most limited intelligence among those it is addressed to. Consequently, the greater the mass it is intended to reach, the lower its purely intellectual level will have to be. But if . . . the aim is to influence a whole people, we must avoid excessive intellectual demands on our public, and too much caution cannot be exerted in this direction."[143]

The new technique consists of ruling the masses as they want to be ruled. To quote another of Hitler's remarkably frank statements: "Like a woman, whose psychic state is determined less by grounds of abstract reason than by an indefinable emotional longing for a force which will complement her nature, and who, consequently, would rather bow to a strong man than dominate a weakling, likewise the masses love a commander more than a petitioner and feel inwardly more satisfied by a doctrine, tolerating no other beside itself, than by the granting of liberalistic freedom with which, as a rule, they can do little, and are prone to feel that they have been abandoned. They are equally unaware of their shameless spiritual terrorization and the hideous abuse of their human freedom. . . ."[144]

However, the same is also true in reverse. Just as the mass found the "leader" it needed in Hitler, so did Hitler find the mass he needed. For, as Nietzsche writes, "The more general and unconditional the influence of an individual or the idea of an individual can be, the more homogeneous and the lower must the mass be that is influenced. . . ."[145] Whoever aims to rule in a totalitarian fashion needs a mass. The horse makes the rider.

The historic field of forces is by no means homogeneous. There are long periods when everything runs straight along well-traveled tracks, where nothing is possible outside the traditional routine, and where would-be innovators and reformers vainly beat their heads against the wall. There are other periods, rarer and usually of briefer duration, when everything seems fluid and where those who see and seize the opportunity can produce major and lasting consequences. These are the occasions of history described by the Greek word *kairos*. Hence to produce the phenomenon of the so-called great man, the "man who shapes history," two elements must coincide: a major opportunity and a person who exploits it.

A widespread notion, since the early romantic period, holds that the exploiter of such an opportunity must be a "genius," a personality of wide scope, a person of original creativity or at least of demonic traits. There may have been great men of the past of whom this was true; but generally the proportion of greatness between a historic opportunity and him who used it has varied widely. Indeed, there is a tension here: the more cultured and highly shaped a personality is, the less chance that its particular shape will fully coincide with the objective requirements of the situation. Such disparities result in difficulties, frictions, and tensions. The great man "fails"—at least in part—and becomes a figure of historic tragedy. Such tragic failure is evidently the less likely the more shapeless and lacking in substance the individual is—the less originality he displays, the less he is a genius, the less scruple or prejudice he feels in adapting to the situation he is about to exploit. These characteristics that lend themselves to the exploitation of the situation also depend on certain innate abilities—but not those normally described as talent, creativity, or genius. Rather, they lie in the direction of cunning, shrewdness, ruthlessness—of those traits with which in normal life pickpockets, speculators, and racketeers tend to be well equipped. *Gelegenheit macht Diebe* ("Opportunity makes the thief") is a proverb that well expresses the relationship.

For those who prefer a more pompous version, we can adduce a well-known saying of Bismarck's: "The statesman can never create something by himself—he can only bide his time and lie in wait until he hears God's step reverberate through the events—then spring forward and grab the edge of his mantle, that is all." Characteristic as this remark is of Bismarck's cast of mind, it applies to himself only in limited measure. His Junker background was not all congruent to the historical situation created by the 1848 revolution. In the further course of events, and after a long wait, he was forced to make concessions to tendencies he considered hostile and repugnant and which, despite these compromises, he did not succeed in curbing or dominating. Thus his career ended on a pronouncedly tragic note.

These are, of course, certain minimal qualifications prescribed for the "great man" by the expectations of those he is to lead. In a hierarchical society these are the demands of members of the elite. In old Athens a person had to come from the social and cultural level of a Cimon or Pericles, in Rome of a Caesar or Augustus, to be considered an effective leader. In mass society, on the contrary—where hierarchical gradations have been obscured and leaders receive their legitimization directly from the masses—the effective candidate has to be on the level of the mass itself, indeed on the lowest and broadest mass level, so as to exploit ruthlessly and fully the historic opportunity. Once again it is now the "opportunity that makes the thief"—in this case not a little pickpocket but a leader, a "Führer," a mass murderer and would-be world conqueror. Only by recognizing this crucial importance of opportunity can we account for the scope of Hitler's historic effect, which stood in such disproportion to the personal banality and hollowness of the man through whom the effect was produced.

His lack of traditional education and inhibitions even benefited Hitler, the ex-corporal, in his later role as supreme commander. The theorists who had created that tradition of military thought which stretches from the great battles of antiquity to the campaigns of World War I had implicitly incorporated into their strategic doctrines many elements of occidental Christian civilization; and, as a result, many paths of action that otherwise might have been highly advantageous were assumed to be foreclosed. A bloody dilettante in strategy as well as in other matters, Hitler was innocent of such conventional inhibitions and scruples. He had at his disposal the most energetic, most highly trained professional commanders and staff officers; he confronted Allied adversaries who at first displayed a striking lack of capability and of courage—hence the spectacular initial successes of his unrestrained insolence and his criminal daring. But, as soon as serious resistance and military reversals began to make their appearance, it became increasingly clear that the insolent corporal in his somnambulent way had thrown to the winds not only the unconscious inhibitions but also the conscious prudence and common sense of centuries of military tradition. Hence the initial successes lasted precisely as long as Hitler's antagonists allowed themselves to be bluffed by his unprecedented (and hence utterly unexpected) unscrupulousness. As soon as the Allied side recovered from its shocked surprise and panic fear—as soon as it rallied its forces for the counterattack and thus called Hitler's bluff—there began the inevitable catastrophe of a well-equipped, efficient, valiant army commanded by a megalomaniac dilettante. As one of Hitler's own generals put it: "The bluff had worked for a long time—until the stronger adversaries became aware of their superiority." "Now all the mistakes of the earlier policy of illusion avenged themselves." "For insolence is of use, if at all, only during the offensive; in the defensive it degenerates into the pure stupidity of the ever repeated 'Führer's orders.' "[146]

Hitler's policies were at first often referred to as "Caesarism" or "Bonapartism"—likening them to the few major analogies that world history offers. Yet neither in the time of Caesar nor that of Napoleon had depletion of the cultural legacy and massification attained anywhere near their present degree. (Napoleon III is somewhat closer to these phenomena of our own time.)

The "guilt" for these developments must be imputed less to those who had the determination and ruthlessness to perceive and exploit the situation, but rather to the lengthy and progressive course of that social pathology which we have called massification. The events of the Nazi period merely ruthlessly brought out into the open the latent tendency of this secular development. It was the acute attack of a disease which in chronic and lingering form had long since been spreading in the body politic and social of the peoples of the West.

l. Catilinarianism

Sociologically speaking, anti-Semitism was only a warming up exercise for the task of superstratification, a method of inculcating national superiority complexes and contempt for other "races" and peoples, and a vehicle for "natural selection" of those most adept at bestial brutality and inhumanity.

After the seizure of power much effort was directed toward solidifying and spreading this criminal countermorality. It was concentrated in the so-called *Ordensburgen* (or training camps) in which the coming generation of the Nazi counterelite were educated. Later, during the war, and with the same intent, all kinds of immoral behavior toward the civilian population of occupied territories (e.g., rape, as well as looting for the sake of individual enrichment) were not only tolerated but encouraged. Indeed, the possibility of personal enrichment was stressed in general orders issued to the soldiers. In his treatment of generals Hitler resorted to outright bribery. Schlabrendorff writes as follows: "In order to bind the officer corps firmly to his person, Hitler paid the high officers from army commander upwards out of his privy purse sums which were not shown in the budget and which were not taxable. Such a gift was a slap in the face for the conception of honor as held by the German officer. Yet Hitler thereby tied his higher generals to a golden guide rope which was no less effective for this reason."[147] There is no recorded case in which such bribes were rejected. On a larger scale, of course, the huge rearmament program, with its unprecedented opportunities for promotion, was nothing but a single bribe handed to the military officers as a class.

Rieckhoff strikingly describes the attitude of the military to Hitler's regime: "To them no doubt a government which cultivated military thinking, which sought to strengthen the armed forces and . . . created better occupational conditions was preferable to any other." The military "suddenly had billions at their disposal. Who could resist this lure? Thus ambition seizes everybody and makes them forbearing toward the man who . . . through his policies creates opportunities for them such as they had not imagined in their boldest dreams. Assuredly, they have their misgivings and their reservations, but in the face of so much 'greatness' . . . they believe they must wink at the weaknesses and inferiorities which they clearly perceive. In this fashion they make of themselves accomplices."[148] Or as the sentence handed down at Nürnberg on 30 September 1946 states (justifying the decision of the tribunal not to declare the German general staff and the Higher Command a criminal organization): "Contemporary German militarism experienced under its most recent ally, National Socialism, a brief flowering more splendid than any it had known in the past."

In normal times of peace, social life appears civilized and moral—not because individuals lack antisocial, immoral urges, but because public opinion condemns, and the police and the courts prosecute, the expression of such urges. In the course of a long process of depletion of the cultural legacy the positive ideals of morality become little more than rigid conventions, and the restraining of the opposite "wicked" urges becomes increasingly a matter of merely external compulsion. This leads to a potentially explosive situation which suggests the possibility of using these explosive forces from the moral underworld for one's own political ends, unleashing them against one's opponents. And this, indeed, is what happened in Nazi Germany, Soviet Russia, and other totalitarian countries. Thus what in petty bourgeois society was mere harmless gossip now became political denunciation; and, generally, free rein was given to sadism, hatred, calumny, and all other hitherto condemned and suppressed base instincts. In a true "transvaluation of values"— Nietzsche's *Umwertung aller Werte*—all these evil instincts were positively rewarded. And with noise and stench the whole pack of them broke loose. All those who were disadvantaged, had flunked out of school or served time in jail, all bankrupts, misunderstood geniuses and frustrated opportunists, all those beset by feelings of inferiority or resentment, or consumed by envy and hatred—they all smelled the scent of a dawning day. All psychopaths and deviants, all shady characters and scoundrels responded to the appeal; people who normally would have been consigned to the madhouse or the workhouse, or who in olden times would have been sent off to the colonies—all sensed that the great hour had struck. All the vermin crawled out of their hiding places and rose like a cloud of locusts, their noxious exhalations poisoning the clean air of Germany. The feeling of release, the gratification of worked-off repression was unmistakable. Nietzsche's demand that "the shabby and the false must come to light" had become everyday reality. To Nietzsche's wistful question "where are the barbarians of the nineteenth century?" the SS could snap to attention, answering "Here!" But release was needed not only for the moral tensions of the preceding regimes: the fascist dictatorships themselves create heavier and more massive pressures which in turn demand the opening of new safety valves. All in all, the systematic cultivation of sadism serves the function of training and of selection; the selective function is of particular importance.

At the pinnacle of this entire pseudoelite stood a one-time unemployed and work-shy peddler of picture postcards, who had knocked about the flophouses of the Vienna lumpenproletariat passing himself off as a misunderstood artist—although, because of his sentimental forelock and coquettish toothbrush mustache, one might have taken him at best for a beach photographer. Even twelve years of unprecedented power and of success on a grand, historical scale did not in the least (anymore than they had in the case

of Napoleon I) "refine" or "raise" this upstart or bring about the development in him of any kind of human traits. The photographs
taken with his stenographer Eva Braun in Obersalzberg suggest the
snapshot of a sergeant with his fiancée, intended for the family
album lined with red velour: to the very end he lost nothing of his
embarrassing vulgarity, of his pervasive inner insecurity which he
made such frantic efforts to compensate for. There are no accounts
whatever of him that would point to even the least trait of greatness, or even of simplicity or human directness. When he had himself photographed with children the effect was that of a badly contrived melodramatic pose intended to appeal to the sentimentality of
German audiences. His unabating, grim seriousness, his horrifying
lack of any sense of humor precluded even those involuntarily comic
situations which gave to the bullfroglike Mussolini an occasional
redeeming feature of clownishness. His German prose in speech and
writing always retained the embarrassing traits of the half-
educated, his rhetorical flights bespoke the successful graduate of
an evening course for party speakers. Only the artful grandiosity of
the sports stadium and his monumental claque secured its success.
The only touch of immediacy in his speeches was the monumental
spite and hatred that now and then erupted in frightening fashion.

Even in his immediate entourage there was no one who genuinely
loved him. Each of them had entrusted their careers and their very
lives to the all-powerful leader of the robber gang; it was his power
in which they sought to participate, which they sought to protect.
They feared his arbitrariness and his lack of self-control. They
speak with ironic contempt of rages that sent him sprawling on the
floor to chew the edges of the nearest rug, of hysterical fits of weep-
ing and shrieking, of grotesque fear of poisoning or assassination. It
fully fits into this picture that the absurd fear of an imaginary
stomach cancer should have hastened the insane pace of his would-
be world conquest. Even his suicide at the eleventh hour lacks any
trait of greatness or dignity: not even death could ennoble this
mauvais sujet. Rather, the repulsive ugliness of this last scene of the
fifth act of the melodrama that he himself had staged was a monstrous expression of his self-hatred and self-contempt. This end, in
which the stench of gasoline mixed with that of charred flesh, which
only its triviality prevents one from calling infernal, was suitably
transformed into the pompous radio announcement, read to strains
of Wagnerian music: "Our Führer Adolf Hitler has been killed in
battle. The German people bows in deepest grief and reverence. . . .
At the end of his struggle and his unerringly straight path of life

stands his hero's death in the capital of the German Reich. His whole life was spent in the service of Germany." Even his will, with its undignified tone, still echoes beyond the grave his hate-filled shrieking and slobbering.

The devil himself had assigned to this repulsive psychopath the task of ruining Germany as rapidly and as thoroughly as possible, and it could hardly have been accomplished more effectively.

Since his youth Hitler had been marked as one of those well-known psychopathic types whose excessive self-appraisal stands in grotesque contrast to his failure in real life. Scrawny and unsightly in appearance, sternly treated by a morose father, spoiled by a mother widowed early in life, he felt, as do so many people of his type, a calling to "higher things"—though fate had made him the sixth child of a low-ranking Austrian customs official.

In school he made a good start but became increasingly a bad and lazy pupil. Sensing in himself a genius for painting and architectural drawing, he twice presented himself with "proud self-assurance" for the entrance examinations of the Vienna Academy, but each time failed miserably. He felt himself a great architect but was only an "indifferent draftsman." Weak, frigid, and shy—as depicted in a convincing portrait sketch of a fellow student around 1904—he was denied any compensation by way of erotic success. He remained determined, despite it all, to become a great man—yet meanwhile he had squandered his orphan's pension and an allowance given him by an aunt, so that he landed, as a ragged, louse-infested, half-starved itinerant peddler in a public shelter.

At last the outbreak of war in 1914 promised to put everything to rights. Failing to report for service in Austria, he enlisted enthusiastically as a German volunteer and surely already felt the marshal's baton in his knapsack. But even in the army he could advance only as far as corporal, the rank he finally received shortly before the end of the war as a consolation prize, since his company commander could not justify a promotion to sergeant.

Thus, from the day he left the nursery to his thirtieth year, he underwent an unbroken chain of the most grievous fiascoes, disappointments, and humiliations. And, as is characteristic of men of his type, the more he failed, the higher soared his daydreams and aspirations. The distance between reality and self-appraisal became ever more grotesque, this indeed is the only dimension of his life that could truly be called "great." Equally notable, of course, is the tenacity with which he did not give up the struggle despite its utter hopelessness; and the fact that he did not seek escape, as do so many others, in suicide or narcotics.

Then came the German collapse of 1918. It opened for him at last a path for which no prescribed training and no examinations were required and which, nevertheless, could lead to the pinnacle of success: the path of the demagogue and politician. Like others who had failed in life he now threw himself into this career—though few had failed as completely and abjectly as he.

Poorly endowed by nature and poory treated by life all emotions in him had long since died except for the smoldering, egomaniac desire both to prove himself to the world and to avenge himself on it—to place reality itself in the wrong, to show to the real world that his boundless self-appraisal had been justified after all—and to punish that very reality by destroying it. His pathological single-mindedness in concentrating on this dual egotistic goal explains the uncanny quality of his character. Such concentration of all energies of the intellect and the will upon such an inhuman and unnatural goal is indeed diabolic, and it makes a demonic impression. It removes the subject so far beyond all humanity, all normal human conventions and assumptions, all emotional ties, inhibitions, and scruples that he can pierce with a look of icy sharpness through realities that remain mercifully hidden to others, and calculate possibilities others dare not think of. The result is that his very inhumanity can be acknowledged as superhuman by insecure persons who feel a need for self-abasement and idolatry. There is something demonic about such inhumanity.

Sigmund Freud once sketched the psychopathology of the criminal as follows: "Two features are essential for the criminal, boundless egomania and a strong destructive tendency: common to both, and a prerequisite for their manifestations, is lovelessness, the lack of an affective valuation of the [human] object."[149] This characterization fits Hitler word for word.

His all-consuming dual need had reached boundless proportions and had to be gratified in two opposite ways: through overwhelming success and through annihilating destruction. There was one way in which both of these could be attained: a go-for-broke game with the highest engagement of all energies and without any caution or restraint, a precipitous rise followed by a calamitous fall that carries all into the abyss.

His nature as a desperate gambler explains his extreme physical fitness at all moments of extreme danger—up until the assassination attempt of 20 July 1944. It also accounts for his astounding, lightninglike initial success: none of his antagonists was prepared for such absolute unscrupulousness. A normal person who finds his satisfaction in success—however tempestuously or brutally he may be bent on it—will combine boldness with caution and guard as far as possible against setbacks or failures. But someone to whom success and failure are the same because he cares only about the gigantic dimensions of each, can and will go to extremes of ruthlessness, increasing the stakes at each turn. Even his favorite opera, Wagner's *Götterdämmerung*, glorified an ending in terror.

For Hitler there never was a "right time" for quitting while he was ahead, for pausing, for compromising. He felt a "total repugnance to defensive measures."[150] This was the hidden meaning of the catastrophe of Stalingrad, which a more circumspect strategy could readily have avoided, and of the militarily absurd Führer's order that prohibited any retreat. Triumph or annihilation for him were the only alternatives; nothing that ranged between these was to him of the slightest account.

This basic nature of Hitler also accounts for his deep misanthropy, his enmity toward all and sundry, the death sentences he meted out to his closest friends. Hence his profound disgust with the whole world—and, in the final account, his disgust with and hatred against himself, his urge to self-destruction, which makes the final catastrophe for Germany in World War II look like mass suicide. Hence also the inexorable logic of his own suicide at the time of the collapse—for the final aim had now been attained, and survival would only have meant a resumption of the old chain of humiliations. And hence, finally, the conviction, to which Speer testifies from firsthand knowledge (but which otherwise would be quite incomprehensible) "that for Hitler personally his own death is history's last word"—a sharp contrast to the boastful official chatter about the "thousand-year Reich."

His years as a tramp and vagrant had accustomed Hitler to a frugal, ascetic life. But all his suppressed urges did not scatter themselves in this or that tabooed object of desires; rather they were all concentrated on the single passionate aim of *revenge*. Hitler fully identified with this utterly compressed yet homogeneous shadow of his own personality; indeed, he enthroned it, instead of a conscience, in the seat of the superego. There was no higher aim than this: not Germany, not national socialism, not anything else. Hitler did not intend the realization of national socialism or greatness for Germany; he had no objective aims whatever. He did not wish to attain anything for Germany, only for himself; both Germany and national socialism, like all else, were mere means to an end, and the end was purely egocentric.

Herein lies the difference between Hitler and all other comparable figures in history, such as Napoleon, Lenin, Stalin, or Mussolini. All of these pursued some supreme objective goal—glory and greatness for their nation, or victory for the world revolution. Even Marxism, in inculcating the notion in its adherents that brutality is a duty in the service of the dictatorship of the proletariat, thus subordinates brutality to a higher goal. The unleashing of brutal instincts is not absolute or unconditional. Such purposeful subordination provides it with some genuine potential for social integration, for the higher goal of world revolution can and must be pursued in common with others. Hitler, by contrast, cared about nothing but himself and his own macabre triumph. This bestowed on him a single-mindedness, an effectiveness and willpower, a sleepwalker's surefootedness—qualities he never stopped boasting about. And the night through which he moved in his sleep was the night of evil, the hell of his inner self in which he felt thoroughly at home.

This frightening egocentric unity of his exclusive concentration upon a single, criminal, ultimate goal accounts for his total unscrupulousness and lack of inhibition, which is not characteristic of any otherwise comparable person. He wished to heighten his power to the utmost so as to drag everything down in a fall of utmost precipitousness. The very depth of the fall was the final aim, to which the height of the earlier rise was a mere means.

All other dictators in the pursuit of the particular supreme goal which they meant to serve and therefore could not afford to endanger, had to weigh risks and chances—and the magnitude of any risk for them was a negative factor. But Hitler was bent on maximizing the risks, and in his calculations he added absolute quantities regardless of plus and minus signs. Hence he did not flinch before any risk, there was nothing with which he was not willing to gamble. In a purely quantitative sense of excess here was singular testimony to his "greatness." Any other statesman, however bold and dauntless, weighs risks and chances. For Hitler there was, in the end, no risk whatever.

Hence his utter loneliness, his absolute and icy isolation from other human beings, the fact (so often attested) that no one, even from his innermost circle of associates, had any real influence on him and his decisions. Reflection and deliberation in common with others presuppose a common goal. But Hitler's ultimate end was so purely subjective and egotistic, so grotesquely pathological and infantile, that there could be no commonness with others. The egocentric insanity that had seized him alone he could not possibly share with any other human being.

Hence also his breathless haste, his desire that all must be done in his own lifetime. He wanted, after all, to be around to witness his own triumph over the world and his revenge on it; nothing else mattered.

And this measure of triumph he did attain: he saw the world at his feet, he smashed Europe into pieces, he destroyed Germany—truly this humiliated and deeply injured individual exacted from this world a terrible revenge!

CHAPTER 3

Conclusions

To cure the social pathology of domination and unfreedom that is due to superstratification there are, in principle, two methods. The first is to proceed consciously against all recognizable forms of the sickness—and this is a task with which the stream of history seems to be confronting us today, so that it depends on us whether and to what extent the problem is soluble. The other is to proceed half-consciously through a series of palliatives and attenuations, by way of checks and balances within the structure of domination. This was the course pursued by Western history, a course that attained its peak in the Middle Ages. Spiritual and secular claims to dominion were in close balance, with the scales tipping now this way and now that; the rights and duties arising from innumerable relations of superordination and subordination were tightly interwoven in a many-colored tapestry; the peasants at the base of the structure, although technically not enjoying the status of freemen, enjoyed in their family enterprises a sphere of freedom that was in practice immune from outside interference; and in the towns the family enterprises of the craftsmen had successfully struggled to have their spheres of liberty legally recognized. The remnants of unfreedom which lingered throughout this structure were neutralized by the prevalent notion of their legitimacy, of their being in accord with God's design.

Since then historical reality in any number of directions has slipped away from this optimum situation attained in the late Middle Ages. Instead domination and unfreedom have become ever more pronounced so that the entire structure of superstratification has reemerged with increasing sharpness.

Yet even as real freedom was diminishing there was a corresponding and opposite increase in human consciousness of, and demand for, freedom. Both of the major elements of Western civilization contributed to this result: the tradition of classical antiquity, which was an enemy to domination and no longer accepted it even in attenuated or disguised form; and Christianity, whose demand for neighborly love was secularized and generalized into a sense of social compassion and social responsibility. This same combination of the liberalism of antiquity with Christian social consciousness also made possible the sort of critical self-assessment of our civilization that would reveal the origins of our historic condition in super-stratification.

The mounting tension between the reality of increasing unfreedom and the ideal demands for increasing freedom was bound to express itself in a series of crises—and today we find ourselves in the midst of the last and the most severe of these.

The same internal checks and balances and traditional inhibitions that gave medieval government its relatively humane character also reduced its effectiveness in dealings both at home and abroad—much to the dismay of rulers lusting for domination. As the personal and institutional restraints on this lust for power diminished, there ensued a development toward a political absolutism, supported by advances in the technique of organization and of warfare, and thus spurred on by the consciousness and the results of its rapidly increasing efficiency. These developments put their imprint not only on the politics of the following centuries, but also on their art, science, and philosophy.

The shift from religious absolutism to enlightened absolutism implied a further unleashing of power urges, since concepts of humanity provided far weaker ties than had those of Christianity. Constitutionalism and parliamentary government transformed the universality of absolutism into a system of domestic and global pluralism whereby the state became the servant of shifting alliances of economic interests at home and a competitor among imperialist nationalisms abroad, deriving new increments of power on both fronts.

Meanwhile, absolutism was transformed into such phenomena as Jacobinism and Bonapartism—a shift that paralleled the evolution of political theory from Hobbes to Rousseau. The final step was modern totalitarianism, the most extreme form of governmental absolutism, which for its purposes of domination makes the fullest use of all available means of modern technology: terror and secret police, control of the news media, control over weapons of unprecedented offensive power, and a controlled, centralized economy. All these devices of communication, organization, and weapons technology potentially can reach around the globe. The technical means for unifying the world are thus already available. The unprecedented possibilities that they open up are sure to exercise such irresistible attraction that they will not remain untried for long. The only questions are who will seize this opportunity and in what spirit: our side, in a spirit of cooperation, democracy, and peace, or the other side through superstratification, totalitarianism, and violence.

To exploit these enormous possibilities in a totalitarian fashion requires corresponding unscrupulousness and total singleness of purpose. These were characteristic of the original superstratifiers—who, however, disposed of only the most primitive technical means of implementation. And ever since, all cultural and intellectual progress has had for its noblest task the dampening and restraining of this original superstratifying spirit. A new, titanic unleashing of this painfully tamed lust for power—its renewed espousal and glorification—came about only as a reaction, as a defiant response to this progressive softening. Among the earliest instances in our Western history of this reawakening are the reactionary regime of Lycurgus in Sparta after the catastrophe of 546 B.C., among its earliest literary expressions are the *Melian Dialogue* of Thucydides and the figure of Callicles in Plato's *Gorgias*. From Machiavelli to Nietzsche we have encountered other spokesmen for such unrestrained lust for power, such a *Wille zur Macht*. Their intellectual level has varied, and the development has not proceeded uniformly or without interruptions; yet the ascending trend is unmistakable.

Fascism in its several varieties originated in a blend of this titanic glorification of violence with the more traditional forms of imperialist nationalism. The totalitarian means of domination were by now available for renewed attempts at superstratification; yet to the pluralism of imperialist nationalisms in foreign policy corresponded a plurality of fascisms, each aspiring to an expansion of its power that would ultimately have led to global domination—but each of which, by its inherently particularistic character, saw itself precluded from attaining such a universalist goal. No national fascism, after all, could expect of any other nation that it would spontaneously submit to its domination—yet none could hold out any different promise. As a result, no fascism could pose any lasting global danger, least of all national socialism, that centered wholly around the person of a single psychopath. Only under the suggestive power of Hitler's pathological self-aggrandizement did the world allow itself to be bluffed into corresponding overestimation.

Logically, a truly global danger could arise only from a universalist totalitarianism which could arouse the desires and stimulate the enthusiasm of peoples beyond its original national borders. And such a universalist totalitarianism, unfortunately, has indeed arisen.

The heightened domination of absolutism had found its earliest and most brutal field of application in colonial imperialism since the age of discovery and circumnavigation. We used to look on this era boastfully as an instance of courageous advance, of unquenchable thirst for knowledge, and of an indefatigable urge for discovery that penetrated to the most remote and inaccessible regions of our planet. Yet thirst for knowledge and urge for discovery were by no means the strongest and most effective motives. Greed, lust for power, and sadism swept over continents whose inhabitants could offer no effective resistance to the firearms or cavalry of the new superstratifiers. A differential of military technology comparable to that of the superstrafications of antiquity brought about similar sociological consequences—except that the unrestrained bestiality of the *conquistadores* this time stood in sharpest contrast to their professions of Christianity and the values of their Western civilization. To justify themselves they at first even denied that the victims of their subjugation and violence were human beings or had souls. But even after the church disproved such assertions and cautioned against such practices, the colonial conquerors continued to trample on the human dignity of the colonial peoples and even began hypocritically to complain of their "white man's burden." To be sure, pious missionaries and humane administrators often did their utmost. To be sure, the natives received not only the benefits of alcohol and syphilis but also of catechisms, of reading and writing, and of a minimum of technical civilization (including medicine and public hygiene—which, however, produced overpopulation and famine as their side effects). To be sure, from the benefits of technical accomplishments like the Suez Canal even the inhabitants of adjoining regions could not be excluded. Yet it would be senseless, stupid, and not wholly honest to keep invoking these positive accomplishments of which there doubtless were many. In the scales of history these weigh light as feathers against the crushing weight of countless crimes, brutalities, and inhumanities. And in the consciousness of the peoples concerned even the benefits of colonialism are like a sum in brackets preceded by a minus sign, and this minus sign converts even the alleged benefits of colonialism into so many negative factors.

The five centuries of Western colonial imperialism are a bloody stain on the historic record of humanity, an endless chain of gravest crime against humanitarianism, a chain that even in the twentieth century was by no means broken. On non-European continents these five centuries of colonial imperialism have evoked inconceivable amounts of hatred and vengefulness, not all of which are yet ready to explode, but which only await the spark of bolshevism to be detonated at what for us may prove the most inconvenient time.

The prevalent form of enterprise in the realms of colonial imperialism was the slave plantation or the slave-operated ore mine, and this form of economy, as we saw, was also transplanted to Europe itself, especially to eastern Europe, where the peasant lower class was degraded to serfdom within a new system of agrarian feudalism.

Meanwhile, technical progress with the onset of the Industrial Revolution had substituted for the family enterprise of the craftsman the factories of large entrepreneurs, depressing the urban masses to the status of proletarians—with numerous reinforcing influences from agrarian to nascent industrial feudalism.

The social structure of superstratification, which in the medieval West had been reduced to a minimum, thus was sharpened and expanded in the age of absolutism, colonial imperialism, and agrarian and industrial neofeudalism—at the very time that traditional compromises were increasingly rejected and the demands for freedom voiced by the intellectual elite were becoming ever more radical. The tension that in this fashion increased from both sides offered an enormous opportunity for a titanic spirit who would unleash the latent energies. To have recognized and seized this unique opportunity was the brilliant and fateful accomplishment of Karl Marx.

Marx's analysis started with the superstrafication situation of urban industrial feudalism which had just then reached a pinnacle and which was most readily susceptible to the influence of a radical urban intelligentsia. His revolutionary doctrine of salvation was, as we saw, a synthesis of the most radical and unsparing titanism with a passionate appeal directed to all the "disinherited of this earth," all those who found themselves deprived of rights, subjugated, and suppressed, to take vengeance, to reverse the roles of anvil and hammer, to "expropriate the expropriators." Marx followed prevalent nineteenth-century tastes in couching his doctrine in a set of pseudoscientific proofs and entering in its behalf the claim of inevitability according to the laws of nature. At the same time he revived one of the oldest themes of Judeo-Christian eschatology, with the classless society as a secularized version of the kingdom of God on earth.

And this universal pseudoreligion, with its unsurpassed menace, today is professed by two global powers, the Soviet Union and Communist China, which between them dominate one-fourth of the land surface and one-third of the population of our planet.

What already encompasses a great portion of the earth and threatens the remainder is nothing but a countersuperstratification, a new superstratification of unprecedented dimension and intensity. Never in the preceding centuries could even the most violent superstratification threaten more than a part of a continent, never could it chain all its subjects with such inescapable brutality, and thus absolutely, to its despotism. Only this new superstratification has taught us to recognize past superstratifications as examples of the same predatory species, sharing the same mentality, the same sociological structure, and the same means of exercising domination and enforcing subjugation—although the earlier members of the species were far behind in their technical efficiency.

What can we oppose as a counterbalance to the pseudoreligious ideology of bolshevism, upon which its dynamism and momentum in no small measure rest? The answer surely is: our Western cultural tradition, derived from classical antiquity and Christianity. But Marxism and bolshevism also originated in this tradition, which in any case no longer possesses that compact character and common orientation that would make an effective counterpoise to bolshevism. Is there any counterconviction? Has the West an idea?[1]

That idea is the ideal of humanity that requires freedom for its full unfolding. Bolshevism in the last analysis must be condemned for its inhumanity, its total repression of freedom, without which humaneness becomes impossible.

It is one of the many serious symptoms of degeneracy of the nineteenth century that the idea of humanity, already passed on in somewhat anemic form from the eighteenth century, had faded into the ideal of humanitarianism—a sentimental, superficial, vague notion of kindness. What is here intended instead is humanity in the fullest and most vital sense of embracing everything that makes men fully human, from the biology of their bodily existence to the psychic, intellectual, ethical, and religious spheres. And if bolshevism in the Marxian system has at its disposal a comprehensive intellectual foundation, laying claim to a scientific character, on our side a new anthropology is forming as a scientific analysis and justification of the idea of humanity with an equally wide, indeed a wider radius; in it all relevant disciplines from biology to history and comparative religion are collaborating, and it promises to fill the idea of humanity with richer, more concrete and more secure content. Our human nature, however capable of reacting differently to different circumstances, gives evidence of an amazing constancy—a constancy without which indeed understanding and agreement among human beings would not be possible. These are the fleshly tablets that, in the great words of Saint Paul, the creator has engraved in the heart of every man without distinction. The new task that has been assigned to anthropology and in the fulfillment of which all of us are cooperating, is faithfully to decipher this human script with the aid of our *lumen naturale*, our natural light.

The most elementary principles of humanity, of course, need not await such full scientific explanation. Rather, they belong to the intellectual legacy of mankind, which can be obscured only under rare and extreme conditions. The insight that the idea of humanity involves an attitude of reciprocity also belongs to these principles: I can and may recognize and treat someone else as a human being only if he in turn treats and recognizes me as a human being. That fundamental, self-evident proposition leads to no difficulties as long as human beings who deliberately exclude themselves from this reciprocity do not exist or exist only as isolated examples—preferably behind prison bars.

Today, however, we must confront the fact that a third of mankind is ruled by men whose credo expressly denies such humane reciprocity to us and others who do not share their own beliefs, which makes inhuman conduct, free from humane restraints, into an ideological or pseudoreligious duty, which boasts of such inhumanity, and which condemns and despises any other conduct as cowardice and culpable weakness.

An assertion going so counter to any human feeling is in need of demonstration.

In one of Lenin's canonical writings, his speech on "The Tasks of the Youth Leagues," delivered at the Third All-Russian Congress of the Young Communist League on 2 October 1920, we read as follows: "We reject any morality based on supranatural or extra-class concepts. . . . We say that our morality is entirely subordinated to the interests of the class struggle of the proletariat. . . . Communist morality is that which serves this struggle." And in *Left Wing Communism, An Infantile Disorder*: "We must be able to stand up to all this, agree to make any sacrifice, and even—if need be—to resort to various strategies, artifices and illegal methods, to evasions and subterfuges, as long as we get into the trade unions . . . and carry our communist work within them at all costs."[2]

And in further proof that this "new morality" is not a mere theory, William C. Bullitt, the first American ambassador to the Soviet Union, reports the following in his memoirs: "In an elated vodka mood the Soviet marshals Voroshilov and Budyeni at a state dinner boasted about the capture of Kiev during the civil war. Voroshilov told the ambassadors that there were 11,000 Czarist officers with their wives and children in the city, while the communists had only about 2,000 men. 'We would have never been able to take the city. Therefore we utilized propaganda.' With the promise of safe-conduct the two marshals induced the officers of the opposing side to lay down their arms. And then? 'Quite simple,' said Voroshilov; 'we shot the men and their small children and stuck the women and girls in houses for our soldiers.' "[3]

Let us not forget that this is the enemy we are facing. Diabolic is too mild an expression for such a degree of inhumanity, for the devil, however grudgingly, recognizes God's supremacy. Yet bolshevism explicitly denies all superior norms that would stand above its own goals, so that the end, in the grimmest sense of the phrase and without exception, justifies the means.

This imposes on us the heavy duty of drawing the logical, negative conclusion from the immanent rule of reciprocal humanity— that is, resolutely to oppose such ideological activism of principled inhumanity, to fight it mercilessly as long as it exists. There can be no peaceful coexistence between humanity and inhumanity. Against superstratifying inhumanity bent on further superstratification there is not only a right but a duty of resistance, a duty incumbent on every individual without exception. The youthful Antoine de Saint-Just (1767-1794) was right when in 1792 he proclaimed that "All men have the secret task of stamping out domination in all countries."

We must be aware how difficult it is to maintain such an attitude, how much it runs counter to our own human nature. This is precisely why we must lend every effort to overcome the situation that forces this attitude on us. Nor must we allow the other side to appeal to our own feelings of humanity and use them as a fifth column.

The same unnatural world situation also imposes on us a duty to defend and arm ourselves. War is inhuman, immoral, and ultimately senseless; pacifism is an indisputable demand of humanity. From this follows the human duty to work for the creation of a world situation that precludes the possibility of war. But as long as one part of mankind is highly armed, ready to commmit any act of inhumanity in its thirst for superstratification, and threatens the freedom of the rest of mankind, it is our foremost duty to resist this threat and to arm our selves at least to an equal level.

There is no doubt that in an atomic Third World War there will be no victors but only vanquished. It is, of course, by no means certain whether this insight will be sufficient to restrain all parties from using atomic weapons—but just as long as this assumption does hold, the outcome of wars will be decided by superiority in conventional weapons. And since the West demonstrated its reluctance to use atomic weapons in a local war such as that in Korea, there is the danger that an artfully and unscrupulously designed series of such small wars would be sufficient for world conquest.

As Franz Böhm has said, "The most serious danger that confronts us today is not . . . the atom bomb but . . . the totalitarian state which . . . makes us tremble at the danger of the atom bomb."[4] Between 1945 and 1949, when the United States alone had nuclear bombs, no one felt threatened. But what would have happened if instead the Russians for years had had a nuclear monopoly? Does anyone seriously believe that they would have shown equal restraint?

The demand for parity between the West as a whole and the Bolsheviks in both nuclear and conventional weapons is a demand imposed by the extreme possibilities of the situation in order, precisely, to prevent such extreme possibilities. Meanwhile and short of this extreme, everything depends on how successfully the West can combat the monopoly (or Russian-Chinese duopoly) of a totalitarian leadership whose rule is independent of any domestic public opinion. Why have we, time and time again, failed to exploit the weak points of the antagonists, left them time to recover from their failures, or matched their mistakes with mistakes of our own? The answer is that in countering the strategy of the other side we have pursued mere tactics. Bolshevism never loses sight of the grand goal of world dominion and subordinates, as best it can, all other measures to this one goal. In contrast, the governments of the free world pursue a large number of partial goals that are by no means always being subordinated to the demands of the global situation. We have not yet learned to ask in judging any particular policy whether it strengthens or weakens the position of the free world vis-à-vis bolshevism.

Foremost among the historic causes that brought humanity to the present global crisis is colonial imperialism, and if we are to overcome the crisis we must put an end to it at once. The most difficult remnant of colonialism, of course, is the situation in South Africa, where the white settlers, resident for many generations, are imbued with a Calvinist sense of mission in their role of superstratifiers.

But beyond the end of colonialism there is a fundamental question from the sphere of political science, a discipline which, looking back on a history in the West of 2,500 years, these days seems to be in the midst of a resurgence. The question is what form of government we can offer to the liberated colonial peoples as an alternative to the imposing model of Bolshevik dictatorship? Surely not the Anglo-Saxon model of parliamentarism, which outside the English-speaking countries of its origin has never and nowhere functioned adequately even in Europe—not in France and not in Italy—and at present in the Federal Republic of Germany is working only on the basis of a special and exceptional configuration. Would any political scientist seriously maintain that this highly delicate and complex form of government would be appropriate for newly liberated colonial peoples? But if not this model, what remains for them to choose but the overly simple countermodel of Bolshevik dictatorship, which is so attractive to would-be dictators? Would it not be an urgent task for our political science to cooperate with intellectuals of those people themselves to elaborate an appropriate model that would combine the dictatorial freedom of action that in their situation is indispensable with a secure anchoring in a minimum of democratic freedom? And should they succeed in such a task would not we ourselves be able to benefit from this lesson?

Understandably, the liberated colonial peoples have no passionate desire to attain our cultural and industrial level as quickly as possible. And since they would need both guidance, help, and investment capital, Point IV of Truman's program—making available what they needed in order to prevent them from turning to the Russians—was an obvious and persuasive idea. However, the difficult problem confronting these people is how to leap over centuries in a few years, without shattering all their social, ideological, and moral integration and thus making themselves vulnerable to primitive Bolshevik salvation doctrines and hate feelings. This question, which for each of these peoples poses itself in different form, has barely been formulated, let alone answered. Naïve optimism and premature zealousness can both cause irreparable harm; yet time is of the essence.

A rapid liquidation of the remnants of Western colonialism would not only deprive the Bolsheviks of one of their most convenient and dangerous propaganda talking points, but conversely provide an opportunity for exposing the highly virulent and still ascendant Bolshevik version of colonial imperialism, which was so barefacedly demonstrated in all its brutality in Hungary in 1956.

But the final liquidation of the most obvious remnants of Western superstratification abroad is not by any means sufficient. Our own governments and societies in the West all originated in superstratification, and their domestic social and economic structure has by no means been cleansed of the effects of this original sin of human history. The relapse which was brought about by the Industrial Revolution, to be sure, is being overcome in the social sphere. But in our economies we are still very far from having attained true equality of opportunity. To attain it will require long and arduous efforts, including extensive theoretical research. It seems all the more essential to adopt such measures as are already feasible—the easiest of these being the establishment of equal educational opportunity—that is, the abolition of all educational privilege based on wealth. Faced with a virulent threat of renewed superstratification we must at least recognize and eliminate the remnants of superstratification in our own civilization.

The economy of the free world enjoys the enormous advantage of a market economy and its competitive performance. Its superior productivity by comparison with any totalitarian planned economy is so obvious in practice and can be so convincingly demonstrated in theory that little more need be said on the subject. Equally beyond question is the inevitable relationship that exists between command economy and totalitarian dictatorship on the one hand, and market economy and democratic freedom on the other. It is a rare good fortune for humanity that the only form of economy which is compatible with democratic freedom in the social and political spheres also has proved itself by far the most productive of all known forms of economic order—and it behoves us to be more conscious and to prove ourselves more worthy of that good fortune. Even economic crises, which once were considered an inherent and fatal flaw of market economies, have been tackled successfully in the economies of the West, and it would seem that the ideal of avoiding economic crises while maintaining full employment is attainable both in theory and practice.

A prime objective of social and economic policy both in the West and in the developing countries must be the maintenance and further development, in viable competitive conditions, of a healthy farming economy based on one-family enterprises. Bolshevism consciously and with malice aforethought works to uproot the peasant family economy, which indeed is one of the strongest bulwarks against totalitarianism. The countries of the free world, in contrast, pursue an unhealthy and corrupt agrarian policy which, in the alleged interest of the farmers, undermines the family character, independence, and self-reliance of the farm enterprise instead of employing the many available technical means to enable the farmers to resort to self-help.[5]

The vulnerability of the capitalist market economy to the crises of the business cycle and its poor performance in respect to social justice are ultimately attributable to the palaeo-liberal principle of *laissez-faire*; both are now more or less being overcome in the civilized countries of the West. These advances, however, are generally made in the form of compromises with socialism or as discrete interventions in specific situations—the result being generally an unplanned hybrid economy. Only the Federal Republic of Germany has a uniform and consistent economic policy that can be held up against the communist program of economic planning. This policy, known as *Soziale Marktwirtschaft*, social market economy, has only been applied since 1948 and has had to struggle against powerful economic interest groups; yet it has already registered spectacular successes.[6]

But the crucial criteria in economic policy are not, as was often assumed in the nineteenth century, mere measurable quantities. Man lives not by bread alone; quality is above quantity. This implies the demand for what I have called *Vitalpolitik*[7]—a policy for enhancing the quality of life. *Vitalpolitik* consciously considers all aspects on which the human sense of self, on which human contentment and happiness in fact depend; its aim is to create a life worth living and worth fighting for. One of its major ingredients is a deliberate policy of town and country planning.

Further along the way we encounter the difficult problem of asceticism in those spheres of social life whose origins in superstratification were traced earlier in this work. Protestant populations in particular are susceptible to an attitude of "innerworldly asceticism" that is an indirect legacy of the Reformation. People who have long been accustomed to forego the simple, natural enjoyments of life have a hard time rediscovering them and accepting them with gratitude. It is not enough to dismantle the unjustified traditional prohibitions and taboos: the real inhibitions are more deep-seated. When the German youth movement took up the struggle against the sexual prudishness of the late nineteenth century, its members expected that from the broken bars of the cage there would ascend a mighty eagle; in reality what often came out was merely a plucked chicken. New freedoms require firm grounding in new social ties. Herein lie difficult and vitally important problems toward the solution of which the new anthropology has already made significant contributions.

One often hears these days that a future elite must demand of its members a measure of asceticism. It is obvious that any above-average achievement in one sphere demands a corresponding readiness for sacrifice in other spheres. But as any sportsman knows, such forms of abstinence have nothing to do with asceticism based on taboos or inhibitions. Rather, the aim should be an attitude of simple enjoyment and the discovery, by trial and error, of the minimum effort that makes possible a rich, full, and productive life.

The need for individuals and families to shape their own lives has as its social converse the rejection of all ostentation, conspicuous consumption, and anxious comparison with the living standards of others—social vices that in Germany especially seem to have become nothing short of endemic. Naïve enjoyment concentrates on a goal close at hand; social competition by contrast is a race without a goal, one that leaves no time or strength to enjoy what one already has attained—too often it degenerates into self-narcotization, with the inevitable hazards to health which such a senseless way of life brings with it. The idolization of the material living standard, so often lamented, must be fought, however, by example rather than preachment; it is, after all, nothing but a bit of superstratification mentality that has slid down the social scale. What we need to do is to find a sensible middle way between austerity and instalment plan buying. The result will be a thoroughgoing change in our attitude and our entire style of life.

We have seen that massification, isolation, and underintegration constitute the most difficult and most widespread social-pathological sequels of superstratification, and that totalitarianism opposes these with its own violent overintegration. An urgent task, therefore, is to discover the healthy optimum of social integration. Unfortunately, there is no magic recipe: this illness, like others, has no panacea. We must learn to judge all public policies on their integrative and disintegrative effects, and miss no opportunity to provide for a salutary increase in integration. This is an important area of research for political science and the new anthropology.

What has just been outlined is a program of change that will take much time to plan and yet more time to take effect; it might therefore be objected that we do not have much time, that something must be done at once. There are two answers to this objection. First, what needs to be done cannot be done quickly, just as a doctor cannot as a rule satisfy his patient's desire for an instant cure. But if it is objected further that the situation is then hopeless, because history will scarcely grant us the time needed for the cure of our disease, then we can find consolation in a second answer. For if the task of restoring health herein demanded could be tackled in earnest, along the whole front; if the aims that everyone vaguely senses, could be clearly formulated; and if everyone could see that step by step we are moving toward these aims—then indeed we would be over the hump and our cause would already be victorious.

The German Federal Republic, with its frontier on the amputated Soviet occupation zone of Germany and its bridgehead in Berlin, finds itself on the easternmost front of the free world. And this frontier between West and East that runs athwart Germany is also the one place where the iron curtain can least be made airtight. Hence the comparison of conditions on either side readily suggests itself: after all, there are Germans in both places whose differences in condition and quality of life can derive only from the difference in their political situations and their political systems. And this very comparison is our most potent weapon in the cold war.

We are in the midst of the great decisive struggle between the free and the totalitarian halves of the world. Bolshevism, there is no doubt, is after our freedom and our very lives, and considers itself entitled—indeed, obliged and called upon—to establish world domination. The struggle thus is one of life and death in which there can be in the long run no coexistence.

For the time being this struggle is being fought in the form of a cold war, and we must do all in our power to bring about an outcome in our favor without letting it convert into a hot war. Essentially so far we have waged this cold war only defensively. Instead we must aim to win, and engage our full strength to do so. It is entirely possible that we will win peacefully—indeed, our superiority in the cold war contest is far greater than it would be in a hot war; but we must bring that superiority fully into play.

The very situation of the world confronts us inescapably with radical decisions. The path instinctively chosen by the Middle Ages of attenuating the evils of superstratification and thus making them tolerable is no longer open to us; it is too far from the road of ever increasing consciousness that humanity has pursued since.

Whereas nothing more than a considerable dampening of the pattern of domination created by superstratification has been attained in past times, the present situation forces us—on pain of death through the threat of Bolshevik countersuperstratification—to seek a radical cure, which though always in our best interests, did not hitherto command a sufficient endogenous motive. If all goes well, necessity will have forced us into our salvation. What is thus needed is not a palliative but surgery. Just as with a cancer operation all depends on whehter intellectually and politically we cut deeply enough. Before we do so we must ever anew examine our consciences and control our impulses as individuals to see that we are inwardly free of any remnant of lust for power, of *cupido dominandi*, in our professional and family life, even in our attitude to our own person. The front of the cold war against superstratification runs invisibly through every factory and office, every family, and every individual. This cold war must be conducted both within and without. The more honestly we conduct it within, the better can be our conscience in conducting it outwardly in the completion with bolshevism in creating a superior human life situation.

Once we attain this aim of victory in the cold war, there will be no possibility of its turning into a hot war. Today we are all inwardly consumed by fear of a third world war, all anxiously ask whether we are not totally impotent and helpless in the face of the terrible threat of this calamity. We are not. Each of us, knowingly or not, day in and day out, stands at the very frontline of the cold war, and any square foot of territory won by any individual in this struggle gets us closer to victory. But once the victory is won, once it is established beyond doubt that the human life situation on our side is superior to that on the other side, this very fact will have a relentlessly corrosive effect on the totalitarian structure of domination and on the enforced certitude of belief of its subjects. And at that point the other side will no longer be able to wage the cold war. Here then is the way in which each of us can for his part continually work to prevent a third world war and to bring about the peaceful victory of freedom.

The saying of Ecclesiastes that "there is nothing new under the sun" is usually invoked by those who, in the last analysis, would shirk their responsiblity and lapse into defeatism and discouragement. For better or worse there *are* new things under the sun. Today, for the first time since the beginning of human history, all of humanity constitutes a single entity—albeit rent in two. Today for the first time we inhabit One World. At no time since the existence of the earth has any of the creatures upon it unleashed forces of superplanetary magnitude. Today and never before the fate of all human beings without exception hangs in the balance. No generation before ours carried the responsibility for the entire future of humanity on its shoulders—indeed the responsibility for whether there *would* be a future of humanity.

An unbiased observer would not get the impression that the present generation is equal to such a responsibility. And after all we did not, heaven knows, seek out such responsibility—anything but that! But now, quite against our wish and desire, there it is on our shoulders, and we have no choice but either to stand up under it—or else to fail, with all the unthinkable consequences that would imply.

All religious dogma, all notions of theology, all magic beliefs aside, there is the sober, empirically demonstrable fact that humanity today finds itself in a unique situation, unprecedented and impossible of repetition—an eschatological situation in the full apocalyptic sense of the word.

Without superstratification and its historic consequences throughout less than ten thousand years there would not have been the remotest chance of the technical and other preconditions for One World coming together. If we should succeed to cleanse this One World of the poison of superstratification, then the blessing of the sin would be freed from its curse. The decision facing us is whether the superstratification cycle of world history will close for evil or for good.

If our Free World should after all be granted its victory—however hard and scant a victory it might be—then the magnitude of the prize will be commensurate with the enormous toils of the preceding struggle and with the catastrophe threatened in the event of defeat. The inevitable result would be that unity of all mankind in freedom and peace longed for by the prophets and seers of all ages. Such a state will come about very soberly and without pathos as an automatic result of the disappearance of totalitarianism. All of us, though sorely exhausted, will be cheerfully and in common tackling a plethora of new tasks. But these tasks will be solvable—solvable after the fashion given to us humans, where each solution begets ever new problems and tasks.

Such a self-realization of the One World—no longer split in two—will have as one consequence among many others that there will be not longer any foreign, but only domestic, policy. This will put an end to the primacy of foreign policy, which ever and again has disrupted domestic politics. Above all, it will thereby remove that basic defect of any liberal democracy of being made at bottom for domestic policy alone and thus being structurally as unsuited as can be to foreign policy—the very feature that constituted democracy's chief handicap in its competition with totalitarianism.

Free mankind will thus be able to renounce those military and dictatorial necessities that today are forced on it by the opposing threat of totalitarian dictatorship and which stand in basic contrast to its structure and ethos. Man's federative tendency will have the widest possible room for development; no authentic special structure, no matter how small, will have to live in fear because of its lack of physical power. Expenditures for armament, which hitherto have consumed nearly half of the social product of all economies, can be rechanneled into peaceful purposes—an instant and effortless doubling of our national incomes. All forces hitherto directed against each other could be directed to fruitful cooperation. This beautiful earth could be made into a garden for all mankind—just as soon as we stop making it a hell for each other, wilfully, for no earthly reason, and against all sense. Such an estimate reflects an utterly sober and realistic form of utopianism.

Such a time is, to be sure, still in the remote future, for we are still in the agony of a divided world. All the more important that in the decisive struggle that has been forced upon us we derive our courage not just from the unimaginable terrors of defeat but from the inspiring prospect of the prize for our perseverance. All is at stake. The decision rests on each of us.

NOTES

ALEXANDER RÜSTOW (1885-1963): A BIOGRAPHICAL SKETCH

1. "Die geistesgeschichtlich-soziologischen Ursachen des Verfalls der abendländischen Baukunst im 19. Jahrhundert," *Archiv für Philosophie* 2 (Istanbul, 1947):123-190; "Lutherana Tragoedia Artis," *Schweizer Monatshefte* vol. 39, no. 9 (1959), pp. 891-906.

2. On Radek's activity see Otto-Ernst Schüddekopf, "Karl Radek in Berlin," *Archiv für Sozialgeschichte* 2 (1966):87-166. Another of Rüstow's favorite anecdotes was about the mutinous marine battalion occupying the Berlin imperial palace in the winter of 1918-1919—the soldiers carefully protecting the windowsills with newspaper before emplacing their machine guns. "What kind of a revolution," he would cry out indignantly, "do you suppose *that* was?"

3. Gerhard Colm taught at the University of Kiel and after 1933 briefly at the New School for Social Research in New York; he then served in a variety of government posts in Washington, including the Bureau of the Budget and the Council of Economic Advisers. Adolf Löwe (Adolph Lowe) taught at the University of Frankfurt am Main, at Manchester, and, from 1940 until his retirement, at the New School. Eduard Heimann also spent most of his exile at the New School, but on his retirement returned briefly to teach at the University of Hamburg.

4. Arthur Rosenberg was a classical philologist at Berlin, radical politician, and later contemporary political historian of socialism. In his *Entstehung der Deutschen Republik* (Frankfurt, 1930; *Imperial Germany: The Birth of the German Republic*, trans. F. P. Morrow, Boston, 1964), he castigates the German Social Democratic party of the pre-1914 period for relying on the strong arm of the Prussian police state to protect it from any untoward consequences of its own revolutionary rhetoric. Herbert Tingsten was a close adviser to Sweden's Social Democratic premier, Per Albin Hanson, until about the time of publication of his major work, *Den svenska socialdemokratiens idéutveckling* (Stockholm, 1941); he subsequently became editor of Sweden's leading liberal daily, *Dagens Nyheter*. He once complained sarcastically that the Nationalization Commission (*socialiseringsnämnd*), which the first Social Democratic government had appointed as early as 1920, over the next decade became something of an institution for the protection of the ineffable mysteries of nationalization. Rüstow admired Rosenberg's work; I suspect that, without knowing him, he shared many of Tingsten's attitudes.

Years later, Rüstow was to describe his friend Alfred Weber's opposite evolution, culminating in membership, late in life, in the Social Democratic party, as follows: "With the general attitudes and tendency of 'academic socialism' (*Kathedersozialismus*) Alfred Weber had always identified from his earliest publications. . . . But from that to active membership in the SPD was a long road, along which many reservations and inhibitions had to be overcome. They were overcome not slowly, step by step, but through a bold leap—one is tempted to say through a headlong jump—in a decision to which he felt morally committed, and on the basis of an attitude that William James once described as the 'will to believe.' " (See the obituary entitled "Alfred Weber," *Zeitschrift für Politik* 5 [1949]:4.) Rüstow never took out membership in any party, but when he spoke of bold leaps, moral commitments, and a will to believe he was not speaking of experiences alien to himself.

5. See particularly his monograph *Schutzzoll oder Freihandel?* (Frankfurt, 1925), and his article (going back to a paper presented at a professional meeting) "Freie Wirtschaft—Starker Staat: Die staatspolitischen Voraussetzungen des wirtschaftspolitischen Liberalismus," *Verein für Sozialpolitik* 187 (1932):62-69.

6. For an estimate of the VDMA's activities, in the context of the associational politics of the Weimar Republic, as they developed under the leadership of Karl Lange (the director) and Rüstow (as head of the research division), see Gerald D. Feldman and Ulrich Nocken, "Trade Associations and Economic Power: Interest Group Development in the German Iron and Steel and Machine Building Industries, 1900-1933," *Business History Review* vol. 49, no. 4 (Cambridge, Mass., winter, 1975), pp. 413-445, esp. pp. 436-442. "Well-reasoned economic arguments, supported by the appropriate statistical analysis and presented in easy-to-understand graphical form, became a major tactical tool of the VDMA in its attempt to counterbalance the good political and bureaucratic connections and prestige of the iron and steel industry" (pp. 436f). "The VDMA, through Rüstow, was able to establish a good working relationship with the three most important liberal, bourgeois papers. . . ." (p. 437). "In the early 1930s, the VDMA tried to expand its political influence by . . . lobbying for liberal economic and political policies and especially directing its attacks against the various movements favoring autarky" (p. 440). "In effect, the VDMA had developed into what Galambos has called a policy-shaping association . . . 'distinguished by outstanding leaders, a well-defined and carefully articulated ideology, and formidable cooperative programs. It was a semi-autonomous economic institution with an identity clearly distinguished from its members' " (p. 441). In contrast, the authors note in conclusion, "it was only in 1933 that the machine-building industry in the United States was able to form a unified association of its many branches and could, therefore, be compared to the VDMA" (p. 442).

7. See pt. 3, chap. 2, sec. 12(ii)c and n. 132 thereto.

8. "General Sociological Causes of the Economic Disintegration and Possibilities of Reconstruction," appendix to Wilhelm Röpke, *International Economic Disintegration* (London, 1942), pp. 267-283. "Zu den Grundlagen der Wirtschaftswissenschaft," *Revue de la Faculté des Sciences Economiques de l'Université d' Istanbul* 2 (1941):105-154; "Die Konfession in der Wirtschaftsgeschichte," ibid. 3 (1942):362-389.

9. *Das Versagen des Wirtschaftsliberalismus als religionsgeschichtliches Problem*, Istanbuler Schriften no. 12 (Istanbul, 1945; 2d ed., Bonn-Bad Godesberg, 1960).

10. "Zur soziologischen Ortsbestimmung des Krieges," *Die Friedenswarte* 39 (1939):81-94; "Die . . . Ursachen des Verfalls der . . . Baukunst . . . ," op. cit. (n. 1); "Der moderne Pflicht- und Arbeitsmensch," *Revue de la Faculté des Sciences Economiques de l'Université d' Istanbul* 5 (1944):107-146; "Vereinzelung: Tendenzen und Reflexe," ibid. 8 (1946-1947):1-39, reprinted in revised form in *Gegenwartsprobleme der Soziologie: Alfred Vierkandt zum 80. Geburtstag* (Potsdam, 1949), pp. 45-48. When a mutual friend sent a copy of this last to Thomas Mann, Mann responded with a letter of critical appreciation, which said, among other things: ". . . I have the distinct feeling that it would have been very good if I had read this essay while I was writing *Doktor Faustus*. But we have in different ways and different forms what at bottom are the same ideas—which is not after all to be called 'individual isolation' (*Vereinzelung*)." See the German edition of this work, 3:581.

11. Several earlier drafts of the *Ortsbestimmung*, together with many boxes of correspondence, extensive especially for the Istanbul years, are deposited in the West German Federal Archives in Koblenz.

12. Only three days before his death, in his last lucid conversation with me from his hospital bed, he asked himself in some anguish whether German history had taken its decisive wrong turn in 1525, with Luther's vicious condemnation of the peasant uprising, as he had long believed, or rather much earlier during the "investiture conflict" between Emperor Henry IV (1056-1106) and the papacy.

13. Rüstow's lecture "Diktatur innerhalb der Grenzen der Demokratie," delivered at the Deutsche Hochschule für Politik in 1929, and the following discussion in which Theodor Heuss and others took part, was printed with a brief commentary by W. Besson, "Zur Frage der Staatsführung in der Weimarer Republik," *Vierteljahrshefte für Zeitgeschichte* (January, 1959):85-111.

14. *Wirtschaft und Kultursystem*, ed. Gottfried Eisermann (Erlenbach-Zurich, 1955).

15. "Worin bestand die geschichtliche Leistung des Freiherrn vom Stein?" reprinted in *Universitas: Zeitschrift für Wissenschaft, Kunst und Literatur* 17 (1962):489-502. Although Rüstow had a lifelong aversion, even loathing, for the representative Prussian figures, from Frederick the Great through Bismarck to the last Hohenzollern emperor, he much admired men

like Stein and Clausewitz—not least for their courage in choosing exile, and even service for an "enemy" government, when political conditions at home no longer left them "any air to breathe."

16. "Lutherana Tragoedia Artis"; "Von Abraham bis Paulus: Alt- und Neutestamentliches in profangeschichtlicher Sicht," *Schweizer Monatshefte* (January, 1963):1-21; this is a prepublication of a passage added to the second edition of volume 2 of *Ortsbestimmung*; see pt. 2, sec. 18.

17. *"Entos humōn estin*: Zur Deutung von Lukas 17:20-21," *Zeitschrift für die neutestamentliche Wissenschaft* 51 (1960):197-224, where the quotation is from p. 208. Luther's translation, like the later King James version, has Jesus saying to the disciples that the kingdom of heaven is "inside within you" (*inwendig in euch*); Rüstow proposes that it should be *"among* you"—a communal as against individualist interpretation of the Christian promise of salvation, which he buttresses with a complete catalog of instances in classical and post-classical Greek where *entos* means "among" and not "within"—and, in commenting on the preceding similes, by a technical discussion of the distinction between lightning bolts and sheet lightning. For a complete list of Rüstow's published writings, see Alexander Rüstow, *Rede und Antwort* (Ludwigsburg, 1960), pp. 350-364.

Author's Foreword (1949)

1. Thus I once wrote in justifying a colleague who found himself in a comparable situation; see my essay "Die Konfession in der Wirtschaftsgeschichte," *Revue de la Faculté des Sciences Economiques de l'Université d'Istanbul*, vol. 3, nos. 3-4 (1942), p. 383.

2. Alfred Weber, *Kulturgeschichte als Kultursoziologie* (Leiden, 1935), 2d rev. ed., 1950.

3. Georg Wilhelm Friedrich Hegel, letter to Niethammer, 26 October 1808.

4. Johann Wolfgang von Goethe, "Tages- und Jahreshefte zum Jahre 1811," *Werke* (Propyläen ed.), 38:382.

5. 2 Cor. 3:3 and Rom. 2:14-15.

6. Johannes Kühn, *Die Wahrheit der Geschichte und die Gestalt der wahren Geschichte* (Oberursel, 1947), pp. 68f; the first sentence quotes Johann Georg Hamann.

7. "Eireusai ta t'eonta ta t'essomena prot'eonta," "telling of things that are and that shall be and that were aforetime." Hesiod, *Theogony*, v. 38 (trans. H. G. Evelyn-White, Loeb Classical Library, London, 1914, p. 81).

Introduction

1. "Wer nicht von dreitausend Jahren/ Sich weiss Rechenschaft zu geben,/ Bleib' im Dunkeln unerfahren,/ Mag von Tag zu Tage leben." Goethe, *West-Östlicher Divan*, "Buch des Unmuts," 13:13-16.

2. Goethe, *Zur Farbenlehre*, sec. "Baco von Verulam," Propyläen ed., 22:140; and letter to Georg Sartorius, 4 February 1811, ibid. 23:67.

3. Marie-Jean-Antoine-Nicholas de Caritat, Marquis de Condorcet (1743-1794), *Esquisse d'un tableau historique des progrès de l'esprit humain* (1794; Paris, 1880), 1:54.

4. Ludwig Gumplowicz, *Der Rassenkampf*, 3d ed. (Innsbruck, 1928); and the following writings of Franz Oppenheimer: *System der Soziologie* (vol. 2, *Der Staat*, Jena, 1926; vol. 4, *Abriss einer Sozial- und Wirtschaftsgeschichte Europas*, pts. 1-2, Jena, 1929-1933), and the article "Machtverhältnisse," in *Handwörterbuch der Soziologie* (Stuttgart, 1931), pp. 338-348.

5. Richard Thurnwald, *Lehrbuch der Völkerkunde*, ed. Preuss (Stuttgart, 1937), pp. 323 and 268.

6. Fritz Kern, *Die Anfänge der Weltgeschichte* (Leipzig, 1933), pp. 119, 124, 125.

7. Karl Mannheim, "Rational and Irrational Elements in Contemporary Society," *Hobhouse Lectures*, no. 4 (London, 1934), pp. 24f.

PART 1, CHAPTER 1: THE RISE OF HIGH CULTURES

1. Adolphe Coste, *Principes d'une sociologie objective* (Paris, 1889), pp. 154-156.

2. Alfred Weber, *Das Tragische und die Geschichte* (Hamburg, 1943), pp. 99f.

3. H. J. Nieboer, "Slavery as an Industrial System," *Ethnological Researches* (The Hague, 1910), 2:438.

4. Cited in Albrecht Goetze, "Kleinasien," *Kulturgeschichte des alten Orients: Handbuch der Altertumswissenschaft* (Munich, 1933), p. 187.

5. Wilhelm Schmidt, *Rassen und Völker* (Lucerne, 1946), 1:326, n. 183. Schmidt has the merit of having repeatedly stressed this extraordinarily important point of view.

6. Egon Freiherr von Eickstedt, *Rassenkunde und Rassengeschichte der Menschheit* (Stuttgart, 1934), p. 328.

7. Alfred Weber, "Kultursoziologie," *Handwörterbuch der Soziologie*, ed. Alfred Vierkandt (Stuttgart, 1931), pp. 287f.

8. Schmidt, *Rassen und Völker*, 2:12.

9. In the words of Diodorus (bk. 19, sec. 94.3), a Sicilian historian of the first century B.C. who in this instance follows the report of Jerome of Cardia, leading chronicler of the half century after the death of Alexander the Great.

PART 1, CHAPTER 2: STRUCTURAL ELEMENTS OF
HIGH CULTURES AS CONDITIONED BY
SUPERSTRATIFICATION AND FEUDALISM

1. Fritz Kern, *Die Anfänge der Weltgeschichte* (Leipzig, 1933), pp. 114f.

2. Jacob Burckhardt, *Weltgeschichtliche Betrachtungen* (1868-1871;

Force and Freedom, trans. James Hastings Nichols, New York, 1943, pp. 111, 112).

3. Friedrich Nietzsche, fragment no. 198, written 1870-1871 (Musarion ed. 3:385).

4. Nietzsche, *Zur Genealogie der Moral* (1887), ibid., 15:385; *Works*, trans. Horace B. Samuel, New York, 1964, pp. 102ff. Nietzsche, it will be recalled, accepted a post at the University of Basel in 1869 and in the winter of 1870-1871 enthusiastically attended Burckhardt's lecture series, which later was published as *Weltgeschichtliche Betrachtungen*.

5. Sigmund Freud, *Die Zukunft einer Illusion*, in *Gesammelte Schriften* (12 vols., Vienna, 1924-34), 11:413.

6. Aristotle, *Politics*, bk. 6, sec. 1.4, 1318b 4-5.

7. Adam Smith, *An Inquiry into the Nature and Causes of the Wealth of Nations* (1776), bk. 1, chap. 2, par. 2 (Cannan ed. 1:16).

8. Emile Durkheim, *Le Suicide: Etude de sociologie* (Paris, 1897).

9. Fritz Künkel, *Angewandte Characterkunde*, 6 vols. (Leipzig, 1935-1942).

10. Cf. Alexander Rüstow, "Vereinzelung (Tendenzen und Reflexe)," *Gegenwartsprobleme der Soziologie: Alfred Vierkandt zum 80. Geburtstage* (Potsdam, 1949), pp. 45-78; an earlier version appeared in Turkey in 1946-1947.

11. Herbert Spencer, *Principles of Sociology* (London, 1879-1896), 2:302.

12. Rousseau, *Contrat social*, bk. 1, chap. 2.

13. Johann Gottlieb Fichte, *Werke* (1845), 6:309.

14. Wilhelm Gerloff, in his *Die öffentliche Finanzwirtschaft* (Frankfurt, 1942), p. 121, speaks of the "circulation of bandits."

15. Wilhelm Weber, "Der alte Orient," in *Der Orient und Wir* (Berlin, 1935), pp. 24f.

16. The title of an essay by William James.

17. Adolf Erman, *Die Religion der alten Ägypter* (Berlin, 1934), p. 129.

18. Hanns-Joachim Rüstow, "Unsere Lage," unpublished lecture (Göttingen, 1946).

19. S. R. Steinmetz, "Das Verhältnis zwischen Eltern und Kindern bei den Naturvölkern," originally published in 1899, in his *Gesammelte kleinere Schriften zur Ethnologie und Soziologie* (Groningen, 1930), 2:28f.

20. Sigmund Freud, "Über die allgemeine Erniedrigung des Liebeslebens" (1912) in his *Gesammelte Schriften*, 5:198-211.

21. Ernst von Aster, *Die Psychoanalyse* (Berlin, 1930), pp. 239f.

22. Fritz Kern, "Natur- und Gewissensgott," *Festschrift für Walter Goetz* (1927), p. 416.

23. Walter Gottschalk, *Das Gelübde nach alter arabischer Auffassung*, dissertation (Berlin, 1919), p. 64.

24. Isa. 14:2; 49:23; 54:3; 63:1-6. The first passage belongs to the period 746-701 B.C., the second and third to the period 550 to 538 B.C., the fourth to that of 538-510 B.C. or possibly earlier.

25. John 10:16.

26. Friedrich Schiller, "Unterschied der Stände."

27. Plato, *Republic*, 459a-d.

28. Käthe Bauer-Mengelberg, "Der Bauer," *Kölner Vierteljahrshefte für Soziologie* 11 (1932-1933):256, citing Adolf Münzinger, *Der Arbeitsertrag der bäuerlichen Familienwirtschaft* (Berlin, 1929).

29. Egon Freiherr von Eickstedt, *Rassenkunde und Rassengeschichte der Menschheit* (Stuttgart, 1934); a second edition, planned in two volumes, began with vol. 1 (Stuttgart, 1937), but was discontinued because the author was not inclined to compromise with the racial doctrines then current in Germany. (*Editor's note*.)

30. Honoré-Gabriel Riquetti, comte de Mirabeau, cited by Wilhelm Röpke, *Die Lehre von der Wirtschaft*, 5th ed. (Zurich, 1949), p. 41.

31. See Walter Eucken, *Die Grundlagen der Nationalökonomie* (Jena, 1940); 6th ed. (Godesberg, 1949); and my detailed appraisal, "Zu den Grundlagen der Wirtschaftswissenschaft," *Revue de la Faculté des Sciences Economiques de l'Université d'Istanbul*, vol. 2, no. 2 (1941), pp. 105-154.

32. Hyacinthe Hecquard, *Voyage sur la côte et dans l'intérieur de l'Afrique occidentale* (Paris, 1853), p. 313, as cited by Nieboer, loc. cit. (n. 3), p. 422.

33. Fritz Rörig, "Die europäische Stadt," *Propyläen-Weltgeschichte* (Berlin, 1932), 4:352.

34. Herodotus, *The History of Herodotus*, trans. George Rawlinson, 2 vols. (London, 1910), 2:2; Aristotle, *The Politics of Aristotle*, trans. Ernest Barker (Oxford, 1946), bk. 1, sec. 8, p. 20.

35. Wilhelm Schmidt, *Gesellschaft und Wirtschaft der Völker* (Regensburg, 1924), p. 346.

36. Diehl, *Anthologia Lyrica Graeca*, 2:128.

37. Cicero, *De re publica* 3.9.15 (trans. Clinton Walker Keyes, London, 1928, p. 197).

38. Tacitus, *Germania* 14.4 (*Works of Tacitus*, revised Oxford translation, London, 1901, 14:305).

39. See pp. 151-154 of my essay cited in n. 31 above.

40. Aeschines, bk. 3, 132.

41. Vergil, *Aeneid*, bk. 1, v. 278.

42. See Heinrich Cunow, "Zur Zusammenbruchstheorie," *Neue Zeit*, vol. 17, no. 1 (1898), pp. 424-430; Rosa Luxemburg, *Die Akkumulation des Kapitals: Ein Beitrag zur ökonomischen Erklärung des Imperialismus* (Berlin, 1913), 2d ed., 1923; Fritz Sternberg, *Der Imperialismus* (Berlin, 1926). The basic idea of this theory had already been expressed by Marx in the *Communist Manifesto*: "The need for ever-wider markets for its products drives the bourgeoisie to the far ends of the globe. . . . How does the bourgeoisie overcome these crises? Through the conquest of new markets" (pars. 19 and 27).

43. Rudolf Hilferding, *Das Finanzkapital* (Vienna, 1910), 2d ed. 1923.

44. Joseph Schumpeter, "Zur Soziologie der Imperialismen," *Archiv für Sozialwissenschaft und Sozialpolitik* 46 (1918-1919):1-39, 275-310.

PART 1, CHAPTER 3: TRANSFEUDAL MOTIVE FORCES OF HIGH CULTURES

1. Justinus Kerner (1786-1821), "Der reichste Fürst."

2. Goethe, *Faust* 2.10.252f (*Faust*, trans. Bayard Taylor, 2 vols., New York, 1912, 2:236).

3. Aristotle, *Athen. Pol.* 3.1 and 3.6.

4. Hesiod, *Erga* 313.

5. *Théâtre italien* (1685) 1:271.

6. Theognis, 1117f.

7. Joseph-Marie-Anne Gros de Besplas, *Les Causes du bonheur public* (1744), 2:74 and 411, as cited in Bernhard Groethuysen, *Die Entstehung der bürgerlichen Welt- und Lebensanschauung in Frankreich* (Halle, 1930), 2:114.

8. Werner Sombart, *Der moderne Kapitalismus*, 2d ed. 1928, 2:507.

9. Hesiod, vv. 3-8.

10. Helmut Berve, "Ionien und die griechische Geschichte," *Neue Jahrbücher für Wissenschaft und Jugendbildung* 3 (1927):513-23; the quoted passage is on p. 522.

11. Cf. Alexander Rüstow, "Worin bestand die geschichtliche Leistung des Freiherrn vom Stein?" *Universitas* 17 (1962):489-502. (*Editor's note.*)

12. Cited by Herman Kees, *Ägypten* (Munich, 1933), p. 193.

13. Alexander Rüstow, "Der moderne Pflicht- und Arbeitsmensch, Herkunft und Zukunft," *Revue de la Faculté des Sciences Economiques de l'Université d' Istanbul* 5 (1944):107-136.

14. Oswald Spengler, *Der Untergang des Abendlandes*, 2 vols. (Munich, 1918-1922), 1:18f.

PART 2. THE PATH OF FREEDOM

1. Oswald Menghin, *Weltgeschichte der Steinzeit* (Vienna, 1931).

2. Ernst Howald, *Kultur der Antike* (Potsdam, 1935), p. 7.

3. Fritz Kern, "Die Welt worein die Griechen traten," *Anthropos* 25 (1930):202.

4. James G. Frazer, *Lectures on the Early History of Kingship* (London, 1905); and *The Golden Bough*, 13 vols. (London, 1935-1936). Leo Frobenius, *Erythräa* (Berlin, 1930).

5. This is the title of two essays by the universal historian Fritz Kern: "Die Welt worein die Griechen traten," *Anthropos* 24 (1929):109-168, and 25 (1930):195-207.

6. Ernst Kornemann, *Die Stellung der Frau in der vorgriechischen Mittelmeerkultur*, Orient und Antike series no. 4 (Heidelberg, 1927), p. 59.

7. Tyrtaeus, fr. 8.5, in Hermann Diels, ed., *Fragmente der Vorsokratiker* (5th ed. Walther Kranz, 3 vols., Berlin, 1934-1937).

8. W. Kraiker, "Die Zeitenwende in Griechenland," in Kraiker and Kübler, *Keramikos I: Die Nekropolen des 12. bis 10. Jahrhunderts* (Berlin, 1939), p. 168.

9. Ibid., p. 175.

10. Berve, "Ionien und die griechische Geschichte," p. 522.

11. These statements, some amusing and some frightening, of leading thinkers of the period from 1876 to 1902, have been compiled by Eduard Stemplinger, *Antike Technik* (Munich, 1924), p. 5.

12. Goethe, *Gespräche mit Eckermann*, 24 November 1824, par. 2.

13. Edward Gibbon, *History of the Decline and Fall of the Roman Empire* (1776-1788), chap. 53.

14. Bruno Keil, "Griechische Staatsaltertümer," in *Einleitung in die Altertumswissenschaft*, ed. Gercke and Norden (Leipzig, 1923), 3:315.

15. Aristotle, *Politics*, bk. 3, sec. 10.7; 1286b 8-20.

16. Jacob Burckhardt, "Griechische Kulturgeschichte," *Gesamtausgabe* (Stuttgart, 1929—, 1:77; *History of Greek Culture*, trans. Palmer Hilty, New York, 1963, pp. 14f). The quotations in the next two paragraphs are from the Stuttgart edition, 1:80 and 1:83f, and do not appear in the Hilty translation.

17. References to the ideal of "living as one pleases" have been compiled by Max Pohlenz, *Staatsgedanke und Staatslehre der Griechen* (Leipzig, 1923), p. 160, nn. 19 and 20. The statement about Sparta is by Plutarch (*Lycurgus*, 24), that from Simonides in fr. 53 (Diels-Kranz).

18. Bruno Snell, *Die Entdeckung des Geistes*, 4th ed. (Hamburg, 1955), p. 338.

19. Goethe, *Faust*, v. 3274.

20. Robert J. Bonner, *Aspects of Athenian Democracy* (Berkeley, 1933), pp. 140, 145.

21. Lactantius, *Inst*. 4.3.

22. Johann Gottfried Herder, *Werke*, ed. Suphan (Berlin, 1877-1913), 17:352.

23. Archilochus, fr. 6 (Diels-Kranz).

24. Hesiod, *Erga*, vv. 637-638.

25. Timon, fr. 43 (Diels-Kranz). Cf. Pindar, *Pyth*. 2.52.

26. Martin P. Nilsson, *Geschichte der griechischen Religion*, vol. 1, 2d ed. (Munich, 1955); vol. 2 (Munich, 1950).

27. Jacob Burckhardt in his first sketch (1869) for the *Griechische Kulturgeschichte* (*Gesamtausgabe*, Stuttgart, 1929—, 8:xviii).

28. Seneca, *De ira* 3.56.

29. Friedrich Meinecke, *Die Idee der Staatsräson* (Munich, 1924), p. 272. Meinecke is describing Hegel's philosophy, but the characterization would apply equally well to Heraclitus, and indeed shows how much Hegel was a Heraclitian.

30. Plato, *Theaetetus* 176B.

31. Marcus Aurelius, 12.18.2.

32. Xenophanes, fr. 34; I follow Plutarch's reading of vv. 1 and 4.

33. Thucydides, bk. 2, chap. 65 (*The Peloponnesian War*, trans. Foster Smith, New York, 1919, pp. 375, 377).

34. Ibid., bk. 2, chap. 37 (trans. Smith, pp. 323, 325, 331).

35. H. T. Wade-Gery, "The Question of Tribute in 449/8 B.C.," *Hesperia* 14 (1955):212-229.

36. Wilhelm Schmid, *Untersuchungen zum gefesselten Prometheus* (Stuttgart, 1929), p. 94.

37. Protagoras, fr. 4 (Diels-Kranz).

38. Hippocrates, frs. 22 and 18 (Diels-Kranz).

39. Sophocles, *Antigone*, vv. 454-457 (*The Tragedies of Sophocles*, trans. R. C. Jebb, Cambridge, 1957, pp. 141-142).

40. Wilhelm Nestle, *Euripides, der Dichter der griechischen Aufklärung* (Stuttgart, 1901).

41. Euripides, fr. 1047 (ed. Nauck).

42. Democritus, fr. 247 (Diels-Kranz).

43. Alcidamas, fr. 1 (ed. Sauppe).

44. Diogenes Laertius, 6.63.

45. Ibid., 6.72.

46. Zeno, fr. 262 in *Stoicorum veterum fragmenta*, ed. von Arnim, 4 vols. (Leipzig, 1903-1924), vol. 1.

47. Francisco de Vitoria (*Relectio de potestate civili*) and Francesco Suárez (*De legibus* 2.19.9) as cited by Joseph Höffner, *Christentum und Menschenwürde* (Trier, 1947), p. 241, n. 1, and p. 234, n. 44. Hugo Grotius, *De iure belli ac pacis*, bk. 2, chap. 20, par. 14; and prolegomena, pars. 17 and 23.

48. On Dante see Fritz Kern, *Humana civilitas: Eine Dante-Untersuchung* (Leipzig, 1913). The quotation from Christian Wolff is from his *Ius gentium* (1749), par. 21.

49. Georges Cottier in *Nova et vetera* (Fribourg), April-June 1944.

50. Plato, *Laws*, bk. 12, 951a (*The Dialogues of Plato*, trans. Benjamin Jowett, 2 vols., New York, 1937, 2:785).

51. The passages referred to are in Plato's *Laws*, bks. 5 (expulsion: 735e; currency and travel: 742a-b), 11 (slaves and foreigners: 915b, 920a), 8 (rejection of physical work: 846d; control of imports: 847c), 12 (foreign travel: 950d-953c), 7 (censorship: 802b), 10 (atheists: 907e-909a), and 2 (political lies: 663d—cf. *Republic* 3.414b).

52. Plato, *Republic* bk. 3, 21; 414b (trans. Jowett, 1:679).

53. Friedrich Nietzsche, *Wille zur Macht* 2:202 (Musarion ed., 18:148).

54. Werner Jaeger, *Aristotle* (trans. Richard Robinson, Oxford, 1934, p. 378).

55. Gustav Senn, *Die Entwicklung der biologischen Forschungsmethode in der Antike und ihre grundsätzliche Förderung durch Theophrast von Eresos*, Veröffentlichungen der Schweizerischen Gesellschaft für Geschichte der Medizin und der Naturwissenschaften no. 8 (Aarau, 1933), pp. 109, 114, 125.

56. Parmenides, fr. 7.3-5 (Diels-Kranz).

57. Democritus, fr. 125 (Diels-Kranz).

58. Democritus, fr. 116 (Diels-Kranz).

59. The first phrase is that of Gustav Droysen, the second that of von Gutschmid.

60. Aristotle, *Politics*, bk. 3, 1284a (trans. Barker, p. 134).

61. The reference is to Goethe's *West-Östlicher Divan*: "Höchstes Glück der Erdenkinder/ Sei nur die Persönlichkeit" ("Buch Suleika," no. 20, vv. 3-4). (*Editor's note.*)

62. Heinrich Gomperz, *Die Lebensauffassung der griechischen Philosophen und das Ideal der inneren Freiheit*, 2d ed. (Jena, 1915).

63. Epicurus, *Kyriai Doxai*, xv.

64. Ibid., x-xii.

65. Michael Rostovtzeff, *The Social and Economic History of the Hellenistic World* (Oxford, 1941), 2:1312.

66. Cicero, *Brutus* 73.254; Horace, *Epodes* 2.1.156.

67. H. Dessau, *Inscriptiones Latinae Selectae* (1892-1916), no. 8393.

68. Michael Rostovtzeff, *The Social and Economic History of the Roman Empire*, 2 vols. (Oxford, 1927), 1:49.

69. Ibid., 1:135f.

70. Ibid., 1:370.

71. Tertullian, *De anima* 30.

72. Vergil, *Aeneid*, bk. 6, vv. 847-853 (*The Aeneid of Vergil*, trans. C. J. Billson, London, 1906, p. 305).

73. Cf. Ferdinand A. Hermens, *Democracy or Anarchy?* (Notre Dame, 1941), and Dankwart A. Rustow, "Some Observations on Proportional Representation," *Journal of Politics*, vol. 12, no. 2 (February, 1950), pp. 107-127.

74. Max Weber, *Wirtschaft und Gesellschaft*, 4th ed. (Tübingen, 1956, 2:467; *Economy and Society*, trans. Guenther Roth and Claus Wittich, 3 vols., New York, 1968, 2:802).

75. Rostovtzeff, *Roman Empire*, 597.

76. Cassius Dio, 76.15.2.

77. Ibid., 77.10.4.

78. Rostovtzeff, *Roman Empire*, 607.

79. Ibid., 374.

80. Lactantius, *De mortibus persecutorum* 7.

81. Rousseau, *Contrat social*, bk. 2, chap. 9.

82. Pseudo-Aristides in his *Address on Kingship*, fr. 105.

83. These are the fundamental distinctions drawn in the treatise of my friend Walter Eucken, *Die Grundlagen der Nationalökonomie*, 6th ed. (Heidelberg, 1950), pp. 79-87.

84. Juvenal, *Sat.* 8.83f.

85. Ludwig Mitteis, *Aus den griechischen Papyrusurkunden* (Leipzig, 1900), p. 34.

86. Cyprianus, quoted by Hermann Schnitzler, *Mittelalter und Antike* (Munich, 1948).

87. Franz Cumont, *Les Religions orientales dans le paganisme Romain*, 4th ed. (Paris, 1929), p. 49.

88. Related by the Neoplatonist Iamblichus (d. ca. 330 A.D.), *Protreptikos*, 21.

89. Ernest Renan, *Les Evangiles* (1877), p. 408.

90. Tertullian, *De carne Christi*, 5: "Credibile, quia ineptum est." Saint Augustine says of the Manichaeans: "Tam multa fabulosissima et absurdissima quia demonstrari non poterant credenda imperari" (*Conf.* 6.5).

91. Ernst Buschor, *Vom Sinn der griechischen Standbilder* (Berlin, 1931), p. 53.

92. H. Koch, *Probleme der Spätantike* (1930), p. 60.

93. Cf. Alexander Rüstow, "Archaisches Weltbild und archaische Weltherrschaft," *Studium Generale* 14 (Heidelberg, 1961):539-546.

94. Gerhard von Rad, *Der heilige Krieg im alten Israel* (1951), pp. 39, 49; and *Die Josephsgeschichte*, 2d ed. (Neukirchen, 1956), pp. 8-9.

95. Martin Noth, *Geschichte Israels*, 4th ed. (Göttingen, 1959), p. 203.

96. Ibid., pp. 300, 310.

97. Elias Bickermann, *Der Gott der Makkabäer* (Berlin, 1937), p. 64.

98. Ibid., p. 134.

99. Ibid., pp. 138 and 92.

100. Hans von Soden, "Die Krisis der Kirche," in *Urchristentum und Geschichte*, vol. 1 (Tübingen, 1951).

101. Hans Lietzmann, *Das Problem Staat und Kirche*, Abhandlungen der Akademie der Wissenschaften (Berlin, 1940), p. 6.

102. Saint Augustine, *De civitate Dei* 4.4 (*The City of God*, trans. Marcus Dods, New York, 1950, pp. 112-113).

103. Ernst Troeltsch, *Gesammelte Schriften* (Tübingen, 1925), 4:822; Desiderius Erasmus, *Opus epistolarum*, ed. Allen, ep. 1381, 300.

104. Bernard le Bovier de Fontenelle, *Eloge de Sir Isaac Newton*, cited in Paul Hazard, *La Crise de la conscience européenne* (Paris, 1935), 2:113.

105. Adolf Harnack, *Lehrbuch der Dogmengeschichte*, 4th ed. (Tübingen, 1910), 3:356.

106. Henri Pirenne, *Les Villes du moyen-âge* (Brussels, 1927), p. 56.

107. Gerhard Ritter, *Die Heidelberger Universität* (Heidelberg, 1936), 1:12.

108. Eberhard Gothein, *Wirtschaftsgeschichte des Schwarzwaldes* (Strasbourg, 1892), 1:62-63.

109. Georg Voigt, *Die Wiederbelebung des klassischen Altertums oder das erste Jahrhundert des Humanismus* (1859).

110. Alfred von Martin, *Soziologie der Renaissance* (Stuttgart, 1932), pp. 44-45.

111. Erich Auerbach, *Mimesis: Dargestellte Wirklichkeit in der abendländischen Literatur*, (Bern, 1946, p. 263; *Mimesis: The Representa-*

tion of Reality in Western Literature, trans. Willard R. Trask, Princeton, 1953, p. 276).

112. Friedrich Nietzsche, *Menschliches, Allzumenschliches* (1876-1878), 2:5, 237 (Musarion ed., 8:211-213): "Renaissance und Reformation" (*Collected Works of Frederick Nietzsche*, ed. Oscar Levy, trans. Helen Zimmern, New York, 1924, 6:222).

113. Cited by Georg Dehio, *Geschichte der deutschen Kunst* (Leipzig, 1926), 3:8.

114. Cited by Jan Huizinga, *Erasmus*, trans. W. Kägi (Basel, 1936).

115. Ibid., pp. 213, 183.

116. From the Protocol of Kammeryk, 1411.

117. "Gespräch zwischen einem Christen und einem Juden," in *Flugschriften aus den ersten Jahren der Reformation*, ed. O. Clemen (Halle, 1906), vol. 1, no. 10, p. 27.

118. Dürer's well-known engraving of 1513, entitled "Ritter, Tod und Teufel," was, as is generally known, inspired by Erasmus's *Enchiridion militis Christiani* ("Handbook of the Christian Soldier"); hence the otherwise startling reference to the quiet scholar as a "knight of Christ."

119. Etienne Gilson, *Les Idées et les lettres* (Paris, 1932), p. 174.

120. Gerhard Ritter, *Die Weltwirkung der Reformation* (Leipzig, 1941), p. 48.

121. Martin Luther, *Werke*, Weimar edition, 11:265, 270.

122. Ibid., 18:299, 293f.

123. Ibid., 18:361, 360, 358, 361.

124. Ibid., 18:292, "Ermahnung zum Frieden" (1525).

125. Ibid., 11:257, "Von weltlicher Obrigkeit" (1525).

126. Ibid., vol. 30, pt. 2, pp. 173 and 192f.

127. Gerhard Ritter, *Luther*, 3d ed. (Munich, 1943), pp. 226f.

128. Ritter, *Weltwirkung,* p. 195.

129. Luther, *Werke*, 11:264.

130. Ibid., 15:219; 18:298.

131. Ritter, *Luther*, p. 211; *Weltwirkung*, p. 187.

132. Cf. Alexander Rüstow, "Lutherana Tragoedia Artis," *Schweizer Monatshefte*, vol. 39, no. 9 (1959), pp. 891-906.

133. Luther, "Vom ehelichen Leben" (1522) *Werke* (2d ed.), 10:304.

134. For "Lutherana tragoedia," see Erasmus, *Opus epistolarum*; ep. 1156, 9 (letter to Conrad Peutinger, 9 November 1520).

135. Luther, in a letter of 1 March 1517.

136. In the words of Walther Köhler.

137. *Corpus Reformatorum*, 68:685. The allusion is to Juvenal, *Sat.* 6.223: *Hoc volo, sic iubeo, sit pro ratione voluntas* ("This I wish and thus I command: let will stand for reason.")

138. This is the judgment of Oskar Pfister, a Protestant theologian and psychoanalyst. See his study *Calvins Eingreifen in die Hexer- und Hexenprozesse von Peney 1545* (Zurich, 1947).

139. In the words of the late Ernest Jones, leading English psychoanalyst and biographer of Freud, in a letter to the author.

140. Henri Hauser, *La Modernité du XVIe siècle* (Paris, 1930), p. 34.

141. Cited ibid., p. 72.

142. Domitius Ulpianus, *Institutiones*, bk. 1, pt. D, sec. 1, par. 4.

143. Pseudo-Augustinus, *Quaestiones veteris et novi testamenti*, 91, 8 (in CSEL, 50, 157, 23).

144. Friedrich Meinecke, *Die Idee der Staatsräson*, p. 331; and James I, *True Law of Free Monarchies* (1604).

145. Louis XIV, *Oeuvres* (1806 ed.), 2:283.

146. Thomas Hobbes, *Leviathan*, pt. 2, chap. 30, pars. 20 and 14; my emphasis.

147. Otto Hintze, "Staatsverfassung und Heeresverfassung" (1906), in his *Gesammelte Abhandlungen* (Leipzig, n.d.), 1:57-59. A similar thesis was expounded by my granduncle Wilhelm Rüstow, *Geschichte der Infantrie* (1857; 2d ed., Nordhausen, 1864), vol. 1.

148. Cited by Paul Hazard, *La Crise de la conscience européenne* (Paris, 1935), 2:67.

149. Georg Friederici, *Der Charakter der Entdeckung und Eroberung Amerikas durch die Europäer*, 3 vols. (Stuttgart, 1925-1936).

150. Georg Friedrich Knapp, "Die Landarbeiter in Knechtschaft und Freiheit" (1891), in his *Ausgewählte Werke* (Munich, 1925), 1:69.

151. Luther, "Ermahnung zum Frieden" (1525), *Werke*, 18:323. In a similar context belongs Luther's translation, unfortunately untenable on philological grounds, of Luke 17.21: "Denn siehe, das Himmelreich ist inwendig in euch." See my essay, "Entos humōn estin: Zur Deutung von Lukas, 20-21," *Zeitschrift für neutestamentliche Wissenschaft* 51 (1960): 197-224.

152. Alexander Rüstow, "Die Konfession in der Wirtschaftsgeschichte," *Revue de la Faculté des Sciences Economiques de l'Université d'Istanbul* 3 (1941-1942):376f.

153. Blaise Pascal, *Pensées*, ed. Tourneur, 262, 5 (trans. H. F. Stewart, New York, 1958, p. 321).

154. René Descartes, *Discours de la méthode* (1637, pt. 6, par. 4; trans. Elizabeth Haldane and G.R.T. Ross, Cambridge, 1968, 1:123).

155. Bernard Le Bovier de Fontenelle, *Eloge de . . . Newton*, cited in Hazard, *Crise de la conscience*, 2:112.

156. Sebastiano Castellio, "De arte dubitandi" (1562) and "De arte confidendi, ignorandi et sciendi" (1563), ed. Elisabeth Feist-Hirsch, in Reale Accademia d'Italia, *Studi e documenti* 2:307-340.

157. Louis Joseph Delaporte, as cited in Gerhard Hess, *Pierre Gassend: Der französische Späthumanismus und das Problem von Wissen und Glauben* (Jena, 1939), p. 110.

158. Hess, ibid., p. 19.

159. Troeltsch, *Gesammelte Schriften*, 4:289.

160. Pascal, *Pensées* (trans. Stewart), p. 396; Charron, *De la sagesse*, bk. 1; Jean Barbeyrac, . . . *De dignitate et utilitate juris* (Lausanne, 1711).

161. Saint-Evremond, *Véritables Oeuvres* (London, 1706), 4:2-3, cited by Gerhard Hess in *Romanische Forschungen*, vol. 52, no. 2/3 (1938), p. 262.

162. Voltaire, *Lettres écrites de Londres sur les Anglais (Lettres philosophiques)*, 1733-1734, no. 6: "Sur les presbytériens," par. 6, end.

163. Cited in Hippolyte Taine, *Les Origines de la France contemporaine* (Paris, 1876), 2:128.

164. Friedrich Meinecke, *Die Entstehung des Historismus* (Munich, 1936, 1:112; *Historicism*, trans. J. E. Anderson, London, pp. 80-81).

165. Ernst Cassirer, *Die Philosophie der Aufklärung* (Tübingen, 1932, p. 296; *The Philosophy of the Enlightenment*, trans. Fritz C. A. Koeller and James Pettegrup, Princeton, 1957, p. 221).

166. Burlamaqui, *Principes du droit naturel* (Geneva, 1747), p. 2.

167. Alexander Rüstow, *Das Versagen des Wirtschaftsliberalismus* (Istanbul, 1945; 2d ed., Munich, 1950).

168. Hobbes, *Behemoth, Or the Long Parliament*, p. 116, cited in Ferdinand Tönnies, *Hobbes*, 3d ed. (1925), p. 20.

169. Goethe, *Faust*, pt. 2, vv. 11,441-46 (*Faust*, trans. Bayard Taylor, 2 vols., New York, 1912, 2:289).

170. Bernard Mandeville, *Fable of the Bees*, 5th ed. (1729), 1:2; and Saint-Evremond, cited by Hazard, *Crise de la conscience*, 2:76.

171. Adam Smith, *The Theory of Moral Sentiments* (London, 1759), pt. 2, sec. 2, chap. 4, par. 12.

172. Pierre Bayle, in his periodical *Nouvelles de la République des Lettres*, April 1684, article 11; cited by Hazard, *Crise de la conscience*, 2:118.

173. Wilhelm Dilthey, *Gesammelte Schriften*, 12 vols. (Leipzig, 1914-58), 3:133.

174. Claude Gibert, *Histoire de Caléjava, ou l'isle des hommes raisonnables* (1700); cited by Hazard, *Crise de la conscience*, 1:205.

175. From a memorial document of 1784 found in the tower of the Church of Saint Margaret in Gotha; cited in Hermann Hettner, *Literaturgeschichte des 18. Jahrhunderts* (Braunschweig, 1893-94), pt. 3. The following year Schiller wrote his "Ode to Joy."

176. Jeremy Bentham states as his "fundamental axiom" in the *Introduction to the Principles of Morals and Legislation*, 1789 (*Works*, 1:227), that "the greatest happiness of the greatest number is the measure of right and wrong." But, contrary to widespread belief, this concept did not originate with Bentham but with the great Italian Enlightenment thinker Cesare Bonesana, marchese di Beccaria (1738-1794), who, in the foreword of his treatise *Dei delitti e delle pene* (1764) speaks of "La massima felicità divisa nel maggior numero."

177. Fontenelle, in a satirical piece on Lamotte-Houdar.

178. Albert Schweitzer, *J. S. Bach*, 6th ed. (Leipzig, 1928), p. 209.

179. Rousseau, *First Discourse*, pt. 1, par. 7 (*The First and Second Dis-*

courses of Rousseau, trans. Roger A. and Judith R. Masters, New York, 1964, pp. 37-38).

180. Rousseau, *Rousseau juge de Jean-Jacques*, 3d dialogue, par. 58; *La Nouvelle Héloïse*, pt. 3, letter 18; *Discours sur l'inégalité*, 1.

181. Rudolf Unger, *Hamann und die Aufklärung; Studien zur Vorgeschichte des romantischen Geistes im 18. Jahrhundert* (Jena, 1911), 1:576-578.

182. As Friedrich Heinrich Jacobi said in his letter to Hamann, 4 September 1786.

183. Cassirer, *Philosophie der Aufklärung*, pp. 311f. (Koeller and Pettegrup, p. 233).

184. H. A. Korff, *Geist der Goethezeit* (Leipzig, 1923), 1:2 and 32.

185. Goethe, Sophien-Ausgabe, 53:11, no. 12.

186. Goethe, *Winckelmann*, "Antikes," par. 2.

187. Gaetano Filangieri, *La scienza della legislazione*, 8 vols. (1780-1788), introduction.

188. Michael Freund, *Die grosse Revolution in England: Anatomie eines Umsturzes* (Hamburg, 1951), pp. 511f. For the opposite thesis, see my "Revolution zur Freiheit oder Revolution zur Knechtschaft?" *Du* (Zurich, March 1952).

189. Voltaire, *Esprit des nations*, chap. 121. The next quotation is from his letter to the comte de Lewenhaupt, 1768 (*Correspondance* 13:131, no. 7180).

190. Anne-Robert-Jacques Turgot, *Oeuvres*, ed. Gustave Schelle (Paris, 1923), 5:454-455.

191. Martin Göhring, *Geschichte der grossen Revolution* (Tübingen, 1950), 1:382 and 1:3.

192. Jean Bodin, *De la république*, 4:3; Charles-Louis de Secondat, baron de La Brède et de Montesquieu, *Lettres Persanes*, lxxix; Paul-Henri-Thierry, Baron de Holbach, *Système social, ou principes naturels de la morale et de la politique, avec un examen de l'influence du gouvernement sur les moeurs*, 3 vols. (London, 1773), 2:2; Rousseau, *Discours sur l'inégalité*, dedication; Rousseau, *Préface aux oeuvres de l'abbé de Saint-Pierre*.

193. Rousseau, *Contrat social*, 2:8, par. 4.

194. Aristotle, *Politics*, bk. 8, sec. 3, 1337b 31.

195. Antoine Aulard, *Histoire politique de la révolution française*, 4th ed. (Paris, 1909), p. 3.

196. Ibid., p. 780.

197. Pierre Caron, *Les Massacres de septembre* (Paris, 1935).

198. Hans Thieme, *Das Naturrecht und die europäische Privatrechtsgeschichte* (Basel, 1947), p. 39.

199. Goethe, in letters to F. B. von Buchholtz (14 February 1814) and to Zelter (18 March 1811 and 1 January 1829).

200. Immanuel Kant, *Vom Streit der Fakultäten*; first published 1798.

201. August Ludwig von Schlözer, in his journal *Staats-Anzeigen* 13 (December, 1789).

202. Letter to Friedrich Heinrich Jacobi, 11 September 1792.

203. Kant, *Vom Streit der Fakultäten* (1798), 2:7.

204. Georg Wilhelm Friedrich Hegel, *Vorlesungen über die Geschichte der Philosophie* (1830-1831); in his *Sämtliche Werke*, ed. Glockner (Stuttgart, 1928), 11:557f.

205. Goethe, *Campagne in Frankreich*, 4th par. from end, and entry for October 20.

206. Schiller, *Das Lied von der Glocke*, vv. 378-381.

207. Karl Marx, *Zur Kritik der Hegelschen Rechtsphilosophie* (1844), introduction.

208. Friedrich Meinecke, *Weltbürgertum und Nationalstaat*, 3d ed. (Munich, 1915), pp. 219-222, referring to Haller's *Handbuch der allgemeinen Staatenkunde* (1808) and *Restauration der Staatswissenschaft* (1816-1825).

209. Adam Müller, *Elemente der Staatskunst* (1809), 1:75.

210. Karl Bergbohm, *Jurisprudenz und Rechtsphilosophie* (1892), 1:190.

211. In Franz Oppenheimer's definition; see his *System der Soziologie* (Jena, 1922), 1:4ff.

212. Jacob Burckhardt, in a letter to Gottfried Kinkel, 13 June 1842; see his *Briefe* (Basel, 1949), 1:201.

213. Goethe, in conversation with Riemer; see *Goethes Gespräche*, ed. Flodoard Freiherr von Biedermann (Leipzig, n.d.), no. 719.

214. Eduard Fueter, *Geschichte der neueren Historiographie*, 2d ed. (Munich, 1925), p. 416.

215. Ludwig Klages, *Der Geist als Widersacher der Seele*, 3 vols. (Leipzig, 1921-1932), 1:4.

216. Ernst Cassirer, in the preface to *Die Philosophie der Aufklärung* (Tübingen, 1932), p. xv.

217. Goethe, in a letter to Zelter, 6 June 1825.

218. Thomas Mann, in an address on Ricarda Huch in 1924, in his *Bemühungen* (Berlin, 1925), p. 254.

219. Cf. Alexander Rüstow, "Die geistesgeschichtlich-soziologischen Ursachen des Verfalls der Baukunst im 19. Jahrhundert," *Archiv für Philosophie* 2 (Istanbul, 1947): 123-190.

220. Kant, *Prolegomena* (1783), preface; and *Reflexionen* (ed. Benno Erdmann), 2:153; and "Träume eines Geistersehers erläutert durch Träume der Metaphysik" (1766), in *Werke* (ed. Cassirer), 2:367.

221. Friedrich Wilhelm Schelling, "Über den nationalen Gegensatz in der Philosophie," *Sämtliche Werke*, pt. 1, vol. 10, p. 193.

222. Voltaire, *Traité de métaphysique*, chap. 3, first par.

223. Gerhard Ritter, *Machtstaat und Utopie* (Munich, 1940), p. 137.

224. Nietzsche, "Antichrist," no. 10 (Musarion ed., vol. 18, p. 178). In Nietzsche's own case, a protestant parson was the philosopher's father.

225. Fichte, *Nachgelassene Werke* (Bonn, 1834), 2:198. It would be amusing to compile all the slanderous remarks that the leading German philosophers made about one another, and to note that all of them were justified.

226. Kant, "Von einem neuerdings erhobenen vornehmen Ton in der Philosophie," *Werke* (ed. Cassirer), pars. 2, 11, 1, and 10 (note).

227. Henrik Steffens, *Lebenserinnerungen aus dem Kreis der Romantik*, ed. Friedrich Gundelfinger (Jena, 1908).

228. Goethe, diary entry, 8 August 1806.

229. Johann Gottlieb Fichte, "Zweite Einleitung in die Wissenschaftslehre," *Sämtliche Werke* (Berlin, 1845), 1:467.

230. Fichte, *Reden an die deutsche Nation*, 2d address, pars. 3 and 4.

231. Hegel, *Geschichte der Philosophie*, 11:65.

232. Rudolf Haym, *Hegel und seine Zeit* (Berlin, 1857), p. 4; Alexis de Tocqueville, letter dated 12 January 1858.

233. Ernst Troeltsch, "Die Restaurationsepoche am Anfang des 19. Jahrhunderts," lecture delivered in Riga in 1913, in his *Gesammelte Schriften* (Tübingen, 1925), 4:613.

234. Wilhelm Röpke, *Die Gesellschaftskrisis der Gegenwart*, 5th ed. (Zurich, 1942), p. 91.

235. Lytton Strachey, *Eminent Victorians* (1918), preface.

PART 3, CHAPTER 1: RATIONALIST TENDENCIES

1. Medard Boss, *Der Traum und seine Auslegung* (Bern, 1953).

2. Hippolyte Taine, *L'Ancien régime* (Paris, 1876), p. 250.

3. See Isa. 26:14; 38:18-19; Ps. 6:6; 30:10; 88:11-13; 115:17; Eccles. 3:19-21; 9:4-6; Ecclus. 17:25-26 (cf. Ps. 104:29) and 17:1-2.

4. Leibniz published this tract containing a "Sample of Political Proofs for Electing the King of Poland" in Königsberg in 1669—with a title page pretending that the author was called Georgius Ulricus Lithuanus and that publication had occurred in Vilna in 1659.

5. Fontenelle, "De l'utilité des mathématiques et de la physique," *Oeuvres* (Paris, 1818), 1:34.

6. Blaise Pascal, *Pensées*, ed. Tourneur, no. 349 (trans. H. F. Stewart, New York, 1950, p. 497).

7. Etienne Bonnot de Condillac, *Oeuvres* (Paris, 1821), 22:146, 149.

8. Fries, *System der Logik*, 3d ed. (Heidelberg, 1837), pp. 302f., and *Neue oder anthropologische Kritik der Vernunft*, 2d ed. (Heidelberg, 1828), 1:67.

9. In our Göttingen student days we used to tease Nelson, saying that he was a follower more of Apelt than of Fries. What attracted me to Fries, in contrast to Apelt, was his sense of morphology and anthropology. This aspect of Fries later bore fruit in the work of Rudolf Otto (1869-1937). In 1904, when Otto was serving as a *Privatdozent* in Göttingen, Nelson and I succeeded in converting him from a rather anemic form of neo-Kantianism to a followership of Fries. Otto's magnificent book *Das Heilige* (Breslau, 1917), which elaborated the fundamental concept of "numinosity," would hardly have been possible except for his close acquaintance with Fries's philosophy.

10. Friedrich A. von Hayek, *The Counter-Revolution of Science: Studies on the Abuse of Reason* (Glencoe, Ill., 1952).

11. Letter to Charlotte von Stein, 15 June 1786.

12. Rudolf Unger, *Hamann und die Aufklärung* (Halle, 1911), p. 10, quoting Gildemeister, *Hamanns Leben*, 5:228.

13. Francis Bacon, *Novum organum scientiarum* (London, 1820), 2:4.

14. Nietzsche, *Wille zur Macht*, nos. 493, 455, 534.

15. Goethe, *Vermächtnis* (1829).

16. Alfred C. Kinsey et al., *Sexual Behavior in the Human Male* (Philadelphia, 1948); and *Sexual Behavior in the Human Female* (Philadelphia, 1953).

17. Voltaire, *Traité de métaphysique* (1734), chap. 5, par. 9.

18. Pierre-Jean-Georges Cabanis, cited by Hermann Hettner, *Geschichte der französischen Literatur im 18. Jahrhundert*, 4th ed. (Braunschweig, 1881), pp. 379f.

19. Plato, *Charmides*, 168 d-e.

20. Saint Augustine, *De libero arbitrio*, 2:23; Aquinas, *Summa contra gentiles*, 2:74.

21. John Locke, *An Essay Concerning Human Understanding*, bk. 2, chap. 4, par. 4; Kant, *Kritik der reinen Vernunft*, 1, para. 6b.

22. Roger Bacon, *Meditationes sacrae de haeresibus*.

23. Gustav Hübener, "Theorie der Romantik," *Deutsche Viertel-jahrs-schrift für Literaturwissenschaft und Geistesgeschichte* 10 (1932):244f.

24. Ernest Renan, cited by Wilhelm Röpke, *Civitas Humana* (Zurich, 1944), p. 138.

25. Ernst Hass, *Des Menschen Thron wankt: Eine naturwissenschaftliche Kritik des modernen Lebens* (Munich, 1955), p. 64.

26. Goethe, *Sprüche in Prosa*, Loeper ed., no. 11.

27. Oswald Spengler, *Der Mensch und die Technik* (Munich, 1931), p. 75.

28. Wilhelm Röpke, "Der Kult des Kolossalen," in *Die Gesellschaftskrisis der Gegenwart*, 5th ed. (Erlenbach-Zurich, 1948), pp. 103-118.

29. Hayek, *The Counter-Revolution of Science*.

30. Alexander Rüstow, "Der Weg durch Weltkrise und deutsche Krise," *Europäische Revue*, vol. 6, no. 12 (Berlin, December, 1930), p. 874.

31. E. A. Thompson, *A Roman Reformer, Being a New Text of the Treatise "De rebus bellicis"* (Oxford, 1942).

32. Cited in Pierre-Maxime Schuhl, *Machinisme et philosophie* (Paris, 1938), p. 22.

33. Cited by Arthur Waley, *Three Ways of Thought in Ancient China* (London, 1939).

34. Goethe, *Dichtung und Wahrheit*, pt. 3, bk. 11, par. 90.

35. Goethe, *Wilhelm Meisters Wanderjahre oder Die Entsagenden*, second version, 3:13.

36. Wilhelm Röpke, "Versuch einer Neufassung des quantitativen Be-

völkerungsproblems," in *Festschrift für O. Engländer* (Brno, 1936), pp. 197ff.

37. Karl Jaspers, *Vom Ursprung und Ziel der Geschichte* (Munich, 1949, pp. 149, 153f., 160f.; *The Origin and Aim of History*, trans. Michael Bullock, New Haven, 1953, pp. 115, 119, 125).

38. Koran, Sura 80, 34-37.

39. *Vita Wolframni episcopi senonensis.*

40. Luke 14:26-27; Matt. 10:37, 8:21-22; and Luke 9:59-60; John 2:4.

41. Bernard de Clairvaux, Epistola 322 (Migne, *Patrologia latina* 182:527).

42. Max Weber, *Gesammelte Aufsätze zur Religionssoziologie* (Tübingen, 1920), 1:93f.

43. Ibid., pp. 99 and 97, citing *Christian Directory* 4:253; and Bunyan's *Pilgrim's Progress*.

44. Pascal, *Pensées*, no. 553.

45. In Heinrich Rommen's phrase.

46. Novalis (Friedrich Freiherr von Hardenberg), "Die Christenheit oder Europa," par. 11, in *Schriften*, ed. Paul Kluckhohn, 2:77.

47. Sigmund Freud, "Das Unbehagen an der Kultur" (1930), in *Gesammelte Schriften*, 12 vols. (Vienna, 1924-34, 11:43; "Civilisation and Its Discontents," in *The Standard Edition of the Complete Psychological Works of Sigmund Freud*, trans. James Strachey, 24 vols., London, 1966-1974, 21:77).

48. Lao-tse, *Tao-te-king*, ch. 5 (trans. Victor von Strauss, Manesse ed., p. 62).

49. Adam Ferguson, *An Essay on the History of Civil Society* (London, 1966), cited by Friedrich Meinecke, *Die Entstehung des Historismus* (Munich, 1936), 1:285.

50. Kant, *Idee zu einer allgemeinen Geschichte in weltbürgerlicher Absicht*; Arthur Schopenhauer, *Parerga und Paralipomena*, 2:400.

51. *Rousseau juge de Jean-Jacques*, 3d dialogue, par. 58 (Rousseau, *Oeuvres* [Paris, 1822], 16:414).

52. Goethe, *Die Leiden des jungen Werthers*, bk. 1, 17 May and bk. 2, 20 January (trans. Elizabeth Mayer and Louise Bogan, New York, 1973, pp. 10, 84); *Zur Farbenlehre*, Historischer Teil, Materialien zur Geschichte der Farbenlehre, sec. 2.

53. Edmund Burke, *Reflections on the Revolution in France*, in *Works* (World's Classics ed., 4:105).

54. Friedrich Engels, *Condition of the Working Class*, 2d German ed. (Stuttgart, 1892), p. 24.

55. Nietzsche, *Schopenhauer als Erzieher*, in *Werke* (Musarion ed.), 7:71.

56. Fëdor Dostoevski, *The Brothers Karamazoff*, trans. Constance Garnett (New York, n.d.), pp. 317-318.

57. Erich Auerbach, *Mimesis: Dargestellte Wirklichkeit in der abendländischen Literatur* (Bern, 1946), p. 435 (*Mimesis: The Representation of Real-*

ity in Western Literature, trans. Willard R. Trask, New York, Doubleday, 1957, p. 431).

58. Albert Schweitzer, *J. S. Bach*, 6th ed. (Leipzig, 1928), p. 152. (The work first appeared in 1908.)

59. Carl Gustav Jung, *Seelenprobleme der Gegenwart* (Zurich, 1946), pp. 402-404 (*Modern Man in Search of a Soul*, tr. W. S. Dell and Cary F. Baynes, New York, 1947, pp. 227-228).

60. Maurice Halbwachs, *Les Causes de suicide* (Paris, 1930).

61. Søren Kierkegaard, *Repetition* (1843) (tr. Walter Lowrie, Princeton, 1941, p. 104).

62. Luther, *Werke*, Weimar ed., 19:217.

63. Karl Barth, *Der Römerbrief*, 6th ed. (Munich, 1933), p. 241.

64. The first quotation is from O. F. Bollnow, *Existenzphilosophie*, 4th ed. (Stuttgart, 1955), p. 24; the second is from Martin Buber in the journal *Philosophia* 3 (Belgrade, 1938):306, 301, 308.

65. Karl Jaspers, *Philosophie*, 3:6.

66. Jean-Paul Sartre, *L'Existentialisme est un humanisme* (Paris, 1946), pp. 9, 22, 78, 55, 22, 37, 62, 81.

67. The first quotation is O. F. Bollnow, "Existentialismus," *Die Sammlung*, vol. 2, no. 11 (November, 1947), p. 660; the second is from Werner Krauss, "Nationalismus und Chauvinismus," *Der Aufbau* (Berlin, May, 1947), no. 5, p. 455.

68. Sartre, *L'Existentialisme*, pp. 94, 36, 52.

69. Kurt Badt, in a review of the London exhibition of works by Picasso and Matisse, 1945-1946, *Deutsche Blätter*, vol. 4, no. 31 (Santiago de Chile, 1946), p. 48.

70. J. Schneider-Lengyel, "Vom Impressionismus zum Surrealismus," *Prisma*, vol. 1, no. 4 (Munich, 1947), p. 37.

71. Auerbach, *Mimesis*, p. 491 (Bern), p. 487 (Doubleday).

72. Ibid., p. 492 (Bern), p. 487 (Doubleday).

73. Franz Kafka, "Er," in the posthumous volume *Beim Bau der chinesischen Mauer* (Berlin, 1931), pp. 215f.

74. Auerbach, *Mimesis*, p. 493 (Bern), p. 488 (Doubleday).

75. Friedrich Engels, *Die Lage der arbeitenden Classe in England*, 2d ed. (Stuttgart, 1892, pp. 24f; *The Condition of the English Working Class*, trans. Florence Kelley Wischnewetzky, London, pp. 23-25). In the preface to the second edition of this work, which was originally published in 1845, Engels as an old man emphasizes that he still believes in the opinions he had expressed at that time.

76. Willy Hellpach, *Mensch und Volk der Grosstadt*, 2d ed. (Stuttgart, 1952), p. 73.

77. Ferdinand Tönnies, *Gemeinschaft und Gesellschaft*, 8th ed. (1935), p. 242 (*Community and Society*, trans. Charles Loomis, East Lansing, Mich., 1957, p. 227).

78. René König, in *Gewerkschaftliche Monatshefte* (August, 1956).

79. Helmuth Plessner, "Nachwort zu Ferdinand Tönnies," *Kölner Zeitschrift für Soziologie und Sozialpsychologie*, vol. 7, no. 3 (1955), p. 341.

80. Ibid., p. 344.

81. Ibid., p. 345.

82. Gerhard Colm, "Masse," *Handwörterbuch der Soziologie*, ed. A. Vierkandt (1931), pp. 354, 358.

83. Walter Hegemann, *Vom Mythos der Masse* (Heidelberg, 1951), p. 103.

84. Helmut Schelsky, "Ist der Grossstädter wirklich einsam?" *Offene Welt*, no. 44 (August, 1956), pp. 326-330.

85. René König, "Die Begriffe 'Gemeinschaft' und 'Gesellschaft' bei Ferdinand Tönnies," *Kölner Zeitschrift für Soziologie und Sozialpsychologie*, vol. 7, no. 3 (1955), p. 406.

86. Ibid., pp. 381 and 410.

87. Ferdinand Tönnies, *Zur Einleitung in die Soziologie*, 1899, pp. 71f. (*Ferdinand Tönnies on Sociology* . . . , trans. Werner J. Cahnman and Rudolf Heberle, Chicago, 1971, p. 82).

88. Alexander Rüstow, *Das Versagen des Wirtschaftsliberalismus als religionsgeschichtliches Problem*.

89. Hedwig Hintze, *Staatseinheit und Föderalismus im alten Frankreich und in der Revolution* (Berlin, 1928), p. 181.

90. Ibid., pp. 188f.

91. Ibid., pp. 185f., 195; the quotation from Burke (*Reflections on the Revolution in France*, 5th ed., pp. 268f.) is on p. 63.

92. Frédéric Bastiat, *Oeuvres complètes* (Paris, 1854), 4:330-333.

93. Alexis de Tocqueville, *De la démocratie en Amérique* (Paris, 1835).

94. John Foster Dulles, *War, Peace, and Change* (New York, 1939), p. 124.

95. Otto Gierke, *Naturrecht und Deutsches Recht* (Frankfurt, 1883), p. 11.

96. Alexander Rüstow, "Die staatspolitischen Voraussetzungen des wirtschaftlichen Liberalismus," address at the annual meeting of the Verein für Sozialpolitik, 28 September 1932; printed in its *Schriften*, 187:62-69.

97. Heinrich Grewe, "Parteienstaat—oder was sonst?" *Der Monat*, vol. 3, no. 36 (Berlin, 1951), pp. 563-577.

98. Novalis, "Fragmente und Studien" (1798), pt. 4, no. 99, in *Schriften*, ed. Kluckhohn, 2:335.

99. Friedrich Christoph Dahlmann in the Frankfurt parliament, 22 January 1849, as cited by Friedrich Meinecke, *Die Idee der Staatsräson* (Munich, 1924), p. 493.

100. Cited, ibid., p. 497, n. 1.

PART 3, CHAPTER 2: IRRATIONALIST COUNTERTENDENCIES

1. Alfred von Martin, "Weltanschauliche Motive im altkonservativen Denken," *Friedrich Meinecke zum 60. Geburtstag* (Munich, 1922), p. 344.

2. The pamphlet, entitled *Peri tes Athenaion politeias* ("On the Commonwealth of the Athenians"), was written in 432 B.C., and is part of the *Corpus Xenophonteum*.

3. Edmund Burke, *Reflections on the Revolution in France* (1790).

4. Novalis, "Fragmente und Studien," pt. 6, no. 100, in *Schriften*, ed. Kluckhohn, 2:335.

5. Friedrich Julius Stahl, *Philosophie des Rechts*, 3d ed., 2 vols. in 3 (Hamburg, 1830-1837), vol. 2, pt. 2, p. 254.

6. Eberhard Gothein, "Wilhelm Heinrich Riehl," *Preussische Jahrbücher* 92 (1898):4.

7. Karl Holl, *Die Bedeutung der grossen Kriege für das religiöse und kirchliche Leben innerhalb des deutschen Protestantismus* (Tübingen, 1917), pp. 58, 56.

8. Goethe, *Gespräche mit Eckermann*, 24 January 1830.

9. Goethe, *Campagne in Frankreich*, Pempelfort, November 1792, and Duisburg November 1792 (cf. *Campaign in France*, trans. Robert Farie, London, 1949, p. 211).

10. Erich Kaufmann, *Zur Problematik des Volkswillens* (Berlin, 1931), p. 11.

11. Carl Gustav Jung, *Die Bedeutung des Vaters für das Schicksal des Einzelnen*, 2d ed. (Leipzig, 1926), preface.

12. Krista Rauhut, *Ursprüngliche Erziehung und ihre Entartung*, dissertation, Heidelberg, 1955, pp. 113f (citing Charlevoix, *Histoire de la Nouvelle France*, 1744).

13. *Blätter für die Kunst*, vol. 5 (1900-1901).

14. Robert Boehringer, *Mein Bild von Stefan George* (Bonn, 1951), pp. 53, 92.

15. Friedrich Wolters, *Herrschaft und Dienst*, 2d ed. (Berlin, 1920), pp. 58, 9, 11, and 31; italics in original.

16. Edgar Salin, *Um Stefan George* (Bonn, 1948), p. 191.

17. Ibid., p. 277.

18. Stefan George, "Der Siebente Ring," *Gesamt-Ausgabe der Werke* (Berlin, 1928, vols. 6 and 7, p. 258; "The Seventh Ring," *The Works of Stefan George*, trans. Olga Marx and Ernst Morwitz, Chapel Hill, N.C., 1949, p. 239).

19. Salin, *Um Stefan George*, pp. 269, 275, 207, 249.

20. George, "Goethes letzte Nacht in Italien," in "Das Neue Reich," *Gesamt-Ausgabe*, 9:9; in *Works* (Marx and Morwitz), p. 280.

21. George, "Der Dichter in Zeiten der Wirren," *Gesamt-Ausgabe*, 9:39; in *Works* (Marx and Morwitz), p. 296.

22. As is well known, George for many years had been using the swastika as the emblem of his publishing house, until the Nazis forbade its further use in that way.

23. George, "Zeitgedicht," in "Der Siebente Ring" *Gesamt-Ausgabe*, vols. 6 and 7, p. 6, 208; in *Works* (Marx and Morwitz), pp. 156, 239.

24. George, "Dritter Jahrhundertspruch," ibid., p. 208; in *Works* (Marx and Morwitz), p. 182.

25. George, "Einzug," ibid., p. 63; in *Works* (Marx and Morwitz), p. 291.

26. Salin, *Um Stefan George*, p. 184.

27. The author was the Germanic philologist Hans Naumann (1886-1951); his book actually was not without merit.

28. Lutz Graf Schwerin von Krosigk, *Es geschah in Deutschland* (Tübingen, 1951), p. 347.

29. Eberhard Zeller, *Geist der Freiheit: Der Zwanzigste Juli*, 2d ed. (Munich, 1954), pp. 374, and 159.

30. See above, pt. 2, sec. 14.

31. Goethe, *Campagne in Frankreich*, Münster, November 1792.

32. Gerhard Wesenberg, *Verträge zugunsten Dritter* (Weimar, 1949), p. 112.

33. Joseph Unger, as cited by Wesenberg, p. 128.

34. Georg Jellinek, "Die Politik des Absolutismus und die des Radikalismus (Hobbes und Rousseau)," in his *Ausgewählte Schriften und Reden* (Berlin, 1911), 2:13, 10.

35. J. W. Gough, *The Social Contract: A Critical Study of Its Development* (Oxford, 1936), p. 107.

36. Hans Nef, "Jean Jacques Rousseau und die Idee des Rechtsstaates," *Schweizer Beiträge zur Allgemeinen Geschichte* 5 (Aarau, 1947):170.

37. J. L. Talmon, *The Origins of Totalitarian Democracy* (London, 1952), p. 3.

38. Rousseau, *Confessions,* bk. 9, par. 6 (van Bever ed.), 2:241.

39. Rousseau, *Contrat social*, bk. 4, chap. 1 (*The Social Contract*, trans. anon., ed. Charles Frankel, New York, 1947, p. 93).

40. Ibid., bk. 4, chap. 2 (Frankel, p. 94).

41. Ibid., bk. 3, chap. 2.

42. *The Political Writings of Jean Jacques Rousseau*, ed. C. E. Vaughan (Cambridge, Mass., 1915), vol. 1, p. 462.

43. Rousseau, *Contrat social*, bk. 4, chap. 1; bk. 2, chap. 6; bk. 1, chap. 7; bk. 2, chap. 3 (Frankel, pp. 93, 35, 17).

44. Ibid., bk. 2, chap. 6, my emphasis (Frankel, p. 35).

45. Luigi Einaudi, in an impressively modest address he gave after serving as president of the Republic of Italy: "Jean Jacques Rousseau, les théories de la volonté générale et du parti-guide, et les tâches des universitaires." *Kyklos*, vol. 9, no. 3 (Basel, 1956), pp. 289-298.

46. Rousseau, *Considérations sur le gouvernement de Pologne*, chap. 6.

47. Rousseau, *Contrat social*, bk. 3, chap. 6 (Frankel, p. 67).

48. See Carl Joachim Friedrich, *The New Belief in the Common Man* (Brattleboro, 1942); an expanded 2d ed. was published under the title *The New Image of the Common Man* (Boston, 1950).

49. Rousseau, *Contrat social*, bk. 1, chap. 7 (Frankel, p. 17).

50. Ernst Rudolf Huber, *Verfassungsrecht des grossdeutschen Reiches* (Hamburg, 1939), p. 361.

51. Rousseau, *Contrat social*, bk. 1, chap. 6 (Frankel, p. 15).

52. Ibid., bk. 2, chap. 4 (Frankel, p. 27).

53. *Sur l'origine de l'inégalité parmi les hommes*, pt. 2, third par. from end.

54. Rousseau, *Contrat social*, bk. 3, chap. 2 (Frankel, p. 56).

55. Ibid., bk. 3, chap. 7, my emphasis (Frankel, p. 37).

56. Ibid., bk. 4, chap. 2 (Frankel, p. 96).

57. Ibid., bk. 1, chap. 7 (Frankel, p. 18).

58. "Mon imagination ne laissoit pas longtemps déserte la terre ainsi parée. Je la peuplois bientôt d'êtres selon mon coeur." Third letter to Malesherbes, 26 January 1762, in Rousseau, *Correspondance générale* (Paris, 1927) 7:72.

59. Einaudi, *Kyklos*, vol. 9, no. 3, pp. 292f.

60. Hegel, *Vorlesungen über die Philosophie der Geschichte* (Berlin, 1822-1831), pp. 71, 44, 71, 63 (*Philosophy of History*, trans. J. Sibree, New York, 1944, pp. 39, 33).

61. Hegel, *Grundlinien der Philosophie des Rechts* (1821), pars. 257f, 331 (*Philosophy of Right*, trans. T. M. Knox, Oxford, 1942, pp. 155, 156, 56, 279, 212).

62. Ernst von Aster, *Psychoanalyse*, p. 203.

63. The above passage appeared earlier in Alexander Rüstow, "Zu den Grundlagen der Wirtschaftswissenschaft," *Revue de la Faculté des Sciences Economiques de l'Université d'Istanbul* 2 (1941):124f; and "Der Idealtypus als Gestalt und Norm," *Studium Generale*, vol. 6, no. 1 (Heidelberg, 1953), p. 57.

64. Rousseau, *Considérations sur le gouvernement de Pologne*, chaps. 3, 12, 13 (*Rousseau's Political Writings*, trans. and ed. Frederick Watkins, New York, 1953, pp. 168, 169, 244).

65. Voltaire, *Annales de l'Empire*.

66. Rousseau, letter to Coindet, 27 April 1765, *Correspondence générale*, 13:265.

67. Goethe, "Des Epimenides Erwachen," final stanza added for the performance in Berlin celebrating the victory over Napoleon, and published posthumously among the *Zahme Xenien*.

68. Hermann Gunkel, *Schöpfung und Chaos in Urzeit und Endzeit*, 2d ed. (Göttingen, 1921).

69. Engels, in his preface to the 3d ed. of Marx's *Civil War in France* (1891).

70. Engels, *Herrn Eugen Dührings Umwälzung der Wissenschaft*, pt. 3, sec. 2, par. 22 and last par. (*Anti-Dühring*, trans. Emile Burns, New York, 1939, p. 309).

71. "Die Deutsche Ideologie III: Sankt Max" (1845-1846) in *Marx-Engels-Gesamtausgabe*, pt. 1, vol. 5, pp. 415, 417, 270; "Privateigentum und Kommunismus" (1844), ibid., pt. 1, vol. 3, pp. 118, 166.

72. Ibid., pt. 1, vol. 5, p. 417; vol. 3, p. 121; vol. 5, pp. 22, 373.

73. Marx, *Das Kapital*, vol. 3, ed. Friedrich Engels (Hamburg, 1894), p.

355 (*Capital*, New York: International Publishers, 1967, 3:820); my emphasis.

74. Marx, *Zur Kritik der politischen Ökonomie*, preface, 4th par. (1859).

75. Ibid.

76. Werner Sombart, preface to the third volume of *Der moderne Kapitalismus* (1928), pp. xvii-xxii.

77. R. H. Tawney, *Religion and the Rise of Capitalism* (London, 1933), p. 36.

78. Marx, in the *Neue Rheinische Zeitung*, 6 November 1848.

79. Paul W. Annienkow, "Eine russische Stimme über Marx," *Die neue Zeit* 1 (1883):237-241. This is a translation by Dr. Julie Zadeck-Romm of an article published in 1880 in the Russian review *Viestnik Ievropy*.

80. Carl Schurz, *Reminiscences*, 3 vols. (New York, 1907-1908), 1:139f.

81. Karl Marx, *Herr Vogt* (London, 1860), pp. 42f.

82. N. Rjasanoff, "Marx' 'Bekenntnisse,'" *Die neue Zeit*, vol. 31, pt. 1 (1931), pp. 854-862.

83. *Marx-Engels-Gesamtausgabe*, pt. 1, vol. 1, p. 609; emphasis in the original.

84. Arthur Prinz, *Das Marxsche System in psychologischer Betrachtung*, unpublished dissertation (Berlin, 1923), sec. 5.

85. *Das Kapital*, vol. 1, chap. 24.

86. Fritz Naphthali, ed., *Wirtschaftsdemokratie: Ihr Wesen, Weg, und Ziel* (Berlin, 1928).

87. Friedrich A. von Hayek, *The Road to Serfdom* (Chicago, 1944).

88. Ernst Troeltsch, *Die Sozialphilosophie des Christentums* (Zurich, 1922), pp. 14f.

89. Bertold Spuler, *Die Goldene Horde: Die Mongolen in Russland, 1224-1502* (Leipzig, 1943), p. xiv.

90. P. S. Hudson and R. H. Richens, *The New Genetics in the Soviet Union* (Cambridge, Imperial Bureau of Plant Breeding and Genetics, 1946), p. 23.

91. Ibid., p. 24, quoting N. A. Berdyaev, *The Origins of Russian Communism* (London, 1937).

92. Heidi Fritz-Niggli, "Einordnung der Naturwissenschaft in das kommunistische Weltbild," *Neue Zürcher Zeitung*, 22 November 1948.

93. E. Karelsky, *Sowjetbürger* (Aarau, n.d.), p. 43.

94. Ibid., pp. 55f.

95. N. A. Berdyaev, "Alte und neue Wege des Humanismus," *Theologische Zeitschrift* vol. 2, no. 2 (Basel, 1946), pp. 124-137; the quoted passages are on pp. 137 and 125.

96. Alexander Rüstow, "Kreuzworträtsel Moskau," *Deutsche Kommentare*, 11 April 1953 (also in *Heidelberger Tageblatt*, 20 March 1953).

97. Johann Gottfried Herder, *Ideen zu einer Philosophie der Geschichte der Menschheit* (1790), bk. 16, chap. 4.

98. Erwin von Beckerath, *Wesen und Werden des faschistischen Staates* (Berlin, 1927), p. 25.

99. Mussolini, as cited by Hermann Heller, *Europa und der Faschismus* (Berlin, 1929), pp. 39, 53, 39.

100. Mussolini at the Naples Congress, shortly before the march on Rome, cited ibid., p. 46.

101. Hermann Jahrreiss, in his expert's opinion given to the Nürnberg Tribunal in 1946; see *Der Prozess gegen die Hauptkriegsverbrecher* (Nürnberg, 1948), 17:531.

102. The remark by the sixteenth-century Jesuit Georg Scherer is cited by Ricarda Huch.

103. Julius Ebbinghaus, *Zu Deutschlands Schicksalswende* (Frankfurt, 1946), pp. 33-35.

104. Fritz Wagner, "Friedrich Wilhelm I: Tradition und Persönlichkeit," *Historische Zeitschrift* 181:79-95, esp. pp. 92, 90, 94.

105. *Memoiren der Markgräfin Wilhelmine von Bayreuth*, 10th ed. (Leipzig, 1899), 2:210.

106. Gerhard Ritter, *Europa und die deutsche Frage* (Munich, 1948), p. 31.

107. Crane Brinton, "A Decade of Revolution, 1789-1799," in *The Rise of Modern Europe*, ed. William L. Langer (New York, 1934), p. 99.

108. Gerhard Ritter, *Staatskunst und Kriegshandwerk: Das Problem des "Militarismus" in Deutschland* (Munich, 1954), 1:127.

109. Wilhelm von Kügelgen, *Lebenserinnerungen des alten Mannes in Briefen an seinen Bruder Gerhard*, ed. Otto von Taube (Leipzig, 1942), pp. 216f. Kügelgen was court painter to the duke of Anhalt-Bernburg; his letter is dated 27 September 1848.

110. Gerhard Ritter, "Die neue Geschichte im Unterricht," *Die Sammlung*, vol. 2, no. 8 (Göttingen, August, 1947), p. 458. Ritter, surely, is above any suspicion of being a liberal.

111. Goethe, *Die Wahlverwandtschaften* (1807-1809), pt. 2, chap. 7.

112. Professor Emil Strohal, in his address celebrating the twenty-fifth anniversary of the Reichsgericht; see *Deutsche Juristenzeitung* (1904), p. 925.

113. Gerhard Ritter, *Europa und die deutsche Frage* (Munich, 1948), pp. 80f, 84.

114. Gerhard Ritter, *Der Schlieffen-Plan: Kritik eines Mythos* (Munich, 1956), p. 93.

115. Ibid., p. 71.

116. Gerhard Ritter, *Geschichte als Bildungsmacht* (Stuttgart, 1946), p. 29.

117. Ritter, *Schlieffen-Plan*, p. 96, quoting a statement of Friedrich von Holstein, a high official in the German foreign office, of May 1900. Holstein's statement explicitly inverts the healthy relationship between policy and strategy.

118. Ibid., p. 101, quoting Theobald von Bethmann-Hollweg, *Betrachtungen zum Weltkrieg*, 2 vols. (Berlin, 1919-21), 2:7.

119. Karl Barth, " 'Und vergib uns unsere Schuld,' " *Die Weltwoche* (Zurich), 14 September 1945.

120. Friedrich Meinecke, *Die deutsche Katastrophe* (Zurich, 1946), pp. 22, 84f, 156f.

121. Hans Bernd Gisevius, *Bis zum bittern Ende* (Zurich, 1946), 1:10.

122. H. J. Rieckhoff, *Trumpf oder Bluff? 12 Jahre deutsche Luftwaffe* (Geneva, 1945), p. 148.

123. Karl O. Paetel, "Deutsche innere Emigration," in *Dokumente des Anderen Deutschland*, ed. Friedrich Krause (New York, 1946).

124. Alfred Vierkandt, *Staat und Gesellschaft in der Gegenwart* (Leipzig, 1916), pp. 156f.

125. Hellmut Becker, "Jugendbewegung und Diplomatie," *Merkur*, vol. 5, no. 44 (Stuttgart, 1951), p. 985.

126. Gisevius, *Bis zum bittern Ende*, 1:147.

127. Ibid., 1:141f.

128. Werner Krauss, "Nationalismus und Chauvinismus," *Der Aufbau* (1946), no. 5, p. 455. This brilliant formulation reflects the fact that the author, a Marburg professor and a Communist, sees national socialism both from the closeness of affinity and the distance of enmity.

129. Rieckhoff, *Trumpf oder Bluff?* pp. 231, 271, 285.

130. Fabian von Schlabrendorff, *Offiziere gegen Hitler* (Zurich, 1946), p. 127.

131. Meinecke, *Die deutsche Katastrophe*, p. 127, quoting an unnamed friend.

132. The author adds parenthetically in the text: "On the list of intended victims the writer of these presents was obligingly placed." In a note he explains that "even the latter-day Nürnbergers were able to hang no one unless they caught him first." This last is an allusion to the proverb based on Till Eulenspiegel's legendary escape from Schilda and its irate citizens: "Die Schildbürger hingen keinen, sie fingen ihn denn." Alexander Rüstow had participated in last-minute efforts to prevent the formation of the Hitler cabinet in January 1933, had had his home searched by the Gestapo in March 1933, and by October 1933 had left Germany to accept a position as professor of economics at the Univesity of Istanbul, where he was to spend sixteen years in political exile. See Biographical Sketch.—*(Editor's note.)*

133. Ebbinghaus, *Zu Deutschlands Schicksalswende*, p. 96.

134. Gerhard Ritter, *Carl Goerdeler und die Widerstandsbewegung*, 3d ed. (Stuttgart, 1956), p. 423.

135. Gisevius, *Bis zum bittern Ende*, 1:372.

136. Hitler, *Mein Kampf*, trans. Ralph Mannheim (Boston, 1943), pp. 36, 35, 82, 35.

137. Hermann Rauschning, *Gespräche mit Hitler* (Zurich, 1939), as cited by Franz Jetzinger, *Hitlers Jugend* (Vienna, 1956), p. 34.

138. Ibid., pp. 25f, 33.

139. Ibid., pp. 33f.

140. Ibid., p. 34.

141. See Alexander Rüstow, "Radikalismus und Arbeitslosigkeit," *Kölnische Zeitung*, 10 March 1932. The statistical correlation was graphically presented with the help of a statistician, Johann Sebastien Geer.

142. Hitler, *Mein Kampf* (Mannheim), p. 642.

143. Ibid., p. 180.

144. Ibid., p. 42.

145. Nietzsche, *Die fröhliche Wissenschaft* (3:149; *Gay Science*, trans. Walter Kaufmann, New York, 1977, p. 195).

146. Rieckhoff, *Trumpf oder Bluff?* pp. 291, 229f, 201.

147. Schlabrendorff, *Offiziere gegen Hitler*, pp. 57f.

148. Rieckhoff, *Trumpf oder Bluff?* pp. 42, 41.

149. Freud, *Gesammelte Schriften*, 12 vols. (Vienna, 1924-1934), 12:8. Of course Freud, in writing this, did not have Hitler in mind.

150. G. Barraclough, review of Asher Lee's *The German Air Force* (London, 1946), in *Erasmus* 2 (1949):297-303.

PART 3, CHAPTER 3: CONCLUSIONS

1. Alexander Rüstow, in *Hat der Westen eine Idee?* Aktionsgemeinschaft Soziale Marktwirtschaft, *Tagungsprotokoll Nr.* 7 (Ludwigsburg, 1957).

2. Lenin, *Ausgewählte Werke*, 2 vols. (Moscow, 1947), 2:788-790, 701.

3. William C. Bullitt's *Memoirs*, as excerpted in *Die Weltwoche* (Zurich), 30 November 1956.

4. Franz Böhm in *Hat der Westen eine Idee?* p. 43.

5. Alexander Rüstow, "Die weltgeschichtliche Bedeutung des Bauerntums in Vergangenheit, Gegenwart und Zukunft," *Zeitschrift für Agrargeschichte und Agrarsoziologie*, vol. 5, no. 1, pp. 1-13.

6. Alexander Rüstow, "Die geschichtliche Bedeutung der sozialen Marktwirtschaft," in *Wirtschaftsfragen der freien Welt* (Frankfurt, 1957), pp. 73-77.

7. Alexander Rüstow, "Vitalpolitik gegen Vermassung," in *Masse und Demokratie*, ed. Arnold Hunold (Zurich, 1957), p. 237.

INDEX

LIBRARY OF CONGRESS CATALOGING IN PUBLICATION DATA

Rüstow, Alexander, 1885-1963.
    Freedom and domination.

    "Abridged translation of Ortsbestimmung der
Gegenwart."
    Includes bibliographical references and index.
    1. Civilization—History.   I.   Rustow, Dankwart A.
II.   Title.
CB88.R84213   909   80-10575
ISBN 0-691-05304-5